Lenin's Political Thought

Neil Harding

PUBLISHERS' NOTE

In order to make this book available in paperback at a reasonable price, the two original hard cover editions of volumes 1 and 2 have simply been put together between one set of covers.

Each volume is paginated separately, each with its own Contents, Acknowledgements, Introduction, Notes and References, Chronology and Index. The Bibliography for volume 1, which was superseded by that published in volume 2, has been omitted from this edition.

Lenin's Political Thought

THEORY AND PRACTICE IN THE DEMOCRATIC AND SOCIALIST REVOLUTIONS

NEIL HARDING

Unabridged paperback edition in one volume

Haymarket Books
Chicago, Illinois

Volume 1 first published in 1977 by MacMillan; volume 2 first published in 1978 by St. Martin's Press. First published in a combined paperback edition in 1983 by Humanities Press.
© 1977, 1978 Neil Harding

This edition published in 2009 by Haymarket Books
P.O. Box 180165
Chicago, IL 60618
773-583-7884
info@haymarketbooks.org
www.haymarketbooks.org

Trade distribution:
In the U.S. through Consortium Book Sales, www.cbsd.com
In the UK, Turnaround Publisher Services, www.turnaround-psl.com
In Australia, Palgrave MacMillan, www.palgravemacmillan.com.au
In all other countries, Publishers Group Worldwide,
www.pgw.com/home/worldwide.aspx

This book was published with the generous support of the
Wallace Global Fund.

Cover design by Rachel Wilsey

ISBN-13: 978-1931859-89-9

Printed in Canada by union labor on recycled paper containing
100 percent post-consumer waste in accordance with the guidelines
of the Green Press Initiative, www.greenpressinitiative.org.

The 1983 edition of this book was cataloged by the Library of Congress.

2 4 6 8 10 9 7 5 3 1

Lenin's Political Thought

Volume 1

THEORY AND PRACTICE IN THE DEMOCRATIC REVOLUTION

Contents

Acknowledgements

My thanks in the first place to the Centre for Russian and East European Studies of the University College, Swansea, for travel funds which enabled me to pursue sources in British and European libraries. Thanks next to my colleague Richard Taylor and to Timothy Fox at Macmillan, whose meticulous reading of different stages of my manuscript eliminated at least some of its infelicities. Thanks, too, to Mary Ghullam, who helped me considerably in obtaining source materials. To Pat Rees, Pat Yates and Judith Gilbody, my admiration for their skills in producing an intelligible typescript from my manuscript. Finally, thanks to my wife and five boys, who had to put up with my solitary delvings for too long.

Glossary of Russian Terms

Bakuninist, follower of M. A. Bakunin (1814–76), ideologist and examplar of anarchism.

Batraki, farm labourers, poor peasants.

Bolsheviki/Mensheviki, men of the Majority/Minority; so called as a result of the votes on constituting the Central Committee and the Central Organ of the R.S.D.L.P. at its Second Congress in 1903.

Bund, the General Jewish Workers' Union of Lithuania, Poland and Russia. Founded in Vilna in 1897, joined R.S.D.L.P. at First Congress, withdrew in 1903, reaffiliated in 1906.

Bundist, adherent of the *Bund*.

Chto delat?, *What Is To Be Done?* Lenin's pamphlet of 1902 and the title of a novel by Chernyshevsky.

Desyatin (or **dessiatine**), measurement of area: 2.7 acres.

Duma, a representative assembly summoned by the Tsar. First Duma, April–July 1906. Second Duma, February–June 1907. Third Duma, 1907–12. Fourth Duma, 1912–17.

Golos Sotsialdemokrata, *The Social-Democrat's Voice.* Organ of the Mensheviks abroad. Geneva, Paris, February 1908 to December 1911.

Iskra, *The Spark.* Illegal journal of the 'orthodox' Marxists. Editorial board (up to August 1903) G. V. Plekhanov, P. B. Akselrod, V. I. Zasulich, V. I. Lenin, L. Martov, and A. N. Potresov. At the Second Congress the editors were reduced to three, Plekhanov, Lenin and Martov. Martov refused to serve and issues 46–51 were edited by Plekhanov and Lenin. Thereupon Plekhanov insisted on the restoration of the old editorial board, Lenin resigned, and from issue 52 the Bolsheviks referred to it as 'the New Iskra'. Leipzig, Munich, London, Geneva, December 1900 to December 1905. 112 issues.

Iskrist, an adherent of *Iskra*, particularly before and during Second Party Congress.

Kadets, Kadeti or Cadets, members of the liberal Constitutional Democratic Party, founded in October 1905.

Kruzhok (plural *kruzhki*), circle, specifically a workers' circle devoted to in-depth propaganda.

Kulak, wealthy peasant.

Kustarnichestvo, handicraft methods; outmoded and inefficient manner of proceeding. Sometimes rendered as 'amateurish'.

Lavrist, follower of P. L. Lavrov (1823–1900), a prominent ideologist of Russian Populism.

Luch, *The Ray.* Legal Menshevik daily. St Petersburg, September 1912 to July 1913. 237 issues.

Mir, *see* **Obshchina.**

Muzhik, peasant.

Nachalo, *The Beginning.* (*a*) Journal of the 'legal Marxists'. St Petersburg, 1899. (*b*) Menshevik daily paper. St Petersburg, 13 November to 2 December 1905. 16 issues.

Narodism, Russian Populism.

Narodnaya Volya, People's Will. Terrorist/Jacobin offshoot of *Zemlya i Volya* founded in 1879; responsible for assassinating Tsar Alexander II, 1 March 1881; thereafter movement decimated by the government.

Narodnichestvo, the ideas and organisations associated with *Narodism.*

Narodnik, Populist (from *narod*, people). A Russian socialist, adherent of the ideas of Herzen, Bakunin, Lavrov, Chernyshevsky *et al.* A believer in the peasant commune as *the* stepping-stone to socialism in Russia.

Narodovolets (plural *Narodovoltsi*), adherent of *Narodnaya Volya.*

Nekulturny, uncultured, but having overtones of uncivilised.

Obshchina (or **Mir**), peasant commune responsible for periodic redistribution of allotments of land, control of crop rotation, organisation of services and collection of communal payments due to landlords and state.

Otzovists (from *otzovat*, to recall). Left-wing Bolsheviks who demanded that Social Democratic deputies to the Third Duma be recalled.

Praktiki, The Practicals; specifically the workerphile opponents of the political line of the *Stariki* and the Emancipation of Labour Group.

Pravda, *Truth.* (*a*) Social Democratic journal. Moscow, 1904–6. (*b*) Menshevik/Trotskyist organ. Lvov, Vienna, 1908–12. 25 issues. (*c*) Bolshevik daily, obliged to change name frequently, generally *Pravda* with various prefixes. St Petersburg, April 1912 to July 1914. Recommenced publication March 1917, again with varied titles, until October 1917, when it resumed the title it has rejoiced under to date.

Proletarii, *The Proletarian.* (*a*) Central organ of the R.S.D.L.P. (predominantly Bolshevik). Geneva, May to November 1905. 26 issues. (*b*) Illegal Bolshevik newspaper. Vyborg, Geneva, Paris, August 1906 to November 1909. 50 issues.

Pud (or *Pood*), measurement of weight: 36 lbs, 13.6 kg.

Rabochaya Gazeta, *The Workers' Paper.* (*a*) Organ of the Kiev Social Democrats adopted as the organ of the R.S.D.L.P. at its First Congress, March 1898. Kiev, August and December 1892. Two issues. Attempt to re-establish it in 1899 occasioned three important articles by Lenin. (*b*) Organ of Bolsheviks and 'pro-party' Mensheviks. Paris, October to July 1912. Nine issues.

Rabochaya Mysl, *Workers' Thought.* First two issues published by Petersburg workmen, subsequently the organ of the economist-dominated Petersburg Committee of the R.S.D.L.P. St Petersburg, Berlin, October 1897 to December 1902. 16 issues.

Rabochee Delo, *The Workers' Cause.* (a) Projected organ of the *Stariki.* Copy prepared, edited and largely written by Lenin, seized by police in extensive arrests of the group in December 1895. (b) The organ of the Union of Russian Social-Democrats Abroad. Geneva, April 1899 to February 1902. 12 issues.

Rabotnik, *The Worker.* An occasional miscellany published by the Union of Russian Social-Democrats Abroad. Geneva, 1896–9. Six issues.

Rech, *Speech.* Daily newspaper, principle organ of the Kadets. St Petersburg, February 1906 to October 1917.

Russkoe Bogatstvo, *Russian Wealth.* Radical *narodnik* monthly. St Petersburg, 1876–1918.

Sotsial Demokrat, *The Social Democrat.* (a) Literary/political review published by the Emancipation of Labour Group. London, Geneva, 1890–2. Four issues. (b) Name given to the group founded by Plekhanov, Akselrod and Zasulich in May 1900 after the split in the Union of Russian Social-Democrats Abroad. (c) Central Organ of the R.S.D.L.P. Geneva, October 1904 to October 1905. St Petersburg, September to November 1906. Seven issues. Paris, Geneva, February 1908 to January 1917. 58 issues.

Sovremennik, *The Contemporary.* (a) Radical monthly founded by Pushkin. St Petersburg, 1836–66. (b) Literary/political monthly. St Petersburg, 1911–15.

Stariki, the old men or veterans; specifically the group of Petersburg Marxists (many of them ex-students of the Technological Institute) who joined forces with Martov's group in late 1895 to form the Petersburg Union of Struggle for the Emancipation of the Working Class. The original group included G. B. Krasin, G. M. Krzhizhanovsky, A. A. Vaneev, N. K. Krupskaya, V. A. Shelgunov, M. Silvin, S. I. Radchenko and V. I. Lenin.

Tkachevist, follower of Peter Tkachev (1844–85), a prominent Russian Jacobin.

Trudoviks, *Labourites.* Title taken by large group of radical peasant deputies in the Dumas. Group formed after convocation of First Duma.

Vperyod, *Forward.* (a) Illegal Bolshevik weekly. Geneva, December 1904 to May 1905. 18 issues. Succeeded by *Proletarii.* (b) *Vperyod* Group. Left Bolshevik opponents of Lenin, active from 1909 to 1913 and led by Bogdanov and Aleksinsky.

Zarya, *The Dawn.* Theoretical organ of 'orthodox' Marxists on the *Iskra* editorial board. Stuttgart, 1901–2. Four issues.

Zemlya i Volya, Land and Freedom. Organisation of revolutionary populists formed in 1876, split in December 1879 into two factions, *Cherni Peredel* (Black Repartition) and *Narodnaya Volya* (see above).

Zemstvo (plural *Zemstva*), local government bodies set up in the central regions of Russia in 1864.

Zhizn, *Life.* Marxist monthly periodical 1897–1902.

VII

Introduction

There is a conventional wisdom which runs through almost all Western commentary, criticism and biography of Lenin. This line of interpretation (let us call it the basic position) has it that the nature of Lenin's genius is his ability to grasp the potentialities of a situation and turn them to his own advantage so as to maximise his power. As an instinctive politician, as a practitioner of revolution, he is incomparable. As a theorist of Marxism, however, he is inconsistent, unorthodox and vacillating and by these tokens comparatively unimportant.[1] Edmund Wilson has provided us with the classic formulation of the basic position, which many a subsequent commentator has quoted or echoed:

> The theoretical side of Lenin is, in a sense, not serious; it is the instinct for dealing with the reality of the definite political situation which attains in him the point of genius. He sees and he adopts his tactic with no regard for the theoretical positions of others or for his own theoretical position in the past; then he supports it with Marxist texts.[2]

Lenin, in this gloss, is pre-eminently a practitioner, not a theorist of revolution. Appropriately enough, what innovations he did make to Marxism are held to relate almost exclusively to the organisational sphere. The questions which galvanise him are: how can the Party be created, moulded, disciplined and controlled? What are the mechanisms through which the forces hostile to the existing regime can be co-ordinated to disrupt it and overthrow it? The more basic theoretical questions relating to the determining factors in the Marxist account of the revolutionary process – the level of development of productive forces, classes and consciousness, the conception of the new world of socialism that lies in the future – these are not his real concern.

1

Lenin's Political Thought

On these first-order problems in the Marxist tradition, Lenin, according to an imposing consensus of commentators, presents little that is original and less that is coherent. He shifts his ground too frequently, he departs from the canons of orthodoxy too flagrantly, and is too absorbed with immediate polemical objectives to treat theoretical constructs with anything but manipulative intent.

The basic position has then, in the opinion of most commentators, been established and authoritatively settled for quite some time. There remain, none the less, significant problems to deal with. Lenin clearly thought he was dealing with problems of Marxist theory; the language and justificatory arguments of Marxism spring readily to his lips. The central problem which now emerges is intelligible only as a derivative of the basic position. If Lenin in his thought and activity cannot be made intelligible simply qua Marxist, what were the motivational drives that led him on to the paths of heterodoxy and deviation? What, in other words, is the source of the accepted bifurcation within his thought and activity? A rich vein of material – historical, intellectual, personal and psychological – has been opened up, quarried and extended by academics and others in search of answers.

For some, Lenin's brand of revolutionism is best explained in terms of the formative influence of his apprenticeship in revolutionary politics, which, it is argued, deeply influenced his whole subsequent career. As a young Russian Jacobin, so the story goes, Lenin assimilated precepts and attitudes of mind which he later tried to graft on to the unreceptive stock of orthodox Marxism. Lenin is presented as a Jacobin out of a long and illustrious line of Russian Jacobins. His early exposure to Russian Jacobinism and the enduring imprint it left upon him provide us with a plausible explanation of his impatient voluntarism which jars too frequently against the Marxism in which it is couched. In this light we can understand his precocious description of Russia as already capitalist in 1893, his rejection of the democratic revolution as the immediate objective, his call for a party of professionals to make the revolution as proxy for the proletariat, his engineering of a socialist revolution in a backward uncongenial environment – all of this can be comprehended as a persistent pattern of imposing the imperious will of the dedicated disciplined group upon a recalcitrant historical process. It is, in short, the classical Jacobin formulation.[3]

2

Complementary in many ways to this resolution of the problem deriving from the basic position is the psycho-historical explanation which discerns deep within Lenin's psyche impulses which he rationalises and explains to himself in the conventional terminology of Marxism. For some the crucial factor in understanding Lenin (that is, in understanding why he went off the rails as a Marxist, for that is the assumption that makes the explanation necessary) is his unsatisfactory relationship with his elder brother – the hanged would-be regicide – Aleksander. Lenin's whole career is presented as a 'search for Aleksander', an attempt 'to expiate his guilt for having failed to understand Sasha and for having frequently ridiculed him'.[4] Others in similar vein conclude that all Lenin's inconsistencies, his extraordinary vehemence about seemingly innocuous issues, really arose from a 'tension between fantasy and reality' in his psychological make-up.[5] Marxism and its dialectical pattern, according to the psycho-historians, was no more than a precarious salve for Lenin's neuroses.

At a rather less sophisticated level, but perhaps none the worse for that, there is the explanation that Lenin, like all politicians, sought power but that in him this proclivity was raised to an unnatural, even monstrous, degree so that his actions and his thoughts were all directed towards his search for complete and total domination. As Soviet interpretations see Lenin as God, this interpretation presents him as the Miltonic Satan of the contemporary world, a perversely heroic being flawed by overweening pride and bent on universal destruction. 'His fanaticism was only the outward form of a demon-driven ego intent upon dominating the processes of destruction and of rebuilding.'[6] Lenin, it seems, made the Russian revolution, created the Communist International, directed all his policies with one aim in view, the elevation of Vladimir Ilich Ulyanov as the paragon of the revolutionary world. Lenin, in this interpretation, was constantly admiring his image in the mirror of the world revolutionary movement. His abiding flaw was vanity and consummate revolutionary narcissism.

Finally, the problem deriving from the basic position may be solved by demonstrating that Lenin *was* a Marxist in the meaningful but qualified sense that he was a 'primitive' Marxist; an enthusiast for the 'Blanquist period' of Marx's thought, particularly of the period 1848–51. 'The new "Leninism", in fact, was a primitive Marxism in two senses. It was the Marxism of the early Marx.

3

And it was the Marxism of a backward Europe.'[7] This line of approach has of course the merit of being compatible with recognising the impact of Russian Jacobinism upon Lenin's reception of Marxism. Once again the whole roster of Russian Jacobins is pressed into service to demonstrate striking similarities of thought and disposition and to show the 'sources' whence Lenin culled his ideas.[8] Lenin, in this guise, is portrayed as a very peculiar and partial kind of Marxist who evaded the determinist constraints of the mature Marx and who imported the aggressive activism of the Russian revolutionary tradition into his own brand of the doctrine.

What all these interpretations have in common is their acceptance of the basic position. The question is not *whether* Lenin was inconsistent and unorthodox in his Marxism, it is *why* he was so. The bulk of modern scholarship on Lenin has been devoted to exploring, often in ingenious and plausible ways, the large variety of explanations of this question. The objective of this book is to question the adequacy of the basic position itself and, therefore, to dispute the point of pursuing the derivative question at all. Manifestly, if we are led to question the assertions that Lenin was inconsistent or unorthodox, the pursuit of the *sources* of his inconsistency or unorthodoxy becomes quite redundant.

The general argument which runs through both volumes of this study is that Lenin's economic and social analyses provide the clue to coherence or consistency in his more expressly political strategies. My justification for swelling the already vast number of studies on Lenin with two more fat tomes is that the various exponents of the basic position as well as, more surprisingly, Soviet and Marxist accounts of Lenin quite fail to develop this connection which is so intrinsic to Lenin's thought as a whole.[9] Both sets of interpretations concentrate upon the search for coherence, originality or orthodoxy at the level of political tactic and organisational principle, to the virtual exclusion of the theoretical analyses from which these 'political' recommendations are explicitly derived. They either fail to appreciate the importance, or even go so far as to deny the very existence of, Lenin's basic economic and social analyses.[10]

The rationale for presenting the study in two volumes proceeds from the general argument that Lenin, at different periods of his life, elaborated two quite distinct economic and social analyses which entailed two quite differring political strategies with radically different objectives in view. These two moments in the development of Lenin's theoretical views with their derivative implications for revolutionary practice will be dealt with in separate volumes.

The first was completed by the turn of the century and was summarised as *The Development of Capitalism in Russia*. It was precisely this thoroughgoing theoretical analysis which provided the basis for Lenin's practical politics right up to 1914, in that it indicated the patterns of growth and decline of social classes in Russia and showed which had an objective interest in the preservation of autocracy and which were for its overthrow. It demonstrated the weakness and instability of the Russian bourgeoisie and pointed to the proletariat as the 'natural representative of all Russia's exploited', duty-bound to articulate the grievances of *all* wage-earners, including the landless peasantry and artisans. The theoretical basis equally dictated the limitations to Social-Democratic objectives. It explained why nothing but the most absurd and reactionary conclusions would attend any attempt to overstep the objective determinants and canvass permanent revolution or an immediate turn to socialism. The level of development of the productive forces, therewith of social relations in Russia, could not, according to Lenin's theoretical findings, support such policies.

Lenin's early theoretical analysis provided not only an account of classes in their development and their likely alignments in the various stages of the democratic revolution, it also gave him a methodology which he applied to the development of class consciousness and working-class organisation. Thus, just as capitalism moved through a series of phases to its developed and essential expression, so too did consciousness and party organisation. Each partook of a progression through discernible stages to its mature and adequate form. The idea of the revolutionary process moving through phases of development towards its consummation is crucial to Lenin's early thought and the clue to this progression is given in his ostensibly economic writings, which have been so neglected by interpreters of his thought.

All of Lenin's writings in this period must be seen against the broader background of an existing Russian Marxist orthodoxy, which Plekhanov and the Emancipation of Labour Group had earlier established. By the time Lenin became a Marxist the main lines of strategy and the bases for distinguishing Marxists from rival revolutionary groups had long been laid down. Part of the objective of the book is, therefore, to establish what this orthodoxy of Russian Marxism consisted of. It has to be reconstructed before we can even attempt to judge the degree of Lenin's originality or orthodoxy. Too often elements of Lenin's thought are represented as peculiar unorthodoxies or innovations of his own coinage which, on further examination, turn out to be denominations of the general currency of Russian Marxism.

Finally, and perhaps obviously, Lenin's thought, particularly his immediate tactical recommendations, have to be seen in the context of the demands of the rapidly evolving Russian labour movement.

Throughout the period up to 1914 Lenin's theoretical analysis and, consequently, its entailments for practice referred almost exclusively to the particular situation of Russia. In 1914, however, inescapable new problems emerged which his earlier economic and social analysis could not accommodate. Lenin consequently undertook a new theoretical analysis which found completed form in *Imperialism the Highest Stage of Capitalism*.[11] The economic and social structure of capitalism had, according to Lenin's new analysis, become a global, monopolistic and degenerate system. Just as capitalism in its imperialist phase could be appraised only on a global basis, so too the balance of class forces had to be assessed on a similarly international plane. From the new theoretical analysis, elements of which were, as we shall see, beginning to emerge in the period 1908–14, a totally new international strategy was elaborated by Lenin.

Put briefly, Lenin's first theoretical analysis demonstrated Russia's ripeness for a radical democratic revolution. Its derivative recommendations on practice were, therefore, concerned with developing the consciousness and organisation of the anti-autocratic forces in Russia to secure the optimum realisation of this objective. The relation between theory and practice in this earlier period of the democratic revolution is the subject of the present volume.

Lenin's second theoretical analysis demonstrated that capitalism in its monopolistic imperialist stage had exhausted its progressive potential and, at the same time, had created the necessary objective and subjective conditions for socialist revolution on an international scale. Lenin's new ideas on practice were, consequently, derived from and justified by the new theoretical analysis and were concerned with the role of international proletarian organisations and of the socialist state in preparing for and realising properly socialist relations on a world scale. The relationship between theory and practice in this later phase of Lenin's intellectual development will be the subject of the second volume of this study.

CHAPTER 1

Samara 1889–93 : The Making of a Marxist

According to his sister the years which Lenin spent in Samara were 'perhaps the most important years in the life of Vladimir Ilich: this was the time when his revolutionary physiognomy was constructed and decisively formed itself'.[1] Our problems begin when we attempt to unravel what is intended by this statement and which of the rival interpretations of the precise constitution of Lenin's 'revolutionary physiognomy' best fits the evidence. Put briefly the question is, was Lenin a Marxist or Jacobin during this period? From this, evidently, two further questions would follow: what sort of a Jacobin or Marxist was he, and what was the importance of this 'formative period' on Lenin's subsequent thought?

The whole question of how we are to characterise Lenin's thought has been projected back to the period of his adolescence and early manhood. Lenin's early writings, according to many accounts, only become intelligible when viewed against the background of his youthful career; they stand as it were as testaments to the traumas he suffered in adolescence – the sudden death of his father and the execution of his elder brother. According to others, an understanding of Lenin's early apprenticeship in revolutionary politics during the so-called Samara period is crucial if we are to interpret his later writings correctly and understand the origins of Bolshevism in proper perspective. Within the mature Marxist, it is contended, there is always the youthful Jacobin struggling to break out.

If Lenin's later alleged 'deviations' or 'voluntarist revisions' to Marxism are in some way explained by, or stand in some sort of causal relationship to, his early apprenticeship in revolutionary politics, we have no option but to begin our survey of the develop-

ment of Lenin's theory of revolution with an examination of the
character his thought assumed during this period. We clearly cannot
escape the task of reconstructing his early intellectual biography.

EARLY YEARS

There are, thankfully, some elements of our story which are not
disputed. Lenin was born into a comfortably off, contented and
well-respected family residing in Simbirsk (now Ulyanovsk) in
1870. He was the second son of a relatively important government
official of enlightened if moderate views, who rose to the post
of provincial inspector of schools and therewith acquired noble
status. Lenin's early years were, by all accounts, perfectly happy.
Certainly he lacked neither the love and affection of an adoring
mother and brothers and sisters, nor the security of a well-ordered
bourgeois provincial home. At school he was a studious and
diligent pupil, if a trifle reserved, who seemed likely to emulate the
outstanding academic records of his elder brother, Aleksander and
his sister, Anna. There was nothing whatever in Lenin's schoolboy
career that could, even under the microscopic enlargement of hind-
sight, be construed as portentous of the future revolutionary. From
the first form to his graduation from the Simbirsk gymnasium he
was always top of the class. With almost monotonous regularity
his tests and examinations registered the highest mark in every one
of the subjects he took. He displayed a special partiality, amounting
almost to a passion, for Latin, and his headmaster, Kerensky-père,
felt certain that it was as a classical scholar that Vladimir would
make his mark upon the world. As Deutscher puts it in his sketch
of these early years:

> There was not even a hint of the rebel about him, not a flicker of
> that restiveness and not a trace of that 'maladjustment' which
> marked the adolescence of so many men who later in life settled
> down quite happily to philistine respectability. He was growing
> up in almost perfect harmony with his environment. His relatives
> and schoolmates, some of whom tried later to ante-date his re-
> volutionary development could not remember a single act of
> insubordination at school.[2]

In 1886 the domestic tranquillity and happiness of the Ulyanov household suffered its first severe blow. In that year Lenin's father died and the comfortable security of the family was abruptly shattered. Maria Aleksandrovna was left in rather desperate straits with her eldest son, Aleksander, and daughter Anna both studying in St Petersburg and dependent upon her for support, as well as the three who had not yet left home, Vladimir, Olga and Dimitry. Eventually she obtained a moderate pension from the state and this, together with the income from letting part of their large Samara house, somewhat restored the family's financial equilibrium.

In the following year the family, struggling to define a new normality, suffered an almost unimaginable trauma. On 1 March 1887 Aleksander was arrested for planning and preparing to assassinate the Tsar. The eldest and best-loved, a scholarly, modest and brilliant youth of whom all the memoirists speak with genuine affection and admiration, had, since the previous summer, been reading Marx. Returning to university he cautiously began to engage in politics; not, initially at least, with any revolutionary intent, but more to protest with what slender means were available against the strangulation of all autonomous organisations within the universities, the omnipresent censorship and the remorseless whittling down of the Zemstva prerogatives, and the regime of perfervid reaction which Nicholas and Pobedonostsev had un-leashed on Russia as a kind of retribution for the assassination of Alexander II by the *Narodnaya Volya* (People's Will – hereafter translations of Russian terms will not generally appear in the text as they are given in the Glossary at the end of the book).

Swiftly Aleksander and his friends realised that there was no way through the stifling censorship, no possible way of reaching or influencing public opinion. 'Under these circumstances con-spiracy appeared to the students as the only way out – the alternative was utter passivity.'[3] It was a familiar predicament and the reaction of Aleksander Ulyanov's group to it, however pathetically amateur in organisation and technical preparation, carried with it at the same time a large element of the heroism and nobility of spirit of the Russian intelligentsia.

The group with which Aleksander was involved had been in existence for less than two months prior to the arrests and comprised some fifteen people who called themselves 'The Terrorist Section of the *Narodnaya Volya*', out of homage to the heroes of 1881 whose deed they hoped to emulate on the sixth anniversary of the assassination of Alexander II. There certainly is no evidence that any of the new conspirators had any organisational link with the original group. On the very eve of the attempt the plot was fortuitously discovered by the police and the main participants were arrested. Even Anna, Lenin's elder sister, who was also studying in St Petersburg but who certainly was not privy to any of Aleksander's plans, was incarcerated on the grounds of presumed guilt by association.

From the time of his arrest to the moment of his execution Aleksander unflinchingly took upon himself the main responsibility for the conspiracy. In fact both 'the initiator and the organizer, in accordance with a previous plan, had fled from St Petersburg. Ulyanov, in the correct testimony of the prosecutor, "took the place of both ringleaders of the conspiracy".'[4] His part in the plot had been to help prepare the bombs and to draft the manifesto which the group hoped to promulgate after the assassination. There was no doubt that he had been one of the most active and dedicated of the conspirators, and yet a timely confession and supplication for mercy might have saved him, for he at least was not caught, as the others were, with bombs and guns in his possession. According to the plan he was to have had no part in the actual process of dispatching the Tsar and this could no doubt have been a factor in his defence.

Aleksander, however, wanted no easy way out; he was, from the moment of his arrest, bent on martyrdom. Perhaps it would be more accurate to say that both morally and prudentially he felt that his own execution was now the best outcome. Morally, as he put it to his grief-stricken mother, whose hair had whitened in the space of a week, it was proper that he, who had intended taking the life of another, should now have his own life taken. Prudentially the only option that a plea for mercy could bring would have brought a lingering living death, incarcerated in solitude in the notorious Schlusselburg fortress, where so many brave and heroic men had been totally broken.

He resolved therefore to take upon himself the main burden of guilt for the conspiracy, even encouraging his weaker comrades to do what they could for their own salvation by disclaiming their complicity in pointing the finger at him. Aleksander Ulyanov it was who, on 18 April, read to the court an impressive statement of the principles which had guided the conspirators and, in the process, arraigned the autocracy and its ministers as the real culprits in the eyes of the Russian people and the civilised world.[5] To the last his resolution never faltered. Once convinced of the rectitude of his course of action Aleksander pursued it unswervingly to its ultimate conclusions.

A brief account of the circumstances surrounding the death of Aleksander has been necessary because, in the opinions of many, Lenin's association with his brother, and the manner of his death, left a lasting imprint on his political attitudes. In fact Aleksander himself became a committed revolutionary only in the last few months of his life, which he spent exclusively in St Petersburg. There was no opportunity for him to have inducted his brother into his ideological universe and since he gave his sister, to whom he was much closer and who was actually in St Petersburg at the time, no inkling of his commitment and plans, it is extremely unlikely that he would have disclosed them to his schoolboy brother four years his junior. Trotsky, who has given us the fullest account in English of this episode, concludes:

> The now generally accepted thesis that Vladimir received his first revolutionary impulses from his terrorist brother appears so obvious from all circumstantial evidence as to require no proof. In reality, that hypothesis is also false. Aleksander introduced no member of his family into his inner world, and least of all Vladimir.[6]

It might well be, of course, that Vladimir from this time onward nurtured an especial hatred for the autocratic government and a commitment to do what he could to overthrow tsarism. It would be surprising if that were not the case. This supposition (and it is a supposition, since neither Lenin nor any of those closest to him at the time have left any reliable testimony of the impact his brother's death made upon him) is no more than a reasonable assumption about a general attitude of mind and a disposition; it can in no way provide us with a pointer to the particular character which Lenin's thought eventually assumed.

Shortly after his brother's death Vladimir graduated from the Simbirsk gymnasium with the gold medal as the most outstanding student of his year. Olga, who took her graduation examinations at the same time, followed in the footsteps of Aleksander, Anna and Vladimir; she too was awarded the gold medal. It is perhaps worth pausing to reflect on the circumstances in which the seventeen year old and his sixteen year old sister prepared for and sat their exams; they could scarcely have been more harrowing. Their mother, now slighted and shunned by polite society, was away in St Petersburg pleading with all the influence and persistence she could command for the life of her eldest son and the release of her daughter. Throughout the examination period, Aleksander's trial was in progress and was, obviously, *the* story in the national newspapers. On the very morning of his brother's execution, Vladimir was sitting an examination. Meanwhile preparations were made to sell the house and, by the time the oral tests arrived, the family was in the process of selling the furniture from the big house in Simbirsk and preparing to remove to outside of Kazan. In these circumstances the resolve and self-control of Vladimir and Olga must have been tested to the utmost. It speaks volumes to their inner strength of character that they came through it all with such brilliant results.

On the strength of his academic record and the glowing testimonial he received from Fyodor Kerensky, his headmaster,[7] that his behaviour and his scholarship left nothing to be desired, Vladimir was admitted to Kazan University. He had been there for less than a term when he too fell foul of the authorities. Following the execution of Aleksander Ulyanov and his four comrades, students at St Petersburg had organised a demonstration protesting against the disgraceful servility with which the University's rector had condemned his ex-students. In the Christmas term disturbances again began in the universities and spread out from Moscow to reach Kazan by early December. After a modest demonstration in which the students had refused an instruction to disperse and had insisted upon presenting the dean with a list of rather moderate demands regarding the running of the University, Vladimir was arrested as an alleged ring-leader.[8] There can be little doubt that from his very first day as a university student, Vladimir had been a marked man, subjected to the zealous attention of police agents who did not hesitate to impute to his every action the most lurid and extravagant objectives.

'The truth was', as Robert Payne puts it 'that Vladimir was guilty by association – with his dead brother.'[9] On the basis of police reports concerning his involvement in this affair, Vladimir was sent down from Kazan and forbidden permission to re-apply for admission. According to the regulations he should have been obliged to return to his 'home town', but by this time the Ulyanov family had severed its links with Simbirsk and Vladimir was allowed to return, with the rest of the family, to Kokushkino where his mother had inherited a share of an estate which had belonged to her father. It was to Kokushkino, too, that Anna had eventually been banished.

It was during the winter of 1887–8 that Lenin first became acquainted with the radical literature of the 1860s and 1870s, which he discovered gathering dust in the library in Kokushkino. This accidental collection he would supplement with materials from the Kazan public library so that by the end of the summer he had acquired an impressive grasp of the social and political ideas of Russian populism. It was now, in the spring and summer of 1888, that Lenin first came upon Chernyshevsky, starting with his uncompromising articles in the *Sovremennik* and then moving on to his novel *What Is To Be Done?* which, according to one account, he read and reread five times in the space of this summer. It is, of course, hardly surprising that Lenin read Chernyshevsky's novel, for it had enjoyed a *succès de scandale* even among liberals and moderates. However, according to a chorus of commentators who cite Valentinov as their authority, *What Is To Be Done?* had a seminal and lasting influence on Lenin. Chernyshevsky is the key to explaining Lenin's impatient voluntarism: it was he who 'transformed Lenin's mind'.[10]

Lenin's own extreme reticence in autobiographical matters and the absence of detail in his sister's account of his intellectual evolution at this time leaves the field wide open for speculative reconstructions, too often based upon flimsy foundations. The fact that Lenin entitled one of his early works *What Is To Be Done?* might imply homage to Chernyshevsky, but no one has ever undertaken any rigorous analysis of the connection, if any, between the set of ideas there expressed and those of Chernyshevsky. We should distinguish between Lenin's admiration for Chernyshevsky as a person, as a symbol of revolutionary steadfastness, and his indebtedness to him in the realm of ideas.

When Lenin later praised Chernyshevsky (and he did so frequently), he had a clear immediate polemical purpose. Like Plekhanov, he always distinguished between the heroic and admirable phase of *revolutionary* populism in the sixties and

15

seventies and the passive, petty-fogging Legal Populism of the eighties and nineties. Chernyshevsky thus became a symbol in a polemical battle; he was held up as the paradigm examplar of total revolutionary commitment regardless of personal cost. He displayed par excellence that intransigent opposition to autocracy and barbarism characteristic of the Russian intelligentsia, a tradition abnegated by the Legal Populists, and taken up anew by militant Marxism. It is in this sense that Lenin appropriated Chernyshevsky; he was a militant, an intransigent, who refused to be seduced by the easy, comfortable illusions of gradualism. He was not, however, Lenin's chief mentor in the realm of ideas.[11]

In the autumn of 1888 Maria Aleksandrovna finally obtained permission for the family to return to Kazan to live and it was now that Lenin's contacts with the revolutionary movement in Russia first began. Perhaps it is something of a misnomer to refer to a 'movement' at all, for what we are concerned with were rather amorphous, ill-defined and short-lived groups which formed themselves on a very local basis around a prominent individual. They were relatively loosely organised circles, comprised almost exclusively of intelligentsia members of differing, and often very vague, political views. Invariably they had few, if any, contacts with other groups in their own locality, let alone with any regional or national association. We should remember that there was, at this time, no nationally or even regionally organised revolutionary party of any kind in Russia. After the assassination of the Tsar in 1881 government persecution had thoroughly decimated the *Narodnaya Volya*. All that was left were isolated veterans who attracted the radical youth with tales from the heroic period of revolutionary populism. One such veteran was Chetvergova, a celebrated *Narodovolets*,[12] whom Lenin regarded with considerable sympathy and whose circle in Kazan he occasionally frequented in the winter of 1888–9.[13] The fact that Lenin was, at this stage, more closely involved with the Jacobin, *Narodnaya Volya* veteran Chetvergova rather than with the explicitly Marxist circle in Kazan led by Fedoseev, has led some commentators to conclude that this was indicative of Lenin's whole ideological disposition and prophetic of his subsequent pattern of ideas. We should again beware of such over-simplified extrapolation for there are numerous scraps of evidence which point in another direction. We know, for instance, that Lenin's association with Chetvergova's

16

group coincided with the beginnings of his study of the first volume of Marx's *Capital*.[14] It seems probable indeed that it was precisely through one of the members of this circle, a student called Mandelshtam, that Lenin first heard an account of the views of the emigré Marxist Emancipation of Labour Group.[15] There is certainly nothing incongruous about a future Marxist beginning his revolutionary career in close contact with revolutionary populists. This was, after all, the milieu in which Plekhanov, Akselrod, Zasulich, Deich, Martov and Potresov, in short all the luminaries of Russian Marxism in the eighties and nineties, began their revolutionary activity. Far from being an exceptional beginning, this was the norm. Even as a fledgeling Marxist he would in any case have found a sympathetic hearing, for the *Narodovoltsi* were, and always had been, eclectics in their political and social views and were quite prepared to acknowledge Marx's eminence as a theorist of socialism. We should beware, therefore, of anachronistically reading back a definite ideological or organisational cleavage between the Social Democrats and the *Narodovoltsi* at this time.

Moreover, it may not have been at all easy for Lenin to gain entrance into Fedoseev's group; the Social Democrats in Russia were, until 1905 at least, obliged to be as secretive and conspiratorial as the *Narodovoltsi* themselves. *Agents-provocateurs* and spies had to be guarded against. Recruitment to the circles was generally through the recommendation of existing members. If Lenin knew none of the Social Democrats personally, and he certainly did not know Fedoseev,[16] he was unlikely to get in. As his sister Anna puts it:

> At that time . . . there were in Kazan a number of circles. But to unify them or even to meet together was impossible due to the contraints of conspiratorial activity.[17]

We would, in any case, be wrong to attach too much importance to Fedoseev's organisational activities at this period. At the time of his arrest Fedoseev was only eighteen and had been engaged in revolutionary activity among the youth of Kazan for less than two years.

It seems likely that at least one of the motives for the family move from the university town of Kazan to the more somnolent

city of Samara, in May of 1889, was to distance Vladimir from
the turbulence of revolutionary student politics which had already
claimed the life of the eldest son. Another reason might well
have been that the authorities were begining to move in real
earnest against the revolutionaries. Shortly after Lenin's departure
from Kazan, Fedoseev and his closest associates were arrested and,
at about the same time, even some members of Lenin's group
were taken into custody. Lastly, Lenin was preparing for the law
examinations at St Petersburg University where he had finally been
allowed to register as an external student. Lenin seems to have
spent the next year dividing his time between his legal studies
(which he completed with the equivalent of a first-class honours
in 1891[18]) and study of the classics of Marxism. He read Engels's
Condition of the Working Classes in England in 1844,[19] made an abstract
of Marx's *The Poverty of Philosophy*[20] and translated *The Communist
Manifesto*[21] into Russian. The manuscript of Lenin's translation was,
it seems, read in the revolutionary circles of Samara,[22] with which
he swiftly became associated. It is not extant. According to his
sister, Lenin was also reading in English the economic works of
David Ricardo and in Russian translation the many volumes of
The History of Civilisation in France by Guizot.[23]

THE SAMARA PERIOD: 1889–93

There can be little doubt that Lenin, by the time he arrived in
Samara at the age of nineteen, was already a Marxist. According
to Polevoi's thoroughly documented account, 'It ought not to be
forgotten, that, arriving in Samara, Lenin here found himself to
be the first and only Marxist'.[24] This may perhaps be something
of an exaggeration. According to the memoir material available,
it is none the less clear that the political exiles in Samara, who
dominated revolutionary circles, were exclusively Narodniks
influenced by Vorontsov, Yuzhakov and Mikhailovsky.[25] They therefore viewed Social Democracy as an alien implant without any
real basis in Russian conditions. None the less, according to Lenin's
sister there were some Social Democrats in Samara at that time,
though they were weak in numbers and mainly youngsters.[26]
Vodovozov, one of Lenin's antagonists of the time, recounts Lenin's
solid and wide-ranging knowledge, his linguistic abilities and his

understanding of *Capital* and a wide range of Marxist literature: 'He showed himself to be a convinced Marxist.'[27]

What little we know of Lenin's attitude towards the great famine of 1891–2 lends substance to this appraisal. Throughout Russia socialists of every hue made common cause with all the liberal and philanthropic elements of society to collect money and organise relief work for the starving peasantry. Almost alone of Samara radicals, Lenin disparaged this philanthropic do-gooding.[28] According to Vodovozov, Lenin asserted that the famine was an inevitable and necessary outcome of the development of capitalism in agriculture, which, objectively, the famine could only promote and accelerate by drawing into the cities the redundant surplus labour of inefficient peasant farming. Furthermore, the famine would compel the peasantry to contemplate the realities of capitalist society and would undermine its faith in the system capped by tsarism.

> It is easy to understand the desire of so-called 'society' to come to the assistance of the starving, to ameliorate their lot. This 'society' is itself part of the bourgeois order. The famine threatens to create serious disturbances and possibly the destruction of the entire bourgeois order. Hence the efforts of the well-to-do to mitigate the effect of the famine are quite natural. Psychologically this talk of feeding the starving is nothing but an expression of the saccharine sweet sentimentality so characteristic of our intelligentsia.[29]

Shub and others, maintain that here, for the first time, is the authentic voice of Lenin; so it might have been, but this was also the authentic voice of Plekhanov speaking through his lips. Plekhanov's analysis of the famine, *The Tasks of the Russian Social Democrats in the Famine (O zadachakh sotsialistov v borbe s golodom v Rossii)*,[30] followed exactly the same line; indeed, one is tempted to believe that perhaps Vodovozov's memory deceived him and that he attributed to Lenin the views of Plekhanov which the former was unlikely to be aware of at that time, though Plekhanov's pamphlet did not take long to arrive in Samara.[31] On Lenin's attitude towards the famine we can agree with Wolfe: 'Ulyanov was not making a policy of his own in any case, merely following his new leader, Plekhanov, of whom he was even then in the process of becoming a disciple.'[32]

19

Lenin swiftly entered into the life of the revolutionary circles in Samara obtaining introductions from his brother-in-law, Mark Timofeevich Elizarov, who was a local man and had, in fact, been a close friend of Aleksander Ulyanov in St Petersburg.[33] There is plenty of evidence that, from the start, Lenin began criticising the predominant Narodnik viewpoint and attempting to convert the leaders to his position. Within a fairly short period he had won over the most prominent leader of the Samara revolutionary youth to his cause – A. P. Sklyarenko, sometimes also known by his real name, Aleksei Vasilevich Popov. By early 1892 Lenin had managed to establish quite an impressive group around him, a group which emerged as a definite and cohesive force in Samara revolutionary politics. So successful indeed was the work of this group, led by the 'Troika' of Lenin, Lalayants (who had but lately arrived in Samara) and Sklyarenko, that, according to Belyakov's memoirs, by early 1892 'it was difficult to find a Narodnik circle since almost all of the young had become Marxist'.[34] This achievement should, however, be seen in proper perspective. In the first place the Narodniks though numerically pre-eminent in revolutionary circles in Samara at this time (as everywhere else in Russia) were in no sense a cohesive group. Not even the so-called adherents of *Narodnaya Volya* had any solid organisation; their 'adhesion' amounted to little more than vying with one another in recounting exciting episodes to the radical youth. In the second place it must be remembered that even Lenin and his group restricted themselves entirely to literary and scholarly endeavours. They made no attempt to proselytise beyond the ranks of the democratic intelligentsia and the youth. Their activity consisted essentially of self-education and public, but quite polite, debates with their Populist rivals.[35]

The self-education activities of the circle were, it seems, somewhat haphazard and extemporised, as Chuev admits: 'The circle had no defined programme of work.'[36] Sometimes the meeting consisted of no more than talk over tea, sometimes there would be a reading from and discussion of illegal literature, sometimes a member would read a paper, or give an abstract of a book. The circle defined itself and coalesced primarily by preparing for and participating in debates with other revolutionaries. Those who point to Lenin's association with prominent Populists and *Narodovoltsi* as evidence of his Jacobinism quite fail to understand the milieu in which he was operating at the time. Lenin and Sklyarenko were obliged to carry the battle of ideas into the Populist camp. They were, to an extent, dependent upon the good offices of Populists like Vodovozov in obtaining a wider audience and a chance to confront nationally known visiting Populists with their critique. Only by combating the most prominent Populist publicists could they solidify their own arguments, assuage the doubts of those with lingering Populist inclinations and win a more extensive following. There is, then, nothing incongruous about Lenin's contact with Populists, Jacobins and *Narodovoltsi*, notorious or otherwise. They formed the revolutionary milieu in Samara at that time, and they were the first targets for conversion by the young Marxists. The alternative for Sklyarenko and Lenin was for their circle to become an hermetically sealed, incestuous and ineffectual group.

That Lenin did swiftly emerge as the *enfant terrible* of the Samara Marxists in debate with the Populists cannot seriously be questioned. Those who hold that Lenin was at this time essentially a Jacobin Populist are obliged to ignore a very considerable volume of evidence which their accounts cannot accommodate. In particular, it was during this period that Lenin took on in open debate some of Russia's most prominent Populist spokesmen.

He first entered the lists, to considerable effect it seems, against M. V. Sabunaev who came to Samara in late December 1889 to establish a firm local basis for the attempt to revive the *Narodnaya Volya* party as the unifying umbrella for all revolutionary groups in Russia.. To this end he read to the Samara gathering a draft programme of 'The Union of Russian Social-Revolutionary Groups'. According to Belyakov, Sabunaev had little to say in response to Lenin's withering critique.[37] In pursuit of the same objective another prominent *Narodovolets*, Rosinovich, visited Samara in March 1891 and again Lenin led the Marxist critics, advancing a mass of carefully prepared statistical evidence to demonstrate that the so-called 'people's industry' had long become the breeding ground for capitalist development.[38]

Later, in the autumn of 1891 Maria Petrovna Golubeva (Yasneva), another veteran *Narodovolets*, arrived in Samara on the same mission. Her memoirs are freely utilised as evidence of Lenin's Jacobin position at this time. According to Yasneva, Lenin was greatly interested in the dictatorship of the proletariat and problems of the seizure of power – hardly astonishing interests for a revolutionary, particularly since Marx had himself appropriated elements of the Blanquist Jacobin teaching on these matters. It is rather unfortunate that those who cite Yasneva's memoirs in this connection invariably end their quotations before she outlines Lenin's objections to the Jacobin position. Yasneva recounts in particular his long discussions with her on the shadowy and inadequate class analysis of *Narodnaya Volya*.

> He could, however, in no way comprehend on what sort of 'people' we expected to base ourselves, and he began to explain at length that the people was not some kind of single and undifferentiated entity, that the people was comprised of classes with differing interests, etc.[39]

Yasneva's memoirs, far from being convincing evidence of Lenin's Jacobinism show him to be interested in those aspects of Jacobinism with which revolutionary Marxism had long associated itself while equally conventionally, condemning it for its obscurity in matters of class analysis.

Finally, in the second half of May 1892, the most celebrated Populist of the time, N. K. Mikhailovsky, came to Samara to stay with the Vodovozovs. Lenin and Sklyarenko were among the twenty or so leading Samara radicals invited to attend an impromptu lecture on 'The Narodnik Road to Socialism' which Mikhailovsky agreed to deliver. Again it was Lenin who was given the job of replying on behalf of the Marxists, and again he came well-prepared with statistical evidence demonstrating the collapse of the peasant commune and the growth of capitalism in peasant agriculture, concluding from this that the possibility of transforming the commune into the centre-piece of an egalitarian system had long since passed by. That Lenin's critique made a considerable impact upon Mikhailovsky is clear from the assessment he gave to Vodovozov after the meeting.

> Ulyanov is, without doubt, a very able individual, a powerful opponent. The clarity of his thought, the strength of his logic and his statistical preparation mark him out as a Marxist very dangerous to *narodnichestvo*. And that simplicity of exposition could in the future make of him a very important propagandist and writer.[40]

22

Mikhailovsky's prophecy was to come true more swiftly perhaps than he anticipated. Significantly Lenin's first venture into print was precisely the development of his critique of Mikhailovsky, published as Part I of *What the 'Friends of the People' Are* . . .

It was in the course of these debates that the Marxist group in Samara found its identity, and, through the successes of Lenin, Sklyarenko and Lalayants, began to secure a firm following. It is not disputed that Lenin 'spent the first six years of his revolutionary apprenticeship in close contact with some of the most outstanding Jacobin radicals in the Russian revolutionary movement'.[41] What is important is to tell a credible story from the evidence available about Lenin's *relations* with these people. There is, to say the least, powerful evidence to support the view that Lenin, by the end of his stay in Samara, had emerged as a thorough and unremitting Marxist critic of all brands of populism. Indeed, it was from this period that Lenin himself dated the commencement of his Social-Democratic activity. Filling in a questionnaire circulated to delegates at the Tenth Party Congress, Lenin replied to the section headed 'Participation in revolutionary movement' with the cryptic autobiographical comment, '1892–1893 Samara. Illegal Social-Democratic circles'.[42]

Lenin set himself three main tasks in this 'Samara Period': (1) the building up of an active specifically Marxist circle to take the initiative from the Narodniks and to win over the revolutionary youth of the region; (2) the deepening of his own, and his new colleagues', understanding of the theoretical bases of Marxism; (3) the application of Marxist theory to concrete conditions in Russia – the detailed study of economic statistics to confront the linchpin arguments of the Narodniks, their assertion that the commune was alive and flourishing and was the main hope for socialism in Russia.

We have briefly examined Lenin's attempts to realise the first of these tasks, his practical work in winning over adherents to the Marxist cause. We have also mentioned that Lenin undertook a translation of the *Communist Manifesto* and abstracts of some of the 'classics', which were circulated in manuscript and discussed in study sessions of the circles. In addition Lenin and his colleagues were clearly anxious to build up as comprehensive a library of socialist literature as was possible in Russia at that time. We know that Lenin utilised his visits to St Petersburg in 1890–92 in connection with his law exams to obtain materials for the Samara group. On the arrest of Sklyarenko in December 1893, much of this literature was seized by the authorities; it comprised an impressive collection with which we must suppose Lenin was quite familiar.

The police list of this library included, among other materials, the following:

The Manifesto of the Communist Party, The Rules of the International Working Men's Association, Capital, The Poverty of Philosophy, Marx's *Speech on Free Trade, Wage Labour and Capital*, Engels's *Socialism Utopian and Scientific*, Kautsky's, *The Economic Teaching of Karl Marx*, Jules Guesde's *Collectivism*, Blagoev's *Rabochii*, no. 1, of 1885 and a hectographed edition of *The Erfurt Programme*, publications of The Emancipation of Labour Group including Plekhanov's *Our Differences, Our Narodnik Men of Letters*, and *The All-Russian Destruction* and according to Lalayants, Engels's *Anti-Dühring* and his *Condition of the Working Class in England*, as well as many pamphlets from the journal *Neue Zeit* which were also readily available in Samara at that time.[43]

We not only have circumstantial evidence of what Marxist sources were *available* to Lenin at this time, we also have the internal evidence of Lenin's extant writings to confirm the view that Lenin was, by 1893, as thoroughly versed in Marxism as almost anyone in Russia at that time.

Lenin's first writings reflect his preoccupation with the third task he set himself – that of demonstrating the applicability of Marx's economic analysis to Russian conditions and, in the process, confronting the Populists on their chosen ground by challenging their conception of the peasantry as an homogeneous mass bound together by basically socialist inclinations and institutions. Lenin, and the group around him in Samara, were unique among Russian Marxists at that time in stressing the necessity of a close and detailed analysis of all the appropriate economic statistics relating to these problems. He set himself in particular to the study of agrarian economic statistics on the polarisation of the peasantry into kulaks and wage-labourers and the consequent break-up of the peasant commune. According to his sister:

Lenin busied himself now with studying materials for the application of that knowledge [of Marx and Engels] to Russian reality – the reading of statistical researches into the development of our industry, our land ownership, etc. Works of that generalising character hardly existed: it was necessary to study primary sources and on the basis of them to construct one's own conclusions.[44]

Lenin's brother has a similar confirmatory account of Lenin's interests at this time.

During these years Vladimir Ilich worked a lot on the statistics of peasant economy. The statistical evidence (the distribution of peasant households into groups according to the number of draught animals, the extent of their crops, rented land and suchlike) indicated a growth of economic inequality among the peasantry, the stratification of the peasantry into a well-to-do, economically strong group and a poor one, into a rural bourgeois and proletarian or semi-proletarian mass of peasants. These conclusions gave the lie to the Narodnik utopia of the homogeneity of the peasantry; they demonstrated the obvious fact of the development of capitalism in Russia. These conclusions confirmed the correctness of the Marxist political line of the Russian revolutionaries.

Ilich's comrades – Sklyarenko, Lalayants and Ionov – were also at that time occupied, as much as Vladimir Ilich himself, with the elaboration of statistical material on these questions.[45]

Lenin's access to the appropriate statistics on peasant life, perhaps also his lifelong insistence upon the tidy and proper arrangement of statistical data, owed not a little to a certain Ivan Markovich Krasnoperov who was a veteran of the Narodnik revolutionary movement of the 1870s, a personal friend indeed of the legendary Dobrolyubov[46] and now employed as head of the statistical bureau of the Samara Gubernia administration. Krasnoperov was no longer active in revolutionary circles but was a frequent visitor to the Ulyanovs.[47] It is reasonable to suppose that it was from him that Lenin imbibed his life-long regard for proper statistical preparation – an enduring trait in his writings, which, as we have seen, Mikhailovsky had already noted. (Lenin's works are spattered with angry outbursts against slipshod statisticians, tsarist and Soviet.)

There can be little doubt that Lenin distinguished himself by the seriousness and assiduousness with which he participated in these concrete attempts to apply Marxism to specific conditions in Russia. According to Semenov's recollections of the earnest meetings in Sklyarenko's rooms,

> Here he [Lenin] read us his papers, dealing, for the most part, with the questions of the economic development of Russia. Here we would examine the works of Nikolai . . . on [N. Danielson], Postnikov . . . and criticise from the Marxist standpoint the works of V.V. [V. P. Vorontsov], Karishev and other pillars of *Narodnichestvo* . . . For a long time I kept some of Vladimir Ilich's papers until they were confiscated in the recent series of searches. The pages of these papers were covered in small neat handwriting with numerous tables, with which at that time Vladimir Ilich was very fond of illustrating his account.[48]

The memoir material is again confirmed by reference to the *writings* of Lenin and Sklyarenko in this period. They submitted their first articles for publication in 1893. Both took as their subject the economic situation of the peasantry and factual evidence of economic differentiation within it. Lenin's effort (the earliest of his texts extant) was a review of V. I. Postnikov's book, *The Peasant Economy of South Russia* and was entitled *New Economic Developments in Russian Peasant Life*.[49] Sklyarenko published his piece, 'On the influence of bad harvests upon the distribution of horned cattle in peasant farming in Samara Uezd', in the *Samara Vestnik*.[50] Whether Lenin himself actually *initiated* this move towards a concrete and detailed study of Russian economic conditions by the Samara group is impossible to establish and perhaps fruitless to pursue. What is important for our purpose is that there is ample evidence to demonstrate that from the time of his *début* as a publicist of Marxism, Lenin seized upon the vital importance of demonstrating the correctness of his world view in the light of the particularities of Russian economic life. Until the turn of the century this task almost permanently absorbed him. The continuity of his pre-occupations in this respect can be traced in the titles of his major works of the period culminating in his *The Development of Capitalism in Russia*.[51] From the outset Lenin recognised that if Marxism was to prevail over the dominant Narodnik views, it would have to establish its *bona fides* as an explanatory and predictive model of Russian society in a far more scrupulous, detailed and refined manner than Plekhanov's generalised analyses of the 1880s had done.

Almost all of the memoirs of this period also speak of the importance of Lenin's more political and polemical papers against prominent Narodnik theorists which were circulated in manuscript in Samara and discussed in the revolutionary circles.[52] Lenin continued working on these papers in the summer of 1893, until the eve of his departure for St Petersburg.[53] These papers which Lenin wrote attacking Yuzhakov, Vorontsov and others, formed the basis of Part II of his first really important work, *What The 'Friends of The People' Are and How They Fight the Social Democrats*, published in hectographed edition in three parts (of which only two survive) in St Petersburg in 1894. The first part, which was an immediate reply to Mikhailovsky's critique of Marxism published in *Russkoe Bogatstvo* in 1884,[54] bore all the marks of hasty composition. Lenin was mainly concerned to score points off his opponent by exposing his inconsistencies. This first part showed little of the progression of Lenin's *own* viewpoints and was not very well thought out or presented. By comparison with Part III it was light-weight stuff and this largely because this third section had been thoroughly prepared over a period of two years in Samara. As his sister Anna noted, 'Lenin's papers on the works of V. V., Yuzhakov, and Mikhailovsky, read in the Samara circles, having later undergone some editing, comprised the three notebooks published under the general title: *What The 'Friends of the People' Are and How They Fight the Social Democrats*.[55] We may justifiably regard the very important third part of this work as the product of Lenin's Samara period, of those years, when he was already elaborating the principle themes which ran through all his later writings.

CONCLUSION

The objective of this chapter has been to dispute the widely accepted view that Lenin began his revolutionary career as a Jacobin. I have argued that the evidence obliges us to believe that early on Marxism became his principal, almost exclusive, intellectual obsession. (Eighteen is young enough, in all conscience, to take on volume one of *Capital*!) We know from the public disputes he was engaged in, from the testimony of his antagonists, from what we know of his reading habits, from his earliest writings and, finally, from what those closest to him at the time tell us of his preoccupations, that Lenin was, by 1893, an unremitting critic of Russian populism and an unusually erudite Marxist for one so young.

As to the question of the particular character of Lenin's Marxism at this time, that is, understandably, more difficult to demarcate, for his thought had obviously not yet fully matured. There are, nonetheless, some distinctive characteristics that had already emerged in this Samara period. There was in the first place Lenin's absorption with collecting and classifying data on Russian economic life, particularly in the sphere of agriculture. He was, from the outset of his career as a Marxist, concerned above all to attempt to demonstrate as rigorously as possible the quantitative growth of capitalism in Russia in order to rebut the Populists' contention that Russian economic life was still firmly based on the principles of natural economy. His economic analysis in turn provided confirmation of Plekhanov's contention that the Russian bourgeoisie was peculiarly weak and that therefore the proletariat would have to take over its role as the principal force in the struggle for democracy in Russia.[56] Finally, Part III of Lenin's *What The 'Friends of the People' Are . . .* already contains the bare bones of his singular and central idea of the proletariat as the vanguard and natural representative of all Russia's exploited, an idea which allowed him to formulate, from within the precepts of Russian Marxist orthodoxy, the potent notion of a proletarian–peasant alliance. In many respects, therefore, Lenin's stock of pivotal ideas had already been arrived at. Later chapters show how they were integrated, developed and refined.

By the time that Lenin left Samara for St Petersburg in the autumn of 1893 he had already undertaken a considerable theoretical apprenticeship in the texts of Marx, Engels and Plekhanov; he was also practised in the conspiratorial arts of revolutionary circle activity. He had commenced his career as a Marxist publicist and was committed to the detailed application of the general theory of Marxism to Russian economic conditions. For a man of twenty-three years this was, as his St Petersburg colleagues quickly realised, a formidable combination of talents.

CHAPTER 2

The Background of Orthodoxy

I have maintained that the evidence obliges us to believe that Lenin early identified himself, and was regarded by his contemporaries, as a Marxist. We can now move on to consider a more interesting problem. To say that Lenin, at the time of his arrival in St Petersburg, was a convinced and practised Marxist does not, of itself, tell us a great deal about the structure of his ideas. We need to go beyond this to ask the questions, what *sort* of a Marxist was he and what were the distinctive characteristics of his interpretation of the doctrine? In answering these questions it is equally clear that we must first establish the basic outlines of the stock-in-trade of ideas which Lenin accepted as orthodox Marxism. To know whether there was any originality or deviation in Lenin's ideas in his early years as a Marxist we must first of all attempt, however briefly, to re-establish *the conception of Marxism that was current at that time and in that milieu.*

I have emphasised the contextual setting since it seems that commentators too frequently take an hypostatised version of the 'essence' of Marxism to which an equally abstracted Leninism is counterposed, and they frequently conclude from this exercise that Lenin was less than a Marxist. It is as if we, from the standpoint of the 1970s, were to condemn Lenin for his one-sided version of Marxism because he took no stock of the *Paris Manuscripts* or the *Grundrisse*. Marxism as an academic enterprise alters in its emphases over time every bit as much as does Marxism as an operational code. The history of the spread of Marxism is also an object lesson in how doctrines and ideologies change their character not merely temporally but also spatially. The set of generalised formulae have to be applied to time and place, the particularities of the new milieu have to be satisfactorily explained and integrated into the theory. Marxism, moreover, sets out not simply to explain but to change

29

the world, and so an integral part of this application to time and place must be the positing of a plan of action, a strategy to achieve change. Marxism in this sense cannot be construed as a a static body of classical texts; it is, like all doctrines, subject to change, adaptation and new emphases. Our points of reference in considering Lenin's degree of orthodoxy are not so much the texts of Marx and Engels as those of his Russian Marxist predecessors and contemporaries considered by the Russian movement to be unimpeachably orthodox.

It would be useful at this point to recall the distinction made earlier between the basic theoretical analysis of Russian Marxism and the practical political recommendations which were derived from it. We are concerned here with the two levels upon which Marxism operated, the level of theory and that of practice, and it would be as well to specify what is intended when these terms are used.

At the primary level Russian Marxism had long established the main outlines of its theoretical posture. It had undertaken an analysis of economic trends and class configurations within Russian society and defined the particular position of the working class vis-à-vis other classes. It had specified the stage of evolution arrived at by the working class and shown the degree of capitalist development in Russia. On the basis of this theoretical assessment the founding fathers of Russian Marxism early established the appropriate objectives of Social-Democratic practice. The theoretical appraisal defined the parameters of the possible in practical political terms. It demonstrated the particular strengths of the proletariat, but set limits to the objectives at which it could reasonably aim given the comparative backwardness of capitalism in Russia.

By the time that Lenin arrived in St Petersburg this dual task, of applying Marx's economic analysis to Russian conditions and teasing from the findings of theory appropriate practical policies had been going on for a decade. Clear guidelines on theory and practice had already been established. The Emancipation of Labour Group had been responsible for this and subsequent generations of Russian Marxists did not, of course, begin with a clean sheet of infinite possibility. They inherited a tradition and consciously identified with its assumptions, its axioms and its mode of discourse, for that was what being a Russian Marxist meant. The disciples could, of course, amplify and extend the theoretical findings and practical prescriptions but, as with all acolytes of an ideology, they had to recognise certain limits. They recognised certain tenets of Russian Marxism which defined it as an autonomous political tendency, i.e., distinguished it from all competing tendencies. These characteristic and distinctive ideas of theory and practice I refer to in this chapter and subsequently as the 'orthodoxy' of Russian Marxism.

Russian Marxists working in exile had, since the 1880s, been concerned with precisely the task of applying Marxism to Russia. For ten years they had continued their theoretical labours in virtual isolation from any sympathisers in Russia until the early nineties, when groups of Marxists began to emerge in the major cities. Their contact with Russia was, to say the least, sporadic and episodic. Samuel Baron puts it succinctly: 'In the decade 1883–93, the few organisations in Russia that sought to mobilise industrial workers arose independently of the emigré Marxists.'[1] It was not in fact until the emigrés encountered Lenin that they had any regular or systematic relations with activists in Russia. As Akselrod recounts, 'with the appearance of Ulyanov on our horizon we finally established more or less regular relations with Russia'.[2]

PLEKHANOV'S CONTRIBUTION

If we are searching for the common stock of ideas which united and defined a Marxist in Russia in the 1890s, we need look no further than to Plekhanov's works of the 1880s and early 1890s. The position of Plekhanov as the fountain-head and guardian of the orthodoxy of Russian Marxism throughout the nineteenth century was unassailable. He was respected and renowned for his reputation as a convinced revolutionary before becoming a Marxist. As a Russian Marxist he was the first on the field and confirmed his pre-eminence by his enormous erudition, his urbanity and wit, his association with Engels and subsequently with the pope of European socialism, Karl Kautsky himself. To the Russian Marxists of the nineties he was regarded as a demi-god – a living link with the original masters, a Russian accepted by them as an equal. Lenin recounted the reverential awe with which he set off on his pilgrimage to Geneva to be inducted into the presence: 'Never, never in my life, had I regarded any other man with such sincere respect and veneration, never had I stood before any man so "humbly".'[3] Other memoirists of this period tell the same tale; in their intellectual development Plekhanov was the brightest star in the firmament for he had first illuminated the way out of the impasse at which Russian socialism found itself at the beginning of the eighties. The naive hopes of instinctive peasant revolutionism had foundered in the 'Going to the People'; the Jacobin Tkachevist alternative of individual terror had, if anything, proved even more counter-productive.[4] Was there then no hope for that freedom and social justice which the broad-natured Russian intelligentsia had so long held before them as sacred goals? Hope there was, Plekhanov replied, but the road would be long and hard: success could not come at a stroke and the attainment of the great ideals would demand a total reorientation of the old economic, social and political analyses. It would demand, in short, the espousal of the integrated Marxist world-view in its relation to Russia.

The main outlines of Plekhanov's translation of Marxism to Russian conditions are clearly established in the first major pamphlets he wrote as a Marxist, *Socialism and the Political Struggle* (1883) and *Our Differences* (1885). They remained, throughout the nineteenth century, the most authoritative texts of Russian Marxism.[5] For those in the emergent Marxist groups of the nineties the ideas contained in these pamphlets were eagerly seized upon and refurbished to serve in the perennial struggle of ousting the predominant Populist and Neo-Populist position. They consciously identified themselves as disciples of Plekhanov's ideas. Martov, Lenin and the rest of the St Petersburg circle known as the *stariki* considered themselves no more than popularisers and developers of Plekhanov's original position. Their writings throughout the nineties returned time and again to the themes and theses of the master, which he continued to set before them in such works as *A New Champion of Autocracy*, *The Tasks of the Russian Social Democrats in the Famine* and his authoritative *The Development of the Monist View of History*.

We must begin our short examination of Plekhanov's contribution to the orthodoxy by outlining his economic analysis of Russian society. Plekhanov's own intellectual biography, as well as the Marxism he came to espouse, make this the obvious starting point. In terms of his intellectual biography it was two rather specialised monographs on Russian economics that raised in him serious doubts about his Populist faith in the peasant commune. Economic doubts led him to Marxism, and, in the logical structure of Marxism, the designation of the economic level of any society was the basis from which all analyses of class, consciousness, ideology and politics in general were held to proceed.

As a Populist Plekhanov had staked his faith in the peasant commune. It was the commune, with its periodic redistribution of land according to size of family and need, that was the institutional expression of the peasants' search for social justice and socialism. The continued existence of a system of natural economy, localised and self-sufficient, producing for immediate consumption and not for the market, was preserved by the communal land-holding system. This communalistic system was the mark of Russia's uniqueness and of her grand destiny. Russia's uniqueness consisted in the fact that, alone among the nations of Europe, the commune had saved her people[6] from all the baneful attributes of capitalism. The cleavage into rich and poor, the self-seeking narrowness of bourgeois culture, its division of labour, its division between town and country – from all this atomisation and tawdry dehumanisation in spiritual as well as in material terms, Russia had been spared by the grace of the commune. The Russian people, through their institutions, preserved a sense of integral community. They refused to tolerate the proletarianisation of the great majority in the interests of the few; they remained an homogeneous mass. The instincts and institutions of primitive communism survived, and herein was the pointer to Russia's great destiny. Russia's mission was, in view of this happy conjunction of circumstances, to show the world the path to socialism, and her peasants were the force which would effect the transition.

The economic and sociological basis of this Populist ideal derived from Haxthausen's massive study of the commune, published in the late forties and early fifties.[7] Haxthausen's work may indeed be claimed as a main source of the initial formulation of Populist thought in that it certainly inspired Herzen to reconsider his view of the commune.[8] Subsequent major theorists of Populism, Bakunin, Petrashevsky and Chernyshevsky,[9] all leaned heavily upon Haxthausen in vindication of their belief in the continued vitality of the commune in Russia. It would not be too much to maintain that the economic analysis of Populism, the 'objective reality' in which its ideals were grounded, was supplied largely

33

by Haxthausen and was in this sense completed by the early 1850s and remained, subsequently, articles of faith rather than a set of hypotheses that needed constantly to be checked anew.

Plekhanov, in common with most Populists at the end of the seventies, felt the need for his ideal of socialist revolution to be firmly rooted in the objective reality of Russian life. He accepted the determining influence of the prevailing mode of production on social and political life. Indeed, in an essay written in late 1878, 'The Law of the Economic Development and Problems of Socialism in Russia',[10] he used this Marxian hypothesis to confirm the rectitude of his Populist creed. The self-sufficient peasant commune (or *obshchina*), with its collectivist land-holding system was, he contended the main productive unit in Russia and therefore the future of Russia would be based on the extremely decentralised collectivism of autonomous productive units. Bakunin's slogan of the free federation of self-governing communes becomes in this metamorphosis not a negation of historical materialism but an accurate reflection of its operation in Russia. Plekhanov cited the example of the Don Cossacks in evidence of his thesis; there the land was held by separate *obshchinas* but nonetheless any member could move from *obshchina* to *obshchina* and retain his right to an allotment of land. 'And such a land [holding] federation of *obshchinas* is conceivable in any country, where the *obshchina* principle is not distorted by countervailing influences.'[11] It was his opinion that these countervailing influences had not as yet had any great impact on Russia. The vast majority of the population were peasants holding land of the *obshchina*. 'Therefore, so long as the majority of our peasantry adhere to the land-holding *obshchina*, we cannot maintain that our homeland has set off on the course of that law according to which capitalist production would be an essential stage in its path to progress.'[12] There were, of course, manufacturing centres in Russia, and agitation among the wage-workers in these centres must become a focal point for the activities of the revolutionary. The workers in manufacturing industry were, however, not conceived of as a quite separate stratum of the population, but were viewed as urban peasants still primarily absorbed with the question of land ownership. These urban peasants were worthy of special attention since their very concentration in large work units made them more amenable to organisation and their separation from conservative family and village ties made them more susceptible to radical agitation. They were destined, therefore, to become the catalysts through which socialist ideas spread outwards to the villages.

> The agrarian question, the question of the independence of the *obshchina*, land and freedom, are equally close to the heart of the worker, as to the peasant. In a word he is not estranged from the peasant mass, but a part of this very peasantry. Their task is one and the same – their struggle can and must be one and the same.[13]

Plekhanov in 1878 was still steeped in the pure stuff of Populism. The land question remained the paramount question; its full communalisation and democratic distribution would be the implementation of socialism. This realisation of socialism would be carried out by the peasants led by their most accessible and conscious detachment – the peasant-workers of the manufacturing centres.

Within two years Plekhanov was obliged to alter this scenario for revolutionary change almost beyond recognition. A causal factor in this metamorphosis was the publication of Orlov's *Communal Property in the Moscow District*. This painstaking study was, in effect, the first detailed analysis of the economic and social composition of the commune since Haxthausen's work. Admittedly M. M. Kovalevsky's earlier study had adduced general sociological evidence from the decline of the commune in many countries, to suggest that economic differentiation, and the clash of interests this produced, was something inherent within the structure of the commune and was the main cause of its decline. What Orlov did was to point to evidence which vindicated this general precept in the particular experience of the Russian commune. Differentiation of the Russian peasantry was proceeding and was increasing in tempo; it was at once symptom and result of the tendency for the period of time between redistributions of the land to get longer and longer. The rich peasants were consolidating their holdings, renting land from the poorer peasants, employing them and their draught animals for appallingly low return. The idyll upon which Populism had been based for so long was exposed for what it was. The peasant commune, according to Orlov, was already degenerating, riven into hostile groups, its natural economy succumbing to the advances of capitalist agriculture and manufacture. 'It is scarcely to be wondered at that Orlov's work "strongly shook" Plekhanov's populist convictions, as he himself later reported.'[14]

Within three years Plekhanov had not only rejected the central tenets of his old faith, he had also arrived at a new one and had spelled out the tactical implications of Marx's general theories in their application to Russia. This he did in a lengthy essay published in 1883 entitled *Socialism and the Political Struggle*,[15] the themes of which were amplified in its even lengthier sequel of two years later, *Our Differences*.[16]

THE ECONOMIC ANALYSIS OF RUSSIAN SOCIETY

The methodology Plekhanov bequeathed to the Russian movement was to become one of its most characteristic distinguishing features. Following him the Russian Social Democrats took the dialectic far more seriously than their West European counterparts. This may perhaps be explained by the fact that throughout the nineteenth century, arguably until 1917, Russian Social Democracy remained almost exclusively an intelligentsia movement. In the absence of a strong labour movement or a mass party with all their countervailing pressures and tendency to seek for partial reforms, the intelligentsia needed the security, or could afford the luxury, of proper method and undiluted theoretical orthodoxy. The orthodox were indeed, as we shall see later, self-consciously aware of the very real threat of eclecticism and the search for partial ameliora-tion which the very emergence of a strong labour movement posed to them. As a movement of intellectuals, Russian Social Democracy displayed, as many have pointed out, an obsessive concern with 'fundamentals'. In their analysis of Russian economic conditions, and in the way in which they regarded the situation of differing classes, one sees continuously the methodological predisposition to search out contradictions. They were, too, far more preoccupied with *movement* than Western Social Democrats appeared to be. They were concerned to demonstrate how the phases of the evolution of industry or class consciousness succeed one another in the progress towards final *dénouement*. Many see all of this as evidence of the continued vitality of eschatological trends in the Russian tradition; it can equally well be seen as what it declared itself to be – the conscious application of Marxist dialectics.

Plekhanov, in his analysis of Russian economic life, stressed time and again the all-importance of Marxist and Hegelian dialectical method. He argued that the task of the social scientist (and by implication of the Marxist revolutionary) was not merely to register the *existing* economic and social dispositions, but rather to demarcate a *process* of development. The revolutionary must be interested in dynamics, not statics; he must consider social and economic relations not as they are, but as they are becoming.[17] This forward look, with its implied teleology, was to be as fundamental to Lenin's world-view as it was to Plekhanov's. It was a feature of the orthodox in general that they assessed each phase of the evolution of industry, or of consciousness, in the proportion that it contributed to the unfolding of the next phase – a viewpoint that was to have profound implications for their practical political recommendations.

Plekhanov, in his analysis of Russian economic life, was sensitive to the repeated Populist charge that the Marxists were merely appropriating universal formulae and traducing Russian reality in forcing the facts to fit them. He retorted that there was nothing supra-historical about Marx's so-called 'inevitable laws', and their dialectical operation. They did not claim an absolute and necessary sovereignty over the course of development in all countries. What they did suggest however was that, once a country had commenced on the road towards capitalism, *then*, unless countervailing forces were sufficiently powerful, its course of development would adhere to certain known processes. As Plekhanov expressed it later, in another classic of orthodoxy, *The Development of the Monist View of History*:

The dialectical materialists 'reduce everything to economics'. We have already explained how this is to be understood. But what are economics? They are the sum-total of the actual relationships of the men who constitute the given society, in their process of production. These relationships do not represent a motionless metaphysical essence. They are eternally changing under the influence of the development of the productive forces, and under the influence of the historical environment surrounding the given society. Once the actual relations of men in the process of production are given, there fatally follow from these relations certain consequences. In this sense social movement conforms to law, and no one ascertained that conformity to law better than Marx. But as the economic movement of every society has a '*peculiar*' form in consequence of the '*peculiarity*' of the conditions in which it takes place, there can be no 'formula of progress' covering the past and foretelling the future of the economic movement of *all* societies.[18]

Plekhanov's main methodological attack on the Populists was that they failed to apprehend this movement and inter-connection in the process of development. The commune was the repository of all their ideals and they were blind to the forces which were acting to undermine it. They saw the principles of the commune and those of capitalism as totally separate and incompatible. They may be incompatible, Plekhanov retorted, but they were far from separate. In the actual processes that took place in Russia, it was clear that they were dialectically inter-related; in fact capitalism grew out of the peasant commune.

The task which Plekhanov set himself in his early works was a many-faceted one. It involved, as he put it, the rendering down of Marx's algebraic general formula to its more specific arithmetical tenability in Russian conditions.[19] When this had been accomplished, and if it were discovered that Russia had entered the early phases of capitalist development, then certain general predictions about its future economic development could be made. The economic analysis carried with it certain conclusions about the evolving configuration of class relationships. It would be found that certain classes were waning, others coming into being and growing in numbers. The task of the Social Democrat was to register and be aware of the future evolution of these processes and to formulate political tactics accordingly.

In his new economic analysis of Russian society Plekhanov had no hesitation in declaring that already in the early 1880s 'not only the immediate future but the present of our country, too, belongs to capitalism',[20] that 'our capitalism can become, and we have seen that it is becoming, the exclusive master in Russia'.[21] Russia, Plekhanov insisted, will 'finish the school [of capitalism] she has *already begun*'.[22] The crucial factor in prompting this development was, according to Plekhanov, the 1861 Reform emancipating the serfs. The emancipation of the serfs was not, Plekhanov contended, to be viewed simply as an act of enlightened and benevolent despotism; its motive was far more mundane and pressing. The emancipation was occasioned by the state's need for money to sustain the bureaucracy, army and police upon which the regime depended for its future existence.

> To maintain the institutions which Peter had introduced into Russia the need was, first, money, second, money, third, money. By the very fact of squeezing this money out of the people, the government was contributing to the development of commodity production in our country. Then, in order to maintain those same institutions, there had to be at least some kind of factory industry.[23]

The transmutation of labour service obligations into cash obligations was to set in train a host of consequences all destructive of the ancestral economy of the commune. The emancipation proved to be the swan song of the old self-sufficient natural economy because it introduced for the first time the necessity for the peasants to obtain cash to meet their redemption payments. The peasants were now obliged to produce goods for the market; they became commodity producers for the first time. Some, inevitably, failed to meet their redemption payments and they rapidly became indebted to the richer peasants and were forced, as their only means of repayment, to sell their labour power to the kulaks and to let their allotments to them.

The mode of repayment of redemption monies stood, Plekhanov argued, in flagrant contradiction to the communalistic principles of the *mir*. *Collective* landholding could not for long survive the enormous tensions resulting from the enforcement of *individual* assessment and responsibility for repayments. The larger peasant households which received proportionately more of the land, who therefore were the richest members of the village communities, quite naturally contributed most towards the communal redemption obligations. By this very token they exerted all their powerful influence to prevent frequent redistributions of the land which might deprive their families of lands, which had, in a real sense, been paid for and redeemed by decades of hard work by their families.[24] The fact of payment, of paying to the communal redemption fund for a clearly demarcated plot gave rise to a kind of *de facto* right, a natural feeling that having faithfully paid the instalments on the goods for so long, some kind of title to the goods was established. The richer peasants naturally did

39

everything they could to prevent the commune redistributing the lands, which had cost them so dear, to some ne'er-do-well who had contributed not a kopek to their redemption.

The designs of the rich peasants found support among the poorest peasants, for they, too, from economic desperation, were compelled to strive for the dissolution of the communal land-holding system. The small allotments they received no longer served as a means of preserving their independence. On the contrary they became an encumbrance to them, forcing them into ever greater dependence on usurers and the rich peasants. For the twenty-five per cent of peasant households without horses, the ideal of agricultural self-sufficiency and independence was, Plekhanov argued, totally illusory. They had neither the capital to farm their land nor could they afford the repayments on it demanded by the commune; legally they could not renounce their share, nor could they move to another village in search of employment. They were in the impossible situation of being quite unable to cultivate their plots and equally impotent to renounce their title to them.[25] Indeed, many communes demanded substantial payment in return for allowing a peasant to renounce his land, and this they were obliged to do since in many instances the repayments demanded considerably exceeded, sometimes almost doubled, the net income from the land. 'Hence it follows that the poor peasant "released by the *mir*" [that is, by the commune] must in the majority of cases pay a certain sum every year for the right to give up their plot and be free of movements.'[26] The poor peasants who remained in the villages were obliged to seek outside employment, either in labour service to rich peasants, or in local manufactories, simply in order to be able to meet the redemption payments demanded of them. In this way there was created a vast mass of rural semi-proletarians who had to sell their labour power if they were to exist. The class objectives of the trading and merchant classes and rich peasantry were achieved and the intrusion of money led inevitably to pressure to increase the mobility of individual property and labour.[27] The preconditions for the advance to the phase of manufacture, the 'release' of vast numbers of workers on to the labour market, had been achieved at the cost of the progressive loss of financial independence for great numbers of the peasantry. Many millions of peasants were obliged to sell their labour, not all on a regular basis perhaps, but their conversion to full-time paid hands of capitalist agriculture or manufacture was but a matter of time.[28] It was of no avail bemoaning the process, Plekhanov argued; it existed and would proceed according to known laws. Indeed, the sooner the process of alienating the peasant and handicraftsman from the land was accomplished, the better it would be – better first in the sense that being grouped together as workmen in capitalist enterprises, their material conditions would improve, and better in a more profound sense in that they would escape the narrow horizons, the conservativism and mindless existence of 'toiling machines' to which life within the isolated communes had reconciled them. The industrial revolution, Plekhanov maintained, enthusiastically endorsing Engels, 'tore the workers out of their "apathetic indifference to the universal interests of mankind" and "drew them into the whirl of history" '.[29] They emerged, in short, as a 'world historical' class sharing common interests with their brothers in other lands.

The uprooting of the peasantry was, in this sense, the necessary first phase in the onward march of capitalism. As such it was progressive for it liberated new forces of production, pre-eminently labour power itself, without which capitalist manufacture would be impossible. By depriving the peasants of their independence it simultaneously created a national market of dimensions previously unimagined. What the peasant previously produced for immediate consumption, he had now to purchase on the market. The scene was set for the advent of the phase of manufacture; the fate of the commune was already sealed by the irreversible consequences of the advent of a money economy. To indulge in romantic illusions about the possibility of resuscitating it as a basis for socialist advance, as the populists contrived to do, was to consign oneself to the futility of utopianism. Plekhanov had made the final breach with the past, his judgement on the commune was final and irrevocable.

All the principles of modern economy, all the springs of modern economic life are irreconcilably hostile to the village community. Consequently, to hope for its further independent 'development' is as strange as to hope for a long life and further development of a fish that has been landed on the bank.[30]

In similar fashion the independence of the peasant handicrafts-men was disrupted by the incursion of commodity production. Whereas previously the handicraftsman made to order for a specific client, now he produced for an anonymous market.[31] The handi-craftsmen, too, became indebted to the more wealthy peasants and to the merchants who marketed their produce.

> The handicraftsmen have not yet felt competition from big indus-trial capital, but the role of exploiter is fulfilled with distinction by their peasant brothers or the merchants who provide them with raw material and buy up their finished product.[32]

From this situation it was but a small step to the stage where the handicraftsman became merely a wage-labourer or piece worker for a manufacturer engaged in 'the domestic system of large-scale production', a situation already arrived at by large numbers of handicraft weavers who had now completely lost their old independence.[33]

What Plekhanov was seeking to demonstrate was that capitalism in its nascent phases of development was not at all a phenomenon isolated in the major industrial and manufacturing centres. It had, on the contrary, penetrated the economic relationships of even the smallest village and had disrupted the ancestral economy of the peasant commune. The degree of capitalist penetration was to be measured not by the prevalence of large-scale factory production but by the existence of wage labour. The creation of a mass of wage-labourers, involving the erosion of the inde-pendence of artisan and peasantry, was a necessary prerequisite to the further progress of capitalism and it occurred long before factory production *per se* had become dominant. It occurred *par excellence* in the manufacturing period.

The 'manufacturing period' had, for Plekhanov, certain definite connotations; it was one of the early phases in the evolution of capitalism to which certain special features attached. According to Plekhanov's analysis, and that of the orthodox generally, it was precisely this phase of capitalism which Russia was undergoing in the 1880s and 1890s. Akselrod, in his authoritative *Present Tasks and Tactics*, located the general situation of Russia as already firmly within the phase of 'manufacturing capitalism', though some sectors still had not completed the process of 'primitive accumulation'.[34]

Plekhanov cited and relied heavily upon Marx's description of the period of capitalist manufacture in part seven of the first volume of *Capital,* where Marx concluded that the main object and result of this phase was to produce

> a new class of small villagers who, while following the culti-
> vation of the soil as an accessory calling, find their chief
> occupation in industrial labour, the products of which they sell
> to the manufacturers directly, or through the medium of
> merchants.
>
> Modern industry alone, and finally, supplies in machinery,
> the lasting basis of capitalistic agriculture, expropriates
> radically the enormous majority of the agricultural population,
> and completes the separation between agriculture and domestic
> industry.[35]

Plekhanov's conclusion was that 'At present we are going through that very process of the gradual conquest of our national industry by manufacture.'[36] The stage of manufacture in its turn was eventually displaced by factory production proper where the marginal 'independence' of the peasant/wage-worker was finally eclipsed. At first the peasants' entitlement to small plots was to the advantage of the manufacturer. He was able to pay incredibly low wages since part of the subsistence of the workers was eked from their agricultural work. As they and their lands became increasingly impoverished, as they must, the situation changed. The manufacturer was obliged to increase wages

> to the level of the famous minimum of the workers' requirements.
> Then it is more profitable to exploit the worker in the factory,
> where the productivity of labour increases by its very collective-
> ness. Then comes the era of large-scale machine industry.[37]

Certain branches of Russian industry had already entered this phase of capitalist production, notably spinning and weaving, and

> the phenomena observed in more advanced branches of industry
> must be considered prophetic as regards other spheres of industry.
> What happened there yesterday can happen here today,
> tomorrow or in general in a not distant future.[38]

Throughout we must notice how consistently Plekhanov adhered to his stated methodology. The Social Democrats, he argued, must see things not as they are but as they are becoming. In its application to the study of economics this dialectical precept clearly enjoined upon the Social Democrats a study of the laws and tendencies of capitalist development as they had been experienced elsewhere and summarised in *Capital*. It also obliged them to view Russian economic life as a process of development with its own in-built teleology. Capitalism revealed itself in many ways, each of its early phases was but a necessary, if temporary, premise for advance to the next phase. All of this, given adequate knowledge of the appropriate laws, was a predictable and necessary process culminating in the socialisation of labour and complementary concentration of capital on a vast scale. Throughout the Social Democrats must take as their yardstick conditions in the most advanced sectors of industry. Knowledge of the laws of capitalist development, foreknowledge, therefore, of the evolving social composition of the population, gave the Social Democrats immense advantages over their opponents. They were endowed with a kind of prescience in ascertaining the future configuration of things.

> For us, what *is coming into being* is the necessary result of what *is becoming obsolete*. If we know that *such a thing*, and *no other* is coming into being, we are indebted for this to the objective process of social development, which prepares us to know *what is coming into being*.[39]

I have dwelt on Plekhanov's economic analysis at some length, not only because doubts over the validity of his earlier economic analysis *prompted* his conversion to Marxism, but also because *as a Marxist* the new economic analysis of Russian society was the theoretical basis from which class analysis and political strategy and tactics were explicitly derived. For all that, there is about Plekhanov's attempts at economic analysis a certain question mark. He did not pursue the more explicitly 'economic' aspects of his thought at any great length. There is nowhere in the very extensive publications he put out in the eighties and nineties any detailed study of Russian economic conditions. His arguments tend to convince more by the bold authority with which they were pronounced than by the volume of data substantiating them. The gaps in his

early economic analysis are no doubt largely explicable in terms
of the absence of reliable statistical data upon which to work.
It was not until the mid-eighties and the nineties that the Zemstvo
statisticians began to produce impressive abstracts of reliable data
on the situation of the peasant farmers and handicraftsmen. That
Plekhanov did not make a great deal of use of this new material
to update his analysis was however, due more to temperamental
disinclination than to circumstantial reasons. He was not particularly enamoured of economics; he was quite willing to leave
to others, in particular to Lenin, the difficult and detailed work
of amassing the substantive evidence for the schema he had roughly
outlined.

CLASS ANALYSIS AND THE LOCATION OF THE PROLETARIAT AS THE DRIVING FORCE OF THE DEMOCRATIC REVOLUTION

Plekhanov's economic analysis led him to the conclusion that
capitalism was evolving within Russia and that in accordance with
the laws of its evolution manufacture would give way to large-
scale factory production – the peasant dependent upon outside
employment would give way to the wage-worker pure and simple.
The proletariat was, therefore, the class of the future in Russia;
its plight was prophetic of the fate of huge numbers of peasants
and handicraftsmen as the earlier economic analysis made plain.
The proletariat was the 'special and essential product' of modern
industry; 'the other classes decay and finally disappear' in face
of it.[40] Plekhanov utilised here Marx's equally prophetic and teleological formulations from the *Communist Manifesto* and applied
them to Russia. Russia was clearly set upon the capitalist path.
This meant that the twin processes of the concentration of capital
and socialisation of labour would progressively erode the
economic bases of all other classes save the proletariat and the
bourgeoisie. The general law of capitalist development specified
that 'industrial progress is constantly accompanied by a relative
increase in constant capital which is extremely harmful to small
producers'.[41] The small man, the peasant or handicraftsman, later
the small-scale merchant and manufacturer were forced out of
business and precipitated into the ranks of the proletariat. The
strategic implication of this was that the Social Democrats, with
their foreknowledge of this development, could distribute their

45

forces accordingly and concentrate their major attention on the proletariat which was emerging as the dominant class of Russian society. To it, rather than to the peasant, the future belonged.

'In the conception of the Social Democrat the working class is a powerful, eternally mobile and inexhaustible force which alone is able now to lead society to progress.'[42] For the first time there had emerged, out of what Herzen had lamented as the 'prostrate crowd' of the Russian people, a dynamic historical actor, a Promethean force which would finally shake Russia out of its Asiatic barbarism and complete its Europeanisation.[43] The passive, condescending view of the Utopian Socialists of the proletariat simply as the 'most suffering class'[44] must be entirely jettisoned for, according to Plekhanov, the proletariat was the only force capable of bringing the autocracy to its knees.[45]

It was a crucial element of the orthodoxy of Russian Social Democracy that the revolutionary movement against autocracy and for the democratisation of Russian life could attain success only under the leadership of the proletariat. *This was the central precept of the political strategy of orthodoxy upon which Plekhanov, as much as Lenin, was insistent.* 'In conclusion I repeat – and I insist upon this important point: the revolutionary movement in Russia will triumph only as a *working-class movement* or else it will never triumph!'[46] Plekhanov's formulation of the leading role of the proletariat in the democratic revolution was endorsed and emphasised in virtually all the main programmatic statements of the R.S.D.L.P. in the 1890s. In the *Programme of the Social-Democratic Emancipation of Labour Group*,[47] it was expressed in this way: '. . . our socialist intelligentsia has been obliged to head the present-day emancipation movement, whose direct task must be to set up free political institutions in our country . . .'. Even more forcibly the manifesto of the First Congress of the R.S.D.L.P. insisted that due to the weakness, cowardice and baseness of the bourgeoisie in Russia the

Russian working class must and will carry on its powerful shoulders the cause of achieving political liberation . . . The Russian proletariat will itself throw off the yoke of autocracy in order to continue with greater energy to fight against capitalism and against the bourgeoisie to the complete victory of socialism.[48]

The same insistence upon the leading role of the proletariat in overthrowing autocracy can be found in Akselrod's influential *Present Tasks and Tactics*. Akselrod insisted that

> if there is no possibility of assigning to the Russian proletariat an independent, pre-eminent role in the struggle against police-tsarism, autocracy and arbitrariness, then Russian Social Democracy has no historical right to exist. [49]

It was hardly fortuitous that it was to be Akselrod who first coined the phrase 'the hegemony of the proletariat in the democratic revolution', first used in the spring of 1901 and meaning, according to the gloss he put to it, 'our party will become the liberator *par excellence*, a centre toward which all democratic sympathies will gravitate and where all the greatest revolutionary protests will originate'. [50]

I have stressed the central point of the political strategy of orthodoxy almost to the point of labouring it and this for the good reasons that it was the bed-rock of the political tactics of Russian Social Democracy in this period, and that it was also to be the *idée fixe* of Lenin's political strategy till 1914. It was in the name of the leading political role of the proletariat in the democratic revolution that Lenin and the orthodox inveighed against the economists at the turn of the century. It was in the name of this principle that Lenin excoriated the Mensheviks who, he alleged, moved progressively away, from orthodoxy from 1903 onwards to the point where, in 1905, they were prepared to accept the ignoble role of merely 'assisting' the treacherous bourgeois in prosecuting the democratic revolution.

In Plekhanov's works and in those of the orthodox in the 1890s, the Russian bourgeoisie was consistently portrayed as weak, vacillating and cowardly, incapable of any real political initiative.

> Only in very rare cases were they the first to raise the banner of revolt even in Western Europe: for the greater part they have undermined the hated system little by little and reaped the fruits from the victory of the people . . . [51]

Time and again Plekhanov and the orthodox returned to the history of Europe, the experience of 1848 and more latterly to that of

47

Italian independence and unity to point up the moral that the bourgeoisie was an unreliable and unscrupulous political ally in the fight with absolutism. They themselves made no sacrifices, rarely assisted the struggle in the initial and dangerous phases. Only when victory was certain did they enter the lists to take the glory, and the power, for themselves. Having taken power in the name of democracy they proceeded to renege on their democratic principles the moment they were threatened from the left:

> West European history tells us most convincingly that whenever the 'red-spectre' took at all threatening forms, the 'liberals' were ready to seek protection in the embraces of the most unceremonious military dictatorship.[52]

The very first programmatic statement agreed upon by the movement in Russia, the *Manifesto of the Minsk Congress*, began by reminding its readers of the history of bourgeois treachery in 1848, when the bourgeoisie 'betrayed both itself and the cause of freedom into the hands of reaction'.[53] The history of 1848 stood out to the orthodox as the story of working-class heroism and gullibility; it proved a cataclysmic if glorious failure of proletarian strategy which must never be repeated. Their view of, and preoccupation with, the events of 1848 was clearly and explicitly derivative of Marx's histories of the time.

In his analyses of the progress and results of the 1848 revolution in France, *The Class Struggles in France 1848 to 1850* and *The Eighteenth Brumaire of Louis Bonaparte*,[54] Marx traced in detail the treacherous role the bourgeoisie had played. The proletariat, arms in hand, had secured the revolution in the name of freedom and the social republic. The bourgeoisie swiftly consolidated its political power and began to rally its forces against the 'dangerous class', the acolytes of red rebellion. They settled accounts and demonstrated their gratitude in the wholesale slaughter of the Paris proletariat in the July insurrection (provoked by the government). The protection of order and property was the pretext for narrowing down the suffrage and was, finally, the pretext upon which the military adventurer, Louis Bonaparte, established his bureaucratic dictatorship.

By repudiating universal suffrage, with which it hitherto draped itself and from which it sucked its omnipotence, the bourgeoisie openly confesses, *'Our dictatorship has hitherto existed by the will of the people; it must now be consolidated against the will of the people'*.[55]

Marx's analysis of the 1848 revolutions made a profound impression on his Russian disciples. They argued that their awareness of the political role of the European bourgeoisie in the past, provided the Social Democrats with the foresight to anticipate what the Russian bourgeoisie would do in the future. The history and experience of the working-class movement in other countries at other times must not be lost upon the emergent Russian proletariat. They must use this experience to avoid the mistakes and pitfalls which had beset the movement in the West.

If *Capital* portrayed the path of capitalist development in the West that Russia was fated to traverse, then Marx's historical works were seen as prophetic with regard to future political dispositions. In the light of their superior knowledge of Western politics and economics, it was pre-eminently the intelligentsia who performed the function of guiding the Russian proletariat. This historical prescience invoked by the orthodox was, of course, fully consonant with the dialectical methodology they embraced and which was discussed above. It was not merely their knowledge of economic laws but also their awareness of the likely *political* behaviour of the bourgeoisie, which conferred upon the intelligentsia the right and the duty of leading the working class.

THE INTELLIGENTSIA/SOCIAL DEMOCRATS, THE PARTY AND THE LABOUR MOVEMENT

Plekhanov's estimation of the vital importance of the intelligentsia in interpreting and hastening the advent of democracy and socialism was a central element of his thought. We have seen how, in his eyes, the economic, social and political processes of development were all dialectically linked in a very complicated way. The adequate direction of the labour movement and of Social Democracy presupposed knowledge of all those multiple interconnections. It was indeed the prescience that this knowledge conferred which was the basis of the right of the intelligentsia to lead the movement. The intelligentsia alone could bring to the labour movement the two crucial elements it manifestly lacked

– knowledge and organisation. Plekhanov insisted that it would fall to the intelligentsia Social Democrats to initiate the revolutionary movement.[56] They would draw up the main outlines of the programme[57] and they would bring consciousness into the working class.[58]

> The strength of the working class – as of any other class – depends, among other things, on the clarity of its political consciousness, its cohesion and its degree of organisation. It is these elements of its strength that must be influenced by our socialist intelligentsia. The latter must become the leader of the working class in the impending emancipation movement, explain to it its political and economic interests and also the interdependence of those interests and must prepare them to play an independent role in the social life of Russia.[59]

They stood, it seems, very much *in loco parentis* over the infant workers' movement. It is clear that, from the outset, Plekhanov did not believe that a united revolutionary movement of the working class could emerge in Russia without the determined activism of the intelligentsia. In the first *Programme of the Social-Democratic Group* this was forcefully underscored. Plekhanov contended that 'even the mere possibility of such a purposeful movement of the Russian working class depends in a large degree upon the work referred to above being done by the intelligentsia among the working class'.[60]

Plekhanov inclined indeed, to a positively instrumental view of the working class. Often in his writings the proletariat was conceived of as but the chosen instrument of *intelligentsia* designs; its historical role was to help and assist the intelligentsia. He talked of the intelligentsia securing 'the powerful support' of the industrial workers[61] and through them they acquired also 'that support of the *"people"* which they have not had until recently'.[62]

We are presented with what appears to be something of a paradox. On the one hand, as we have noticed, Plekhanov counterposed to the Populist conception of the passive crowd a vision of the proletariat as a Prometheus, a vital historical actor. On the other hand, it is equally clear from Plekhanov's writings that it was the intelligentsia which virtually created the working-class movement in its conscious form. It brought it science, revolutionary theory and organisation. The proletariat in this latter scenario appear to be almost bereft of self-activity. The view of the relationship between the proletariat and the intelligentsia that Plekhanov consistently adopted seems strikingly similar to the one implied in Marx's famous formulation: 'as philosophy finds its material weapons in the proletariat, the proletariat finds its intellectual weapons in philosophy'.[63] The tactical implication of this was interpreted by Plekhanov, and the Russian Marxists generally, to suggest that the job of the intelligentsia was not simply to go among the proletariat, absorb its strivings and aspirations and help in their realisation; its job was rather to win over the proletariat and to raise proletarian consciousness to intelligentsia level. The Social Democrat 'will bring *consciousness* into the working class and without that it is impossible to begin a serious struggle against capital'.[64]

If the worker was impotent without the intelligentsia, so too was the intelligentsia without the worker. The marriage between them must take place and was accomplished through the instrumentality of the party.

> The workers' party alone is capable of solving all the contradictions which now condemn our intelligentsia to theoretical and practical impotence . . . Secret workers' organisations will solve this contradiction by drawing in to the political struggle the most progressive sections of the people.[65]

Here again the problems were posed in a way oddly reminiscent of the young Marx. The motive for the party would appear to be the overcoming of intelligentsia isolation; it would be the instrument through which *their* ideals would be actualised.

The ideals and objectives of the intelligentsia were essentially political ones. Their first objective was the overthrow of autocracy and the implementation of legal and constitutional freedoms, the programme in fact of the 'democratic' revolution. The ultimate objective was the seizure of state power by the proletariat who would administer a transitional dictatorship to build the basis for socialism. The Social-Democratic Party in Russia would therefore wage a war on two fronts simultaneously, one against the tsarist, autocratic system of government, the other against the owners of capital.[66] The realisation of both these objectives demanded from the proletariat a considerable development of its political consciousness. Plekhanov argued that only in the proportion that the proletariat recognised that it must emerge as a political force – as a political party – did it properly become a class: 'Only gradually does the oppressed class become clear about the connection between its *economic* position and its *political* role in the state.'[67]

The stages of the evolution of proletarian consciousness were established by Plekhanov in a very important section of *Socialism and the Political Struggle*.[68] Initially the worker conceived of the struggle as one with a particularly rapacious local employer. Only gradually did he realise that the confrontation was not local and particular but a generalised class struggle. Even then the proletariat strove, at first, for limited and partial reforms which would aid it in the final confrontation.

> Only by going through the hard school of the struggle for separate little pieces of enemy territory does the oppressed class acquire the persistence, the daring, and the development necessary for the decisive battle . . . What is called the revolution is only the last act in the long drama of revolutionary class struggle which becomes conscious only in so far as it becomes a *political* struggle.[69]

The cynical might maintain that the Marxist intelligentsia Plekhanov was speaking for were playing a rather transparent definitional game with the proletariat. They emerged as a class, according to Plekhanov, only in so far as they appreciated the necessity for the overthrow of autocracy and the eventual seizure of power to implement socialism. They emerged as a class only in so far as they represented themselves politically on a national plane through the agency of a political party. In short it might be said they emerged as a class only in so far as they lived up to the expectations of the intelligentsia and accepted the necessary means to implement their ideals. Arguments of this sort were pressed by Plekhanov's Populist opponents, but if they were pressed against Plekhanov they had their foundation too in Marx. Plekhanov, was being quite consistent with the master, who expressed himself more emphatically than Plekhanov dared in the *Manifesto*, where he set the objective as the 'organisation of the proletarians into a class, and consequently into a political party'.[70] Marx had earlier developed this idea in *The Poverty of Philosophy*, a favourite text for Plekhanov and Akselrod (later too for Lenin), since it dealt in great detail with the ideas of Proudhon which enjoyed considerable vogue among their Populist opponents. At the end of his philippic, Marx expanded upon the way in which the class first began to coalesce in purely economic and defensive combinations. Then because of the grouping together of their capitalist opponents and the intervention of the state to support the latter, these combinations were obliged to assume a political character. Indeed the passage cited from Plekhanov seems to be almost a paraphrase of Marx.

> Economic conditions had first transformed the mass of the people of the country into workers. The domination of capital has created for this mass a common situation, common interests. This mass is thus already a class as against capital, but not yet for itself. In the struggle, of which we have pointed out only a few phases, this mass becomes united, and constitutes itself as a class for itself. The interests it defends become class interests. But the struggle of class against class is a political struggle.[71]

Repeatedly Marx emphasised that the sharing of a common economic mode of existence was certainly a necessary attribute of a class but was in no way a sufficient condition for the existence of a class. In *The Eighteenth Brumaire* he remarked that the peasants in France did share a similar mode of economic existence and in that weak sense they did form a class, but

> In so far as there is merely a local interconnection among these small-holding peasants, and the identity of their interests begets no community, no national bond and no political organisation among them, they do not form a class.[72]

It was a central axiom of Marx's position, and one that was enthusiastically endorsed by the Russian orthodox, that classes attained their adequate expression only as political groupings. In this political confrontation the economic antagonism inherent within the fabric of bourgeois society found its most generalised and clear representation. The bourgeoisie in becoming quite openly the masters of the state machine, and in utilising its coercive force in

53

defence of their partial economic interests, provided a clear target and a profound educative experience for the proletariat. With all of this the orthodox concurred. As Plekhanov put it: 'Sharply defined economic relations determine no less sharply defined political groupings; the antagonism between labour and capital gives rise to the struggle between the workers' and the bourgeois parties.'[73] The task of the Social Democrat was, he contended 'to organise the workers into a separate party in order thus to segregate the exploited from the exploiters and give political expression to the economic antagonism'.[74]

The insistence upon political action as a prerequisite of *class* activity was undoubtedly at the core of Russian Marxist orthodoxy. It was for this reason that some of the orthodox, Plekhanov and Akselrod in particular, shied away from the policy of economic agitation pursued in the mid-nineties, and it explains why those who did embrace this tactic regarded it only as a preparatory phase to the political struggle proper. Later the bond of unity among the orthodox in opposition to the 'economists' and 'revisionists' was precisely the same preoccupation with the political role of the party and the proletariat, their fears that the pre-eminence of the party in the political struggle with autocracy was threatened by over-concentration on the specific economic grievances of the workers.

The forward political role assigned to the proletariat was justified by Plekhanov in a number of ways. In the first place he argued that because the proletariat had emerged as an organised force with a political mouthpiece at the very beginning of the struggle for a democratic constitution, it had pre-empted bourgeois initiative. In any case, as we have noticed, Plekhanov considered the Russian bourgeoisie to be politically weak and vacillating; its more enlightened spirits would be drawn alongside the proletariat and its party as the bearers of progress for all society.[75] Finally, in conditions of autocracy, only the secret groupings the workers had established could form the organisational nexus from which a broader political ferment could grow. These clandestine groupings would overcome the isolation from which the movement had hitherto suffered by 'drawing into the political struggle the most progressive sections of the people'.[76] A prime task of the intelligentsia in creating the party was 'to organise the workers in our industrial centres, as the foremost representatives of the whole working population of Russia in secret groups with links between them and a definite social and political programme . . .'[77]

Plekhanov, and the orthodox generally, in stressing the paramount significance of the political role of the party, were unanimously generous in their praise of the *Narodnaya Volya* for having begun the difficult task of deflecting the Russian revolutionary movement away from its anarchic political abstentionism. It was to the great credit of the activists of *Narodnaya Volya* that they had recognised the necessary connection between economic and political power; to them belonged 'the honour of giving new scope to our movement'.[78] Their advocacy of the 'democratic political revolution' as the most reliable 'means of social reform'[79] represented, according to Plekhanov, a fundamental corrective to, or rather a decided negation of, earlier Populist strategy. They remained, of course, in a state of theoretical confusion and eclecticism, unable even to appreciate the elementary fact that the democratic and socialist revolutions were totally distinct in character. Nonetheless, Plekhanov and the orthodox were quite clear that, in terms of practical politics, the *Narodovoltsi* stood closer to Marxism than any other Russian group.

The eight-point programme which Plekhanov outlined setting forward the immediate tasks of the party was notably moderate in its stress upon democratic constitutional demands. Its object was to purge Russia of the remnants of feudalism and Asiatic barbarism, and to introduce a modern 'European' political order where the freedoms of speech, press and association were guaranteed, where civic equality was asserted and universal suffrage and payment of representatives introduced. The law was to apply equally to all and the person and home of citizens declared inviolate.[80] The only item which appeared discordant was the demand for the abolition of the standing army and its replacement 'by general arming of the people', but this too, at the time, was a general radical demand rather than one specifically identified with socialism.

The programme was the programme of the democratic revolution and stood in sharp contrast to the programme Marx sketched in the *Communist Manifesto* as appropriate to the first phase of *socialist* construction, with its calls for land nationalisation and the centralisation of the commanding heights of the economy in the hands of the state.[81] Plekhanov and the orthodox were quite clear that this phrase of the struggle was still a long way off in Russia: 'We must admit that we by no means believe in the early possibility of a socialist government in Russia.'[82] The immediate objectives of the Social Democrats in Russia were ineluctably constrained by the level of economic development in Russia. The objective economic and social basis for an advance to socialism, Plekhanov argued, had not yet emerged – and this followed from his economic analysis. It was on exactly these grounds that the orthodox were to criticise the utopian illusions of *Narodnaya Volya* and later the Legal Populists. The economic preconditions can neither be decreed by a revolutionary provisional government nor inflenced by the moral exhortations, however admirable, of 'the friends of the people'; the facts remain the facts. 'In other words', Plekhanov concluded, 'socialist organisation, like any other, requires the appropriate basis. But that basis does not exist in Russia'.[83]

With the development of the productive forces, the phase of advance to socialism would of course, present itself on the agenda and the surest guarantee that the proletariat would emerge successful from this *future* battle was that in the *present* fight for emancipation and democracy they should lead the way.

> That is why our socialist intelligentsia has been obliged to head the present-day emancipation movement, whose direct task must be to set up free political institutions in our country, the socialists on their side being under the obligation to provide the working class with the possibility to take an active and fruitful part in the future political life of Russia.[84]

The proletariat needed political freedom for its development – its full emergence as a class demanded, as we have seen, an open political struggle with the bourgeoisie. Only the freedoms enunciated in the programme would allow the working class to spread and consolidate its political influence. In the words of the *Minsk Manifesto*:

> But what does the Russian working class need? It is completely deprived of things that are enjoyed without let or hindrance by its foreign comrades; participation in government, freedom of the spoken and the printed word, freedom of organisation and assembly – in a word, of all those weapons and means whereby

the West European and American proletariat is improving its position and with which it is fighting for its final emancipation, against private property – for socialism. Political freedom is as necessary to the Russian proletariat as fresh air is to healthy breathing. It is the fundamental condition for its free development and the successful struggle for partial ameliorations and final emancipation.[85]

CONCLUSION

It might be as well for us now to make a brief resumé of what has been said above on the basic precepts of Russian Marxist orthodoxy in the nineties. The first proposition is that Russia was already pervaded by capitalist relations and the tempo of capitalist advance had increased dramatically ever since 1861. There is agreement, however that Russia as a whole was still at an early phase of capitalist development and that consequently the potentialities for further capitalist development were very far from being exhausted. Consequently, in terms of politcal action, restraints were placed upon the strategy of the Marxists. There could be no possiblility of an early advance to socialism; the immediate political objectives were far more modest. The initial task was the creation of a cohesive and conscious political party without which nothing could be accomplished on the national plane. The objectives of the party were two-fold. First, it must strive for the implementation of democratic freedoms which alone could establish the necessary preconditions for broadening the influence of the party both within the proletariat and upon other classes. Democratic freedoms and the struggle for them were, moreover, vital educative means for deepening the political consciousness of the proletariat. The party and the proletariat were obliged to assume the leadership of the democratic revolution for circumstantial and prudential reasons. The economic development of Russia demonstrated the peculiar circumstances of extreme bourgeois weakness; it could not be relied upon to pose as the champion of democracy. A prudent awareness of the history of other countries demonstrated, moreover, the way in which the proletariat was betrayed on the morrow of the democratic revolution for want of assertiveness and cohesion.

Considerable attention has been given in this chapter to the notion of the leading role of the proletariat in the democratic revolution. Most commentators would agree that this was perhaps the central tenet of orthodoxy. Many, however, proceed to attempt to reconcile this with a quite distinct and discordant proposition which has it that the 'orthodox' should render assistance to the bourgeoisie in the struggle for democracy. Thus Baron, in his book on Plekhanov, immediately after citing Plekhanov's utterance that 'political freedom will be won by the working class or not at all', proceeds 'In his mind, there existed no question about the desirability of lending proletarian support to the campaign against absolutism'.[86] The position of the orthodox, as argued in this chapter, suggests that this formulation should be inverted. The proletariat supported no one; on the contrary, as the unequivocal leader of the struggle it behoved other groups and strata to support *it*. Unless this is grasped, then the rationale for Lenin's *What Is To Be Done?* and the whole policy of *Iskra* becomes incomprehensible.

The second objective specified that the party, while assuming the leadership of the all-class assault on the autocracy, must simultaneously prepare the proletariat for socialism. It must ensure that it developed into a cohesive and conscious historical actor, aware of the economic antagonism inherent in capitalist society and its reflection in the operation of the state. The raising of proletarian consciousness to the level where it clearly perceived the necessity of seizing state power in order to realise socialism as the only remedy for its grievances – this degree of proletarian consciousness could not arise spontaneously out of the day to day economic struggle. This *political* and *revolutionary* consciousness must be introduced into the workers' movement by the intelligentsia Social Democrats.

Both of the political tasks of the party, the winning of the battle for democracy and the forging of the instrument for socialist advance, presupposed and demanded the energetic activism of the socialist intelligentsia. The adequacy of their organisational ability and, coincidentally, their theoretical clarity, would in large measure determine the degree of success the party attained in realising its objectives.

CHAPTER 3

St Petersburg :
The Emergence of a Leader

Lenin arrived in St Petersburg in the winter of 1893. He was to spend just over two years at liberty in the capital and some months thereafter in prison before being sent into exile.[1] These were important years for Lenin. They were in the first place the only years prior to the revolution when he was, more or less continuously, in immediate contact with workers' groups. Out of this experience he formulated a view of the phasal development of working-class consciousness which was to be profoundly important in the subsequent evolution of his thought. Understanding this experience and Lenin's reflections on it is a crucial factor in establishing the context of *What Is To Be Done?* They were, secondly, years when Lenin began to impress his stamp upon the Marxist movement. It was at this time that Lenin emerged as an important leader, perhaps the single most important leader of the movement in Russia. As a consequence he began to assume the responsibility for spelling out the programmatic and tactical precepts of Russian Social Democracy.

So long as Marxism remained merely the creed of a section of the radical intelligentsia the problems of the political programme and tactics of the movement remained academic; the Marxists did not dispose of sufficient forces to parade themselves on the political arena. They remained absorbed with the literary debate with Populism, establishing the theoretical foundations of Russian Marxism. After the famine of 1891–2 which brought deep disillusion to many of the Populists (not so much at the government, but at the stoic passivity of the peasants) and when the rapid advance of industrialisation, especially in the South, demonstrated the strength and staying power of Russian capitalism, at that stage in the early nineties the Marxists began to win a more sympathetic hearing in intelligentsia circles. However, they still had not accomplished the transition from being an intellectual coterie to being a significant political force. For this to happen, and for the Social Democrats to realise their own stated objectives, they would have to win over to their cause at least a section of the industrial working class. The period 1893–6 signalled the beginning of this transition. The Marxist movement came to look more like a Social-Democratic movement (though the stigmata of its origins as an intellectual coterie were never completely expunged). Haltingly and self-consciously the movement began to 'build bridges' to the workers. The young proselytes went forth in search of converts.

At first they viewed their worker groups simply as apprentice intelligentsia groups and treated them to lofty disquisitions on economic and political theory. With the rise of the strike movement in 1895–6 the Social Democrats for the first time directly involved themselves in mass action. Whether the Social Democrats did, in any meaningful sense, 'lead' this strike movement is for the moment unimportant.[2] What is important is that the new 'awakening' of the Russian working class, its new combative mood, the host of organisations it now threw up, demanded a precise and forthright response from the Social-Democratic leadership. Issues of political practice now presented themselves as matters of pressing urgency and Lenin as a leader of the movement was obliged, indeed eager, to take them up. His works in this period (up to 1900) reflected his twin preoccupations. He continued his economic work and his attacks on the social, economic and political theory of Populism on the one hand; on the other he now began to draft proclamations and leaflets, programmes for the party and tactical directives. Writing in 1897 Lenin self-consciously outlined the recent change of emphasis:

> At the present time . . . the most urgent question, in our opinion, is that of the *practical* activities of the Social Democrats. We emphasise the *practical* side of Social Democracy, because on the theoretical side the most critical period – the period of stubborn refusal by its opponents to understand it, of strenuous efforts to suppress the new trend the moment it arose, on the one hand, and of stalwart defence of the fundamentals of Social Democracy,

on the other – is now apparently behind us. Now the *main and basic features* of the theoretical views of the Social Democrats have been sufficiently clarified. The same cannot be said about the *practical* side of Social Democracy, about its political *programme*, its methods, its tactics.[3]

In the remainder of this chapter we shall turn to Lenin's personal involvement in the movement during this period and his reflections and recommendations on its practice.

LEADERSHIP OF THE ST PETERSBURG MARXISTS

By the time of his arrival in St Petersburg at the end of August 1893, Lenin had already established numerous, direct and indirect contacts with the Marxists there. He had, as we have seen, earlier visited St Petersburg in April and May of 1891 and he returned to sit more exams in September of that year. He went to see the Marxist Professor Iaven at the Technological Institute and doubtless was at that time introduced to other student Marxists of the Institute who were to form the nucleus of the *stariki*. We know that during this stay Lenin came to know Radchenko, one of the most prominent St Petersburg Marxists, and even, according to one account, attended illegal workers' meetings in his company.[4] En route for St Petersburg in 1895, Lenin stopped off in Nizhni Novgorod for a time, to talk with the celebrated Marxist academic P. N. Skvortsov whom he knew from his articles in the *Iuridicheski Vestnik*. Lenin also became acquainted with some of Skvortsov's more revolutionary comrades, in particular the foremost Moscow Marxist C. I. Mitskeevich. Mitskeevich, in his memoirs, recalled the powerful impression Lenin made upon the Nizhni group and together they discussed at length the necessity for establishing firm links between the scattered Marxist groups in Russia.[5] It was in Nizhni too, that Lenin first began to articulate his critique of Populism to a wider audience, began in other words, to establish himself as a theorist of the Russian Marxists. He read a paper (which he took with him to St Petersburg and which was incorporated into *What the 'Friends of the People' Are . . .*), criticising Vorontsov's *The Fate of Capitalism in Russia*.[6] Finally it was in Nizhni Novgorod that Lenin met M. A. Silvin,[7] a prominent member of the group of Marxists centred on the Technological Institute in St Petersburg. It was Silvin who provided Lenin with his letter of

61

introduction to the Marxist circles of the capital. En route for St Petersburg Lenin broke his journey in Moscow for a few days with his sister Anna and her husband, Mark Elizarov, where they, too, had established themselves with the local Marxists.

Lenin did not therefore arrive in St Petersburg unknown and unannounced save for his brother's reputation, as some would have us believe. From his contacts he must have known of most of the prominent activists there and must have been known to them, if only by repute. Krupskaya and others recall that talk of the theoretical prowess of the man from Samara preceded his first meeting with the St Petersburg group.

It was in Silvin's flat that Lenin first met the group led by Krassin which was comprised almost entirely of students and ex-students of the Technological Institute. This group had only been in existence for a year or so prior to Lenin's arrival and it conducted its affairs in a very similar manner to the circle Lenin had lately left in Samara. It was, of course, an exclusively intelligentsia group; no workers were admitted to its ordinary sessions. The group was bound together by a common creed, and, as importantly, by ties of personal friendship and common educational background. Consequently 'its organisation was extremely loose, "primitive", amateur, and accidental in nature and lacking any widespread organisation among the workers'.[8]

According to Soviet textbooks Lenin single-handedly and immediately revolutionised this careless, dilettante approach to the work. Some at least of the memoirs present a more credible analysis. As a preliminary Lenin had to establish his authority within the group and this he swiftly did when, in November 1893, he participated in a session in Radchenko's apartment, attended by almost all the prominent St Petersburg Marxists and at which Krassin read a paper 'On Markets'. Lenin had read the paper prior to the meeting and came armed with reservations and corrections bolstered by masses of statistical data and references which, cumulatively, demolished Krassin's case and established Lenin as the principal theorist of the group. It has been well said of Lenin that throughout his life his authority was essentially that of a schoolmaster. It was certainly by dint of his prowess in theory that he established himself as a leader, nor could it have been otherwise in a milieu where the movement was almost wholly comprised of intellectuals.

It is curious that commentators consistently and almost unanimously disparage the seriousness of Lenin's theoretical contributions which were precisely the contributions most valued by his colleagues and through which he established himself as a leader and maintained his leadership. All the memoirs are agreed that it was at this meeting and by means of his superior knowledge and Marxist erudition that Lenin established himself as the foremost theoretician of the St Petersburg Marxists; 'This paper of G. B. Krassin, "On Markets", was a turning-point in the life of our circle. Krassin's leadership was toppled'.[9] Krzhizhanovsky and Krupskaya both recounted their amazement at the young man's grasp not only of the basic theoretical postulates but more especially of his command of detail and concrete data in applying theory to Russian conditions. There is no need to doubt the authenticity of these memoirs. Lenin was, after all, playing to his strong hand. His earlier studies had, as we have seen, led him in this direction. That Lenin had emerged as the leading theorist of the group is further confirmed by the fact that early in 1894 the St Petersburg Marxists nominated him to deliver the counter-blows to Mikhailovsky's critical articles on Marxism. This Lenin did in his *What the 'Friends of the People' Are . . .*, a lengthy pamphlet which the St Petersburg group threw all its meagre resources into publishing and distributing.[10] This pamphlet confirmed Lenin's pre-eminence; he had established himself not only over Krassin, but as a competitor in prestige to Plekhanov himself. Mitskeevich recounts the great need that was felt among Russian Marxists for a riposte to the journalistic campaign against Marxism. Neither in the legal nor illegal press, he maintained, was there an adequate theoretical exposition of the position of the Russian Marxists. Plekhanov's works had, he contended, by this time become outmoded. They were concerned to answer the theorists of revolutionary Populism who had long ago been dropped by the contemporary spokesmen of 'small-deeds' Legal Populism. Lenin's work filled the gap and became, according to Mitskeevich, the theoretical and programmatic statement of Russian Marxism.[11] Its impact was immediate and extensive; it rapidly spread to Marxist circles throughout the empire, to Moscow, Nizhni Novgorod, Vladimir, Penza, Rostov on Don, Vilno, Riga, Kiev, Chernigov, Poltava, Tomsk and Tiflis.[12]

WHAT THE 'FRIENDS OF THE PEOPLE' ARE...

The contemporary significance of this work was clearly very considerable. The significance attached to it today by many commentators is rather different and it would be as well, at this point, to examine briefly the case made for regarding this work as some kind of harbinger of Bolshevism, where Lenin already displayed marked signs of his future 'voluntarist' revisions of Marxism. We will not deal here with Lenin's finding that Russia was already capitalist in structure at this time. In Chapter Two the case was made for regarding this as a perfectly orthodox position for a Russian Marxist to adopt. Indeed, Lenin himself pointed out in *What the 'Friends of the People' Are* . . . that ten years previously 'a separate group of socialists appeared who answered in the affirmative the question of whether Russia's evolution was capitalist'.[13] Far from being a departure from Marxism this was, as Lenin rightly argued, the *central* precept distinguishing Russian Marxists from other Russian socialists. ' "Mr Critic" must surely know that the Russian Marxists are socialists whose point of departure is the view that the reality of our environment is capitalist society.'[14] He pointed out that what *united* Social Democrats was precisely their agreement 'on the fundamental and principal thesis that Russia is a bourgeois society'.[15] This can only be properly understood in terms of Lenin's account of the phasal evolution of capitalism, which was developed for the first time in the *What the 'Friends of the People' Are*. . .

Actually, the organisation of our 'people's' handicraft industries furnishes an excellent illustration to the general history of the development of capitalism. It clearly demonstrates the latter's origin, its inception, for example, in the form of simple co-operation . . . it further shows that the 'savings' that – thanks to commodity economy – accumulate in the hands of separate individuals become *capital*, which first monopolises marketing ('buyers-up' and traders), owing to the fact that only the owners of these 'savings' possess the necessary funds for wholesale disposal, which enables them to wait until the goods are sold in distant markets; how, further, this merchant capital enslaves the mass of producers and organises capitalist manufacture, the capitalist domestic system of large-scale production; and how, finally, the expansion of the market and increasing competition lead to improved techniques, and how this merchant capital becomes industrial capital and organises large-scale machine production.[16]

For contemporary commentators to argue from this that Lenin there-fore imagined that capitalism had run its full course and exhausted its potentialities, leaving the stage clear for a socialist revolution, is a grossly misleading and unwarranted extrapolation. Lenin at no time prior to 1916 ever suggested that capitalism in Russia had exhausted its potential. On the contrary he repeatedly pointed out that Russia was, as a whole, in the early phases of capitalist accumu-lation and this fact set severe limitations on the kinds of goals appropriate to the Marxist movement.

'Substantive' evidence of Lenin's Jacobinism is often culled from *What the 'Friends of the People' Are . . .* to the effect that as a con-sequence of his precocious estimation of Russia as already capitalist, Lenin concluded that (1) socialist revolution was on the immediate agenda and therefore (2) the time for alliance with liberals and democrats was long passed. In evidence of (1) Lenin's ringing conclusion is sometimes cited as follows: 'The Russian *worker*, leading all democratic elements will bring down absolutism and will lead the *Russian proletariat* (together with the proletariat of *all countries) by the direct road of open political struggle to the triumphant Communist Revolution.*'[17] The very italicisation is said to denote Lenin's burning impatience to get on with the job. If, however, we read the whole of the passage from which this is taken, we must I think emerge with a rather different view of how careful Lenin was in interspersing his ringing phrases of inspiration to the converted with a nice balance of caveats and conditional clauses. He says that the Social Democrats must 'concentrate all their attention' on the working class and

when its advanced representatives have mastered the ideas of scientific socialism, the idea of the historical role of the Russian worker, when these ideas become widespread, and when stable organisations are formed among the workers to transform the workers' present sporadic economic war into conscious class struggle – then the Russian *worker*, rising at the head of all the democratic elements, will overthrow absolutism and lead the *Russian proletariat* (side by side with the proletariat of *all countries*)

65

along the straight road of open political struggle to *the victorious Communist Revolution.*[18]

We are presented with a timetable, a sequence of prerequisites necessary to final triumph, which is quite clearly spelt out and stringent in its specifications. Lenin's readers, both within the movement and without, would have needed no telling that the preliminary tasks he specified of (a) propagandising the working class leaders, (b) disseminating the ideas of scientific socialism more widely, (c) creating stable working-class organisations, had barely been commenced by the Russian Marxist intelligentsia. They were, as we shall see, at this time taking their first faltering steps in setting up workers' study circles. Even when the preliminary conditions were realised, the overthrow of tsarism was made contingent upon the workers 'rising at the head of all the democratic elements' – no more than a reassertion of the orthodoxy of Russian Marxism bequeathed by Plekhanov and Akselrod, specifying the hegemony of the proletariat in the democratic revolution. Finally, and quite consistent again with Plekhanov (and Marx), the realisation of the communist revolution in Russia was parathetically bound to the international extension of the revolution where the Russian proletariat marched 'side by side with the proletariat of *all countries*'. To represent all this as evidence of Lenin's early expression of voluntarist tendencies seems to rest both on a capricious reading of the text and a blithe ignorance of Lenin's constant insistence upon the realisation of the democratic revolution as the immediate goal of Social Democracy in Russia.

The case for (2) – Lenin's early dismissal of an alliance with the liberals and his rejection of democracy as the immediate goal – is hardly more substantial. It rests upon an equally capricious interpretation of one passage from *What the 'Friends of the People' Are. . .,* where Lenin specified that 'a *complete* and *final rupture* with the ideas of the democrats is *inevitable* and *imperative!*'[19] Conclusive evidence of the Jacobin interpretation it would seem. That is until we read a little more of the pamphlet. Throughout, Lenin was concerned to demonstrate that the so-called socialists of the Legal Populist hue, were no more than radical democrats, intent on partial amelioration and utopian schemes of social reconciliation. Throughout, Lenin utilised a distinction cited by Chernyshevsky to the effect that behind the banner of democracy these liberals were serving the interests of plutocracy;[20] heart and soul they eschewed all revolutionary means of transforming society. The 'friends of the people' have, in short, under the guise of socialism and democracy, reneged on the revolutionary goals of Narodism. Objectively these liberal democrats no longer stood (as the 'fathers' did) on the side of the revolutionaries and on the side of socialism. Chernyshevsky in contrast was 'a democrat of that epoch, when democracy and socialism were undivided'.[21] Now, Lenin maintained, it was essential to distinguish between the liberal – 'friend of the people' – the Narodnik-democrat and the working-class socialist. The first group had, in Lenin's estimation, now become positively reactionary *in so far as they posed as socialists and spokesmen of the working class.* In short, what Lenin was attempting to do was to point out that once upon a time it was proper and natural to view the Populists as the authentic spokesmen of socialism and of the exploited. The situation had, however, changed and they were now to be regarded simply as radical democrats intent upon patching up the holes in the structure of capitalism. As radical democrats it was, however, extremely important for the Social Democrats to enlist the aid of the Populists in the battle for democracy.

It is difficult to see how it is possible to miss this constantly repeated distinction which is the basic message of *What the 'Friends of the People' Are*. . . . It is equally difficult to see how Lenin could have been more emphatic in pointing out to his supporters the need to reject the Populists *qua socialists* while supporting them and spurring them on *qua democrats*. The whole of the last section of his pamphlet was concerned with conveying this message.

I ask you also to note that I speak of the need for a break with petty-bourgeois ideas about *socialism*. The petty-bourgeois theories we have examined are *absolutely* reactionary *inasmuch* as they claim to be socialist theories. . . . we must ask: *what should be the attitude of the working class towards the petty-bourgeoisie and its programmes?* . . . It is progressive in so far as it puts forward general democratic demands, i.e., fights against all survivals of the mediaeval epoch and of serfdom; it is reactionary in so far as it fights to preserve its position as a petty-bourgeoisie and tries to retard, to turn back the general development of the country along bourgeois lines. . . . A strict distinction should be drawn between these two sides of the petty-bourgeois programmes and, while denying that these theories are in any way socialist in character, and while combating their reactionary aspects, we should not forget their democratic side. I shall give an example to show that, although the Marxists completely repudiate petty-bourgeois theories, this does not prevent them from including democracy in their programme, but, on the contrary, calls for still stronger insistence on it. [22]

The allegation that Lenin had already rejected democracy as the immediate goal of Russian socialists and had therefore rejected as inappropriate an alliance with bourgeois and petty-bourgeois democrats cannot be seriously sustained from a reading of *What the 'Friends of the People' Are* . . . . Lenin conformed completely to the orthodox standpoint of commitment to the democratic revolution as the first and necessary step in creating conditions of political freedom for the further progress of the workers' movement:

The worker needs the achievement of the general democratic demands only to clear the road to victory over the working people's chief enemy, over an institution that is purely democratic by nature, *capital*, which here in Russia is particularly inclined to sacrifice its democracy and to enter into alliance with the reactionaries in order to suppress the workers, to still further impede the emergence of the working-class movement. [23]

It was indeed because of this vacillating attitude of the Russian bourgeoisie and petty-bourgeoisie that the proletariat was compelled to assume the leadership of the democratic revolution, to pre-empt and paralyse the instability of the bourgeoisie. This again was orthodoxy of the most pure. Even though the democratic revolution would, objectively, aid the bourgeoisie even more than the proletariat, nonetheless it was vital to impress upon the working class the necessity of achieving political liberty:

The workers must know that unless these pillars of reaction are overthrown, it will be utterly impossible for them to wage a successful struggle against the bourgeoisie, because so long as they exist, the Russian rural proletariat, whose support is an essential condition for the victory of the working class, will never cease to be downtrodden and cowed, capable only of sullen desperation and not of intelligent and persistent protest and struggle. And that is why it is the direct duty of the working class to fight side by side with the radical democracy against absolutism and the reactionary social estates and institutions . . .[24]

We have here, in brief compass, the main elements of Lenin's revolutionary strategy which emerged in sharper outline in 1905 and which was retained until 1914. The immediate struggle was with the autocracy for the implementation of a radical democratic programme. Only if this were realised would the conditions be realised for the Russian proletariat (urban and factory) to accomplish its mission of rallying *all* the exploited, especially the rural proletariat behind it.

Lenin's idea of the proletariat as the natural representative of all Russia's exploited population was, as we will outline in Chapter Four, a crucial one. It was, significantly enough, amplified for the first time in *What the 'Friends of the People' Are* . . .[25]

The prevalent notion that Lenin, early in his career, rejected the peasantry as a quiescent or reactionary group quite fails to understand Lenin's economic as well as his political thought at this time. His economic work contained, as one of his main thrusts against the Populists, a detailed account of the break-up of the peasantry into hostile groups. His entire argument was to demonstrate from the available data the polarisation of the peasantry into wage-labourers and hirers of labour, into a rural bourgeoisie and a rural proletariat. It was the responsibility of the proletariat and its party to bring consciousness to the latter and to represent them on the national political plane, but this could be done only in and through the securing of democratic freedoms. When, in alliance with all the democratic forces of society, the autocracy has been toppled, when the proletariat has become in fact the representative of the whole working population of Russia, only then would it be able to undertake the battle for socialism.

We see then that Lenin's economic or theoretical ideas on the nature and class dispositions of Russian capitalism and his ideas on political practice, not only complemented each other but were inextricably bound together. In neither sphere did his ideas represent in any way a violation of the orthodoxy bequeathed by

Plekhanov and Akselrod. They did, no doubt, constitute in some ways an extension of that orthodoxy, particularly with regard to Lenin's ideas on the vanguard role of the proletariat and its consequent relationship with the rural proletariat and artisans. It is certainly true that by comparison with Plekhanov, Lenin was already looking more to the rural proletariat for support than to the Russian bourgeois radicals but, as has been indicated this was a consequence of his more diligent economic researches which were themselves conducted on an impeccable Marxist foundation.

It is clear that the key to Lenin's whole strategy was his view of the factory proletariat as the advance guard both of the immediate democratic tasks of the revolution as well as of the eventual fight for socialism. Whereas the rural proletariat was dispersed and scattered, unable therefore to unite and generalise from its experience, unable of its own to emerge as a class, the factory proletariat was exposed to very differing conditions.

> Large-scale capitalism . . . inevitably severs all the workers' ties with the old society, with a particular locality and a particular exploiter; it unites them, compels them to think and places them in conditions which enable them to commence an organised struggle. Accordingly, it is on the working class that the Social Democrats concentrate all their attention and all their activities.[26]

There were, of course, other reasons why the Social Democrats chose to concentrate their activities in the main urban centres. Reasons of logistics dictated this course. With such pitifully weak forces available it would have been useless to spread them thin throughout the vast breadth of Russia. In the second place the forces available were, as we have seen, almost exclusively from the intelligentsia. Apart from being naturally drawn to the university and urban centres, they needed the size and relative anonymity of the larger cities to be able to carry out their clandestine work. Finally, in the urban centres and among the factory proletariat, the Social Democrats did have something, if not much, to build upon. Even if the workers had had little experience of durable working-class organisations, there had been earlier attempts by the *Zemlya i Volya* and more latterly by the remnants of *Narodnaya Volya* to organise and politicise the workers in the main centres.

70

Autonomous workers' associations had indeed been created in the past; those associated with the names of Blagoev, Tochissky, Brusnev and Shelgunov spring to mind. These groups derived their influence largely from the dynamism of these individuals and when they were each in turn arrested, imprisoned and exiled, the organisations they had formed invariably fell apart. Although all of these attempts attained only limited and generally fleeting success, they had at least produced a feeling among some industrial workers that organisation was important to them. They had also produced a generation of activists who were important to the Social Democrats in 'building bridges' to the working class.

'PROPAGANDA' IN THE WORKERS' CIRCLES

It was in the Nevsky Gate district of St Petersburg that Nikolai Petrovich (for such was the conspiratorial name under which Lenin rejoiced at the time[27]) first went among the workers. The esteem with which Lenin was already regarded by his fellow Marxists can be adduced from the fact that this group embraced some of the most intelligent and talented of the worker-activists in St Petersburg, among them Babushkin, Kniazev, Borovkov, Gribakin and Zhukov.[28] Lenin's mode of approach in inducting the workers under his charge into the toils of socialist theory followed the lines already established by the St Petersburg Marxists. The tactic consisted of treating the workers as fellow-students; it was merely a matter of taking the study circles out of the technical institutes and universities and into the workers' quarters. Philosophy, economics and history was the strong diet Lenin prepared for his workers in order to build up their intellectual strength so that they, in their turn, would go among their workmates as fully trained propagandists. The presupposition behind this kind of work was that the road to working-class consciousness lay through education of a rather formal and bookish kind. The appropriate education would induct the worker into the texts of Marxism and then into an understanding not only of the causes of exploitation but of the necessary connection between economic and political power as well. Perhaps even this underestimates and narrows down too far the elevated tasks the Social-Democratic propagandist set himself, for to understand Marxism and modern socialism it was necessary to show the workers how they were emanations of the whole corpus of modern culture in the broadest sense. According

71

to the testimony of one of the members of these workers' circles, the Social Democrat taught them that

> to be an organiser of the working class, it is necessary first of all to be honest in all relations oneself, secondly, to be a worthy comrade, and finally, a cultivated person to whom others could turn with questions, and from whom they could receive definitive answers. Therefore it is necessary to discipline and cultivate oneself. It is necessary to learn by a definite programme . . . A good propagandist must be able to answer such questions as why there is day and night, seasons of the year, and eclipses of the sun. He must be able to explain the origin of the universe and the origin of the species, and must therefore know the theories of Kant, Laplace, Darwin and Lyell. In the programme must be included history and the history of culture, political economy, and the history of the working class.[29]

Part of the reason for the success of the Marxists in supplanting the Populists as organisers and leaders of the urban working class was precisely their willingness patiently to instruct and broaden the horizons of the working-class activists. Unlike the Populists they did not exhort their supporters to immediate, and generally catastrophic, open revolutionary activity. Calls for terrorist activity were eschewed by the Marxists as counter-productive and inappropriate to the primitive level of development of consciousness and working-class organisation. The revolution, as all Social Democrats recognised, was still a long way off; in the meantime the gradualist watchwords of Liebknecht summarised their activity: 'studieren, propandieren, organisieren.' Krzhizhanovsky later recounted with some pain how students like himself, 'Marxists to the point of pedantry . . . tormented our first working-class friends with the "frock coat" and the sackcloth from the first chapter of *Capital*'; how he was 'firmly convinced that no good would ever come of anyone who had not gone through Marx's *Capital* two or three times'.[30]

Lenin seems to have agreed with Krzhizhanovsky, and with Plekhanov's conviction that *Capital* should be made a Procrustean bed for all would-be Marxists to lie upon. 'Vladimir Ilyich read with the workers from Marx's *Capital* and explained it to them', according to Krupskaya.[31] The current Soviet *Short Biographical Sketch* of Lenin is more fulsome about Lenin's pedagogic abilities: 'he was able simply and intelligibly to explain the most complicated problems of Marx's thought.'[32] The memoirs of the worker students themselves are sometimes more candid. Kniazev, a prominent pupil of the then Nikolai Petrovich, confesses that often the lecturer was a little difficult to understand.[33] The incomprehension was no more than we might expect. This was after all the first contact of a twenty-three-year-old intellectual with the workers in a country where the cultural gulf between these two groups was greater than anywhere else in Europe. His pupils had precious little in the way of elementary education. Some admittedly had benefited from the official literacy classes to learn how to read and write, but beyond that their education generally ceased. The official literacy classes and adult education institutes had, by this time, been infiltrated by Marxists, particularly women, who used these open forums to get the workers to think about their own situation and attempted to cream off the best and most active workers and direct them into Social-Democratic circles. Many of Lenin's students had in this way graduated from the 'Smolensk' Sunday evening school in the Nevsky Gate area – the school at which Krupskaya and Z. P. Nevzorova, both convinced Marxists, were teaching[34] – to Marxist discussion circles. There was, as Krupskaya puts it 'a silent conspiracy' afoot. 'Workers belonging to our organisation went to the school in order to observe the people and note who could be brought into the circles or drawn into the movement.'[35] The tactic of utilising open and legal forms of association as initiation and recruitment centres for clandestine revolutionary activity was, of course, an old Blanquist tactic which was imposed upon the Marxists by the conditions of illegality in which they worked.

It seems clear that Lenin, in his classes, was concerned not only with impressing the Marxist point of view upon his students, but also with obtaining from them concrete information about working and social conditions among the industrial proletariat. This certainly conforms to the pattern of Lenin's Samara days, when he already recognised the importance of amassing detailed and accurate data on economic matters. Babushkin[36] and Kniazev[37] both recount how Lenin, after the strong dose of theory which comprised the first half of his class, would press them for detailed information on rates of pay, extent of fines and other deductions, housing conditions, child and female labour, etc. Lenin later got up a model questionnaire on such topics which was duplicated and utilised by other St Petersburg groups.[38] No doubt part of his motive in soliciting this information was to have a detailed and precise knowledge of working-class life in order that he might better demonstrate to his students the reality of the theories he was trying to convey. He knew, as all adult education teachers know, that a general point of theory is illuminated far more quickly by an apt example drawn from the current problems of his audience, than by an exposition of its validating rationale. Soon, however, the mass of data he was acquiring was to be put to a new purpose; unwittingly Lenin was preparing himself as a major spokesman within Russian Marxism of the new tactic of 'agitation'.

Up to this point in his career (i.e., to 1895) Lenin, in common with other Russian Marxists, had been engaged in the tasks of 'propaganda'. He had devoted most of his energies to the literary and polemical crusade against Populism in general, and more specifically against its contemporary spokesmen, V. V. (V. P. Vorontsov), Nikolai . . . on (N. Danielson), Yuzhakov and Mikhailovsky. It is no exaggeration to maintain that *all* of Lenin's early works are concerned with combating Populist ideas on economics, history, class and the role of individuals, political action and the role of the state, etc.[39] It is, on the face of it, rather curious that Lenin, who was already leading the underground life of a professional revolutionary, should have devoted so much time and energy to this literary work; the more so since the chances of legal publication were slender. Lenin's writings of this period, if they were published at all, were circulated either in handwritten duplicates of the original or in limited hectographed editions. Lenin's most important work of this period, *What the 'Friends of the People' Are* . . ., for instance, was initially produced in an edition of not more than 50 copies, though it was swiftly recopied by local groups. The audience was almost exclusively the radical intelligentsia already drawn towards Marxism by the legal publication of works by Plekhanov, Struve and Tugan-Baronovsky. To educated society at large, and obviously to the workers, these theoretical writings of Lenin were almost entirely inaccessible. Lenin was, of course, aware of all this; his objective in writing these works was to draw deep into the active movement those who were already interested. His object was to keep up a running critique of Populism to bolster the faith of the committed, and, hopefully, to convert some of the enemy. In particular his concern was to capture the minds of the radical youth in universities and institutes for he recognised that, without a nucleus of dedicated and trained activists schooled in theory, it would be impossible to begin any large-scale proselytising among the working class. In all of this Lenin was doing no more than following the guidelines laid down by Plekhanov in the 1880s. There the 'Master' had insisted that the essential preliminary task in winning the working class to Marxism was the winning over and proper induction of the radical intelligentsia. Like Lenin he stressed the importance of *proper* induction – no wavering, no eclecticism, no dilution of the class struggle and revolutionary commitment. Both were aware of the dangers the infant Marxist movement faced on the theoretical plane; mistakes in this crucial period might cause it to become permanently disfigured. It was therefore essential to expose at every turn the errors of competing groups and especially those which pretended to be socialist. It was no less important to guard against any ideological deviation within the Marxist camp, to bring to task those rather mechanistic determinists, like Stuve, who failed to appreciate the dynamic importance of class struggle.[40] From the outset Lenin was as insistent as Plekhanov upon the necessity of absolute theoretical rectitude.

Some of this severity no doubt carried over into Lenin's meetings with the workers' circles. The theoretical clarity and level of induction into the elements of Marxism of the members of these circles would have to be commensurate with the huge role they were intended to play in the movement. According to the strategy of the St Petersburg Marxists at this time, the urgent task of the movement was to train a force of worker intellectuals who, armed with theory, would return to the working class to act as the catalysts in an ever-broadening schema of working-class enlightenment. They would train new worker activists and theorists who would, in turn, spread the word further; and so on, *ad infinitum* in geometric progression, until the whole class became conscious of its place and destiny in history. It was what we might term a chain-letter tactic for the generation of socialist consciousness.

In fact, things worked out very differently. Some, no doubt, of the worker intellectuals did their best to carry out the tasks expected of them, but in general the results of this so-called 'propaganda' period of spreading theroretical knowledge through workers' study circles, proved disappointing to the Russian Marxists in the mid-nineties. The worker members of the circles were, in general, not very flattered by their role as leaven to the proletarian lump. They were concerned with their own self-improvement and, having sampled a tantalising bite of the benefits of literacy and the cultural horizons it opened up, were loathe to return to convert their untutored and unappreciative comrades. Far from building bridges to the proletariat, the Social Democrats discovered that they were in danger of creating a rather precious worker élite, concerned as far as possible to distinguish and isolate itself from the '*nekulturni*' mass.

Lenin became sharply aware of this at the end of 1894 when a strike and disturbances broke out at the Semyannikov works, which was in the Nevsky Gate district in which he operated. It happened that some of Lenin's worker students were from this works and yet they gave the Social Democrats no advance warning, no presentiment that grievances were building up to boiling point. Indeed, it is clear that the worker intellectuals themselves were against militant action. They argued that the time had not come when it was desirable to broaden the movement; for the moment the movement should deepen itself and fortify its existing bases.[41] Lenin no doubt berated his pupils for their failure to participate in, and to assume the leadership of, this popular movement of industrial discontent going on under their very noses. He must too have agreed with Silvin that 'Once more it was confirmed that the worker members of our Circles were remote from the masses'.[42] Takhtarev, writing about the same strike, bemoaned the fact that ' "our" workers played no part whatever in the whole affair'.[43] To remedy the situation, Lenin set about collecting materials on conditions at the factory and the substance of the workers' demands, which he wrote up as a leaflet, an appeal to the strikers and a presentation of their grievances. This leaflet, written at the very beginning of 1895[44] which does not seem to have been translated into English, proved to be the humble beginning of a new policy orientation of the St Petersburg Social Democrats – the beginning of the 'agitation' phase. It was a very modest and rather ineffective beginning since the Social Democrats at that time had no facilities either for printing or for ensuring the proper distribution of agitational leaflets. Krupskaya was frank about their weaknesses in these respects at that time:

I remember that Vladimir Ilyich drew up the first leaflet for the workers of the Semyannikov works. We had no technical facilities at all then. The leaflet was copied by hand in printed letters and distributed by Babushkin. Out of the four copies two were picked up by the watchman, while two went round from hand to hand.[45]

Even this modest effort was accounted a great success. Whether Lenin's leaflet preceded or ante-dated the discussion among the St Petersburg Marxists of the brochure *On Agitation* is difficult to establish from the conflicting testimony available. According to Krzhizhanovsky, Lenin, from the time of his arrival urged 'a change-over from "over-profound" study with a small circle of selected workers to activity influencing the broad masses of the St Petersburg proletariat – that is, a transition from propaganda to agitation'.[46] This account hardly tallies with what we know of Lenin's activities in these years gleaned from other sources. The bulk of the evidence suggests that the brochure *On Agitation* arrived in St Petersburg and was read and formally discussed at a special meeting of Social Democrats in the spring of 1895, though not finally adopted as the policy of the St Petersburg group until the autumn of that year.[47] Such was the importance ascribed to the proposed new tactic that worker representatives were invited to participate. Indeed, it would appear from Silvin's account that almost all of the prominent Marxist activists in St Petersburg were present – Lenin, Silvin, Krupskaya, Krassin, Starkov, Zaprozhets, Radchenko, Yakubova, Shelgunov, Babushkin, Merkulov and some other circle members. Lenin, it seems, was the principal spokesman for the new tactic and was supported by the worker representatives. Krassin and Radchenko were the main opponents, arguing that the new tactic would involve a down-grading of revolutionary political work and the pursuit of trifling everyday matters. They argued moreover that attempts by the Social Democrats to mobilise the masses on the basis of their economic grievances would lead to swift police retribution and the smashing of the emergent circle movement. The majority of the participants were, however, in favour of the transition from propaganda to agitation.[48] We must later establish the significance of this new tactic, what it consisted of and how it influenced the activities of St Petersburg Marxists in general and Lenin's ideas on practice in particular. This will be pursued in Chapter Five.

Before moving on to discuss Lenin's ideas on the political strategy and tactics of Russian Social Democracy it is of crucial importance that we first examine the basic economic and social analysis of Russia which he was simultaneously elaborating. This painstaking economic and social analysis was not, of course, to be completed until 1899 with the publication of *The Development of Capitalism in Russia*. Many of its leading themes, however, we have already remarked upon in his earliest writings and, particularly, in Part III of *What The 'Friends of the People' Are* . . . It would not be entirely anachronistic, therefore, to bring together the strands of what we may term Lenin's theoretical analysis before going on to examine his ideas on practice. It is, indeed, the central contention of this book that we cannot begin to make sense of Lenin's ideas on practice unless we have first grasped the theoretical basis which underlies them. Sadly this also happens to be the area of greatest (one is almost tempted to say total) neglect in studies of Lenin's thought.

CHAPTER 4

Theoretical Basis – The Economic and Social Analysis

Plekhanov, as we have seen, had done Herculean work to establish the *bona fides* of Marxism in Russia. He made it intellectually respectable. He attended above all to the large questions which had traditionally absorbed the intelligentsia. Philosophy of history and Russia's destiny, literary criticism and the role of the artist, the evolution of social and political thought, the role of the individual in a determinist world outlook – his disposition was towards these very broad problems and his value to the cause of Marxism in Russia was that he brought the weight of his great erudition to bear upon them. But if Plekhanov had established a general outline for the interpretation of Marxism in Russia, the problems posed to those in the emergent practical movement of the nineties were nonetheless daunting. From Plekhanov's very generalised sketch they had to descend by logically related steps to the setting of immediate Party tasks.

The problem of putting a recognisable outline to Plekhanov's skeletal sketch was nowhere more apparent than in the field of the economic analysis of Russian society. At the highest level of philosophical generality Plekhanov, in his *Development of the Monist View of History*,[1] argued the cogency of scientific materialism and the determining influence of the economic substructure of society more fully than even Marx himself had attempted. He had also asserted the relevance of these principles to Russia, maintaining that Russia was already embarked upon the progress of capitalist development described by Marx.[2] The phases of this progress were, however, alluded to only briefly and they had been no less briefly expounded by Marx.

Lenin took upon himself the enormous task of establishing the

79

concrete nature and, more important perhaps, the inter-relationship of these early phases of capitalist development as they were actually taking place in contemporary Russia. He was obliged to develop and extend the insights which Plekhanov had retailed from Marx and to demonstrate the progression from feudalism to industrial capitalism as a necessary and law-bound process, to colour it moreover with the particularities of Russian economic development. This task was a momentous one in several respects. It was the first serious attempt by a Marxist scholar to chronicle and fill out Marx's account of the development of capitalism out of feudalism, to demarcate with reliable data how the progression actually occurred. It remains the fullest account in the literature of Marxism on this subject and reflects the many years of Lenin's intellectual prime devoted to its thorough completion. In the second place the conclusions which Lenin arrived at from this analysis were to have profound effects upon his whole political strategy up to 1914, with regard especially to the objectives he considered appropriate for the Party to pursue. The economic analysis was the theoretical basis which set the limits to the practical objectives at which the Marxists could aim. Finally, the methodology he utilised to examine the evolution of capitalism was directly related to the way in which he later analysed the development of consciousness and of the Party: each partook of a similar phasal development with a changing organisational mode appropriate to each phase. This methodological parallel was, as we shall see, consciously evoked by Lenin. He repeatedly employed the language and terminology of the economic analysis in his discussions of political phenomena. He clearly viewed both the economic and political as partaking of a directly comparable progression.

Each phase was significant and important only in so far as it contributed to the final dénouement, be it of advanced machine production, a cohesive national party, or full Social-Democratic consciousness. In this respect Lenin was clearly in the Plekhanov mould; the key element of his thought was a dialectical teleology. The main difference between him and Plekhanov is that he was far more anxious to demarcate as precisely as possible the stages of growth involved. The sorts of questions Lenin addressed himself to were, how, why, and at what exact point have the potentialities of one stage been exhausted? How can the Social Democrats best anticipate this evolution and make the necessary adjustments in their propaganda and organisation to promote and reap the greatest advantage from the stage which is coming into being?

From this rather generalised preamble the impression may have been created that Lenin, arriving in St Petersburg in 1893, came ready equipped with a dossier of questions and all the necessary proofs to validate his replies. Such, of course, was not the case. He developed his arguments on the economic structure of Russia largely in polemic with the still dominant Populist interpretation, a polemic which absorbed the greater part of Lenin's energies in the first six years of his political life.

THE NEO-POPULISTS AND 'THE FATE OF CAPITALISM IN RUSSIA'

The 'Controversy over Capitalism', as this debate has been called,[3] took up many of the issues which Plekhanov imagined he had settled in his pamphlets of the eighties. The Populists (or Neo-Populists as the later publicists were sometimes called) re-emerged undeterred and strengthened, so they believed, by a new' and convincing economic expertise. This expertise was supplied by the two principal exponents of Populism in the late eighties and early nineties, the economists V. P. Vorontsov and N. K. Danielson. Lenin's analysis of capitalism in Russia was explicitly counterposed to this Populist viewpoint. It was this more sophisticated exposition of the Russian socialist position which to a great extent prompted him to refine and extend the earlier work of Plekhanov. To understand Lenin's case and his preoccupations, we must first reconstruct, in outline at least, the arguments of his opponents. We shall deal here, for the sake of brevity, and also because he was arguably the most coherent, and certainly the most prolific of the Populist spokesmen, with the ideas of V. P. Vorontsov.[4]

Vorontsov sought to demonstrate that not only was capitalism undesirable, narrow, mean, selfish, divisive and all manner of other things abhorrent to the 'broad nature' of the Russian soul, it was also (more damning in a 'scientific' age) theroetically and practically impossible. 'The people's party would stand to gain a great deal', Vorontsov maintained, 'if to its faith in the vitality of the foundations of peasant life was added a conviction of the historical impossibility of the growth of capitalist production in Russia'.[5]

The arguments which Vorontsov adduced to support this conviction were first developed in an article written in 1880.[6] By 1882 he had developed his thought into an integrated and comprehensive explanation of why capitalism was doomed in the Russian environment. His book, *The Fate of Capitalism in Russia*, rapidly became the authoritative handbook of the Legal Populists.

Leaning heavily upon Sismondi, Vorontsov argued the thesis of a necessary disparity between production and consumption, the impossibility in other words of an adequate home market. Given the fact that the workers were paid far less than the value of their products, there arose a surplus which could only be disposed of abroad.[7] The home market could not absorb the products of home industry under advanced capitalism, and there ensued a fierce competition for overseas markets which, once saturated, necessarily produced crisis and breakdown in the metropolitan capitalist countries. Given this intense competition for foreign markets among advanced industrial states, how could a backward nation intent on developing capitalism hope to dispose of its goods? If foreign markets were virtually closed, the prospects were no more rosy for the development of an internal market. Here the appropriation of the latest technique typical of capitalist production would merely exacerbate the problem by reducing the number of workers (and therefore the purchasing power of the market) in proportion to the goods produced. The very creation of a viable market was, on these general grounds, disputed. More specific and particularly Russian considerations were brought in to ramify his argument. The creation of a home market on the national scale demanded by large-scale capitalist production could only be effected by an efficient system of transport. Such a system Russia did not possess and the burden of creating one would so severely handicap Russian capitalism as to render it unable to compete with foreign goods on the home market. Likewise, the inordinate freight charges involved in hauling goods across the breadth of Russia and then to distant foreign markets, would evidently render them uncompetitive compared with goods produced in countries with a more advantageous geographical situation and with a denser, more compact population easing the problem of transportation. As if this were not enough, Russia's severe climate demanded outlays on fuel, clothing, shelter and food far beyond the norm of West European countries.[8] Furthermore, wages suffered general inflation because of the peasant's passion for the land and possession of it; to lure him away high wages would have to be paid. Finally, Russia had for centuries isolated herself from western civilisation. Her people were ignorant and primitive, untouched by scientific culture; where then were the technical and administrative personnel to come from?[9]

Weighed down by such disadvantages it was, Vorontsov argued, small wonder that government-sponsored capitalism had floundered so inauspiciously. The attempt had been made to introduce large-scale production into Russia; that such plants *existed* was not at issue. The point at issue was whether the capitalist relations of production which they typified were increasing their hold on the economy generally, whether they were in any sense the *dominant* economic relations. In settling these problems Vorontsov took evidence of the socialisation of labour as his infallible yardstick for ascertaining the prevalence of the capitalist system. Socialisation of labour for him represented the particular differentia of capitalist production; an examination of its extensiveness was at the same time an examination of the development of capitalism. When he undertook this study Vorontsov emerged with the conclusion that capitalism, far from burgeoning, was actually in the process of decline. The number of workers employed in large-scale 'socialised' plants showed a tendency to decline. From this he concluded that in spite of massive government subsidies, capitalism was collapsing due to the basic inhospitability of Russian conditions.

This economic theory of the Populists provided the foundation for their attack on the political practice of the Social Democrats. With some force they could argue that, given the fact that the Russian proletariat was numerically tiny (and declining in numbers), with its consciousness still extremely ill-developed, it would be foolhardy to premise one's whole political strategy on illusory hopes of its future dominance. The Marxists were grossly in error in designating the proletariat as *the* revolutionary class of the future, the most important anti-autocratic force in the country. Their error proceeded from an inappropriate transposition of Marx's conclusions to an alien context. Russia was not England; in particular, the persistence of communal land tenure preserved the peasantry from the incursion of capitalism and therefore from its social contradictions. Marx's schema was in other words, inapplicable to Russia however apposite its analysis might be to advanced industrial capitalism. If the economic analysis was in error, *ipso facto* the political prescriptions designating the proletariat as *the* revolutionary class, *the* vehicle of general emancipation, were also all awry.

According to Vorontsov, and the Neo-Populists generally, the economic salvation of Russia and the alleviation of the evident and widespread deprivation, was intimately bound up with the fate of the peasant commune. Only by revitalising the commune could the lot of the vast peasant majority of the Russian people be improved. Present governmental policies, they contended, were the main cause of the dissolution of the old natural economy made painfully manifest in the mass famine of 1891. The government-inspired importation of industry had to be paid for and it was the peasants who largely did the paying. The transport system necessary to industrialisation was similarly funded. The peasants, therefore, were burdened not merely with excessive redemption payments for the land they tilled, not merely with having to sustain an expensive parasitic nobility and a vast and privileged bureaucratic machine, but they also had to foot the bill for a programme of forced industrialisation which, far from benefiting them, resulted in higher imposts and the ruination of their handicraft enterprises. Small wonder then that the economy of the commune had been disrupted; the wonder was that it had survived at all. The tasks in hand, as the Neo-Populists conceived them, were, first, to bring pressure to bear to make the government aware of the foolhardiness of its policies, and second, to serve the people's welfare by helping to attenuate the corrosive influence of these mistaken policies, to mitigate in particular the more oppressive aspects of capitalist advance.

The position of the Neo-Populists with regard to industrialisation was certainly not one of unqualified opposition. Danielson, Mikhailovsky, and even the minimalist[10] Vorontsov, favoured the advance of manufacture and machine industry in so far as they improved the conditions of life of the mass. The development of industry was, however, only practicable, and, more emphatically, ethically desirable, on the basis of a simultaneous improvement in the standard of living of the peasantry. Only if this occurred was industrialisation to be welcomed; only in these circumstances, moreover, was, it *possible*, for without a mass market, without peasant well-being and purchasing power, industrialisation was doomed to collapse. This setting of the tasks of Populism raised, however, the enormous problem of *how* to introduce a planned, humane, socialist society given the existing political conditions. The credibility of the Populists in the nineties was closely tied to their ability to answer this question; the rapid decline of Populist fortunes can be seen as symptomatic of their failure to do so.

LENIN: THE NATURAL HISTORY OF CAPITALISM

The fundamental error of the Populists' appraisal of capitalism was, according to Lenin, their failure to view it as an organic process of growth characterised by differing features at differing stages of its evolution.

They characterised capitalism simply in terms of the typical contradictions of advanced industrial capitalism. They argued that if the worker was not alienated from the land, if there was little evidence of large-scale production involving machinery and therewith the socialisation of labour, little evidence therefore of an extensive proletariat, properly so-called, then it could not be contended that capitalism was the preponderant form of economic relations in Russia. The key to Lenin's response to the Populists was his extremely perceptive and original application to Russia of the stages of development of capitalism described by Marx in *Capital*.

Lenin's argument, briefly stated, ran as follows. The full-blown and typical contradictions of advanced *industrial* capitalism were not immediately apparent in the earlier phases of capitalist evolution. They were immanent within the whole course of its evolution but only *realised* in proportion as capitalism advanced towards the consummation of its highest phase. That capitalism must *eventuate* in the displacement of hand techniques by machine production, in supplanting small-scale artisan and peasant production by extensive plants developing the socialisation of labour and the division of labour to its utmost, all this Lenin accepted from Marx's exposé of its internal and necessary dynamic. The extension of the market from local and regional to national and international scale, with its corresponding expropriation of peasant and artisan; increased efficiency developing with the division of labour, utilisation of machinery and economies of size; the emergence of class contradictions and social polarity – this gamut of the characteristic features of capitalism were all reciprocally connected. They necessarily proceeded hand in hand towards their developed expression in large-scale machine industry. They were, however, developed only in the course of a long progress from usury to merchants' capital, and from this to manufacturing capital which in turn led on to the highest stage of industrial capital employed in production by machine. In terms of this fluid and sophisticated analysis Lenin undertook to reveal how the so-called 'people's industry' or 'Russian system' was by no means proof against the incursions of capitalism; on the contrary it was the basis upon which the nascent forms of capitalism were nurtured.

Lenin's approach was the natural history approach of starting with primitive forms of the evolution of capital in order the better to explain its fully mature form. 'The social process', Lenin remarked in 1894, 'is a process of natural history'.[11] Plekhanov, in contrast, tended to start at the top and work downwards arguing from a more abstracted notion of historical necessity. He accepted the fact that large-scale machine industry had been established in the urban centres and proceeded to analyse, in very general terms, the disruptive impact this had upon the traditional structure of natural economy in the peripheral hinterland. Lenin took on the far more demanding task of outlining the historical process of capitalist accumulation in the agrarian hinterland itself. He showed the process of growth of commodity economy out of natural economy, moving from its nascent forms to its developed expression in time, and from the countryside to the town in place. His account is, therefore, far more convincing than Plekhanov's as an explanatory model of the genesis and development not only of capitalist production, but also of the progressive socialisation of labour, the alienation of the peasantry and artisans from their own forces of production and the class formation of the proletariat.

Plekhanov's account provided no real answer to the constant Populist claim that capitalism was a harmful alien implantation, the introduction of which was exclusively to blame for the signs of collapse of Russia's natural economy. Indeed, Plekhanov yielded hostages to fortune by insisting that a main error of the

Populists was that they rather ignored the vital importance of government intervention in fostering capitalist development and protecting the home market by tariff barriers particularly in its early phases.[12]

Lenin's analysis confronted the Populists on their own chosen field of battle by demonstrating that the erosion of natural economy *in the countryside* was a spontaneous process which was entirely explicable without the need of invoking 'extraneous' factors like the intrusion of foreign capital or the role of the Russian state in 'artificially' promoting or protecting capitalist production.[13]

Crucial to Lenin's whole position in the controversy was his minimal definition of capitalism as no more than that particular stage of commodity production at which 'not only the products of human labour, but human labour-power itself becomes a commodity'.[14] Where men were employed for wages in order to produce goods for sale on the market – there capitalism existed. This definition was of considerable importance to Lenin's whole analysis since it allowed him to side-step a semantic problem which could potentially have called it into serious question. The problem was this: Lenin was setting out to describe Russian economic life as *capitalist* in terms of economic structures which Marx explicitly described as *pre-capitalist*. The chapter of Volume One of *Capital* where Marx discussed the role of usury and merchant's capital is entitled 'Pre-Capitalist Economic Formations'. The question might therefore arise: wasn't Lenin pulling a fast one introducing these self-same forms as evidence of capitalism? What Lenin was implying was that Marx accidently slipped into the same trap as the Narodniks, reserving the term capitalism only for the most advanced phase of a long process. That this was inconsistent is demonstrated by applying Marx's own definition of capitalism to these earlier phases. Utilising this definition Lenin went on to demonstrate with massive documentation that the presence of labour power as a commodity (*ergo* the presence of capitalism) was evident long before the development of a national market, extensive division of labour, large-scale machine production, etc. These latter characteristics were indeed dependent upon, and presumed the prior existence of, labour power as a commodity. To cite these evidences of a highly developed capitalist market structure and technology as typical of capitalism *tout court* was to fail to notice that 'capitalism exists both where technical development is low and where it is high; in *Capital* Marx repeatedly stresses the point that capital first subordinates production as it finds it, and only subsequently transforms it technically'.[15]

THE PHASES OF CAPITALIST DEVELOPMENT

The error of the Narodniks arose, according to Lenin, from their lack of historical sense. They quite failed to understand that the capitalism of machine industry, with its developed division of labour, had its own history. It represented certainly the apex of capitalist development but it was only an apex which rested upon and presumed a vastly more extensive infrastructure. This infrastructure was gradually built up through the various stages of capitalist growth. Only gradually were the small producers expropriated, only gradually was the old natural economy of feudalism subordinated to the power of capital.

> The subordination begins with *merchants* and *usury capital*, then grows into industrial capitalism, which in its turn is at first technically quite primitive, and does not differ in any way from the old systems of production, then organises manufacture – which is still based on hand labour, and on the dominant handicraft industries, without breaking the tie between the wage-worker and the land – and completes its development with large-scale machine industry. It is this last, highest stage that constitutes the culminating point of the development of capitalism, *it alone* creates the fully expropriated worker who is as free as a bird, *it alone* gives rise (both materially and socially) to the 'unifying significance' of capitalism that the Narodniks are accustomed to connect with capitalism in general, *it alone* opposes capitalism to its 'own child'.[16]

The Narodniks always described things as though the worker separated from the land was a necessary condition of capitalism *in general*, and not of machine industry alone.

Let us now turn to an examination of Lenin's account of this process. As he usually represented it, it consisted of a temporal progression of four stages though, as he was at pains to point out, the rate of progress in different branches of industry and in different regions of the empire was very uneven and variegated.

The stages he set out were, of course, similar to those outlined by Plekhanov but Lenin was able, thanks largely to the availability of a great volume of reliable data recently collected by Zemstvo statisticians, to fill out far more convincingly the Russian mutation of the Marxian position. Above all, he was able to establish the interconnection between these stages through case studies of particular industries and regions. In what follows, the very considerable data which Lenin assembled to validate his theme has to be omitted; only the general progression which constitutes the organisational principle of his early economic works is set out.

Usury was the first and most primitive form of capital as it emerged within the old economic order. Echoing Marx, Lenin maintained that usury (or kulak) capital represented the domination of capital in its primary forms.[17] Its basis lay in the natural differentiation (size of family, hence of allotment) of peasant households into relatively well-to-do and impoverished, a differentiation which greatly increased in post-Reform Russia due to the obligation of all households to contribute cash to the communal redemption payments. The intrusion of cash payment into the old natural economy carried with it enormous repercussions. It necessitated commodity production on the part of the small producer; it obliged him to produce increasingly for the market in order to obtain cash. Not only did it act to stimulate the growth of the market, it also provided the basis for the growth of usury capital. The usurer followed in the baggage-train of the tax collector. As Marx put it,

> Every payment of money, ground-rent, tribute, tax, etc. which becomes due on a certain date, carries with it the need to secure money for such a purpose. Hence from the days of ancient Rome to _those of modern times, wholesale usury relies upon tax collectors.[18]

Some were obliged to borrow money from their better-off neighbours against the security of the sole commodity of value remaining to them – their labour power. At this stage the power of money became the power of capital in that it was employed in the purchase of labour power, having as its objective the securing of surplus value. The kulaks became the beneficiaries of the labour service rendered by the poorer and middle peasants, profiting from the latter's every misfortune to press ever more usurious terms upon them.[19]

Lenin saw bondage (through mortgage or long-term debts) as invariably associated with usury; indeed, the two terms were often identified. 'The Russian *muzhik* knows only too well what bondage is! From the scientific standpoint this concept covers all contracts which entail elements of *usury*.'[20] The conditions of personal dependence and bondage attaching to labour service as a primitive rent for land, or repayment of a loan, was emphasised too by Marx. Labour-rent, he maintained, appeared as 'a direct relation of lordship and servitude, so that the direct producer is not free; a lack of freedom which may be reduced from serfdom with enforced labour to a mere tributary relationship'.[21]

The more precarious the situation of the 'independent' peasant farmer, the more he was forced into a situation of comprehensive dependence and bondage to the kulak. Indeed, the very fact of his vaunted 'independence' was itself a major element in this enslavement for, in his struggle to retain his status, the 'independent' allotment-holding peasant was obliged from time to time to borrow money or grain from his more wealthy neighbours undertaking 'to work off either the entire loan or the interest on it'.[22] Typically he undertook to perform a specified job utilising his own implements and draught animals, often at the very time when these were most needed on his own allotment, which consequently went further into decline. The very fact that he possessed a measure of independence in his own allotment in turn reduced the wages the kulak and landowner were obliged to pay, so that the returns for work performed were usually less than half those under 'free' capitalist hire.[23] 'The allotment in such cases, continues to this day to serve as a means of "guaranteeing" the landowner a supply of cheap labour.'[24] The less viable 'independent' farming became, due to the competition of 'commercial' agriculture (which itself presupposed the on-going process of conversion of the 'independent' producer into a wage-labourer), the more the poorer and middle peasantry were forced, in order to preserve their vestigial 'independence', to resort to usurious conditions of labour-service – the more, in other words, they became wage-labourers assisting the progress of that very capitalist agriculture that was engulfing their independence.

Lenin was arguing that a complicated and harsh dialectical process was at work. The more desperately the peasants struggled to retain their independent status, the more surely they contributed to their own ruin since, at least in its early stages, capitalist agriculture parasitically relied upon a measure of peasant 'independence'. It was dependent upon the plentiful source of cheap labour power, implements and draught animals supplied by the impoverished allotment-holding peasantry. They formed a convenient reservoir not only of labour but also of 'capital goods' (implements, draught animals and their pasturage) enabling capitalist farming to commence and to extend its sway with the minimum possible outlay on constant capital.[25]

Lenin expressly derived his analysis of labour-rent and its subsequent transmutation into money-rent from Chapter Forty-seven of Volume Three of *Capital*. There Marx outlined the essential characteristics of labour-rent as follows:

> If we consider ground-rent in its simplest form, that of *labour-rent*, where the direct producer, using instruments of labour (plough, cattle, etc.) which actually or legally belong to him, cultivates soil actually owned by him during part of the week, and works during the remaining days upon the estate of the feudal lord without any compensation from the feudal lord, the situation here is still quite clear, for in this case rent and surplus-value are identical.[26]

The whole system, according to Marx, was necessarily dependent upon the most extreme ties of personal bondage, i.e., complete dependence upon the local lord or usurer which might result either from legal obligations or from the pressure of immediate economic need. In either case, Marx concluded, 'conditions of personal dependence are requisite, a lack of personal freedom, no matter to what extent, and being tied to the soil as its accessory, bondage in the true sense of the word'.[27]

The effects of usury capital were, to a large extent, regressive. Following Marx's analysis Lenin argued that there must be an accentuation rather than diminution of bondage, particularly the most pernicious forms of personal bondage and dependence,[28] adding further inhibitions to the mobility of the peasant population. Nor did it have anything to commend it with regard to improvements in the mode of production; on the contrary it was based upon primitive hand-labour technique and stereotyped cultivation. The isolation of the separate and tiny units of production and the immobility of the peasantry, which usury accentuated, limited the possibilities of innovation, limited social intercourse among the peasantry and limited, too, the extent of the market. Consequently the peasant was unable to conceive of the oppression of capital as systematic; he saw it rather as adventitious and proceeding from the machinations of 'tricksters' and 'shrewd people'.[29] The conditions of dependence and exploitation under usury capital were peculiarly personal ones, based upon the social immobility of the countryside and dispersed small-scale production – conditions which, as Lenin approvingly noted, Marx had pointed to in explaining the low level of class consciousness among the peasantry.[30]

The role of usury capital was none the less important in that it initiated the process whereby the independent cultivator progressively became a wage-labourer – a necessary condition for the further evolution of capitalist agriculture. Its technical base, however, remained reliant upon ancestral technique, and its limitation of the market for labour power and other commodities militated against the further development of commercial agriculture and therefore it had to be supplanted.

That Lenin's account of the dual character (the 'contradictory elements') of usurer's capital squared with that of Marx can be readily observed by pursuing his references[31] to the *locus classicus* of his ideas on 'Usurer's Capital', Volume Three of *Capital*:

> Usury centralises money wealth where the means of production are dispersed. It does not alter the mode of production, but attaches itself to it like a parasite and makes it wretched . . . Usury has a revolutionary effect in all pre-capitalist forms of property on whose solid foundation and continued reproduction in the same form the political organisation is based.[32]

Merchant capital was the next stage in the progress; it emerged from usury capital with which, in many instances, it was inextricably connected. With the growth of commodity production, and therefore of the market, the small producer was increasingly distanced from his customer. He no longer had either the requisite knowledge or the volume of goods to undertake the marketing of his own

commodities. Conditions were created for the emergence of an entre-
preneurial class whose initial function was simply to see to the
marketing of the commodities of the small producer on the vastly
extended market which the development of the railway had produced.[33] The merchant had both a knowledge of the market and
the necessary bridging finance to undertake to purchase goods on
a regular basis from the small producer for resale on the market.

Merchant capital entered the countryside in the seemingly
innocent person of the buyer-up. The merchant, however, was not
slow to capitalise upon his effective monopoly of knowledge of
the market and upon the fact that he swiftly became 'the only
person to whom the peasant can regularly dispose of his wares,
and then the buyer-up takes advantage of his monopoly position
to force the price he pays to the producer down to rock bottom'.[34]
The peasant or artisan was increasingly forced to borrow money
and repay his debt with goods (needless to say at a considerable
discount). The connection between merchant's and usury capital
was made manifest; the merchant/usurer took every opportunity of
profiting from the misfortunes of his 'clients' to increase their
dependence and indebtedness. Finally, the merchant realised the
advantages that could accrue not only from disposing of the finished
commodities but also from the supply of raw materials, a profit
being secured at both ends of the process. 'Having cut off the
small industrialist from the finished-goods market, the buyer-up
now cuts him off from the raw materials market and thereby brings
him completely under his sway.'[35] From this it was but a short
step to begin actually to pay the small producer for finished
goods with raw materials. Imperceptibly this phase of the internal
development of merchant's capital was transformed into the system
where

> the buyer-up directly hands out materials to the handicraftsman
> to be worked up for a definite payment. The handicraftsmen
> becomes *de facto* a wage-worker, working at home for the capita-
> list; merchant's capital of the buyer-up is here transformed into
> industrial capital.[36]

So long as the entrepreneur was concerned merely to take over
the marketing of the goods of the peasants or handicraftsmen, later
the bulk purchase of raw materials for resale to them, his capital

remained within the domain of merchant capital. However, as soon as he proceeded to employ the peasants or artisans to utilise implements or to work up raw materials belonging to *him*, merchant capital was transformed into manufacturing capital.

The transformation into manufacturing capital was, of course, far from being clear-cut. It was, at first, intermingled with the existing forms of merchant and usury capital. Similarly its level of technical development would, at first, be quite primitive and virtually indistinguishable from that which preceded it. Merchant's capital clearly signalled an extension of the market and the growing pre-eminence of commodity production, but it did not entail, in its early forms at least, improvements in technique, socialisation of labour, or even the alienation of the peasantry from the soil. It was this comparatively early stage of capitalist development at which Russian agriculture of the 1890s found itself, at the stage of transition from merchant's to manufacturing capital. Capital, in other words, was just beginning to be applied directly to the productive system instead of merely being concerned with the appropriation and marketing of its produce.[37]

Manufacture was the third and penultimate stage in the evolution of capital, a primitive form of industrial capital. The initial form typically adopted by industrial capital was that of capitalist domestic manufacture. The previous phases of capitalist development, by expropriating part of the peasantry and making large numbers of the earth-scratching allotment-holders increasingly dependent upon outside industrial employ, created a great reservoir of unemployed or underemployed labour to be tapped by the domestic system. The existence of this surplus population was itself a necessary prerequisite for the further progress of capitalism.[38]

The hesitant beginnings of manufacturing capital were to be seen in the establishment of manufactories producing half-finished goods which were sent out to be worked up at home for a fixed price by the rural surplus population. In this way as Lenin (following Marx) pointed out, great economies were produced not only in that demands on capital for premises and implements were thereby reduced, but the costs of supervision and of labour power generally were reduced to the barest minima. In many ways this was directly comparable to the labour-service system in agriculture; it was motivated by similar considerations – the maximum extraction of surplus value from the lowest outlay on constant capital. Its results, too, were almost exactly similar to those noticed prevailing under this system in agriculture. The workers were 'scattered, disunited, and less capable of self-defence'.[39] They were subject to the depredations not only of the entrepreneurs but of the multitudes of subcontractors who sprang up, so that a double tribute was exacted from their labour. The conditions of work were universally appalling, the hours of work prodigious and all the usurious tricks learnt so well by now – the truck system, sweating system and payment of wages in goods – were visited upon the benighted workers.[40] They were subjected to 'not only robbery of labour, but also Asiatic abuse of human dignity that is constantly encountered in our countryside', conditions of bondage which arose out of the immobility of labour.[41]

In its early development even manufacture represented no technical advance. It concentrated production to some extent but still utilised untransformed hand technique; it was but handicraft industry writ large. The advantages of size and the benefits that could accrue from developing a degree of specialisation and division of labour within the manufactory were, however, gradually developed. Increased competition, a function of the growth of the market, led to increased specialisation of the individual workshops or, as Lenin would have it, a more highly ramified 'social division of labour'.[42] The whole development and importance of capitalist manufacture might indeed be characterised by its intense development of the division of labour between workshops and within the workshop. 'Manufacturing industry splits up into separate, quite independent branches, each devoted exclusively to the manufacture of one product or one part of a product.'[43] The erstwhile artisan was progressively reduced from an omni-competent skilled worker to a mere detail-worker, exclusively concerned with the repetitious performance of one specialised part of his trade. The technical basis of manufacture was still hand labour, but through the division of labour and the accompanying specialisation of the tools and instruments utilised, a great increase in productivity was attained.[44] It was precisely this involved division of labour within manufacture that prepared the way for the final phase of large-scale machine industry, for it reduced the complex intricacies of hand labour to its simplest component parts, to the detail-labour of repetitive mechanical operations. The simplest of these operations was gradually taken over by machinery, which only gradually extended its sway within the productive process. The workman, as detail-labourer, became unable any longer to work on his own account, his skills atrophied and he was able to produce only as an operative in a socialised labour process. As a productive being he was trained to dependence upon the factory; he was trained to accept the fact that he could exist now only as a wage-labourer. Manufacture was, in all senses, a transition period to the stage of large-scale machine industry. It created the necessary agglomerations of capital and further developed the expropriation of the 'independent' artisan and handicraftsman, extending the mass of underemployment and unemployment so vital to the development of machine industry. Yet even at this stage the separation of industry from agriculture was not completely effected nor was the small producer finally extinguished.[45] Manufacture, in some of its phases, still found the vestigial 'independence' of these small producers a useful adjunct to its own power.[46]

Though evidently not yet fully realised, the essential contradictions of machine industry already began to manifest themselves in the phase of capitalist manufacture. The growth of large workshops and socialisation of labour 'begins the transformation of the mentality of the population'.[47] The objective conditions for the emergence of class consciousness and social polarity were emerging even if still partially obfuscated.

> The gulf between the one who owns the means of production and the one who works now becomes very wide . . . . But the multitude of small establishments, the retention of the tie with the land, the adherence to tradition in production and in the whole manner of living – all this creates a mass of intermediary elements between the extremes of manufacture and retards the development of these extremes.[48]

Polarity, open struggle of the differences, had not yet emerged but things were moving towards their maturation. The essential contradictions of capitalism, immanent in its earlier phases of development, were here being realised – albeit imperfectly. Only the full development of large-scale machine industry would finally eliminate 'the intermediary elements'.

Lenin's whole analysis rested upon his location of the contradictions immanent within capitalism being actualised in proportion as capitalism advanced through the several phases of its evolution. They attained their quintessential expression only in the highest and culminating phase. This notion came through forcibly in his rebuttal of a favourite Populist argument that machine industry was but an adventitious and geographically restricted growth (a mere 'corner'), artificially promoted by mistaken government policies and having no contact with the prevailing 'people's industry' of the independent self-sufficient peasant and artisan.

> If we take even the smallest producers in agriculture or in industry, we will find that the one who does not hire himself out, or himself hire others, is the exception. But here again, these relationships reach full development and become completely separated from previous forms of economy only in large-scale machine industry. Hence, the 'corner' which seems so small to some. Narodniks *actually embodies the quintessence of modern social relationships,* and the population of this 'corner', i.e., the proletariat, is, in the literal sense of the word, the vanguard of the whole mass of toilers and exploited. Therefore, only by examining the whole of the present economic system from the angle of the relationships that have grown up in this 'corner' can one become clear about the main relationships between the various groups of persons taking part in the production, and, consequently, trace the system's main trend of development.[49]

Here was the yardstick for examining the earlier phases of capitalist evolution, the extent to which its typical quintessential characteristics were realised. Only in proportion as this realisation occurred were the conditions created for the growth of modern classes and their consciousness – the preconditions of final emancipation.

At last we arrive at the characteristics of advanced machine industry. If the existence of a profusion of petty self-contained and isolated markets was typical of the early phases of capitalist development, the era of industrial capitalism proper brought with it the boundless extension of the market's limits commensurate with its prodigious output of commodities. The market was now national and unified: indeed, it became an international market. A prime condition for the growth of the home market (and here Lenin diametrically confronted the Sismondian underconsumption arguments of the Populists[50]) was precisely the final expropriation of the peasantry and handicraftsmen. Their alienation from their own forces of production obliged them to purchase on the market what hitherto they had themselves produced or acquired through barter. This expropriation was finally accomplished through the utilisation of agricultural machinery, rendering obsolete the old parcellated and antiquated mode of peasant farming and releasing great numbers of the peasantry, making them 'available' to the growing need for labour of machine industry. Thus, only at this, the highest stage of capitalism was the separation of industry from agriculture, the final expropriation of the peasant, accomplished. The very growth of the market was indeed partly based upon the necessity of larger numbers of wage-workers purchasing the articles of consumption they previously produced for themselves.

Lenin's theory of the growth of the market under capitalism was without doubt a great improvement on Plekhanov's and was based on his reading of Volumes Two and Three of *Capital* which were, of course, unavailable to Plekhanov when he formulated his ideas. Plekhanov had very little to say on the theoretical problems of the growth of the market under capitalism, but for Lenin the issue was inescapable since, as we have seen, the Legal Populists based their whole argument on the impossibility of an adequate home market developing in Russia to absorb the product of capitalist industry. In 1893 Lenin had already elaborated a sophisticated and detailed Marxist account of the way in which the progressive phases of capitalist accumulation must expand the market. His article, 'On the so-called Market Question',[51] demonstrated an impressive grasp not only of the statistical evidence of the differentiation proceeding among the peasants and artisans and the growth of manufacture in various trades and regions of Russia; it also showed how thoroughly conversant Lenin was with Marx's arguments in Volume Two of *Capital*.

> Part III of Volume II of *Capital*, in which Marx discussed the so-called theory of realisation or the reproduction scheme, is the basis from which Lenin starts his whole argument. He probably understood the implications of Marx's scheme better than any other man; and also the limitations of the theory of realisation too.[52]

Lenin's argument was that there was evidence in plenty to demonstrate the rapid growth of differentiation and specialisation both within and between the various trades or sectors of commodity production. Each advance in the social division of labour necessarily caused an extension of commodity production and a commensurate increase in the volume of goods the artisans and peasants were obliged to purchase on the market. 'The concept "market" is quite inseparable from the concept of the social division of labour.'[53] This in no way inferred, however, that the standard of living of the wage-workers was increased. On the contrary, Lenin would agree with the Legal Populists that it tended, in fact, to depress their living conditions to the barest minimum, and often below that. The issue at stake was not whether the early phases of capitalist accumulation created greater popular well-being, but whether they obliged the peasants and artisans to purchase an ever-increasing volume of their immediate requirements on the market rather than, as under natural economy, producing them for themselves. Lenin could point to an impressive volume of Russian evidence to support Marx's general finding that while the level of consumption of the peasants and artisans had declined, none the less the quantity of goods purchased on the market had increased. The impoverishment of the mass, far from being an impediment to the growth of the market and of capitalist accumulation, was an essential condition for both.

> The second conclusion is that 'the impoverishment of the masses of the people' (that indispensable point in all the Narodnik arguments about the market) not only does not hinder the development of capitalism, but, on the contrary, is the expression of that development, is a condition of capitalism and strengthens it. Capitalism needs the 'free labourer' and impoverishment consists in the petty producers being converted into wage-workers. The impoverishment of the masses is accompanied by the enrichment of a few exploiters, the ruin and decline of small establishments is accompanied by the strengthening and development of bigger ones; both facilitate the growth of the market: the 'impoverished' peasant who formerly lived by his own farming now lives by 'earnings', i.e. by the sale of his labour-power; he now has to purchase essential articles of consumption (although in a smaller quantity and of inferior quality). On the other hand, the means of production from which this peasant is freed are concentrated in the hands of a minority,

are converted into *capital*, and the product now appears on the market.[54]

The main impetus for the growth of the market was not, however, production of the means of consumption. It was production of the means of production, i.e., of tools and machinery, buildings and the production of raw materials that go into their composition, that predominantly accounted for the growth of the market. It was the historical mission of capitalism, Lenin argued, not to maximise consumption but rather to maximise accumulation and the more rapidly accumulation proceeded, the more intense, consequently, was the development of that department of capitalist production which manufactured products not for personal but for productive consumption.[55] This, Lenin contended, was a necessary and inherent contradiction of capitalism which became most fully apparent in its highest stage of development.[56] It was a necessary concomitant of the progressive role of industrial capitalism in immeasurably augmenting the power and effectiveness of the productive forces of society.

THE FORMATION OF THE PROLETARIAN CLASS AND ITS VANGUARD ROLE

Accumulation and the unending necessity of expanding production presumed the exploitation of labour on a vast scale and its concentration, or socialisation, in large numbers. Large-scale machine production and a sophisticated division of labour necessarily entailed the aggregation of workers into ever larger units. All of this evidently presupposed the availability of larger and larger numbers of wage-labourers who not only *needed* to sell their labour power but who also were not restricted in travelling by legal impediment or local ties.[57] The constraints of machine industry, therefore, very greatly increased the mobility of the population and Lenin made impressive use of statistics to demonstrate the existence of vast numbers of migrant labourers leaving the agricultural areas to seek work in the urban centres or rural industrial settlements.[58] These vast legions of migrant workers, recruited from the reserve army of the unemployed 'released' by the expropriation of the peasantry and 'liberation' of the artisans and handicraftsmen, could not but have the effect of breaking down the web of personal, patriarchal, communal and local ties which had so long enslaved the peasant – ties of bondage, which, as we have seen, were accentuated rather than diminished in the early phases of capitalism and had succeeded in reducing the peasant to the level of a barbarian accustomed to Asiatic abuse and lack of civil rights, a creature with extremely low cultural level and expectations. His wanderings across the face of Russia, the variety of jobs he undertook, the large groups with whom he could compare and share experience, all combined to break down the feudal incubus which had so restricted his social, political and material expectations. This, Lenin argued was the beginning of the process of class formation.[59]

The rural proletarian becoming an industrial worker was, Lenin maintained, confronted with new perspectives, and this arose from the very different social relations of production in which he was involved. The isolated mode of production in agriculture, with its ill-elaborated division of labour, was supplanted by an eminently social and co-operative productive process with a highly refined division of labour. The industrial worker was brought willy nilly into productive and social relations with countless others. Means of communication with his fellows was facilitated by (was, indeed, a prime condition of) industrial production, and his urban environment. The conditions were thereby created for associations of the wage-workers, the beginnings of organisations of self-help and mutual defence, the beginnings of the consciousness that they formed a separate and distinct class.

Part of the historic role of industrial capitalism, according to Lenin, was to accomplish the

> shattering to the very foundations the ancient forms of economy and life, with their age-old immobility and routine, destroying the settled life of the peasants who vegetated behind their medieval partitions, and creating new social classes striving of necessity towards contact, unification, and active participation in the whole of the economic (and not only economic) life of the country, and of the whole world.[60]

Therewith was created 'a special class of the population totally alien to the old peasantry and differing from the latter in its manner of living, its family relationship and its higher standard of requirements, both material and spiritual'.[61] This growth of expectations and insistence upon a measure of human dignity on the part of the industrial worker signalled a new beginning of social and political relations in Russia. The exploited people were no longer quiescent in their dismal lot. The socialisation of labour gave them confidence in their combined strength. Indeed, the very processes of industrial capitalist production themselves organised and disciplined the proletarians for their struggle and began to forge their consciousness into an awareness of their class position.[62] Confronted as they were with exploitation in its classically pure form,[63] *sans phrases* and unencumbered by the entanglements of personal ties that accompanied exploitation in the nascent phases of capitalism, the relationship of the workers to their employers was made crystal clear. They realised, Lenin contended, that it was founded on callous cash payment and the market.[64] The veil which had hitherto shrouded the essential nature of capitalism was rent asunder. The developed contradiction between social production and individual appropriation was fully realised. Here, Lenin was confident, dreams were no longer possible.[65] The social polarities immanent within all the earlier phases of the development of capitalism were progressively realised within its several stages of evolution. The task of theory had been to elucidate the precise stage at which various branches of Russian industry found themselves, hence the extent to which social polarities were realised.

In the early phases, of course, these contradictions were ill-developed and difficult to discern even by those most intimately caught up in them. To explain how and why the evolution of capitalism led necessarily to the self-evident contradictions of developed capitalism was Lenin's main object. Given that theory accepted that the evolution of capitalism from one stage to the next was a law-governed process, it became possible for (it was, indeed, incumbent upon) the theorist to be aware beforehand of the configuration of social contradictions, not only as presently existing but as they were likely to appear in the stage that was coming to be. Throughout his career, whether Lenin was examining the development of capitalism, working-class consciousness, the Party or the activities of the Soviet State, this sense of movement towards an end, the notion of *progressive and demarcated stages of advance* remained constant. We have seen how this applied to Lenin's economic studies: it applied every bit as much to his overtly political analyses. He was, throughout, insistent upon the obligation of the theorist to judge the moment when a particular phase had exhausted its potentialities, an obligation which carried with it the task of supplying the theoretical and organisational realignments appropriate to the coming phase. This was, in brief, Lenin's conception of the role of the Marxist theorist in a revolutionary movement.

It is in this general context that we should understand Lenin's characterisation of the proletariat as the vanguard class leading the struggle of the exploited against autocracy and eventually against capital. They were the vanguard class not simply because Marx said so, but because they alone were in a position to come to an adequate understanding of exploitation. Here the socialisation of labour, its stark confrontation with massive wealth, its convenient lines of communication, etc. formed, as we have seen, the objective and necessary conditions for the growth of class consciousness. Only in the factory were these conditions adequately developed:

> The very capitalism that is underdeveloped in the village and, therefore, abounds in usury, etc., is developed in the factory: the very antagonism existing in the countryside is fully expressed in the factory: here the split is complete, the question cannot be posed in the half-hearted way that satisfies the small producer ... *Here* dreams are not possible.[66]

The peasantry and the handicraftsmen suffered no less from capitalist exploitation; in a way, as we have seen, they suffered more, but the nature of their exploitation was more diffuse and diverse and their mode of production restricted mobility and lines of communication. Their indebtedness was to particular persons, and against these persons rather than against a system of exploitative relations their animosity was directed. Oppressed and exploited they certainly were, but they could not apprehend the nature of their exploitation, they could not articulate their grievances nor organise themselves for their redress; they lacked in short, the fundamental prerequisites of a class properly so-called.

For these reasons the proletarian alone was in a position to articulate the grievances of *all* the exploited strata; he 'is the sole and natural representative of Russia's entire working and exploited population'[67] – 'natural' in that his life situation was already that which the life situation of the other strata must become, 'natural' in terms of an almost Aristotelean teleology where the developed and already realised characteristics of the proletarian life situation were but immanent in the life situation of the other exploited strata,

> Natural because the exploitation of the working people in Russia *is everywhere capitalist in nature*. . . . But the exploitation of the mass of producers is on a small scale, scattered and un-developed, while the exploitation of the factory proletariat is on a large scale, socialised and concentrated. In the former case, exploitation is still enmeshed in medieval forms, various political, legal and conventional trappings, tricks and devices, which hinder the working people and their ideologists from seeing the essence of the system which oppresses the working people, from seeing where and how a way can be found out of this system. In the latter case, on the contrary, exploitation is fully developed and emerges in its pure form, without any confusing details. The worker cannot fail to see that he is oppressed by *capital*, that his struggle has to be waged against the bourgeois *class* . . . the class which oppresses and crushes the working people not only in the factories, but everywhere. That is why the factory worker is none other than the foremost representative of the entire exploited population.[68]

Lenin had here arrived at a momentous idea. In the first place, in broad theoretical terms he had greatly refined the somewhat sketchy notion of the proletariat as a vanguard class. He offered a sophisticated rationale for it, more in keeping with Marx's method than Marx's own estimation of the proletariat. Marx himself never fully escaped from a rather Romantic conceit of the proletariat as a class standing outside civil society, a class with radical chains whose mission was to realise philosophy. This conception also coloured Plekhanov's rather patrician attitude towards the proletariat. In the case of both men their initial location of the proletariat as a revolutionary instrument stemmed more from a Romantic dialectic – a desire to find a totally alienated group which would rejuvenate a degenerate civilisation – than from a more positive conception of the determined life situation of the proletariat as preparing it for the leadership of all those exploited by capital. Marx, especially, portrayed it as the most oppressed, poorest, most alienated and, therefore, most *indignant* class – almost, it would seem, in exile from society.[69] Lenin's location of the proletariat as a vanguard class owed nothing to these conceptions. His view, as we have shown above, stemmed directly from an application of Marx's later economic methodology. He made explicit what was merely inferred in Marx's teleology of capitalist development, by pointing out that just as machine industry represented the apogee of capitalist development and a portent of the development of capitalism in general, so its product, the proletariat, represented the *essential* predicament of all wage-earners.

Secondly, Lenin not only made this inference from Marx explicit, he also was to make it the corner-stone of his whole political strategy. As we shall see presently, Lenin, having arrived at this view of the role of the proletariat, did not hesitate to draw what he considered to be the logically necessary consequences from it. The proletariat, in his analysis, was duty-bound to act not only on its own behalf, but on behalf also of all the millions of wage-working peasants and artisans, the semi-proletarians whose cause was intimately linked with their own. The proletariat was duty-bound to represent them in the historical process for the good reason that theory had demonstrated why they, though severely exploited, were unable to represent themselves. In its political role especially, the proletariat must bear the enormous responsibility of: (1) convincing the semi-proletarians of the identity of interest shared with the proletariat, (2) representing *all* the exploited in the national, hence political, domain and (3) clarifying and making more apparent the essential polarity into which society was riven. It is clear then that for Lenin the proletariat could not adopt a passive stance of awaiting a proletarian 'majority' before committing itself to purposeful political action. On the contrary, the educative lead of the proletariat in clarifying and polarising social and political life was the key element in *producing* majority support for the cause of the emancipation of the exploited. The responsibilities and obligations of the vanguard role of the proletariat entailed in Lenin's view were staggering. That Lenin took them totally seriously is beyond doubt. We shall not understand his later vehemence, nor his whole political line especially from 1903 to 1905, unless we grasp how his view of the proletariat as the 'natural representative' of all Russia's exploited reinforced and considerably extended the precedence given in the orthodoxy to the proletariat's role in the democratic revolution. The democratic revolution would be won by the proletariat, Lenin insisted, not primarily in association with the bourgeois liberals, but in association with the rural semi-proletarians who were part petty-bourgeois and part proletarian. Their class position alone could guarantee, in association with the proletariat, an un-ambiguous and radical conclusion to the battle for democracy. Only in this way would the proven treachery of the bourgeoisie proper be forestalled.

The importance of Lenin's economic theory for an understanding of his politics cannot be over-estimated; the two elements are inextricably bound, especially in his early works. His analysis of the economic and social conditions of emergent capitalism led him directly to the unique potentialities of a proletarian–peasant alliance which he was to canvass so aggressively in 1905 and 1917. Those who maintain variously that either Lenin had never bothered to undertake an analysis of Russian society or that he opportunistically appropriated the analyses of others – the agrarian programme of the Socialist Revolutionaries is often cited – are equally wide of the mark. These interpretations do not fit the known facts. We know, for instance, that Lenin was beyond doubt the best-informed of all Russian Social Democrats on the economic and social situation in Russia. Neither Plekhanov nor Martov or Akselrod, nor certainly Deich and Zasulich could come close to him in this respect. It was Lenin who was given the task of formulating the crucial agrarian programme of the Russian Social Democratic Labour Party (R.S.D.L.P.), and almost alone of the prominent leaders of the Party, he was able to contribute a great deal to the day-to-day agitational literature of the mid-nineties, which demanded a detailed knowledge of Russian conditions.

It was no accident that Lenin first established his reputation as a theorist in the economic sphere with his sharp critique of Struve's *Critical Remarks on the Subject of Russia's Economic Development*.[70] Struve, he contended, interpreted Marx too mechanically, too fatalis-tically; he quite failed to appreciate the dynamic importance of class struggle. Having disposed of Struve, who was his only serious contender in the sphere of economic analysis within the Party, Lenin consolidated his position with a ceaseless stream of articles and monographs culminating in his massive study, *The Development of Capitalism in Russia* (1899).[71] This was the product of all his earlier studies and of a prolonged and arduous period of study while in prison in St Petersburg and exile in Shushenskoye.

This book is arguably the most important he ever penned. The volume of work which went into its production is staggering. Some idea of the volume of material Lenin got through in this period can be gleaned from his letters to his family and to comrades detailing long lists of abstracts, Zemstvo and government publications, monographs and reports of commissions of one sort or another. He consulted and digested more than 500 of the most important books on all aspects of Russian social and economic conditions.[72] The labour of sifting, tabulating and integrating this material into his theoretical structure was no less exacting, as his notes and drafts make apparent.[73] That Lenin was constantly aware of the all-importance of an adequate appraisal of Russian economic life, is clear from his continuing detailed attention to the new literature and source materials which became available after 1899 and which he utilised for the numerous alterations and additions made to the second edition in 1908.

The Development of Capitalism in Russia remains the fullest, best-documented and best-argued examination of the crucial period of the evolution of capitalism out of feudalism in the literature of Marxism. It is, indeed, somewhat surprising that Lenin's later acolytes in under-developed countries, faced, it would seem, with analagous social and economic problems, made no attempt to transpose his insights and methodology to their own environments. By comparison with the weight of Lenin's researches, Mao's *Analysis of the Classes in Chinese Society*[74] for instance, seems flimsy and un-sophisticated. In Russia Lenin's book quickly became the standard authoritative source for Russian Marxists on the modern development of their society and economy. It is symptomatic of the state of contemporary scholarship on Lenin that almost all the commentators ignore this work, or give it the most cursory attention in spite of the fact that Lenin constantly insisted upon the integration of his economic and political analyses. Nowhere, indeed, is this more apparent than in his Preface to the Second Edition of *The Development of Capitalism in Russia* (1908):

The analysis of the social–economic system and, consequently, of the class structure of Russia given in this work on the basis of an economic investigation and critical analysis of statistics, has now been confirmed by the open political action of all classes in the course of the revolution. The leading role of the proletariat has been revealed. It has also been revealed that the strength of the proletariat in the process of history is immeasurably greater than its share of the total population. The economic basis of the one phenomenon and the other is demonstrated in the present work.[75]

CONCLUSION

The minimum objective of the present chapter has been to demonstrate that Lenin did work out a thoroughgoing analysis of Russian economic and social conditions. He was indeed, even in the 1890s, the foremost theorist of the Russian Marxists in this respect, and his work was accepted and extensively utilised by the orthodox. That Lenin was accepted as an important contributor to the orthodoxy is hardly surprising, for, as we have demonstrated, Lenin appropriated and expanded Plekhanov's sketch of capitalist development, giving it new cogency in supplying a mass of corroborative data and new sophistication in locating and describing the interaction of the various phases of its evolution. To this extent it was Lenin and not Plekhanov who was primarily responsible for routing the Neo-Populists by a detailed and concrete application of Marxism to Russian conditions. Lenin, too, was entirely in accord with the principal political tenet of orthodoxy – the leading role of the proletariat in the democratic revolution. He was the first to give this notion an economic justification in Marxist terms. From his economic analysis he demonstrated why the proletariat must emerge as the representative and leader of all Russia's exploited. The political implications of this formulation were to be very considerable and we may justifiably regard it as Lenin's most significant extension of the orthodoxy he inherited.

CHAPTER 5

From Economic Agitation to Political Agitation

It was in the mid-1890s and in the period extending up to the turn of the century that Lenin began to evolve an integrated and distinctive set of views on the practice of Social Democracy and on the revolutionary process. His major preoccupation in this period was the working out of a consistent tactic for Social Democracy, one which would attend to the needs of the moment yet, at the same time, guide them in the direction of the ultimate objective. Just as Lenin's theoretical work is intelligible only in terms of the internal teleology which informs it, so too with his ideas on practice. If each step in the development of capitalism was to be measured in terms of its contribution to the final phase of industrial capitalism, by an exactly similar reasoning each advance in working-class consciousness and organisation was appraised in terms of its contribution to the full development of that degree of Social-Democratic consciousness and organisation necessary for the socialist revolution. Just as the growth of capitalism demanded changes in its organisational structure, so too with the labour and Social-Democratic movements. Each phase of advance had, according to Lenin, its appropriate division of labour, its proper degree of centralisation and specialisation of function. The important thing for Lenin was, as we shall see, the ability to recognise when a particular phase had exhausted its progressive possibilities, when, therefore, it was necessary to inaugurate a new phase of advance in consciousness and so to establish a new organisational basis for the movement.

The development of capitalism and that of Social Democracy ran parallel in a dual sense. Historically and chronologically the one gave birth to the other. Notionally they partook of the same process of realising their essential character in proportion as they moved through the phases of their evolution. Lenin's teleological notions had, therefore, to stipulate some kind of timetable, or at least a specified progression towards an end. To this extent his early propaganda work, which envisaged raising the workers straight from a very primitive level of consciousness to Social-Democratic consciousness at one blow, was a false start. Lenin's early programmatic statements similarly reflected this absence of a specified progression. If we compare *What the 'Friends of the People' Are . . .* with Lenin's writings of some three or four years later, the differences are striking. *What the 'Friends of the People' Are . . .* is very general, exhortatory in tone and providing very little in the way of concrete organisational proposals. The presumption that adequate revolutionary consciousness would dawn on the working class appeared to be rooted in an act of faith or in an extrapolation from historical determinism – the ways, means and phases of this metamorphosis were not broached. From the middle of the 1890s the whole tenor of Lenin's recommendations on practice underwent a marked change, a change that derived its impetus from the large-scale strike movement which broke out at that time and his related acceptance of the tactics of *On Agitation*.

The strike movement which began in late 1894 gathered force and momentum in 1895 and reached its apogee in the huge St Petersburg textile strikes of 1896. It was this movement which obliged the Social Democrats, Lenin foremost among them, to revise their tactics. The strikes were in general rather anarchic affairs, ill-prepared, ill-organised and financed, lacking in leadership, and they almost invariably voiced very limited demands arising from particular abuses with regard to hours of work, payment of wages, piece-work rates, etc. This, it must have appeared, was petty and rather mundane stuff. The pursuit of trivial and local ameliorations must have seemed almost retrogressive when measured against the radical systemic change Social Democracy envisaged. The danger existed that the socialists might by lured by the prospect of fleeting popularity into participating in this movement and thereafter becoming prostituted into mere trade union leaders. On the other hand, there lay the equally grave danger of the Social Democrats becoming quite alienated from the labour movement – from the struggle, however primitive and limited, that the workers were already beginning to undertake. We have already seen how evidence of the alienation of the worker-intelligentsia at the Semyannikov factory had left its impress upon Lenin.

'ON AGITATION'

It was the brochure/programme *On Agitation* which provided Lenin with the necessary perspective to set a course which (he hoped) would avoid both the threat of degeneration into trade unionism and the danger of hermetic isolation from the working class. It was the mutually reinforcing influences of the strike movement and the brochure *On Agitation* that made Lenin realise the vital importance of the notion of practice in the development of revolutionary consciousness. When this notion is integrated with Lenin's theoretical analysis – especially his formulation of the idea of the proletariat as vanguard class – the skeleton of his whole theory of revolution is laid bare.

On Agitation was the product of the then much more advanced Jewish workers' movement in the Pale of Settlement (i.e., those regions in the western and southern provinces of the empire to which Russian Jews were confined). At this time the Jewish workers were much better and more extensively organised than were the Russians. They had already organised large-scale strikes and street demonstrations and had established a firm organisational nexus which was later to be formalised in the *Bund*. It was two prominent activists of the Jewish movement operating out of Vilna, who, reflecting on the experience gained in the strike movement, penned the brochure *On Agitation*. They were Julius Martov and Arkadi Kremer. The latter was, in fact, responsible for formulating the leading ideas of what came to be known as the 'Vilna Programme'. Martov's task, according to his memoirs, was purely editorial; he simply produced a polished version of Kremer's original paper.[1] The central conclusion that emerged from their reflections, which they voiced in the very first paragraph of the pamphlet, was 'that the first steps of the Russian Social Democrats were incorrect and that, in the interests of the cause, their tactics must be changed'.[2] Later in the pamphlet the criticism is amplified into a sweeping censure of the old, in-depth, small discussion groups characterising the period of 'propaganda'. By creaming off the best-educated and

111

most militant elements of the working class the Social Democrats (it was argued) merely produced men who 'understand the conditions of activity of Western Social Democracy better than the conditions of their own activity'.[3] Their activity was not simply useless for being so academic; it was more positively harmful in that the very men who should have emerged as the natural leaders of the workers in their everyday struggles were taken out of their class environment and this of itself retarded the development of the workers' struggle:

> Propaganda has a directly harmful side – it weakens the intellectual strength of the mass. Creating a worker socialist intelligentsia, alienated from the mass, we harm the cause of the development of the proletariat, we harm our own cause.[4]

The final indictment was becoming increasingly self-evident to the impatient activists in St Petersburg, but the bluntness with which it was uttered must have shocked them, as all home truths do. 'With propaganda in the circles great sacrifices were necessary for the achievement of insignificant results.'[5]

The crucial significance of this brochure for the subsequent evolution of Lenin's thought lay in its diagnosis of where the movement had gone wrong. It argued two closely related propositions. The first was that proletarian consciousness arose not out of theoretical induction and the educational work of intellectuals and worker-intellectuals: it had its origins, and was refined and developed, in the course of the very struggle for existence of the working mass. Secondly, it argued that it was utopian and unhistorical to imagine that the mass, even if blessed with cohorts of worker-intellectuals, would emerge directly from its pristine darkness into the full light of Social-Democratic consciousness at one blow. It argued that, on the contrary, the process of self-education through its own activity must take the working class through a series of transitional stages before this could be realised. Each stage built the basis for, and was the necessary precondition of, the next and higher phase in the development of consciousness. The idea of there being discernible stages in the evolution of working-class consciousness became, as we shall see, a central point of Lenin's theory of revolution; it seems clear that *On Agitation* provided him with the germs of it.

Kremer and Martov repeatedly insisted that before political consciousness became widespread among the workers, that is, before they could appreciate the importance of securing democratic liberties, they had first of all to solidify themselves and become aware of a community of economic interest.

The idea of political freedom is neither simple nor obvious, the more so in a politically backward country, the working class cannot be imbued with it so long as it remains suffocated in the present political atmosphere . . .[6]

The workers would, it was argued, be led to political awareness only in and through the economic struggle, only when experience had taught them the futility of attempting to achieve a general amelioration of their condition without statutory guarantees. Only experience would teach them that the struggle for improvements in working conditions and pay must become a struggle, not merely with particular employers, but with the whole bourgeois class and with the state which supported the capitalist order of things.

The consciousness of the opposition of interests must precede political class self-consciousness. The opposition of interests, then, will be recognised when this opposition appears in the life of the proletariat.[7]

On this basis, the struggle for petty and initially, very local demands would produce, according to the pamphlet, a resurgence of working-class energy.

It prepares and promotes individual persons who until then were lost in the mass, and it gives to other workers the example of how to 'fight successfully with the owners. In the struggle even for petty demands, the workers must willy nilly join together, satisfying themselves in practice of the necessity and possibility of uniting. This practice means much more in the education of the mass, it is more convincing than books speaking about the same thing.[8]

Only in and through continuous *economic* struggle was the class unified and prepared for the next *political* phase. The objectives of

113

the first phase were to develop 'a class, organised by life itself, with a strongly developed class egoism, with a consciousness of a community of interests of all workers and their opposition to the interests of all others'.[9]

On Agitation not only pointed to the importance of recognising the several phases of development of working-class consciousness, it also implicitly recognised the need for a change in the organisational structure of the labour and socialist movements appropriate to their changing objectives. It is worth quoting this rather unobtainable document at length.

> The first phase of the struggle for petty demands, towards which an easily understood calculation pushes the worker – the exploitation of the owner having been explained without difficulty – demands from the workers a certain level of energy and unanimity. In the second phase, when the task has to do with the whole bourgeois class, which the government will immediately hurry to help, a greater level of endurance, solidarity and courage will be demanded, together with the ability to connect its interests with the interests of other workers of the same branch of production, some times even of another, but such consciousness can be formed only when the worker comes by his own experience to the conclusion that success is impossible on the basis of localised struggle for the interests of workers of separate factories. The struggle with separate owners will form in the working class a degree of stability and endurance, of unity, a sense of independence and class self-confidence, which it will need when the necessity of the class struggle in the proper meaning of the word will arise before it. On entering this stage the workers' movement will begin little by little to assume a political colouring.[10]

It was, of course, an axiom of Marx's view of the role of the proletariat in history that for it to constitute a class properly so-called, it needed national organisation and a political party to express its interests. In the *Communist Manifesto* and elsewhere Marx was quite clear that the non-ownership of the means of production was a necessary but not a sufficient element in the definition of class. The 'organisation of the proletarians into a class, and consequently into a political party'[11] tells us something more about

114

Marx's definition of class, as does the watchword from Marx which Plekhanov chose as his preparatory text for *Socialism and The Political Struggle*: 'Every class struggle is a political struggle.'[12] The Russian Marxists were, of course, familiar with these texts; what they were unsure about was the best means of assisting an emergent proletariat along the road to political and Social-Democratic consciousness. For some of them *On Agitation* resolved their problems and there can be no doubt that the progression it suggested left a deep impression upon Lenin's theory of revolution. It helped resolve the dilemma inherent in Marxism between quiescent determinism and *praxis* by coming down firmly in favour of the latter. It taught (against the prevalent German Social-Democratic view) that the road to proletarian self-awareness lay through the experience of struggle – first against a local employer, then against the employers as a class and, finally, against the state which supported and sustained that class. Consciousness would be the product of determined mass practice. At first, this would take the form of economic or industrial practice; later the transition to political practice would be signalled.

POLITICS VIA ECONOMICS

That these ideas were turning over in Lenin's mind as a result of his exposure to the theses of *On Agitation* there can be little doubt. A glance at his extremely important *Draft and Explanation of A Programme For the Social Democratic Party*,[13] written shortly after his imprisonment, in late 1895 or early 1896, shows Lenin quite self-consciously working out these precepts into an integrated and consistent strategy. Most of the ideas expressed in this document were repeated and amplified in his programmatic statement of 1897, *The Tasks of the Russian Social-Democrats*.[14] These two texts constitute Lenin's most important contributions to the practice – the strategy and tactics of Russian Social Democracy prior to the publication of *What Is To Be Done?* in 1902. To assess whether what Lenin wrote in this latter work was consistent with what he wrote earlier, we must pause and consider Lenin's tactical recommendations in the period up to 1897.

Lenin took as his basis his theoretical findings on the nature and extensiveness of Russian capitalism. The orthodox Russian Marxist view that Russia was already dominated by capitalism,[15] that therefore the majority had become reliant upon wage-labour,[16] led him to his conclusion that the majority of Russians, the wage-earners, were amenable to the leadership of the proletariat and its party. He recognised, however, that the development of capitalism in Russia was very uneven and that, consequently, the development of the working class was differentially affected. Only the urban proletariat was in a position to articulate the grievances and begin the struggle common to the working class as a whole.

> The big factories are creating a special class of workers which is enabled to wage a struggle against capital, because their very conditions of life are destroying all their ties with their own petty production, and, by uniting the workers through their common labour and transferring them from factory to factory, are welding masses of working folk together.[17]

This 'special class', which was concentrated and united by advanced industrial capitalism, had to take it upon itself to mobilise and spur on the more backward sections of the working class. 'Agitation among the advanced sections of the proletariat is the surest and the only way to rouse (as the movement expands) the entire Russian proletariat.'[18] For these reasons Social Democracy must, said Lenin,

> concentrate its activities on the industrial proletariat, who are most susceptible to Social-Democratic ideas, most developed intellectually and politically, and most important by virtue of their numbers and concentration in the country's large political centres.[19]

All of this was hardly new; it was a repetition of Lenin's view of the vanguard role of the proletariat which he had arrived at from his economic or theoretical analysis. What was new to Lenin's analysis was his outline of the process whereby the proletariat became conscious of its duties. In his appraisal of the several phases through which the proletariat moved towards adequate consciousness, the role of practice was now given a pre-eminent position in Lenin's thought and it was no accident that he linked this more or less explicitly with the 'transition' to the programme of *On Agitation*.

116

This transition of the workers to the steadfast struggle for their vital needs, the fight for concessions, for improved living conditions, wages and working hours, now begun all over Russia, means that the Russian workers are making tremendous progress, and that is why the attention of the Social-Democratic Party and all class-conscious workers should be concentrated mainly on this struggle, on its promotion. . . . We have said that the Russian workers' transition to such struggle is indicative of the tremendous progress they have made. This struggle places (leads) the working-class movement on to the high road, and is the certain guarantee of its further success. The mass of the working folk learn from this struggle, firstly, how to recognise and to examine one by one the methods of capitalist exploitation, to compare them with the law, with their living conditions, and with the interests of the capitalist class. By examining the different forms and cases of exploitation, the workers learn to understand the social system based on the exploitation of labour by capital. Secondly, in the process of this struggle the workers test their strength, learn to organise, learn to understand the need for and the significance of organisation. The extension of this struggle and the increasing frequency of clashes inevitably lead to a further extension of the struggle, to the development of a sense of unity, a sense of solidarity – at first among the workers of a particular locality, and then among the workers of the entire country, among the entire working class. Thirdly, this struggle develops the workers' political consciousness. The living conditions of the mass of working folk places them in such a position that they do not (cannot) possess either the leisure or the opportunity to ponder over problems of state. On the other hand, the workers' struggle against the factory owners for their daily needs automatically and inevitably spurs the workers on to think of state, political questions, questions of how the Russian state is governed, how laws and regulations are issued, and whose interests they serve. Each clash in the factory necessarily brings the workers into conflict with the laws and representatives of state authority.[20]

In the first paragraph of this quotation Lenin outlined the concrete practical tasks falling to the Social Democrats in the period of 'agitation', and he was himself a prominent publicist of this tactic in Russian Social Democracy. He produced at this time a whole series of agitational leaflets and pamphlets. Some of them were addressed directly to the workers and were intended to point up the abuses prevalent in particular factories, like his early address to the Semyannikov workers[21] and his *To the Working Men and Women of the Thornton Factory.*[22] Others were explanatory brochures in which Lenin leaned on his legal expertise to unravel the intent behind tsarist legislation affecting the workers; his *Explanation of the Law on Fines Imposed on Factory Workers*[23] and *The New Factory Law*[24] were detailed and thorough explanations of this sort, containing a rich quarry of material for agitators. Others were more overtly political, again intending to provide agitators and workers with convincing evidence of how the government always came to the aid of the employers and generally served the interests of the bourgeoisie. *What Are Our Ministers Thinking About?* and *To The Tsarist Government* are examples of this latter type. It is significant that Lenin was almost alone among the prominent intellectuals of Russian Social Democracy in concerning himself with agitational literature of this sort. In spite of insistent requests from the activists in Russia as well as from the émigré Marxists, Akselrod and Plekhanov studiously, one should perhaps say contemptuously, refused to sully their pens with such ephemera. According to Ascher, Akselrod

> had no taste for the work, preferring to devote himself to more theoretical writings. He confided to Plekhanov that the union [The Union of Russian Social Democrats Abroad] could publish 'such literary caricatures as the "leaflets"' without his help.[25]

At least Akselrod made some attempts, even if they did not come to fruition, even he had to concede that he entered into the work 'without inner fire, but, on the contrary, often with repugnance'.[26] Plekhanov was, however, uncompromising in his desire to remain in the pure realms of thought. This is, indeed, a strange position for men like Plekhanov and Akselrod who, according to the mythology in which the study of Russian Marxism is swathed, are credited with far more faith in the creative spontaneity of the working class than Lenin possessed.

In the second paragraph of the quotation from the *Draft and Explanation of a Programme* Lenin committed himself to the view

118

that in the development of consciousness the permanent struggle of the working class to secure its existence was the crucial formative factor. The struggle was, initially, a struggle between the proletariat and their employers, in the course of which the proletariat, under the guidance of the Social-Democratic intelligentsia, emerged with an awareness of the incompatibility of their economic interests with those of their employers. They emerged, as Lenin said, with a well developed class egoism. The form of struggle typifying this phase of struggle was, of course, the strike. 'Every strike', Lenin maintained

> concentrates all the attention and all the efforts of the workers on some particular aspect of the conditions under which the working class lives. Every strike gives rise to discuss about these conditions, helps the workers to appraise them, to understand what capitalist oppression consists of in the particular case, and what means can be employed to combat this oppression. Every strike enriches the experience of the entire working class.[27]

It was, according to Lenin, out of this strike movement, out of the struggle for petty demands, that there emerged a sense of unity, a shared recognition of community of purpose which was a definitional prerequisite of *class* activity in Marxist terms. 'Thus, out of the isolated revolts of the workers grows the struggle of the entire working class.'[28] It was because the industrial workers were so concentrated, had easy lines of communication and job mobility which allowed them to compare experience, that they had to undertake the leadership of the entire working class in defending its interests against capital.[29]

This phase of working-class struggle we refer to as 'industrial practice'. It began on the basis of localised and often petty demands having to do with partial amelioration of the workers' lot. In one place it would take the form of the simple demand that wages be regularly paid. (Russian workers often had to wait months between pay days – in the meantime, of necessity, they had to obtain credit at company truck stores where inferior commodities were sold at premium prices; out of the permanent debt incurred the worker virtually became an indentured man.) Elsewhere, the workers undertook defensive strikes to protest at the reduction of wages or piece-work rates. However minor and petty the grievances were, however orderly and peaceably the workers conducted themselves, often in pursuit of demands which appeared to be guaranteed to them by law, Lenin recognised better than most that, in Russia at least, such manifestations of working-class mobilisation would have immediate political consequences. In a country where participation in a strike was considered so serious an offence as to merit imprisonment and exile, where membership of a trade union was similarly punishable by law, the organisation of the labour movement was clearly perceived as a threat to state power. If in other countries such relatively minor everyday disputes could be left to the private negotiations of workers' representatives with their employers, in Russia the autocratic power was too sensitive to the dangers of allowing such autonomy to the private sphere. It was as afraid of the danger from the political designs of the liberal manufacturing and trading classes as it was of the threatening turbulence and anarchy of the labouring classes. The autocracy was, therefore, very much *engagé* in the matter of labour unrest and conceived it vital to protect its prerogatives and edicts in this sphere.

Lenin was quick to seize upon the political consequences that the strike movement would necessarily give rise to in the Russian situation. He realised that, given the disposition of the government and the autocratic laws governing labour matters, every outbreak of discontent would be viewed as a threat and would have to be met with the force of the state. 'Each clash in the factory necessarily brings the workers into conflict with the laws and representatives of state authority.'[30] Each clash in the factory, each, strike would elicit immediate response from the government. The reality of the interconnection of economic and political power was made manifest to the workers in the physical presence of gendarmes and Cossacks at the factory gates and in the workers' quarters. The task of impressing upon the workers the Marxist proposition regarding the inseparability of the economic struggle and the political struggle of the workers was considerably simplified. This proposition dawned upon the *mass* of the workers not as a result of theoretical induction or from a study of the history of Western Europe; it was demonstrated to them by the immediate facts of their daily life.

The socialists give strikes a political character! Why, before any socialist did, the government itself took all possible measures to give the strikes a political character. Did it not set about seizing peaceful workers, just as though they were criminals? Did it not arrest and deport them? Did it not send spies and provocateurs all over? Did it not arrest all who fell into its hands? Did it not promise to help the factory owners in order that they might not yield? Did it not prosecute workers for simply collecting money in aid of the strikers? The government itself was ahead of everybody else in explaining to the workers that the war they were waging against the factory owners must inevitably be a war against the government. All that the socialists had to do was to confirm this and publish it in leaflet form. That is all.[31]

Lenin's argument was basically the same as that set out in *On Agitation*. He maintained that the industrial practice of the working class was important not only in that it mobilised the class, threw up new organisations and new leaders, helped, in short, to solidify it as a group; it was also important because eventually this industrial practice would cause the masses of the workers to think about problems of power and control over the laws and the state.

Thus the struggle of the factory workers against the employers inevitably turns into a struggle against the entire capitalist class, against the entire social order based on the exploitation of labour by capital.[32]

Politics came via economics, problems of state power necessarily arose out of the industrial practice of the working class. Political consciousness, the minimum expression of which was the recognition by the workers that they needed a national party to represent their common position, arose, according to Lenin, only in and through the economic struggle.

The class consciousness of the workers means the workers' understanding that to achieve their aims they have to work to influence affairs of state, just as the landlords and the capitalists did, and are continuing to do now.
By what means do the workers reach an understanding of all this? They do so by constantly gaining experience from the very struggle that they begin to wage against the employers and that

increasingly develops, becomes sharper, and involves larger numbers of workers as big factories grow.[33]

It was only in the course of prosecuting their demands for the immediate and pressing necessities of life – for food, shelter, warmth and a degree of security – that the workers, according to Lenin, became aware of their total lack of political rights. They were, he maintained, harried and oppressed for daring to lay claim to the satisfaction of their most basic needs as human beings. They could neither gather together to discuss their affairs, still less organise themselves to prosecute their demands and publish their grievances.[34] So long as this situation prevailed, the workers would, according to Lenin, come to recognise that whatever minimal protections they were granted by law were quite useless. So long as the workers were denied the rights of organisation, assembly and publication of their grievances, the laws would be ignored wholesale, or at best, be distorted piecemeal by totally irresponsible bureaucrats or factory managers. Lenin, as we have noticed, devoted considerable energies to pointing out in detail how the laws were thus manipulated to subserve the interests of the employers; how paper guarantees were rendered worthless; how the 'officials are on the side of the factory owners, and that the laws are drawn up in such a way as to make it easier for the employer to oppress the worker'.[35]

Lenin's argument was that the workers did not have to have come to socialist consciousness in order to acquire political consciousness. They did not have to be aware of the necessity of doing away with wage-labour itself; it was sufficient for them to present unified demands for better conditions in which to sell their labour power. Their struggle *to improve their lot as labourers* must, according to Lenin, impress upon them the necessity of organisation, of establishing mutual aid and strike funds and of publishing their demands – yet all these things were proscribed by law. The very attempt at economic amelioration was, and would be seen to be, greatly hampered by political and legal restraints. The workers would come to recognise that the economic struggle was, by necessary extension, a political struggle. In this progression

the achievement of political freedom becomes the '*vital task of the workers*' because without it the workers do not and cannot have any influence over affairs of state, and thus inevitably remain a rightless, humiliated and inarticulate class.[36]

The logic of the objective situation of the Russian workers, according to Lenin, compelled them progressively to realise their existence as a class in Marxist terms. Initally this consisted of a shared awareness of immediate economic interest achieved through their industrial practice. Industrial practice gradually impressed upon the workers the necessity of influencing the state and its laws. When this point was arrived at, the signal was given for transition to a new practice and new organisational modes appropriate to the new tasks which, according to Lenin, necessarily presented themselves. The vanguard section of the proletariat had, at this stage, to undertake the leadership of the entire movement for democratic reform.

HEGEMONY OF THE PROLETARIAT IN THE DEMOCRATIC REVOLUTION

The imperative to work for political reform, for the realisation of democratic freedoms, was in this way shown to be no mere abstract formulation of the orthodoxy of Russian Marxism; it proceeded rather from the everyday struggle of the working class. It was an imperative which was all the more vital for the proletariat because it, unlike the bourgeoisie, was entirely devoid of influence upon the state and the formulation of laws. The bourgeoisie, through its professional associations, its family links with the governing bodies, its press, its ability to bribe and distribute favours, had a myriad means of making its voice heard. Its influence was often indirect; it was, Lenin argued, generally covert pressure which it exerted behind locked doors in private consultations at national and at local levels. Partly no doubt for this reason the bourgeoisie was, Lenin maintained, somewhat prevaricating in its attitude towards democracy. It would certainly have liked *more* power, *more* influence on affairs of state, yet, at the same time it found a certain advantage in ruling yet not being seen to rule. The fiction of an autocratic government standing above class was still a potent influence upon the popular mind and too valuable a protective shell for capitalism to be scrapped lightly.

> Although the government, according to law, possesses absolute and independent power, actually the capitalists and landowners possess thousands of means of influencing the government and affairs of state. They have their own social-estate associations – noblemen's and merchants' societies, chambers of trade and manufacturers, etc. – recognised by law. . . . In their societies they discuss laws of state, draft bills, and the government usually consults them on each issue, submits draft bills to them with a request for their views. [37]

'The employers', Lenin concluded, 'have thousands of ways of exerting pressure on the government'. [38]

While certain progressive elements of the bourgeoisie were finding autocratic rule increasingly dysfunctional to advanced capitalism, they were at one with their peers in fearing the tumult and disorder, the threat to property which might be unleashed by its radical overthrow. The attitude of the bourgeoisie towards democracy was, like the attitude of all other classes, determined, according to Lenin, by its place in the prevailing structure of ownership relations. Only the working class was totally without rights and totally without property. The other classes, the bourgeoisie and petty bourgeoisie held property, however precariously, and exerted their influence, however covert and limited, upon government. Lenin's thesis, which he frequently bolstered by reference to the past history of Western Europe, especially to the France of 1848–51, was that the propertied classes had always played an ambiguous political role. On the one hand, they could not but strive for their own ascendancy over monarchical and feudal power. On the other, they were compelled to defend their property. This ambiguity had, Lenin maintained, frequently proved fatal to the cause of democracy for, at that point in the struggle when the monarchical and feudal power was prepared to yield to the larger part of their demands, the propertied classes had demonstrated their preparedness to jettison the full implementation of democracy. They had, Lenin maintained, repeatedly shown themselves ready to do a deal with the status quo, to enlist the support of the coercive agencies of the old state apparatus to put down potential threats to property.

For all these reasons Lenin was led to a forceful restatement of the orthodox position that the proletariat, from the very commencement of its independent political activity, must assume hegemony over the struggle for democracy in Russia. He took up Plekhanov's and Akselrod's earlier insistence that only the proletariat could be 'the vanguard fighter for democratic institutions'.[39]

> . . . in the fight against autocracy, the working class must single itself out, for it is the *only* thoroughly consistent and unreserved enemy of the autocracy, *only* between the working class and the autocracy is no compromise possible, *only* in the working class can democracy find a champion who makes no reservations, is not irresolute and does not look back. The hostility of all other classes, groups and strata of the population towards the autocracy is *not unqualified*; their democracy always looks back. The bourgeoisie cannot but realise that industrial and social development is being retarded by the autocracy, but it fears the complete democratisation of the political and social system and can at any moment enter into alliance with the autocracy against the proletariat. The petty bourgeoisie is two-faced by its very nature, and while it gravitates, on the one hand, towards the proletariat and democracy, on the other, it gravitates towards the reactionary classes, tries to hold up the march of history, is apt to be seduced by the experiments and blandishments of the autocracy . . . is capable of concluding an alliance with the ruling classes against the proletariat *for the sake of* strengthening its own *small proprietor* position.[40]

In order that the proletariat be seen to be *in fact* the leading force in the struggle for democracy, it must become the vehicle par excellence of every strata and group which nursed a grievance against the autocracy. If it was *in fact* to assume responsibility for unifying all the disparate trickles of discontent into one great torrent to sweep away the autocracy, then, argued Lenin, it must in this phase of its political activity drop its class exclusiveness and concentration upon the particular grievances of the working class. The proletariat, particularly its Social-Democratic publicists, must assume new responsibilities and new functions. In this political phase of the struggle they must appear as the tribunes of all the discontent welling up over the whole breadth of Russia.

In agitation, this support will be expressed by the Social Democrats taking advantage of every manifestation of the police tyranny of the autocracy to point out to the workers how this tyranny affects all Russian citizens *in general*, and the representatives of the exceptionally oppressed social estates, nationalities, religions, sects, etc. in particular; and how that tyranny affects the *working class* especially. Finally, in practice, this support is expressed in the readiness of the Russian Social Democrats to enter into alliances with revolutionaries of other trends for the purpose of achieving certain particular aims . . .[41]

Already, by 1897, Lenin was insisting upon a distinction which was to become a commonplace in his thought and which formed the main fabric of his much misinterpreted *What Is To Be Done?* The distinction was between economic and political agitation. At this juncture we need to fill in a few salient facts from the history of the labour movement in Russia from Lenin's imprisonment in December 1895, to the time of writing *The Tasks of the Russian Social Democrats* in late 1897.

At the beginning of this period the dissemination of Social-Democratic literature of an agitational kind had barely got off the ground in St Petersburg. Admittedly earlier progress had been made in other centres, notably in Poland and Lithuania, where they anticipated the St Petersburg conversion by some nine months or so.[42] Initially worker unrest typically took the form of machine wrecking and the looting and destruction of factory premises, warehouses and stores. The events at the Semyannikov works were typical of this spontaneous destructivism. By the summer of 1896 the St Petersburg workers were conducting a quite orderly mass general strike in the textile industry with sympathetic strikes in other branches of industry, presenting a clear and forthright statement of their demands to the government and employers. They were pressing not simply for the rectification of abuses in their particular industry, but for a statutory restriction of the working day to ten and a half hours for all workers. The government promised concessions: the Minister of Industry, Count Witte, assured the strikers that the government was 'deeply concerned to improve the lot of the workers'. When, however, the government showed little dispatch in giving these assurances concrete form, the combative Petersburg workers called for a new strike in January 1897. This time the very threat of a general strike had its effect; it was announced that as of April the working day would be limited to eleven and a half hours. The workers remained unsatisfied; the strike movement spread throughout the early months of 1897 in an attempt to wring more favourable concessions from the government. The seriousness with which the government regarded the burgeoning strike movement can be gauged from the rapidity with which it moved to promulgate the New Factory Law of 2 June 1897, conceding many of the workers' demands. The very fact that the autocracy had been seen to capitulate to the demands of a section of the Russian people was something almost unique in Russian history. The lesson was not lost upon Lenin. In his pamphlet on *The New Factory Law* he pointed out repeatedly that it was only the determined initiative of the advance guard of the Petersburg workers, who drew others into the fray, that secured legal concessions for all workers. Only continued activism would ensure that the guarantees were actually implemented.

It was only by struggle, by a conscious and staunch struggle, that the workers secured the *passage* of this law. Only by struggle will they be able to secure the actual enforcement of the law and its enforcement in the interests of the workers. Without a stubborn struggle, without the staunch resistance of the united workers to every claim the employers make, the new law will remain a scrap of paper.[43]

The *Statistics of Disputes in Russia*, published by the Ministry of Trade and Industry, tells part of the tale of these years of labour turbulence. In 1895, the year of the first general strike of textile workers in St Petersburg, 31,195 workers in factories covered by the factory inspectorate (approximately half of Russian factories) were directly involved in strikes. In 1896 the figure was 29,527 and in 1897 it rose to 59,870.[44] According to Wildman, whose picture of this period in Chapter Three of his book[45] is evocative and thorough, the years 1896–7 saw a profound change in the temper of the industrial working class of St Petersburg.

The workers of the capital had undergone an extraordinary shift in temperament in the space of a single year. Having overcome their awe of the authorities and their mistrust of socialists, they

127

were now prepared to risk direct clashes with the full force of government authority for what they felt to be their legitimate demands. [46]

This difference in attitude is reflected in the differing styles with which the May Day Manifestos of 1896 and 1897 were presented. That of 1896 is rather amorphous and sloppy in its generalised formulations, that of 1897 clearly and forthrightly specifies the attainment of political liberties as an immediate goal. [47]

For Lenin the momentous events of these years culminated in what he took to be the recognition of the advanced section of the proletariat that the struggle was now a properly class and, therefore, political struggle. This signified that the time was ripe for the proletariat to assume the leading role in the struggle for democracy. His view was based on the fact that the workers had recognised the necessity of confronting not merely individual employers or groups of employers but had taken on the government. They had taken the crucial step of demanding a change in the law as the only means of securing their economic position. By this token the proletariat had, for the first time in Russia, declared itself a political force. The lessons of the great strikes of 1896 and 1897 had revealed among other things that 'the Russian Government is a far worse enemy of the Russian workers than the Russian employers are'. [48]

Lenin was arguing that the Social Democrats must recognise that the events of 1895 to 1897 marked a new turning-point in the development of the movement. The commencement of the independent political activity of the proletariat had been signalled and had won a conspicuous early victory. There must, Lenin argued, be no letting up, no resting on the laurels of a quick and rather minor success. The real fight, he maintained, had barely been joined for, unless it was able to secure democratic liberties, the advance guard of the proletariat would be prevented from realising its historical role of rousing and directing the struggle of all of the wage-workers. 'Russia's advanced workers', Lenin argued, 'must do their utmost to draw the more backward workers into the movement. Unless the entire mass of Russian workers is enlisted in the struggle for the workers' cause, the advanced workers of the capital cannot hope to win much.' [49] The process of struggle for democracy would, of itself, draw an increasingly broader spectrum of the working class into political life and class awareness, but for the whole mass of rural proletarians without adequate lines of inter-communication, the securing of democratic liberties appeared as a prior condition for their mobilisation. Lenin's position was, then, that for the proletariat to achieve even a significant improvement in its material conditions of life it must mobilise all of Russia's exploited alongside it. In order to do this, however, it needed to be able to reach the scattered millions of wage-workers. It needed freedom of association, organisation and publication.

The insistence upon the need for democratic rights was so integral to Lenin's strategy, was so central to the orthodoxy he inherited and was repeated almost *ad nauseum* by him in virtually all of his programmatic statements, that it is almost inexplicable to find a chorus of commentators asserting that Lenin had jettisoned the struggle for democracy as the immediate strategic task. In his *Draft and Explanation of a Programme* of 1895–6 Lenin specified precisely a list of nine basic democratic freedoms and rights which Social Democracy placed 'first and foremost' of its objectives.[50] The 'first aim' of the Russian working class was stated to be the achievement of political liberty. The debilities from which the Russian working class suffered in the absence of these rights was outlined[51] and, as if the message needed repeating, Lenin left nothing to chance and obliged with italics:

That is why the most urgent demand of the workers, the primary objective of the working-class influence on affairs of state must be *the achievement of political freedom*, i.e., the direct participation, guaranteed by law (by a constitution), of all citizens in the government of the state, the guaranteed right of all citizens freely to assemble, discuss their affairs, influence affairs of state through their associations and the press. The achievement of political freedom becomes the *'vital task of the workers'* because without it the workers do not have and cannot have any influence over affairs of state, and thus inevitably remains a rightless, humiliated and inarticulate class.[52]

As we have seen above, even Lenin's explicitly agitational leaflets, like *The New Factory Law* written in the summer of 1897, did not hesitate to rub home the lesson that without political freedoms the workers would be helpless. He resorted there, as elsewhere, to comparing the 'abnormal' situation of the Russian worker to that of his foreign comrades:

> In all other countries, the workers, in their 'search for the means of subsistence', have the right to organise unions, mutual benefit societies, to openly resist the employer, to present their demands to him, to conduct strikes; in our country this is not allowed.[53]

The whole of this pamphlet was thereafter concerned to demonstrate how fatuous it was to trust in 'protective' laws dispensed from above in the absence of any rights for working-class, self-protective associations. In this situation the workers must always lose out when 'discretion' was exercised by those responsible for executing the law.

> The employer has thousands of ways of exerting influence on the factory inspectors and of forcing them to do what he wants. The workers, however, have no means of influencing the factory inspectors, and cannot have such means as long as the workers do not enjoy the right of free assembly, the right to form their unions, to discuss their affairs in the press, and to issue workers' newspapers. So long as these rights are withheld, no supervision by officials over the employers can ever be serious and effective.[54]

In his *Tasks of the Russian Social Democrats* of late 1897 Lenin, for fear that any should have misunderstood his earlier insistence, returned to the theme stressing the necessity of bearing in mind not only the struggle against the employers for the ultimate realisation of socialism, but also the immediate task of 'winning political liberty in Russia and democratising the political social system of Russia'. He reminded his audience of the dual objectives laid down in the orthodoxy by Plekhanov, that the Social Democrats 'have always insisted on the inseparable connection between their socialist and democratic tasks'.[55] The democratic tasks referred to were then shown in their inter-relation to the ultimate socialist objectives.

> Russian Social Democrats set themselves the task of propagating *democratic ideas* among the working-class masses; they strive to spread an understanding of absolutism in all its manifestations,

of its class content, of the necessity to overthrow it, of the impossibility of waging a successful struggle for the workers' cause without achieving political liberty and the democratisation of Russia's political and social system.[56]

Lenin went on to show, as we have noticed above, how and why the working class was the only unswerving and resolute champion of democracy in Russia.

It was precisely because of Lenin's belief in the necessity of going over to the political struggle for democracy that he began, in 1897, to urge the formation of a cohesive all-Russian socialist political party. Without such a party it would not be possible to build upon the successful initiation of the proletariat into politics signalled by the strikes of 1896 and 1897. The advance guard of the proletariat, Lenin was now arguing, had already shown itself capable of taking this step in its class development; the leadership should not lag behind. Without such an all-Russian unified structure the pretensions of the Social Democrats and the proletariat to assume the leadership of the democratic revolution would lapse by default. As a necessary preliminary, Lenin argued, the Social Democrats had to get their own house in order. Before presuming to lead the all-Russian, all-class onslaught on the autocracy they must evidently secure their *own* national cohesion.

Russian Social Democrats have much to do to meet the requirements of the awakening proletariat, to organise the working-class movement, to strengthen the revolutionary groups and their mutual ties, to supply the workers with propaganda and agitational literature, and to unite the workers' circles and Social-Democratic groups scattered all over Russia into a single *Social Democratic Labour Party*![57]

Lenin's was, of course, only one of the voices simultaneously pressing for the establishment of a unified party, an aspiration which was realised, at least formally, in March 1898 when the First Congress of the Russian Social Democratic Labour Party (hereafter R.S.D.L.P.) was convened in Minsk. Already, however, in 1897, Lenin was beginning to formulate a view of the structure of the Party which was later to become so central an issue for his contemporary critics and later commentators.

In a very short and important appendix to his *The Tasks of the Russian Social Democrats*, Lenin argued that the success of the strike movement had put the Goverment on its guard. It had recognised the power of the Social Democrats over the working class by

> steadily developing the size and range of the activities of those of its lackeys who are hounding revolutionaries, is devising new methods, introducing more provocateurs, trying to exert pressure on the arrested by means of intimidation, confrontation with false testimony, forged signatures, planting faked letters, etc. etc.[58]

Consequently, with the new tasks before them of confronting the autocracy on the all-Russian political plane, the Social Democrats must tighten up their organisation, they must become skilled in the arts of concealment.

> Without a strengthening and development of revolutionary discipline, organisation and underground activity, struggle against the government is impossible. And underground activity demands above all that groups and individuals specialise in different aspects of work and that the job of co-ordination be assigned to the central group of the League of Struggle, with as few members as possible.[59]

Lenin's argument, it must be remembered, would not have struck his audience as particularly innovatory. This after all had long been the mode of procedure of the locally-based Leagues of Struggle throughout Russia. A central group of activists had co-ordinated the activities of the 'peripheral' circles through designated intermediaries known only by their revolutionary sobriquets. The peripheral groups were kept ignorant of any knowledge of neighbouring groups for fear that one man might compromise many. Such were the elements of underground activity in the socialist and labour movements imposed by the illegality in which they worked in Russia. Lenin invoked a similar rationale for the structure of the all-Russian Party. He argued that allocation to specific jobs would enable individuals and groups to become expert at them, would prevent the inadvertent compromising of others, would enable the centre to replace 'agents and members who have fallen' and would generally make the job of the police that much more difficult.[60] Such specialisation of function clearly demanded centralised control for without a clearly specified allocation of function the detail-labour of the individual parts would be rendered meaningless. Lenin argued that without specialisation and professionalism the Party would be unable to exist under conditions of illegality and oppression.

Here then, in 1897, before Lenin had come upon the 'perversions' of 'tailism', 'revisionism' and 'economism', was the embryo of the ideas later to be expressed at such length in *What Is To Be Done?* Before moving on to consider that document it would be as well to recapitulate Lenin's ideas on practice and to present them in annotated form.

CONCLUSION

1. Orthodoxy had demonstrated that the bourgeoisie was a vacillating force in the democratic revolution and that hegemony must devolve upon the proletariat. Lenin's economic analysis confirmed this finding and formulated a view of the proletariat as the vanguard and natural representative of all Russia's exploited.
2. The Social Democrats must mobilise the proletariat, cause it to solidify as a group with a shared community of economic interest through the tactic of agitation. Out of economic agitation, or industrial practice, the recognition of the necessity of political agitation would arise.
3. Part of the objective of the democratic revolution must be to break the economic and political power of the now outmoded feudal structure of land ownership – the central prop of an equally outmoded autocracy. This was necessary for the capitalists to assume unveiled dominance over the state in order that, in the next phase of the struggle, the proletariat might recognise its true enemy. Economic polarity here assumed its political expression.
4. The democratic revolution was necessary for the legal guarantees it afforded to the proletariat. Without the rights of association, organisation and publication, the proletariat was prevented from becoming conscious of its ultimate objectives. It was prevented also from realising the task (given by Lenin's theoretical analysis) of rallying to its side all the other exploited layers of the working class: rural proletarians and handicraftsmen; wage-labourers of all kinds.

5. To secure the democratic revolution the proletariat had to assume the leadership of all those strata and groups which had grievances against the autocracy. It had therefore, to appear as the political tribune of *all* these elements and must not restrict itself to expressing the particular demands of the workers. It had to appear as the most steadfast, resolute and influential party in a general coalition, unifying and prodding forward all the less resolute elements. Lenin here restated the arguments of Plekhanov and Akselrod.

6. To accomplish the all-Russian task of unifying and urging on all opposition elements in the battle for democracy, while at the same time preserving the particular socialist objectives of the proletariat, a cohesive all-Russian party structure was necessitated, one moreover which was skilled in the practical functions called forth by these tasks, and vigilant in its theoretical outlook.

In the following chapters we shall see how constant these themes remained in Lenin's political thought. Time and again he returned to them; indeed his writings up to 1908 were almost wholly concerned with their elaboration. In Chapter Seven we shall present *What Is To Be Done?* not as a primer on how to construct a conspiratorial party but as a specification of the objectives and responsibilities of Social Democracy in the democratic revolution. Lenin's statement of the political tasks confronting the Marxists in this situation is of primary importance; the organisational particulars are held to be of secondary concern. They are purely derivative. They are the appropriate and only practicable means for realising the tasks enjoined by orthodoxy and confirmed by Lenin's theoretical analysis and his ideas on the phases of evolution of working-class consciousness.

CHAPTER 6

Turn-of-the-Century Crisis – The Threat To Orthodoxy

We turn now to what is probably the most contentious period of Lenin's political thought. It was a period when, according to the dominant interpretation, Lenin finally and explicitly forsook orthodox Marxism and identified himself as a Jacobin or Blanquist. As a consequence of this voluntarist deviation, so the legend goes, the Russian Social Democratic Labour Party split into two warring sections, the Mensheviks holding fast to orthodox economic determinism, and the Bolsheviks asserting the creative historical rôle of a determined and disciplined group of professional revolutionaries. This orchestration is complemented in all essentials by the prevailing Soviet and Marxist interpretations of Lenin's achievements during these years. There it is argued that Lenin, beset about by hydra-headed revisionism, reformism and economism, found, initially at least, some fair-weather friends who, as the battle progressed, themselves succumbed to opportunism. (In the prevailing Western interpretation they were temporarily duped by Lenin.) It suits Soviet and most Marxist interpretations as much as it does Western ones, to represent Lenin as the genius (benign or evil as the case may be) of the piece. Single-handedly it seems, he hewed the foundations of Bolshevism, the party of professional revolutionaries, the party of a new type – secret, activist, disciplined and dedicated, inspired and guided by its newspaper and ultimately responsible to the editor-in-chief himself – Lenin. We are in the somewhat anomalous position that imposing generalisations are made and generally accepted on Lenin's thought in this period without anyone feeling obliged to do the background research. In the period we are examining for instance, a period accepted by all as being of considerable if not crucial importance in the evolution of Lenin's thought, there exists no authoritative edition which explains the text of Lenin's *What Is To Be Done?* in the fullness of its context.[1] The larger part of *What Is To Be Done?* is concerned to rebut the arguments of rival claimants to the leadership of the R.S.D.L.P. and precisely for this reason Lenin subtitled the book *Burning Questions of Our Movement*. Unless the main arguments of the protagonists to these disputes and the situation within the movement to which they referred are reconstructed, we cannot hope to understand Lenin's text.

PARTY ORGANISATION – THE PHASES OF DEVELOPMENT

In his 'Conclusion' to *What Is To Be Done?*, Lenin outlined a periodisation of the movement's progress to date. The first period he located as 'the period of the rise and consolidation of the theory and programme of Social Democracy'; it extended from 1884 to 1894. The second period ran from 1894 to 1898; 'In this period Social Democracy appeared on the scene as a social movement, as the upsurge of the masses of the people, as a political party.'[2] The creation of the Party in the spring of 1898 was, according to Lenin, 'the most striking and at the same time the *last* act of the Social-Democrats of this period'.[3] The years up to 1898 were, in Lenin's view, years of consistent and steady advance. The activists had schooled themselves thoroughly in theory and had assiduously rebutted the theoretical and practical notions of their opponents. They had succeeded in rousing and drawing into the movement significant sections of the working class and had taken the first steps towards creating a disciplined, united all-Russian political party.

The years of consistent advance from a lower form of organisation (the isolated study circle) to a form appropriate to the elevated tasks of Social Democracy (the national political party) ran *pari passu* with the changing mode of struggle, from theoretical disputation within the intelligentsia to mobilising the masses of the proletariat. Throughout *What Is To Be Done?* and other writings of this period, Lenin insistently drew the parallel between the dislocated and localised mode of operation of the study circles and the beginnings of manufacture in small-scale handicraft workshops. Circle activity was consistently characterised by Lenin as *kustarnaya promyshlenost* or *kustarnichestvo*. In the English translations this is generally represented as 'amateurism' or 'primitiveness',[4] but Lenin was employing this term in its specific and direct economic meaning. He was employing a teleology of advance for the party so directly comparable to that of the development of industry that the same terms were employed to describe each. *Kustar* production (handicraft, domestic production) was to circle methods and activity what factory production was to the unified national Party.

. Lenin's argument was that the tasks which theory had outlined to the movement, in particular the responsibility of leading the all-Russian onslaught against autocracy, could only be fulfilled by co-ordinating the activities of all local groups and by devising a more efficient division of labour within the Party. The task, for instance, of producing and distributing a national newspaper, which would act as the vehicle of the party's hegemony within the democratic movement, was quite beyond the 'handicraft' resources of scattered local groups.

> . . . the publication of an *illegal* newspaper, however small its size, requires an extensive secret apparatus, such as is possible with large-scale factory production; for this apparatus cannot be created in a small, handicraft workshop. It requires professionally well-trained revolutionaries and a division of labour applied with the greatest consistency.[5]

Lenin's plaint is precisely that 'the movement has not yet developed the forces for large-scale production, continues to flounder in amateurism [*kustarnichestvo* – handicraft methods]'.[6] We have here an explicit analogy between Lenin's teleology of the development of capitalism and the development of the Party. Each passed through successive phases of advance, the significance of which was derived from the contribution each made to the evolution of a more efficient and productive system. Each phase broadened the base of activities, involved new organisational forms, new extensions of the division of labour and imposed ever-increasing 'productive targets'. As with the development of capitalism, so, too, with the revolutionary movement – in competition with others it had either to adapt its 'productive mechanism' to the demands of the time, or suffer bankruptcy. The obligation of the Party, as Lenin conceived it, was to ensure that the dispersed and isolated revolutionary workshops were brought together to work according to a common plan. Its primary function was to ensure that the enormous duplication and therefore wastage of effort, which had prevailed hitherto, should be eliminated by introducing a clear and authoritative division of labour. Just as with industry, the scope and extensiveness of the Party's tasks determined its organisational mode. Social Democracy must, if it was in fact to carry out the tasks stipulated by theory, change over from handicraft to factory methods so that

> A study circle that has not yet begun to work, but which is only just seeking activity, could then start, not like a craftsman in an isolated little workshop unaware of the earlier development in 'industry' or of the general level of production methods prevailing in industry, but as a participant in an extensive enterprise that *reflects* the whole general revolutionary attack on the autocracy.[7]

We have seen how, according to Lenin's periodisation of the movement, it began to emerge from primitive handicraft methods and a narrow scope of activity during the second period. The great success of the second period was indeed the signal given by the creation of the Party for a transition to broader activity and unified organisation. The start was never consolidated. On the contrary, in Lenin's view the movement had relapsed into the parochialism of local groups whose scope of activity shrank and whose objectives became commensurately petty and narrow.

The third period, prepared in 1897 and definitely cutting off the second period in 1898, was, according to Lenin, characterised by disunity and vacillation and the dissolution of Party ties. It represented a relapse into the outmoded techniques and restricted scope of *kustarnichestvo*. It was characterised above all by the lag of the leadership of Social Democracy behind the masses. The third period represented 'the combination of pettifogging practice and utter disregard for theory'.[8] The broad perspectives of Social Democracy were increasingly jettisoned and the movement inclined towards eclecticism and revisionism; that is, in Lenin's view, it sought to justify its organisational backwardness and *kustarnichestvo* 'by all manner of high-flown arguments'.[9]

Before considering in greater detail Lenin's diagnosis of the causes and symptoms of malaise from which the movement was suffering, we must first establish what Lenin's position was within the movement at this time, who were his allies and who his opponents.

ORGANISATIONAL CRISIS AND RIVAL TACTICS

The two years from 1897 to 1899 were relatively uneventful ones in Lenin's life. After the frenzy of activity of his years in St Petersburg, Lenin settled down easily, almost one could say with a certain relief, to the pleasures of the countryside around his place of exile in Shushenskoye and to the luxury of two years of uninterrupted study. He spent his time preparing his *magnum opus, The Development of Capitalism in Russia,* and translating the Webbs' *History of Trade Unionism* with his new wife Nadezhda Krupskaya. In summer his day was divided between walking, hunting and studying; in winter between skating, playing the odd game of chess and studying. Occasionally there were trips to visit neighbouring groups of exiles and, less frequently, some would visit him. Lenin was, at this period, probably more relaxed than at any other time of his adult life. He reconciled himself to his lot and threw himself into his researches. He would later look back with some nostalgia upon these years as a gentleman scholar in the country. There was, in any case, little that Lenin could do but reconcile himself to his position. The St Petersburg *stariki* had, as we have seen, been effectively decimated by the arrests of late 1895 and 1896 and the Moscow organisation had been smashed in like manner. The foundation Congress of the Russian Social Democratic Labour Party in Minsk, March 1898, brought a brief ray of hope to the Marxists, but it proved a false start. The remaining Marxist veterans who participated at the Congress were swiftly rounded up and imprisoned along with more than five hundred of the most prominent Social-Democratic activists in centres throughout Russia.[10] The movement was effectively crushed: the whole leadership echelon disappeared almost overnight. All that survived of the attempt to found an all-Russia socialist party was a manifesto written by Peter Struve. Lenin was, therefore, to all intents and purposes, left high and dry, with no organisational base upon which to operate. It was hardly surprising then that during these years he rarely concerned himself with organisational matters – a reflection of the fact that there was precious little left to organise.

The labour movement admittedly continued to grow and solidified its position, albeit in a rather more humdrum way after the climacteric of the great strikes of 1895 to 1897. In any case, new men had taken over the leadership of the workers' movement after the imprisonment and exile of the veterans. They were younger men with a more practical bent, concerned more with the immediate bread-and-butter problems of the young labour movement than with the grander, more long-term perspectives of the veterans. With the failure of the Party organisation to get off the ground, these men, the *praktiki*, the 'worker-phile' intellectuals or the 'youngsters' (as they were variously called), saw themselves as having little option but to assist in strengthening the localised self-help organisations and strike-funds which had emerged among the workers in the mid-nineties. Lenin, already in 1897, had been made aware of the potential danger of this orientation. At a meeting in St Petersburg, shortly before going into exile, he and the veterans, the orthodox we may call them, had argued long with the youngsters who were to replace them. The latter, it appeared to Lenin, regarded economic agitation not instrumentally, i.e., as a means to prepare the workers for a higher phase of *political* consciousness, but rather as an end in itself. For the moment, indeed for the next two years, Lenin did not appear to be terribly peturbed at this trend; no doubt he felt that these men could at least hold the fort until the old leadership returned out of exile to lead the faithful back along the straight road.

By 1899 there were already straws in the wind which indicated that Lenin's working assumptions were somewhat optimistic. Indeed, by the turn of the century the evidence seemed to suggest that Russian Marxism was decomposing into coteries of hostile groups. The old guard of orthodoxy, the Emancipation of Labour Group, found itself isolated and in a minority among the emigré Russian Marxists. In Russia itself the workers appeared to be intent upon pursuing their own path to purely economic progress, and some were stridently calling for a break from the tutelage of the intellectuals. The Social-Democratic groups which, in a flush of enthusiasm to greet the first Congress had lately changed their title from 'League of Struggle' to 'Committee of the R.S.D.L.P.', acknowledged no Party centre, no leading or authoritative spokesman for the Party as a whole. They had lapsed back into unco-ordinated localised work and had neither the inclination nor the resources to pursue the broader objectives laid down in the Party Manifesto.

The split in the Union of Social Democrats Abroad was the first indication Lenin must have had that the movement was falling into disarray and factionalism. The Union had been founded by the Emancipation of Labour Group in Geneva in 1894 as a some-what dubious means of providing an organisational focus for the increased number of Social-Democratic emigrés, while, at the same time, preserving the exclusiveness and leading role of the Emancipation of Labour Group, which insisted on supervising the activities of the larger organisation and editing its publications. The younger emigrés were, naturally, offended by this rather patrician treatment and their sense of injury was deepened by Plekhanov's disparaging attitude towards them and his withering references to their literary and theoretical shortcomings. On their part they justifiably criticised the exiled veterans for their lamentable failure to produce popular agitational literature and their general organisational incompetence. By the end of 1898 the 'youngsters' were in a clear majority within the Union and, after a series of acrimonious and bitter disputes, the Emancipation of Labour Group announced its refusal to edit any more of the Union's publications. At the Second Congress of the Union in April 1900 the Emancipation of Labour Group formally withdrew from the Union and founded the autonomous organisation *Sotsial-Demokrat*. When, therefore, the Union of Social Democrats Abroad decided in late 1898 to establish a journal, the Emancipation of Labour Group was left high and dry. It was the 'youngsters' who assumed responsibility for editing the new *Rabochee Delo* (Workers' Cause), which began publication in March 1899. Lenin must have been perturbed at this situation, but, for the moment at least, there was no hard evidence that the young opposition to Plekhanov was anything but orthodox in its outlook.

KUSKOVA'S 'CREDO'

The chance to attack them on this score came almost fortuitously to Lenin. His sister sent him a copy of a manuscript by I.D. Kuskova entitled *Credo*. Its main message was that, in common with the historical experience of labour movements throughout Europe, the Russian labour movement would operate along the 'line of least resistance' to achieve its objectives. In Russia this meant, according to Kuskova, recognising that political struggle, indeed the creation of an independent working-class-party, represented the 'transplantation of alien aims and alien achievements to our soil'. 'For the Russian Marxist', she concluded, 'there is only one course: participation in, i.e., assistance to, the economic struggle of the proletariat, and participation in liberal opposition activity.'[11] According to Kuskova, out of the struggle for partial, economic goals, there would dawn upon the Russian Marxists the realisation that gradual change for practical reforms brought greater lasting benefit than the pursuit of a revolutionary seizure of power.

> Intolerant Marxism, negative Marxism, primitive Marxism (whose conception of the class division of society is too schematic) will give way to democratic Marxism, and the social position of the party within modern society must undergo a sharp change. The party *will recognise* society; its narrow corporative and, in the majority of cases, sectarian tasks will be widened to social tasks, and its striving to seize power will be transformed into a striving for change, a striving to reform present-day society on democratic lines . . . The concept 'politics' will be enlarged and will acquire a truly social meaning, and the practical demands of the movement will acquire greater weight and will be able to count on receiving greater attention than they have been getting up to now.[12]

Kuskova did not doubt that advocacy of this overall strategy of the workers seeking immediate and palpable economic benefit as their main preoccupation while, in the political sphere, aiding the liberals, would inevitably rouse the protest of the orthodox Marxists.

For Lenin her challenge was irresistible. Kuskova's *Credo*, even if intended for purely private distribution, was a heaven-sent opportunity to implicate the young opposition to Plekhanov in the corporative sin of economism. 'This statement', Lenin declared, 'was such an excellent weapon against economism that, had there been no *Credo*, it would have been worth inventing one'.[13] Her views were influential with the editors of *Rabochaya Mysl* and were

142

shared by her husband S. N. Prokopovich, who 'for a brief moment swayed younger Social Democrats in the Berlin colony who were seeking ideological ammunition to vent their grievances against Plekhanov'.[14]

It was Prokopovich who had had the temerity to specify the exact nature of his reservations to Plekhanov's theoretical views. This he did at the request of the Emancipation of Labour Group in a pamphlet which immediately aroused Plekhanov's ample wrath for the critique it contained of the Emancipation of Labour Group's 'Draft Programme'. This 'Programme', in Prokopovich's estimation, gave too much emphasis to the role of the intelligentsia, placed too much emphasis on their role as political mobilisers of the working class and paid insufficient attention to the workers' own defensive organisations, which would articulate the genuine grievances of the workers, not the goals attributed to them by the intelligentsia.

These arguments Plekhanov took up in his *Preface to the 'Vademecum' for the Editorial Board of Rabochee Delo*.[15] With all the vehemence of wounded pride he rounded on the 'youngsters' who had so effectively raised the flag of revolt against the veteran Emancipation of Labour Group. These 'narrow-minded pedants' and 'political castrates',[16] barely out of nappies, with scant literary attainment and the most rudimentary theoretical training, how could they presume to tell Akselrod and Plekhanov what the workers *really* wanted? In actual fact what the young *praktiki* were doing was merely sanctifying the *present* level of working-class consciousness, taking *present* demands as the only proper or feasible ones to pursue.[17] According to their logic, Plekhanov went on, the Social Democrats must restrict themselves to the interests and objectives of which the workers were already conscious. They were therefore renegades to the ideals and final goals of socialism just as surely as Bernstein was. They renounced the central obligation of Social Democrats to utilise present-felt grievances to *develop* the consciousness of the working class into a comprehensive and revolutionary critique of capitalist society. There was, Plekhanov concluded, precious little either of socialism or of democracy in the social democracy of the 'youngsters' who dominated the Union.[18]

The workers, Plekhanov insisted, did not and could not know the full nature of their position and their objectives within society.

There was, in his view, a lag of working-class consciousness behind the development of objective conditions within society. Only the determined activity of the 'revolutionary bacilli', conscious Social Democrats from the working class or the intelligentsia, could overcome the lag of consciousness.[19] It was precisely the job of the Social-Democratic agitator to open up the eyes of the workers to these ways and means of improving their situation which had not yet occurred to them. In particular it was his job to demonstrate from the struggle itself how economic improvement was intrinsically bound to political change and political action.[20] Plekhanov's argument was the same as the one which Lenin was later to employ so centrally in *What Is To Be Done?* Unless economic agitation was used as a means to produce political consciousness, it had no Social-Democratic content – it was but economism, a variant of revisionism. All particular and partial strategies acquired their meaning and Social-Democratic significance only in so far as they contributed to the final goals of the movement. Unless political agitation was immediately taken up as the main preoccupation of the movement, unless the workers were welded into an independent political party, then they would shortly become but the political tool of the radical bourgeoisie.[21]

Plekhanov's prognosis was the same as Lenin's and was based upon the same implacable Marxist logic. This was the first shot in the battle, fired by the veterans of the Emancipation of Labour Group roused to new-found enthusiasm by Lenin's unequivocal support for their position against the 'youngsters' in his *Protest*. It was, of course, a battle which *Iskra* was to take up, *What Is To Be Done?* was to summarise and the Second Party Congress was summoned to terminate.

Lenin's *Protest by Russian Social Democrats*, like all his polemics up to 1902 had a number of intertwined objectives. He was seeking, obviously, to cut the ground from under incipient revisionism within the Russian movement. Coincidentally, this involved attacking those who had attacked Plekhanov. At the very beginning of the *Protest* Lenin made an identification which must have been obvious to anyone in the movement. He complained about those who

. . . depart from the fundamental principles of Russian Social Democracy that were proclaimed by its founders and foremost fighters, members of the Emancipation of Labour Group . . .

The *Credo* reproduced below, which is presumed to express the fundamental views of certain ('young') Russian Social Democrats, represents an attempt at a systematic and definite exposition of the 'new views'.[22]

In this his first sally into the controversy over revisionism, Lenin's intention was made crystal clear. Quotation follows quotation from the sacred texts of the 'old current'. With each Lenin lent the power of his pen to the beleaguered forces of orthodoxy. Lenin had committed himself to a cause he was to pursue remorselessly for the next three years. Along with Potresov and Martov he had thrown in his hand with the veterans of the Emancipation of Labour Group; this combination, Lenin had decided, must take upon itself the reorganisation and reconstruction of the R.S.D.L.P. To those who insist that Lenin was, throughout, an opportunistic power-seeker, this decision is difficult to explain. By 1899 Plekhanov was, to all intents and purposes, a spent force. He had precious few connections and still less control over the movement within Russia. In the world of the Russian socialist emigrés he found himself almost friendless. His intolerance and personal vindictiveness even threatened to alienate those who had been with him since the early 1880s. It took all the considerable resources of self-abnegation of Akselrod and Zasulich to sustain the trinity. No doubt the prestige and editorial and literary resources of the three entered into Lenin's considerations, but still there is little doubt that Lenin and his group could have achieved pre-eminence *without* the Emancipation of Labour Group. That they chose to ally with them, and were prepared to suffer in silence Plekhanov's personal prickliness and *hauteur*, signifies above all that they felt a strong ideological kinship to this group and to this group alone.[23]

RABOCHAYA MYSL, RABOCHEE DELO AND ECONOMISM

All the rest of the groups competing for pre-eminence within the movement were, in Lenin's opinion, unequal to the responsibilities which leadership of the movement entailed. Above all they were tainted in varying degrees with opportunism. Of none was this more true than of the most prominent group during these years, for which the newspaper *Rabochaya Mysl* (Workers' Thought) was the spokesman. Until the appearance of *Iskra* in December 1900,

Rabochaya Mysl was far and away the most successful and regular Russian socialist publication. For two and a half years before the appearance of *Iskra* it held sway, preaching the consistent message of 'workers save yourselves'. The project had indeed been initiated, and the first two issues had been produced, entirely by the St Petersburg workers. After arrests destroyed this workers' group, the venture was taken over by August Kok, then living in Berlin and himself an ex-worker and Bernstein sympathiser. Throughout the period up to 1900 *Rabochaya Mysl* hewed to a consistently 'economic' line. It proclaimed the object of the workers' movement as the satisfaction of their immediate economic and professional demands. It saw little place for the struggle for political rights and none at all for the formation of an illegal revolutionary political party of the working class. As Takhtarev expressed it in his editorial for the seventh issue:

> The organisation by intellectuals of small circles of leading workers for the overthrow of the autocracy – seems to us a theory which has long outlived its time, a theory abandoned by all in whom there is the least sensitivity to and understanding of reality.[24]

According to Lenin, *Rabochaya Mysl*, with its prominence as a self-styled spokesman of labour, represented the apogee of the economist trend in Russia and demonstrated, in the course of its own evolution, the potentially fatal conjunction of economism with revisionism. By economism Lenin had in mind simple pragmatism, bowing to the immediate bread-and-butter demands of the working class. Economism rested upon a mistaken self-denying ordinance of the intelligentsia who, interpreting Marx in a purely fatalistic way, considered that only those demands were appropriate of which the mass of the workers were *already* conscious. For them the objective development of social relations, in particular the self-organisation of the working class, itself determined the proper tasks. The role of the intelligentsia was therefore to collect, publish and help to articulate the grievances and objectives as stated by the workers themselves. True to this interpretation of the proper function of the intellectuals in assisting the workers, the columns of *Rabochaya Mysl* were chock full of workers' letters declaiming against fines, reduction of holidays, extension of hours of work, reduction of rates of pay, manipulation of piece-work rates, housing, sanitation and the activities of managers, police and factory inspectors. Almost invariably the complaints and grievances had to do with a particular plant or factory; only rarely did they broach more general problems pertinent to the trade or whole region.

It was not part of Lenin's case to accuse the Economists of total neglect of the political struggle; he was prepared to concede that 'Rabochaya Mysl does not altogether repudiate the political struggle',[25] but he maintained that the sort of politics it embraced could in no way be viewed as Social-Democratic politics. The Economists restricted themselves to 'Lending the economic struggle itself a political character', striving to secure satisfaction of their trade demands and improving working conditions in each separate trade, by means of 'legislative and administrative measures'.[26] The politics of the Economists, according to Lenin, did no more than directly subserve their essentially trade-union activity of negotiating better terms for the workers in the sale of their labour power. Lenin's appraisal of the *Rabochaya Mysl* attitude towards politics was certainly not without foundation.

The issues of *Rabochaya Mysl* which appeared up to 1901 consistently stressed the subordination of politics to the economic struggle. Political activity was viewed as an immediate and direct extension, an auxiliary arm of a basically trade-union struggle. This position was pointedly sustained against the orthodox in the one venture into theoretical disputation (normally *Rabochaya Mysl* cultivated a lofty disdain for the airiness of theoretical controversies) it allowed itself. Takhtarev and Kok decided to publish a 'Separate Supplement' in which they would express the underlying theoretical rationale upon which their practical recommendations rested. The 'Separate Supplement' was an explicit attempt to settle accounts with the orthodox veterans. This 'Separate Supplement' to *Rabochaya Mysl*, no. 7 became, for Lenin, the *locus classicus* of Russian revisionism. Its appearance in 1899 must have been like a red rag to a bull for all the orthodox Russian Marxists. Bernstein himself contributed an article, and, fearing perhaps that some would miss his somewhat guarded expression of his position, the editors published another under the euphemistic title 'A New Trend in German Social Democracy', where Bernstein's critique of orthodox Marxism was elaborated. It was, however, in the long lead article 'Our Reality' that the views of the editors were most fully and consistently expressed.

The author (K. M. Takhtarev[27]) began by analysing the actual state of development of the Russian working-class movement consequent upon the spread of large-scale factory production. Due to the uneven development of industry the movement in different centres found itself at differing levels. Its present objective, therefore, must be to consolidate stable organisations (such as the Jewish workers had already achieved) throughout Russia.

> The tasks of the movement at the present moment, the objective which emerges from the present unsatisfactory situation of the Russian workers, actually reduces itself to the improvement of this situation by all the possible ways and appropriate means of the workers' independent social activity: by means of the struggle (militant strike organisation), mutual aid (mutual aid societies), self-help (consumer and educational societies).[28]

A little further on Takhtarev contended that the establishment of such organisations had barely commenced in many centres and that the present period must be one of consolidation and patient building up of self-defence and self-help unions. 'The development among the workers of organisations, in our opinion, is the most immediate task of the movement.'[29] Only in and through such organisations could they voice their grievances and organise for their redress. According to *Rabochaya Mysl* the most pressing and keenly felt demands and grievances of the Russian working class were those which flowed directly from its abject economic situation. These demands, it conceded were, invariably, localised and particular demands, but they could not be on that score discounted. On the contrary, it was the demands expressed by the workers themselves that must determine the character and objectives of the movement; they were 'the most characteristic indicator of the direction of our movement'.[30]

> The most immediate particular demands of the workers are an increase in wages, the shortening of the working day, the abolition of fines [and] of the harshness and oppression of the administration, the right to have electoral representatives, workers' deputies in all cases of conflict with the owners, with their administration and the police . . . and other particular demands depending

on the local, particular conditions of life and labour of given workers. The most immediate general-political demands still remain the legislative shortening of the working day (to 10 hours) and the restoration of the holidays abolished by the law of the 2nd of June 1897. But here we are accused of heresy by those who expose the narrowness of our orientation; the revolutionaries who call us the representatives of the lower strata of the proletariat.[31]

According to *Rabochaya Mysl* the independent political role of the working class should, for the present, be restricted to 'the legislative defence of labour'. The article looked forward to the progressive democratisation of Russian life as each class in turn asserted its right to share in the administration of the country. Each phase of this process would afford new channels through which the working class could itself permeate the administrative structure and secure the eventual socialisation of the means of production.

Throughout the article there was a strong smack of the inevitability of gradualness, of the objective development of industry and society necessitating political change. In like fashion, socialism was seen as an inevitable eventual outcome of the growing extensiveness and maturity of the working class; it would arise as an efflux of the movement itself. 'In conclusion – a few words about our conception of socialism. We see it in the workers' improvement itself, in the present and future development of the social and political development of the workers' organisations.' Socialism would, in short, arise naturally out of 'the participation of the workers in public self-government and finally in the representative institutions of the country'.[32] The whole tone of the article suggested, however, that the dawning of socialist consciousness was still a long way off. The worker readers were advised not to lose heart, not to be concerned about the problems their grandchildren would have to solve; rather they should take heart from the irreversible forces making ultimately for democracy and socialism. In the meantime, they should prosecute their present fight for more immediate physical needs, for that was the part which they could play in the unfolding drama. They were unequivocably advised not to be seduced by nebulous distant vistas but to fight the present fight which was the only possible and therefore the only desirable fight.

> What sort of struggle is it desirable for the workers to conduct?
> Isn't the desirable struggle the only one which they are able to
> conduct in present circumstances? And in present circumstances
> isn't the possible struggle the one which they are in fact
> conducting at the present time?[33]

This was the work which, in Lenin's view, 'expresses the ideas
of the Economists more consistently than any other'.[34] It was, in
Lenin's view, the paradigm statement of a trend of which *Rabochee
Delo* also formed a part, albeit at a more inchoate and less-
developed stage. Both took their stand, according to Lenin, on
the primacy of the economic struggle. For *Rabochaya Mysl*, as we
have seen, the economic struggle was almost sufficient in itself.
Its politics during the hey-day of its success amounted to no more
than canvassing the legislative enactment of trade demands. *Rabochee
Delo* in its *Programme*,[35] while far more positive in its commitment
to the political struggle, still based itself in all essentials upon
the programme of *On Agitation*. Politics, it tirelessly repeated,
would come via economics. The growth of the labour movement
would inevitably bring it into conflict with the autocracy and out
of that conflict there would dawn the realisation of the necessity
of securing the all-important rights of freedom of association,
freedom of the press and the inviolability of the person.

> The life activity of the working class leads it into political
> struggle. The constraints of the plain economic struggle oblige
> the workers to put forward political demands and to fight for
> political freedom. The political struggle of the working class is
> but the most highly developed, the broadest and most valid form
> of the economic struggle. The most immediate political demands
> of the working class in Russia are: freedom for unions, for
> strikes, and meetings, [freedom of] expression and the press and
> the inviolability of the person. Those political rights are the
> essential conditions for the further all-round development of the
> workers' movement. They are as necessary to the Russian
> proletariat in its fight for emancipation as light and air. The
> struggle of the working class for these rights comprises the
> immediate content of its struggle with tsarist autocracy .... [36]

In the eyes of Lenin and the orthodox there was little to choose between the programmes of *Rabochaya Mysl* and *Rabochee Delo*. According to them, both demeaned the role of Social-Democratic leadership, both failed to understand the political role of Social Democracy as the leader of the democratic revolution. They failed to recognise that the leadership of this movement necessarily entailed the creation of an organisation and of a press that would articulate the demands not only of the proletariat but of all groups and social strata opposed to the autocracy. More importantly, both groups failed to prosecute and to act on the demands this leadership role entailed. The primary task of consolidating the start made at the First Congress of the Party had been abnegated in favour of purely local work. The localised unco-ordinated work of the groups was, in itself, both cause and symptom of a narrowness of horizons in theoretical and political matters. Each group went its own way, each, according to Lenin, duplicating the activities of the other in a most uneconomic way and each falling prey to the same errors as the other. There existed no division of labour, there existed no common stock of shared experience and no continuity of work. It was, Lenin argued, impossible to presume to lead even the workers on the basis of this ramshackle chaos, let alone pretend to lead other potential allies in a revolutionary upsurge.

'TAILISM' V. PARTY LEADERSHIP AND PROLETARIAN HEGEMONY

The basic cause of this disarray was, in Lenin's view, the lag of the so-called 'leaders' behind the spontaneous mass movement. In his analysis the Russian working class had consistently and almost instinctively groped forward ever since 1898 to engage the autocracy directly in the streets. The May Day demonstrations which grew apace after 1899 were evidence enough of this. Greater numbers of workers were continually being brought into the movement and the advanced workers were leading them into open conflict with the authorities. Meanwhile the leadership slumbered in the comfortable aphorisms of *On Agitation* or helplessly intoned the message of trade union consolidation. The apostasy of 'leaders' of this ilk was the more shameful, in Lenin's eyes, precisely *because* the working-class movement was growing apace and was *already*, without any Social-Democratic assistance, undertaking sporadic political demonstrations and demanding an end to the autocracy. The premise of *What Is To Be Done* (and, historically speaking, the occasion for it) was that the demands made upon the leadership did not diminish with the growth of the labour movement; they became, on the contrary, enormously greater.

> The greater the spontaneous upsurge of the masses and the more widespread the movement, the more rapid, incomparably so, the demand for greater consciousness in the theoretical, political, and organisational work of Social Democracy.
> The spontaneous upsurge of the masses in Russia proceeded (and continues) with such rapidity that the young Social Democrats proved unprepared to meet these gigantic tasks. This unpreparedness is our common misfortune, the misfortune of *all* Russian Social Democrats . . . Revolutionaries, however, *lagged behind* this upsurge, both in their 'theories' and in their activity; they failed to establish a constant and continuous organisation capable of *leading* the whole movement.[37]

We must turn now to Lenin's diagnosis of the dangers posed by this crucial failure of leadership to the nascent Social Democratic Party in Russia. His diagnosis followed, in all essentials, Akselrod's projections in his *Present Tasks and Tactics* of 1898. Throughout this period Lenin repeatedly came back to this text; he was obviously captivated and disturbed by the dialectical choice posed by the two perspectives Akselrod outlined. In the second part of this work Akselrod set out two possible lines of advance for Russian Marxism and the Russian labour movement – one leading to eventual disaster and the other to eventual triumph.

> I conceive of two perspectives for the not too distant future:
> The workers' movement does not leave the narrow course of purely economic clashes of the workers with the employers, and in itself is, on the whole, devoid of political character. In the struggle then for political freedom, the advanced strata of the proletariat support the revolutionary circles or fractions of the so-called intelligentsia. In a word, the emancipation movement proceeds the same way in one very important respect, if not entirely, as in more distant times in the West, when

monarchic–bureaucratic tyranny still held sway; the working masses do not play an independent political role, they support the bourgeois intelligentsia and fight for freedom not under their own banner but under that of somebody else.

The other perspective: Social Democracy organises the Russian proletariat in an independent political party, fighting for freedom, partly alongside and in association with the bourgeois revolutionary factions (in so far as such exist), but partly also drawing directly into its ranks or dragging along behind it the most democratic [people-loving] and revolutionary elements of the intelligentsia. Obviously, this latter perspective requires from the workers a much higher level of political consciousness and self-consciousness, than the first, in which representatives of the bourgeois classes would be the leaders of the revolutionary movement, and the proletariat would only be a guided mass, blindly supporting them.

Does Russian life possess the means necessary for the development within the Russian workers of such political consciousness and self-activity, which would enable them to be organised into an independent and leading revolutionary party? Such therefore, is the first, one might say fundamental, question on the solution of which the future destiny of Russian Social Democracy depends. If there are not such means, in other words, if there is no possibility of supplying the Russian proletariat with an 'independent' leading role in the struggle against the tsarist-police autocracy and arbitrariness, then Russian Social Democracy forfeits its historical right to existence. In such an eventuality devoid of any vitality it would by its very existence rather impede the growth of the revolutionary movement than promote it.[38]

Throughout this extremely important pamphlet Akselrod was concerned to warn the Russian movement about the consequences of becoming intoxicated with the programme of economic agitation. The question was not, he maintained, simply one of expanding the strike movement and drawing ever-larger numbers into it. That process would no doubt proceed unchecked. The question was, what direction and what character would the movement assume. The answer to this latter question was not, in his estimation, to be settled simply by letting things take their course or by letting the workers' demands, as expressed by them, dictate the policy of the Social Democrats. On the contrary, as the R.S.D.L.P.'s expert on the history of the western labour movement, Akselrod was at pains to point out how, in the West, the economic struggle of the working class, however extensive, however consolidated its organisational base, did not automatically lead to a growth of *political* consciousness. If political strivings did emerge among the workers they almost invariably fell under the sway of the bourgeoisie.[39] His conclusion was that the political *potential* of the workers' movement could only be tapped, could only develop into kinetic energy, under the influence of energetic Social-Democratic activity.[40] Even the gradual spread of organs of self-government were unlikely to have much impact in themselves, unless the Social Democrats intervened and brought their ideas to the workers. 'But it goes without saying that these conditions, without the energetic influence of the Social Democrats, may cause our proletariat to remain in its condition as a listless and somnolent force in respect of its political development.'[41]

The critical factor, for Akselrod, as for Plekhanov, was the decisive intervention of the socialist intelligentsia into the workers' movement and their ability from the very start to inject into that movement a social and political ideal. Akselrod was as categorical as Lenin ever was in *What Is To Be Done?* that, spontaneously and organically, the workers' movement could not produce a galvanising ideal which would spur it into an independent political and class existence. If this were not the case then the intervention of Social-Democratic intellectuals would, after all, be superfluous. Akselrod was quite explicit;

> The proletariat, according to the consciousness of the Social Democrats themselves, does not possess a ready-made, historically-elaborated social ideal. 'The economic struggle' with its employers remains the path whereby it slowly formulates such an 'ideal' in its consciousness – to speak more plainly – it prepares the workers' understanding for the definitive goals of socialism.[42]

The 'one-sided' infatuation with the strike movement for immediate economic demands had, according to Akselrod, more present dangers; in particular this struggle was exclusively a struggle of wage-labourers. It was a struggle which they fought alone against the combined resources of the bourgeoisie and the state, a battle in which the nascent labour movement could not expect assistance from other social strata. It was, moreover, a struggle which, in Russia, was fraught with more dangers than in any other country in Europe.[43] The danger existed that, in this unequal trial of strength, the young proletariat would exhaust itself in this 'one-sided' activity and, out of exhaustion, become disillusioned with Social Democracy. Their only possible salvation, at least until their forces were more extensive and more cohesively organised, was to attract the sympathy of other social classes by undertaking the leadership of a broader, political struggle with the autocracy. Unless the movement was continually bolstered by recruitment from the radical intelligentsia and by winning the sympathy of other strata opposed to the autocracy, the movement might well wear itself out. To win this support, however, the movement must switch the main emphases of propaganda and practical work away from the localised class-bound economic struggle towards the 'general-democratic tasks of our movement and in this way to popularise its general-national significance for contemporary Russia'.[44]

It was on the basis of these impeccably orthodox propositions that Lenin began his own assault on the Economists and revisionists in 1899. In article after article he paid homage to Akselrod's insights and developed them into the stock of ideas which were later drawn together in *What Is To Be Done?*

Like Akselrod and Plekhanov, Lenin located the primary error of his opponents in their failure to lead, their failure in particular to undertake the role of Social Democracy, at the head of the labour movement, as the advance guard in the fight for democracy. The failure of the leaders, their willingness to plod patiently along behind the mass movement, to follow its tail, and then *de post facto* to justify and to hold up as theory what the proletariat had already achieved, this for Lenin was tantamount to treachery. It represented theory as retrospection not as prescience. In practical matters this 'cringing to spontaneity' and 'tailism' left the door wide open for bourgeois democrats to usurp the role of Social Democracy and not only intrude themselves as the leaders of the general-democratic struggle but also, as Akselrod had warned, to take the political strivings of the workers under bourgeois direction. The lag of leadership behind the mass movement, its failure to provide positive guidance and adequate organisation for the increasingly militant and political spontaneous movement, constituted the cardinal cause of the crisis in Social Democracy. Into the political vacuum created, and indeed boasted about, by the Economists, would step the representatives of bourgeois radicalism. The flood-gates, it seemed to Lenin, were already half-open, the conditions were maturing exactly as Akselrod had specified, for the first disastrous scenario he had outlined.

> The reason lies in the fact that we failed to cope with our tasks. The masses of the workers proved to be more active than we. We lacked adequately trained revolutionary leaders and organisers possessed of a thorough knowledge of the mood prevailing among all the opposition strata and able to head the movement, to turn a spontaneous demonstration into a political one, broaden its political character, etc. Under such circumstances, our backwardness will inevitably be utilised by the more mobile and more energetic non-Social-Democratic revolutionaries, and the workers, however energetically and self-sacrificingly they may fight the police and the troops, however revolutionary their actions may be, will prove to be merely a force supporting those revolutionaries, the rearguard of bourgeois democracy and not the Social-Democratic vanguard.[45]

We should note at this point that Lenin consistently located the source of the crisis within the leadership of the movement. It was the Social Democrats who had proved unequal to their tasks and *not* the mass movement. I am aware, of course, that the majority of commentators assert the reverse. It is argued that Lenin, during this period, 'lost faith' in the spontaneous mass movement, despaired of it ever attaining socialist consciousness and concluded that the revolution would have to be engineered by a professional élite. This interpretation has the attraction of being simple and consistent with the Lenin-as-Jacobin interpretation; it raises, however, considerable, indeed insuperable, problems for anyone who actually reads and attempts to make sense of Lenin's writings. What, for instance, are we to make of Lenin's repeated insistence that the spontaneous movement had far outstripped the leadership in terms of taking the initative in directly confronting the government? What are we to make of his assertion that 'no one, we think, has until now doubted that the strength of the present-day movement lies in the awakening of the masses (principally, the industrial proletariat) and that its weakness lies in the lack of consciousness and initiative among the revolutionary leaders'.[46] Even more emphatically the

> 'spontaneous' protest against the autocracy is *outstripping* the conscious Social-Democratic leadership of the movement. The spontaneous striving of the workers to defend the students who are being assaulted by the police and the Cossacks surpasses the conscious activity of the Social-Democratic organisation![47]

It is nonsense to suggest that Lenin *despaired* of this spontaneity; on the contrary he, more than anyone, anticipated this upsurge and appreciated its revolutionary potential. What he *did* despair of was the possibility of converting that revolutionary potential into a cohesive political force given the current dominance of *praktiki* and Economists at the grass roots of the movement. We cannot make sense of the passages quoted and cited in the notes by imputing to Lenin a lack of faith in the revolutionary potential of the working class. On the contrary the whole point of the plan he elaborated from 1899 onwards was that the escalating revolutionary upsurge had to be harnessed by Social Democracy, organised on a national basis if it was to have a hope of success. Unless this was done the workers would be cut down piecemeal in their sporadic and unco-ordinated attempts to bring down the autocracy. It was, as we have already noted, *precisely the 'awakening' of the mass* which imposed new theoretical and practical obligations upon the leadership, obligations which they had lamentably failed to fulfil.

The failure of the Economists resulted, according to Lenin, from a theoretical or methodological lapse on their part. They failed to comprehend the process whereby consciousness developed within the mass, and they gravely *underestimated* the pace with which it could proceed. It was, in Lenin's opinion, they, not the orthodox, who underestimated the revolutionary capacity of the masses and, because of their disparaging conception of proletarian ability, set the tasks far too narrowly. Like the terrorists, the Economists demonstrated in their practice a lack of faith in the working class:

> . . . both the terrorists and the Economists *underestimate* the revolutionary activity of the masses despite the striking evidence of the events that took place in the spring [the large-scale street

157

demonstrations which began in spring of 1901], and whereas the one group goes out in search of artificial 'excitants', the other talks about 'concrete demands'. But both fail to devote sufficient attention to the development of *their own activity* in political agitation and in the organisation of political exposures.[48]

The Economists, according to Lenin, misread the situation because they failed to understand that it was always the most advanced section which determined the character of the movement. The Economists took as their norm of development the average or more backward sections of the working class and tried, as it were, to lead from below – attempting to organise and instil a primary awareness of a set of shared economic interests amongst these groups. They committed the error of tailoring the tasks and policies of the movement as a whole to the demands of its least developed sections. '*Rabochaya Mysl* . . . is moving backwards and fully justifies the opinion that it is not representative of advanced workers, but of the lower, undeveloped strata of the proletariat.'[49] 'Our Economists, including *Rabochee Delo*, were successful because they adapted themselves to the backward workers.'[50] Their whole position, according to Lenin, amounted to a total renunciation of Social Democracy's role even vis-à-vis the proletariat. The Economists did not concern themselves with problems of theory or future strategy for to do so would involve dictating to the movement, which would itself, in due course, elaborate its new policies. The implication was that socialism was immanent within the labour movement and the experience of the working class would progressively lead them to articulate it. Some indeed (like *Rabochaya Mysl*), went even further and asserted that 'socialism is merely a further and higher development of the modern community'.[51] Such views rested, in Lenin's opinion, on a dangerous misconception of the genesis of socialism and the manner in which socialist consciousness developed in the working class. Into these turbulent waters, with natural trepidation, we must in the next chapter launch ourselves.

CONCLUSION

The crisis which Russian Marxism faced at the turn of the century was, in the opinion of many commentators, no real crisis at all.

It was invented by Lenin and the Iskrists as a convenient way of attaching pejorative labels (economist, revisionist, etc.) to their competitors for the leadership of the Party. It is suggested that Lenin invented a straw man when he accused the *Rabochaya Mysl* and *Rabochee Delo* adherents of abstaining from the political struggle. Lenin's view, they say, would not withstand an impartial examination of the evidence, for, particularly after 1901, even *Rabochaya Mysl* advocated a distinctly political line.

In considering these charges there is, I think, one major point which rather tends to be overlooked but which cannot be stressed too forcibly in our conclusion. The struggle within the movement was not so much a battle for control over an existing established party, for, as we have seen, there did not exist a Russian Social Democratic Labour Party in any meaningful sense of the word. It was, rather, a more elemental battle about how the R.S.D.L.P. should be constituted, a battle about what sort of party Russia needed. It was fundamentally a fight between two clearly distinct trends. On the one hand there were the Iskrists, who reaffirmed the central idea of Russian Marxist orthodoxy, that the class struggle was, definitionally, a political struggle and that in Russian conditions the proletariat would have to assume hegemony over the democratic revolution. To fulfil the role of leading all anti-autocratic strata, the party of the proletariat had to assume awesome organisational tasks which, in turn, demanded a centralised all-Russian party structure. On the other hand the *Rabochaya Mysl* and *Rabochee Delo* adherents considered the gradual piecemeal improvement of the workers' material conditions to be the proper centre of Social-Democratic activity. They did not deny that politics could be a useful adjunct of this work but they *did* deny Iskrist politics in the sense that they never aspired to establish proletarian hegemony over the democratic movement. The difference of orientation between these two trends was not, as many commentators suggest, lacking in historical foundation. It certainly would not be traducing the evidence to contend that the Iskrists emphatically orientated themselves towards revolutionary politics whereas their opponents, equally emphatically, considered that the ·gradual winning of economic reforms was the appropriate focus for Party activity at this time and in the foreseeable future.

The fact that there was no party in existence is of cardinal importance in understanding the passion and earnestness of Lenin and the orthodox in getting an undiluted, revolutionary, Marxist programme adopted for the reconstituted R.S.D.L.P. The situation in the Russian movement was such that they felt they could not afford to allow a large minority (perhaps even a majority) of avowed revisionists a prominent role in deciding the composition of the programme and the governing organs of the Party. It was, they felt, imperative that the programme, which defined the ethos and long-term objectives of the Party, and would therefore determine its strategy for decades to come, must reflect the expressly political revolutionary strivings of the Russian proletariat. The German Party could, in Lenin's view, afford the luxury of a large revisionist minority within its ranks only because it had a clearly defined Marxist programme, authoritative leaders, an established Party press and settled traditions for resolving disputes. In Russia *none* of those conditions prevailed. Worse still the effect of police persecution had been to deprive the movement of virtually all its experienced and theoretically-trained leadership cadres, leaving it easy prey to the green enthusiasm of ill-informed and ill-prepared youngsters infatuated with immediate bread-and-butter problems. It was unthinkable to Lenin and Martov, even more unthinkable was it to Plekhanov and Akselrod, that such men should be entrusted with drafting the programme and defining the whole future orientation of the Party, which they were all trying to re-establish.

CHAPTER 7

The Reaffirmation of Orthodoxy – Social-Democratic Consciousness and the Party

The ideas which Lenin set out in *What Is To Be Done?* were, as we have seen from the previous chapter, inextricably connected with the power struggle proceeding within the R.S.D.L.P. in the years from 1899 to 1903. The bulk of the pamphlet is quite unintelligible if divorced from this immediate context. In 1907 Lenin insisted that the arguments and organisational principles of *What Is To Be Done?* were not intended as general statements of everlasting applicability but were, on the contrary, pertinent to a particular situation faced by the Russian movement at a particular moment of its development.

> Concerning the essential content of this pamphlet it is necessary to draw the attention of the modern reader to the following.
> The basic mistake made by those who now criticise *What Is To Be Done?* is to treat the pamphlet apart from its connection with the concrete historical situation of a definite, and now long past, period in the development of our Party.[1]

The whole purpose of the book, Lenin went on, was to provide 'a controversial correction of Economist distortions and it would be wrong to regard the pamphlet in any other light'.[2] Its elements of exaggeration were, in Lenin's later considered view, very necessary since seemingly minor differences of orientation at the beginning of this new work, at the beginning of the Social-Democratic movement 'would very substantially affect propaganda, agitation and organisation'.[33] The significance of *What Is To Be Done?* was, therefore, that it 'straightens out what had been twisted by the Economists'.[4]

The primary goal of Lenin's pamphlet was to state the orthodox case that the Party, at the forthcoming 'constitutive' Congress, should commit itself to a frankly revolutionary political strategy in which the proletariat and its Party would feature as the vanguard of the democratic movement against autocracy. It was, in this sense, primarily a statement about the proper goals of Social Democracy at this time – an orthodox insistence that economic goals be subordinated to political goals and not vice versa. Put in another way, Lenin was asserting that the strategic transition from economic agitation to political agitation had been signalled by the actions of the masses and could no longer be delayed.

Lenin's ideas on organisation and consciousness were derivative of his basic objective. The argument was that if the Party was to lead all the democratic forces in a concerted all-Russian revolutionary movement to topple autocracy then it must have an appropriately cohesive and efficient all-Russian structure. The general pattern of the organisation was, therefore, according to Lenin, entailed by the specification of the objectives appropriate to the Party – the one was a function of the other. Demonstration of this truth was, for Lenin, afforded by the attitude of the Economists to this question. Their specification of the Party's primary objective – improving the economic lot of the workers – inevitably led them to recommend a loosely structured Party where local committees had to enjoy ample initiative to pursue the specific local conditions of employment, pay, fines, housing, etc.

SOCIAL-DEMOCRATIC CONSCIOUSNESS AND THE DEVELOPMENT OF SOCIALISM

Part of the reason why the Economists set the objectives of the movement at so low a level, and, consequently could rest content with a primitive 'handicraft-type' organisation, lay, in Lenin's view, in their inability to understand the history of the development of socialism and of working-class consciousness. The Economists' belief that socialism was immanent within the workers' movement and would ineluctably work its way through quite unaided, was based, in Lenin's view, on a gross misconception about the history of socialism as a tradition of thought and a no less inadequate grasp of the history of the workers' movement – notably in England. Fundamentally the Economists failed to grasp the dynamic relationship between theory and practice. Lenin, in his reflections on consciousness, was doing no more than restating the perfectly orthodox proposition developed long previously by Plekhanov, that the duty of the Party was always to be one step ahead of the workers' movement. Its theoretical prescience must so guide the practice of the workers' movement as to encourage it to achieve the next phase of the ascent towards fully socialist consciousness – otherwise the Party had no *raison d'être*.

To clarify this position, we must examine more closely Lenin's account of the development of 'Social-Democratic consciousness'. Our first step, quite clearly, is to discover quite what Lenin intended by this phrase. True to his didactic temperament Lenin provided us with a lengthy definition:

The consciousness of the working masses cannot be genuine class-consciousness unless the workers learn, from concrete, and above all from topical, political facts and events to observe *every* other social class in *all* the manifestations of its intellectual, ethical, and political life; unless they learn to apply in practice the materialist analysis and the materialist estimate of all aspects of the life and activity of *all* classes, strata and groups of the population. Those who concentrate the attention, observation, and consciousness of the working class exclusively, or even mainly, upon itself alone are not Social Democrats; for the self-knowledge of the working class is indissolubly linked up, not solely with a fully clear theoretical understanding – it would be even truer to say, not so much with the theoretical, as with the practical, understanding – of the relationships between *all* the various classes of modern society, acquired through the experience of political life. . . .

In order to become a Social Democrat, the worker must have a clear picture in his mind of the economic nature and the social and political features of the landlord and the priest, the high state official and the peasant, the student and the vagabond; he must know their strong and weak points; he must grasp the meaning of all the catchwords and sophisms by which each class and each stratum *camouflages* its selfish interests and its real 'inner

163

workings'; he must understand what interests are reflected by certain institutions and certain laws and how they are reflected.[5]

We noticed earlier that Lenin's style was often that of a head-master; he was, quite clearly, a headmaster who demanded a very great deal from his pupils. His specification of what constituted adequate class or Social-Democratic consciousness was extra-ordinarily rigorous and severe. Intrinsic to it was his insistence that the essential character of Social-Democratic activity was to represent the workers on the national political plane, i.e. it represented the working class 'not in its relation to a given group of employers alone, but in its relation to all classes of modern society and to the state as an organised political force'.[6] This, of course, followed from the orthodox axiom which has earlier been noted, that the working class began to emerge with its essential attributes only when it constituted itself a political party and articulated the general-national demands of the class. To this extent Lenin's severe specification of the constituents of adequate consciousness was no more than an elaboration of what was entailed in the phase of *political* activity of the working class. The obligation to be aware of the economic, social and political situations of all other classes and strata was, of course, heightened by the equally orthodox insistence that the leadership of all the varied groups comprising the democratic movement in Russia must devolve upon the pro-letariat, with Social Democracy as its political representative. In other words the level of consciousness demanded was that appropriate to, and flowing from, the political tasks the Russian Social Democrats were duty bound to carry out.

Let us notice for the time being that Lenin's account of Social-Democratic consciousness was extremely broad and demanding, involving as it did a total composite picture of the social sub-divisions of contemporary Russia. The problem which emerged was, was it reasonable or indeed possible for the worker to acquire *such* consciousness from the economic struggle for existence? Could political and Social-Democratic consciousness arise, in Lenin's view, from what we have termed the *industrial practice* of the working class? Lenin answered, unequivocally, in the negative.

The sphere of activity of industrial practice was too narrow, its confines too restrictive, for the worker to be able to come to adequate political consciousness. Within the economic sphere the clash was exclusively between those who hired themselves as wage-labourers and their employers. At its broadest this could amount only to a clash between the whole class of labourers and the owners of capital. Even at this maximum extension the owners were confronted precisely as such, as a group disposing of capital; they were not typically confronted as disposers of political power allied with other classes and groups.

> Consequently, *however much we may try* to 'lend the economic struggle itself a political character', we *shall never be able* to develop the political consciousness of the workers (to the level of Social-Democratic political consciousness) by keeping within the framework of the economic struggle, for *that framework is too narrow.*[7]

According to Lenin the advanced workers were already discontented with the economic struggle. They already recognised the necessity for decisive and unified political activity but of themselves lacked a national organisational focus and lacked the necessary knowledge to elaborate an independent political strategy. Lenin's imaginary worker in *What Is To Be Done?* became the mouthpiece of the advanced workers now chaffing against the short rein on which they were held by *Rabochaya Mysl* and *Rabochee Delo.*

> . . . We are not children to be fed on the thin gruel of 'economic' politics alone; we want to know everything that others know, we want to learn the details of *all* aspects of political life and to take part *actively* in every single political event. In order that we may do this, the intellectuals must talk to us less of what we already know and tell us more about what we do not yet know and what we can never learn from our factory and 'economic' experience, namely, political knowledge. You intellectuals can acquire this knowledge, and it is your *duty* to bring it to us. . .[8]

Lenin's position with regard to the development of consciousness at this time was quite clear and intelligible. He made no attempt to dissimulate; on the contrary, he stated his position openly and systematically. He contended that the experience of the economic class struggle of the proletariat could not, of itself, lead to

165

adequate political consciousness because political consciousness demanded a knowledge of all classes and strata in their inter-relationships. The economic 'spontaneous' struggle of the workers could not lead to Social-Democratic consciousness for that entailed *leading* all other classes and strata in the democratic revolution. It necessarily involved, therefore, knowledge of the political interests, strengths and weaknesses of every opposition group. It involved, further, a national political organisation to co-ordinate *all* anti-autocratic manifestations, and the creation of a vehicle of systematic national propaganda and agitation through which the grievances of all groups and classes could find an outlet. Interests must be generalised, must be articulated, must be seen in relation one with another before consciousness could dawn upon the masses.

We should be clear at this stage that Lenin's evaluation of the immediate tasks confronting the movement was shared by all the orthodox. Plekhanov and Akselrod were stating the same position, Potresov and Martov were in complete accord. Furthermore, they all believed that those tasks could not be accomplished by relying upon the localised, and therefore weak, Social-Democratic Groups in Russia. More significantly, perhaps, they were at one with Lenin in believing that the expansion of consciousness among the workers, which the implementation of these tasks demanded, could not issue from the narrow compass of Economist politics. At the very least none of the orthodox registered any disapproval of Lenin's thesis that, *left to themselves* the workers would only develop trade-union consciousness, i.e., an awareness of a shared set of economic interests.

In view of the forcefulness with which he put his position, and in view of the almost universal opinion that Lenin was here departing from Marxist orthodoxy, it is more than surprising that the recognised guardians of that orthodoxy in Russia should have entered no reservations at the time. Nor can it be maintained that Lenin suddenly and unexpectedly sprang this upon his colleagues, throwing them into temporary confusion. In the very first number of *Iskra*, Lenin's editorial, *The Urgent Tasks of Our Movement*, set out quite clearly the orthodox position with regard to the development of consciousness. We must regard this as a joint statement of the whole editorial board – both Akselrod and Plekhanov as fellow-editors had seen and approved the article.

In it Lenin contended that the mischief wrought by the Economists consisted primarily in splitting the working class from its connection with the broader goals of socialism through concentrating almost exclusively on localised work and the economic struggle. 'Isolated from Social Democracy', Lenin contended 'the working-class movement becomes petty and inevitably becomes bourgeois. In waging only the economic struggle, the working class loses its political independence; it becomes the tail of other parties ...'[9] The task of the Social Democrats was stated quite clearly: it was 'to imbue the masses of the proletariat with the ideas of socialism and political consciousness and to organise a revolutionary party inseparably connected with the spontaneous working-class movement'.[10] Unless this were done, that is, unless the Social-Democratic intelligentsia brought consciousness and organisation to the workers,

> the proletariat will never rise to the class-conscious struggle; without such organisation the working-class movement is doomed to impotency . . . . Not a single class in history has achieved power without producing its political leaders, its prominent representatives able to organise a movement and lead it.[11]

We have seen in Chapter Two, how Plekhanov repeatedly emphasised the responsibility of the Social-Democratic intelligentsia to bring consciousness and organisation into the labour movement. We have seen above how Akselrod insisted that without the determined intervention of the Social Democrats the labour movement was doomed to subserve the interests of bourgeois politics. Lenin's formulations in polemic with the Economists might well have been sharper but they were hardly innovatory. Lenin himself had insisted in 1899 that it was a gross error to identify the strivings of the labour movement with socialism. The two were, he maintained, distinct, though each needed the other. Social Democracy as a movement of men and ideas could only exist, in Lenin's view, as a fusion of the two; he maintained that 'Social Democracy is not confined to simple service of the working-class movement'; it represented '*the combination of socialism and the working-class movement*' (to use Karl Kautsky's definition which repeats the basic ideas of the *Communist Manifesto*).[12] Earlier still, in 1894, Lenin had emphatically rejected the 'fatalistic' interpretation foisted on to Marx by 'cowardly petty-bourgeois' interpreters who asserted that working-class political and socialist organisations were the spontaneous product of capitalist development. This contention Lenin argued:

> is refuted by all the activities of the Social Democrats in all countries; it is refuted by every public speech made by any Marxist. Social Democracy – as Kautsky very justly remarks – is a fusion of the working-class movement and socialism.[13]

The distinction which Lenin invoked in *What Is To Be Done?*, between the labour movement and Social Democracy, was, as we have seen, intrinsic to the position of all the orthodox. None of them had rebuked him earlier for drawing attention to it, nor were they to do so in 1902–3.

It was indeed to the impeccable authority of Karl Kautsky that Lenin again appealed when he maintained in *What Is To Be Done?* that socialism was not purely and simply a product of the labour movement, but arose as a body of ideas within the intelligentsia. He cited from Kautsky's recently published *Programme for the Social Democratic Party of Austria*[14] in defence of his position:

> The vehicle of science is not the proletariat, but the *bourgeois intelligentsia* [K. K.'s italics]: it was in the minds of individual members of this stratum that modern socialism originated, and it was they who communicated it to the more intellectually developed proletarians who, in their turn, introduce it into the proletariat class struggle where conditions allow that to be done. Thus, socialist consciousness is something introduced into the proletarian class struggle from without [von Aussen Hineingetragenes] and not something that arose within it spontaneously [urwüchsig]. Accordingly, the old Hainfeld programme quite rightly stated that the task of Social Democracy is to imbue the proletariat [literally: saturate the proletariat] with the *consciousness* of its position and the consciousness of its task. There would be no need for this if consciousness arose of itself from the class struggle.[15]

Many present-day students of Marxism might well see some large theoretical problems emerging from Kautsky's assessment of the evolution of consciousness but what cannot be denied is that, at

168

this time Kautsky was unquestionably regarded as the guardian and oracle of Marxist orthodoxy. Those who dispute Lenin's conclusions on the genesis of socialist consciousness must it seems, also dispute Kautsky's claim to represent Social-Democratic orthodoxy for Lenin's elaboration of this theme in *What Is To Be Done?* was but an exegesis of Kautsky whose views were, as we have seen, very closely similar to those of the other orthodox within the Russian movement.[16]

The rest of Lenin's analysis of consciousness in *What Is To Be Done?* was no more than a development of Kautsky's views in the Russian context. He used Kautsky's conclusions as a lever to demonstrate the untenability of his opponents' views. One of these views, widely canvassed by *Rabochee Delo*, commended 'tactics as process'. This suggested that, through the dialectics of its own development the workers' movement would, in time, come to political and Social-Democratic consciousness. The implication of this was again that socialism was immanent within the strivings of the working class, and would be actualised by it quite unaided. For Lenin, this position stood in flat contradiction to Kautsky's insistence that socialism could only be introduced from without.[17] The position of the 'tactics as process' men was not only theoretically incorrect, it raised great practical dangers for the movement. Lenin's argument might have appeared rather strange, but it did have a certain implacable logic. Given that the workers, of themselves, could not evolve socialist ideas, given that they could not articulate an independent and consistent political strategy of their own, it followed that simply to sit by waiting for the impossible to occur, meant, in practice, delivering them into the hands of bourgeois politicians. This must follow because in the first place bourgeois ideology was much older and better established; secondly, the bourgeoisie controlled the media for the dissemination of ideas; and, finally, its task would be greatly eased in Russia because the workers' movement was so young and ill-organised.[18]

Part of Lenin's case rested upon Marx's own analysis which we have already broached. Marx's economic and historical analysis pointed in particular to the emergence of class polarity within society. Since ideologies and parties expressed, more or less adequately, class interests, these must reduce themselves to two totally opposed political courses – bourgeois or proletarian. There could be no middle way, for all intermediary classes and ideologies were progressively swept aside. Given the fact (which none of the orthodox disputed) that the working class of itself could not elaborate an independent political standpoint, the choice presented was clear – *either* it would be won over by the bourgeoisie (who, as Lenin noted, had many advantages in the struggle) *or* it would be won over to the socialist views and organisation outlined by the intelligentsia Social Democrats.

> Since there can be no talk of an independent ideology form-
> ulated by the working masses themselves in the process of their
> movement, the *only* choice is either bourgeois or socialist
> ideology. There is no middle course (for mankind has not
> created a 'third' ideology, and, moreover, in a society torn by
> class antagonisms, there can never be a non-class or above-class
> ideology). Hence, to belittle the socialist ideology *in any way, to
> turn aside from it in the slightest degree* means to strengthen
> bourgeois ideology. There is much talk of spontaneity. But the
> *spontaneous* development of the working-class movement leads to
> its subordination to bourgeois ideology, *to its development along
> the lines of the Credo programme*; for the spontaneous working-class
> movement is trade-unionism, is *Nur-Gewerkschaftlerei*, and trade-
> unionism means the ideological enslavement of the workers by
> the bourgeoisie. Hence, our task, the task of Social-Democracy, is
> *to combat spontaneity to divert* the working-class movement from
> this spontaneous trade-unionist striving to come under the wing
> of the bourgeoisie, and to bring it under the wing of revolutionary
> Social Democracy.[19]

Lenin's position here did not differ in any essentials from the viewpoint of Akselrod cited above; it was a position which Plekhanov had himself expressed in his *Preface to the 'Vademecum' for the Editorial Board of Rabochee Delo*. There Plekhanov similarly insisted that the policy of trusting the workers to elaborate their own political strategy, of concentrating on the economic struggle and of utilising only those legal outlets of representation available to the workers, would, in the absence of a strong party guided by the revolutionary bacilli of the intelligentsia, be tantamount to delivering the workers up to the radical or liberal bourgoisie who would fashion them into a pliant tool of their

The Reaffirmation of Orthodoxy

political objectives.[20] The same argument was pursued at length in his *Once Again Socialism and the Political Struggle* where he introduced an argument which is also crucial to *What Is To Be Done?* and Lenin's whole account of the development of consciousness in the mass.

Plekhanov insisted that a main cause of the Economists' dereliction of duty was their failure not merely to keep one step ahead of the workers in general, but of the *advanced workers* in particular. As far as the *Party* was concerned it must distinguish levels of consciousness within the working class and it must seek always to be one step ahead of its leading stratum in defining the immediate tasks of the movement.

> In the words of the author the agitator should always be one step ahead of the masses. So let it be. But precisely which stratum should the party be ahead of? Precisely which stratum should we precede by one step? If it is the most advanced one, then the moment of transition to the political struggle has probably arrived . . . All these difficulties disappear as soon as we remember that it is one thing for the whole working class, and another for the Social-Democratic Party to represent itself as the most advanced section of the working class, even if, at the outset [that section is] small in numbers.[21]

Plekhanov made it quite clear that, for the Party the base-line had to be the most advanced section of the working class and that section was already groping towards revolutionary politics. Unless the Party acted as the guide for this section, unless also it reorganised itself on a cohesive basis, then the danger existed, for Plekhanov, as for Lenin and Akselrod, that the whole movement would be deflected into the political camp of the bourgeoisie. This indeed, was the logical outcome, in Plekhanov's opinion, of the Economist tactic.

> But such an outcome is, as far as we are concerned, totally undesirable. If in the struggle which must begin in Russia – in the struggle for political freedom – our workers, among whom class-consciousness is already awakening, come out as the vassals of others, alien to the party, then the advantage will accrue to

no one except the bourgeoisie. Let the ideologist of the bourgeoisie try to lead the workers along that path. We, Social Democrats, will try to move them along another.[22]

Clearly, for Plekhanov, as for Lenin, as for Kautsky and Akselrod, there was no necessary determinism at work which ineluctably propelled the working class towards socialism. The emphasis of all Plekhanov's works at this time was the same; only the determined intervention of the Social-Democratic intelligentsia, only the infusion of socialism into the working class, only the creation of a strong centralised party, could prevent the workers becoming the tool of bourgeois politics. It is on this note that he ended his *Once Again Socialism and the Political Struggle*, invoking Akselrod's two perspectives.

> The triumph of the 'economic' trend would lead to the political exploitation of the Russian working class by the democratic and liberal bourgeoisie.
>   The tactic which I defend in this article would as inevitably give to Russia Social Democracy – to that most advanced section of the Russian working class – the political hegemony in the struggle for emancipation from tsarism.[23]

It is hardly to be wondered-at that Plekhanov, neither at the time nor for some time after its publication, criticised *What Is To Be Done?* Its basic theses were his own.

Let us now consider the reorientation of Social-Democratic activity which Lenin thought necessary for the evolution of properly socialist consciousness. The assumptions which formed the basis of his view were in every respect similar to those we have already encountered in discussing Lenin's ideas on 'industrial' or economic practice. Even in that primary phase of the solidification of the working class, the workers did not *commence* the struggle with their employers with anything like adequate consciousness of the irreconcilability of their respective economic interests. They did not, even at this stage, comprehend their situation theoretically. Comprehension came only in and through practice; it came from experience of strikes and economic struggle. For the broad mass even the first steps towards a recognition of shared economic interests did not come from books; it came from following the

172

advanced workers into the actual struggle. The chain of consciousness which Lenin presented was roughly as follows. The Social
Democrats, armed through theory with the ability to generalise,
undertook relentless exposures of the nature of Russian capitalism
by seizing upon particular keenly felt abuses and demonstrating
their general significance. The *advanced* workers responded to the
Social-Democratic call to action and drew with them the mass of the
workers. In the course of the struggle the *mass* too came to
appreciate the general nature of the system of exploitation. This,
we have contended, was Lenin's view of the way in which the
primary elements of class *economic* solidarity were forged. An
exactly similar progress was invoked in the case of *political* and
Social-Democratic consciousness. The process would be the same,
only the object of attention and the focus of activity had to change.
In an article written at the end of 1899[24] Lenin quite explicitly
emphasised that his conception of the growth of this second phase,
or political consciousness, followed the same path as his analysis
of the first or economic phase. In both it was the advanced workers
who were crucial; with Plekhanov he agreed that they determined
the character of the movement.

> It is the task of Social Democracy to develop the political con-
> sciousness of the masses and not to drag along at the tail-end
> of the masses that have no political rights; secondly, and this
> is most important, it is untrue that the masses will not understand
> the idea of the political struggle. Even the most backward worker
> will understand the idea, provided, of course, the agitator or
> propagandist is able to approach him in such a way as to
> communicate the idea to him, to explain it in understandable
> language on the basis of facts the worker knows from everyday
> experience. But this condition is just as indispensable for
> clarifying the economic struggle; in this field too, the backward
> workers from the lower or middle strata of the masses will
> not be able to assimilate the general idea of economic struggle;
> it is an idea which can be absorbed by a few educated workers
> whom the masses will follow, guided by their instincts and
> their direct, immediate interests.
>
> This is likewise true of the political sphere, of course; only
> the developed worker will comprehend the general idea of the
> political struggle, and the masses will follow him because they

have a very good sense of their lack of political rights . . . and because their most immediate, everyday interests regularly bring them into contact with every kind of manifestation of political oppression. In no political or social movement, in no country has there ever been, or could there ever have been, any other relation between the mass of the given class or people and its numerically few, educated representatives than the following: everywhere and at all times the leaders of a certain class have always been its advanced, most cultivated representatives. Nor can there be any other situation in the Russian working-class movement.[25]

The main emphasis of the work in the second phase, must, in Lenin's view, be shifted from economic exposure to political exposure. This imperative arose not only because the advanced workers were already engaging in political demonstrations but also because political exposures touched upon the conditions of life of all opposition sections of the populace. Only by becoming acquainted with these broader issues could the proletariat attain consciousness and impress its leadership.

The Social Democrats must change their role from being trade-union secretaries to becoming tribunes of the whole people.[26] The working class as a whole could come to adequate consciousness only by being led into the struggle, by themselves participating in every aspect of the democratic revolution, by encountering in practice the dispositions of *all* social strata.

It is not enough to *explain* to the workers that they are politically oppressed (any more than it is to *explain* to them that their interests are antagonistic to the interests of the employers). Agitation must be conducted with regard to every concrete example of this oppression (as we have begun to carry on agitation round concrete examples of economic oppression). In as much as *this* oppression affects the most diverse classes of society, in as much as it manifests itself in the most varied spheres of life and activity – vocational, civic, personal, family, religious, scientific, etc. etc. – is it not evident that *we shall not be fulfilling our task* of developing the political consciousness of the workers if we do not *undertake* the organisation of the *political exposure* of the autocracy *in all its aspects*?[27]

Repeatedly Lenin made the same point: only by participating in the broader democratic struggle, by fusing itself with Social Democracy, would the mass of workers acquire adequate consciousness.

> A basic condition for the necessary expansion of political agitation is the organisation of *comprehensive* political exposure. *In no way* except by means of such exposures *can* the masses be trained in political consciousness and revolutionary activity. . . . Working-class consciousness cannot be genuine political consciousness unless the workers are trained to respond to *all* cases of tyranny, oppression, violence, and abuse, no matter *what class* is affected.[28]

Unless this were done then Social Democracy might as well in Lenin's view, concede its leading role and cease pretending to assume hegemony over the democratic movement.

> Those who refrain from concerning themselves in this way . . . in actuality leave the liberals in command, place in their hands the political education of the workers, and concede the hegemony in the political struggle to elements which, in the final analysis, are leaders of bourgeois democracy.[29]

The road to mass political consciousness lay, according to Lenin, through political practice under the guidance of the Social Democrats. This view which is intrinsic to *What Is To Be Done?* had been formulated, like so many of Lenin's other arguments there, some three years earlier. In 1899 he had already come to his conclusion.

> Surely there is no need to prove to Social Democrats that there can be no political education except through political struggle and political action. Surely it cannot be imagined that any sort of study circles or books, etc., can politically educate the mass of the workers if they are kept from political activity and political struggle.[30]

At about the same time that Lenin formulated this view he was also evolving his conception of the appropriate organisational mode for conducting the cross-class democratic struggle. The linchpin here was, of course, the rather singular importance accorded to the Party newspaper.

THE ROLE OF THE NEWSPAPER

Lenin's project for a newspaper, whose function was to serve as a 'proto-party', first appeared in rounded form in some of the articles he prepared for *Rabochaya Gazeta* while he was still in Siberian exile. Although these articles remained unpublished until 1925 they are of outstanding importance in establishing the continuity of Lenin's thought during the period 1899 to 1902. In the first of them, *Our Immediate Task*, the characteristics and functions of the newspaper were already set out in fully-developed form. 'The founding of a Party organ that will appear regularly and be closely connected with all the local groups'[31] was discerned by Lenin as the most urgent task confronting the movement. Without it local work would remain amateurish and narrowly conceived. Furthermore:

> An economic struggle that is not united by a central organ cannot become the *class* struggle of the entire Russian proletariat. It is impossible to conduct a political struggle if the Party as a whole fails to make statements on all questions of policy and to give direction to the various manifestations of the struggle. The organisation and disciplining of the revolutionary forces and the development of revolutionary technique are impossible without the discussion of all these questions in a central organ, without the collective elaboration of certain *forms and rules for the conduct of affairs*, without the establishment – through the central organ – of every Party member's *responsibility* to the entire Party.[32]

All the movement's resources and organisational ability must, Lenin insisted, be concentrated on this objective. In default of such an organisational and theoretical focus of the movement, local work, in Lenin's opinion, lost nine-tenths of its significance. Moreover, the creation of an illegal newspaper was particularly vital to the development of *Russian* Social Democracy since all other organisational means enjoyed by the movement in other countries, were proscribed.

In his next article, *An Urgent Question*, Lenin sought to demonstrate how the constraints of producing the newspaper, collecting material for it and ensuring its efficient distribution, would, of themselves remedy the abuses of localism, disorganisation and inefficient distribution of forces from which the labour movement and Social Democracy so palpably suffered. Specialisation and division of labour would have to be introduced to ensure the efficient production and distribution of the paper. Such detail-labour was even more necessary in conditions of illegality. Specific and limited functions could be allocated to particular groups; the legal, semi-legal and illegal aspects of the work could then proceed in a co-ordinated way and, moreover, the minimum number of people would have to expose themselves to real risk. Lenin already broached an idea which was later to become a bone of contention at the Second Party Congress – the distinction between 'active' Party members and those who 'assist' the Party in legal and semi-legal activities; these latter Lenin referred to here as the 'reserve'. Talking of the advantages of a functional division of labour he maintained that

> making affairs of this sort the specific function of a special contingent of people would reduce the strength of the revolutionary army 'in the firing line' (without any reduction of its 'fighting potential') and increase the strength of the reserve, those who replaced the 'killed and wounded'. This will be possible only when both the active members and the reserve see their activities reflected in the common organ of the Party and sense their connection with it.[33]

Finally, the creation of a regular Party newspaper would be, in Lenin's view, the indispensable means for realising the hegemonic role of the proletariat vis-à-vis other classes in the democratic revolution. The newspaper in its editorial emphasis must undertake the leadership of the whole political opposition to tsarism and the nature of this task set it way beyond the capacities of local groups. 'Only a common Party organ, consistently implementing the principles of political struggle and holding high the banner of democracy will be able to win over to its side all militant democratic elements and use all Russia's progressive forces in the struggle for political freedom.'[34] The local organisations had neither the financial resources nor the organisational ability and literary expertise to create such a paper.

The fundamental characteristics of the Party organisation which Lenin was later to elaborate in *What Is To Be Done?* were clearly present in these articles of 1899 – functional division of labour, with the more hazardous functions reserved to the 'active' forces, and the broader, legal ones to the 'reserve'. Specialisation, in turn, presupposed unification and a centralised body with the authority to allocate functions and the right to expect the membership to be accountable for their performance – all of this was already developed in Lenin's mind. To this extent his ideas on the newspaper were inseparable from his ideas on the Party. The two became almost identified, particularly since Lenin argued that the foundation of a Party organ was a vital precondition for the reconstitution of the Party itself.

Only through its columns and through open controversy over theory and strategy was it possible, he maintained, for the bases of a principled unity to be elaborated. Lenin was quite clear, however, that the unity sought for could not be the unity of the lowest common denominator; it could not for him be a consolidation of compromises worked out by the representatives of the movement in its current state of dissolution and theoretical wavering. On the contrary, in Lenin's words, unity 'must be worked for'.[35] By this he meant that the competing trends must first openly declare their views and expose their differing standpoints so that the movement might clearly appreciate what was at issue.

> Before we can unite, and in order that we may unite, we must first of all draw firm and definite lines of demarcation. Otherwise our unity will be purely fictitious. . . . We do not intend to make our publication a mere store-house of various views. On the contrary, we shall conduct it in the spirit of a strictly defined tendency. This tendency can be expressed by the word Marxism. . . . Only in this way will it be possible to establish a genuinely all-Russian, Social-Democratic organ. Only such a publication will be capable of leading the movement on to the high road of political struggle.[36]

Lenin was here speaking in the name of the whole editorial board of *Iskra*, for by this time (September 1900) the Russian trio of Lenin, Potresov and Martov, had teamed up with the émigré trinity of Plekhanov, Akselrod and Zasulich to pursue the scheme which Lenin had conceived a full year earlier. They were now jointly and explicitly engaged on an audacious enterprise. The objective of that enterprise may be simply stated as the capture of the Social-Democratic and labour movements in Russia by the orthodox – by the ones whom Lenin described with characteristic gall as the representatives of *Marxism*. It was they who explicitly took upon themselves the establishment of a Party centre comprised of orthodox veteran Social Democrats able to give, through their newspaper, authoritative guidance to all sections of the Marxist and labour movements in Russia. In choosing to focus all their attention on the newspaper the veterans chose judiciously. Not only would they have a vehicle for the expression of their views, they would also build up an organisational network bound to them by ties of personal loyalty. In choosing to hazard all on the newpaper they knew full well that they were playing to their strong hand. Theirs were the big names; they had the theoretical, literary and financial advantage over their opponents. They had the connections (via Akselrod and Plekhanov) with the German Social Democrats through whose good offices the venture of large-scale publication could be commenced.

It would be naive to imagine that their enterprise did not involve personal factors and the bids of differing factions to establish their pre-eminence. Disagreements about political principle are always intertwined with issues of political leadership; that has ever been the case with political parties and we should not be surprised to find that it was so with the Russian Social Democratic Party. When the *stariki* and the Emancipation of Labour Group found their position of hitherto unchallenged pre-eminence being eroded at the end of the nineteenth century, when they were faced with the old dread and terror of the Russian intelligentsia – becoming alienated and isolated – they responded as one might expect seasoned politicians anywhere to respond. They restated their principles as the orthodoxy of the movement and did their best to associate their rivals with heresy and betrayal – especially to emphasise their rivals' connections with, and indebtedness to, Bernstein. They indulged in intrigue, they rigged conferences and congresses to their own advantage, above all they used their newspaper as their main weapon in the struggle. In short they used every trick in their considerable repertoire of political wiles to re-establish their pre-eminence. We must again be clear that Lenin

179

was by no means the only one to pursue this strategy. He was certainly in the thick of the struggle and increasingly assumed the role of main polemicist and publicist for the old orthodoxy, but he did so with the support and collaboration of *all* the *stariki*, of *all* the Emancipation of Labour Group.

For the *Iskra* board the newspaper was to be the nucleus of the Party; its network of agents were to be tied to them. The plan of the newspaper involved specialisation of function. Therefore it presumed a centre to allocate function; it presumed professional revolutionaries; it presumed leadership of all the scattered groups and expected them to respond to directives. The newspaper was to be (as Lenin quite openly expressed it in *Iskra*, no. 4) 'not only a collective propagandist and a collective agitator, it is also a collective organiser'.[37] The newspaper was, in the context of Russian Marxism at that time, consciously setting out to establish its organisational centre, *its* power-base against all comers. The editorial board gave notice that it sought to establish 'a network of agents' to

form the skeleton of precisely the kind of organisation we need – one that is sufficiently large to embrace the whole country; sufficiently broad and many-sided to effect a strict and detailed division of labour; sufficiently well-tempered to be able to conduct steadily *its own* work under any circumstances.[38]

This network would, through its newspaper, consolidate and co-ordinate the activities of all the scattered groups so that Social Democracy (the Editorial Board) would be in a position to harness the forces necessary for its leading role in the democratic struggle, to 'provide a tribune for the nation-wide exposure of the tsarist government, . . . That tribune must be a Social-Democratic news-paper'[39] Finally, and with no trace of false modesty, Lenin in his lead article revealed the final advantage:

If we join forces to produce a common newspaper, this work will train and bring into the foreground, not only the most skilful propagandists, but the most capable organisers, the most talented political party leaders capable, at the right moment, of releasing the slogan for the decisive struggle and of taking the lead in that struggle.[40]

This was no more than a plea for a vote of confidence in what had already been decided. The newspaper had already been established. Its guiding spirits were well-known. The invitation amounts to no more than an invitation to work under them and to admit past errors. In the context of Russian Marxism at that time the message of Lenin's article must have been crystal clear. It stated unashamedly that the paper was in the hands of the orthodox and most capable leaders. They would direct their agents within the labour movement, they would decide Social-Democratic policy and they would, by dint of that fact, become the leaders of the democratic revolution. It is not too much to maintain that *What Is To Be Done?* merely reiterated these claims to hegemony: the hegemony of the Editorial Board within Social Democracy, the hegemony of Social Democracy over the labour movement, the hegemony of the revolutionary proletariat within the democratic movement as a whole.

ORGANISATIONAL PRINCIPLES AND OBJECTIVES

In view of all that is alleged about *What Is To Be Done?*, actually reading the text must come as a grave disappointment to revolutionaries expecting to discover a primer on revolutionary conspiracy. Far from codifying rules of conspiratorial procedure, or specifying precisely the chain of command and lines of communication from central directorate down the pyramid to the primary cells (as, for instance, Buonarotti did in his *Conspiration des Egaux*), Lenin's 'manual' contained not even a recipe for invisible ink. His organisational principles were developed only in the most general terms. *What Is To Be Done?* was the embodiment of Lenin's attempt to express in a systematic way the principles of party-building long expressed in the editorials of *Iskra*. It was intended to reinforce the Editorial Board's claim that the Party should be reconstituted under its aegis and in its image. There is no doubt that it was used by all the Iskrists in their struggle to establish their pre-eminent position at the Second Party Congress.[41]

In Lenin's view of things the principles upon which the reorganisation of the Party must be based were determined directly by the tasks confronting the Party. For him these organisational principles and these tasks stood in a one-to-one relationship; to assent to the tasks was to assent to the organisation. It was for this reason that by far the greater part of *What Is To Be Done?* was not concerned at all with organisational questions *per se*. The first three chapters were concerned with restating the urgency of assuming the role of vanguard fighter in the democratic revolution and criticising in turn each of the heretics who had departed from this course. The first three chapters represented no more than a summary compilation of *Iskra's* case against Economists and terrorists, a case which had been consistently advanced over the previous two years, the outlines of which we are already familiar with.

Only in the fourth chapter, 'The Primitiveness of the Economists and the Organisation of the Revolutionaries', did Lenin move on to consider the organisational entailments of actually fulfilling the 'vanguard role'. Even here his method was more negative than prescriptive. *His* ideas on organisation were broached only after demonstrating the deficiencies in the organisational notions of his opponents. Their incorrect ideas on organisation were seen as a function and necessary reflection of their restricted view of the tasks confronting the Party. At the very beginning of Chapter IV, in controversy with *Rabochee Delo*, Lenin emphatically stated the interconnection of the two elements.

> The 'economic struggle against the employers and the government' does not at all require an All-Russian centralised organisation, and hence this struggle can never give rise to such an organisation as will combine, in one general assault, all the manifestations of political opposition, protest, and indignation, an organisation that will consist of professional revolutionaries and be led by the real political leaders of the entire people. This stands to reason. The character of any organisation is naturally and inevitably determined by the content of its activity.[42]

The question which now needed to be settled was, given Lenin's description of the 'content of activity' appropriate to the Party, what was the nature of the determination this exercised upon the organisational precepts it should have embraced? How, in other words, did the tasks set dictate the Party's organisation?

The Party's primary and immediate task, according to all the orthodox, was to assume the leading role in the democratic revolution. They were equally agreed that it must therefore be an all-Russian task, in the sense that the Party must recognise its obligations to represent all classes, all groups, all regions hostile to the autocracy and to co-ordinate all manifestations of discontent. As Lenin put it in *What Is To Be Done?*:

> *We* must take upon ourselves the task of organising an all-round political struggle under the leadership of *our* Party in such a manner as to make it possible for all oppositional strata to render their fullest support to the struggle and to our Party.[43]

To articulate and to co-ordinate all these elements of discontent the Party had to have an all-Russian newspaper. The creation of this newspaper was, however, as we have seen, beyond the capabilities of scattered Social-Democratic groups.[44] Their resources must therefore be pooled and utilised to prevent duplication of effort. A centralised allocation of the scarce resources available to the Party was, in Lenin's view, virtually entailed in the full elaboration of party tasks.

The main justificatory argument Lenin leaned upon in *What Is To Be Done?* for the kind of organisation he proposed, was that the winning of mass support for the struggle against the autocracy had to be achieved in conditions of utmost danger and illegality. Part of his argument was that while many groups and individuals might be hostile to the autocracy, they were understandably loath to expose themselves to the severe penalties attaching to organising opposition activity. These reservations became hardened almost into abstention from the struggle whenever attempts to organise were seen to founder through lack of preparation, expertise, secrecy or co-ordination on the part of Social-Democratic groups. There was evidence, already, according to Lenin, that sections of the advanced workers were becoming alienated from the Party because they considered that their heroic actions had issued in disaster because of such organisational amateurism.

> Things had indeed reached such a pass that in several places the workers, because of our lack of self-restraint and the ability to maintain secrecy, begin to lose faith in the intellectuals and to avoid them; the intellectuals, they say, are much too careless and cause police raids![45]

There was a huge credibility gap, in Lenin's opinion, between the pretensions of the Party to lead the onslaught against autocracy, and the seriousness with which it trained and organised its forces to perform this role. Until the gap was closed, until the Social Democrats could minimise the risks entailed in political opposition – for all sections of the opposition movement – they could not hope to gain the necessary mass support. Lenin's point was that there must be gradations of skill, expertise and conspiratorial training appropriate to the levels of risk involved in each facet of oppositional activity. At each level the degree of risk could be minimised by introducing specialisation of function, so that, at no matter what level, activists would have the opportunity to become expert and efficient in dealing with their particular and restricted aspect of the work. At the lower levels this division of labour would serve a number of functions. It would increase efficiency through specialisation. It would make the task of the police more difficult since each activist, even if he volunteered evidence, would only be in a position to expose a relatively small area of activity. It would prompt more people to come forward and be active since they would realise the difficulties the authorities would have in making a case out against them for the 'minor' roles they played.

At the higher level, the domain of co-ordinating the activities of a multiplicity of groups, maintaining and establishing contacts, re-establishing groups after arrests, seeing to the nation-wide distribution of the newspaper and maintaining contact with the emigré centre, far more developed skills and expertise were called for. Here, according to Lenin, nothing but professionals would do. Cadres would have to be trained who were conversant with the wiles of the political police who would, obviously, concentrate their main attention on the big fish, the co-ordinators and planners: 'The struggle against the *political* police requires special qualities; it requires *professional* revolutionaries.'[46] These cadres must be skilled in conspiratorial technique, skilled that is, in minimising the risks to themselves (through proper use of codes, avoiding surveillance, arranging contacts, etc.) and, more importantly, skilled in minimising the risks run by the groups they served. The professionals were never conceived by Lenin as an end in themselves, as a self-sufficient revolutionary force. On the contrary, their justification was that they alone had the requisite skills and knowledge to co-ordinate and guide the mass of semi-legal and illegal oppositional groupings scattered throughout Russia. The whole *raison d'être* of the corps of professional revolutionaries was to serve as a medium of communication and as an inspiring force to the growing mass movement of political discontent. It was the workers, the 'average people of the masses', who, in Lenin's estimation, 'are capable (in fact, are alone capable) of *determining* the outcome of the movement'.[47] The revolutionaries were not to 'usurp' the functions allotted by history to the mass; on the contrary, Lenin was insistent that the emergence of mass political unrest was the *occasion for* and *object of* his organisational plan.

> The active and widespread participation of the masses will not suffer; on the contrary, it will benefit by the fact that a 'dozen' experienced revolutionaries, trained professionally no less than the police, will centralise all the secret aspects of the work – the drawing up of leaflets, the working out of approximate plans, and the appointing of bodies of leaders for each urban district, for each factory district, and for each educational institution, etc. . . . Centralisation of the most secret functions in an organisation of revolutionaries will not diminish, but rather increase the extent and enhance the quality of the activity of a large number of other organisations, that are intended for a broad public and are therefore as loose and as non-secret as possible, such as workers' trade unions; workers' self-education circles and circles for reading illegal literature; and socialist, as well as democratic, circles among *all* other sections of the population; etc., etc. We must have such circles, trade unions and organisations everywhere in *as large a number as possible* and with the widest variety of functions; but it would be absurd and harmful to *confound* them with the organisation of *revolutionaries*, to efface the border-line between them, to make still more hazy the all too faint recognition that in order to 'serve' the mass movement we must have people who will devote themselves exclusively to Social-Democratic activities, and such people must *train* themselves patiently and steadfastly to be professional revolutionaries.[48]

The professional revolutionaries were, in Lenin's view, necessary if the Party was to fulfil its vanguard role *in Russian conditions.* How else except secretly and conspiratorially were groups which were themselves illegal and semi-legal to be organised in Russian conditions? The primary oppositional groupings must, however, if the objective of leading the masses was to be attained, be as broad and open and non-secret as was possible within the narrow constraints of autocracy.

> The workers' organisation must in the first place be a trade-union organisation; secondly, it must be as broad as possible; and thirdly, it must be as public as conditions will allow (here, and further on, of course, I refer only to absolutist Russia). On the other hand, the organisation of the revolutionaries must consist first and foremost of people who make revolutionary activity their profession. . . .[49]

At the primary level, then, the organisations must be diffuse, as broadly based as possible, loose in organisational structure to make them more difficult for the police to crack. Preferably they should be legalised, thus freeing the revolutionaries for other work.[50] In Russian conditions it would, Lenin argued, be suicidal to make a fetish of the organisational mode of procedure current in other Social-Democratic parties and the West European labour movement. 'Only an incorrigible utopian would have a *broad* oganisation of workers, with elections, reports, universal suffrage, etc., under the autocracy.'[51] The very conditions for operating democratic principles within the party likewise did not exist. For inner-party democracy to be meaningful there must, Lenin said, be 'first, full publicity, and secondly election to all offices'.[52] To advance the slogan of a democratic party, while simultaneously being obliged to recognise the impossibility of establishing the preconditions for it, amounted, in Lenin's view, to deceit. It made 'broad democracy' into 'nothing more than a *useless and harmful toy*'[53] – a demagogic device utilised by the worker-philes. It was a recipe for exposing the movement to the depredations of the police. A democratic structure might be appropriate in Germany,[54] Lenin argued, but even there the leadership rejected the sort of primitive democracy insisted upon by some Russians, and preserved the prerogatives of the professionals.[55]

From these arguments, Lenin concluded that in Russia 'the only serious organisational principle for the active workers of our movement should be the strictest secrecy, the strictest selection of members, and the training of professional revolutionaries'.[56] Only in this way, given the conditions of illegality in which they worked, could the Social Democrats hope to co-ordinate, provide stability and a cohesive national plan for all opposition groups – for what we would now term the front organisations. But, and on this Lenin was clear, it was the mass movement and only the mass movement which would eventually decide the outcome. The *raison d'être* of the professional was, as we have seen, to expand and organise the mass of political opposition – not to displace it but to enhance it and give it coherence. This was Lenin's justification for his conception of the nature of the Party at this juncture. It stemmed directly from his understanding of what was involved in Social-Democratic hegemony over the democratic revolution in the conditions of tsarist autocracy.

That Lenin laid claim to being a spokesman· for the old orthodoxy in all his writings up to and including *What Is To Be Done?* should not surprise us. Certainly none of his contemporaries disputed his claim, and it was one which was insistently made in virtually all his writings during this period. Constantly he held up Plekhanov's writings as the guide for Russian Marxists and lambasted the temerity of youngsters presuming to improve upon Plekhanov.[57] The texts of orthodoxy, Akselrod's *Present Tasks and Tactics*,[58] the *Minsk Manifesto*,[59] the *1885 Draft Programme*[60] of the Emancipation of Labour Group, were all pointedly utilised to show how the political line of the veterans (and, evidently of Lenin) has always been correct, and to show how the Economists had strayed from the foundation theses of Russian Marxism.

We must conclude that Lenin's views of the Party as presented in his writings from 1899 to 1902 are not to be regarded as extraordinary, innovatory, perverse, essentially Jacobin or unorthodox. On the contrary, they had long been canvassed in *Iskra* and accepted by Lenin's co-editors who were the only ones who could reasonably be described as having a claim to expressing the orthodoxy of Russian Marxism. Recondite references to Nechaev or playing Tkachev's phrases off against Lenin's, the whole industry of delving into the history of Russian Jacobinism to discover 'the origins' of Bolshevism', are all alike misconceived and to no effect unless they can be established as central to the context in which Lenin and his co-editors were working. Lenin's pamphlet was read and discussed by them all; there is no evidence of any significant contemporary disagreement within the *Iskra* camp on his main themes. 'Plekhanov and Akselrod merely made minor suggestions in the draft which Lenin adopted.'[61]

It is equally certain that, in the intrigues which preceded the convocation of the Second Party Congress, it was precisely *What Is To Be Done?* which was used as the touchstone of orthodoxy in nominating, selecting or electing delegates. Adherence to it was seen as a measure of adherence to *Iskra* policies. According to Lepeshinskii, '*Iskra* prevailed in Moscow and in other centres of the revolutionary movement only because the *Iskra* agitators had in their hands *Chto Delat?* [i.e., *What Is To Be Done?*]'.[62] Even Valentinov, one of the main contributors to the Lenin-as-Jacobin interpretation, conceded that at the time of its publication, *What Is To Be Done?* was regarded as quite unexceptional in its political line and was enthusiastically welcomed as a résumé of the *Iskra* position. 'We took *What Is To Be Done?* as a catechism and we welcomed it for the lead it gave us in practical and organisational matters.'[63] On the basis of the available evidence it is difficult to deny the accuracy of the summary Lenin made some five years after his pamphlet had been published:

> *What Is To Be Done?* is a *summary* of *Iskra* tactics and *Iskra* organisational policy in 1901 and 1902. Precisely a '*summary*', no more and no less.[64]

It is, of course, generally contended that *What Is To Be Done?* far from representing the orthodoxy of Russian Marxism is, rather, 'a most un-Marxian work and its implications are fully in tune with a premature – by Marxist standards – advocacy of proletarian revolution'.[65] The insuperable problem for this line of interpretation is that what are alleged to be the most significant and outrageous revisions ever to be introduced into Marxism went unnoticed and uncontested by Plekhanov and Akselrod. Akselrod's biographer, who retains the axiomatic character of Lenin's Jacobinism as a dramatic foil for Akselrod's more 'Western' and optimistic Social Democracy, concedes that his failure to oppose Lenin's ideas is indeed a very considerable puzzle.

One of the most puzzling aspects of this period in the history of Russian Social Democracy is the failure of the older Marxists publicly to voice serious criticisms of Lenin's ideas on the organisation of the party, which he had first developed in 1900 but elaborated most extensively in 1902 in *What Is To Be Done?*[66]

He admits that: 'When all the bits of evidence indicating that Akselrod objected to *What Is To Be Done?* are pieced together, they still amount to a meek protest'.[67] Unfortunately we are not told when even *these* shreds amounting cumulatively to a 'meek protest' were made, or of what they consisted.

We are asked to believe that on such fundamental issues as Lenin's alleged 'commitment to permanent tutelage of the proletariat by the intelligentsia', his 'lack of faith in the capacity of the proletariat as a class ever to attain that degree of consciousness necessary for it to take a decisive part in the coming revolutionary events without outside leadership' – on such fundamental issues as these Akselrod and Plekhanov held their peace. Had they ever before tolerated such theoretical enormities to pass uncontested? Were they ever to do so again? The actions were not in keeping with the men. On earlier and on subsequent occasions they used the full weight of their dialectical and polemical skills in ruthless critiques of far more trivial deviations. We are asked to believe too much. Such an explanation is none at all; it is a total mystery. The only way to dispel the mystery is to accept *What Is To Be Done?* for what it represented at the time – a restatement of the principles of Russian Marxist orthodoxy.

THE BOLSHEVIK/MENSHEVIK DISPUTE

During the years 1899 to 1903 Lenin, as we have seen, concentrated all his attention on the internal crisis confronting the Party and the Russian labour movement. In common with the other editors of *Iskra* he firmly believed that the Second Congress of the Party to be summoned in 1903 under their aegis would at last put to rout the heretics of various hues and firmly implant the principles of orthodoxy and its veteran exponents in their deserved places at the leadership of the movement.

For much of the Congress things proceeded according to plan. The Economists' objections to Lenin's organisational plan were, despite the cogent pleadings of Martynov and Akimov, rejected out of hand by the *Iskra* caucus.[68] The same fate befell the claims of the *Bund* to be admitted into the Party as an autonomous unit with full jurisdiction over the Jewish labour movement. In Lenin's view the application of the principle of autonomy within a federal Party, which the *Bund* desired, would not only harm the unity of the Social-Democratic Party in Russia it was also harmful to the Jewish cause since 'it *sanctions* segregation and alienation, elevates them to a principle, to a law'.[69] The Iskrists were again unanimous in opposing any dilution of the Party's centralism by the federalist concessions which the *Bund's* claim entailed.

It was not until the debate on the Party Statutes that the unanimity of the *Iskra* caucus was abruptly and unexpectedly shattered. There had already been some heated discussions in the *Iskra* closed sessions with regard to the composition of the Praesidium of the Congress. Martov wanted a body of nine which would include representatives of the *Bund* and the journal *Rabochee Delo*. Lenin and Plekhanov however persuaded the majority of the Iskrists to opt for a smaller exclusively Iskrist Praesidium of three. In a way the controversy which now erupted reflected a similar controversy; the crucial difference was that it took place not behind locked doors in the *Iskra* caucus meetings, but in heated exchanges on the conference floor.

Lenin and Martov proposed differing drafts of Article 1 of the Party's Rules, the object of which was to define the qualifications for Party membership. According to Lenin's formulation a party member was one 'who recognises the Party's programme and supports it by material means and by personal participation in one of the Party's organisations'. According to Martov a member 'recognises the Party's programme and supports it by material means and by regular personal assistance under the direction of one of the party organisations'. The difference between these drafts may perhaps seem as insignificant to the contemporary reader as it did to many rather bemused delegates to the Congress, but out of such mole-hills, politics, particularly revolutionary politics, has a talent for creating great mountains. There was perhaps a difference between 'personal participation in one of the party's organisations' and 'regular personal assistance under the direction of one of the party's organisations' and a great deal of ink has been spilt on elaborating it, yet it must have struck many of the delegates as an extremely fine one. What sort of candidate for membership would be excluded by the first formulation yet accommodated by the second? How in actual practice would committees of the Party be able to decide that a man was rendering 'regular personal assistance under the direction of a party organisation' and yet was not 'personally participating' in it?

Lenin himself, at the Second Congress, maintained that his formulation

> . . . narrows this concept [of a party member], while Martov's expands it, for (to use Martov's own correct expression) what distinguishes his concept is its 'elasticity'. And in the period of Party life that we are now passing through it is just this 'elasticity' that undoubtedly opens the door to all element of confusion, vacillation, and opportunism.[70]

There can be no doubt that Lenin believed that this was the essence of the matter; all his subsequent moves at the Congress confirm that he did feel that this was an issue of considerable importance. And yet, simply examining the wording of the rival drafts one is hard put to it to understand how Lenin could put so decisive a construction upon the dispute. A good case could indeed be made out for the argument that, of the two formulations, Martov's was the more exclusive in that its specifications might be regarded as more demanding. 'Regular assistance' which is, moreover, expressly 'under the direction of one of the Party's organisations' seems to entail at least as much commitment and activism as 'personal participation in' a Party organisation. We should, in any case, be clear that neither specification had in mind the sort of broad open Social-Democratic Party of the West where the only condition of Party membership amounted to the token payment of dues.

In the event the delegates voted twenty-eight to twenty-two for Martov's revision to the *Iskra* draft which Lenin and Plekhanov defended. It was, as Lenin was later to put it, no great disaster for the Party – certainly not a matter of life and death. Even at the Second Congress he declared that 'we shall certainly not perish because of an unfortunate clause in the Rules'.[71] None the less Lenin, Plekhanov and the majority of the Iskrists who had endorsed Lenin's Article 1 against Martov's (Akselrod and Zasulich had, significantly, voted for Martov's) were now doubly determined that this abrupt display of 'softness' be checked. Lenin

191

carefully laid his plans to ensure that the 'widening' of the Party base be compensated by a 'narrowing' of the leading bodies of the Party – the Central Committee and the editorial board of the Party organ (which was, of course, to be *Iskra*).

The 'hard' Iskrists were by this time assured of a majority on the floor of the Congress since the *Bund* representatives as well as the two *Rabochee Delo* men had voted with their feet and departed in umbrage at earlier decisions. At this point the supporters of Lenin and Plekhanov became the majority, the *bolsheviki*, and they used their new-found strength to implement Lenin's two trio plan – a three-man editorial board of *Iskra* to be complemented by a three-man Central Committee. This and not the squabble over Article 1 of the Rules proved to be the great divide.

Issues of wounded pride immediately became inseparable from issues of principle and this was inevitable in a situation where some of the legendary heroes of the movement were being asked to withdraw from the limelight and accept a more humble role. Potresov, Zasulich and Akselrod were wounded to the quick, for Lenin's plan meant their effective demise as leaders of the movement – they were to be retired as editors of *Iskra* and their whole lives were suddenly robbed of meaning. Martov sprang to their defence (though, according to Lenin, he had earlier approved the plan[72]), reviling both Plekhanov and Lenin for their heartlessness and refusing outright to accept the place alongside them on the editorial board which the Congress had allotted him.

If the reactions of Akselrod, Potresov, Zasulich and Martov were quite understandable, so too were Lenin's motives. His proposal did no more than bring into the open in a formal and frank way the situation which had *de facto* prevailed on *Iskra* for some time. As journalists Akselrod, and Zasulich particularly, were disastrous. Their productivity was dismal and their reliability to produce material on time equally so. They had, moreover, no knowledge whatever of the practical movement in Russia and were quite incompetent as organisers. There can be no question that, in terms of proven ability to produce good material inside the deadlines that a regular newspaper necessarily demanded, Lenin's proposed editorial board stood to lose very little from the exclusion of Zasulich, Akselrod and Potresov but stood to gain a great deal in terms of expediting the paper's production with just the three most active editors at the helm.

In his *Account of the Second Congress of the R.S.D.L.P.*, written shortly after it adjourned, Lenin outlined some of his reasons for insisting on a trio – with powers, if necessary, to co-opt additional members.

> The old board of six was so ineffectual that *never once in all its three years* did it meet in full force. That may seem incredible, but it is a fact. *Not one* of the forty-five issues of *Iskra* was made up (in the editorial and technical sense) by anyone but Martov or Lenin. And *never once* was any major theoretical issue raised by anyone but Plekhanov. Akselrod did no work at all (he contributed literally nothing to *Zarya* and only three of four articles to all the forty-five issues of *Iskra*). Zasulich and Starover [Potresov] only contributed and advised; they *never* did any actual editorial work.[73]

The best composition of the editorial board was, Lenin rather naively felt, 'as clear as daylight' to everyone at the Congress – it could only be Plekhanov, Lenin and Martov. To suggest as many have done, that this proposal was further evidence of Lenin's desire to impose his personal dictatorship upon the Party is to betray volumes of ignorance on the characters of his proposed fellow-editors. Plekhanov was an imperious prima donna who had always insisted on his own star-billing and his absolute right to criticise everyone around him. Martov, as the earlier proceedings of the Congress had demonstrated, had a mind of his own and was far from being a pliant tool of Lenin. Lenin's naivety, and his evident surprise at the uproar which greeted his proposal, stemmed from his inability to appreciate that many of the delegates found it impossible to view the matter in his cold rational way – what was best for the Party was demonstrated 'as clear as daylight' by past experience of a board of six and the actual performance of the old editors, and there was an end to it.

What Lenin failed to take into account was the immense emotional and psychological hurt that this entailed for Akselrod and Zasulich in particular. Earlier, in the debate over Article I, Plekhanov had openly ridiculed Akselrod's objections to Lenin's formulations, pouring public scorn on the man who had, for so long, been his friend and who had been so utterly dependent upon him. Now the final blow was to deprive him of that one mark of prestige which might have given him sorely-needed esteem in the eyes of the movement and recognition of a life-time devoted to it. Much the same would have applied to Zasulich and Potresov and many more felt the awful embarrassment of having to tell them that they were almost superfluous to the Party's needs. Martov rallied to their defence, as they had earlier supported him, and categorically refused to serve on the editorial board which was, none the less, ratified by the majority.

The party had no sooner been re-established than it split. In the aftermath of the Congress the bitterest enemies of a few months previously suddenly found common purpose. Menshevik Iskrists rapidly forgot the great divide which separated them from the Economists and joined forces against the 'state of seige' which Lenin and Plekhanov were enforcing on the Party. The victory of the Bolsheviks proved short-lived. The Foreign League of Russian Social Democracy at its conference in October 1903 saw the first rallying of the varied Menshevik camp which secured a small majority to condemn many of the decisions of the second Congress and the 'bureaucratic centralism' from which the Party suffered. In the following month Lenin suffered an even more severe setback. Plekhanov insisted on restoring the old editorial board of *Iskra* in spite of the decision of the Congress. Lenin resigned, the Mensheviks appeared to have secured the only objective which united them, the arch-villain had been ousted. He had, however, clearly emerged as the single most important leader of the Russian movement and the Mensheviks had, paradoxically, assisted his rise to pre-eminence by concentrating all their fire upon him.

> By constantly attacking Lenin as would-be dictator as well as crude, tactless, ruthless and intolerant, the Mensheviks augmented his importance. No Russian Social Democrat could doubt any longer that he was a figure to be reckoned with. The concentration on personal vilification further played into Lenin's hands by seeming to confirm his insistence that the Mensheviks were motivated not by principle but wounded feelings, hurt pride and private resentments.[74]

It happens to suit both left and right to read back the subsequent divide between Social Democracy and Communism to its 'roots' at the Second Congress of the R.S.D.L.P., where, it is made to appear, two starkly contrasted sets of principles were first fully exposed. On the one hand was the Menshevik, open, democratic, Western-style party, placing its trust in the spontaneous socialist strivings of the working class; on the other, Lenin's vision of a strictly disciplined party of the 'new type' in which the professional revolutionaries were to play the role of the working class in history. The great confrontation of pluralism versus totalitarianism is seen at its inception and with such great causes on the march it is hardly surprising that much of the historical evidence gets trampled.

There is, for instance, the evidence of Akselrod himself who had, in all conscience, reason enough to feel piqued and humiliated at Lenin's actions and was well enough versed in theory to find the slightest chink in his defences. And yet when attempting to explain the dispute to Kautsky he was obliged to confess that the issue was not one of principle but of personality.

> As late as May 1904 Akselrod wrote that there were 'still no clear, defined differences concerning either principles or tactics', that the organisational question itself 'is or at least was' not one of principle such as 'centralism, or democracy, autonomy, etc.', but rather one of differing opinions as to the 'application or execution of organizational principles . . . we have all accepted'. Lenin had used the debate on this question 'in a demagogic manner' to 'fasten' Plekhanov to his side and thus win a majority 'against us'.[75]

Kautsky's response was that since the controversy was one of political expediency rather than one of principle, the adoption of Lenin's organisational plan would cause far less harm than continuing dissension, particularly since, as he understood it (Akselrod being his main informant), 'the Bolsheviks did not explicitly repudiate any of the central tenets of orthodoxy'.[76]

Curiously enough the Mensheviks themselves appear to have accepted Kautsky's conclusion that the organisational question was entirely peripheral to the dispute. In late 1905 sitting in conference they formally rejected Martov's version of Article 1 and accepted Lenin's.[77] Subsequently, at the Fourth (or Unity) Congress of the R.S.D.L.P., which they dominated, Lenin's formulation was adopted unanimously.[78]

Paradoxically, as we shall see, by this time Lenin was insisting upon a far more open party organised from top to bottom on the elective principle, which conditions of political freedom now, for the first time, made possible. He remarked ironically that *none* of the prominent Mensheviks in late 1905 or early 1906, when conditions of political life were freer than they had ever been, chose to do away with the underground or relax the centralised structure of the Party.

There is, finally, no evidence that after 1903 the Mensheviks did in actual practice make the local committees they controlled any more 'democratic', 'open' or 'proletarian' in composition than those of their Bolshevik opponents. Indeed, the one thorough study we have of the organisational structure and social composition of the two factions concludes that:

> The Menshevik élite was, on average, forty-five years old –
> fifteen years older than the local leaders, whereas the top
> Bolsheviks, whose average age was thirty-four, were only seven
> years older. Unlike the Menshevik organisational structure, the
> Bolshevik was more open. The young Bolsheviks were able to
> advance rapidly to positions of authority – which may help to
> explain the faction's more radical activity. [79]

We must conclude that the 'organisational question' has been given a position of unwarranted importance as the occasion for the Bolshevik/Menshevik dispute which much of the evidence will not support. It was not until 1905 and especially 1906 that clear differences between the factions, in political strategy and understanding of the objectives of the democratic revolution, first became apparent.

CHAPTER 8

1904–7: Revolution and Counter-Revolution

At the end of 1904 there was in Russia an almost unanimous conviction among all the articulate sections of society that radical political change was necessary and was imminent. For some years students and workers had, with increasing temerity, mounted political strikes and demonstrations explicitly calling for democratic liberties and constitutional rights. The Zemstvo Unionists, the men behind the local government machinery, had, in a campaign of banquets culminating in a national conference in November, taken up the old demand that the Tsar should 'crown the edifice' of local representative institutions by convening a national rep-resentative assembly. As the war with Japan wore on, and as, with each day, fresh news of military defeat and administrative ineptitude seeped through, the mood became increasingly radical. Lenin was not alone in believing that 'the capitulation of Port Arthur is the prologue to the defeat of tsarism'. His sentiments were shared by many liberals for whom Miliukov spoke expressing the hope that 'the idol autocracy be overthrown in the waters of the Yellow-Sea'.[1] Revolts in the army and mutiny on the Potemkin convinced him and many others that the fate of the Romanov dynasty would be settled in a matter of months rather than years.

In these heady days of late 1904 even the Menshevik *Iskra* fully shared the conviction that great deeds were at hand which called for the utmost audacity and revolutionary commitment.

The time has come fearlessly and with all our might to support the courageous rising of the forces. Boldness will win . . . Seize the branch offices of the State Bank and the munition stores and arm the people. Establish contact between the individual towns and between town and country; let the armed citizens hasten to each other's help wherever such help is needed. Seize the prisons and let out the fighters for our cause; they will reinforce our ranks. Proclaim everywhere the overthrow of the tsarist monarchy and the establishment in its place of a true democratic republic. Rise citizens! The hour of liberation has arrived. Long live the democratic republic! Long live the revolutionary army! Down with tsarism![2]

At the Menshevik Conference of April–May 1905 the insurrectionary ardour still ran hot as the resolution 'Concerning an Armed Uprising' made quite clear.

Regarding as its task the preparation of the masses for an uprising, the Social-Democratic party will strive to bring the rising under its own influence and leadership in order to serve the interests of the working class . . . The Social-Democratic Party, in preparing the way for an uprising, must above all: . . . strengthen the masses awareness of the inevitability of revolution, the need to be ready for armed resistance at all times and the possibility of transforming it into a rising at any moment.[3]

Many of the most prominent Menshevik leaders in Russia went even further and, together with Trotsky and Parvus, asserted that the bourgeois and proletarian revolutions would run into each other, that therefore the task in hand was to prepare for a workers' government. The strange spectacle now emerged of arch-moderates like Martynov and Dan (who had, a year previously, vehemently attacked Lenin's 'Jacobin' policies and wilfulness) joining company with Trotsky and Parvus posturing now as apostles of the theory of permanent revolution, which pervaded the lead articles of their journal *Nachalo*.

Lenin was not an advocate of permanent revolution at this time. He could, indeed, hardly have been more insistent in denying the possibility of jumping stages and positing socialist goals for immediate achievement. Lenin insisted that there could, at this stage, be no talk of a government of working-class democracy which will be a Social-Democratic government.[4] There must be a clear distinction between the democratic and socialist phases of the revolution and these could not coincide. 'If Social Democracy sought to make the socialist revolution its immediate aim, it would assuredly discredit itself.'[5] The degree of Russian economic and social development made such objectives impossible of attainment and therefore made those who canvassed them irresponsible utopians. He talked of

> the absurd and semi-anarchist ideas of giving effect to the maximum programme, and the conquest of power for a socialist revolution. The degree of Russia's economic development (an objective condition), and the degree of class consciousness and organisation of the broad masses of the proletariat (a subjective condition inseparably bound up with the objective condition) make the immediate and complete emancipation of the working class impossible.[6]

The economic analysis, or theory, set the parameters of the politically possible and it was on this sure ground that Lenin, throughout 1905, rejected the idea of workers' government, dictatorship of the proletariat, immediate advance to socialism dispensing with the democratic phase, or any similar notion. 'Whoever wants to reach socialism by any other path than that of political democracy, will inevitably arrive at conclusions that are absurd and reactionary both in the economic and political sense.'[7]

'Marxism', he asserted, 'has irrevocably broken with the Narodnik and anarchist gibberish that Russia, for instance, can bypass capitalist development, escape from capitalism, or skip it in some other way other than that of the class struggle, on the basis and within the framework of the same capitalism.'[8] Only after the period of democratic revolution had come to an end in Russia would it be proper to discuss the nature of the next phase. 'When that time comes we shall deal directly with the question of the socialist dictatorship of the proletariat.'[9] Clearly that time was no closer, in Lenin's eyes, in mid-1906 when he wrote that 'we are incomparably more remote than our Western comrades from the socialist revolution'.[10]

Lenin recognised, however, that in so far as immediate objectives were concerned, there was little that divided Social Democrats in Russia in late 1905 and early 1906.

> The Mensheviks together with the Bolsheviks clamoured for a strike and an uprising then. They called upon the workers not

to quit the fight until they had seized power . . . Differences arose only in regard to details in the appraisal of events.[11]

In view of the close identity of both factions on what they perceived as the immediate tasks, it is small wonder that at the local level their committees rapidly forgot the old disputations and collaborated closely. In many places, St Petersburg for instance, the two factions merged to form a single Social-Democratic committee.[12] The mood of the local committees and the urgency for practical co-operation in organising the uprising made the formal separation of the factions impossible to sustain. In April–May 1906 they came together once again at the Unity (or Fourth) Congress of the Party which the Mensheviks dominated but which was, none the less, a frankly revolutionary gathering which gave short shrift to the pleas of Plekhanov and Akselrod for more moderate policies.

Meanwhile the popular demands for a representative assembly were made more precise and radical by the widely-canvassed 'four-tail' formula calling for universal, free, equal and direct suffrage. The liberal Zemstvo men and the Union of Unions representatives who began by calling the Tsar's attention to the popular mood and loyally suggesting reforms which alone, in their view would stave off revolution, met with nothing but rebuffs, disdain and contempt for their projects. They came slowly to the conclusion that they would have to use the power of the people to wrest power from the autocracy. Revolution was in the air and nowhere more so than in the salons of the well-to-do and the deliberations of professional men.

It was in this atmosphere of growing public discontent that the priest, police-agent and workers' organiser, Gapon, decided to organise a peaceful mass demonstration of St Petersburg workmen to petition the Tsar for redress of their economic grievances, and, in uncompromising terms, to demand a popular, elected assembly. The awful massacre of the innocents before the Winter Palace on Bloody Sunday, 9 January 1905, in which the peaceful march ended, sent its reverberations throughout the length and breadth of Russia. The strike movement began again in earnest and was strengthened by peasant riots. Society was outraged; the students left the universities and took up the cry of the marchers of 9 January – freedom or death. Russia was torn apart by civil strife – it seemed that civil war was on the immediate agenda. To many, Lenin among them, it seemed that the Tsar had, in fact, already proclaimed a war upon his people.

Lenin's instant reaction to the news was that the government 'deliberately drove the proletariat to revolt, provoked it, by the massacre of unarmed people, to erect barricades, in order to drown the uprising in a sea of blood'.[13] Overnight the people's naive faith in the Little Father had been broken, they were abruptly transformed from supplicants to insurrectionaries. 'It was very difficult for the workers to go over to the armed combat. The government has now forced them to it. The first and most difficult step has been taken.'[14] The conclusion they were compelled to arrive at was, therefore,

> . . . *à la guerre comme à la guerre*. The working-class masses, and, following their lead, the masses of the rural poor, will realise that they are combatants in a war, and then . . . then the next battles of our civil war will be fought according to plan.[15]

If it was to be war, if the day of actual physical confrontation with the autocracy had finally dawned, then, clearly, a revolutionary leader had to prepare himself for it. Lenin reacted to the news of Bloody Sunday in a way that was entirely predictable and entirely unlike the reactions of any other Russian Social Democrat. He went straight to the Public Library in Geneva to consult with von Clausewitz and, of course, Marx and Engels on the military strategy of revolutionaries in 1848 and 1871. Not until October of 1905 did he return to Russia; the months of waiting were spent in self-preparation and feverish attempts to prepare his followers in Russia for the task of leading the coming revolution.

Throughout the spring and summer of 1905 opposition continued to grow and Russia became one gigantic seething cauldron wherein just about every major grouping in the multifarious Empire suddenly found the courage to voice grievances nurtured for generations. The professional men grouped themselves into unions with a central Union of Unions. The Zemstvo liberals, under Miliukov's astute leadership, formed themselves into a political party, the Constitutional Democrats or 'Kadets' as they were popularly known. Strikes, conferences, proclamations and constitutional demands followed each other thick and fast from the most varied segments of the population, and it was against this background that the Government, in early August published its 'All-Highest Manifesto on the Establishment of a State Duma'.[16] It was to be indirectly elected on the basis of separate franchises for each social estate and each of the four principal social estates were to sit separately in different committees and were to have no more than a consultative voice. The proposals satisfied no one, least of all the professional men of town and country and the urban industrial workers who were, without doubt, the best-organised and most resolute supporters of a democratic regime. Under the terms of the Tsar's proposals, both groups would have been almost totally disenfranchised since neither was recognised as a social estate.

Through the late summer and autumn of 1905 the opposition grew in intensity and extensiveness. Large parts of the Empire became, to all intents and purposes, autonomous self-governing units as peasant insurgency and the movements of national minorities forced the administration and police to retreat. Mutiny in the fleet and in some army detachments added to the regime's problems while the universities in the main cities became huge forums for increasingly radical open political meetings.

In late October things finally came to a head. The Government arrested all the delegates to the Railwaymen's Congress. The whole union went on strike, and was promptly joined by all the other industrial and professional unions. A general strike of proportions unprecedented at any time or in any country of the world now gripped Russia. The whole of 'society' followed the lead of the industrial workers – the teachers closed the schools and even the bankers walked out joining 'the barristers and the judges, the clerks of the town councils and of the audit offices. The strike soon spread to every place that could be reached by rail or wire.'[17] According to Treadgold 'the fate of the country now in effect passed out of the hands of the authorities and descended into the hands of the striking workers'.[18]

In order to co-ordinate the strike movement and to press their demands for a constituent assembly based on universal free and equal suffrage, the unions, prompted by the Mensheviks, set up a 'Soviet', or council of elected delegates, in St Petersburg which convened for the first time on 27 October. The stage was clearly set for a showdown with the Government. The days of autocracy

202

appeared to be almost over and every articulate section of society appeared to be united behind the political demands of the Soviet.

On 30 October 1905 the Tsar finally, and reluctantly, acceded to many of the popular demands by issuing a manifesto promising wide extensions of the franchise for the Duma and the powers it was to enjoy. The Duma was now to have full legislative rights and control of the budget. Again it appeared that the Tsar had conceded too little and too late. The more radical liberals insisted that the crucial ingredient of a constitutional government, the accountability of the ministry to the legislature, had not been granted. The socialist parties for their part were outraged by the electoral law which still left a large proportion of the proletariat and the poor peasantry disenfranchised. There can be no doubt, however, that the granting of the October Manifesto was the turning-point in the 'revolution' of 1905. For the right-wing (who now honoured the Manifesto by dubbing themselves Octobrists), it struck the proper balance between the preservation of a stable and strong monarchy while acknowledging the right of responsible 'society' to be heard on questions of policy. Some of the moderate liberals, for their part, voiced their dissatisfaction regarding many of the Manifesto's provisions, but most were prepared to accept it as a promising first step.

> The October Manifesto raised the question of whether the satisfaction of the Kadet programme still necessitated revolutionary change. In general, the Kadets appear to have believed at first that the revolution they needed had indeed taken place and now only had to be consolidated.[19]

The administration had, in this way effectively isolated the committed revolutionaries and lost no time in consolidating its forces to move against them. By this time many of the leading Social Democrats (Plekhanov and Akselrod were the notable exceptions) had returned to Russia and all alike were gripped with revolutionary fervour. Both Bolsheviks and Mensheviks were at this time agreed that the October Manifesto was quite worthless since it left the coercive power of the state exclusively in the Tsar's hands. They agreed, therefore, that only the revolutionary overthrow of the autocracy and the inauguration of a democratic republic could save Russia from the reaction. Together they attempted to steel the Soviets and to prepare the urban working class for the final struggle, but by this time revolutionary enthusiasm was already beginning to wane. Many of the workers no doubt felt that their main demands had already been conceded, others were becoming aware of a growing mood of resentment towards the pretensions of the Soviets. Only comparatively few were effectively organised by Social-Democratic committees and were prepared to fight.

On 16 December the entire St Petersburg Soviet was arrested and its call for a general strike and a rising of the workers met with little response. On 20 December the Moscow Soviet made the same appeal under the joint names of the Soviet, the Bolsheviks, the Mensheviks and the Socialist Revolutionaries. It was, however, the Bolsheviks, who provided the organisation and most of the fighting detachments for the insurrection which followed. Initially the insurgents were helped by a large part of the city's population which had been outraged by the excesses of the military in dealing with a previous strike in Moscow. When, however, the troops began to mass and when artillery was drawn up with the clear intention of ruthlessly suppressing the rising, support swiftly evaporated. A contributory factor in the decline of general support for the rising was the fact that in its early stages the Tsar, yielding once again to Witte's advice, agreed to extend very considerably the franchise for the Duma. The fighting continued for a week, waged largely by mobile guerrilla bands confronting an infinitely superior military force. The insurgents' only hopes of success lay in the possibility that some detachments of the army might come over to them, or that their example would be followed on a wide scale throughout the country. In the event both hopes proved ill-founded and they were mercilessly put down.

With his two capitals now secure, the Tsar moved to consolidate his position in the provinces. All opposition was ruthlessly crushed, large areas were put under martial law, punitive military and police reprisals for earlier opposition demoralised the revolutionary forces. In the space of a few months the initiative had, against all expectations, been seized by the autocracy. Under Witte's able guidance the regime now moved on a whole number of fronts to reconsolidate its positions. Constitutionally it promulgated 'clarifications' of the October Manifesto which effectively deprived the forthcoming Duma of any real power.

Parts of the budget were 'iron clad' and exempted from public criticism; loans and currency were put under the uncontrolled jurisdiction of the Minister of Finance; the army and navy, with all that related to them, were retained as prerogatives of the crown. The council of State, so far nominated by the sovereign, was now strengthened for legislative purposes by an equal number of persons elected from the higher institutions of the country, including stock exchanges, universities and Zemstva. It became the Upper House and received the same legislative rights as the Duma; if the two Houses disagreed as to the budget, the government might choose whichever of the two figures it preferred; if no budget were passed, the government might take the estimates of the preceding year.[20]

For fear that even these measures might not be entirely watertight, Witte negotiated an immense loan from France with the express intent of making the regime financially independent of the Duma.

It was in this unpromising atmosphere that the First Duma eventually convened in May 1906. Lenin, in common with almost all of the Social-Democratic leaders, Bolshevik and Menshevik, had advocated a boycott of the elections and only when they were almost over did he, and the majority of the R.S.D.L.P., agree to allow local organisations to put up candidates, whose sole objective should be to use the Duma as a vehicle for revolutionary propaganda. (By this time the only remaining elections were in the Caucasus where the strong Menshevik organisations secured more than twice as many votes for its men as all other candidates put together.) The Kadets had an absolute majority in the Duma and the only other group of any significance was a radical peasant group of some seventy members who came to be called *Trudoviks*. The Kadets, confident that the power of public opinion which they represented was an irresistable force, determined to use it to compel the Tsar to extend the power of the Duma until it resembled an English-style parliament. At this time,

the Kadets still cherished the thought that they themselves would be appointed to ministerial positions. Besides, they very much valued even a rump Duma as a public forum for it was the primary vehicle through which Russia as a whole might be politically educated.[21]

The more conciliatory line of the Kadets was mirrored almost exactly in Akselrod's conclusions which, though by no means dominant among Menshevik activists in Russia, were already beginning to gain ground. 'We cannot, in absolutist Russia', he maintained, 'ignore the objective historical requirement for "political co-operation" between the proletariat and the bourgeoisie.'[22] 'I will venture to say', he went on, 'that even the most wretched caricature of a parliamentary system offers immense advantages compared with the useless means that have so far been at our disposal.'[23] Lenin, as we shall see, was not slow in seizing upon the similarity of positions and the abdication of the leading role of the proletariat that Akselrod's proposals clearly involved. That there was an abrupt and fundamental change in Menshevik thought at this time cannot seriously be questioned. Leonard Schapiro summarises it well enough:

> One of the casualties of 1905 was the menshevik belief in the 'hegemony' of the proletariat which, with the emergence of the liberals as an active and independent force, ceased to have much relation to facts . . . the mensheviks faced with the evident fact that the *Kadety* were going to think and act for themselves . . . quietly abandoned their once cherished doctrine. Trotsky described 'hegemony' as 'hypocrisy', and Plekhanov as 'absurd'.[24]

Plekhanov had, from the outset, condemned the Moscow rising as a *putschist* adventure, the effect of which would be to alienate the sympathy and support of the middle-class radicals and thereby weaken the revolutionary movement. The Social Democrats, Plekhanov insisted, must immediately drop their infatuation with insurrection. They should, rather, extend a hand to the radical intelligentsia and grant them their legitimate role in the revolution as the most Left-inclined section of the bourgeoisie. The Social Democrats must see them as their most reliable ally; the peasantry, by contrast, was an insignificant and unreliable force in the revolution. Lenin's distrust of the bourgeoisie was paralleled, if not equalled, by Plekhanov's distrust of the peasants. 'In his writings of the revolutionary years, save for an occasional jab of ridicule, there is scarcely a mention of the Socialist Revolutionary Party.'[25] Do not alienate the sympathy of society,

206

do not reject the intelligentsia, do not raise the spectre of red revolt and peasant uprising, rest content with the role of extreme opposition in the stage of the revolution and the surety of victory in the next. Such was Plekhanov's message.

The whole tenor of the Menshevik position, according to Lenin, reflected their irresolution and vacillation. After an initial insurrectionary rush of blood, now that the Duma had been convoked, more sober councils prevailed upon the Mensheviks. Their argument that the bourgeoisie must play its part in the leadership of the democratic revolution and must form the government of the new regime, demonstrated how far they had strayed into the camp of Economism. The new *Iskra* now accepted the very ideas which the old *Iskra* was created to destroy, in particular the idea that the vanguard role in the democratic revolution must be left to the bourgeoisie with the proletariat and its party featuring as the 'extreme opposition'. Lenin was not slow in seizing upon what seemed to him a total dereliction of the hegemonic role of the proletariat sanctified in the old orthodoxy. Nor he maintained, was it entirely accidental that the man who formulated the Menshevik notion of the proletariat meekly following the bourgeoisie as its 'opposition', was the arch-Economist Martynov – the persistent antagonist of orthodoxy as expressed by the *Old Iskra*.[26]

> Just as the Economists were constantly falling into the fallacy that the economic struggle is for the Social Democrats, while the political struggle is for the liberals, so the new-*Iskra* supporters, in all their reasonings, keep falling into the idea that we should modestly sit in a corner out of the way of the bourgeois revolution, with the bourgeoisie doing the active work of carrying out the revolution.[27]

It was the Mensheviks who had forgotten the central political precept of the old orthodoxy which they themselves first formulated: the hegemony of the proletariat in the democratic revolution. Now, in the actual heat of the struggle they demonstrated in practical affairs the instability and vacillation evident in their theoretical views ever since 1903. They were, for instance, in favour of the slogan of preparing the insurrection, but were against setting their organisaion to work actively to procure arms and to train men in the use of them. They declared themselves for an insurrection but were resolutely opposed to co-ordinating the forces which alone could accomplish one. They were *for* a constituent assembly and *for* a radical agrarian programme, but could not or would not explain how either could be achieved without overthrowing the autocracy, without i.e., organising the physical force that would topple the regime.

> These vulgarisers of Marxism have never given thought to what Marx said about the need to replace the weapon of criticism by the criticism of weapons. Taking the name of Marx in vain they, in actual fact, draw up resolutions on tactics wholly in the spirit of the Frankfurt bourgeois windbags, who freely criticised absolutism and deepened democratic consciousness, but failed to understand that a time for revolution is a time of action, of action from both above and below. By turning Marxism into sophistry they have turned the ideology of the advanced, the most determined, and energetic revolutionary class into an ideology of its most backward strata, of those who shrink from difficult revolutionary-democratic tasks, and leave them to Messrs. the Struves to take care of.[28]

Lenin knew full well that he had pricked the raw nerve of Menshevism and he returned again and again to assault them for throwing the old orthodoxy overboard. That orthodoxy, Lenin correctly insisted, had envisaged the bourgeoisie supporting the proletariat, not vice versa. It had insisted that the bourgeoisie was a weak and cowardly force in Russia, that it would betray. And yet Plekhanov insisted that the proletariat restrain itself *for fear that* the bourgeoisie turned to the counter-revolution. He never, in the words of his biographer 'took into his calculations the possibility that the bourgeoisie might be disinclined to participate in revolutionary action with a group which openly avowed its intention to destroy bourgeois society'.[29] Moreover, his repeated insistence that Social Democrats could play no part in constituting the provisional government which they must leave to the bourgeoisie to establish, amounted to a recognition of a political capacity and resolution within the bourgeoisie which his previous theoretical analysis considered impossible. To Lenin, and to Kautsky, this self-denying ordinance of the old philosopher-king seemed not only impractical and unreal but positively mischevous. 'It is impossible to fight while refusing victory in advance', wrote Kautsky in direct rebuttal of Plekhanov's views. For Kautsky, as for Lenin, the proletariat had to fight in 1905 with or without the bourgeoisie. For them both the only ally could be the peasantry which Plekhanov so contemptuously disregarded. For both of them 'it made no sense whatever to fight unless the leaders were prepared for power. To engage the enemy only if the bourgeoisie did, and unconditionally to forswear power, added up to political bankruptcy.'[30]

Plekhanov's reputation as a practical leader of the R.S.D.L.P. was finally broken in 1905 and Lenin's persistent critiques had not a little to do with his extinction. 'He continued to enjoy esteem for his past contributions, but more and more he was regarded as a kind of historic monument. And he himself was painfully aware of being out of step.'[31] By contrast Lenin's star was rising; 1905 made him unquestionably the most important single figure in Russian Social Democracy. His clarity, his persistence and his enormous capacity for work singled him out from his rivals. 'Indeed for the first time', Ulam concedes, 'he dwarfed the other figures: the venerable veterans Plekhanov and Akselrod, Mensheviks Dan and Martov, were but secondary figures in the drama'.[32]

The Kadets prepared for the First Duma by drawing up a broad programme of fairly moderate reforms which, they felt, they had a mandate to put through. This package of reforms was incorporated into the 'Address to the Throne' which, in imitation of British procedure, they drew up in response to the Tsar's speech welcoming the Duma representatives. The Kadet Address, duly endorsed by unanimous vote of the Duma, was sent to the Tsar and his ministers for their consideration. After making his contempt for the Duma, its officers, its programme and its pretensions abundantly clear, the Tsar simply announced that its proposals were inadmissable. After tolerating its existence for ten days the Tsar, without warning or consultation of any kind, proclaimed its dismissal and ordered a new Duma to be summoned in March 1907. In such summary fashion were all the extravagant hopes for a new age of freedom and democracy in Russia rudely dashed. The response of the Duma representatives was to withdraw to Viborg in Finland and issue a call for passive resistance – non-payment of taxes – until the Duma was restored. They had, however, made no prior arrangements to co-ordinate resistance; indeed it was impossible for the Kadets to do so since they almost entirely lacked even a rudimentary party organisation through which to channel opposition. Their appeal fell flat and their real power to lead resistance to the autocracy was shown to be quite nugatory.

The effect of the summary dismissal of the Duma upon the Kadets proved very similar to the effect that the Moscow rising had upon the Mensheviks. Confrontation, it was persuasively argued by the more moderate elements within their ranks, had produced nothing but discredit for the parties promoting radical reform and had actually strengthened the autocratic grip on the country. It would, moreover, have been tactically disastrous to admit that the Duma was quite impotent since the Social Democrats, particularly the Bolsheviks, had always insisted that impotence had been written into its whole constitution. The Kadets consequently were committed to the negative policy of keeping the Duma alive. As one commentator puts it: 'The underlying reason for Kadet acquiescence is obvious with even a cursory reading of memoirs and party reports and has been pointed out in many places: the Kadets feared the violence of a new revolutionary wave.'[33] This, for Lenin, was the betrayal which their whole class position drove them to and which the orthodoxy had always anticipated.

There was without doubt a very considerable shift in Menshevik and Kadet thinking during 1906. Both parties toned down their attitude of intransigent opposition and accommodated their policies to what they took to be the new realities of the power situation in Russia. They both accepted the fact that they would have to live with autocracy for a good deal longer than they had expected and that they would have to make the best possible use of whatever legal channels existed to promote the political education of the Russian masses. What was now needed, they both in their differing ways concluded, was a patient programme of mass political education within the existing constitutional framework so that when the next challenge to the autocracy took place, they would have the organisation and the support to guarantee lasting change.

In March 1907 after an electoral campaign in which the authorities had openly intervened by arbitrary proscription of candidates (all the signatories to the Viborg appeal were, for instance, disqualified), rigging of elections, narrowing of the franchise and wholesale intimidation, the Second Duma eventually convened. In spite of government harrassment during the elections its composition was a good deal more radical than the First Duma in that the radical peasant group, the Trudoviks, had some two hundred representatives, the Social Democrats fifty-four and the Socialist Revolutionaries thirty-five. The representation of the Right had, too, considerably increased. The Octobrists together with groups to the right of them numbered approximately eighty. The main loser in this polarised situation was, of course, the liberal centre which saw its representation shrink to 123. Nonetheless, they attempted to play a conciliatory, statesmanlike role: 'chastened by their experience, [they] were anxious to avoid endangering the survival of the Duma by provoking further conflicts'.[34] The atmosphere was, however, far too bitter and partisan. The Right was spoiling for an opportunity to arraign the Socialists for treasonable activities and to secure the Government's aid in putting them down. The Left for its part was committed to using the Duma purely and simply as a convenient medium for revolutionary propaganda and no more. They were accused of plotting the assassination of the Tsar, then, when this could not be made to stick, the Social Democrats were accused of plotting mutinies in the army. On this pretext Stolypin demanded the exclusion of all Social Democrats from the Duma which the Duma refused to do without examining the evidence. While they were about to start doing so the Duma was unceremoniously dismissed and the Social-Democratic representatives arrested and exiled.

The Tsar now delivered the final sledge-hammer blow to all the great expectations and signal victories of 1905. On 3 June he issued a Manifesto accusing the Duma of fomenting plots against the regime and of being unrepresentative of the wishes of the people. Revisions to the electoral law were therefore promulgated under which most of the towns lost their separate representation and were merged with the provinces. Property qualifications were greatly increased and a devious system of indirect election was to leave the country gentry with the final say on which peasant candidates would be allowed to enter the Duma. The urban working class was to all intents and purposes disenfranchised. All of this was, of course, flagrantly unconstitutional in that the 'inviolable' Fundamental Laws, which the Tsar himself had promulgated, reserved the right of alteration of the electoral law exclusively to the Duma. It was, moreover, entirely obvious that the measure had been well-prepared in advance and that the regime had been bent upon engineering a pretext to introduce it. It was an openly avowed *coup d'état,* which was immediately followed by widespread arrests of socialists throughout the Empire. The Tsar had now successfully clawed back all the concessions he had been forced to make and had made abundantly clear the narrow limits in which he was prepared to accept the counsel of the land. Censorship was restored, martial law reigned over large parts of the Empire, reaction rode triumphant and there was none left to challenge it.

CHAPTER 9

Theory and Practice in the Democratic Revolution

THE RIVAL FORMS OF THE DEMOCRATIC REVOLUTION

The issue in Russia, throughout the period 1904–7 was not *whether* democracy was the objective. On the general desirability of radical democratic change virtually the whole population, including the big bourgeoisie and not a few grand dukes, were agreed. The question for Lenin related to the form the democratic revolution would take. Would it radically destroy the autocratic system of government and the economic and political power of the feudal landlords upon which that system was based, or would it stop half-way with some shoddy compromise which the reaction could subsequently use to restore itself to full power once more?

The theoretical reasoning behind this stark dialectical choice we will come to later; for now let us look more closely at Lenin's analysis of the two possible outcomes, the two rival strategies of the democratic revolution as he conceived them in early 1905.

We should notice that from the outset the democratic revolution connoted, to Lenin, as much an economic programme as a political programme. His argument was a consistently Marxist one – that constitutional tinkering to alter the political balance of forces in the country would be meaningless and futile without a simultanous assault on the economic basis which had so long sustained the autocracy. The question of the democratic revolution was, in his mind, the question of whether the proletariat could dispose of sufficient real force to prevent the bourgeoisie, the landlords and the autocracy from compacting together to represent marginal *political* changes as the accomplishment of the democratic revolution. Such a dénouement boded nothing but ill for the proletarian cause. It left the proletariat and its allies easy prey to the forces of reaction. For Social Democrats, Lenin insisted, the democratic revolution must be an expressly anti-feudal revolution. Its objective in history was to smash the economic, social and political power of landlordism and autocratic monarchism. If these elements were allowed to survive, then four things would follow: (1) the power of the reaction would be greatly augmented; (2) capitalism, especially in agriculture would be greatly retarded in its development; (3) consequently the emerging and natural polarity of economic life, mirrored in consciousness and political formations, would remain hidden and disguised; (4) hence the prospects for socialism would be delayed.

The fundamental political issue which, according to Lenin, necessarily followed from this appraisal, was the issue of *who* would convoke the constituent assembly. Would the Tsar, with an eye to the interest of the landowners and big bourgeoisie, be allowed to do so? If so, then the revolution could not attain its objects; it would prove as disastrous as those of 1848. Or would the revolutionary people arms in hand, led by the proletariat, establish their own provisional revolutionary government on the ashes of the old regime and *then* convoke a constituent assembly?

To make his points more graphically Lenin frequently resorted to historical parallels to demonstrate his case that there were two entirely different possible outcomes for the democratic revolution in both political and economic terms. These were:

(a) radical republic of the 1789 type, and
(b) constitutional monarchy with separation of powers of the 1848 type.

Lenin explained the difference between these two types and the class composition of their respective leadership groups:

> . . . the bourgeois-democratic revolution carried out by France in 1789, and by Germany in 1848, was brought to its consummation in the first case, but not in the second. The first ended in a republic and complete liberty, whereas the second stopped short without smashing the monarchy and reaction. The second proceeded under the leadership mainly of the liberal bourgeoisie, which took the insufficiently mature working class in tow, whereas the first was carried out, at least to a certain extent, by the revolutionarily active mass of the people, the

workers and peasants, who, for a time at least, pushed the respectable and moderate bourgeoisie aside.[1]

These alternative political models have their corresponding economic bases, the first allowing a full and unimpeded development of capitalism, the second retaining substantial elements of feudal economic relations, especially in agriculture, and thereby frustrating the development of new forms of production and class development. Corresponding therefore to the political forms (a) and (b) above, Lenin posited the economic forms:

(1) of the American type encouraging unfettered capitalist production in all areas of the economy, and

(2) of the junker type preserving labour-service and bondage, retaining the economic, social and therefore political power of the landlords.

Lenin again explained the difference between these rival forms;

One alternative is evolution of the Prussian type – the serf-owning landlord becomes a junker; the landlords' power in the state is consolidated for a decade; monarchy; 'military despotism, embellished in parliamentary forms' instead of democracy; the second alternative is evolution of the American type – the abolition of landlord farming; the peasant becomes a free farmer; popular government; the bourgeois-democratic political system; the greatest equality among the rural population as the starting point of, and a condition for, free capitalism.[2]

The former road would pauperise and enslave the peasantry, the latter would greatly benefit at least a section of them; it was, therefore, 'the form of bourgeois-democratic revolution most advantageous to the peasants'.[3] The central economic question of the democratic revolution in Russia related not to the fate of urban machine industry – its fate was not threatened. It related rather to the agrarian question and the basis of the landlords' power.

The pivot of the struggle, we repeat, is the feudal latifundia. The capitalist evolution of these is beyond all dispute, but it is possible in two forms: either they will be abolished, eliminated in a revolutionary manner by peasant farmers, or they will be gradually transformed into Junker estates (and

215

correspondingly, the enthralled *muzhik* will be transformed into an enthralled *Knecht*).[4]

'There cannot be the least doubt', Lenin argued, 'that a tremendous increase in the productive forces, a tremendous rise in the technical and cultural level will inevitably *follow the break-up of the feudal latifundia in European Russia*'.[5] As he had earlier expressed it, the whole mission of the democratic revolution in Russia was to 'cleanse it of the slag of feudalism'.[6]

THE PEASANTS AND THE AGRARIAN QUESTION

It is quite clear that for Lenin a radical solution of the agrarian problem was the fundamental economic objective of the democratic revolution and that his political strategy is quite unintelligible unless this is borne in mind. The question was, which classes and political groups in contemporary Russia had an objective interest in the destruction of landlordism and which would strive to preserve it. Lenin's own theoretical analysis had long provided him with the answer – only the proletariat and the poor peasantry were wholeheartedly committed to the destruction of landlordism. The bourgeoisie would prevaricate, make concessions, but would ultimately side with the landlords because they were bound to them by innumerable economic, social and family ties.

The revolution demonstrated in practice to Lenin the correctness of his theoretical analysis which had foreseen the conjunction of interests between the proletariat and the poor peasants. The peasant deputies in the Dumas insistently and stridently declared that they had come with one object and one object only – to secure the land, all of the land, for the peasants by any means. In so doing they were, according to Lenin, announcing the incompatibility of their economic and political objectives with anything the bourgeoisie had in mind. What the Social Democrats had to do, in order to establish the proletariat as the vanguard of all Russia's exploited, was to convince the peasants that their economic objectives were only attainable within the framework of the political programme of Social Democracy. In particular it had to be demonstrated that the sole political structure which could guarantee the peasants' economic objectives was a democratic republic governed by the proletariat and the peasantry.

216

The nationalisation of all landlords' lands became the centre-piece of Lenin's strategy throughout this period. It was, in the first place, the only measure which could eliminate the substantial social base of autocracy. It was, in the second place, the only measure which could promote the fullest and freest development of capitalist relations in agriculture. Lenin's argument, which had unimpeachable sources in Marx's own thought, was that private ownership of the land impeded rather than assisted the development of capitalist productive forces in agriculture. Under the present system, Lenin argued, the farmer had to expend an enormous pro-portion of his total available capital on the purchase of land to cultivate. Inevitably, therefore, his capacity to take advantage of the most advanced agricultural machinery and technology was very greatly reduced. Lenin maintained that in a situation where the state became the universal landlord, letting land at moderate rent, a tremendous volume of capital would be released from unproductive purchase of the land and channelled into improve-ments in technology and agricultural technique. In this way the capitalist development of Russian agriculture would be enormously accelerated and, therewith, the open class struggle between capitalist farmers and wage-earning rural proletarians would be rapidly clarified.

It was on these grounds that Lenin clearly distinguished the Bolshevik agrarian programme from that of the Socialist Revolu-tionaries. It was utopian, in his view, to argue that the peasants could be saved from the baneful impact of capitalism. The object of the democratic revolution could not be, as the Socialist Revolutionaries imagined, some half-way house to socialism, the aim of which was to arrest the progress of capitalism and save the peasant commune as a *point d'appui* for the leap to socialism. On the contrary, Lenin's whole economic analysis had demon-strated that the commune was already hopelessly doomed. The economic programme of the democratic revolution had to face this fact and promote not retard the development of capitalist relations in agriculture. Only then would the reality of emergent class polarity in the countryside be clarified and the web of bondage which still ensnared the majority of Russian peasants be swept away.

The Socialist Revolutionary ideal was to reunify the peasantry through the socialist measures of a revolutionary government. The Bolsheviks saw their objective as that of promoting capitalist development in the Russian countryside via land nationalisation which would accelerate the process of splitting the peasants into frankly warring class groupings. The advance to socialism could only be contemplated after the wage-earning landless peasants, the *batraki*, had been freed from feudal bondage, exposed to the reality of capitalist exploitation and organised under the leadership of the urban proletariat.

Just as the proletariat must understand the centrality of binding the peasantry to advancing the revolution through an *economic* measure which ostensibly benefited only the latter, so, too, the peasantry must come to understand that they would be secure in their newly-won possessions only if they insisted upon the *political* programme vital to the proletarian interest. They must recognise that to rely upon the present administration and its officials to supervise the huge redistribution of land they insisted upon, would lead to inevitable disaster.

> Hence – we will explain to the peasants – if the land is to be transferred to the whole people in a way that will benefit the peasants, it is necessary to ensure that all government officials without exception are elected by the people. Hence my proposal for nationalisation, with the proviso that a democratic republic is fully guaranteed, suggests the right line of conduct to our propagandists and agitators; for it clearly and vividly shows them that discussion of the agrarian demands of the peasantry should serve as a basis for political propaganda in general, and for propaganda in favour of a republic in particular.[7]

In the fight for the republic and for confiscation or nationalisation of all landlords' land, the interest of proletariat and peasantry coalesced. They went far beyond the most radical bourgeois programmes and were quite unacceptable to the autocracy. They were the objectives for which these classes would fight and for which they must frankly be told they would have to fight.

THE ROLE OF THE BOURGEOISIE

We should not expect Lenin in 1905 to set aside his earlier judgements about the role of the bourgeoisie in the democratic revolution, nor did he. Nothing that occurred during the period 1905–7 caused him to alter by one iota his view that the bourgeoisie could not be trusted with the leadership of the democratic revolution. They did have democratic aspirations, and, to a certain extent, were anti-autocratic; but only to a certain extent. At a moment propitious to themselves they would, if allowed to, conclude a pact with the Tsar and establish a constitutional monarchy with a complicated constitutional division of powers in which they would retain the whip-hand. By its class nature the bourgeoisie was bound to vacillate. It needed the proletariat as a battering ram to force concessions from the autocracy. At the same time it feared the militant claims of proletarian socialism and, against these latter, it sought to preserve the coercive power of the old state intact. In short it did not aspire to radical republican democracy, nor, because of its fellow feeling with the landlords, did it want a radical extirpation of the remnants of feudal economic relations in the countryside. Its object, therefore, was to seduce the proletariat and the peasantry with slogans of apparent universality, and commitments on paper to all sorts of radical change, whereas in fact its very class situation obliged it to do a deal with the autocracy and arrest the revolution half-way. These ideas concerning the weakness, cowardice and instability of the bourgeoisie were not new either to Lenin's political thought, nor to the Russian Marxist tradition. We have seen in Chapter Two that the thesis that the Russian bourgeoisie could not be trusted with carrying out the democratic revolution was the single most important precept of Russian Marxist orthodoxy.

Lenin knew that the bourgeoisie would betray the revolution and refuse to redeem its easily-given pledges. His economic analysis had confirmed this finding of orthodoxy and it was, in any case, reinforced by Marx's judgements on the bourgeois betrayals of 1848 exemplified by 'the abortive, unfinished semi-revolution in Germany in 1848 . . . which we shall never tire of recalling'.[8] Everywhere, throughout this period, Lenin's writings were haunted by Marx's analysis of the false hopes, illusions, unpreparedness and subsequent disasters the proletariat entertained and suffered. How then could the treacherous instability of the bourgeoisie be stymied? That was the basic tactical problem of the revolution. Lenin answered that, on its own, the proletariat was insufficiently strong to withstand the future alliance of the bourgeoisie with the autocracy. Only if the proletariat preserved absolute independence of action, only if it made the fullest possible use of each and every occasion of bourgeois wavering to clarify the situation, only, finally, if it won over the revolutionary section of the peasantry to its cause would it be able to prevent the revolution being arrested by bourgeois betrayal.

The vagueness and vacillation of the bourgeoisie was, in Lenin's view, a function of its objective class situation. It must act as an intermediary between the autocracy and the insurgent people.

> . . . the gist of the bourgeoisie's political position is, as we have frequently pointed out, that it stands between the Tsar and the people and would play the part of the 'honest broker' and steal into power behind the back of the militant people. That is why the bourgeoisie appeals to the Tsar one day, and to the people the next, making 'serious' and business-like proposals for a political deal to the former, and addressing empty phrases about liberty to the latter.[9]

The essence of the bourgeois dilemma was that it needed the people against the Tsar, yet, at a slightly later date, it knew that it would need the Tsar against the people.

> . . . its class instinct enables it to realise perfectly well that, on the one hand, the proletariat and the 'people' are useful for *its* revolution as cannon fodder, as a battering-ram against the autocracy, but that, on the other hand, the proletariat and the revolutionary peasantry will be terribly dangerous to it if they win a 'decisive victory over tsarism' and carry the democratic revolution to completion.[10]

The bourgeoisie was, therefore, compelled to play a nicely balanced game. It recognised that, of its own resources, it commanded no real force to frighten the Tsar into concessions; it recognised further that only such force would impress the Tsar. It must, therefore, turn to the people, to the proletariat, the petty bourgeoisie and the peasantry, but in exciting them to assume an anti-autocratic stand, in drawing them into the maelstrom of revolutionary politics, it could have no guarantee of being able to prevent them turning anti-bourgeois. Its role of inducting the masses into political consciousness might be quickly usurped by the more radical Social Democrats, a potentiality which Lenin fully appreciated. 'Let the bourgeoisie stir up those that are most backward; let it break the soil here and there; we shall untiringly sow the seeds of Social Democracy in that soil.'[11]

Always, in confronting the autocracy, the bourgeoisie had one fearful eye fixed on the threat from below. Even during the heat of the democratic revolution the bourgeoisie could never feel secure, and for that reason, it could not advocate the complete destruction of autocracy nor any sudden and final destruction of feudalism in the countryside. It was too sensitive to its own insecurity and weakness not to realise that elements of the old regime would have to be preserved so that, when the bourgeois goals had been achieved, it would be able to cry halt to the revolutionary upsurge and have the power to ensure a speedy return to order.

> . . . it is to the advantage of the bourgeoisie to rely on certain remnants of the past, as against the proletariat, for instance, on the monarchy, the standing army, etc. It is to the advantage of the bourgeoisie for the bourgeois revolution not to sweep away all remnants of the past too resolutely, but keep some of them, i.e., for the revolution not to be fully consistent, not complete, and not to be determined and relentless.[12]

By contrast,

> the very position the proletariat holds as a class compels it to be consistently democratic. The bourgeoisie looks backward in fear of democratic progress which threatens to strengthen the proletariat. The proletariat has nothing to lose but its chains but with the aid of democratism it has a whole world to win.[13]

It followed, therefore, from Lenin's analysis of the respective positions of proletariat and bourgeoisie, that only the former was unreservedly and frankly democratic in its goals, only it wanted a clean and complete break with feudalism and autocracy, for only then could class alignments on a national scale be clarified and brought to the consciousness of the masses. Hence it followed that 'the more complete, determined and consistent the bourgeois revolution, the more assured will the proletariat's struggle be against the bourgeoisie and for socialism'.[14]

The political programmes of the bourgeois parties mirrored the complexity and deviousness of their tactic of playing the people off against autocracy and autocracy against the people. Their

221

constitutional proposals came dressed in all the luxuriant verbiage of the universal objectives of democracy. They appeared replete with carefully drafted paper guarantees of the rights of the citizen and the limitations to be set upon the executive arm of the government. To Russians starved so long of even the hope of civil liberties and the realisation of a measure of human dignity, their words fell as manna from heaven. The Russian people were, Lenin argued, for good historical and social reasons, particularly and especially prone to the seductions of the siren calls of liberals and Constitutional Democrats (Kadets). The constitutional ideal of the latter was, Lenin maintained,

> that power in the state should be divided into approximately three parts. One part goes to the autocracy. The monarchy remains. The monarch retains equal power with the popular representative body, which is to 'agree' with him on the laws to be passed, and submit its *bills* to him for *approval*. The second part goes to the landlords and the big capitalists. They get the Upper Chamber, from which the 'common people' are to be barred by a two-stage electoral system and a residential qualification. Lastly, the third part goes to the people, who get a Lower Chamber elected on the basis of universal, equal and direct suffrage by secret ballot.[15]

Thus, Lenin maintained, did the bourgeois 'radicals' redeem their promise to fight for the four-tail suffrage, preserving it intact but quite emasculated within the complicated 'classless' political structure which preserved and strengthened the feudal elements and would undoubtedly frustrate any radical economic proposals.

Lenin's prognosis was, for him, confirmed by the Kadet, liberal and Octobrist satisfaction with the constitutional concessions wrung from the Tsar in October of 1905. In jubilation the Kadets cried victory. They assumed immediately the mantle of parliamentarians, calling, especially after their sweeping victory at the polls, for the people's full confidence in the Duma as the instrument of the popular will which would realise liberty in Russia. Flushed with importance, conceiving themselves to be the authentic tribunes of the Russian people, the Kadets, by a huge and illogical flight of fancy, imagined that therefore they *should* exercise power; indeed, they came to think, act and represent themselves as if they *were* a power in the land. Therein lay the danger of this democratic facade of the Duma. It was, according to Lenin, but a flimsy tinsel embellishment, a bit of window-dressing by the autocracy to make its wares appear more palatable to passing public fancy. Or to change the imagery – 'The Duma is to serve as a plaster to draw the heat out of the revolution.'[16] It was, Lenin tirelessly pointed out, only the *real power* of the workers of Russia who had followed the railwaymen's lead in early October 1905 to organise the biggest general strike in Russian (perhaps European) history which had proved at all effective.

The danger was that the *workers*, having *obliged*, the autocracy through their combined force to concede a more democratically elected assembly, would now yield place to the parliamentary adepts of liberalism, waiting patiently in the wings, polishing their prose and anxious to play their roles as soon as the melée was over. Theirs, Lenin argued, must be a fantasy world which must slough off the uncomfortable but real truths of the situation of their assembly. The Tsar treated it with undisguised contempt. His ministry was in no way responsible to the elected representatives. The Duma was powerless to control the executive. Most importantly, the coercive power of the state remained firmly in the Tsar's hands. Yet the Kadets postured and played out the charade not as if it were a game but as if it were for real. Therein lay the danger of their game. Unless ruthlessly exposed they would persuade a credulous Russian people to believe what they wanted to believe, namely, that the fight was over, that democracy was already established and the realm of freedom was at hand. The Kadets fostered the illusion that the people at large had *already* asserted control over their own destiny, that through the Duma they could progressively realise the ideals of social justice and free democracy so ardently and universally espoused. All of this was but a soporific, Lenin argued. It reflected the half-instinctive, half-conscious awareness of the bourgoisie that the revolution had reached its optimum point of development as far as bourgeois interests were concerned. The Tsar has been forced to concede a representative assembly of sorts. It did not, admittedly, incorporate the initial demands made by the bourgeois parties, but none-theless they had been the main beneficiaries in that their party, the Kadets, had won overall control of it. To go further at this point, to incite the people into demanding a fully democratic representative body and a responsible ministry would provoke a direct clash with the autocracy. Such a course would be fraught with dangers. It would invite an uncontrollable holocaust and oblige the Kadets to relinquish leadership to the expressly revolutionary parties. It would, moreover, produce in the popular masses expectations of radical change in *their* interests commensurate with *their* contribution.

Any· deepening of the revolution would, however, prejudice bourgeois interests. Their class position dictated that they should cry halt, that they should therefore present the shoddy compromise of an emasculated Duma and irresponsible ministry as the accomplished revolution. They presented their own interest as the general interest and reneged on all their ealier loftier pledges. At this stage the bourgeoisie betrayed the revolution, they sold out for whatever mess of pottage the Tsar beneficently ladled out.

Lenin had, as we have seen, expected and predicted this betrayal. The whole theoretical background of Russian Marxism, his reading of Marx on 1848–51, his earlier class analysis of Russian society, all insisted that the bourgeoisie always reneged on its general revolutionary declarations when its particular interests had been satiated and that historical generalisation was especially true of the Russian bourgeoisie. In July 1905 Lenin pointedly reminded Social Democrats of this crucial theoretical finding.

> The bourgeoisie in the mass, will inevitably turn towards counter-revolution, towards the autocracy, against the revolution, and against the people, as soon as its narrow, selfish interests are met, as soon as it 'recoils' from consistent democracy (*and it is already recoiling from it!*). There remains the 'people', that is, the proletariat and the peasantry.[17]

After the critical moment of betrayal, after the bourgeoisie had identified itself with the Tsar's small concessions, and agreed thereby to preserve the autocracy and the landlords' power, there could be no way forward except *against* the bourgeoisie. The democratic revolution had to be consummated against both Tsar and bourgeoisie which now, objectively, had moved over to the counter-revolution.

At this point the class composition of the frankly democratic camp changed substantially in character. At this stage, according to Lenin, only the proletariat and the rural proletariat and rural petty bourgeoisie had a vital interest in seeing the revolution through to its completion. Therefore at this point the tactics, the organisational basis, the slogans and objectives of Social Democracy had to be changed. The issues which had now to be brought to the fore were not the issues which *united* bourgeoisie, petty bourgeoisie and proletariat. Such policies were appropriate in the first phase of the revolution but would be disastrous in the second phase for they did but strengthen the carefully cultivated bourgeois illusions that *everybody's* best interest was secured by the road of patient peaceful advance via the Duma. The Mensheviks, therefore, who argued that the revolutionaries must beware of alienating the bourgeoisie, must moderate their policies 'lest the bourgeoisie recoil'[18] and join the counter-revolutionary camp, quite failed to recognise that this had already occurred. In their moderation the Mensheviks lent credence to the Kadets' demands for patience and restraint and confidence in the people's elected representatives. The Mensheviks objectively assisted them in peddling soporifics, lulling the proletariat into a false sense of security which would leave them quite defenceless when the bourgeois/autocratic alliance moved to physical repression of the revolutionaries as it surely would.

A constituent assembly or even a properly democratic representative assembly could only be meaningful or significant, in Lenin's view, if it were convened *after* the destruction of the autocratic power. Any playing at parliamentarism, drafting of ambitious bills, establishing of committees for this and that, within the framework of the Tsar's projected representative assembly, amounted to an idle pretence that the Russian Duma was an English Parliament or a groundless optimism that it would *develop* into such.

By constitutional illusions we mean deceptive faith in a constitution. Constitutional illusions prevail when a constitution seems to exist, but actually does not: in other words, when affairs of state are *not* administered *in the way* parliament decides. . . . The liberal bourgeois, dreading the extra-parliamentary struggle, spreads constitutional illusions even when parliaments are impotent. . . . Social Democrats stand for utilising the parliamentary struggle, for participating in parliament; but they ruthlessly expose 'parliamentary cretinism', that is, the belief

225

that the parliamentary struggle is the *sole* or *under all circumstances the main* form of the political struggle.[19]

The Social Democrats had to insist that so long as the autocracy remained undisturbed in its power, so long as the Duma remained 'a fig-leaf for the autocracy',[20] and so long as the popular movement was growing in extensiveness and depth, the main object of attention must be the active preparation of an armed uprising. Repeatedly Lenin insisted that it was the obligation of Social Democrats to be the first in the field to give out the slogan of an uprising; they must also be the last to leave it for lower, less developed forms of struggle. Only when the revolution had quite exhausted itself and spent its forces, only when the tide was ebbing was it permissible for Social Democrats to make what use they might of emasculated parliamentary forms. This was, according to Lenin, Marx's policy in 1848–51.[21] It was the policy which Kautsky recommended to the Russians Marxists arguing that they should boycott the Duma and 'fight in order to wreck the Duma and to secure the convocation of a constituent assembly'. In this way,

> the peasants and the proletariat will more and more vigorously and unceremoniously push the members of the Duma to the left, will steadily strengthen its *Left wing*, and steadily weaken and paralyse their opponents, until they have utterly defeated them.[22]

THE ORGANISATION OF REVOLUTIONARY FORCE AND THE REORGANISATION OF THE PARTY

The battle for the democratic revolution was, in Lenin's analysis, one which concerned the vital interests of every major class of Russian society. It was, therefore, resolvable only through violent confrontation; 'great historical issues can be resolved only *by force*, and, in modern struggle, *the organisation of force* means military organisation.'[23] In such a situation it was illusory and dangerous to imagine that any sort of words, decisions, resolutions or projected constitutions could be of any avail. 'While power remains in the hands of the Tsar all decisions of any representatives whatsoever will remain empty and miserable prattle.'[24] It was precisely the Tsar's forces which had been used in the bloody suppression of peaceful demonstrations and loyal presentation of petitions. Ever since Bloody Sunday, when men, women and children, in peaceful procession to the Winter Palace to supplicate redress of their grievances, were shot down in their hundreds, ever since that time, the autocracy itself had confirmed the Marxist finding that:

> Major questions in the life of nations are settled only by force. The reactionary classes themselves are usually the first to resort to violence, to civil war; they are the first to 'place the bayonet on the agenda', as the Russian autocracy has systematically and unswervingly been doing everywhere ever since 9 January. And since such a situation has arisen, since the bayonet has really become the main point on the political agenda, since insurrection has proved imperative and urgent – constitutional illusions and school exercises in parliamentarianism become merely a screen for the bourgeois betrayal of the revolution.[25]

Force was necessary to 'paralyse the bourgeoisie's instability',[26] and to forestall its attempted sell-out of the revolution.[27] At the same time that insurgent armed power disorganised the opposition, causing elements of its forces to waver or join the popular movement, it also facilitated the expropriation of funds for the revolution.[28]

And so, according to Lenin, insurrection was the order of the day. Only the proletariat could lead such an insurrection and its Party had the clear obligation to prepare it for its task. This was, according to Lenin, a conclusion arrived at not from any imposition of a Jacobin or Blanquist will on the process of history. On the contrary, he argued that 'the conditions of social and economic development' in Russia had matured to the point where the democratic revolution was a matter of urgency. Further it was incontestable that the almost universal awareness of the immediate desirability of democracy gave the revolution a moral force which was

> overwhelmingly great; without it, of course, there could be no question of any revolution whatever. It is a necessary condition, but it is *not sufficient*. Only the outcome of the struggle will show whether it will be translated into a material force sufficient to smash the very serious . . . resistance of the autocracy. The slogan of insurrection is a slogan for deciding the issue by material force, which in present-day European civilisation can

only be military force. The slogan should not be put forward until the general prerequisities for revolution have matured, until the masses have definitely shown that they have been roused and are ready to act, until the external circumstances have led to an open crisis. But once such a slogan has been issued, it would be an arrant disgrace to retreat from it . . . No, once the die is cast, all subterfuges must be done with, it must be explained directly and openly to the masses what the practical conditions for a successful revolution are at the present time.[29]

This was an important formulation of Lenin's ideas on revolution. He specified three necessary conditions which had to be satisfied before a call to arms should be given out: (1) the maturation of social and economic conditions for the revolution, which finds its reflection in (2) the moral preponderance of the revolutionary idea, which, in turn, must be reflected in (3) the consciousness of the desirability of the change and evidence of preparedness to act to accomplish it.

All of these were necessary but not sufficient conditions for the triumph of the revolution. To the three necessary conditions there must be added a fourth before the issue could even be brought to a test: the organisation of the requisite material force. Revolutionaries, if they were seriously committed to the triumph of the revolutionary cause, if they genuinely wished to realise the role of leading the struggle, without prevarication, without any looking back, had to commit themselves wholeheartedly to the task. *En la guerre comme à la guerre*, the task in hand was now to prepare, co-ordinate and direct the activities of those who were ready to *fight* for a radical democracy. Down with those who belittled the revolutionary energy of the working class;[30] down with those pedants who disdained an alliance with militant armed proletarian groups on the grounds that their theoretical preparation was insufficient;[31] down with those who failed to comprehend the potent revolutionary forces in the countryside and the crucial importance of an alliance with the peasantry.

The tasks which Lenin set the Party followed on from his specification of its duty and obligations. He defined them early on in the revolution and continued to propound them long after the failure of the Moscow uprising in December 1905. This was how he outlined them in April 1905:

1. To explain to the proletariat by means of propaganda and agitation, not only the political significance, but the practical organisational aspect of the impending armed uprising.

2. To explain in that propaganda and agitation the role of mass political strikes, which may be of great importance at the beginning and during the progress of the uprising;

3. To take the most energetic steps towards arming the proletariat, as well as drawing up a plan of the armed uprising and of direct leadership thereof, for which purpose special groups of Party workers should be formed as and when necessary. [32]

Under 1., the Party had to demonstrate that real political liberties would be attainable only *after* the destruction of the autocracy, that therefore only the establishment of a provisional revolutionary government, only a republic could guarantee the people's rights. These objectives were the proper objectives precisely because the bourgeoisie had not accepted them and perhaps could not accept them. They must be pressed and insisted upon precisely because they '*advance* the revolution, take it beyond the limits to which the monarchist bourgeoisie advances it'. [33] These objectives tsarism could not possibly concede; therefore, they were the appropriate ones. These objectives clearly stated the proletarian case, prevented the big bourgeoisie from 'striking a huckster's bargain with tsarism' [34] and obliged the liberal and radical bourgeoisie to declare its interest – for the Tsar or for the people, for an arrested revolution and the triumph of the reaction, or for complete victory for the democratic cause.

In this situation, Lenin argued, it would be the utmost folly for Social Democrats to be assailed by qualms about the people's theoretical or organisational preparedness for the role allotted to them. Was it not evident, many of Lenin's own supporters argued, that substantial parts of the proletariat followed the Mensheviks and were even seduced by Kadet propaganda? Furthermore, the peasantry as a mass gave its support not to the Social Democrats, not even to the frankly socialist, if utopian, Socialist Revolutionaries – but to a party which was more an accidental congerie of half-baked populists – the Trudoviks. What then could one do with people whose theoretical awareness was so little developed and whose organisational basis was so amorphous and ill-elaborated?

Lenin's response was disarmingly simple. Yes, these people are as you describe; their theoretical awareness is in a lamentable state when viewed from the heights of achieved Social-Democratic consciousness. Yes, they are presently ill-organised. What can we do about this situation? We can and must lead them, insist repeatedly upon our radical demands, begin organising the insurrection, polarise the political life of Russia. In this very process consciousness would become immeasurably more extensive, infinitely more profound. In the very activity of mass political strikes to press their demands, the proletariat would establish its own organisational basis for the insurrection. The peasants, too, would establish their own committees to see to the distribution of expropriated land and to organise the revolution. To all the faint-hearted who would stand aside from the struggle Lenin cried – draw near with faith in the enormously compressed educative experience of the revolutionary period which will 'rouse the vast masses to active life, to heroic efforts, to "fundamental historic creativeness"'.[35]

Open political activity would purge the masses of their illusions. The shallow words of the bourgeois liberals as well as the deviations of Mensheviks would be as chaff blown away by the revolutionary whirlwind. Proletarian and peasant action would inevitably produce commensurate reaction from the forces of order. The more resolutely and radically the revolutionaries pursued their aims, the more cohesive and distinct the forces of reaction became: '. . . revolution progresses by giving rise to a strong and united counter-revolution, i.e., it compels the enemy to resort to more and more extreme measures of defence and in this way devises ever more powerful means of attack.'[36] The defenders of autocracy would be obliged openly to declare themselves, the waverers to choose sides. In the breach of blood that civil war produced there could be no neutrals.[37]

Lenin's conception of the accelerated growth of consciousness during revolutionary periods was intimately linked with his changing ideas on the proper structure of the party. The ascent of the mass to a heightened level of consciousness must, Lenin argued, be reflected in the composition of all party organisations so that 'the greatest possible number of workers capable of leading the movement and the Party organisations be advanced from among the mass of the working class to membership on the local centres and on the all-Party centre'.[38] Paradoxically it was precisely *Lenin* who felt constrained to answer those critics in the Party who maintained that 'the Party would be dissolved among the masses, it would cease to be the conscious vanguard of its class, its role would be reduced to that of a tail'.[39] Nonsense! Lenin retorted, culpable nonsense, for the organisation *must* be appropriate to its objectives and if they entailed assault on autocracy and command over a large army of fighters, then that required a large organisation however theoretically naive many of its members might be. Only the faint-hearted, only those who lacked confidence in the theoretical and strategic analysis of Social Democracy, could fear the revivifying effect of large numbers of new recruits upon a Party which

> has stagnated while working underground . . . The 'underground' is breaking up. Forward, then, more boldly; . . . extend your bases, rally all the worker Social Democrats round yourselves, incorporate them in the ranks of the Party organisations by hundreds and thousands. Let their delegates put new life into the ranks of our central bodies, let the fresh spirit of young revolutionary Russia pour in through them. So far the revolution has justified all the basic theoretical prepositions of Marxism, all the essential slogans of Social Democracy.[40]

Confidence in the theoretical adequacy of the Party's position was the premise for confidence in the revolutionary spirit of the masses, for the process of revolution itself *demonstrated* the correctness of theory and the appropriateness of derivative slogans. It was the workers, Lenin reminded the Party, who 'act, and transform drab theory into living reality'.[41] Not only must the fresh revivifying forces of the revolutionary youth be *admitted* into the Party, they must be given a weight in Party councils to match their numbers. The time had come, Lenin insisted, for the Party thoroughly to apply the elective principle to its whole organisational structure. In his article 'The Reorganisation of the Party', written in November 1905, Lenin made it quite clear that the old *modus operandi* of the underground no longer sufficed. Its secretive hierarchical structure was a necessary response to conditions of police persecution and absence of freedom to publicise and canvass. However, conditions had changed and the movement had extended itself enormously. Candidates for office were known because in the course of the revolutionary events they had been able to step out openly and publicly proclaim their stance. Open Party meetings were now a possibility in the more relaxed political atmosphere. Therefore the Bolsheviks appealed 'for the immediate application and introduction of the elective principle'.[42]

So fulsomely did Lenin support his newly-coined organisational theme of 'democratic centralism' that one wonders what had become of the insistence, in *What Is To Be Done?*, on the elements of unanimity, discipline and accountability of all Party organs to the Centre. In the new organisational scheme he talked of the precedence of *local* organisations. Indeed this emphasis upon the initiative of the local committees seems to encapsulate a good deal of what he intended by the term democratic centralism. The organisational tasks confronting every Social Democrat were:

> to apply the principles of democratic centralism in Party organisation, to work tirelessly to make the local organisations the principal organisational units of the Party, in fact and not merely in name, and to see to it that all higher-standing bodies are elected, accountable, and subject to recall. We must work hard to build up an organisation that will include all conscious Social-Democratic workers, and will live its own independant political life. The autonomy of every Party organisation, which hitherto has been largely a dead letter, must become a reality.[43]

Lenin's vision now was of a Party built from below upwards with the higher organs deriving their powers from, and directly accountable to, the lower ones. There could, in this organisational framework, be no question of the Central Committee or Central Organ issuing irrefragible directions. Always and at all times democratic centralism, in Lenin's conception at this time, entailed the right of dissent; it 'implies universal and full *freedom to criticise*, so long as this does not disturb the unity *of a definite action*'.[44]

Lenin in his italicised phrase commending 'freedom to criticise' was, of course, inviting a direct comparison of the organisational principle of 'democratic centralism' compared with that of *What Is To Be Done?*. In the latter, protestations about the 'freedom to criticise' were dismissed by him as thin disguises for the right of introducing bourgeois ideology into the working class and its Party.

At *that time*, Lenin insisted economism and Bernsteinism represented a real threat to the workers' movement *because* there was no central Party organisation of any sort capable of rebutting it. *At that time*, moreover, the workers had not had a chance to learn from their own experience of political struggle the true class structure of capitalist society. They were in the infancy of their evolution as a class, as a conscious and politically organised class, and were, therefore, especially prone to the comfortable undemanding line of revisionism. By 1905–6, however, the situation had changed almost beyond recognition. The orthodox Marxists had established their pre-eminence in the Party. The Party had been effectively constituted at the Second Party Congress. The workers had, moreover, ever since 1902, undergone an important educative experience in mounting mass political strikes and demonstrations. In the revolutionary days of 1905 their degree of consciousness grew with the extensiveness of their activity and the clarity with which it obliged all other classes of society to declare their interest. The working class was becoming conscious, was, with amazing rapidity, becoming organised under the leadership of Social Democracy. The revolution, moreover, was daily confirming the adequacy of the Social-Democratic theory and slogans. In this new situation, Lenin argued, the organisation had to enlist members by the hundreds and thousands. It had to have the confidence in its own theoretical prescience that events would confirm its diagnosis. The illusions, deviations and deficiencies of the new recruits would be purged through observing the progress of events themselves for these events ruthlessly exposed society's polarities, the treachery of the bourgeoisie and the necessity for a seizure of power to effect radical democracy. Lenin's confidence in the proletariat, his recommendations to broaden the Party, to encourage 'wide and free discussion of Party questions, free comradely criticism and assessment of events in Party life', his insistence on democratic centralism which connoted 'guarantees for the rights of minorities and of all loyal opposition . . . the autonomy of every Party organisation . . . recognising that all Party functionaries must be elected, accountable to the Party and subject to recall'[45] – all of this was derived from the theoretical conviction that the immanent polarities were working themselves out, were impressing themselves on the minds of the masses, and would sweep away all deviations and hesitations.

Revolution teaches: and we believe that practical unity in the struggle of the Social-Democratic proletariat throughout Russia will safeguard our Party against fatal errors during the climax of the impending political crisis. In the course of the fight, events themselves will suggest to the working masses the right tactics to adopt.[46]

Again and again Lenin preached the same message – have faith in the rectitude of Bolshevik theoretical prognoses, have confidence in the prescience of Marxism whose predictions were being realised with breath-taking rapidity.

We must remember that our 'doctrinaire' faithfulness to Marxism is being reinforced by the march of revolutionary events, which is everywhere furnishing *object lessons to the masses* and that all these lessons confirm precisely our dogma.[47]

It might well be, of course, that part of Lenin's motive in re-formulating his ideas on the proper organisation of the Party, was to win control for himself and for his Bolshevik faction over the whole Party. He knew that the Mensheviks, because of their rather confused self-denying stance on the revolution had lost the support of many of the younger Party militants. The most enthusiastic and dedicated of these were coming over to Lenin's camp. As one of these, who later became a Menshevik, recounted: 'I would say that the most dedicated, the most active young Social Democrats became Bolsheviks . . . We couldn't understand the Mensheviks' tactics. And therefore it seemed natural to us to become Bolsheviks.'[48] Lenin, no doubt, hoped, by reorganising the Party, to capitalise on this new-found strength and convert it into Bolshevik dominance over the Central Organ as well as over the Central Committee. In part then, this reorganisation could be seen as a tactical ploy. Even as a tactical ploy, however, its success rested upon events confirming the Bolshevik line and hence confirming their theoretical analysis.

More fundamentally Lenin's proposals for Party reorganisation directly complemented his account of the ascending phases of class consciousness. The progression and interconnection of these elements was clear in his mind. Changes in the extensiveness and direction of working-class activity produced new levels of mass consciousness which in turn required changes in the structure and organisation of the Party.

In the period 1900 to 1902, for instance, the advanced workers began to move towards engaging the autocracy on the political level. They were held back by the mass of the workers and the opposition of Economists, worker-philes and revisionists. What was necessary *at that stage* was, therefore, a disciplined Party centre, professionally trained to activate the masses in conditions of acute police repression, stimulate the workers into political activity in the van of all oppositional forces. Only in the course of engaging in political activity would the mass acquire consciousness. This ascent to mass political consciousness, Lenin argued, had been effected in the years 1902 to 1905. But at that stage the advanced workers began to recognise the necessity of leading and organising the *revolutionary* assault on autocracy. Political consciousness, an awareness of the need to complement economic demands by political ones, grew to *revolutionary* consciousness and, in this situation, the old Party structure became obsolete. At this stage the masses were already politically ·activised by the progress of events themselves. The polarities had worked themselves through to a situation of impending and actual civil war. What was needed at this stage, Lenin argued, was a Party which would accept into its ranks and give due weight to all those prepared to *fight* under its direction for the success of radical democracy.

Intrinsic to Lenin's conception of the Party there was, therefore, a conception of its phasal evolution in every way comparable to the evolution of capitalism and the development of consciousness. Each phase marked a stage of advance in the formation of the class, for this, to a Marxist, was definitional. A class was *defined* in terms of its ability to organise cohesively on a national basis in order to articulate its viewpoint, and eventually to fight for its own predominance. Its organisational form had to be appropriate to the tasks which each successive phase of development imposed upon the class, and had to be based upon the level of consciousness it had attained. This did not, of course, mean for Lenin that the Party simply passively *reflected* an achieved level of consciousness. On the contrary, the Party always took its cue from the *advanced* workers in specifying the tasks that lay ahead, in promoting the struggle from which the mass would emerge with a more developed consciousness.

The crucial point to note, as far as Lenin's writings on the revolution of 1905–6 are concerned, is that he clearly recognised that the Party had reached a vital transitional point in its development. It was entering the third phase of its evolution and this marked the specification of new tasks, and the ascent to a new level of mass consciousness. In March 1905 Lenin self-consciously recognised the need for the Party to lift itself out of the organisational structure and patterns of behaviour appropriate to the second phase.

> The development of a mass working-class movement in Russia in connection with the development of Social Democracy is marked by three notable transitions. The first was the transition from narrow propagandist circles to wide economic agitation among the masses; the second was the transition to political agitation on a large scale and to open street demonstrations; the third was the transition to actual civil war, to direct revolutionary struggle, to the armed popular uprising. Each of these transitions was prepared, on the one hand, by socialist thought working mainly in one direction, and on the other, by the profound changes that had taken place in the conditions of life and in the whole mentality of the working class, as well as by the fact that increasingly wide strata of the working class were roused to more conscious and active struggle.[49]

The culmination of the revolution and its dénouement must, according to Lenin, be violent. There would come a time when the talking stopped, the time when politics as such became a matter of no moment. The political period of the revolution was but that phase in which classes became articulate, differentiated, conscious and organised – that is, attained their essential expression. The political period was, therefore, that period when the polarities revealed themselves and the imperative to choose was posed. It was the period of parley in which the forces of the two sides to the coming physical confrontation, drew themselves up into ranks and prepared themselves for the violent resolution of the conflict. The Party of the proletariat as the leader and organiser of one of the armies had to elaborate an organisational form to meet this situation. It must seek to win over or at least co-ordinate, the activities of *all* who were prepared to fight regardless even of their party affiliation.

> There should be an extremely discreet, tactful, and comradely attitude towards the workers, who are ready to die for freedom, who are organising and arming for the fight, who are in complete sympathy with the proletarian struggle, and who are yet divided from us by a lack of a Social-Democratic world outlook, by anti-Marxist prejudices, and by survivals of superannuated revolutionary views.[50]

Given the tasks, which flowed from Lenin's theoretical analysis, his views in particular of the limitations of politics and its necessary supercession by force, the tactics of the Party followed. It had to undertake the arming and training of all insurgent groups, co-ordinate their activities and attempt to win over sections of the army without whose help no armed insurrection could succeed.[51] All of this amounted not to adventurism, Jacobinism or Blanquism, as the Mensheviks alleged; it was rather a specification of the obligations which, according to Lenin, the revolution would impose upon the Social Democrats and which they would be irresponsible to shun. It follows then that 'in a period of civil war the ideal party of the proletariat is a *fighting party*'.[52]

Lenin's views on party reorganisation must, therefore, be seen in the light of the following factors: (1) the revolution itself had brought the mass to a level of consciousness undreamt of a few years previously. There was, therefore, no danger that they would be waylaid by bourgeois ideologists; (2) the revolution itself had produced *de facto* if not *de jure* conditions of comparative political freedom where the elective principle could realistically operate in Party affairs; (3) following the Second Party Congress a Party Centre had been created which, though split, had created a structure for the organisational coherence and political articulation of the proletarian interest. The further progress of the revolution would purge the Party of Menshevik illusions; (4) the revolution had brought the contradictions in Russian social life to the apogee of their expression which could only be resolved through armed conflict. Civil war had been placed on the immediate agenda, hence the Party had to become a militant fighting party, marching as to war and organised according to the precepts of democratic centralism but retaining its secret underground network.

CLASS FORMATION AND CLASS CONSCIOUSNESS

Lenin's analysis of the revolutionary process was built around a dialectical pattern which he clearly believed was intrinsic to the events he was observing and participating in. Each phase of the process presumed a previous one, yet had to transcend it, raise it to a higher plane. Within each phase two forces were in contestation – revolutionary action whose object was to heighten and develop the process, and counter-revolutionary reaction whose objective was to arrest or reverse the process. Each phase of the struggle heightened and clarified the issues involved, each phase led to a progressive strengthening of the organisational basis and degree of consciousness of the two camps. Within this dialectical pattern revolutionary action was the thesis vying with the antithetical forces of reaction. Out of the struggle emerged, at each transitional stage, a new synthesis of heightened consciousness and more cohesive organisation.

> As this struggle develops, class consciousness and solidarity will inevitably grow in the ranks of the revolution and in the ranks of the reaction, and sharper and more ruthless forms of struggle will inevitably be adopted. Nothing could be more effective than these rapid transitions from 'days of freedom' to 'months of shooting' in diminishing the ranks of the passive and indifferent, in drawing new strata and elements into the struggle, in developing the class consciousness of the masses by throwing into vivid relief first one then another aspect of the autocracy . . . The quicker and the sharper these transitions occur, the sooner will matters come to a head owing to the inevitable preponderance of the social forces on the side of freedom.[53]

It was, according to Lenin, only in the course of the actual struggle for the democratic revolution in Russia, that the economic groupings of society emerged with that degree of organisational cohesion and conscious articulation of their general interests and objectives which alone entitled them to be called classes. Since the economic substructure of capitalist society was dominated by two essential economic groupings, this process was the process whereby the strata or semi-estates which no longer had a central role to play in the productive system, the strata whose existence was continually being eroded by capitalist development, whose situation was therefore marginal – these strata were increasingly obliged to align themselves behind one or other of the essential classes. Their political organs reflected the instability and pre-cariousness of their economic existence; their ideological vacil-lation reflected the marginal and transitory position they occupied in the modern productive process. 'Undoubtedly, the idealogical confusion of the Trudoviks also reflects the extremely precarious position of the small producer in present-day society.'[54] 'That the petty bourgeoisie should display such instability is quite explicable from the economic point of view.'[55] Lenin's whole economic analysis had, after all, pointed to the inescapable and remorseless erosion of the independence of the small peasant and artisan. Thus Lenin could never view the Socialist Revolutionaries or the Trudoviks as constituting a serious threat to eventual Social-Democratic hegemony over the rural proletariat. The peasantry, as such, was a social estate not a class. As a social estate it could not aspire to realise the degree of organisational cohesion or level of articulate consciousness of the proletariat or bour-geoisie. As a social estate it was in the process of being broken down into its proletarian and bourgeois constituents by the progress of capitalism. With the success of the democratic revolution and the rapid acceleration of capitalism, therewith of open *class* struggle in the countryside, the peasants as such would cease to have a role to play.

> Of course, not being a class organisation, the Peasant Union also contains elements of disintegration. The more imminent the victory of the peasant uprising and the fuller that victory, the more imminent will be the disintegration of this Union. But up to the victory of the peasant uprising, and for such a victory, the Peasant Union is a mighty and viable organisation.[56]

The process of the democratic revolution was, for Lenin, the process in which, for the first time, the differences *between* classes attained conscious expression and refined themselves, and it was the process in which the differences *within* the two essential classes were pared down to relative insignificance. All the owners gradually coalesced around one political centre and so did the non-owners.

In a society based upon class divisions, the struggle between the hostile classes is bound, at a certain stage of its development, to become a political struggle. The most purposeful, most comprehensive and specific expression of the political struggle of classes is the struggle of parties . . . in the class struggle there can be no neutrals; in capitalist society, it is impossible to 'abstain' from taking part in the exchange of commodities or labour power. And exchange inevitably gives rise to economic and then to political struggle.[57]

The basic economic antagonism of capitalist society must, according to Lenin, work its way through to its achieved articulation in political form.

Lenin's argument about the generation of revolutionary consciousness was along lines familiar enough to us by now. Just as he had earlier argued that the proletariat did not begin the period of strikes or 'industrial practice' with anything like even a shared awareness of economic interest; just as he had earlier argued that first a shared *economic* consciousness then a *political* consciousness arose only from the *practice* of the proletariat, so, now he argued the same case in respect of revolutionary consciousness. The proletariat and peasantry would not, *at the beginning of the revolution*, have any clear view of the irreconcilability of their interests with those of the bourgeoisie or even the landlords. Substantial numbers of them reposed their faith in the utopian constitutional projects of the Kadets or the equally utopian dreams of immediate populist socialism. Only in the actual course of struggle, only from suffering from the treachery of the bourgeoisie, only be observing what policies were endorsed by the political representatives of the different economic groups – only by undergoing this compressed education through action did revolutionary consciousness begin to dawn. The proletariat became aware that its demands could not be realised within the framework of the bourgeois-preferred scheme of power-sharing. The peasantry became aware that the realisation of its demand for the land was incompatible with the survival of the landlords as a class and fell outside the purview of liberal economic ambitions.

We approach at this point the climax of Lenin's early writings. What was but immanent in the fabric of Russian economic and social life, ill-developed and disguised by feudal remnants, was precipitated into the full light of day. The tensions and immanent polarity of the economic basis found their reflection in political groupings, and impressed themselves upon the minds of the masses. The heightened practice of a revolutionary epoch translated theoretical propositions into urgent political strategies, made manifest the whole physiognomy of a society.

> There is not the slightest doubt that the revolution will teach Social Democratism to the masses of the workers in Russia. The revolution will confirm the programme and tactics of Social Democracy in actual practice by demonstrating the true nature of the various classes of society, by demonstrating the bourgeois character of our democracy and the real aspirations of the peasantry.[58]
> All the main social groups in Russia today have already, in one way or another, taken the path of open and mass political activity. Open action relentlessly reveals the basic differences of the interests involved. The parties are seen in their true colours. Events, with an iron hand, sort out the adherents of the various classes and make them decide who is on one side and who is on the other.[59]

The Social Democrats, as we have pointed out above, were able to arrive at the future general trend of development through extrapolation from theory. Their prescient awareness of emerging class patterns, and the history of other countries, was, according to Lenin, the whole source of their strength and the sure basis of their political strategies. The Party learned, became conscious of its role, from analysing the objective economic and social milieu in which it was working and from reflecting upon 'mankind's far wider collective experience which has left its impress upon the history of international democracy and international Social Democracy, and has been systematised by the foremost representatives of revolutionary thought'.[60] Systematised past experience, of economic patterns, social development and the progress of revolutions yields up trends, general laws which operate in specified situations. It produces therefore an ordered accumulation of knowledge of other economies, and other societies, which have earlier traversed the path which Russia was treading. The Social Democrats, therefore, were blessed with the power of prescience. They possessed a key to the portals of the future, a predictive model able to specify, in general terms, the trends which history was striving to realise.

Systematised past experience was, however, accessible as a source of inspiration only to exceptional and relatively privileged individuals, for

> . . . while society is based on the oppression and exploitation of millions of working people, only the few can learn directly from that experience. The masses have to learn mostly from their own experience, paying dearly for every lesson. The lesson of 9 January was a hard one, but it revolutionised the temper of the entire proletariat of the whole of Russia.[61]

Lenin clearly distinguished between the way in which the Social-Democratic *intelligentsia* came to consciousness and the generation of consciousness *in the mass*. For the mass the road to consciousness was not and could not be through reflection, study and extrapolation. Consciousness was rather imparted sensuously. It was felt in the solidarity and strength communicated to the individual in a mass demonstration or strike. It was communicated empirically, experimentally, through immediate observation of phenomena which the mass encountered and confronted: 'enlightenment is not obtained from books alone, and not so much from books even as from the very progress of the revolution, which opens the eyes of the people and gives them a political schooling.'[62] 'Experience in the struggle enlightens more rapidly and more profoundly than years of propaganda under other circumstances.'[63]

Revolutionary events and the drama of a rapidly changing open conflict of political parties roused the individual from his workaday apathy and concern with his own particular problems. Millions were drawn into the maelstrom of political life and obliged to declare where they stood. In practical terms this means they were obliged to identify with one or other political party.

> We must remember what a tremendous educational and organising power the revolution has, when mighty historical events force the man in the street out of his remote corner, garret, or basement and make a *citizen* out of him. Months of revolution sometimes educate citizens more quickly and fully than decades of political stagnation.[64]

It would purge them of all the many illusions with which they began their political activity, it would inevitably confront them with the coercive power of the reaction and that, as much as Social-Democratic propaganda, would teach them the truths of Social-Democratic theory. The reaction as forcibly as the revolution would teach Social Democracy to the masses. It would, with each blow painfully felt by the revolutionary people, teach them the vital importance of organising, for their own defence, and for an eventual bid for power. In the revolution the organising capacity of the masses was raised, according to Lenin, by a factor of millions. '. . . the organising abilities of the people, particularly of the proletariat, but also of the peasantry, are revealed a million times more strongly, fully and productively in periods of revolutionary whirlwind than in periods of so-called calm.'[65] 'Mention a period in Russian or world history, find any six months or six years, when as much was done for the free and independent organisation of the masses of the people as was done during the six weeks of the revolutionary whirlwind.'[66] It was *par excellence* the period when, for the first time, 'the masses of the people themselves, with all their virgin primitiveness and simple, rough determination begin to make history, begin to put "principles and theories" immediately and directly into practice'.[67]

It was in the sense that revolutionary periods enormously accelerated the development of consciousness and of class organisation that Lenin described them as 'locomotives of history' and 'festivals of the oppressed and the exploited'.[68] They were the locomotives of history in that they distilled in practical activity, and therefore impressed upon the minds of the masses, the essential contradictions of social life long discerned by theory. The nature and fate of the revolution was, as Lenin pointed out,

> determined by the objective combination of the operation of the various social forces. The character of these forces has been defined theoretically by the Marxist analysis of Russian life; at present it is being determined in practice by open action by groups and classes in the course of the revolution.[69]

Revolutionary practice clarified, developed and highlighted class configurations whose nascent form had been uncovered by theoretical analysis.

What Lenin was arguing was that the gradual, almost imperceptible, progress of capitalism in transforming objective economic relations in Russia proceeded almost unnoticed for decades. The economic fact that this progress had eroded the independence of millions of small producers, and severed the tie with the soil of millions more, did not, for a long time, find reflection in popular conceptions or the mass organisation of the dispossessed. Revolutionary periods were precisely those periods when this lag, between objective situation and subjective appreciation of it, was rapidly overcome. The class was enormously extended; millions who in 'normal times' could not stir themselves to conscious consideration of the reality of their situation, or rested content with outmoded explanations of it, were now obliged to reflect where their best interest lay. The class was constantly obliged to define its position to every event, to every other class and to the state. It had to organise to press its general demands and create a political organ to articulate them. It became, in short, a class properly so-called. This was how Lenin reviewed the process:

> The real, definitive and mass separation of the proletariat as a class, in opposition to all other bourgeois parties, can only occur when the history of *its own* country reveals to the proletariat *the entire character* of the bourgeoisie as a class, as a political unit – the entire character of the petty bourgeoisie as a section, as a definite ideological and political unit revealing itself in some open broadly political activities. We must incessantly explain to the proletariat the theoretical truths about the nature of the class interests of the bourgeoisie and petty bourgeoisie in capitalist society. These truths, however, will be driven home to really broad masses of the proletariat only when these classes will have visible, tangible experience of the behaviour of the parties of one class or another, when the clear realisation of their class nature is supplemented by the immediate reaction of the proletarian mind to the whole character of the bourgeois parties.[70]

The masses, according to Lenin, arrived at the consciousness of the need for *revolutionary* activity in precisely the same way as they had earlier acquired an awareness of the need for economic solidarity and, later, political activity. They acquired such consciousness in and through their immediate activity and not through the mediation of abstract theory: '. . . the advanced representatives of the popular masses have themselves arrived, not as a result of theoretical reasoning, but under the impact of the growing movement, at new and higher tasks of the struggle.'[71]

THE REALISATION OF THEORY THROUGH PRACTICE

Let us now, by way of conclusion, attempt to set Lenin's writings on the revolution of 1905 in their relation to his earlier ideas. Clearly Lenin's ideas had changed quite substantially. He elevated certain themes to a central position which hitherto had enjoyed only a marginal significance. Others which once enjoyed the limelight were now held to be inappropriate. To many commentators these are marks of Lenin's inconsistency and incoherence. Hopefully it will be conceded that changelessness is not always the sole, nor most important, characteristic of the coherence of a man's ideas.

What I have argued in this chapter is that Lenin's writings in this period can only be comprehended in the light of his theoretical findings and his 'theoretical' mode of analysis. I am aware that I am using theoretical in a rather esoteric way and it would be as well if I briefly elaborated what I have in mind.

Lenin's early theoretical (or socio-economic) analysis of Russian society had, as we have seen, led him to establish a number of propositions.

1. The independence of the peasants and artisans was being eroded. Their social-estate existence was being destroyed through the process of *class* differentiation consequent on the spread of capitalism. The peasantry was dissolving into its bourgeois and proletarian constituent elements.

2. Plekhanov and Akselrod had demonstrated the weakness of the Russian bourgeoisie as a class, a precept of orthodoxy confirmed by Lenin's theoretical analysis.

3. Due to the low development of capitalist forces of production there could be no question of an immediate advance to socialism. The democratic revolution alone was feasible. The proletariat however, because of 2. above, would have to lead that revolution.

4. In leading the democratic revolution the proletariat would have to rely on other social forces to bring down autocracy. Theory had, in 1. above, demonstrated the objective bonds

between the proletariat and the rural proletariat. The proletariat was 'the natural representative of all Russia's exploited'.

The process of the revolution was, for Lenin, the process whereby these propositions derived from economic or theoretical premises, worked themselves through to the political sphere and impressed themselves upon the consciousness of the masses in the contest first of political parties, then in the physical confrontation of civil war. The polarities which theory abstractly apprehended as immanent in the economic structure of society were revealed and realised in the heightened practice of the revolution.

The revolutionary period became, for Lenin, a sort of nodal point at which economic classes assumed their more or less adequate political expression. The apparent unity of objective at the commencement of the revolution was rudely shattered as each group was obliged to articulate its demands and define its position apropos of all others. Clarity began to emerge, initial illusions were purged, and the further the revolution progressed the more political dispositions were polarised; that is, the more accurately they reflected the basic antagonism of economic life. The centre moved to the right; it betrayed its initial promises, and was progressively dominated by the big bourgeoisie. The actual pusillaminity and cowardice of the bourgeoisie as a whole substantiated therefore, the prognostications of orthodoxy confirmed by theory. The mass who followed the centre and the utopian left democrats (the Socialist Revolutionaries and Trudoviks), learned from this treachery and from the virulence of the reaction which followed it; they were forced alongside the Social Democrats. The irresolution and political waverings of the peasant parties mirrored, in Lenin's view, the precariousness and volatile instability of the peasant economic situation long recognised by theory. Experience of the revolution obliged the peasants to recognise the proletariat as their natural representative and political mouthpiece. Practice again confirmed the insights of theory. The process of the revolution for Lenin, was the process wherein the one fundamental and inescapable contradiction of Russian social life, the contradiction between wage-labour and all forms of exploitation, was refined, made conscious and articulate in the struggle of political parties which increasingly came to represent the standpoints of the contending classes. It was the story of how classes emerged out of the cocoon of mere economic interest groups and fledged themselves in the open light of political practice. From being but congeries of economic interests they became organised, conscious, national, articulate, political and polarised groups. The welter of casual groupings at the commencement of the revolution was pared down to reveal the essential polarity between the party of the exploited and that of the exploiters.

The proletariat would, however, be able to emerge as the acknowledged leader of all Russia's exploited only if it abided by certain conditions, for theory stipulated a general *potential* and not a certitude. It outlined the objective trends but not their specific delineation, the general parameters within which the proletariat could win support; it would not drop spontaneously into its hands. The proletariat must, above all, have faith in the prognosis of emerging class/political polarity and base its whole strategy on this faith. Accordingly at no stage could it concede hegemony to any other group or class, for the root antagonism could only be resolved by force and for this dénouement the people had to be prepared in organisational terms as well as in popular consciousness. Finally, the political phase in which the antagonistic forces of modern society drew up their ranks was supplanted by the phase of civil war. The tasks of the Party altered substantially in nature and its organisational base had to be restructured accordingly.

Just as Lenin's theoretical findings worked themselves out in the practice of the revolution, so too the methodology he utilised in his theoretical work was applied to the cardinal questions of the development of consciousness and Party organisation. The teleology of capitalist development through ascending phases to its apogee or essential expression was matched by Lenin's account of the development of consciousness and of the Party. Each of these progressed through demarcated transitional stages to its consummation. Thus, through the heightened accelerating influence of revolutionary events, in which the essential polarity of modern society was made manifest, and which obliged interests to be declared and sides chosen, the proletariat became conscious of the maximum objectives compatible with the given economic level of society. These maximum objectives became, in the logic of the revolutionary situation, the only appropriate goals. To aspire to less was utopian and would fore-doom the revolution to failure. In the light of these goals, expressing as they did the maximum development of consciousness attainable under the dominion of capitalism, the Party was compelled to organise the proletariat and its allies for their attainment. It was compelled, therefore to become as broad, extensive, representative and militant (in the exact meaning of that word) as the conscious proletariat it represented. It attained its essential expression as a vehicle of class war, albeit in pursuit of goals which could not go beyond the democratic revolution pressed to its most extreme form. Only the most extreme and radical democracy was, in any case, the appropriate goal, for, true to his methodology, Lenin estimated the significance of the democratic phase of the revolution solely in terms of its contribution to the further unfolding of history; that is, its contribution to preparing the bases for the battle for socialism.

Lenin's writings both before and during the revolution of 1905–6 displayed an unswerving consistency of themes and an almost unbelievably dogmatic prediction and appraisal of the way things *must* turn out. It would come much closer to the truth to invert the general finding that Lenin trimmed his theory to suit his actions. It would be more accurate to say that Lenin slotted historical events into a fore-ordained pattern. For Lenin the events of these years were but history's realisation of the prognostications of prior theory. They were not mysterious, chaotic or amorphous events to which one could only react instinctively. They were, on the contrary, only to be understood as manifestations of underlying trends whose basic direction theory had long previously discerned.

In all these respects Lenin's writings on the revolution of 1905 pressed to their logical conclusion all of the themes we have observed in the whole corpus of his earlier works. The potentialities given by the theoretical analysis had been pushed to their ultimate extension. Practice, in Lenin's view, had confirmed and concretely realised the findings of theory. Lenin's structure of thought, constructed around his early economic and social analysis, was complete; it could go no further. What followed was, in more than one sense, an anti-climax, a holding operation, until a new theoretical analysis began to emerge and indicate new potentialities for practice.

CHAPTER 10

1908–11: Problems of Cohesion in a Period of·Reaction

These were hard years for Lenin, the hardest of his life. They were years of exile and wandering, a European round of seedy apartments and spartan living. The movement inside Russia had exhausted itself and its remnants were being methodically cut down by Stolypin's draconian policies. To all intents and purposes the Party as an organised structure had ceased to exist. The situation was even worse than that faced by the *Iskrists* in the 1900–2 period. All the major centres of Social Democratic activity were repeatedly hit by mass arrests followed by an inevitable decline in the number of Party members.[1] In Moscow, for instance, where the Bolsheviks had had 2000 members in 1905, their numbers shrank to 500 by the end of 1908 and by mid-1909 there remained only 260 members of the Party.[2]

Outside Russia the warring Bolshevik and Menshevik factions, after *de facto* collaboration in 1905, fell back into the bitterest recriminations on the causes of failure. The rot went even deeper than this, for the Bolsheviks and Mensheviks were themselves suffering from deep internal divisions which threatened to explode into a host of independent grouplets and factions. Many of Lenin's own most faithful and talented disciples deserted him for one reason or another: Gorky, Bogdanov, Lunacharsky, Aleksinsky, Pokrovsky and Volsky – the intellectual stars in the old Bolshevik firmament – now went their own ways. Zinoviev and Kamenev were the only two he could absolutely rely upon, though Stalin was already beginning to emerge as one of Lenin's principal lieutenants within Russia. As if this were not enough, the nationally-based socialist parties of the empire – the Letts, the *two* Polish parties, the Bund, the Caucasian Regional Committee – having no authoritative, all-national Party centre to look to, became increasingly autonomous and confounded the existing confusion by backing now one side now another in the internecine feud.

The very conditions of exile of course exacerbated these dissensions and in a milieu of hopelessness, bickering, intrigue and the settling of personal scores, the ever present *agents-provocateurs* were given a heaven-sent opportunity for manoeuvre. All this constant, petty in-fighting might have gone on relatively unnoticed in the eyes of the wider world had it not been for the series of melodramatic episodes and scandals which irresistibly attracted curiosity and which, in their turn, provided further grounds for factional squabbles. There were the Bolshevik expropriation squads, for instance, who carried out a series of flamboyant and daring raids on banks, culminating in 1908 in the routing by bombs of an armed detachment escorting a vast sum of government money in Tiflis. There were the curious and dubious negotiations of the Bolsheviks to supply arms, at a considerable profit, to Lbov's bandits in the Urals. There was the infamous affair of the Schmidt inheritance in which the Bolsheviks cozened money from two heiresses by marrying them off to their agents only to find their own agents unreliable. Scandal followed scandal: bombs discovered in Berlin, agents arrested for passing counterfeit notes in diverse parts of Europe, protestations, accusations, suicides, threats and even brawling between factions were symptoms of the deep malaise which threatened the very existence of Russian Social Democracy in this period. Up to the end of 1911 at least, its situation both within Russia and outside was desperate.

There were, for Lenin, some fitful rays of light in these drab years. There were brief interludes of gaiety and relaxation with Gorky in idyllic Capri. There was also Lenin's relationship with the talented and beautiful Inessa Armand of which some make so much from so slender a stock of evidence. No doubt Lenin was infatuated with Inessa, no doubt her charm and comfort sustained him at the darkest moments of those bleak years; we still, however, have no evidence that they were sexually intimate and, even if we did have, it is difficult to see how this could have affected Lenin's political stance at this time.

THE REACTION TRIUMPHANT: 1908–11

The period 1908–11 was, for Lenin, the period of the reactionary offensive. The Tsar progressively clawed back all the concessions the democratic movement had forced him to concede in 1905. When each successive Duma proved too radical to stomach, he resorted to the simple, though illegal, expedient of further narrowing the franchise until the big landowners were assured of an absolute majority. Coincidentally, the *de facto* freedom of the press was whittled away by administrative harassment and proscription. The revolutionary parties were hounded as severely as they had been before the revolution, and even the comparatively pliant and responsible Constitutional Democrats were never accorded a legal existence. 'Stolypin's neckties' dotted the Russian landscape as a gruesome reminder that the regime was out for revenge on the revolutionaries and that any anti-state activity would be met with summary field martial and death on the gallows. Some six hundred were executed in this way in the aftermath of 1905 and thousands more were to suffer arbitrary administrative arrest and exile without trial.

In the countryside Stolypin's agrarian reforms were put into operation with an uncustomary rapidity which signalled the regime's realisation that it had to find more positive measures to consolidate broader mass support for the status quo. In 1905 the Tsar and his ministers had opened the franchise to the peasants as a whole, expecting the great mass of the peasantry to express their ancestral faith in the 'Little Father' and show up the turbulent aggressive urban workers for the small minority that they were. The Trudoviks in the First and Second Dumas rudely shattered these rosy expectations. Their extreme radical sentiments, especially their insistence upon the immediate nationalisation or distribution of the big estates, brought home to the autocracy the impossibility of using the broad peasant masses as a counter-balance to the revolutionary aspirations of the workers. Stolypin's agrarian reforms were, according to Lenin, the economic counterpart of the narrowing of the franchise: both were expressly based upon a policy of building a base for the regime not in the peasantry at large, but among the landlords and the 'strong', the rich peasants. This was to be achieved by implementing two inter-related policies. The first aimed to encourage the development of a class of prosperous peasant proprietors by allowing the peasants (where the commune. had so decided by a two-thirds majority) to leave the commune and claim title to the land hitherto allotted to them in strips as one consolidated holding which was not to be subject to future redistribution. The second attempted to overcome the evident land hunger in the central and southern provinces by opening up vast tracts of land beyond the Urals for resettlement. In this way, it was hoped, the migration of impoverished (and therefore troublesome) peasants eastwards, to be established on homesteads with relatively generous allotments of land which were to be the personal property of the peasants, would provide a solution to endemic agrarian unrest.

THE AGRARIAN QUESTION

Throughout this period Lenin continued to devote to the agrarian question a large part of his considerable energies. He utilised all the available statistical abstracts, government reports, relevant Duma debates, reminiscenses of administrators and Trudovik statements to reinforce and develop his own agrarian programme in the light of changing conditions. Article followed article from his over-fecund pen to impress upon any doubters the fact that the agrarian problem remained the outstanding problem of the democratic revolution. Lenin's continual and painstaking analysis marked him off from his Menshevik opponents and lay at the basis of his whole political strategy. In the Menshevik camp there was no one of any prominence who did anything more than dabble with the complexities of the agrarian question. They had a policy, no doubt, but the programme of municipalisation of the landed estates, to be carried out by popularly elected local committees, was never based upon the same rigorous economic analysis of conditions in the countryside and, more importantly, appeared to have but little bearing on their other tactics orientated towards the workers and the liberals.[3] Municipalisation was, as it were, a policy hurriedly cobbled together to meet an unfortunate but inescapable problem which 'orthodox' Marxists should not really have had to face. Once decided upon, the policy was, occasionally, brought out for a ritual polish then put safely back in store to gather new encrustations.

Lenin, in contrast, had made a proletarian–peasant alliance the linchpin of his strategy in 1905 and saw no reason to change his attitude during the reaction. On the contrary, the Junker solution to the agrarian problem, which Stolypin was hurriedly pushing through, not only made a proletarian–peasant alliance more imperative, it also made it more likely.

The imperative derived from the fact (long recognised by Kautsky) that the liberal bourgeoisie had now become definitely counter-revolutionary and, in tying their coat-tails to the antiquated ox-cart of landlord political domination, had tied themselves to policies which expressly inhibited the development of capitalist relations in agriculture. The objective significance of Stolypin's reforms was not that they were encouraging modern capitalist agriculture by releasing the peasant with land from the commune – that part of Stolypin's reforms was but a *de jure* recognition of what in fact had *already* occurred. It was, rather, that through such devices as the establishment of homesteads and the Resettlement Programme he could preserve the feudal structure of land-lording patterns, therewith the whole nexus of feudal relations in agriculture intact and solid. He therefore preserved, for a time at least, the economic base of a class upon which the autocracy overtly relied. Far from encouraging the free and open development of capitalist agrarian relations, the import of Stolypin's policies was to restrict and curtail them. The fundamental contradiction of the Russian countryside was, in Lenin's view,

> the contradiction between capitalism, which is highly developed in our industry and considerably developed in our agriculture, and *the system of land ownership*, which remains medieval, feudal. There is no way out of this situation unless the old system of land ownership is radically broken up.[4]

In view of the crucial importance which this finding had for Lenin's social and political analysis, we must probe deeper into Lenin's justificatory arguments.

Let us look first at some of the facts to which Lenin repeatedly returns in respect to landholding patterns in Russia at this time. According to his statistics some ten and a half million peasant households, comprising approximately fifty million poor peasants, held in total approximately seventy-five million dessiatines of land. The thirty thousand largest landlords owned only slightly less than the ten and a half million peasant households, their estates totalling some seventy million dessiatines.[5] Lenin's whole analysis of the agrarian problem derived directly from these facts. His argument was that the maintenance of the vast latifundia (the top 700 landlords owned more than 30,000 dessiatines *each*[6]) demanded the retention in the countryside of a huge agricultural reserve army of thoroughly impoverished peasants.[7] The latifundia had to have labour and the way they obtained labour was to rent land or pasturage in return for labour-service. The peasantry, being unable to survive without renting land, were obliged to accept whatever usurious terms were demanded by the landlords. The typical return the landlord exacted for rented land was not cash but an obligation to work his land for a specified period of time. Naturally the peasants worked off their rental obligations with less than enthusiasm and, in any case, brought to their task the worst of techniques and draught animals and the most antiquated implements. The net result of this vicious circle was that the peasants remained totally impoverished, immobile and subject to the most appalling famine. The landlords resorted to ever more usurious terms to squeeze a profit from the bonded peasants[8] and were rewarded consequently with yields falling even below the pitiful productivity of poor peasant farmers.[9] Agricultural technique remained rooted in medieval primitiveness. The scale of production on the latifundia was consequently exceedingly small-scale, the unit of production being no more than the members of a household working off its rental debt on a designated plot of land. All the worst, most antiquated and least efficient aspects of agricultural production were, therefore, concentrated in the large estates. The basic cause of this economic retardation (which, of course, by limiting the home market had a profound effect on all other sectors of industry and commerce[10]) was the continued prevalence of labour-service. Some two-thirds of the Russian peasantry were subject to one or many of the myriad forms which labour-service or bondage assumed.[11] Given the land-holding system, this situation with all its baneful consequences was inevitable. The peasants had to rent land to survive and they therefore had to accept the terms offered by the landlords. Having no cash with which to pay rent they were obliged to bond themselves to work off their debt and in so doing paid triple the price.[12] The landlords for their part had to rely upon what amounted to an indentured work-force. Being unable or unwilling to introduce efficient capitalist agricultural techniques and machinery, they were unable to offer the wages which the free competitive hiring of labourers demanded. They, therefore, had a direct interest in retaining a vast pool of surplus poor peasants obliged through pressing necessity to accept bonded conditions of hire.

We are led, finally, to Lenin's alternative to Stolypin's Junker policy. It can be encapsulated in one phrase: nationalisation of the landed estates. This, Lenin argued, was the only measure which would, once and for all, break the power of the feudal landlords and pre-empt the possibility of an autocratic restoration. It was the only measure which would satisfy the poor peasants for, at one stroke, their holdings could be doubled.[13] It was, furthermore, the only measure which could provide the much-needed stimulus to the development of capitalism in Russian agriculture.[14] Land would be made available by the state for a reasonable cash rent, not for labour-service. This would itself enormously boost commodity production and the home market. Moreover, the agriculturalist, having access to land for a modest rent, would thereby be encouraged to spend his available capital on the purchase of modern agricultural machinery and the hiring of efficient free wage-labour rather than, as hitherto, disperse it all on the purchase of land. Nationalisation and the free availability of land to rent would, therefore, free an enormous volume of agricultural capital to pursue its proper ends – raising productivity through improved technique and modern machinery. It would enormously extend the development of capitalist relations in the countryside and thereby accentuate the emergent class polarity and transform the mentality of agrarian workers.[15] The agrarian wage-workers freed from bondage and exclusively relying upon the sale of their labour power would be forced to recognise that, apart from the closest unity with the urban workers, they would have no future.[16]

Nationalisation of the landed estates was emphatically not a socialist measure in Lenin's considered and oft-repeated view.[17] It was a radically anti-feudal measure.

> There is nothing more erroneous than the opinion that the nationalisation of the land has anything in common with socialism, or even with equalised land tenure. Socialism, as we know, means the abolition of commodity economy. Nationalisation, on the other hand, means converting the land into the property of the state, and such a conversion does not in the least affect private farming on the land.[18]

This democratic solution, even if all the land is transferred to the peasants without compensation, does not and cannot in the least encroach on the foundations of capitalist society – the power of money, commodity production, and the domination of the market.[19]

On this basis, Lenin clearly and emphatically distinguished the intent of his agrarian programme from that of the Socialist Revolutionaries and Trudoviks. No state decrees could 'legislate' an equalisation of land tenure or an advance into socialism, for, as long as commodity production and the hiring of wage-labour prevailed in the countryside, any paper equalisation would swiftly be eroded just as all the elaborate restrictions on renting or alienating of communal allotment land had been ignored wholesale. As long as Russian capitalism remained relatively under-developed and ill-elaborated there could be no talk of an advance to socialism. The largest single factor retarding Russia's general capitalist development was agrarian impoverishment, itself inseparable from the continued vitality of feudal relations in agriculture which, in turn, derived from the structure of land ownership. The elimination of the landlords and their supercession by the state as a universal landlord was, in Lenin's analysis, an objective requirement for the fullest and freest development of capitalist productive forces and of the class struggle within the countryside. It was, therefore, the solution to the agrarian problem most advantageous to the proletariat. It would oblige the bourgeoisie to come out openly as the masters of the country-side and of the state and would deprive them of the ability to hide behind the coat-tails of the landlords, as they had done hitherto in both these spheres.

ASSESSMENT OF THE LIBERALS

As far as external threats were concerned, the principal danger to the 1905 synthesis came from the liberals. The main enemy was not the hard Right but the flabby Centre. Barely a week went by in this whole period which did not see an article or extended reference by Lenin demonstrating the correctness of his 1905 analysis of their role. He followed remorselessly their every tactical shift and every major policy statement, distilling from each the message he never tired of repeating: the bourgeoisie was counter-revolutionary; it had long since ceased to be democratic; it has indeed lapsed into degeneracy. With each confirmation, his contempt grew and his epithets became more loaded and savage. He talked of 'the honeyed lies . . . of the spineless and unprincipled liberal oligarchy' of the Constitutional Democrats.[20] They were, he maintained, craven, grovelling, spineless and base.[21] His imagery became on occasions quite inhuman – he talked of 'the liberal pig, which deems itself educated, but in fact is dirty, repulsive, overfat and smug'.[22] The liberals had become mere trash, feckless, cowardly and fat – the Billy Bunters of the revolution, full of schemes but incapable of following them through, yelping and squealing whenever chastised from on high.

Their weakness and servility was a product of their class situation. Caught between revolution and reaction, fearing the former more than the latter, they had made common cause with the Right. Having delivered themselves up to the Right by foreaking the revolutionary movement in the expectation of reaping the rewards of its 'responsible' stand, they had reaped the inevitable reward of being treated with contempt by the autocracy and reduced to insignificance even in the Duma by the progressive narrowing of the franchise. This, for Lenin, described the ineluctable progress of the liberals and Kadets during this period. It was, in his view, a brilliant demonstration of his analysis at the beginning of 1905, which was itself modelled on Marx's analysis of 1848–51. The old regime made token concessions to buy off the liberals. The revolutionaries were isolated and dealt with. The regime then moved against the liberals, progressively withdrawing the sops earlier dispensed and reducing them to impotence. It was this situation, according to Marx, which provided the basis for the rise of Bonapartism.

With the proletarian–peasant democratic movement temporarily exhausted and the bourgeoisie reduced to a political cipher, the regime created a situation in which it had ample space to manoeuvre to use the budget and the franchise to curry favour now with one sectional interest, now with another.

In the science of history, this device of a government which retains the essential features of absolutism is called Bonapartism. In this case, it is not definite classes that serve as a support, or not they alone, and not chiefly, but hand-picked elements, mostly from among various dependent sections of the population.[23]

The whole 3 June System inaugurated and dominated by Stolypin, was, in Lenin's view, a purposefully constructed scheme to keep the power of the Right, Centre, and the bourgeois liberal Left in approximate balance. The regime could, in this way play one group off against another as occasion demanded. There were, he argued, two majorities possible in the Duma, a coalition of the Right with the Octobrists, or a coalition of Octobrists with Kadets. When the government was in a repressive mood it leaned on the former, when it sought to curry popular favour by moderate reforms it cultivated the latter.

> Thus there have been two possible majorities in the Third Duma: (1) the Rights and the Octobrists = 268 out of 437; (2) the Octobrists and the liberals = 120 and 115 = 235 out of 437. Both majorities are counter-revolutionary.[24]

The whole essence of the 3 June System rested upon the regime's manipulation of this situation of approximate parity – the classic condition for the rise of Bonapartism.

> It is due to a balance between the forces of the hostile or rival classes . . . the government may – provided there is a certain balance between the forces of these rivals – gain *greater* independence (within certain, rather narrow, limits, of course) than when either of these classes has a decisive superiority.[25]

Lenin's general argument had the great merit, as Geoffrey Hosking concedes in his study of the relationship between Government and Duma in the period, 'of demonstrating at one and the same time (as no Western work has yet done) both the government's urgent desire for co-operation with certain sections of society in passing reforms, and also the depth of political polarisation which made such co-operation ultimately impossible'.[26]

Stolypin's agrarian programme, therefore, became, in this analysis, an aspect of autocratic Bonapartism. It represented the autocracy's attempt to build up an agrarian kulak class as a counterbalance to the urban workers and as a substitute for the urban bourgeoisie which still entertained ideas above its station. The post-1908 regime in Russia had, in Lenin's view, become a frankly Bonapartist regime. Russia had arrived at the end of the classical cycle of reaction established by Marx. It had now exhausted all the techniques of maintaining the feudal political superstructure independent of the actual major class forces in Russia, but its techniques of manipulation were, at the same time, indicative of the fragility of the regime. Bonapartism could survive only as long as the revolutionary-democratic classes of the population were kept atomised and alternately cowed into submission or flattered with concessions. It was walking a tight-rope which would and must snap because the very policies of Bonapartism served to accentuate class divisions and served to heighten consciousness of the necessity for its revolutionary overthrow.

Bonapartism was, then, the necessary outcome of the bourgeoisie forsaking its pretensions to political power in order the better to defend its economic interest, which it saw threatened by the revolutionary movement. In France this had happened during an epoch when there had existed a situation of approximate parity in terms of the strength of the bourgeoisie and the proletariat. The bourgeoisie, being unable to resist the proletarian striving for socialism unaided, had handed power over to a military adventurer – it could not then expect the trappings of power. The situation in Russia was different to the extent that the bourgeoisie was unable to lead a *democratic* revolution. Hegemony, therefore, fell to the proletariat and, consequently, the democratic revolution assumed such a radical character that the bourgeoisie was unwilling to see it consummated. Like the French bourgeoisie almost half a century before, it became a Party of Order and to this end was prepared to countenance the almost untrammelled dominance of the executive. Pointedly Lenin drew the parallel between his appraisal of the Russian bourgeoisie and Marx's estimate of the French bourgeoisie of 1848; it was not only counter-revolutionary[27] but also 'toadying, vile, foul and brutal'.[28]

Lenin's attacks on the liberals were savage even by his permissive standards of impassioned polemic. His savagery is explained not so much by the fact that the liberals were counter-revolutionary for, after all, his class analysis had long previously told him they would be. It is, rather, because the Kadets still sustained the *pretence* of being a radical force. They kept up a facade of

259

pressing for democracy and popular freedom yet in *practice* were prepared to accept, albeit with some whimpers, every arbitrary restriction imposed by the executive. Lenin's contempt for their lachrymose snivelling and whimpering[29] is, at time, very reminiscent of Sorel's fearsome moral condemnation of the *fin-de-siècle* bourgeoisie as a class which had lost its nerve, lost its manliness and heroism, could no longer lead, could not, indeed, properly defend its own interests and no longer had a *raison d`être*. Lenin certainly shared Sorel's view that the liberals had become a corrupt force, a group which could only corrupt popular consciousness by continuing to peddle its utopian project of an organic gradual development towards constitutional freedoms when it knew full well that the whole course of Russian politics after 1905 irrefragably demonstrated that the exact opposite had occurred. To admit this, however, would be to admit its own apostasy in 1905 and to concede that the prognosis of the revolutionaries had been exactly fulfilled. Liberalism preferred to live a lie. In its head it was wedded to the old liberal ideals, yet in its stomach and in its pocket it was wedded to autocracy. For these reasons, Lenin argued, the Kadets must be ruthlessly exposed at every turn. For these reasons 'we must be *"Kadet-eaters" as a matter of principle*'[30] for 'without systematic, undeviating, day-by-day criticism of liberalism', the democratic idea could not be sustained.[31]

Lenin's stance with regard to the liberals during this period can come as no great surprise to us. He was, certainly, more venomous, but his general line on their instability and counter-revolutionary strivings had, as we have seen, been a central precept of the orthodoxy of Russian Marxism and had formed the central element of his analysis in 1905. It was not, however, a line which was agreed to by all sections of the Party. On the contrary, the Mensheviks began to distinguish themselves as a definite tendency in Russian Marxism precisely over the question of how to appraise the nature of liberalism and the prospects for a peaceful, legal development of the working-class movement in Russia.

MENSHEVIKS AND LIQUIDATORS

The Mensheviks as a whole certainly had a rosier view of the liberals and of the prospects for legal constitutional development than did Lenin. Like the liberals the Mensheviks believed that

Russia was entering a period of gradual evolution towards civic and political rights and a constitutional regime. The task of socialists, as they saw the situation, was to mobilise the workers and all the democratic elements of Russia in a campaign of gradual encroachment on the autocratic prerogatives. The first, and most vital right to press for was freedom of association. Without legal guarantees of freedom of association the workers would be unable even to group themselves into trade associations let alone political parties. This demand was, moreover, not a divisive one: on the contrary, it could anticipate the support of all the liberal and bourgeois groupings and parties which still had no legal existence. The prominence of the slogan 'freedom of association' in Menshevik propaganda at this time, was itself indicative of a political line which, in the course of these years for the first time sharply distinguished itself from Bolshevism.

The Bolsheviks, under Lenin's inexhaustible leadership, clung to the synthesis of 1905. The objective revolutionary situation still obtained. The revolution had not been consummated. The reaction was building a deeper and broader crisis. Therefore, the re-volutionary slogans of 1905 (for a democratic republic, for nationalisation of the large estates, for the eight-hour day) re-mained on the agenda. Not only were the old demands still appro-priate but the old organisation, firmly based upon the underground Party, remained the only possible vehicle for carrying on *revolutionary* propaganda and preparing for the coming revolution. The Mensheviks, too, accepted the fact that the revolution had not been consummated; they accepted the fact that the reaction had, for the moment, triumphed over an exhausted and demora-lised working class. The conclusions that they slowly arrived at from this stock-taking, though varied and often confused, showed a very distinct difference of emphasis from Lenin's. In general they were for trimming and moderating the demands of the socialists to a level more compatible with the existing very low level of working-class activity. They were conscious, too, of the need to tone down the radical slogans of 1905 which had resulted in the liberals being frightened into an alliance with the Right. With the working-class movement so depressed, it was imperative to secure the support of the radical bourgeois intelligentsia. The dis-location and torpor of the labour movement made a realistic setting of Party goals imperative – it would, they argued, be quite utopian to press for the revolutionary objectives of 1905 in the post-1908 period of strident reaction and working-class passivity. Attention must be directed once again to the immediate economic grievances of the workers. Their primary organisational units, the trade unions, must be built up and legalised as a precondition for convening a broad workers' congress whose task it would be to revivify the shattered Party structure, making it expressly proletarian and democratic, freed at last from the tutelage of the conspiratorial underground. The watchwords given out in the Menshevik press in this period were, therefore, far more modest and 'realistic' than those of the Bolsheviks. They exhorted the Party workers to take every advantage of all legal and quasi-legal openings for mobilising the working class. Particular attention was to be paid to the trade unions. The Party was to be made more open, more democratic and far broader.

Akselrod's idea of a workers' congress was not a new one. It had been floated in the immediate aftermath of the 1903 split as a means of revitalising the Party structure which, in the opinion of many, had atrophied into an intelligentsia élite concerned more with its internecine squabbles than with building a genuine workers' party. It had been taken up in this guise as a main plank of Menshevik propaganda in late 1905. By 1907, however, with the revolutionary wave clearly subsiding, the idea assumed a new, more emphatically radical, form. Akselrod now came to the conclusion that the Party was so degenerate, so rooted in its conspiratorial narrowness, that it was beyond resuscitation. The task of the workers' congress now became a more momentous one – it was no less than that of creating the Party anew.

> Thus it will fulfil its last duty to the proletariat, for it will itself help its advanced elements make a revolution, the aim of which is to eliminate the regime of the intelligentsia's tutelage over the labouring masses awakened to conscious political life and substitute for it the regime of their organised self-government. In this ideally favourable case the workers' congress will play the role of a proletarian constituent assembly, which will liquidate our old party system and initiate a new party regime in the ranks of Social Democracy and the advanced strata of the proletariat. Such a congress would be the greatest triumph for our party.[32]

It was this frank statement, of the need for an internal 'party revolution' which would 'liquidate' the old party system, which gave Lenin his opportunity to lambaste the Mensheviks. Immediately on the appearance of Akselrod's new formulation he carried the majority of the Bolshevik-dominated Fifth Congress of the Party in 1907 behind him, in a resolution condemning the attempt of certain intelligentsia groups 'to liquidate the existing organisation of the R.S.D.L.P. and to replace it with an amorphous association'.[33] Thereafter he developed a multifaceted and utterly remorseless attack on the 'liquidators'. They surpass even the liberals as the principal butt of Lenin's tireless (and, frankly, not a little tiresome) polemical resilience right up to the outbreak of war.

At the basic theoretical level Lenin contended that the whole idea was based upon an opportunist failure to distinguish between party and class. Lenin's point was the same as that made earlier against the Economists who suffered from the same sort of confusion. The Party, Lenin insisted, represented the advanced workers, the conscious and active workers who, through their initiative, spurred the average workers and the class as a whole into class activity, in the course of which the entire class acquired a new level of consciousness. 'The party is the politically conscious, advanced section of the class; it is its vanguard. The strength of that vanguard is ten times, a hundred times, more than a hundred times, greater than its numbers.'[34] With a sure instinct Lenin appropriated to the Bolshevik cause the whole tradition of Iskrist orthodoxy: the battle then, as now, he constantly reminded his audience, was against those who would dissolve the Party in the class. Then they were called Economists; now they were brazen liquidators and both shared a common genealogy reflecting the inevitable invasion of petty bourgeois ideas into the workers' party in Russia. Both trends, according to Lenin, exhibited the consummate dread of the petty bourgeois intellectuals to submit themselves to party discipline. Being unwilling to participate in an organisation which demanded a firm structure and the accountability of the parts to the whole, they had nothing to recommend beyond a purely negative wrecking of the only cohesive national organisation of the proletariat. Their organisational opportunism was matched by an equally contemptuous attitude towards the setting of Party tasks. The liquidators, like the Economists before them, demeaned the grandeur of the Social-Democratic role in the democratic revolution. Like the liberals they were men who had lost their nerve in the temporary dominance of reaction and had reneged on the heroic mission they previously set themselves. The proletariat in Russia, Lenin argued, could never be spurred into a heroic commitment to revolutionary activity to overthrow autocracy with the paltry, accommodative policies of gradual encroachment recommended by the Mensheviks. They would not venture their lives for partial and, in Russia, utopian demands like freedom of association or the convocation of a workers' congress. In a situation of hopelessness, rightlessness and arbitrary repression, proximate, 'realistic', attenuated demands were, by their nature, unlikely to enthuse or produce steadfast determination to fight. If there was to be a fight, then let it be not for a chink of light in the darkness but for the blaze of the sun at noon.

At the level of immediate political strategy Lenin based his ideas on a profoundly pessimistic appraisal of the consequences of 1905. Repression would get worse, the reactionaries would gather strength, the liberals would move to the Right, the 'democratic' gestures of the first phrase of the revolution would be reversed, *de facto* freedoms would be curtailed and eliminated. All of this, of course, had its dialectical counterpart in Lenin's thought: the future revolutionary explosion must be bigger and better than the first.

The Mensheviks shared with the liberals a more optimistic prognosis for the development of freedom in Russia. A start, however humble, had been made. The failure of the Moscow rising proved the impossibility of the workers going it alone, so it was best to recognise the situation of weakness and assist the liberals in fighting the Right and ally with them in securing modest increments to freedom using the Duma and the trade unions as the main levers of the struggle. There can be little doubt that the Mensheviks as a whole hoped for, and expected, a gradual peaceful extension of democratic freedoms. Their whole emphasis during this period, on building a legal broad-based workers' party served by a legal working-class press, emphatically reflected their hopes and expectations – and left them dangerously exposed to Lenin's persistent critique. The liquidators were as utopian as the liberals and were, therefore, just as dangerous as corruptors of mass consciousness. Their political strategy was, according to Lenin, premised upon a gradual expansion of freedoms to approximate political conditions in Western Europe. In fact the reverse process had occurred since 1905. The liquidators were, therefore, simply whistling in the dark, an ill-assorted coterie, a group of wishful thinkers who imagined that, if they wished hard enough, their dreams would come true. They were just playing at European Social Democracy, appropriating its slogans and its mode of organisation in an environment where the essential preconditions for such activity were totally absent. Pointedly Lenin reminded the deviants that by 1908 the working class had been all but disenfranchised. Its earlier Duma representatives were languishing in prison and exile, its militants had been executed or cowed into submission by Stolypin's ruthlessness, its press lived a parlous hand-to-mouth existence and was muzzled by censorship. Even the most moderate demands to establish trade unions with the blessing of employers were turned down by the government. How *could* an open revolutionary party exist in such conditions?

The corollary, for Lenin, of the Menshevik insistence upon a legal 'open' party, was the jettisoning of the frankly revolutionary commitment of the old party. Insistence on the need to overthrow autocracy was obviously incompatible with being granted a legal status by it. Hence, Lenin argued, the liquidators discreetly dropped the slogan of a democratic republic. Similarly the commitment to nationalisation (or municipalisation) of the landed estates could hardly expect to find favour with either the autocracy or the liberals. And so it was again quietly forgotten by the liquidationist newspapers. It was, indeed, openly stated by them that to press for this demand would be inopportune at the present time. What then was left as Menshevik policy – the desire for freedom of association, the legalisation of trade unions and the convocation of a workers' assembly. The policy of the liquidators became, in Lenin's eyes, almost indistinguishable from that of the liberals for the good reason that they put forward only such demands as they knew would be acceptable to the liberals.

No doubt Lenin did rather simplify and therefore distort the variety of opinions hostile to his own within the R.S.D.L.P. The historian looking back on this period will, no doubt, discover that the Mensheviks, Bundists and Caucasians were very far from sharing a common viewpoint on the relative importance of legal as compared with illegal activity. Lenin's polemics, to a very limited extent, did acknowledge divergences, but only in the sense that the dichotomy between a pro-Party stance and that of liquidation was raised in high relief.

Lenin acknowledged, for instance, that Plekhanov, after 1908, rejected Potresov's proposed revolution against the existing party structure, but he played upon Plekhanov's break with his erstwhile friends precisely in order to associate *all* the remaining Mensheviks with Potresov's position or that set out by the newspaper *Luch*. The tactic was the same as that adopted, for instance, in the debate over revisionism. Then Lenin had seized upon the *Credo* as the most extreme (and therefore, illuminating) statement of the case and associated all his opponents with it. The tactic then as later was purposely designed to serve both a positive and a negative function. In the first place, it advertised to the faithful the enormity of the threat posed to orthodoxy. It therefore served to cement their loyalties. In the second place, by seizing upon the most extreme utterances, Lenin was inviting his more 'moderate' opponents in the other camp to dissociate themselves and, by clarifying the nature of their reservations, to sow disharmony in their alliance. It would be, then, as naive to read Lenin's polemics of the time as an accurate historical record of the disputes he engaged in as it would be so to read those of his opponents. The object of polemics, as Lenin candidly admitted on more than one occasion, is not to present rounded historical truth but to destroy one's opponent in the current controversy. It would be wrong to look at Lenin's polemics during this period without bearing this destructive intent in mind. It would, however, be equally wrong to suggest that Lenin's attacks on the liquidators were quite without foundation, that he was inventing a straw man.

It was undoubtedly true that one of the few features that distinguished the Mensheviks during this period was their belief that there was a greater scope for Social Democracy to progress in Russia through legal, 'open' channels than via a concentration upon strengthening and extending the illegal underground party. This conviction was, in the first place, inseparably connected with their general conception of the nature of the epoch they were living through, the balance of class forces, the improbability of a revolutionary outbreak and the necessity of winning over the centre on a programme of moderate reform. The appropriate slogans and demands of Social Democracy were, therefore, in this conspectus, modest and unrevolutionary. Therefore they *might* reasonably expect a degree of toleration from the regime – a period of comparative social peace which the Social Democrats could use to rebuild the party's severed links with the masses and revitalise working-class organisations of all types in preparation for a future (and relatively distant) revolutionary upsurge. Obviously in the comparatively lengthy preparatory period of rebuilding the party, expressly revolutionary slogans would be inappropriate. They would not reflect the feelings of the workers, they were likely to affront the liberals and they would unleash savage governmental repression which would severely injure the Party's and the workers' cause. Lenin was, therefore, essentially correct in his contention that the striving for a legal, open party carried with it its necessary corollary – that the frankly revolutionary programme and slogans of the Party would have to be watered down or, at the very least, kept in obscurity. Certainly an examination of *Luch* and *Golos Sotsialdemokrata* tends to confirm his view that the Mensheviks pressed only those demands which could be accommodated *within* the existing political and economic structure; definitionally, therefore, they were unrevolutionary.[35]

The Menshevik attachment to a legal party stemmed, in the second place, from what was an undoubtedly genuine belief on their part that this was how European Social Democracy, in particular the model S.P.D., ran its affairs. This was the only means of keeping the party firmly accountable to those it professed to serve; it was the only way in which the tutelage of the intelligentsia *over* the working class could be overcome. It was, as Martov put it, the structure which alone could rid the Russian Party of its built-in tendency to regard the workers as mere reserve forces to be mobilised by the Party in times of crises.

> For us the workers' movement is not a spontaneous element which we revolutionaries merely want to 'use' for the destruction of a feudal state, for the conquest of a republic. For us the class-rallying of the working masses is a chief, permanent aim.[36]

Lenin's retort to this attitude we have already touched on. Its essence was that he agreed that in Europe an open, legal party *was* the only appropriate form, but there conditions of freedom for the individual, associations, press, etc. made it possible. In

Russia where none of these freedoms existed and autocracy rode roughshod over its own minimal guarantees, it was positively harmful to pretend that one could carry on as the Europeans did. A final telling point, which Lenin repeatedly returned to, was, why was it that in 1905–6 when conditions *were* free, when *de facto* freedom of association and of the press prevailed, why was it that nobody in the Party had at *that* stage advocated a downgrading of the underground in favour of legal work?

The answer may, perhaps, be provided by the third factor which is no less vital in helping us understand Menshevik attitudes in this period. This is the negative side of their altruistic Europeanism – their unquenchable hostility to Lenin. More than any other factor this united them, far more than Lenin himself gave credit for. As Riazanov noted at the time: 'Only personal hatred for the scoundrel Lenin kept together most of the Mensheviks, Bundists and Trotskyites.'[37] The fact is that Lenin, ever since 1902, had identified himself as the principal apologist of the underground, as guardian of the Party's old traditions (though, inexplicably to some, he had in 1905–6 been the most insistent of all Party leaders on the need to open the Party to as broad a following as possible). It is, moreover, vital to bear in mind that Lenin had, from 1907, been in effective control of the central institutions of the Party. Antagonism to his control became in all conscience difficult to distinguish from antagonism to the Party and its accepted decisions – a fact of which Lenin made the greatest play. In this way he could, with some justification construe attacks on the Bolshevik-controlled underground as attacks upon the Party. It was not, as so many commentators imply, transparently hypocritical of Lenin to insist throughout these years upon the sanctity of the Party organisations and their decisions. It does not help us much either to be reminded time after time that the Mensheviks were the orthodox genuine Social Democrats whereas the Bolsheviks represented a Russian conspiratorial deviation from the norm. These judgements have a simplistic attractiveness, but they beg more questions than they answer. The problem of orthodoxy in particular cannot be settled in such an abstract, ahistorical manner.

It is one thing for commentators to praise the Mensheviks for their support for an open, legal party; it is quite another to represent this as the orthodox stance for Russian Marxists to adopt. To my

268

knowledge never, in any of the resolutions of any of the Congresses of the Party, was this accepted as the primary focus of their work. On the contrary, the Party in its resolutions repeatedly and emphatically warned against any attempts to discredit or undervalue the central importance of its illegal structure. This might well be unpalatable but it was undoubtedly the case. It is equally beyond dispute that the Mensheviks just as repeatedly and just as emphatically *did* deride and discredit the underground and did attempt to set up their separate organisations within Russia which ostentatiously eschewed contact with the Central Committee of the Russian Bureau of the Party. It is difficult to escape the conclusion that the Mensheviks were playing a rather devious game.

Soberly, realistically, they knew that the Party as an organised whole could not for the moment manage without the energy, commitment, finance and contacts of the Bolsheviks. As Getzler puts it, 'they were not equipped to replace the Bolsheviks: they lacked their rivals' self-confidence and thought that they did not command the people and resources necessary to man and run the party'.[38] This was, they hoped, but a temporary deficiency which would be more than made up for when the anticipated upsurge in working-class activity would transform them into a genuine mass workers' party and expose their opponents as isolated sectarian conspirators. For the Mensheviks then, this was a period of tactical marking time, acknowledging their temporary weaknesses but building the independent, 'legal' bases for the mass influx of working-class strength which was their strategic goal. Sustained as they were by this comforting vision, some at least of the Menshevik leaders still acknowledged that the fears of Lenin and Plekhanov were well-founded. Martov at least confided in his private correspondence that the continued Menshevik policy of encouraging non-Party organisations as nuclei of a future workers' congress, carried with it the danger of a relapse into *kustarnichestvo* and the heresy of economism. Great care would have to be taken, he confided, 'not to slip into a real liquidationism of all elements of politics, and consequently of party-mindedness in the fragmented and small-craft-like practical activity of the Mensheviks of the present'.[39] One can almost hear Lenin intoning his amens.

For Plekhanov, too, liquidationism was closely associated with *kustarnichestvo*. The liquidationist Mensheviks, he maintained, had forsaken their revolutionary commitment and lapsed into organisa-

269

tional anarchy. In both respects they put the very existence of the
R.S.D.L.P. *as a revolutionary Party* into the gravest jeopardy.[40] From
1909 to the end of 1911, in his own newspaper as well as in
contributions to the Bolshevik press, Plekhanov urged his
supporters in the pro-Party Menshevik organisations to co-operate
with the Party's Central Committee which, though Bolshevik-
dominated and therefore flawed, remained the *only* national
structure able to arrest a decline into localism, apoliticism and
revisionism.

Wearing their other hat, as members of a faction which derived
much of its unity from a shared hostility to Lenin, the Menshevik
leaders quite simply were not prepared to censure or discipline
any of their supporters who openly flouted Party decisions or
refused to work with the accredited 'Leninist' organs of the Party
or its local cells. To put it more severely, the Menshevik leaders
had a vested interest in *promoting* these attitudes as a means of undermining Bolshevik pre-eminence. They therefore provided justification for Lenin's charge that they were wrecking the Party they could
not themselves control. In this context, as Baron perceptively
concludes,

> 'liquidationism' figured as an attempt of the Mensheviks to sever
> organisational ties that had become intolerable fetters; if they
> remained in the party and subject to its discipline, they would be
> forced to act in ways opposed to their fundamental inclinations.[41]

By 1911 Lenin considered that these people who had for so long
either ignored or acted directly against Party resolutions no longer
had a right to claim title to Party membership. One of the
refreshing ironies of history of which he could now remind his
opponents was that *they* had, in 1906, substituted Lenin's narrower
formulation of Article 1 of the Party Rules in preference to the
looser Martov formulation adopted at the Second Congress. None
the less, it was impossible, according to Lenin, to see how either
specification could embrace people like Akselrod, who annually
revamped his pet project (condemned by Party resolutions) of
a labour congress in order to subvert the *existing* organisation,[42]
or Potresov, who had the effrontery to argue the specious case
that liquidationism could not exist since there was nothing left
of the Party to be liquidated:

I ask the reader whether it is possible that there can exist, in this year of 1909, as something that is actually real and not a figment of a diseased imagination, a liquidationist tendency, a tendency to liquidate what is already beyond liquidation and actually no longer exists as an organised whole.[43]

Potresov's fellow editors of *Vozrozhdenie* (Dan, Martynov, Martov and others) heartily supported him declaring that:

There is nothing left to liquidate and – we for our part would add – the dream of re-establishing this hierarchy in its old, underground form is simply a harmful, reactionary utopia.[44]

For *these* people, by their own admission, Lenin concluded, the Party had ceased to exist.

The liquidators are not only opportunists (like Bernstein and Co.); they are also trying to build a *separate* party of their own, they have issued the slogan that the R.S.D.L.P. *does not exist*; they pay no heed *whatever* to the decisions of the R.S.D.L.P.[45]

The issue now became, for Lenin, that of the very existence of the Party. He had already, in July of 1911, arrived at the conclusion that was organisationally implemented in Prague in 1912 when the Bolsheviks effected their *coup d'état* and assumed the title of the R.S.D.L.P. as their exclusive preserve.

If they could take few crumbs of comfort from Party resolutions to boost their claims to orthodoxy, the liquidationist Mensheviks fared no better in their appeals to its international guardians – the leaders of the S.P.D. The German leaders had, ever since the commencement of hostilities between the Bolshevik and Menshevik factions, been drawn into the dispute as adjudicators who were highly esteemed by both sides. Since 1903 both had wooed the German leadership, with the Mensheviks taking every advantage of their much closer personal relations and private correspondence to secure their support. Kautsky, in particular, was acknowledged by all as the oracle of the International on problems of Marxist theory and strategy, and his response to their new entreaties was almost as devasting as his analysis of the 1905 revolution had been to them. There is, indeed, a sense in which

Kautsky's attitude at that time is directly germane to his attitudes after 1910 when, as a trustee of the bulk of the funds of the R.S.D.L.P., he was reluctantly obliged to arbitrate between the factions.

In 1905, as we have seen, Kautsky unreservedly and in almost every particular endorsed Lenin's views on the nature of the revolution and the appropriate strategy for Social Democracy in Russia. In emphatic opposition to Plekhanov, Martov and many of the Mensheviks, he maintained that the bourgeoisie could not be relied upon as a revolutionary force. It could never solve the basic agrarian question in the radical way that the exigencies of a capitalist development made urgent and would fall prey to the reaction. The only guarantee that the agrarian question could be solved and democracy assured lay in a proletarian alliance with the peasantry which could not stop short at the overthrow of the autocracy but must lead to their taking their share of political power in the state. This was, as we have seen, the analysis which Lenin had arrived at quite independently of Kautsky and it was, in all essentials, the analysis which continued to inform his policies in the years of the reaction. Neither he nor Kautsky altered their appreciation of the driving forces of the democratic revolution in Russia; both admitted that the objective tasks of the revolution were still outstanding. It is hardly surprising therefore that Kautsky, in the period of the reaction in Russia, inclined distinctly towards Lenin's general strategy rather than to that of the Mensheviks. He had, after all, dismissed the bourgeoisie as a credible force in the democratic revolution and he reiterated this view in 1909, declaring them to be incapable of leading the democratic revolution in Russia.[46] He was, therefore, unlikely now to incline towards the Mensheviks who, at this time, had elevated the task of winning over the 'third element' (i.e., the salaried professional employees and members of the liberal professions) and assisting the liberals in a campaign of democratic encroachment rather than concentrating on a revolutionary proletarian–peasant alliance for the overthrow of the autocracy.

This background might perhaps explain Kautsky's seemingly 'permissive' attitude towards the Bolshevik expropriations and the scandalous Schmidt inheritance affair. He acknowledged that they had frequently acted improperly, that Lenin was a difficult man to deal with; none the less, he gave short shrift to those Mensheviks who privately entreated him in 1908 to pronounce a final anathema against Lenin. Later, when Martov in 1911 belatedly raked through the Bolshevik dirty deeds of the past expressly in order to discredit Lenin, he too suffered Kautsky's measured rebuke. His pamphlet *Saviours or Destroyers?* was castigated by Kautsky as a 'detestable brochure'; he 'denounced this washing of dirty linen in public as repulsive' and held that Martov, rather than Lenin, deserved censure for the 'senseless' attack.[47]

Martov's moralising was perhaps rather misplaced for at this very time the Mensheviks were using all their connections and personal ties with the Germans precisely in order to get them to release to *them* some of the proceeds of the Bolshevik expropriations and the infamous Schmidt inheritance. The irony could hardly be nicer – Martov writing a comprehensive dossier on Bolshevik moral turpitude in the matter of obtaining funds, as a weapon in the battle to get the German trustees to hand over the same funds to the Mensheviks.

Personal friendships and persistent canvassing notwithstanding, Kautsky and his fellow trustees voted not a penny to the Mensheviks, but on a number of occasions delivered large sums to the Bolsheviks. Ascher is, no doubt, correct in attributing this partiality to the fact that 'in so far as Kautsky did detect divergences, by this time he seems to have been sympathetic to Lenin's overall strategy . . .'[48] In contrast, the Mensheviks were told, in almost so many words, that their claims to represent the legitimacy and orthodoxy of the Russian movement had been found wanting. 'The fact of the matter – so painful and incomprehensible to Akselrod – was that the Mensheviks still had not convinced most of the leaders of international socialism that they merited support.'[49]

OTZOVISTS, ULTIMATISTS AND GOD-BUILDERS

Lenin's attacks on deviations within his own faction were almost as severe as those on the liquidationists. The deviations involved ranged from extreme left 'otzovism', to slightly more moderate 'ultimatism', to the downright idealism of 'God-building'. The novice to Russian Marxist controversy may feel justifiably appalled at the thought of being precipitated into the controversies raging around these strange-sounding groups, but a brief coverage of them will be necessary in order to establish some important aspects of Lenin's thought at this time.

The otzovists derived their name from the Russian *otzovat* – to recall. The central plank of their platform was an insistence that the Social-Democratic deputies elected to the First and Second Dumas should be recalled. They contended that a consistent application of Bolshevik ideas which exposed the Duma as but a flimsy mask for the autocracy, carried with it the tactical message that revolutionaries should *expose* its hollowness and not participate in elections to it or waste their time on unreal and ineffectual discussion. They took their stand on Lenin's own policy of December 1905, which had stipulated that the R.S.D.L.P. should boycott the elections and press on with preparations for a general uprising. The difference between Lenin and the otzovists was, at heart, a difference of estimating quite when the revolutionary wave was beginning to subside. Lenin, as we have seen, believed that, so long as the revolutionary mass movement remained a vital force, so long as significant uprisings against the autocracy continued, a revolutionary should not yield to parliamentary palliatives. The failure of the Moscow uprising and the failure of the regions to support it, were the first symptoms of the process of decline. The elections themselves and the evident failure of the boycott, confirmed that the rot had set in. It was, Lenin argued, *correct* to try to point out to the masses that so long as autocracy was firmly in the saddle, a circumscribed consultative assembly could not bring the changes they had insisted upon. This was, indeed, the object of the boycott of the early elections to the First Duma. The tactic of the boycott was, therefore an entirely proper one to adopt when the revolutionary movement was still moving forward; it exemplified at that time the attempt by the revolutionaries to warn the masses of the trap that was being laid for them by the tsarist diversion of the movement into peaceful channels.[50] It would, however, be quite absurd to shut one's eyes to the effective failure of the boycott which expressed the widespread hope of the masses that things might still be peaceably settled. The very function of the elections was to contribute to the deflation of revolutionary will in the masses. It was a device by the autocracy to buy time and cool the popular indignation. The successful holding of the elections and the enthusiasm they aroused for the hope of peaceful radical change were *themselves* factors of cardinal

274

importance in causing the decline of the revolutionary movement.

It would, Lenin argued, be foolish and dangerous to ignore this fact and retain the old tactics quite unaltered. The otzovists, in short, failed to appreciate that differing forms of struggle were appropriate at different times.[51] In a period when the revolutionary movement was waning, what Lenin termed 'lower' forms of struggle *had* to be adopted. The Duma had to be utilised as a vehicle of class struggle, as the one legal forum through which Social Democrats could reach the masses.[52] It could, in its own way, become a tribune of the revolution[53] but only on condition that the Duma fraction was held firmly accountable to the Party and only as long as elections and work in the Duma were viewed, not as ends in themselves nor for the negligible results they yielded in the shape of reforms, but as the last legal means available to the Party to clarify class and political relations and dispel the constitutional illusions of the masses. The very form which the Third Duma took (a landlords' Duma solidly supporting autocracy and transparently reflecting the class interests of the land-owners and big bourgeoisie) was itself, according to Lenin, a sufficient guarantee that the democratic movement would have its remaining illusions shattered. The Third Duma, unlike the first two Dumas, accurately reflected in its composition the true class basis of the autocratic regime and this fact could and should be highlighted by the socialist opposition *within* the Duma.

> The Third Duma is a *less* fictitious parliament, because it *more truly reflects* the actual relations between the state authority and the present ruling classes. As long as power is in the hands of the Tsar and the feudalist landlords, there can be no other parliament in bourgeois Russia.[54]

The position of the ultimatists is, perhaps, rather more obscure. They were a short-lived and small group who shared the otzovists' fear that participation in the Duma might contaminate the Social-Democratic representatives and, through the growing prestige of these representatives as popular figureheads of the Party, spread the malady throughout the movement. To meet this danger the ultimatists proposed keeping the Social-Democratic deputies firmly and permanently accountable to the Party, to an extent which seemed to Lenin to deny them any creative initiative. Lenin defined ultimatism as 'the demand that the Social-Democratic group in the Duma be presented with an *ultimatum* to act in a strict Party spirit and obey all the instructions of the Party centres, or else give up their mandates'.[55] Lenin's response to this demand was the commonsense one that such a permanent, meticulous review would be an intolerable restraint on Social-Democratic deputies. They would have to learn from their direct experience of work in the Duma what were the most effective means of making it a tribune of the revolution. Lenin's argument was that the general lines of Party policy and Party slogans had, of course, to be voiced by its Duma representatives, and, to ensure that this was effectively carried out, they would be asked periodically to account for their actions. The Party had to realise, however, that the manner, timing and forum in which Party views could be presented with greatest effect in the Duma, had to be left to its deputies. In spite of these strictures directed against the ultimatists, Lenin himself undertook the task not only of scrutinising and, where necessary, criticising almost every speech by Social Democrats in the Duma, he even went so far as to write whole speeches to be pronounced by his followers from its rostrum.

In Marxist terms Lenin characterised ultimatism and otzovism as ascending steps towards syndicalism and anarchism. They were forms of petty-bourgeois instability which were found to occur when the movement encountered a set-back.[56] This was especially true of Russia whose predominant petty-bourgeois milieu inevitably infiltrated the ranks of the Party. In times of advance, when optimism was easily sustained, the petty-bourgeois element within the Party kept discipline. When, however, the movement was forced to retreat, this element, in Lenin's view, was always the first to break ranks and inevitably fell into primordial apoliticism – an aspect of the despair which reflected its chronic social and economic instability. In Lenin's analysis the apolitical despair of the petty bourgeoisie could assume a wide variety of forms ranging from extreme Left to extreme Right, from Socialist-Revolutionary terrorism, anarchism, syndicalism and otzovism through ultimatism to liquidationism. There was, Lenin argued, liquidationism of the Left as well as of the Right. What both had in common was a basic instability which caused them, at the first rebuff, to seek an easy way out of the arduous task of representing the *revolutionary political* strivings of the working class in a period of reaction.

It was not until mid-1909 that Lenin managed to rout his opponents *within* the Bolshevik faction who had, ever since the December 1905 decision to boycott the Duma elections, continued to dream of a new revolutionary outbreak and continued, moreover, to command a majority against Lenin within Bolshevism. For the most part they were young men, enthusiastic and romantic intellectuals, who had provided Lenin with an enormous boost in the years 1904 to 1905. They were, in their way, more peculiarly Russian than Lenin himself, cosmopolitan in culture, anxious to take on the challenge of assimilating all contemporary trends of knowledge into their basically Marxist world-outlooks. As a group they seemed to have the pretensions of being the 'encyclopaedists' of the revolutionary movement, setting themselves the task of providing for it a new synthesis of history, aesthetics, natural science, philosophy, literature and proletarian culture. For these 'men of the future' it seemed natural to align themselves in the years of Russia's first revolution with the audacious and uncompromising Lenin whose every action and printed line breathed a spirit of enthusiasm and dedication to build a new Russia. No doubt Lenin was at the time flattered and gratified that men of the calibre of Bogdanov, Lunacharsky, Pokrovsky, Bazarov, Gorky and Valentinov had chosen to join him in spurring the revolution to its radical conclusion and assist him with the considerable power of their pens against the Mensheviks. He was aware, quite early on, that his new allies were men of restless, questing intellect and did his best in private correspondence to steer them gently away from the pitfalls of neo-Kantianism which was, in Russia as elsewhere, enjoying a considerable vogue. Lenin must have had, at the back of his mind, the spectre of Bulgakov and Berdyaev who, some years previously, had begun by attempting to 'improve' upon Marx's synthesis by importing an alien ethic and ended up as distinguished theologians. For the moment, however, Lenin proclaimed a policy of Party neutrality in respect to the more abstruse philosophical enquiries of his comrades. In a way he had no alternative, for he needed them even more in these years of reaction when Bolshevik fortunes were at their lowest ebb than he had in 1905. Until Lenin managed to recruit and train new agents to re-establish firm nuclei in Russia, he was obliged to allow his restless 'Left' disciples a comparatively free hand.

By 1908, however, things had come to a head and a direct confrontation with the Left intelligentsia within the Bolshevik faction became imperative on tactical grounds. Things had reached such a pass that in mid-1907, at a Party Conference to discuss the elections to the Third Duma, 'fourteen out of fifteen Bolshevik delegates (all but Lenin!) had been for boycott and they had named Bogdanov instead of him as spokesman for the faction.'[57] More perturbing in the long run were the open attempts being made by the Bogdanov group to establish their pre-eminence not only in the Bolshevik faction in exile but in Russia as well. They began developing their contacts and, more ominously, established a Bolshevik school at Gorky's house in Capri where they began to mould Bolshevik activists from Russia in their own image. To rout the Left wing of his own faction, Lenin *had* to undermine Bogdanov's prestige and authority which, in some ways, had already surpassed his own.

Lenin began in his meticulous way to prepare for the onslaught. Organisationally he began to promote more trustworthy lieutenants like Zinoviev and Kamenev, and, through Krupskaya's redoubled efforts, he began to establish a broader base of support in Russia being able to finance his ventures from the proceeds of the expropriations. To counter Bogdanov's pedagogical venture in Capri, the veteran 'headmaster' established his own 'orthodox' Bolshevik school at Longjumeau near Paris. Tactically he came out with a spate of articles denouncing the boycotters, the ultimatists and otzovists, as deviants from the Party line which had ruled against left as well as right liquidationism. Philosophically he began a major work which would once and for all denounce his Bolshevik opponents (especially Bogdanov) as men who had turned their backs on Marx's militant materialism and gone a-whoring after 'modern' relativist philosophical theories which led them, ineluctably, into fideism and rank religiosity.

The product of Lenin's lengthy endeavours to come to grips with modern philosophical trends as expressed by their Russian Bolshevik epigones was his *Materialism and Empirio-Criticism*. It is a work which, from first to last, bears the imprint of the context in which it was written. It was written against Bogdanov as the most important leader of the Left Bolsheviks who so threatened Lenin's grip on the faction and who were pursuing political tactics which Lenin considered disastrous. It was written against those who would allow one single chink to appear in what Lenin saw as the armour plating of dialectical materialism which was the only philosophical stance that could benefit the proletariat.[58] Indirectly it was written against the Menshevik liquidators, for, having disposed of his own anti-party element, Lenin could make a good deal of political capital by insisting that the Mensheviks did likewise and set their house in order by disciplining all those elements who disavowed the basic tactical line of the Party.

Lenin's objective in *Materialism and Empirio-Criticism* was essentially practical rather than philosophical. He was less concerned with demonstrating that Mach, Avenarius or Bogdanov had false views on epistemology, psychology or natural science than he was to demonstrate that any attempt to assail a conception of philosophy as dialectically riven into two hostile camps – the party of materialism confronting the party of idealism – must *objectively* aid the bourgeoisie. It must *objectively*, whatever its professions to the contrary, end up in fideism or religion.[59] Lenin sought to establish his contention through two arguments which recurred throughout the book and were meant to reinforce each other.

The first argument was that phenomenalism and idealism were, as a matter of historical fact, closely linked with fideism. Those who historically have adopted idealism or phenomenalism as the basis of their philosophical ideas have also, Lenin noted, been believers in God. Lenin cited the cases of Berkeley, Locke, Kant and Hegel in substantiation of his generalisation (though, for good reason, ignoring the 'difficult' cases of Hume and the Utilitarians).

The second argument which Lenin brought to bear was that there was not merely an historical, contingent connection between religion, idealism and phenomenalism, but a necessary logical connection. Here Lenin would appear to be skating on thinner ice. To assert a thousand times the basic materialist proposition that the material world objectively existed independent of a percipient observer and that that world was, in all its complexity and development, possible to comprehend did not, of itself exclude the possibility of a deity having created matter and ordered its development – nor could it. Materialism, therefore, might be consistent with some form of fideism or religion and this, indeed, was the position argued by Lunacharsky and, to some extent by Gorky. The epistemological precepts of phenomenalism by contrast could not by their nature allow of the existence of God, for what would it mean to reduce God to a sense-impression. God, in the conventional sense, as an absolute eternal being existing independently of the world and of ourselves, must by his nature be beyond the range of human sense-impressions. As one commentator pithily presents the case: 'Idealism is radically agnostic, realism may be atheist.'[60]

Lenin's attachment to a straight dialectical either/or in philosophy was, of course, entirely consonant with his social and political views. In the social sphere, as we have seen, Lenin acknowledged the existence of a host of intermediary transitional strata and interest groups, but the whole process of the modern economy must reduce them to two antagonistic classes – all the intermediary groups were progressively broken down into their modern class components. Politics must eventually reflect this process and we have noticed how, in Lenin's analysis, the 1905 revolution produced the imperative to choose between Left or Right; it eliminated the apparent class independence of the Centre. Similarly with philosophy, which, as an element of the superstructure, could not insulate itself from the objective developments of the social and economic bases. It, too, must reflect the polarised class and political groupings and did so in the choice of either materialism or idealism. Beyond this all else, all intermediary schema, all attempts to transcend or reconcile the antagonistic parties, all attempts to dismiss it as outmoded in the light of modern scientific developments – all this was of the bourgeoisie in Lenin's view. Repeatedly and emphatically Lenin made the point with which we are well familiar from his political writings – the party most to be feared was the party of the centre which pretended that it stood above class and transcended the class struggle. It thereby corrupted political consciousness with its spurious reconciliationism and thereby aided the reaction even when crisis situations did not oblige it to go over *openly* to the counter-revolution. The same, exactly, held true for philosophy which, like the class war it at one remove represented, was necessarily partisan. There too, far better the honest idealist to the middle-of-the-roader who sought to combine elements of materialism and idealism or proclaimed both *passé*.

'Of all parties,' our Joseph Dietzgen justly said, 'the middle party is the most repulsive . . . Just as parties in politics are more and more becoming divided into two camps . . . so science too is being divided into two general classes: metaphysicians on the one hand, and physicists, or materialists, on the other. The intermediate elements and conciliatory quacks, with their various appellations – spiritualists, sensationalists, realists, etc. etc. – fall into the current on their way. We aim at definiteness and clarity. . . . If we compare the two parties respectively to solid and liquid, between them there is a mush.'[61]

Throughout the book the same point was tirelessly made: philosophy was inseparable from the class struggle, the opposing parties in philosophy were both products of and weapons in this struggle. As soon as any concessions were made to Lunacharsky's 'deification of the higher human potentialities' or Bogdanov's ' "general substitution" of the psychical for all physical nature',[62] as soon as a threat to 'one basic premise, one essential part' of 'Marxist philosophy, which is cast from a single piece of steel'[63] was allowed to go unchallenged, then the relapses into philosophical idealism and bourgeois politics became inevitable.

What Lenin clearly set out to accomplish was to associate Bogdanov, in spite of his cogent protests to the contrary, with Lunacharsky's overt lapse into a kind of religious anthropomorphism with all the more 'idealist' utterances of Mach and Avenarius, or any of their disciples, in order to demonstrate the un-Marxist character of Bogdanov's basic epistemological presuppositions – which had led him and his group into petty-bourgeois political tactics.

Lenin was not, however, so naive as to imagine that texts from Engels, no matter how numerous, would be sufficient to displace the otzovists and God-seekers from their position of strength in the Bolshevik faction. More practical measures ensured him a majority at an enlarged Editorial Board meeting of *Proletarii* in July 1909 where, finally, he disposed of them. Boycottism, recallism [*otzovism*], ultimatism, God-construction and Machism were all of them 'incompatible with membership in the Bolshevik faction'.[64] Lenin parted company with the brilliant intellectual coterie he had earlier attracted. Their paths were not to meet again until after the Bolshevik Revolution when many returned to the fold to devote their undoubted talents to the building of socialism – until Stalin, one of the men Lenin promoted to fill the gap they now left, cut them down with all the brutality of an insecure parvenu.

1911–14 : Revival of the Labour Movement and Glimmerings of a New Theoretical Analysis

From mid-1911 things began to improve for Lenin. The dissenters within his own faction had been dealt with and had for some time ceased to be a real threat. The Mensheviks were in evident disarray both within Russia and in the emigré movement where they had become the object not only of Lenin's abuse but of Plekhanov's bitter invective as well. In the latter part of 1911 Bolshevik organisational links with the cells and committees were re-established after the earlier arrest of all the Bolshevik members of the Central Committee in Russia.[1] The labour movement showed distinct signs of rebirth even before the infamous massacre of hundreds of striking workers in the Lena goldfields. Once again in this savage act the Government demonstrated its barbarity and its totally irresponsible use of state violence to put down claims even to the modest right of workers to withdraw their labour. The autocracy was serving Lenin's purpose perfectly by giving force to his proposition that, so long as autocracy continued to maintain itself in full control of the coercive agencies of the state, Russia would remain a rightless and barbarised land.

Lenin was convinced that the pattern of the first revolution would repeat itself, only this time the masses would have learned from their mistakes of 1905. According to Lenin's own periodisation, the years of reaction had, as he had long predicted, given way to a new revolutionary period.

The three years 1908–10 were a period of Black Hundred counter-revolution at its worst, of liberal-bourgeois renegacy and of proletarian despondency and disintegration. The number of strikers dropped, reaching 60,000 in 1909 and 50,000 in 1910.

However, a noticeable change set in at the end of 1910 . . . The year 1911 saw the workers gradually going over to the *offensive* – the number of strikers rose to 100,000. Signs from various quarters indicate that the weariness and stupor brought about by the triumph of the counter-revolution are passing away, that once again there is an *urge* for revolution. [2]

Lenin's whole strategy during the period of the reaction was founded upon his belief that the objective tasks of the revolution had not been fulfilled and could not be fulfilled so long as the autocracy backed by the landlords held power. Since 1905 the bedrock of his strategy had been the assertion that, in such a situation, there was no possibility of reforms in contemporary Russia. [3] On this he had committed himself totally. This had been the rationale for retaining the revolutionary slogans of 1905 intact throughout the bleak years up to 1911. Now, at last, it seemed to Lenin that his strategy was beginning to bear fruit. Almost alone among the political groups in Russia, the Bolsheviks had insisted that only a revolutionary movement could achieve the radical objectives of 1905, which still remained outstanding. Now, in 1911, Lenin seized upon the hard data of strike statistics which were, in his view, an infallible chronicle of the class war, [4] to demonstrate the correctness of his views. The sudden and dramatic upsurge of economic and political strikes during this period exposed the hollowness of Mensheviks and liberals and all believers in the possibility of organic change in Russia. [5] The democratic movement in Lenin's view, did not and, in Russia especially, could not proceed in this gradualist way. The liberal and Menshevik assumptions about the way change could be brought about were rooted in a false transference of West European experience to the Russian situation. Of course, in Germany, France and England, where the labour movement and socialist parties were legalised and enjoyed freedom to publish, propagandise and organise, the movement could painstakingly build up its strength and, within limits, achieve its goals. In Russia, however, it was precisely the pursuit of partial ameliorations which events like the Lena massacre had shown to be utopian.

Lenin's usual confidence in the correctness of his political line was boosted by the massive support the Bolsheviks obtained from the revitalised labour movement in Russia. Month by month hard evidence poured in that the working class in all the major industrial centres of Russia overwhelmingly supported the Bolsheviks against their Menshevik competitors. Needless to say, Lenin seized on every scrap of this evidence to discomfort the Mensheviks who had, for so long, pinned all their hopes and premised all their policies on the conviction that this upsurge of the genuine labour movement would leave them as the main beneficiaries. In fact the very opposite occurred and in the years immediately preceding the First World War their fortunes slumped disastrously. In article after article Lenin reported the Bolshevik successes. Their newspaper circulations climbed to 40,000 compared to the Mensheviks 16,000.[6] More importantly, according to Lenin the scale of support from the working class, as demonstrated in collections for the rival presses, showed four-fifths of the workers' groups supporting the Pravdists.[7] (*Pravda* was the main Bolshevik organ at this time.) Furthermore in not a single trade did the liquidationists receive more support than the Pravdists.[8] The Bolsheviks won control of virtually every major trade union in Russia. The same story was told in the returns for the two nation-wide elections which had been held in 1912, the elections to the Fourth Duma and the elections to the All-Russia and Metropolitan Insurance Boards. In the Duma elections the Bolsheviks swept the board in the workers' curia (i.e., in the six industrial centres where the workers were allowed to nominate candidates) – all six deputies elected were Bolsheviks. Similarly in the open election of worker delegates to the Insurance Boards more than eighty per cent of those elected were Bolsheviks.[9] The Mensheviks were left with no crumbs of comfort. On their own chosen field of battle – the struggle for the mass workers' movement – they had suffered a whole series of ignominious defeats. As Getzler puts it, 'The Mensheviks found themselves harassed and beaten in their own favourite areas of activity'.[10]

THE ROLE OF THE ILLEGAL PARTY

Lenin, for his part took the victories as proof positive not only of his frankly revolutionary political line but also of the organisational ideas he had so tenaciously clung to in the darkest period of reaction. In such a period it was, he argued, all the more necessary to preserve the illegal conspiratorial structure of the Party, not, as his contemporary detractors and latter-day commentators alleged, as an end in itself, nor as *the instrument* to make the revolution. At no time did Lenin commit himself to the view that the Party could or should go it alone and engineer a coup. The supreme importance of preserving the illegal structure during the reaction, lay, in Lenin's eyes, in the functions it alone could perform when the working class once more emerged recovered and revitalised from its necessary period of recuperation. The cadres of the Party who had preserved their organisational links with the Party centre, no matter how apparently puny their forces, would then exert an influence over the mass movement out of all proportion, to their numbers. 'There must be an organisation of the advanced elements of the class, immediately and at all costs, even though at first these elements constitute only a tiny fraction of the class.'[11] They, Lenin argued, alone would be in a position to mobilise, encourage and co-ordinate the revolutionary activity of the mass the moment that strikes broke out once more.

The sweeping successes the Bolsheviks won in dominating the 'open' labour movement in the years immediately preceding the First World War appeared to Lenin as a brilliant vindication of his analysis of the proper relationship of the Party to the class. He had, as we have seen, consistently rejected the dangerous notion that the Party could be *identified* with the class. This idea had lain at the centre of the Economist heresy and had been resuscitated by the Mensheviks with their amorphous ideas of merging the Party with a general labour congress. The danger of this confusion Lenin had amplified in earlier disputes, especially in the period 1900–2; essentially it would condemn the Party to appearing as the passive executor of the relatively undeveloped consciousness of the average and backward workers. It would have meant accepting the idea that socialism was a natural and spontaneous outgrowth of purely working-class experience which, as the writings of Kautsky and the experience of England demonstrated,, was a profoundly mistaken idea. It would, moreover, have meant ignoring all the evidence on the evolution of socialist parties not only in Russia but in the advanced Western countries too. In all countries, Lenin maintained, it had taken decades of persistent work by Marxist intellectuals and advanced workers to

285

forge a socialist party. In the West, as Lenin pointed out, even in the countries where socialism was best-developed and organised, the Party still only comprised a small part of the class. 'In Germany, for example, about one-fifteenth of the class is organised in the party; in France about a hundred-and-fortieth part.'[12] These facts, he argued, demonstrated the common-place truth that 'the class' was not an undifferentiated mass; it had within it gradations of consciousness and organisation. 'The class' was composed of a relatively small proportion of conscious and organised workers, the advanced workers. After them came the 'broad section' of average workers, and finally there was the mass of backward and unorganised workers which would, in times of crisis, respond to the activism of the more advanced.

> My argument is that in all countries, everywhere and always, there exists, *in addition* to the party, a 'broad section' of people *close to the party* and the huge mass of the *class* that founds the party, causes it to emerge and nurtures it . . .
>
> The party is the politically conscious, advanced section of the class, it is its vanguard. The strength of that vanguard is ten times, a hundred times, more than a hundred times greater than its numbers.
>
> Is that possible? Can the strength of hundreds be greater than the strength of thousands? It can be, and is, *when the hundreds are organised. Organisation increases strength tenfold* . . .
>
> The political consciousness of the advanced contingent is, incidentally, manifested in its ability to organise. By organising it achieves *unity of will* and this united will of an advanced thousand, hundred thousand, million *becomes* the will of the class. The intermediary between the party and the class is the 'broad section' (broader than the party but narrower than the class), the section that votes Social Democrat, the section that helps, sympathises, etc.[13]

THE MASS STRIKE AND THE REVOLUTIONARY PROCESS

It was perhaps fortuitous that immediately before the period of the upswing in the labour movement Lenin elaborated the role of strikes in the process of revolution. In a masterly article, perhaps the most important he had written for some years, inoccuously entitled *Strike Statistics in Russia*,[14] he was able for the first time to locate and account for the 1905 revolution within the general structure of his thought. Utilising the great mass of official statistics which had become available on the strike movement of 1905–6, Lenin was able to point to objective statistical data supporting the positions he had adopted at that time. The data demonstrated that it was, beyond doubt the advanced workers, the best-organised workers in the largest industrial plants, in particular the metal workers, who had been first into the fray. They had drawn the mass of the average and backward workers into the battle. They had been the first and remained the most persistent in striking for purely political objectives. They had been on strike longer and oftener than any other section of the proletariat, and had forfeited far more than any other section in lost wages. The enormous strain of mobilising the mass and stirring the backward into action had, inevitably taken its toll. The metal workers' pre-eminence lapsed somewhat in 1906. But in 1907 when the movement was beginning to decline it was once again the organised workers of the big establishments, the metal workers of St Petersburg in their vanguard, who rallied once more in an attempt to prevent a collapse of the movement.

The role of the organised advanced workers in mobilising the mass to action and thus to more adequate consciousness could not, in Lenin's estimation, be set too high. Their endurance and tenacity was proved to be incomparably greater than any other section. (The metal workers, for instance, lost three times as much pay from strike activity as the next most prominent group.) Their slogans and demands were far more audacious and spurred the backward sections with confidence to put their own more modest demands. The wave of largely economic strikes, which the average and more backward workers then felt confident enough to mount, served in turn to sustain and give force to the emphatically political strikes of the more advanced sections. Each forward move encouraged new, unorganised sections of the class to seize the chance to improve their conditions and their claims were subsequently generalised and radicalised in the demands of the advanced workers. All sections of the class were shown to stand in a complex chain of relationships. The advanced urged the backward into action, initially in pursuit of purely economic goals. Their economic strikes provided, in turn, the basis of strength on which the advanced could more audaciously and with more credibility generalise the class demands and make them political. The average workers then began to make the transition to political demands as the outlying areas of the country and unorganised sections of the class were drawn into the battle. The advanced section sank back temporarily exhausted only to re-emerge with renewed vigour, to save the movement from decline when the average and backward workers were bought off with improvements in their economic situation and promises of political change.

The essential political lessons confirmed by the strike statistics of the 1905–7 period were, in Lenin's view:

1. That the advanced workers, the organised vanguard of the proletariat, exerted an influence quite out of proportion to their numbers. They had drawn the mass behind them into class action and had thereby immeasurably raised the general level of consciousness. They were the catalysts of general change and the Party's aim, in a revolutionary situation, must be to organise, stimulate and co-ordinate their efforts. From this group and this group alone the Party should take its cue.

2. That the proletariat and it alone was the force which obliged the autocracy to make concessions. The success of the movement in wringing constitutional changes from the Tsar had nothing whatsoever to do with the sympathy of liberals or society as a whole (the Menshevik thesis), still less was it due to any organic gradual transformation. Success was the immediate and direct result of the qualitative and abrupt transformation of the potential energy of the proletariat into enormous organised power. The statistics, Lenin argued, made a nonsense of the schemes of dreamers of organic change. In the entire decade from 1895 to 1904 a little over two million striker-days were registered in the official statistics. In the single year of 1905 the figure exceeded twenty-three and a half million striker-days.[15] Significant change, Lenin could cogently argue, came only in moments of climacteric, at the nodal points when quantity was dialectically transformed into quality.

Lenin returned to all of these persistent themes in his writings in the period of revival which began in 1911. Mass strikes, both economic and political, once more swept Russia and Lenin expected them to follow the pattern of 1905, from economic strike to political strike to street demonstrations and an armed uprising. All the evidence again pointed to the vanguard role of the St

288

Petersburg workers in mobilising the country as a whole and to the metal workers as the advance guard of the capital's workers.[16] This time, he felt the proletariat would win through to final victory. It was, after all, much stronger in numbers and more concentrated than it had been in 1905.[17] It had learnt from its earlier mistakes and would not now be bought off with cheaply given promises.

There were, however, some new and important elements which Lenin added to his earlier analysis. In particular he began to lay much stronger emphasis on the role of mass strikes in winning the sympathy, and if possible, the active assistance of the peasantry and the army. 'It is essential', Lenin argued, 'that the smouldering resentment and subdued murmurings of the countryside should, along with the indignation in the barracks, find a centre of attraction in the workers' revolutionary strikes.'[18] The Party could not, of course, artificially produce mass strikes at will, but it could see to it that

> . . . strikes, meetings and demonstrations should take place con-
> tinuously, that the whole peasantry and the armed forces should
> know of the workers' stubborn fight, and that the countryside
> – even the most out-of-the-way corners of it – should see that
> there is unrest in the towns, that *'their'* people have risen in
> revolt . . .[19]

The progression of Lenin's thought is plain enough. If economic strikes grew into political strikes and demonstrations and were to culminate in a successful armed uprising; if the whole movement was to acquire its proper national democratic significance, then the active assistance of the peasantry and part, at least, of the peasant army were obviously essential. 'Premature attempts at an uprising', Lenin warned

> would be extremely unwise. The working class vanguard must
> understand that the support of the working class by the demo
> cratic peasantry and the active participation of the armed forces
> are the main conditions for a timely, i.e. successful, armed
> uprising in Russia.

Mass strikes in revolutionary epochs have their objective logic. They scatter hundreds of thousands and millions of sparks in all directions – and all around there is the inflammable material of extreme bitterness, the torture of unprecedented starvation, endless tyranny, shameless and cynical mockery at the 'pauper', the 'muzhik', the rank and file soldier.[20]

The general strategy he was to pursue in 1917 had already been fully formed in Lenin's mind.

There is, finally, another element which intrudes itself into Lenin's analysis of the mass strike which is worth remarking. In formulations which are strikingly akin to those of Rosa Luxemburg and Georges Sorel, Lenin openly betrayed a certain historical pessimism. He argued, on occasion, that only the mass political strike was capable of stirring the masses from despair to conscious activity. Only it could save Russia from decay and suffocation.[21] The implications are clear, and, as noticed earlier, are consonant with all Lenin's writings. The revolution would not arrive willy-nilly without conscious preparations; in this sense it was not inevitable in the way that some Marxists optimistically imagined. It was not enough that the ruling classes be incompetent nor that the productive forces be stifled. It was not enough that the oppressed classes desire change. The revolution demanded titanic activity, wholehearted commitment and heroic sacrifice before success could be achieved. The function of the mass strike was, in Lenin's account, to act as the mechanism through which a revolutionary morality embodying these values could penetrate the mass of the working class.[22]

The period up to the outbreak of war was, for Lenin, a period of renewed optimism. The bleak years of exile, with all its usual problems of internecine squabbling made worse by a feeling of hopelessness induced by what appeared to be the complete withdrawal of the labour movement during the reaction, abruptly passed away. The movement had revived, more importantly it had accepted Bolshevik leadership to an extent which, one suspects, even Lenin had hardly dared to dream of. The signs of a new more potent 1905 appeared on all sides and Lenin felt himself once more in his natural element. He returned to his theses of 1905. Open political and physical confrontation would reveal the true nature of objective class patterns which had been maturing for so long, consciousness would make a qualitative leap forward as the experience of struggle taught the masses, the activity of the struggle would itself forge the appropriate values of co-operation, herosim and self-sacrifice so vital to the building of a new society. Even now, however, there was no talk in Lenin's writings of any advance to socialism in Russia for, as we have seen, his ideas on the proper practice for the R.S.D.L.P. remained firmly based on his theoretical analysis of the level of development of *Russian* capitalism.

MONOPOLY CAPITALISM, MILITARISM AND THE
TECHNOLOGICAL BASIS OF SOCIALISM

It was, of course, natural and inevitable that Lenin's prime focus of attention should have been his own country. There was nothing singular or peculiar about this; he was no more ethnocentric than the leaders of the main European parties who rarely had much expertise on the movement in other countries. The great bulk of Lenin's writings in this period, as earlier, reflected his almost exclusive preoccupation with Russian affairs and one is indeed struck by the paucity of references he made to the steadily worsening international situation and preparations for war. There were, none the less, clear signs that, particularly from 1912, Lenin was becoming aware of the need for a broader-ranging structure of economic ideas.

There was, in the first place, the need to establish some kind of Marxist explanation for the continued growth of revisionism within the European labour movement, especially in Britain, the home of capitalism. Lenin's explanation was the one which Hilferding had earlier advanced in more sophisticated terms, that the British bourgeoisie, taking advantage of their monopoly position as manufacturers to the world, had dispersed a small portion of their excess profits to a privileged section of the working class. This privileged section, aided and abetted by Britain's 'near-Socialist intelligentsia' contaminated the labour movement and naturally inclined to reformism and revisionism.

In the middle of the nineteenth century Britain enjoyed an almost complete monopoly in the world market. Thanks to this monopoly the profits acquired by British capital were extraordinarily high, so that it was possible for some crumbs of these profits to be thrown to the aristocracy of labour, the skilled factory workers.

291

This aristocracy of labour, which at that time earned tolerably good wages, boxed itself up in narrow, self-interested craft unions, and isolated itself from the mass of the proletariat, while in politics it supported the liberal bourgeoisie.[23]

This situation, Lenin argued, had already begun to change. Britain's world monopoly had long since disappeared with the advent of German and American competition. Consequently profits had shrunk and wages had been depressed to the minimum once more.

Capitalism in Europe, Lenin argued, had begun to degenerate. It was no longer thrusting, self-confident and progressive. Like the Russian bourgeoisie the European bourgeoisie in general had become reactionary, militarist and obscurantist, ready to clutch at any straw which might save it from the holocaust of revolution it knew to be at hand. 'In "advanced" Europe, the *sole advanced* class is the proletariat. As for the living bourgeoisie, it is prepared to go to any length of savagery, brutality and crime in order to uphold dying capitalist slavery.'[24] It was a class which had outlived its function in the development of the productive forces; it had become obsolescent and idle, grown rich, not from work but from parisitically 'clipping coupons' and fattened on the profits of its share capital.[25] Joint stock companies merely assisted the process of accelerating the concentration of capital in the hands of the big magnates, the directors of the trusts and monopolies.[26] Power, Lenin concluded 'is in the hands of the banks, the trusts and big capital in general'.[27] A year previously, in an equally isolated reference, he had asserted that 'throughout the West power is in the hands of the imperialist bourgeoisie, which is already three-quarters decayed and willing to sell all its "civilisation" to any adventurer for "stringent" measures against the workers, or for an extra five kopeks profit on the ruble'.[28] These propositions, which were to lie at the heart of Lenin's later theory of imperialism remained, as yet, isolated, if striking thoughts. Rudolf Hilferding had, of course, some three years earlier in his *Finance Capital* (1910), elaborated a sophisticated Marxist analysis of the role of banks, cartels and trusts in the new epoch of finance capital, which had displaced industrial capital as the dominant form of capitalist accumulation. He had further shown how capitalism, in this its last degenerate stage as finance capital, was necessarily propelled towards militarism. Lenin followed him (and for that matter followed the 'bourgeois' analyst of imperialism, John Hobson, whose book he had already read), in tracing the connection between monopoly capital and militarism. Lenin's references were again brief and tantalisingly undeveloped, but there were occasional presentiments of his later thought. In one of these, a very short piece on 'armaments and Capitalism' written in May 1913, he pointed to the international capitalist conspiracy reaping vast profit from the promotion of jingoism, national antagonisms and armaments.

> And we find that admirals and prominent statesmen of both parties, Conservative and Liberal, are shareholders and directors of shipyards, and of gunpowder, dynamite, ordnance and other factories. A shower of gold is pouring straight into the pockets of bourgeois politicians, who have got together in an exclusive international gang engaged in instigating an armaments race among the peoples and *fleecing* these trustful, stupid, dull and submissive peoples like sheep.
>
> Armaments are considered a national matter, a matter of patriotism; it is presumed that everyone maintains strict secrecy. But the shipyards, the ordnance, dynamite and small-arms factories are *international enterprises*, in which the capitalists of the various countries work together in duping and fleecing the public of the various countries, and making ships and guns alike for Britain against Italy, and for Italy against Britain.[29]

It is perhaps rather strange that right up to the outbreak of war Lenin made no further references and attempted no fuller account of the nature of monopoly capitalism nor its relation to militarism. Only after the outbreak of war, stimulated by Bukharin's enormously important study *Imperialism and World Economy*, did he seriously begin to apply himself to the study of finance capital in its conjunction with political power.

Just as Lenin gave us but fleeting glimpses of his future account of the degeneration of capitalism in its final finance capitalist phase, so too he only occasionally lighted upon what was to be represented as the dialectical inverse of its moribund nature – the way in which it involuntarily created the basis for an international advance to the era of socialism. Here too Lenin's comments were rather scattered, disconnected and suffused, as we shall see, with not a little technological utopianism.

For all his hard-headedness, the element of the dreamer was never far from the surface in Lenin's make-up. He had indeed much earlier recognised this part of himself and reminded the Party that what it needed was not less but more of dreams.[30] What he meant was that no meaningful revolution could be made without inspiration, without a vision of the better life for the mass of the people. There had to be a way to lighten the intolerable burden of the working class and the Marxist revolutionary was, Lenin asserted, committed to its discovery. Gorky recognised well enough this disposition in Lenin's own make-up.

> I have never met in Russia, the country where the inevitability of suffering is preached as the general road to salvation; nor do I know of, any man who hated loathed and despised so deeply and strongly as Lenin all unhappiness, grief and suffering.[31]

This imperative, undoubtedly well-intentioned and altruistic in its motive, was to lead Lenin, both in power and in the years before the October Revolution, to be waylaid into extravagant optimism on the prospects for immediate short-cut solutions to the proletariat's burden. He became, indeed, almost as fanciful and extravagant as Fourier at times.[32]

Lenin, more than most Marxists of the time, was deeply committed to a heroic view of man the Prometheus ever striving to tap and control the enormous potential of nature, and this general ontology no doubt inclined him towards a pronounced technological optimism. He talked for instance, about the 'enormous revolution in industry', which the development of William Ramsay's method of obtaining gas from coal without the necessity of mining it, would produce.

> Under socialism the application of Ramsay's method, which will 'release' the labour of millions of miners, etc., will make it possible immediately to shorten the working day *for all* from eight hours to, say, seven hours and even less. The 'electrification' of all factories and railways will make working conditions more hygienic, will free millions of workers from smoke, dust and dirt, and accelerate the transformation of dirty, repulsive workshops into clean, bright laboratories worthy of human beings. The electric lighting and heating of every home

will relieve millions of 'domestic slaves' of the need to spend three-fourths of their lives in smelly kitchens.

Capitalist technology is increasingly, day by day, *outgrowing* the social conditions which condemn the working people to wage-slavery.[33]

The point which Lenin wanted to make, a point which figured so largely in his later theoretical analysis, was that the techno-logical prerequisites for socialism had already been forged in the advanced industrialised countries of the West. The potential of electricity to ease the toil of labour, shorten working hours and improve the standard of living of the workers, was, Lenin believed, quite boundless. America could, for example,

by converting the power of waterfalls into electricity . . . immediately obtain an additional *sixty million* h.p.!

Already a land of boundless wealth, it can at one stroke *treble* its wealth, *treble* the productivity of its social labour, and thereby guarantee to *all* working-class families a decent standard of living worthy of intelligent human beings, and a not exces-sively long working day of six hours.[34]

Here, once again, the solution to age-old drudgery and poverty was presented as 'immediately' available; an instant panacea was at hand which could be implemented 'at a stroke'.

Lenin's case was, of course, no more than a contemporary elaboration of the one that Marx had argued, namely that the enormous *potential* of the new productive forces could no longer be accommodated within the framework of capitalist patterns of ownership relations. So long as a small group of the population owned the forces of production and depended on a vast army of wage-labourers to man them, depended, moreover, on the surplus value they extracted from wage-labourers for their profit and the increase of their capital, there could be no hope for any significant or lasting improvement in the living conditions of the workers. The labour theory of value dictated the tendency for their wages to be depressed to the minimum. It therefore enormously restricted the ability of the market to consume the products of capitalist production. The longer capitalism survived the less it could accommodate technical innovation. Consequently the vast productive potential of the new technology and new methods of rationalising the work process (like the Taylor system) could never be adequately developed under capitalism. There arose, in the modern era an enormous and inescapable contradiction between the capacity for general improvement of which mankind was transparently capable, and what was actually being achieved within the framework of capitalism. The present reality of hunger, unemployment, long working hours and appalling living conditions was, Lenin argued, flagrantly at odds with the potential of 'large scale production, machinery, railways, telephone . . . to cut by three-fourths the working time of the organised workers and make them four times better off than they are today'.[35]

To summarise, we can, I think, say that these were comparatively new themes for Lenin. He had not previously presumed to comment much on the conditions for socialism in the world at large. Indeed, his almost exclusive focus of attention had been upon how a radical democratic revolution could be brought to success in Russia. Lenin had, undoubtedly, begun to shift his attention towards a more global analysis but, as yet (i.e., up to 1914), it remained patchy and undeveloped. We should also note that when Lenin referred at this time to the prospects for socialism, he always referred to the advanced countries of the West as being its initiators, not Russia. Finally, we can conclude perhaps that Lenin very considerably over-estimated the speed, ease and extent to which an unfettered development of productive potential could transform the living standards of the mass of the people. This excitation of extravagant expectations in himself and those who followed him was to have a very important bearing on his years in power.

THE NATIONAL QUESTION

An intrinsic part of Marx's account of the development of capitalism, part of its progressive nature, had been its tendency to erode the boundaries between different countries. Capitalism was, Marx argued (especially in chapter one of the *German Ideology*), a world historical force. It was, indeed, the first world historical mode of production in the sense that its very nature drove it to endless expansion and required the subjugation of the whole world to its influence. It must constantly 'nestle everywhere, settle everywhere' in pursuit of new markets for its finished goods and surplus capital and new sources of raw materials to appease its insatiable hunger. It destroyed ancestral immobility based on natural economy and made commodity production vital to the survival of all countries of the world. Capitalism thereby destroyed all particular, localised systems of status; oriental despotism, the caste system and remnants of feudal relations were ruthlessly swept aside and, in their place, the whole world was divided into two social groupings which knew no borders – those who owned the means of production and those whose sole property was their labour power. An international culture was gradually created, international bonds of affiliation among proletarians and bourgeois alike were established and national boundaries became increasingly anachronistic.

Lenin, as we shall see, echoed all of these Marxian ideas; it was, indeed, his detailed study of the national question which directly led him into a more thorough appraisal of monopoly capitalism.

Lenin, true to form, based his analysis of the national question on an account of its place in the development of capitalism. There were, he argued, two moments in the development of capitalism in this respect. In the early phases of its growth capitalism acted as a progressive force in awakening national spirit. It destroyed local, regional boundaries and created, for the first time, mass movements which 'draw *all* classes of the population into politics through the press, participation in representative institutions, etc'.[36] The process of drawing the whole of the population into political groupings was, of course, in Lenin's view simply a *de post facto* acknowledgement of the development of new economic patterns which had riven the country into two antagonistic classes:

> That truth is that *every* mile of railway, *every* new shop that is opened in the village, *every* co-operative society that is formed to make buying easier, *every* factory, and so forth, draws peasant economy into the orbit of commerce. And that means that the peasantry is *breaking up* into proletarians and *proprietors* employing hired labourers.[37]

The progress of capitalism was then the progress of modern class formation and classes articulated themselves for the first time in the course of the democratic revolution as *national* groupings. This grouping of people who shared a common economic situation on a national plane, was, in Lenin's (as in Marx's) view, enormously progressive compared with the petty localism, regionalism and individual bondage that had hitherto prevailed. 'The great centralised state is a tremendous historical step forward from medieval disunity to the future socialist unity of the whole world, and only *via* such a state (*inseparably* connected with capitalism), can there be any road to socialism.'[38]

Lenin's account of the progressive significance of nationalism as a necessary adjunct of capitalism in its early phases of development lay at the heart of his dispute with Rosa Luxemburg on the national question. It was by no means accidental that the differing political conclusions they came to mirrored the differing spheres of their respective economic analyses. Thus, whereas Lenin's main focus had been the evolution of capitalism out of feudalism with particular attention to Russia, Luxemburg, in her *magnum opus The Accumulation of Capital*,[39] had concentrated upon the most contemporary data of the accumulation of capital in the most advanced countries of the West.

From her economic analysis Rosa Luxemburg emerged with the conclusion that the highly ramified international patterns of contemporary trade had finally rendered nationalism redundant, indeed retrogressive. It was retrogressive not only in the historical sense that it ran counter to modern economic relations but also in the directly practical sense that any commitment to national principle would inevitably lead socialists into a position of subordination to bourgeois nationalism. This danger was particularly acute, she argued, in countries where capitalism (and, consequently, the proletariat), was ill-developed; countries like her native Poland. To preach the right of the Polish people to national self-determination was to run directly counter to the myriad economic ties which firmly cemented the polish economy to that of Russia. Worse, it meant delivering up the proletariat to the chauvinism of the Polish aristocracy and bourgeoisie who had long previously staked their claims as the authentic spokesmen of Polish national aspirations.

The objective analysis of the social evolution of Poland leads to the conclusion that the trends towards a re-establishment of a Polish State *at this time* are a petit-bourgeois Utopia; as such, they are suited only to confuse the proletariat's class struggle and lead it astray.[40]

The only salvation for the Polish working class lay in promoting and participating in an all-Russian rising led by the united working class of all national groups within the Empire.[41]

Lenin did not wish to deny that Luxemburg's analysis contained the germs of an important truth. He certainly agreed that *after* the democratic revolution, *after* capitalism had dominated the national market, then it would be inexorably driven, in its more advanced phase, into external expansion and the consequent internationalisation of its economic relations. In this phase capitalism did undoubtedly have a 'world-historical tendency to break down national barriers, obliterate national distinctions and to *assimilate* nations'.[42] Where Luxemburg was in error, he maintained, was in her assumption that policies towards the national question appropriate to *this* stage of capitalist development were of universal application. She failed to grasp the differential rates of advance in capitalist economies and therefore the differences in the objective significance of the national question.

Developing capitalism knows two historical tendencies in the national question. The first is the awakening of national life and national movements, the struggle against all national oppression, and the creation of national states. The second is the development and growing frequency of international intercourse in every form, the break-down of national barriers, the creation of the international unity of capital, of economic life in general, of politics, science, etc.

Both tendencies are a universal law of capitalism. The former predominates in the beginning of its development, the latter characterises a mature capitalism that is moving towards its transformation into socialist society.[43]

Luxemburg's error consisted in her inability to grasp this historical perspective. According to Lenin, 'Rosa Luxemburg has lost sight of the most important thing – the difference between countries where bourgeois-democratic reforms have long been completed, and those where they have not'.[44] In Russia the slogan of the right of self-determination for all the subject nationalities had become a vital ingredient of the unity of the anti-autocratic movement for democracy in Russia. It was, Lenin cogently argued, precisely the autocracy and its Black Hundred supporters who insisted upon the unified integrity of the Empire and the dominance of the minority Great Russians within it. In this situation, at this phase of development, to urge imperial unity would be to align oneself with the most obscurantist and savagely oppressive anti-democratic forces within Russia. It was, of course, essential to bear in mind that Lenin's attitude towards the national question in Russia had to be seen in relation to the consummation not of the socialist revolution but the democratic revolution. The choice therefore was between feudal imperial nationalism or radical bourgeois-democratic nationalism which would guarantee the right to self-determination and secession from Russia.

The national minorities in Russia, who, taken together, comprised the majority of the population, had Lenin argued, been subjected to the most appalling oppression.[45] They would be unlikely, in view of their past experience, to settle for anything less than the right to secede. This did not, however, mean that the area which comprised the Russian Empire would be forever condemned to Balkanisation, the setting up of mutually antagonistic and economically unviable small states. On the contrary, once the element of coercion and oppression had been removed, once the national groupings felt secure in their identity and cultural autonomy, they would recognise the natural advantages that could flow from re-uniting: 'we stand for the *right* to secede owing to reactionary, Great-Russian nationalism, which has so besmirched the idea of national coexistence that sometimes *closer* ties will be established *after* free secession.'[46] The economic interdependence of national groups was the surest guarantee that internationalism would flourish and triumph. An enforced political suzerainty acted merely as an artificial stimulant to national antagonisms.

What we do not want is the element of *coercion*. We do not want to have people driven into paradise with a cudgel; . . . We are convinced that the development of capitalism in Russia, and the whole course of social life in general, are tending to bring all nations closer together. Hundreds of thousands of people are moving from one end of Russia to another; the different national populations are intermingling; exclusiveness and national conservatism must disappear. People whose conditions of life and work make it necessary for them to know the Russian language will learn it without being forced to do so. But coercion (the cudgel) will have only one result: it will hinder the great and mighty Russian language from spreading to other national groups, and, most important of all, it will sharpen antagonism, cause friction in a million new forms, increase resentment, mutual misunderstanding, and so on.[47]

Lenin's case was that *in Russia* the right of self-determination for the oppressed nationalities was indissolubly bound to the radical democratic movement. He never attempted to universalise from the Russian situation; on the contrary, he was anxious to point out that in Austria, where national minorities felt the main threat to their autonomy coming from outside the Austrian Empire, different considerations might well apply. Even as far as Russia was concerned the recognition by Social Democrats of the *right* to self-determination did not mean that in all cases they would *encourage* secessionist movements. In all the resolutions Lenin wrote on the national question there was always a covering clause which in one way or another warned against confusing the stipulation of a right and the expediency of taking advantage of a right. 'The Social-Democratic Party must decide the latter question exclusively on its merits in each particular case in conformity with the interests of social development as a whole and with the interests of the proletarian class struggle for socialism.'[48] These reservations might well seem to suggest a considerable watering-down of Lenin's fulsome support for national self-determination and they were, in the future, to give some Bolsheviks ample room for manoeuvre vis-à-vis claims for autonomy. To Lenin, however, the reservations were no different in principle from those involved in other recognised rights. To support the right to divorce, for instance, did not, he maintained, entail advocating the break-up of all marriages.[49] On the contrary, the very existence of the right served to limit its exercise; its effect was to preserve loving unions and dissolve forced ones.

The resolution of the national question which Lenin envisaged after a successful and radical democratic revolution in Russia would be based upon a full recognition and guarantee by the new republic of the right of all national groups to secede from the Russian state provided that this decision had been democratically arrived at. He clearly hoped, however, that the very existence of this right, together with the immediate devolution of extensive powers to regional parliaments or Diets in the 'autonomous regions', would preserve a unitary all-Russian state organisation. The establishment of autonomous regions in no way involved concessions to the principle of federalism – better a clean break than this recipe for dissension and inaction; it was no more than the granting of specified powers and jurisdiction within a specified area by the central government.[50] There could, in this constitutional structure, be no wrangling over where sovereignty resided.

We should, finally, notice another reservation which Lenin repeatedly made in his programmatic statements on the national question. It concerned the structure of Party organisation and it was, like the reservations mentioned earlier, to emerge as a potent source of conflict when, immediately after the seizure of power, the demands of national groups to secede from Russia became a reality. Just as Lenin was against the federal principle in the state, so too he had fought a long battle against it in the Party, first against the claims of the Jewish *Bund* at the Second Party Congress, and later against the Letts and the majority Polish party, the P.P.S. He insisted that 'the interests of the working class demand the amalgamation of the workers of all nationalities in a given state in united proletarian organisations – political, trade union, co-operative, educational, etc.'[51] The Party as the vanguard of all opposition groups, the channel for all anti-autocratic discontent (including that of the oppressed nationalities), would have to retain its unified centralised structure uniting the proletariat of all national groups. What was to happen to Party ties if a national group opted to secede after the revolution, is not at all clear.

CONCLUSION

The years immediately prior to the Great War were important ones in the development of Lenin's thought. He had by this time managed to integrate his earlier analysis of the role of strikes in the revolutionary process into quite a sophisticated account of the importance of combining political and economic strikes as mobilisers of the mass of average and backward workers into revolutionary activity. General political and economic strikes came to assume a cardinal role in Lenin's conception of how the democratic revolution would be brought to its successful realisation. They acted not only as mobilisers of the mass, but also as the form of activity through which a more heightened political consciousness and revolutionary commitment could be attained. They further provided a demonstration of the power of the proletariat to challenge and dislocate the autocratic regime and, in this way, created the milieu in which the peasants and the soldiers acquired the confidence to organise and to act to remedy their particular grievances. Mass political and economic strikes were not, however, in Lenin's view, to be identified with the revolution itself and here again his reflections differed from those of Rosa Luxemburg. They were crucial ingredients in creating a revolutionary situation but would not, of themselves, lead to the overthrow of the old regime. The mobilisation of the masses and their growing consciousness of the need for revolutionary change must, if the revolution was to succeed, be supplemented by the purposive organisation of an armed force operating in a planned way so that it could bring to bear, in the appropriate places and at the right time, a preponderance of military power. This distinction between creating the conditions for revolution and the actual mechanics or 'art' of organising an uprising to overthrow the old regime was, of course, to be dealt with at greater length by Lenin in his writings on the eve of the October Revolution of 1917.

Lenin's preoccupation with the role of strikes in the revolutionary process was, as we have seen, of long-standing. It dated back at least to 1895 and the implications of the *On Agitation* tactic and had been given renewed force by the experience of 1905. Lenin was, therefore, doing no more than continuing his reflections on the past experience of the Party and the working class and attempting to integrate this into the established structure of his thought. The same can hardly be said about the interconnected themes of monopoly capitalism and the national question which began to appear at this time. It was once again Rosa Luxemburg, who obliged Lenin to enter these fields which, to all intents and purposes, he had hitherto ignored. In order to rebut her case that the issue of national self-determination had become an irrelevance in the modern world, he had also to examine the justificatory argument upon which this case was premised, i.e., that modern capitalism in its international monopolist phase had made national groupings anachronistic. Lenin's response to this challenge was sound enough. He did not challenge the basic contention of Luxemburg and Hilferding that modern capitalism had changed its nature and entered a new and final stage of its development as monopoly or finance capital. All he had to do to establish his own view of the continued importance of the national question as far as Russia was concerned, was to assert that Luxemburg had failed to grasp the uneven pace of capitalist development. The problem in Russia was the problem of the democratic revolution, the removal of the economic and political remnants of feudalism. In this situation, Lenin argued, the orthodox Marxist propositions concerning the progressive nature of movements of national self-determination continued to apply.

There were, none the less, crucial points which Lenin's 'resolution' of the national question did not settle. He was obliged, in the first place to recognise that the patterns of Russian capitalist relations had been outpaced by developments elsewhere. Western capitalism, it appeared, was undergoing a quite new phase of development as monopoly or finance capitalism. The economic theory of finance capital in turn carried with it profound implications for the Marxist analysis of the transformed nature of the imperialist state and its colonialist and militarist policies. It provided a sophisticated Marxist explanation for the obvious preparations being made for an international war and an economic rationale which could account for the spread of reformism and revisionism in the Western labour movement. As we have seen Lenin had already accepted many of these political conclusions in his attempts to explain developments in the West. He was, however, becoming increasingly aware of the fact that the theoretical structure of ideas with which he had been operating thus far could not accommodate these crucially important new phenomena. His own theoretical analysis had been based on purely Russian experience and had located large-scale industrial capitalism as the final phase of capitalist development. Its whole objective had been to demonstrate (against Narodnik arguments to the contrary) that the growth of capitalism out of feudalism and its creation of a national market could be explained as an indigenous and natural process which did not require extraneous factors like foreign trade or foreign capital to explain its growth. Lenin's economic and social theory therefore had to do with Russia and Russia alone. The practical political objectives which flowed from the theory were similarly meant to apply only to Russia. It was the national question which prompted Lenin to examine the limitations of his whole theoretical analysis. If Luxemburg and Hilferding were correct in asserting that capitalism in the West had outgrown the phase of free competition within a national market and had become monopolistic and international by its very nature – then, clearly, Lenin's old theoretical structure would be quite useless as an explanatory model or as a guide to action on an international scale. The argument of the theorists of monopoly capitalism was that the global problems faced by the world on the eve of war had been caused and internationalised by a quite new phase in the development of capitalism. Lenin was forced to acknowledge the truth of many of their propositions and he was also forced to realise that his own theoretical analysis, however effective as an explanatory model and guide to action in the Russian environment, just could not accommodate the new problems. It was too spatially and temporarily limited in that it referred solely to Russia and asserted large-scale machine industry to be capitalism's culminating point.

It was the drift towards war which led Lenin to question the adequacy of his old theoretical analysis and it was the outbreak of the war which imperatively demanded the adoption of a new theory with radically changed implications for practice. Lenin's new theoretical analysis and the political practice which flowed from it will be examined in the second volume of this study.

Notes and References

Full title, place and date of publication is only given when a work is cited for the first time in the notes. Thereafter only the author's surname followed by page number is normally given. In cases where more than one work by the same author are referred to, the author's surname is followed by an abbreviation of the title.

INTRODUCTION

1. I am grateful to the editors of the *European Journal of Sociology* for permission to use in the Introduction some material developed in my article 'Lenin and his Critics: Some Problems of Interpretation', vol. XVII (1976) pp. 366–83.
2. E. Wilson, *To the Finland Station* (London, 1960, first published 1940) p. 390. Exactly similar accounts of Lenin as a theorist can be found in such influential texts as R. N. Carew-Hunt, *The Theory and Practice of Communism* (London, 1950), and J. Plamenatz, *German Marxism and Russian Communism* (London, 1954).
3. This well-worn interpretation originated in Menshevik critiques of Lenin's thought after the 1903 split and is a recurrent theme in subsequent Lenin studies in the West. The fullest recent account is by R. Pipes, 'The Origins of Bolshevism, the Intellectual Evolution of Young Lenin' in R. Pipes (ed.), *Revolutionary Russia* (London, 1968). See also *inter alia*: A. B. Ulam, *Lenin and the Bolsheviks* (London, 1969) pp. 108–9; Carew-Hunt, p. 166; L. B. Schapiro, *The Communist Party of the Soviet Union* (London, 1970) p. 4; S. V. Utechin, Introduction to *What Is To Be Done?* (London, 1963) pp. 28–33 and cf. his *Russian Political Thought* (London, 1964) p. 217; R. Payne, *The Life and Death of Lenin* (London, 1964) p. 30; and R. H. W. Theen, *V. I. Lenin: The Genesis and Development of a Revolutionary* (London, 1974) pp. 38–42.
4. Theen, p. 36; cf. N. Leites, *A Study of Bolshevism* (Glencoe, Ill., 1953) and E. V. Wolfenstein, *The Revolutionary Personality* (Princeton, 1967).
5. L. S. Feuer, 'Between Fantasy and Reality: Lenin as a Philosopher and Social Scientist' in B. W. Eissenstat (ed.), *Lenin and Leninism* (London, 1971) pp. 59–79.
6. S. Page, *Lenin and World Revolution* (N.Y., 1959) p. xix.

7. R. Conquest, *V. I. Lenin* (London, 1972) p. 40; cf. Theen, p. 60: 'Lenin may be understood as the embodiment par excellence of the Jacobin spirit and tendency of early Marxism, i.e., Marxism before 1850.'
8. Consider the strident anachronism of the title (and substance) of A. L. Weeks's book *The First Bolshevik – A Political Biography of Peter Tkachev* (N.Y., 1968).
9. The nearest any Marxist account of Lenin comes to exploring this question is Georges Cogniot's attempt, in the first volume of *Présence de Lénine* (Paris, 1970), to outline the themes of each of Lenin's major texts. Such a catalogue suffers, necessarily, from lack of continuity and brevity of treatment (*The Development of Capitalism in Russia*, for example, merits less than two small pages). Marcel Liebman's scholarly and provocative *Le Léninisme*, 2 vols (Paris, 1973; English edition *Leninism under Lenin*, London, 1975) follows many other studies in appearing to assume that Lenin's significant contributions to the theory and practice of revolution did not really begin until 1902, by which time his early social and economic analysis had long been established. Although Tony Cliff's study, *Lenin* (London, 1975) vol. 1, is more comprehensive and does provide a brief account of Lenin's early intellectual development, it also is concerned (as the sub-title *Building the Party* makes clear) almost exclusively with Lenin's ideas on 'practice'; their 'theoretical' underpinnings emerge only occasionally and accidentally. This applies equally, to Trotsky's otherwise excellent *The Young Lenin* (Harmondsworth, 1974) and Nina Gourfinkel's succinct and attractive *Portrait of Lenin* (re-issued N.Y., 1972).
10. Consider Gregory Guroff's amazing assertion that Lenin 'had little time for comment or analysis of specifically economic problems . . . Lenin did not set forth his own economic views or any observations about the future organization of a Socialist economy' (in Eissenstat, pp. 183–4), and John Plamenatz's contention that 'When he [Lenin] wanted to establish the truth of his opinions, he seldom discussed the relevant facts: he did not study society and government but only what Marxists, orthodox and heretical, had so say about them' (in Plamenatz, p. 248).
11. In V. I. Lenin, *Collected Works* in 45 vols (Moscow, 1960–70) vol. 22, pp. 187–304. Almost all subsequent references to Lenin's writings will be to this English translation of the Fourth Russian Edition of the *Sochineniya*. Subsequent references to Lenin's *Collected Works* will be abbreviated to *CW* and will give only the volume number in bold type followed by the page number in plain type. In this notation the reference given above would be rendered: *CW*, **22**, 187–304.

CHAPTER 1

1. A. E. Ulyanova Elizarova, *'Vospominaniya ob Iliche'* in *Vospominaniya o*

Vladimire Iliche Lenine [hereafter referred to as *Vospominaniya*], 3 vols (Moscow, 1956–60) vol. 1, p. 25.

2. I. Deutscher, *Lenin's Childhood* (London, 1970) p. 30.
3. Deutscher, p. 52.
4. L. Trotsky, *The Young Lenin* (Harmondsworth, 1974) pp. 81–2.
5. An account of Aleksander's speech justifying the conspirators and outlining their political aspirations can be found in the compilation of materials dealing with the last year of his life edited by his sister: A. E. Ulyanova Elizarova, *Aleksandr Ilich Ulyanov i delo 1 Marta 1887 g.* (Moscow, 1927) pp. 330–40.
6. Trotsky, p. 126.
7. Fyodor Kerensky's testimonial is quoted at length in Payne, p. 75.
8. A full account of Lenin's brief career at Kazan University is given in P. E. Nafigov's *Pervyi shag v revolyutsii. V. I. Ulyanov i kazanskoe studenchestvo 80kh godov XIX veka* (Kazan, 1970) ch. 2.
9. Payne, p. 80.
10. N. Valentinov (Volsky), *Encounters with Lenin* (London, 1968) p. 76.
11. I have dealt with this question at greater length in 'Lenin's Early Writings – The Problem of Context', *Political Studies* (December 1975) 442–58.
12. *Narodovolets* (plural *Narodovoltsi*), adherent of the terrorist organisation *Narodnaya Volya* (The People's Will). For an account of the history and ideas of this organisation see Franco Venturi's excellent study *Roots of Revolution* (London, 1964) chs 21 and 22.
13. Richard Pipes, one of the most prominent spokesmen of the Lenin-as-Jacobin interpretive line, has exhaustively catalogued the 'Jacobin' groups and personages with whom Lenin was in any way associated during his early years. See his 'The Origins of Bolshevism: The Intellectual Evolution of Young Lenin' in Pipes (ed.), *Revolutionary Russia*.
14. *Vospominaniya*, vol. 1, p. 19.
15. According to Karl Radek, cited in Trotsky, p. 146.
16. *Vospominaniya*, vol 1, p. 21. See also Lenin's own testimony that he never met Fedoseev, 'A few Words about N. Y. Fedoseev', *CW*, **33**, 452–3.
17. *Vospominaniya*, vol. 1, p. 20.
18. V. I. Lenin, *Kratki biograficheskii ocherk*, 6th edn (Moscow, 1970) p. 15.
19. *Vospominaniya*, vol. 1, p. 21.
20. Ibid., p. 23.
21. Ibid., p. 57.
22. Lenin, *Kratkii biograficheskii ocherk*, p. 13.
23. *Vospominaniya rodnykh o V. I. Lenine* (Moscow, 1955) p. 100.
24. Yu. Z. Polevoi, *Zarozhdenie marksizma v Rossii 1883–1894 gg.* (Moscow, 1959) p. 410; cf. Trotsky, p. 183.
25. V. Chuev in his *V. I. Lenin v Samare* (Moscow, 1960), gives a detailed account of the groups and individuals comprising the exile circles in Samara at this time. See also B. M. Volin, *V. I. Lenin v Povolzhe* (Moscow, 1955) and M. I. Semenov, *Revolyutsionnaya Samara 80–90kh godov: Vospominaniya* (Kuibishev, 1940) for details of Lenin's activities in

propagating Marxist ideas among Populist circles in Samara at this time.

26. *Vospominaniya*, vol. 1, p. 22.
27. See Vodovozov's appraisal of Lenin at this time in the collection *V. I. Lenin v Samare 1889–93* (Moscow, 1933) pp. 98–101; cf. N. Lalayants in *Vospominaniya*, vol. 1, p. 104, and A. B. Ulam, *Lenin and the Bolsheviks* (London, 1969) p. 135.
28. Ulam, p. 138.
29. Quoted in D. Shub, *Lenin* (Harmondsworth, 1966) p. 39; cf. the account given by A. Belyakov in *Yunost Vozhdya* (Moscow, 1958).
30. G. V. Plekhanov, *Sochineniya* [hereafter referred to as Plekhanov, *Sochineniya*, followed by the volume number in bold type and the page number in plain type] 2nd edn, ed. D. Ryazanov, 24 vols (Moscow, 1923–7) 1.
31. Chuev, p. 55.
32. B. D. Wolfe, *Three Who Made a Revolution* (Harmondsworth, 1966) p. 109; cf. the appraisal of Pipes who attributes Lenin's hard line to the influence of a Samara Jacobin, a certain Yasneva.
33. Mark Elizarov's background and subsequent relations with Aleksander Ulyanov and Lenin are traced in P. P. Elizarov, *Mark Elizarov i Semya Ulyanovykh* (Moscow, 1967).
34. Polevoi, p. 412 n.
35. See Ulam, pp. 136–8 for an account of Lenin's first major public debate when he took on none less than Mikhailovsky and scored well.
36. Chuev, p. 26; see also T. Barkovskaya, *Nachlo bolshego puti* (Kuibishev, 1964) pp. 6 et seq, and V. Sutyrin, *Aleksandr Ulyanov (1886–1887)* (Moscow, 1971) p. 67.
37. Sabunaev had been one of the participants at a meeting of veteran *Narodovoltsi* in Kazan in the latter part of September 1889 where this strategic objective had been adopted (Chuev, p. 28). An account of Lenin's public controversy with Sabunaev is given in Belyakov.
38. In *Molodye Gody V. I. Lenina*, A. I. Ivanskii ed. (Moscow, 1958) pp. 380–2.
39. M. Golubeva (Yasneva), 'Moya pervaya vstrecha s Valdimirom Ilichem' in *Lenin v Samare: Vospominaniya Sovremenikov* (Kuibishev, 1969) pp. 103–7. See also her account in *Vospominaniya*, vol. 1, pp. 96–9.
40. Quoted in Semenov p. 108. Belyakov's ample account of the meeting is in Ivanskii, *Molodye gody V. I. Lenina* (Moscow, 1958) pp. 440–9.
41. Theen, p. 44; cf. Pipes.
42. *Leninskii sbornik* (Moscow, 1932) vol xx, p. 51.
43. Polevoi (p. 414) gives a full list of the materials in this library. See also Lalayants's account of its contents in his *U istokov Bolshevizma* (Moscow, 1930) p. 17. Cf. A. B. Ulam's account of the resources of radical literature in Samara at that time: 'Books could be borrowed if one had a friend who was a member of the Merchants' Club, which possessed the only semi-decent library in the town' (Ulam, pp. 142–3). This is at variance with Chuev's account which gives the names of two

libraries in Samara at this time which subscribed to the main journals and also possessed adequate sources on Russian peasant life. The records of Lenin's borrowings from the libraries are, it seems studiously preserved; see Chuev, p. 73. Chuev also tells us that Lenin obtained copies of *Neue Zeit* and other German language materials from Prof. L. I. Yaven in St Petersburg (ibid., pp. 47–8).

44. *Vospominaniya*, vol. 1, p. 22.
45. Ibid., p. 61.
46. Barkovskaya, p. 125.
47. Semenov, p. 14; cf. M. Golubeva (Yasneva), *'Yunosha Ulyanov'* in *Staryi Bolshevik* (1933) no. 5, p. 163.
48. M. I. Semenov, *Staryi tovarishch A. P. Sklyarenko* (Moscow, 1922) p. 11; cf. the account of Krasnoperov's background in *Lenin v Samare*, B. N. Avilkin, ed. (Kuibishev, 1969) p. 62.
49. See *CW* 1, 13–73. According to Lalayants, Lenin also wrote analyses of V. P. Vorontsov's *The Fate of Capitalism in Russia* and of Fedoseev's manuscript articles on the economic reasons for the abolition of serfdom in Russia (*Vospominaniya*, vol. 1, p. 105). According to Lalayants, Lenin stressed the significance of Fedoseev's work 'as the first serious attempt to outline the basic causes for the transition from serfdom from a Marxist point of view' (comment of N. Lalayants to the memoirs of M. I. Semenov in *V. I. Lenin v Samare 1889–93*, p. 52). Fedoseev's three articles dwelt on the economic motives of the wealthier and more efficient landowners in pressing for increased mobility for agricultural labour, hence their opposition to bondage and serfdom (see the short review given in Semenov, pp. 56–7).
50. Polevoi, p. 416.
51. *CW*, 3.
52. Polevoi, p. 419; cf. Lalayants in *Vospominaniya*, vol. 1, p. 105 and Chuev, p. 68.
53. Chuev, p. 88.
54. For an account of Mikhailovsky's arguments see A. P. Mendel 'N. K. Mikhailovsky and his Criticism of Russian Marxism', *The American Slavic and East European Review*, xiv (1955) 331–45.
55. *Vospominaniya*, vol. 1, p. 23.
56. This conclusion considered by Pipes to be 'astonishing' (Pipes, *Revolutionary Russia*, p. 38) and which Berlin maintains is 'extraordinary and extravagant' ('Comment on Pipes', ibid., p. 53) was also the conclusion arrived at by Plekhanov and Akselrod. It was in fact a key concept of orthodox Russian Marxism as I will argue further in Chapter Two.

CHAPTER 2

1. S. H. Baron, *Plekhanov, the Father of Russian Marxism* (London, 1963) p. 135.

2. *Perepiska G. V. Plekhanova i P. B. Akselroda*, 2 vols, ed. B. I. Nickolaevsky, P. A. Berlin and W. S. Woytinsky (Moscow, 1925) vol. 1, p. 275.

3. *CW*, 4, 340.

4. For an excellent account of the ideas of Bakunin and Tkachev and the movements they inspired see Venturi.

5. 'For Lenin *Socialism and the Political Struggle* was to Russia what *The Communist Manifesto* was to the West' A. Rothstein, Preface to Plekhanov's *In Defense of Materialism* (London, 1947) p. 10. *Our Differences* was perhaps even more influential: 'The Soviet historian Pokrovsky merely stated the obvious when he remarked that this work contained "practically all the basic ideas that formed the stock-in-trade of Russian Marxism up to the end of the century".' Baron, p. 89.

6. The 'people' in Populist parlance referred, of course, to the peasants and workers, to the producers and not to the landlords, nobles and bureaucrats.

7. A. von Haxthausen, *Studien uber die inneren Zustände, das Volksleben und insbesondere die ländlichen Einrichtungen Russlands*, 3 vols (Hanover and Berlin, 1847, 1852); translated as *Studies on the Interior of Russia*, ed. S. F. Starr (Chicago, 1972).

8. Venturi, p. 22.

9. Ibid., pp. 60, 84, 151.

10. G. V. Plekhanov, *Sochineniya*, 1. I have used the *Sochineniya* for those writings not included in the far more accessible G. Plekhanov, *Selected Philosophical Works* [referred to hereafter as Plekhanov, *SPW*, followed by the volume number in bold type and the page number in plain type] (Moscow, 1961) 1.

11. Plekhanov, *Sochineniya*, 1, 61.

12. Ibid., p. 61.

13. Ibid., p. 69.

14. Baron, p. 56.

15. Plekhanov, *SPW*, 1, 57–121.

16. Ibid., pp. 122–399.

17. Ibid., pp. 155–6, 173, 184, 185–6.

18. Ibid., p. 760.

19. Ibid., pp. 164–5.

20. Ibid., p. 266. This formulation is repeated almost word for word on p. 308.

21. Ibid., p. 267.

22. Ibid., p. 309.

23. Ibid., p. 442.

24. Ibid., pp. 302–3.

25. Ibid., p. 281.

26. Ibid., p. 280.

27. Ibid., p. 274.

28. Ibid., pp. 257–8.

29. Ibid., p. 214.

30. Ibid., p. 298.

31. Ibid., p. 224.
32. Ibid., p. 257.
33. Ibid., p. 250.
34. P. Akselrod, *K voprosu o sovremennykh zadachakh i taktik russkikh sotsial-demokratov* [hereafter Akselrod, *K voprosu*] (Geneva, 1898) p. 5.
35. K. Marx, *Capital*, 3 vols (Moscow, 1954, 1957, 1962) vol. 1, pp. 748–9.
36. Plekhanov, *SPW*, 1, 261.
37. Ibid., pp. 262–3.
38. Ibid., p. 263.
39. Ibid., p. 475.
40. Ibid., p. 95.
41. Ibid., p. 255.
42. Ibid., p. 421.
43. Ibid., p. 445.
44. Ibid., p. 154.
45. Ibid., p. 445.
46. Ibid., p. 454.
47. Ibid., pp. 400–5.
48. *Manifest Rossiiskoi Sotsialdemokraticheskoi Rabochei Partii* [hereafter, *Manifest*] (Geneva, 1903) p. 3. This Manifesto, written by Peter Struve, was adopted at the First Congress of the Russian Social Democratic Labour Party (R.S.D.L.P.) held at Minsk in 1898. It is often referred to as the Minsk Manifesto.
49. Akselrod, *K voprosu*, p. 20.
50. Quoted in A. Ascher, *Pavel Axelrod and the Development of Menshevism* [hereafter Ascher, *Axelrod*] (Cambridge, Mass., 1972) p. 134.
51. Plekhanov, *SPW*, 1, 240.
52. Ibid., p. 108.
53. *Manifest*, p. 1.
54. K. Marx and F. Engels, *Selected Works* [hereafter, *MESW*] 2 vols (Moscow, 1962) vol. 1. The *Selected Works* have been used for those writings of Marx and Engels not yet covered by their *Collected Works*, detailed in note 63 below.
55. *MESW*, vol. 1, p. 227.
56. Plekhanov, *SPW*, 1, 120.
57. Ibid., p. 118.
58. Ibid., p. 377.
59. Ibid., p. 117.
60. Ibid., p. 404.
61. Ibid., p. 405.
62. Ibid., p. 446.
63. K. Marx and F. Engels, *Collected Works* [hereafter *MECW*] to comprise 50 vols (London, 1975–   ) vol. 3, p. 187.
64. Plekhanov, *SPW*, 1, 377.
65. Ibid., p. 389.
66. Ibid., p. 119.
67. Ibid., p. 89.
68. Ibid., pp. 90–91.

69. Ibid., p. 91.
70. *MECW*, vol. 6, p. 493.
71. Ibid., p. 211.
72. *MESW*, vol. 1, p. 334.
73. Plekhanov, *SPW*, 1, 327–8.
74. Ibid., p. 60.
75. Ibid., p. 425.
76. Ibid., p. 389.
77. Ibid., pp. 403–4.
78. Ibid., p. 71.
79. Ibid., p. 73.
80. Ibid., p. 403.
81. *MECW*, vol. 6, p. 505.
82. Plekhanov, *SPW*, 1, 111.
83. Ibid., p. 112.
84. Ibid., pp. 402–3.
85. *Manifest*, p. 2.
86. Baron, p. 109.

CHAPTER 3

1. A full account of this important period in Lenin's life is given in A. I. Ivanskii, *Lenin, Peterburgskie gody* (Moscow, 1972).
2. See the divergent accounts in R. Pipes *Social Democracy and the St Petersburg Labour Movement 1885–1897* (Cambridge, Mass., 1963); J. L. H. Keep, *The Rise of Social Democracy in Russia* (London, 1963); and A. K. Wildman, *The Making of a Workers' Revolution* (Chicago, 1967).
3. *CW*, 2, 327–8.
4. V. Kapelina, 'Tri Vstrechi' in *Krasnaya Letopis*, no. 1 (Leningrad 1924) pp. 10–11.
5. C. I. Mitskeevich, *Revolyutsionnaya Moskva, 1888–1905* (Moscow, 1940) p. 145.
6. I. Grigorev, *Proletarskaya Revolyutsiya*, no. 8. Cited in Lenin *Sochineniya*, 3rd ed, 30 vols (Moscow, Leningrad, 1926–35) vol. 1, p. 489.
7. See Silvin's account of the meeting in *Proletarskaya Revolyutsiya*, no. 7 (1924); cf. Ivanskii, *Lenin, Peterburgskie gody*, p. 15.
8. M. A. Silvin, 'V. I. Lenin v epokhu Zarozhdeniya partii', *Katorga i Ssylka*, no. 10 (1934) 77.
9. M. A. Silvin in *Katorga i Ssylka*, op. cit., p. 81; cf. the accounts of this meeting in *Vospominaniya*, vol. 1, by C. Nevzorova-Shesterina (p. 142) and G. M. Krzhizhanovsky (p. 152); see also N. Krupskaya, *Memories of Lenin* (London, 1942) pp. 1–2.
10. The surviving First and Third Parts of this work take up some 200 pages in Lenin's *Collected Works* (*CW*, 1, 133–332).
11. *Vospominaniya*, vol. 1, p. 134.
12. N. N. Akimov *et al.*, *Metodicheskie Sovety po izucheniyu proizvedenii V. I. Lenina* (Moscow, 1972) p. 7.

13. *CW*, 1, 267. This was, of course, a reference to Plekhanov's Emancipation of Labour Group.
14. Ibid., p. 197.
15. Ibid., p. 267.
16. Ibid., p. 218.
17. As cited by Pipes, *Revolutionary Russia*, p. 39n.; cf. the distortion, through omission of Lenin's qualifying clauses, in Theen, p. 59.
18. *CW*, 1, 300.
19. Ibid., p. 271; cf. Theen, p. 59 and Pipes, *Revolutionary Russia*, p. 39.
20. *CW*, 1, 282–3.
21. Ibid., p. 280.
22. Ibid., pp. 288–9.
23. Ibid., pp. 291–2.
24. Ibid., p. 291.
25. Ibid., p. 299.
26. Ibid., p. 300.
27. It is perhaps unwise even to broach the topic of Lenin's many pseudonyms which has provided material enough for monographs. The curious may delve into I. N. Volper's authoritative *Psevdonimy V. I. Lenina* (Leningrad, 1965).
28. Krupskaya, p. 5.
29. N. M. Bogdanov, in *Ot Gruppy Blagoeva k Soyuzu Borby 1886–94* (Rostov, 1921), cited in Wildman, p. 35.
30. *Vospominaniya*, vol. 1, p. 150.
31. Krupskaya, p. 7.
32. V. I. Lenin, *Kratkii biograficheskii ocherk,* p. 22.
33. *Vospominaniya*, vol. 1, p. 118.
34. O. G. Kutsentov, *Deyateli Peterburgskogo 'Soyuz borby za osvobozhdenie rabochego klassa'* (Moscow, 1962) p. 8. R. H. McNeal's *Bride of the Revolution: Krupskaya and Lenin* (London, 1973) contains the fullest account in English of the very prominent role played by Marxists in these evening and Sunday schools.
35. Krupskaya, p. 6.
36. *Vospominaniya*, vol. 1, p. 114.
37. Ibid., p. 119.
38. Not included in the Russian editions of Lenin's *Sochineniya* nor in *Collected Works*. Published in L. M. Ivanov (ed.), *Rabochee dvizhenie v Rossii v XIX veke, tom IV chast pervaya 1895–1897* (Leningrad, 1961), pp. 1–2. Ivanov's attribution of this *Questionnaire on the Situation of the Workers* to Lenin is confirmed by Babushkin's memoirs, see *Vospominaniya*, vol. 1, p. 114.
39. The titles of Lenin's works in this period illustrate his preoccupations: *New Economic Developments in Peasant Life, On The So-Called Market Question* (1893), *What the 'Friends of the People' Are and How They Fight the Social Democrats, The Economic Content of Narodism and the Criticism of it in Mr. Struve's Book* (1894), *A Characterisation of Economic Romanticism, Gems of Narodnik Project-Mongering, The Heritage We Renounce* (1897).
40. See Lenin's *The Economic Content of Narodism and the Criticism of it in*

Mr. Struve's Book (The Reflection of Marxism in Bourgeois Literature), written at the end of 1894 and beginning of 1895. *CW*, **1**, 333–507.

41. M. Silvin in *Vospominaniya*, vol. 1, p. 124.

42. Ibid., p. 125.

43. 'Peterburzhets' (pseud. of K. M. Takhtarev), *Ocherk Peterburgskogo rabochego dvizheniya 90kh. godov* (London, 1902) pp. 12–13.

44. The date given in the Third Edition of Lenin's *Sochineniya* (Moscow, 1926) vol. 1, p. 518, is January 1895. Lenin himself (writing in December 1910) in an obituary for Babushkin, recounts how the latter helped to draw up 'the first agitational leaflet put out in St Petersburg in the autumn of 1894, a leaflet addressed to the Semyannikov workers.' *CW*, **16**, 361. This recollection sets the date too early, however, since one of the workers' grievances was the non-payment of their wages immediately before the Christmas holiday. The reason this leaflet does not appear in Lenin's *Collected Works* may perhaps be attributable to the note of confusion as to its authorship introduced by G. M. Krzhizhanovsky who, in a letter to *Letopis Marksizma* (1927, no. 4, p. 140) claimed to have helped to write it.

45. Babushkin's own account of this episode can be found in Ivanskii, *Lenin, Peterburgskie gody*, p. 117; cf. Krupskaya, p. 11 and her account in 'The League for the Emancipation of the Working Class' in *Borba za sozdanie marksistskoi partii v Rossii* (Moscow, 1964) p. 71; cf. T. Kopelzohn in *O Lenine* (Moscow, 1925) p. 21. Only part of this leaflet is extant. It was found in Akselrod's archive and was, presumably, brought from Russia by Lenin himself when he visited Plekhanov and Akselrod in Switzerland in the summer of 1895. The surviving fragment was published for the first time by Boris Nikolaevsky in *Letopis Marksizma*, no. 3 (1927) pp. 61–6. It can be found in the excellent collection of documents, *Nachalo rabochego dvizhenie i rasprostranenie marksizma v Rossii 1883–1894 gody* (Moscow, 1960) and in S. N. Valk's definitive edition of the leaflets produced by the St Petersburg Union of Struggle, *Listovki Peterburgskogo "Soyuza borby za osvobozhdenie rabochego Klassa" 1895–1897 gg.* (Moscow, 1934) pp. 1–6.

46. *Vospominaniya*, vol. 1, p. 152.

47. See the accounts in *Vospominaniya*, vol. 1 of: Shelgunov (p. 116) and Silvin (p. 121). Krupskaya has it that it was Martov and Lyakhovsky who brought the good news of *On Agitation* from Vilno to St Petersburg and this is taken up by subsequent commentators. See her account in 'The League for the Emancipation of the Working Class', op. cit., p. 70. According to Silvin, however, Martov did not arrive in St Petersburg until the autumn of 1895 (*Vospominaniya*, vol. 1, p. 127). Nikolaevsky puts the date of the brochure's arrival and the discussion of it a year earlier than this (*K istorii peterburgskoi sotsial-demokraticheskoi gruppi "Starikov"'*, in *Letopis Marksizma* no. 3 (1927) p. 63). According to Takhtarev, however, the final commitment on the part of the intelligentsia to the new tactic did not occur until the autumn of 1895. Takhtarev's account is quite detailed and has the merit of having been

written not long after the events in question. (See his *Ocherk Peter-burgskogo rabochego dvizheniya*, pp. 16–19.)

48. *Vospominaniya*, vol. 1, pp. 126–7.

CHAPTER 4

1. Plekhanov, *SPW*, 1, 542–782.
2. Plekhanov's main contribution in this respect had been completed by 1884, and was therefore unable to take account of Marx's fuller elaboration of the early phases of capitalist accumulation set out in volumes ii and iii of *Capital*, which were not published until 1885 and 1894 respectively. Plekhanov was, in any case, little inclined to update the economic analysis arrived at in chapters ii and iii of *Our Differences* (*SPW*, 1, 235–310).
3. A. Walicki, *The Controversy over Capitalism* (Oxford, 1969).
4. For a fuller account of the Populist case in this period see: R. Wortman, *The Crisis of Russian Populism* (Cambridge, 1967); A. P. Mendel, *Dilemmas of Progress in Tsarist Russia: Legal Populism and Legal Marxism* (Cambridge, Mass., 1961); and Walicki, op. cit. For once it would appear that history has done justice to the vanquished. We are indeed in the somewhat anomalous position that the most sophisticated and influential Russian Marxist critique of Populism has received precious little historical examination.
5. V. V. (pseud. V. P. Vorontsov), *Sudby Kapitalizma v Rossii* (St Petersburg, 1882) p. 4.
6. V. V., '*K voprosu o razvitii kapitalizma v Rossii*', *Otechestvennye Zapiski*, no. 252, part 2 (Sept. 1880).
7. Cf. Sismondi: 'Owing to the concentration of wealth in the hands of a few proprietors, the home market is contracted and industry must make other outlets for its products in foreign markets . . .' S. Sismondi, *Nouveaux Principes*, 2nd edn (Paris, 1827) p. 361.
8. V. V., '*Iz istorii russkogo Kapitalizma*', *Otechestvennye Zapiski*, no. 259 (Dec. 1881) 216.
9. V. V., '*K voprosu o razvitii kapitlizma v Rossii*', op. cit., p. 7.
10. A. P. Mendel makes a useful distinction between the small-deeds evolutionary socialism of Vorontsov which prevailed through the eighties and the 'maximalist' approach of publicists like Mikhailovsky and Danielson who maintained that time was running out too quickly to afford the luxury of permeative gradualness. The maximalists argued that only a total re-orientation of policy and government in a socialist direction could pre-empt the acceleration of injustice and deprivation which capitalist industrialisation had brought to Russia.
11. *CW*, 1, 411.
12. Plekhanov, *SPW*, 1, 235, 239; cf. I. M. Brover, *Ekonomicheskie vzglyady G. V. Plekhanova* (Moscow, 1960) pp. 67–8.
13. *CW*, 1, 218–9.
14. Ibid., p. 93; cf. pp. 430, 437.

15. Ibid., pp. 437–8.
16. Ibid., p. 438.
17. Ibid., pp. 374–5.
18. Marx, *Capital*, vol. iii, p. 586.
19. Cf. *Capital*, vol. iii, p. 582. 'In the form of interest, the entire surplus value above the barest means of subsistence (the amount that later becomes wages of the producers) can be consumed by usury.'
20. *CW*, 6, 143.
21. *Capital*, vol. iii, p. 771.
22. *CW*, 3, 198.
23. Ibid., p. 202.
24. Ibid., p. 203.
25. Ibid., p. 204.
26. *Capital*, vol. iii, p. 770.
27. Ibid., p. 771.
28. *CW*, 3, 204.
29. *CW*, 1, 373.
30. *CW*, 3, 315 n.
31. Ibid., pp. 183–4.
32. *Capital*, vol. iii, p. 583.
33. *CW*, 1, 428.
34. *CW*, 3, 368.
35. Ibid., p. 368.
36. Ibid., p. 369.
37. See, for example, *CW*, 1, 407, 482; *CW*, 2, 427; *CW*, 3, 204.
38. The genesis of the industrial reserve army had earlier been established by the Marxist Professor of Economics at Moscow University, Nicholas Ziber in his *Ocherki pervobytnoi ekonomicheskoi kultury* (Moscow, 1883) and his influential *David Rikardo i Karl Marks v ikh obshchestenno-ekonomicheskikh issledovaniyakh* (St Petersburg, 1897). Lenin was particularly indebted to Ziber's account of how machine industry arose out of the previous phase of capitalist manufacture. (See his references to Ziber, *CW*, 2, 180, 186–7.)
39. *CW*, 2, 428.
40. Ibid., pp. 428–9, 435.
41. *CW*, 1, 235–6.
42. *CW*, 2, 382.
43. *CW*, 3, 311.
44. Ibid., pp. 351–2.
45. Ibid., pp. 433–4.
46. *CW*, 1, 209; cf. *CW*, 2, 428.
47. *CW*, 3, 435.
48. Ibid., p. 544.
49. *CW*, 3, 585–6 (emphasis added). This general methodology is a consistent strand in Lenin's thought; cf. *CW*, 6, 131.
50. See Lenin's rather laboured polemic *A Characterisation of Economic Romanticism*, *CW*, 2, 129–265 and his briefer and better *On the So-Called Market Question*, *CW*, 1, 79–125.

51. *CW*, 1, pp. 79–125.
52. M. Tanaka 'The Controversies Concerning Russian Capitalism – An Analysis of the Views of Plekhanov and Lenin', *Kyoto University Economic Review*, XXXVI (Oct. 1966) 37.
53. *CW*, 1, 99–100.
54. Ibid., pp. 102–3.
55. *CW*, 2, 158; cf. *CW*, 3, 54, where Lenin presented this as one of Marx's principal conclusions in volume II of *Capital*.
56. *CW*, 2, 159–60.
57. *CW*, 3, 547–8.
58. *CW*, 3, 315–21, 545.
59. *CW*, 1, 106–7, 321; cf. *CW*, 3, 546–7.
60. *CW*, 3, 382.
61. Ibid., p. 546.
62. *CW*, 1, 236, 300; cf. *CW*, 3, 316–17.
63. *CW*, 1, 299.
64. Ibid., pp. 384–5, 403; cf. *CW*, 3, 244.
65. *CW*, 1, 380.
66. Ibid., p. 379–80.
67. Ibid., p. 299; cf. *CW*, 3, 31.
68. *CW*, 1, 299.
69. See in particular Marx's appraisal of the dialectical relationship between capital and labour in *The Holy Family, MECW*, vol. 4, pp. 35–7.
70. *CW*, 1, 333–507, *The Economic Content of Narodism and the Criticism of it in Mr. Struve's Book*.
71. *CW*, 3.
72. Ibid., p. 636 n.
73. V. I. Lenin, *Leninskii Shornik*, vol. XXXIII.
74. Mao Tse-tung, *Selected Works*, 4 vols (Peking, 1961–5) vol. 1, 13–19.
75. *CW*, 3, 31.

CHAPTER 5

1. See Martov's account of the discussion in the Vilna group about the new tactic in his *Zapiski Sotsial-Demokrata* (Berlin, 1922; re-issued Cambridge, 1975) pp. 232–4. According to Getzler, Martov was over-modest about his role in the preparation of *On Agitation*. Getzler credits Martov with the writing of the two-page, 'theoretical' preamble to the pamphlet. See I. Getzler, *Martov: A Political Biography of a Russian Social Democrat* (Cambridge, 1967) p. 23 n.
2. A. Kremer and J. Martov, *Ob agitatsii*, with an Afterword by P. Akselrod (Geneva, 1896) p. 3. *On Agitation* was published, with considerable misgivings, by the Emancipation of Labour Group and did not, in fact, appear until early 1897.
3. Ibid., p. 19.
4. Ibid., p. 21.

5. Ibid., p. 22.
6. Ibid., pp. 7–8.
7. Ibid., p. 12.
8. Ibid., pp. 13–14.
9. Ibid., p. 16.
10. Ibid., pp. 14–15.
11. *MECW*, vol. 6, p. 493.
12. Plekhanov, *SPW*, 1, 58, taken from the *Manifesto of the Communist Party*, *MECW*, vol. 6, p. 493.
13. *CW*, 2, 93–121.
14. Ibid., pp. 323–51.
15. Ibid., pp. 95–6.
16. Ibid., p. 105.
17. Ibid., p. 95.
18. Ibid., p. 331.
19. Ibid., p. 330.
20. Ibid., pp. 114–5.
21. In S. N. Valk, pp. 1–6.
22. Ibid., pp. 6–12; and *CW*, 2, 81–5.
23. *CW*, 2, 33–72.
24. Ibid., pp. 271–315.
25. A. Ascher, *Axelrod*, p. 130.
26. Ibid., p. 154.
27. *CW*, 2, 114.
28. Ibid., p. 104; cf. p. 95.
29. Ibid., p. 103.
30. Ibid., p. 115.
31. Ibid., p. 125.
32. Ibid., p. 107..
33. Ibid., p. 113.
34. Ibid., p. 110.
35. Ibid., p. 72.
36. Ibid., p. 118.
37. Ibid., p. 111.
38. Ibid., p. 289.
39. Ibid., p. 336.
40. Ibid., p. 335.
41. Ibid., p. 334.
42. See note 45 to Chapter Three above for the divergent accounts of when *On Agitation* was adopted by the St Petersburg Marxists. A. K. Wildman in his excellent study *The Making of a Workers' Revolution* (Chicago, 1967) puts the date of the Vilna transition to 'agitation' as winter 1893–4 (p. 41) and that of the St Petersburg *Stariki* as autumn 1895 (p. 61).
43. CW, 2, 290.
44. S. P. Turin, *From Peter The Great to Lenin, A History of the Russian Labour Movement* (London, 1968) p. 189.
45. Wildman, p. 58.

46. Ibid., p. 78.
47. Ibid., p. 83.
48. *CW*, 2, 278.
49. Ibid., p. 278.
50. Ibid., p. 97.
51. Ibid., p. 110.
52. Ibid., p. 118.
53. Ibid., p. 285.
54. Ibid., p. 296.
55. Ibid., p. 328.
56. Ibid., p. 332.
57. Ibid., p. 347.
58. Ibid., p. 349.
59. Ibid., p. 349.
60. Ibid., p. 350.

CHAPTER 6

1. Perhaps the best available edition is J. J. Marie, *Que Faire?* (Paris, 1966). The only English-produced edition, edited by S. V. Utechin (London, 1963), is so little concerned with context that the editor presumes to prune Lenin's text of references to 'forgotten' groups and factions which allegedly add nothing to the work's essential message.
2. *CW*, 5, 517.
3. Ibid., p. 518.
4. See e.g., ch. IV of *What Is To Be Done?*, 'The Primitiveness of the Economists and the Organisation of the Revolutionaries'.
5. *CW*, 5, 484.
6. Ibid., p. 489. The insertion in square brackets is mine.
7. Ibid., p. 507.
8. Ibid., p. 519.
9. Ibid., p. 518.
10. Wildman, p. 187.
11. The *Credo* is published in full as part of Lenin's *A Protest by Russian Social Democrats*, *CW*, 4, 167–82. The reference here is to p. 174.
12. *CW*, 4, 173.
13. *CW*, 5, 364.
14. Wildman, p. 143.
15. Plekhanov, *Sochineniya*, 12, 5–42.
16. Ibid., pp. 13–14.
17. Ibid., p. 25.
18. Ibid., p. 34.
19. Ibid., p. 26.
20. Ibid., p. 30.
21. Ibid., p. 36.
22. *CW*, 4, 171.

23. See Lenin's article *How the Spark,* [i.e. *Iskra*] *was Nearly Extinguished,* unusual among Lenin's writings in that it gives a frank account of the strong emotions of admiration and exasperation which Lenin felt for Plekhanov at the time.
24. Cited in Wildman, p. 139.
25. *CW*, 5, 386.
26. Ibid., p. 404.
27. Wildman gives the author of the lead article of the 'Separate Supplement' as P. A. Berlin (p. 141 n.). L. I. Komissarova however, in her article *'Pokrytyi psevdonim', Istoriya S.S.S.R.,* ii (1970) 169–70, cites letters from Tugan Barnovsky and Zasulich to the effect that the author was a certain Vetrinsky – a widely-known pseudonym for K. M. Takhtarev. I am grateful to Mary Ghullam for drawing this article to my attention.
28. *'Nashe Deistvitelnost',* in *Otdelnoe prilozhenie k Rabochei Mysli* (St Petersburg, 1899) p. 4.
29. Ibid., p. 5.
30. Ibid., p. 5.
31. Ibid., p. 5.
32. Ibid., p. 15.
33. Ibid., p. 14.
34. *CW*, 5, 388.
35. *Programma periodicheskogo organa soyuz russkikh sotsial demokratov 'Rabochee Delo' ottisk iz no 1-go 'Rabochego Dela'* (Paris, n.d. [1899?]. The first issue of *Rabochee Delo* was published in November 1898).
36. Ibid., p. 3.
37. *CW*, 5, 396–7.
38. Akselrod, *k voprosu,* pp. 19–20.
39. Ibid., p. 22.
40. Ibid., p. 22.
41. Ibid., p. 23.
42. Ibid., p. 24.
43. Ibid., p. 27.
44. Ibid., p. 27.
45. *CW*, 5, 438–9.
46. Ibid., p. 373. The same sentiment recurs constantly in Lenin's works of this period. See e.g.: *CW*, 4, 290, 358; *CW*, 5, 19, 316–8, 396–7, 413–6.
47. *CW*, 5, 435.
48. Ibid., pp. 420–1.
49. *CW*, 4, 259; cf. pp. 262 and 274–5.
50. *CW*, 5, 415.
51. *CW*, 4, 275. Lenin is quoting from the 'Separate Supplement' to *Rabochaya Mysl*, No. 7. Almost the whole of his very important article *A Retrograde Trend in Russian Social Democracy* (*CW*, 4, 255–85) is devoted to a critique of the 'Separate Supplement'.

CHAPTER 7

1. *CW*, **13**, 101.
2. Ibid., p. 108.
3. Ibid., p. 106.
4. Ibid., p. 107.
5. *CW*, **5**, 412–3.
6. Ibid., p. 400.
7. Ibid., p. 421. Emphasis in original.
8. Ibid., pp. 416–7.
9. *CW*, **4**, 368.
10. Ibid., p. 369.
11. Ibid., p. 370.
12. Ibid., p. 217.
13. *CW*, **1**, 320.
14. K. Kautsky, 'Die Revision des Programms der Sozialdemokratie in Österreich', *Die Neue Zeit* (1902) band I, pp. 68–82.
15. *CW*, **5**, 383–4. The insertions in square brackets are Lenin's. It is very regrettable that this quotation, the latest word on the question of consciousness by Europe's most respected Marxist, a quote which is clearly central to Lenin's justification of his own position, should be edited out of S. V. Utechin's version of *What Is To Be Done?*
16. Roger Garaudy is one of the few to notice the implications of Lenin's debt to Kautsky on the question of consciousness. It is difficult to dispute Garaudy's conclusion that, in this respect 'les thèses principales sont explicitement empruntées à Kautsky . . . Il n'y a donc rien de spécifiquement léniniste dans ces thèses sur "le Parti d'avant-garde" exposées dans *Que Faire?* Cette conception est celle de Kautsky et Lénine le souligne expressément.' *Lénine* (Paris, 1968) p. 20.
17. At this stage, Lenin could have further bolstered his claim to orthodoxy by quoting the same article by Kautsky in which the Austrian variant of 'socialism as process' – a spontaneous emanation of the labour movement – had been firmly and decisively rounded on. 'In this connection', Kautsky argued,

> socialist consciousness appears as the necessary direct result of the proletarian class struggle. That is, however, false. Socialism as a teaching [*Lehre*] is rooted in any case both in contemporary economic relationships, and in the class struggle of the proletariat, and springs just like the latter from the struggle against the mass poverty and mass suffering that capitalism produces; both arise beside one another and not from one another, and under differing pre-suppositions. Modern socialist consciousness can only arise on the basis of profound scientific insight. In fact contemporary economic science/knowledge [*Wissenschaft*] is as much a precondition for socialist production as contemporary technology, but with the best will in the world the proletariat can create the one as little as it can the other; they both result from the contemporary social process.

This passage immediately precedes the lengthy passage quoted in *What Is To Be Done*; it is to be found in *Neue Zeit*, op. cit., p. 70.

18. *CW*, 5, 386.
19. Ibid., pp. 384–5.
20. Plekhanov, *Sochineniya*, 12, especially p. 36.
21. Ibid., pp. 80–1.
22. Ibid., p. 101.
23. Ibid., p. 102.
24. *CW*, 4, *A propos of the Profession de Foi*, 286–96.
25. Ibid., pp. 291–2.
26. *CW*, 5, 423.
27. Ibid., pp. 400–1.
28. Ibid., p. 412.
29. Ibid., p. 341; cf. p. 319.
30. *CW*, 4, 288.
31. Ibid., p. 218.
32. Ibid., p. 219.
33. Ibid., p. 225.
34. Ibid., p. 226.
35. Ibid., p. 354.
36. Ibid., pp. 354–5.
37. *CW*, 5, 22.
38. Ibid., p. 23.
39. Ibid., p. 22.
40. Ibid., p. 24.
41. Lenin later pointed to the irony of Martov's supporters utilising *What Is To Be Done?* precisely in order to justify *their* formulation of the contentious Article 1 of the Party Rules which defined a Party member (See *CW*, 7, 27).
42. *CW*, 5, 440.
43. Ibid., p. 428.
44. Ibid., p. 484.
45. Ibid., p. 443.
46. Ibid., p. 450.
47. Ibid., p. 450.
48. Ibid., pp. 465–6.
49. Ibid., p. 452.
50. Ibid., p. 455; cf. *CW*, 4, 224–5.
51. *CW*, 5, 459.
52. Ibid., p. 477.
53. Ibid., p. 479.
54. Ibid., p. 478.
55. Ibid., p. 481.
56. Ibid., p. 480; cf. p. 459 and *CW*, 4, 324.
57. See, for example, *CW*, 5, 446. Further approving references to Plekhanov's writings are to be found throughout *CW*, 4 and 5.
58. See, for example, *CW*, 4, 178–9, 267; *CW*, 5, 388, 433.
59. *CW*, 4, 180–1, 323, 366.

60. Ibid., p. 231–2.
61. L. Schapiro, *The Communist Party of the Soviet Union* (London, 1963) p. 39.
62. Cited in Wildman, p. 235.
63. N. Valentinov (Volsky), *Encounters with Lenin* (London, 1968) p. 27.
64. *CW*, 13, 102.
65. J. C. Rees, 'Lenin and Marxism' in *Lenin the Man, the Theorist, the Leader*, ed. P. Reddaway and L. S. Schapiro (London, 1970) p. 102 n.
66. Ascher, *Axelrod*, p. 176.
67. Ibid., pp. 179–80.
68. Akimov's account of the Second Congress is to be found in *Vladimir Akimov on the Dilemmas of Russian Marxism 1895–1903*, edited and introduced by Jonathan Frankel (Cambridge, 1969). Frankel's lengthy introduction is one of the most sophisticated accounts of the development of Russian Marxism during this period.
69. *CW*, 6, 486.
70. Ibid., p. 502.
71. Ibid., p. 501.
72. Whether or not Martov *had* approved the plan, or whether Lenin was lying in asserting that he had, itself became a major issue in the split and was taken up in the bitter debates at the Conference of The Foreign League of Russian Social Democracy in October 1903. See *CW*, 7, 84–90.
73. Ibid., p. 31.
74. Ascher, *Axelrod*, pp. 193–4.
75. Ibid., p. 208.
76. Ibid., p. 213.
77. Schapiro, p. 72.
78. *CW*, 10, 372. See *Resolutions and Discussions of the Communist Party of the Soviet Union*, ed. R. C. Elwood, 2 vols (Toronto, 1974) vol. 1, pp. 93–4.
79. D. Lane, *The Roots of Russian Communism* (Assen, 1968) pp. 214–5.

CHAPTER 8

1. Cited in D. W. Treadgold, *Lenin and His Rivals* (London, 1955) p. 130.
2. Cited in M. N. Pokrovsky, *Brief History of Russia*, trans. D. S. Mirsky, (London, 1933) vol. 2, p. 145.
3. *Otdelnoe prilozhenie k no 100 'Iskry'* (Geneva, 1905) p. 18.
4. *CW*, 8, 291.
5. Ibid., p. 294.
6. *CW*, 9, 28.
7. Ibid., p. 29.
8. Ibid., p. 49.
9. Ibid., p. 86.
10. *CW*, 10, 424.

11. Cited in Shub, pp. 103–4.
12. Schapiro, p. 71.
13. *CW*, **8**, 107.
14. Ibid., p. 108.
15. Ibid., p. 109.
16. Translated in M. Raeff, *Plans for Political Reform in Imperial Russia, 1730–1905* (Englewood Cliffs, New Jersey, 1966) pp. 142–52.
17. Pokrovsky, p. 272.
18. Treadgold, p. 26.
19. J. E. Zimmerman, 'The Kadets and the Duma 1905–07' in C. E. Timberlake (ed.), *Essays in Russian Liberalism* (Columbia, Missouri, 1972) p. 119.
20. B. Pares, *A History of Russia* (London, 1926) p. 437.
21. W. G. Rosenburg, 'The Kadets and the Politics of Ambivalence, 1905–17' in Timberlake, p. 143.
22. A. Ascher, *The Mensheviks in the Russian Revolution* [hereafter Ascher, *Mensheviks in Revolution*] (London, 1976) p. 60.
23. Ibid., p. 62.
24. Schapiro, p. 82.
25. Baron, p. 266.
26. Martynov had, in January 1905, already expressed the formula which inspired Menshevik strategy from mid-1906 onwards: 'We must remember that until the socialist revolution Social Democracy *is and must remain the party of the extreme opposition*, unlike all other parties, which in one way or another, to a greater or lesser extent, can anticipate joining the government of bourgeois society.' (A. S. Martynov, *V dve Diktaturi* (Petrograd, 1905) p. 74.)
27. *CW*, **9**, 90; cf. p. 110.
28. Ibid., p. 96.
29. Baron, p. 271.
30. Ibid., p. 274.
31. Ibid., p. 277.
32. Ulam, p. 318.
33. W. G. Rosenburg, in Timberlake, p. 145.
34. Schapiro, p. 94.

CHAPTER 9

1. *CW*, **9**, 241.
2. *CW*, **12**, 356.
3. Ibid., p. 465.
4. *CW*, **13**, 242.
5. Ibid., p. 252.
6. *CW*, **10**, 76.
7. Ibid., p. 287.
8. *CW*, **9**, 379.
9. Ibid., p. 180–1.

10. Ibid., p. 119.
11. Ibid., p. 181.
12. Ibid., p. 50.
13. Ibid., p. 51.
14. Ibid., p. 50.
15. *CW*, **10**, 215.
16. Ibid., p. 272.
17. *CW*, **9**, 97–8.
18. Ibid., p. 111.
19. *CW*, **10**, 353.
20. Ibid., p. 262.
21. Ibid., p. 262.
22. Ibid., p. 379 n., repeated pp. 452–4. Lenin was quoting from Kautsky's pamphlet, *The State Duma*.
23. *CW*, **8**, 563.
24. *CW*, **9**, 33.
25. Ibid., p. 132.
26. Ibid., p. 100.
27. *CW*, **8**, 467–72.
28. *CW*, **10**, 153–4.
29. *CW*, **9**, 368–9.
30. *CW*, **8**, 539.
31. Ibid., p. 509.
32. Ibid., pp. 373–4.
33. *CW*, **9**, 45.
34. Ibid., p. 45.
35. *CW*, **8**, 291.
36. *CW*, **11**, 172.
37. *CW*, **9**, 204.
38. *CW*, **8**, 410.
39. *CW*, **10**, 31.
40. Ibid., p. 32.
41. Ibid., p. 38.
42. Ibid., p. 38.
43. Ibid., p. 376. The extent to which the Social-Democratic organisations, both Bolshevik and Menshevik, continued in 1905 with the time-hallowed separation of the intelligentsia Party Committee from the working-class periphery, is graphically related in Piatnitsky's memoirs. He recalls a meeting in October 1905 of the Odessa Party organisation with many present, 'a preponderance of women among them. And almost no Russian Workers . . . at succeeding meetings, as well as at those of the Mensheviks and Socialist Revolutionaries, the percentage of Russian workers present was comparatively small'. (O. Piatnitsky, *Memoirs of a Bolshevik* (London, n.d.) p. 86.)
44. *CW*, **10**, 443.
45. Ibid., p. 314.
46. Ibid., p. 315.
47. *CW*, **8**, 217.

48. S. Schwartz, *The Russian Revolution of 1905* (Chicago and London, 1975) p. ix.
49. *CW*, 8, 211.
50. Ibid., p. 509.
51. *CW*, 10, 153.
52. *CW*, 11, 220.
53. Ibid., p. 185.
54. Ibid., p. 227.
55. Ibid., p. 228.
56. *CW*, 10, 259 n.
57. Ibid., p. 79.
58. *CW*, 9, 17.
59. *CW*, 10, 485.
60. *CW*, 9, 147.
61. Ibid., p. 147.
62. *CW*, 8, 287.
63. *CW*, 9, 351–2.
64. *CW*, 8, 564.
65. *CW*, 10, 259.
66. Ibid., p. 258.
67. Ibid., p. 253.
68. *CW*, 9, 113.
69. Ibid., p. 55.
70. *CW*, 13, 73.
71. *CW*, 8, 562.

CHAPTER 10

1. N. Matyushkin ed., *Partiya Bolshevikov v period reaktsii 1907–1910 gody* (Moscow, 1968) p. 5; c.f. the detailed account of the decline of the labour movement in this period in G. V. Knyazeva, *Borba Bolshevikov za sochetanie nelegalnoi i legalnoi partiinoi raboty 1907–1910* (Leningrad, 1964).
2. Matyushkin, pp. 59–60.
3. The Mensheviks' attitude to the redistribution of the land is encapsulated in the very brief Agrarian Programme which was accepted by the Fourth (Unity) Congress of the R.S.D.L.P. in April 1906. It is translated in Ascher, *Mensheviks in Revolution*, pp. 64–5.
4. *CW*, 18, 75.
5. *CW*, 15, 80; cf. p. 159.
6. *CW*, 19, 194.
7. *CW*, 16, 435.
8. *CW*, 15, 86; cf., pp. 97–8 and *CW*, 20, 316.
9. *CW*, 15, pp. 136, 160.
10. *CW*, 20, 317.
11. Ibid., pp. 242–3; cf. *CW*, 15, 84–92; *CW*, 17, 112, 121.
12. *CW*, 15, 86, 97–8.
13. Ibid., p. 159; cf. *CW*, 18, 34–5.

14. *CW*, **15**, 141, 301; cf. *CW*, **18**, 145.
15. *CW*, **15**, 147; cf. *CW*, **19**. 196.
16. *CW*, **19**, 377.
17. *CW*, **15**, 138; *CW*, **17**, 284, 381; *CW*, **18**, 147.
18. *CW*, **15**, 138.
19. *CW*, **17**, 381.
20. Ibid., p. 105.
21. *CW*, **18**, 583.
22. Ibid., p. 313.
23. Ibid., p. 342.
24. Ibid., p. 55.
25. Ibid., pp. 342–3.
26. G. Hosking, *The Russian Constitutional Experiment. Government and Duma 1907–1914* (Cambridge, 1973) p. 250.
27. *CW*, **15**, 397; *CW*, **18**, 330.
28. *CW*, **18**, 26.
29. *CW*, **17**, 302.
30. *CW*, **18**, 297.
31. Ibid., p. 295.
32. Ascher, *Axelrod*, p. 237.
33. *Kommunisticheskaya partiya sovetskogo soyuza v rezolyutsiyakh i resheniyakh*, 7th edn (Moscow, 1954) vol. 1, p. 195.
34. *CW*, **19**, 406.
35. Ibid., pp. 168–9.
36. Cited in Getzler, p. 118.
37. Ascher, *Axelrod*, p. 295.
38. Getzler, p. 132.
39. Martov to Potresov, cited in Getzler, p. 125.
40. See Baron, pp. 281–6 for a useful summary of Plekhanov's views at this time.
41. Ibid., p. 282.
42. *CW*, **19**, 415.
43. Potresov in *Nasha Zarya*, no. 2, p. 61. Cited in *CW*, **17**, 493.
44. *CW*, **19**, 157.
45. *CW*, **17**, 227.
46. See P. Lösche, *Der Bolschewismus im Urteil der Deutschen Sozialdemokratie 1903–1920 (Berlin, 1967)*.
47. Getzler, p. 134.
48. Ascher, *Axelrod*, p. 276.
49. Ibid., p. 288.
50. *CW*, **16**, 381–2.
51. *CW*, **15**, 387; cf. *CW*, **16**, 31–2.
52. *CW*, **16**, 33.
53. Ibid., p. 201.
54. *CW*, **15**, 389.
55. Ibid., pp. 428–9.
56. Ibid., pp. 444–5.
57. Wolfe, p. 562.

58. The immediate occasion for Lenin's counterblast was, as his Preface to *Materialism and Empirio-Criticism* makes clear, the appearance of a collection of essays under the title *Studies in the Philosophy of Marxism*, with contributions from Bogdanov, Lunacharsky, Bazarov, Berman, Helfond, Yushkevich and Suvorov (see *CW*, 14, 19–20).
59. *CW*, 14, 341.
60. M. C. Morgan, *Lenin* (London), 1971) p. 71.
61. *CW*, 14, 339–40.
62. Ibid., p. 345.
63. Ibid., p. 326.
64. Wolfe, p. 568.

CHAPTER 11

1. *CW*, 17, 348–9.
2. *CW*, 18, 102–3.
3. *CW*, 19, 49.
4. Ibid., p. 323.
5. *CW*, 16, 406.
6. *CW*, 20, 506.
7. Ibid., p. 550.
8. Ibid., p. 554.
9. A handy compilation of Lenin's 'Objective Data on the Strength of the Various Trends on the Working-class Movement' appears in *CW*, 20, 381–7; cf. the detailed survey of the rebirth of the labour movement in E. E. Kruze, *Peterburgskie rabochie v 1912–1914 godakh* (Moscow, 1961) pp. 241 et seq.
10. Getzler, p. 134.
11. *CW*, 19, 409.
12. Ibid., p. 407.
13. Ibid., pp. 406–7.
14. *CW*, 16, 393–421.
15. Ibid., p. 406.
16. See, for example, *CW*, 19, 128–9.
17. *CW*, 18, 472.
18. Ibid., p. 477.
19. Ibid., p. 477.
20. Ibid., p. 108.
21. *CW*, 19, 223.
22. See, for example, *CW*, 18, 85.
23. *CW*, 19, 370; cf. *CW*, 18, 360.
24. *CW*, 19, 99; cf. p. 86.
25. Ibid., p. 205.
26. Ibid., p. 203.
27. Ibid., p. 84.
28. *CW*, 18, 400.
29. *CW*, 19, 106–7.

30. *CW*, 5, 510.
31. M. Gorki, *Days with Lenin* (London, n.d.) p. 29.
32. Glimpses of Lenin's flights of fancy in this respect occasionally emerge in Y. G. Feigin, *Lenin i sotsialisticheskoye razmeshenie proizvoditelnykh sil* (Moscow, 1969).
33. *CW*, 19, 62.
34. *CW*, 20, 69.
35. Ibid., p. 154.
36. Ibid., p. 401.
37. Ibid., p. 113.
38. Ibid., p. 46.
39. R. Luxemburg, *The Accumulation of Capital* (London, 1963; first published 1913).
40. Cited in L. Basso, *Rosa Luxemburg. A Reappraisal* (London, 1975) p. 115.
41. On Luxemburg's views on the national question see J. P. Nettl, *Rosa Luxemburg* (London, 1969) Appendix, 'The National Question', pp. 500–19.
42. *CW*, 20, 28.
43. Ibid., p. 27.
44. Ibid., p. 405.
45. *CW*, 19, 243.
46. Ibid., p. 501.
47. *CW*, 20, 72–3; cf. Lenin's cautionary words (*CW*, 19, 499) to an Armenian Bolshevik who was in favour of a compulsory official language. Such an attitude, Lenin warned, ignored the crucially important psychological revulsion that cultural coercion inevitably produced.
48. *CW*, 19, 429.
49. *CW*, 20, 422–3.
50. Ibid., p. 51.
51. *CW*, 19, 428.

Chronology of Major Events and Lenin's Writings and Activities, 1870–1914

Dates given here (and in the main text of this book) are those of the Russian Old Style calendar which is, for the nineteenth century, twelve days behind the New Style adopted in 1918 to bring Russia into line with European practice. In the twentieth century the Old Style is thirteen days behind the New.

1870	10 April	Vladamir Ilich Ulyanov (Lenin) born in Simbirsk.
1874		The 'Going to the People', mass arrests of Populists.
1879		Lenin begins as a pupil in Simbirsk classical gymnasium. The Populist organisation *Zemlya i Volya* (Land and Freedom) split into orthodox Bakuninist *Cherni Peredel* (Black Repartition) and terrorist *Narodnaya Volya* (People's Will).
1881	1 March	Tsar Alexander II assassinated by the Executive Committee of *Narodnaya Volya*.
1883		Formation in Geneva of the Emancipation of Labour Group and publication of George Plekhanov's *Socialism and the Political Struggle*.
1885		Publication of Plekhanov's *Our Differences*.
1886	January	Death of Ilya Nikolayevich, Lenin's father.
1887	1 March	Aleksander, Lenin's elder brother, arrested for participation in plot to kill Tsar Alexander III.
	8 May	Aleksander and his accomplices executed.
	10 June	Lenin graduates from the Simbirsk gymnasium with the gold medal as most outstanding pupil.
	Late June	Family moves to Kazan.
	August	Lenin enters Kazan University.
	December	Lenin participates in student rally, is arrested, expelled from University and exiled to the village of Kokushkino.

1888	October	Lenin permitted to return to Kazan to live.
	Winter	Lenin begins to study Marx; reads vol. 1 of
	1888–9	*Capital*; involved in revolutionary circle led by
		Chetvergova.
1889	May	Family moves to recently-purchased estate at
		Alakeyevka, near Samara.
	October	Family moves to Samara.
1890		Lenin continues his study of Marxism; translates
		the *Communist Manifesto*; teams up with Sklya-
		renko and engages in debates with Populists.
	May	Lenin receives permission to sit Law Exami-
		nations of St Petersburg University as an external
		student.
	Late August–	Lenin's first visit to St Petersburg in connection
	late October	with his legal studies.
1891		Severe famine in this and the following year;
		peasant passivity and disillusion of Populists;
		uncompromising stand of Plekhanov echoed by
		Lenin.
	April–May	Lenin visits St Petersburg to study and sit first
		part of Law Examinations.
	Mid-May	Returns to Samara; continues work collecting
		and collating statistical material on agrarian
		life and preparing for further examinations.
1892		Lenin graduates top of his class with equivalent
		of First-Class Degree in Law from St Petersburg
		University; continues reading of Marxism,
		building a library, preparing papers on agrarian
		question and debating with Populists in Samara.
1893	Spring	Prepares and reads *New Economic Developments in
		Russian Peasant Life* – earliest significant MS.
		extant.*
	May	Takes on N. K. Mikhailovsky in debate in
		Samara.
	Summer	Works on critiques of Yuzhakov and
		Mikhailovsky which were later incorporated into
		What the 'Friends of the People' Are . . . .
	August	En route for St Petersburg, where ostensibly he is
		to practice law, Lenin stops off in Nizhni
		Novgorod to meet local Marxists.
	31 August	Lenin arrives in St Petersburg.
	Autumn	Joins Marxist circle of Technological Institute
		students; criticises Krassin's paper and writes his
		own, *On the So-Called Market Question*.

---

* The authoritative check-list of Lenin's extant writings is the *Khronologicheskii ukazatel proizvedenii V. I. Lenina 1886–1923*, 2 vols plus Index (Moscow, 1959–63).

	Winter 1893–4	Begins work as a leader of workmen's circles in the Nevsky Gate district.
1894	March–June	Lenin writes *What the 'Friends of the People' Are . . .*, much of it based on papers prepared in Samara.
	Late December	Disturbances at the Semyannikov factory; Lenin writes first 'agitational' leaflet to appear in St Petersburg.
1895	February	Lenin at meeting of representatives of Marxist groups from a number of cities held in St Petersburg.
	Spring 1895	Arrival of the brochure *On Agitation* in St Petersburg; long discussions of it and attempts to implement its tactics.
	April	Lenin goes abroad to contact Emancipation of Labour Group.
	May	Meets and greatly impresses Plekhanov and Akselrod; arranges with them for publication of a collection of articles – *Rabotnik* (The Worker).
	May–September	Lenin variously in France, Switzerland and Germany meeting prominent Marxists and studying the European labour movement.
	7 September	Returns to Russia with illegal literature.
	September 7–29	Visits Vilna, Moscow and Orekhovo Zuyevo establishing contacts, commissioning articles, and arranging distribution of *Rabotnik*.
	November	Joint meeting of *stariki*, Martov's group and workers' representatives to unite their activities on basis of the programme of *On Agitation*.
	November 7 or 8	Lenin's leaflet, *To the Working Men and Women of the Thornton Factory*.
	10 November	Disturbances at the Laferme Tobacco Factory.
	November–December	Lenin prepares first issue of illegal *Rabochee Delo* (The Workers' Cause) – edits it and writes a good deal of the copy.
	3 December	Publication of Lenin's pamphlet *Explanation of the Law on Fines*.
	8 December	Lenin and other leaders of St Petersburg Union of Struggle for the Emancipation of the Working Class arrested; material for *Rabochee Delo* seized.
	Late 1895–early 1896	Lenin writes his *Draft and Explanation of a Programme for the Social-Democratic Party*.
1896	Spring	Lenin begins preparations for a study of the development of capitalism in Russia.
	June	Very extensive strike throughout textile industry in St Petersburg; accounted great success for Union of Struggle.
	November	Publication of Lenin's *To the Tsarist Government*.

1897	January	Renewed strike in textile plants in Ivanovo and St Petersburg; government again makes concessions; Lenin exiled to Shushenskoye for three years.
	February 14–17	Lenin given three days to settle his affairs before travelling to place of exile; arranges meeting between *stariki* (the veterans) and the 'youngsters' who are to replace them as leaders in St Petersburg.
	April–July	*A Characterisation of Economic Romanticism* published in instalments.
	8 May	Lenin arrives in Shushenskoye.
	Summer–autumn	Writes pamphlet *The New Factory Law*.
	Winter	Writes *The Tasks of the Russian Social Democrats* and a number of articles on economics – preparatory studies for the *Development of Capitalism in Russia*; in St Petersburg factory workers produce the first issue of *Rabochaya Mysl* (Workers' Thought).
1898	February–August	Lenin works with Krupskaya on a translation of the Webbs' *History of Trade Unionism*.
	1 March	Foundation Congress of the Russian Social Democratic Labour Party convenes in Minsk, its *Manifesto* written by Peter Struve published in July.
	July	Lenin and Krupskaya are married; widespread arrests of Social Democrats throughout Russia.
	August	Lenin completes the draft of his study *The Development of Capitalism in Russia*; publication in Geneva of Akselrod's influential *Present Tasks and Tactics of the Russian Social Democrats*.
	October	Collection of Lenin's writings *Economic Studies and Essays* published under the pseudonym V. Ilin.
	Autumn	Lenin's *The Tasks of the Russian Social Democrats* published in Geneva.
	November	At the First Congress of the Union of Social Democrats Abroad the Emancipation of Labour Group defeated by 'young' opposition and refuses to continue editing the publications of the Union.
1899	Late January	Lenin completes the preparation of the MS. of *The Development of Capitalism in Russia* which is published in March.
	March	First issue of the journal of the Union of Social Democrats Abroad – *Rabochee Delo* (The Workers' Cause); Eduard Bernstein publishes his *The*

Preconditions of Socialism and the Tasks of Social Democracy.

August   Lenin writes *A Protest by Russian Social Democrats* against Kuskova's *Credo* and organises a meeting of exiled Marxists to support his *Protest*; Lenin writes three articles for the proposed *Rabohaya Gazeta* (Workers' Paper).

September   Publication of the 'Separate Supplement' to *Rabochaya Mysl*, no. 7, *locus classicus* of Russian revisionism.

Late 1899   Lenin writes a riposte to the leading article of the 'Separate Supplement' entitled *A Retrograde Trend in Russian Social Democracy.*

1900   January   Lenin's term of exile ends.

February– July   Much travelling between Social-Democratic centres in Russia; Lenin establishes connections and makes detailed arrangements for the publication of an all-Russian 'orthodox' newspaper to counter *Rabochaya Mysl* and *Rabochee Delo* and to prepare the ground for a Second Party Congress.

Spring   Publication of Plekhanov's *'Vademecum' for the Editorial Board of Rabochee Delo.*

May Day   Large-scale open demonstrations and strikes in Kharkov.

August   Lenin in Zurich for discussions with Plekhanov and Akselrod on the publication of *Iskra* (The Spark).

11 December   First issue of *Iskra* appears, edited by Lenin and carrying his leading article, *The Urgent Tasks of our Movement.*

1901   Lenin composes a series of articles for *Iskra* and *Zarya* (The Dawn) outlining the political tasks of the Party and the need for comprehensive reorganisation.

March   Open political demonstrations in many Russian cities.

May Day   Intensive campaign of demonstrations throughout Russia leading to pitched battle of the Obukhov Defense in St Petersburg.

1902   Throughout the year constant work, writing articles for and editing of *Iskra*, organising and instructing *Iskra* agents in Russia in preparation for the Second Party Congress.

January– February   Lenin and Plekhanov in polemics over draft Programme.

March   Publication in Stuttgart of Lenin's *What Is To Be Done? Burning Questions of Our Movement.*

Late March	Lenin and Krupskaya leave Munich for London where *Iskra* is to continue publication.
Mid-June	Lenin moves to Paris.
September	Lenin writes *A Letter to a Comrade on Our Organisational Tasks* – an elaboration of the organisational entailments of *What Is To Be Done?*
November	General strike and open political demonstrations in Rostov; Pskov Conference of Russian Social Democrats to consider the Second Congress of the Party – an Organising Committee for its convocation set up.
1903	Continued editorial and journalistic work for *Iskra* and directives to Organising Committee and Iskrist agents in Russia.
March	Publication of Lenin's pamphlet *To the Rural Poor*.
March–June	General strikes and demonstrations of unprecedented dimensions in most major cities especially in the south of the empire.
June–July	Lenin drafts standing orders and agenda, prepares draft rules and resolutions for forthcoming Congress.
17 July	Second Congress of the Russian Social Democratic Labour Party convenes in Brussels; Lenin elected vice-chairman and member of Praesidium.
20 July	Lenin speaks at sixth session on the place of the *Bund*.
22 July	Speech on Party Programme.
24–9 July	Congress moves from Brussels to London.
29 July	Lenin reports on Party Rules.
31 July–1 August	Lenin speaks several times on the agrarian question.
2 August	Lenin speaks at the 22nd and 23rd sessions of the Congress in support of his formulation of Article 1 of the Party Rules (defining the conditions of membership); Martov's formulation is carried.
2 or 3 August	*Iskra* caucus splits over question of candidates for election to Central Committee.
4–5 August	Lenin speaks on co-option to Central Committee and to editorial board of central organ.
7 August	Fierce debate over composition of editorial board of central organ to which Lenin, Plekhanov and Martov are elected; adherents of Lenin and Plekhanov now emerge as *Bolsheviki* – men of the majority.

	Mid-August	Lenin recovers from nervous exhaustion on walking holiday in Switzerland.
	Early September	Writes his *Account of the Second Congress of the R.S.D.L.P.*
	19 October	Lenin resigns from editorial board of *Iskra* over Plekhanov's decision to expand the board to include the three editors ousted by the Second Congress.
1904	February	Outbreak of Russo-Japanese War; constant polemic within the Party throughout the year; Lenin reviews the crisis in *One Step Forward, Two Steps Back*; his organisational ideas attacked by Rosa Luxemburg in the 'New' *Iskra*; Lenin forms a Bureau of Committees of the Majority and through this and through the Central Committee of the Party, calls for convocation of Third Party Congress.
	November	Zemstvo Conference – Russian liberals begin to stir.
	December	Fall of Port Arthur. General strike in Baku.
1905	9 January	Bloody Sunday; Gapon leads huge peaceful demonstration which ends in mass shooting before the Winter Palace; massive strike movement begins. In a stream of articles in newly-established Bolshevik journal *Vperyod*, Lenin reviews events and calls for determined revolutionary action to overthrow autocracy.
	12–27 April	Third Congress of R.S.D.L.P. in London at which Lenin speaks on the armed uprising, relations with the peasantry and the nature of the future revolutionary government.
	June–July	Lenin writes *Two Tactics of Social Democracy in the Democratic Revolution*, published in October; much editorial work and writing of articles for *Proletarii*.
	August	Government Manifesto instituting an Imperial Duma published and rejected by almost all sections of society.
	October	Arrest of delegates to railwaymen's Congress leads to almost total general strike and formation of Soviets; Tsar is forced to concede 'October Manifesto' apparently granting a democratic constitution.
	7 or 8 November	Lenin arrives in St Petersburg calling for urgent preparation of armed rising and reorganisation of the Party.
	12–17 December	Bolshevik Conference in Tammerfors, Finland, approves Lenin's call for active boycott of

		Duma. General strike and insurrection in Moscow.
1906	January–April	Speeches and articles on boycott of Duma and preparations for Party Congress.
	10–25 April	Fourth (Unity) Congress of R.S.D.L.P. convened in Stockholm; Lenin delivers speeches and reports on the agrarian question, Duma and armed uprising; at the 27th session Article 1 of the Rules as formulated by Lenin is carried by the Congress.
	May–July	Considerable journalistic work for *Volna* (The Wave), *Vperyod* (Forward) and *Ekho* (The Echo), especially on attitude to the Duma.
	8 July	Dissolution of First Duma; Stolypin establishes firm control of the autocracy.
	December	Lenin edits, and writes preface to translation of Kautsky's pamphlet *The Driving Forces and Prospects of the Russian Revolution*.
1907	January–February	Fierce polemic between Lenin and Mensheviks over tactics for election to Second Duma.
	30 April–17 May	Fifth Congress of R.S.D.L.P. convened in London; Lenin main rapporteur on attitude towards bourgeois political parties.
	3 June	Peremptory dissolution of Second Duma – Stolypin's *coup d'état*.
	5–10 August	Lenin, with Martov and Rosa Luxemburg, involved in giving radical sting to resolution 'On Militarism and International Conflicts' adopted by the Stuttgart Congress of the Socialist International; convenes informal conference of Left delegates to the Congress.
	September	Lenin writes an important preface to volume 1 of a three-volume collection of his writings entitled *Twelve Years*.
	December	Lenin goes into emigration again.
1908	January–February	Very active in preparing new Bolshevik journal *Proletarii* and in study of Machism and Bogdanov's 'revisions'.
	March	Second edition of *The Development of Capitalism in Russia* appears in St Petersburg.
	April	Lenin with Gorky in Capri tells Bogdanov and Lunacharsky of his philosophical differences with them.
	April–October	Lenin hard at work on *Materialism and Empirio-Criticism*.
	December	Lenin and Krupskaya move from Geneva to Paris where *Proletarii* is to be published.

1909	January–May	Continued work on philosophy and proof-correcting *Materialism and Empirio-Criticism*.
	8–17 June	Articles against otzovism (recallism); conference of extended editorial board of *Proletarii* at which Bogdanov is expelled from the faction.
	October	Lenin in Brussels attending meeting of International Socialist Bureau.
1910	January–June	Absorbed with polemic within the Bolshevik faction (against otzovists and god-builders) and against the Mensheviks (liquidators).
	18–30 June	Lenin with Gorky on Capri.
	August	In Copenhagen for the Eighth Congress of the Second International.
	September–November	Lenin works on data of *Strike Statistics in Russia* and writes an important article published in two parts, December 1910 and January 1911.
1911	January–June	Lenin joined by Plekhanov in journalistic campaign against the liquidators; stream of articles for *Rabochaya Gazeta* (The Workers' Paper), *Zvezda* (The Star) and *Sotsial Demokrat* (The Social Democrat) on the state of affairs in the Party.
	Spring–summer	Lenin, Krupskaya and Inessa Armand living at Longjumeau where a Party school is held.
	September	Lenin in Zurich for a meeting of the International Socialist Bureau.
	November	Delivers speech at funeral of Paul and Laura Lafargue.
	December	Presides over meeting of Bolshevik groups abroad held in Paris; preparations made for final split from Mensheviks.
1912	January	Bolsheviks organise in Prague a Conference of R.S.D.L.P. at which the liquidators (i.e. majority of Menshevik leaders) are declared to be outside the Party; Lenin's *coup d'état,* appropriating title of R.S.D.L.P. to exclusive use of Bolsheviks.
	February–March	Lenin defends Prague decisions to the International Socialist Bureau and to Social-Democratic groups in Russia and abroad.
	April	Hundreds of striking workers shot down in the Lena goldfields; sympathetic strikes on mounting scale spread throughout industrial centres of Russia; first issue of the Bolshevik daily newspaper *Pravda* (Truth); thereafter prolific output of articles by Lenin on the agrarian situation, strikes, liquidators, Kadets, Fourth Duma and various international issues.

	Late June	Lenin moves from Paris to Cracow to establish more immediate ties with *Pravda* and Bolshevik group in Duma.
1913	January–April	Lenin's intensive journalistic work continues; strikes and demonstrations in Russia grow in size.
	April	Lenin's *Three Sources and Three Component Parts of Marxism* published.
	April–June	Lectures, articles, instructions to *Pravda* and Duma group.
	June	Lectures in Zurich, Geneva, Lausanne and Berne on the national question.
	25 September–1 October	Poronin Conference of Bolsheviks
	October–December	Lenin writes his *Critical Remarks on the National Question.*
	December	Lenin's *The National Programme of the R.S.D.L.P.* published in *Sotsial Demokrat.*
1914	January	Lenin in Paris, Brussels, Liege and Leipzig lecturing on the national question.
	February–May	Writes *The Right of Nations to Self-Determination.*
	May–July	Strikes and demonstrations on a scale unknown since 1905 throughout the major cities of Russia.
	June	Lenin's article *Objective Data on the Strength of the Various Trends in the Working-Class Movement* published.
	July	Brussels Conference of the International Socialist Bureau – convened to settle the attitude of the International to the threatening war; I.S.B. Commission hears reports on situation in R.S.D.L.P., among them Inessa Armand's 'ultimatum' written by Lenin.
	23 July	Social Democratic Party of Germany votes for War Credits in the Reichstag – the collapse of the Second International.
	26 July	Lenin arrested in Nowy Targ (Galicia).
	6 August	Following intervention of Polish and Austrian socialists Lenin released from prison.
	Mid-August	Lenin receives permission to leave Austria–Hungary for Switzerland.
	23 August	Lenin arrives in Berne.

Index

otzovism 273–5, 276, 281

Parvus, A. I. 198
peasants: role of in Populist
thought 33–6; and development
of capitalism 39–45, 46, 59, 69,
84, 85, 97–106; labour-rent and
89–92, 98, 100–1, 103;
Plekhanov's distrust of 206,
209; Lenin on, in 1905 215–18;
unstable economic and political
position of 238–40, 245; and
Stolypin's reforms 251–6;
Lenin on, in 1908–11 252–6,
303
permanent revolution 5, 198–9
Petrashevsky, M. V. 33
Plekhanov, G. V. 5, 15, 17, 24, 27,
63, 70, 72, 74, 130, 245; attitude
to famine of 1891 19, 27, 28;
reputation 31–2; Populist
beliefs 33–6; economic
analysis of Russia 37–45, 79,
86–7, 89, 98, 106, 108; dialectical
methodology 36–8, 44–5; on
leading role of proletariat
45–9, 66, 104–5, 114, 134; on
role of intelligentsia 49–51,
75, 154, 167, 170–2; distaste for
economic agitation 118; and
economism 141, 142–5, 155,
160, 163, 166–7, 170–2, 173, 178,
179, 187, 189; and 1902
split 190–4; moderation of in
1905 200, 203, 206–9, 272;
against liquidationism 266,
269–70, 282; works of: *The Tasks
of the Russian Social Democrats in the
Famine* 19, 32; *The All-Russian
Destruction* 24; *Our Narodnik Men
of Letters* 24; *Our Differences* 24,
32, 36; *Socialism and the Political
Struggle* 32, 36, 52, 115; *A New
Champion of Autocracy* 32; *The
Development of the Monist View of
History* 32, 37, 79; *Preface to the
'Vademecum' for the Editorial Board
of Rabochee Delo* 143–4, 170–1;
*Once Again Socialism and the Political
Struggle* 171–2
Pobedonostev, K. P. 11
Pokrovsky, M. N. 249, 277
Polevoi, Iu. Z. 18

Populism, Populists: Lenin's
controversies with in Samara
20–3, 26–8; commune as basis of
33–6, 38, 59, 60, 66–7, 72, 74;
economic views of 81–5, and
Lenin's critique of 85ff., 97–9
108, 199, 229, 240, 304; *see also*
Legal Populism
Posnikov, V. I. 26
Potresov, A. N. 17, 145, 166, 178,
192–4, 240–1
Prokopovich, S. N. 143
proletariat: orthodox conception
of 34–5, 40–1, 45–58; Populist
view of 34–5, 83–4; stages of
development of 52–5, 234–48;
Lenin's view of leading role of
65–6, 70–1, 116, 123–6, 128,
133–4, 162, 181, 239, 259; genesis
of according to Lenin 100–8; as
natural representative of all
Russia's exploited 103–6, 246;
as leader of democratic
revolution 119, 121–5, 206,
245–7, 259, 288; and peasants in
1905 216–18, 257; and
bourgeoisie 219–26; and consciousness 50–4, 58, 75–6,
112–15, 121–3, 143–4, 151–60,
162–75, 230–48
Proletarii 281
'propaganda', and workers' circles
74–6, 110–12

R.S.D.L.P. (Russian Social Democratic Labour Party): *Manifesto*
of First (Minsk) Congress
46, 48, 56–7, 141, 187; agrarian
programme of 106; First
Congress 131, 139, 151; turn-of-
the-century crisis of 135–8,
140–58, 161, 178–81, summarised
158–60; Second Congress 162,
181, 188, 189–95, 233, 270;
Fourth (Unity) Congress 195,
200; and First Duma 205, 270–1
Rabochaya Gazeta 176
Rabochaya Mysl 142; as exemplar
of Economism 145–51, 158–9,
165
Rabochee Delo: origins 141;
Plekhanov's attack on 143–4,
170–2; Lenin's attack on 150–1,

Lenin's Political Thought

Volume 2

THEORY AND PRACTICE IN THE SOCIALIST REVOLUTION

But we are out to rebuild the world . . .
Yet we are afraid of our own selves. We are loth
   to cast off the 'dear old' soiled shirt . . .
But it is time to cast off the soiled shirt and to put
   on clean linen.

   (V. I. Lenin, concluding words of 'The Tasks
   of the Proletariat in Our Revolution', September 1917, *Collected Works*, vol. 24, p. 88).

Contents

Acknowledgements

My thanks in the first place to the secretaries of the Department of Politics and Centre for Russian and East European Studies, Pat Rees, Pat Yates, Anne Smith and Caryl Johnston, who shared the burden of typing the manuscript, and to my colleague Richard Taylor, who read it all with such care. Thanks too to Michael Levin and John Rees for their helpful comments. Finally, my apologies to Alexander, Gareth, Daniel, Benjamin and Thomas for games of rugby unwatched and stories unread.

Introduction

Writing a book with the title *Lenin's Political Thought* is only a little less presumptuous than writing one entitled *What Marx Really Meant* or *The Meaning of the Testaments*. As there are Marxists and Christians of numberless denominations, so too there are Leninists. And each particular denomination claims exclusive title to the writ. We begin then with the recognition that no single interpretation of Lenin's political thought can hope to satisfy everybody. Lenin's thought is still too potent a force in the contemporary world for anyone to aspire to a definitive account of it. In its terms, the present policies of twenty-seven regimes throughout the world, embracing a total population of more than one and a quarter thousand million, are couched and justified. Here, all too often, the task of interpreting Lenin's thought is pre-eminently a practical matter whose object is to vindicate present policies. Apart from the Marxist-Leninist regimes in power, there are individuals, groups and parties in almost all countries of the world who style themselves 'Leninist'. Each has its particular emphasis, its own distinctive view of the relevance of Lenin's thought and in that distinctiveness lies its claim to exist.

The historian of so sensitive a body of ideas will inevitably tread on toes for his concern is not with relevance nor with justifying or recommending present policies but with telling an intelligible and coherent tale from the evidence available. That is the brief I set myself in these two volumes. My object has been neither to censure nor to recommend Lenin's political ideas, but to render them intelligible. This approach leads to difficulties not merely with the believers, Lenin's self-styled disciples, but with commentators, critics and academic historians who have, too frequently, been concerned to demonstrate that 'It is easy to discover the folly of Lenin'.[1] Why one should seek to discover Lenin's folly is not at all clear. It may be, of course, that part of the unspoken intention

1

of such an exercise is to demonstrate that the policies of states, groups or parties, justified by reference to Lenin's ideas are, *ipso facto*, fallacious. This, clearly, falls into the same a-historical trap. There is another, perhaps more potent if more opaque, rationale which might explain the persistent quest for the folly of Lenin's thought, namely the vindication of Menshevik thought and activity. I am aware that it is hardly prudent simultaneously to invite the wrath of both left and right, but in order to make sense of Lenin's writings one has no option. It is undoubtedly the case that much of what we may call Western scholarship on Lenin's thought bears the heavy impress of the Menshevik critique. There were, after all, in the decades after the October Revolution, very few Europeans or Americans who were familiar with the Russian language and even fewer who were knowledgeable about the complexities of the evolution of Bolshevik thought. With the emergence of Bolshevik Russia as a prominent and threatening actor on the international scene, the demand for experts who could fill in the background and, perhaps, provide guidance on future trends, was spontaneously created. The Menshevik emigrés filled the breach.

Their general line of interpretation has had an enormous impact upon subsequent Western histories, both directly through their books, pamphlets and articles, and through the generations of talented students they have attracted and left their stamp upon. Their contribution to the history of the Russian revolutionary movement has been and continues to be invaluable.[2] It would obviously be more than arrogant to deny that they, through their own personal experiences, their invaluable archives, their familiarity with the recondite disputes which constantly wracked the movement, have made an indispensable contribution. It would, equally, be naive to suppose that the Mensheviks did not have their own tale to tell, that their history would not be an *apologia pro vita sua*. From the time of the Bolshevik/Menshevik dispute in 1903, as I outlined in Volume 1, anti-Leninism became the sole rallying point uniting the diverse Menshevik groups. Lenin was presented as a Jacobin, and Menshevik historians re-wrote history to demonstrate that he had, from the outset of his political career, always been a Jacobin. In Volume 1, I examined the evidence for these assertions, found it wanting and concluded that Lenin owed far more to Plekhanov and Akselrod than either Menshevik or Soviet historiography would (for their differing reasons) have us believe. When Lenin and the Bolsheviks seized power in October 1917, the Mensheviks and, following them, the main current of Western academic literature on the subject, portrayed this as further evidence of Lenin's Jacobinism. The seizure of power and the attempt to inaugurate socialism in such a backward country was, they argued, incapable of being justified in Marxist terms. The Mensheviks, robbed of their heritage and exiled from their land, were understandably very much engagé in writing the history of the Revolution. Little stock was taken then, or later, of Lenin's considerable attempts to provide a cogent theoretical justification for an international revolution. It was simpler, more consistent and more convenient to label the Bolshevik seizure of power a premature coup. Subsequently, after Lenin's death, a major part of Menshevik and Western historiography of the Russian Revolution was concerned with explaining the enormities of Stalinism in terms of its 'origins' in Leninism. Throughout, Lenin is portrayed as the evil genius uniquely responsible for Marxism going off the rails; a ruthless schemer, inconsequential as a theorist but a superb opportunist and organiser. His actions are explained in terms of his Jacobinism, his power mania or simply in terms of his brilliance as a pragmatic politician to alter course as the moment demanded. The general consensus of academic writing on Lenin has therefore been that Lenin's genius was as a political actor and not as a theorist of Marxism. His Marxism, it is widely concluded, was of a peculiarly voluntarist sort and was, in any case, rent with internal contradictions. Lenin's theoretical ventures are therefore viewed as rationalisations for actions already undertaken; they can in no way explain or justify these actions. The argument of this book is that Lenin was, on the contrary, an extraordinarily doctrinaire politician. He was the most doctrinaire of the successful politicians of the twentieth century. By doctrinaire I mean that Lenin altered his political course only after thorough theoretical work had convinced him of the need to do so. Once convinced by his theoretical study, no practical impediment, no consideration of the popularity or 'viability' of his new course would divert him from committing himself totally to its implementation. There is about Lenin the same doctrinaire attitude one finds in Marx – if reality was out of joint with theory, then so much the worse for

3

reality – or as Marx put it, 'It is not enough for thought to strive for realisation, reality must itself strive towards thought.'[3] And so as soon as Lenin, from his study of imperialism and the imperialist state, became convinced that international capitalism was not merely ripe but rotten ripe for socialism and convinced too that only via socialist revolution was it possible to save the world from barbarism, from that moment he was totally committed to preparing himself and his followers for the revolutionary conquest of power. No consideration of the fierce rejection of his views by the populace at large, or even within his own party, distracted him in the slightest. So unique was he in the extreme radicalness of his views that many considered he had finally gone mad. So out of tune with the general mood were his slogans of turning the imperialist war into a civil war that many felt that his own intransigence spelt the end of his political influence. Lenin's activities and slogans for political practice during the war, during 1917, and in the years thereafter, cannot be rendered intelligible by presenting him as a pragmatic politician ever anxious for power and influence. On the contrary, his theoretical findings dictated his practical activity. Lenin's theoretical analysis of imperialism not only showed the world to be ripe for socialist revolution, it also suggested the forms of administration which the socialist revolution would adopt. It gave not merely the imperative to revolution, but the outline of the positive content of that revolution.

The attempt of this second volume is the same as that of the first – to trace the relationship between theory and practice in Lenin's political thought. I will use these terms 'theory' and 'practice' in the same way as they were used in Volume 1, but it might be as well for me to remind the reader of the sense in which they are used. By 'theory' I understand Lenin's economic and social analysis of society. This theoretical structure estimates the level of development of productive forces, division of labour and socialisation of labour within society and gives an account of the relative strengths and weaknesses of its various classes. It also observes regularities in the development of industry and of classes, on the basis of which it is able to formulate laws with predictive capacity. Theory is, in this sense, prescient. It can anticipate economic and social developments and this gives it its claim to advise, guide or lead practical political affairs. It is of course intrinsic to Marxism that the economic substructure of society conditions or determines its entire legal and political superstructure. It also follows that the practical political strategies and tactics of Marxists will be conditioned or determined by their socio-economic analysis of existing society and the projections they make about the future on the basis of laws abstracted from that analysis. In Volume 1, I showed that Lenin's socio-economic analysis of the development of Russian capitalism was both logically and chronologically prior to his elaboration of a consistent strategy and tactic of the *democratic* revolution. In this volume, I seek to show that his economic analysis of international finance capitalism (or imperialism) occupies precisely the same place in his account of the strategy and tactics of the *socialist* revolution. The imperative for the socialist revolution, the strategies recommended to implement it and the forms it would assume are, therefore, not merely intimately connected with Lenin's economic and social analysis, they are quite unintelligible when viewed apart from it.

CHAPTER 1

Social Democracy and the War

Lenin's politics changed radically and permanently in August 1914. Until then Lenin, as we noticed in Volume 1 of this study, devoted comparatively little attention to the development of international affairs and the drift towards war.[1] He was, no doubt, sustained by an optimism, almost universal among socialists, that the power of public opinion, the power of the socialist parties and in particular the massed cohorts and experienced leadership of the S.P.D. (the Social-Democratic Party of Germany), the pride of the International, would not tolerate a European war. It was this optimism which Jaurès, shortly before his tragic death, gave voice to: 'If the Kaiser were to begin a war,' he prophesied, 'four million German Socialists would rise as one man and put him to death.'[2] On 4 August the Kaiser's demand for war credits to the tune of five thousand million marks was met not with a rising but with the unanimous and unconditional assent of the 110 S.P.D. representatives in the Reichstag. It fell to Haase to read the Party's declaration: it began with a disclaimer of any responsibility for the outbreak of the war, which was attributed wholly to the imperialist policies of the great powers, but it continued:

> For our people and its peaceful development, much, if not everything, is at stake, in the event of the victory of Russian despotism, which has stained itself with the blood of the best of its own people. Our task is to ward off this danger, to safeguard the civilisation (*Kultur*) and the independence of our own country. And here we make good what we have always emphatically affirmed: we do not leave the Fatherland in the lurch in the hour of danger.[3]

If the S.P.D. found reason enough to rally to the Fatherland in its hour of crisis, with what greater justification could the French socialists respond to the tocsin cry of *'la patrie en danger'*. *La patrie* was, after all, the land of the revolutionary climacterics of 1789, 1830, 1848 and 1871; it was the land of an illustrious roster of socialist thinkers and activists extending from Babeuf and Saint Simon to Vaillant and Guesde. It was, moreover, a genuinely democratic republic under obvious threat of attack by a quasi-democratic militarist monarchy. The cry of national defence was, as Lenin constantly maintained, a loophole through which virtually any socialist could slide to evade his socialist duty. To the Germans it was represented as the need to preserve civilisation from the marauding Cossack hordes; for most of the other countries of Europe it was couched in terms of saving themselves from Prussian militarism. National defence was the justifying rationale behind the votes for war credits by the S.P.D. and the French and Austrian socialist parties on that fateful day of 4 August. It was the unseen dynamite that blew the International to pieces.

The war undoubtedly brought with it very considerable problems for the leaders of the European socialist parties. The mobilisation of their supporters, militants and officials took away much of their constituency and disrupted their organisation. At the ideological level, they had to face the embarrassing critiques of those few intransigents who accused them of treachery to the cause and pointed to the glaring contradiction between their earlier solemn professions and their present political stances. These were, however, no more than tiny ripples which were quite swept away by the mighty wave of jingoistic patriotism that engulfed the working class every bit as much as the other sectors of society. The workers, gripped by the general mood, had flocked to the colours. On the day before voting for war credits, one S.P.D. representative records:

> I saw reservists join the colours and go forth singing Social Democrat songs! Some Socialist reservists I knew said to me 'We are going to the front with an easy mind, because we know the Party will look after us if we are wounded and that the Party will take care of our families if we don't come home'.[4]

Of what relevance now were the earlier revolutionary pledges and internationalist declarations? To repeat them now and to act upon them would have been interpreted by the mobilised working class as treachery. They would, it was cogently argued, have made short shrift of any leaders who questioned or objected to the war effort for which they were putting their lives on the line. To have taken a firm stand against the war would have resulted in the socialist organisations being swept clean away by popular resentment. And, if popular resentment did not do the job, the war-time governments assuredly would. The S.P.D. knew full well that if it opposed the war, its magnificent organisation, the product of four decades' labour, would be swiftly dismantled. The memory of Bismarck's anti-socialist laws was still fresh in its mind. The French Socialist Party was equally aware that its government had drawn up contingency plans for the arrest of over 2500 labour and socialist leaders (for whom the Minister for War had reportedly threatened the guillotine)[5] in the event of any attempts to mount a general strike or impede the war effort.[6]

The arguments of moderates became, in this situation, enormously seductive. Why hazard all that had been built up for a stand on the principle of proletarian internationalism and the resolutions of the Second International when, clearly, the bulk of the proletariat had been infected with patriotic fervour and would reject the exhortations of the leadership? The social democrats, they could convincingly argue, had done everything that fell within their powers to prevent the outbreak of war. Had not the Second International repeatedly come out against the threatening prospect of European war? Had not the national parties energetically campaigned in their press and in public meetings right up to the outbreak of hostilities against the international blood-letting which was being prepared by their capitalist governments? If, in spite of their valiant efforts, the war had arrived then surely the best course was to retain the integrity and power of the socialist parties as the only voices of sanity in the midst of the chaos and carnage. The task of the socialist parties, the moderates urged, was to bring the war to as speedy a conclusion as possible and to ensure that no punitive peace settlements were imposed. It was also widely believed, if little discussed in the open, that the socialist parties must preserve their structure and influence intact since they would undoubtedly fall heir to political power which the capitalists, by bringing civilisation beyond the

edge of disaster, had clearly forfeited. The war signalled the end
of the old era and the socialists must be on hand to pick up the
pieces and begin to build the new order. Their heritage was at
hand, but it would be theirs only if they acted with the people, not
against them. The great mass of the people in all belligerent
countries were undoubtedly for the war.

If the war brought its perils, embarrassments and disruptions,
it also brought very real advantages to the major socialist parties.
The rewards they reaped from their voluntary decisions to
suspend the class war for the duration of hostilities were very
considerable. In Germany, the *Burgfrieden* – the civil peace –
proclaimed by the S.P.D., met with immediate government
response. Party literature was allowed to circulate in the army, its
newspapers were, for the first time, allowed on to the news-stands
at railway stations, all legal proceedings against trade unions were
dropped, official posts became accessible to Party members and,
most important of all, the government promised electoral reform
in Prussia.[7] These tangible advantages apart, there was also a less
easily defined, but perhaps more potent, feeling that at last the
Party had been accepted. After so many decades it had come in
from the cold, was consulted by cabinet ministers and even
referred to approvingly by the Kaiser. For many there was, no
doubt, a sense of profound elation that the two Germanies – the
official, military and middle-class Germany on the one hand, and
working-class Germany on the other – after living in animosity
and virtual isolation one from another, had at last become one.

In France, the degree of separate development had never been
so pronounced. Persecution of the socialist parties had not been
so persistent; since 1871, France had been a genuinely democratic republic with a ministry responsible to parliament. There was,
therefore, the real opportunity, which had never existed in
Germany, that a socialist government could be peacefully installed by popular vote. France had, after all, been the first country in
which a socialist minister – Millerand – had been given cabinet
office. It was hardly surprising that, in the late summer of 1914,
war produced a universal excitement of patriotic feeling. The
German *Burgfrieden* found its complement in the *union sacrée*
and, typically for France, in the inclusion of socialists, Guesde
amongst them, in a national government.

The Bolshevik section of the Russian Social Democratic Party

(R.S.D.L.P.) had, ever since 1905, been unique amongst the socialist parties of Europe in that it not only believed in the imminence of revolution and laid great emphasis on the enormous educative role of revolutionary activity in raising the consciousness and developing the organisation of the workers – its commitment to revolution was even more unique in that it was not simply theoretical but practical. The Russian Bolsheviks, alone of all the parties of the Second International, took the business of preparing their cadres and, as far as they were able, the masses they led, for the actual physical confrontations that lay ahead. The other parties of the International, whilst theoretically acknowledging that conditions in Europe were ripe for socialist revolution, made no attempts whatsoever in the pre-war era actually to prepare their members or their followers for the physical combat that this would entail. If they had not done so in the years of 'normality' how much less likely was it that they would do so in war-time when the very existence of their countries was threatened. To have advocated a civil war for socialism would, in this situation, have lost them the enormous support they had patiently built up over two or three decades and would undoubtedly have seen them branded as traitors. Even Lenin's own Bolshevik cadres blenched at the prospect of initiating his proposals. Many of them, indeed, adopted an openly defencist stance, arguing the case that Russia was in no way the aggressor and that, moreover, in fighting alongside republican France, Russia was performing a progressive role in defeating reactionary German militarism. Some of Lenin's own principal lieutenants went as far as to join the Russian emigré detachment of the French army.[8]

Within Russia itself, as we noticed in the concluding chapter of Volume 1, the years from 1912–14 had seen a very considerable revival of the Russian labour movement and the Bolsheviks had been far more successful than their Menshevik rivals in harnessing it.[9] The strike movement grew apace in the early months of 1914, beginning with mass strikes and demonstrations commemorating Bloody Sunday in January and culminating in a general strike in St Petersburg in July in which barricades once again went up in the workers' quarter and armed fighting between police and strikers threatened to spill over into a general revolutionary outburst. There seemed to be evidence enough to support Lenin's contention that a new, more powerful and decisive 1905 was at hand which would finally deal the death blow to the autocracy. Russia's declaration of war abruptly changed the situation. 'It suddenly created among the workers a kind of collective impulse to stop the movement in view of an approaching calamity. And the strike movement ceased immediately.'[10] The workers, in common with every other class of Russian society, were overnight transformed into patriots and faithful subjects of the Tsar. The government, for its part, carefully presented the declaration of war as a defensive move reluctantly entered into by Russia to honour her commitments to the Slavs of Serbia invaded by a predatory Austria-Hungary, and to preserve Russia itself from the hostile expansionism of Germany. Astutely, the Tsar consolidated the instinct to rally round the flag by reconvening the Duma which was to express the new-found national unity. At the same time, however, the autocracy moved in to suppress all socialist, trade union and labour organisations throughout Russia. Its sufficient pretext for this was the 'unpatriotic' stance of the Social Democratic group in the Duma which, with an unaccustomed display of solidarity between its Bolshevik and Menshevik wings, refused to vote for the war budget and immediately issued a declaration to all Russian workers which denounced the war and called on the international proletariat to press for its speedy termination.[11] For their pains, the whole Social Democratic group was arrested, in spite of their immunity as deputies, and the Bolshevik faction was subsequently tried, sentenced and exiled to Siberia. The entire socialist press had earlier been closed down. Having disposed of the political leadership, the government immediately turned its attention to the local Social Democratic committees and the trade unions. From late 1914 to the collapse of the autocracy in February 1917 there were virtually no organisations to represent the workers' interest and no press to articulate their demands. As late as December 1916, thirty members of the Duma were moved to declare that the other allied governments recognised and accepted the legitimacy and necessity of strong labour organisations . . . whereas our governments engaged in disorganising our working masses. The labour press is abolished, the trades unions are closed, the health insurance offices are paralysed in their activities.[12]

The very absence of alternative political and trade union

11

organisations was to have an enormous effect on the mushroom growth of soviets in the months after March 1917 and accounts in large measure for the extraordinary influence they wielded. It may, equally, account for the parallel, extremely rapid growth of factory committees during these months with their strident calls for workers' control over production. In the absence of their traditional structures of trade unions and political parties, the workers improvised their own organisations to articulate their demands.

The mood of national conciliation which the outbreak of the war produced was far from being restricted to the workers and the liberal and right-wing parties. It deeply affected many of the most prominent Social Democratic leaders, who now showed themselves to be far from immune to deep-rooted national prejudices. The most spectacular exemplar of this was Plekhanov. In a bemusing about-turn the veteran emigré, the father of Russian Marxism, suddenly effected a spectacular metamorphosis. From being a practising cosmopolitan and dedicated exponent of proletarian internationalism, he became a fervid supporter of the cause of freedom and democracy (represented by the Entente and *therefore* by Russia) against despotism and militarism (represented by the Axis powers). He ardently supported the French socialists in voting for war credits and gave his blessing to their entry into a coalition government. He went a good deal further: he called on Russian emigrés in France to volunteer *en masse* for the French army to do battle for the cause of progressive humanity – a call which even many Bolshevik leaders abroad answered by volunteering.[13] To an astonished visitor, he announced that, were it not for his advanced age, he himself would go to the front in defence of Russia.[14] To an equally amazed and scandalised Angelica Balabanoff, he declared, 'if I were not old and sick I would join the army. To bayonet our German comrades would give me great pleasure.'[15]

Germany was, beyond a shadow of Plekhanov's doubt, the guilty country. It was the leaders of the German Social Democrats, as the representatives of the largest, best organised, most theoretically developed socialist party in the world, who were, in his view, most culpable for wrecking the cause of international proletarian solidarity. In spite of their earlier professions, in spite of the disciplined cohorts they commanded, they had meekly acquiesced in support of the obviously aggressive aims of their government. By their devious actions, they had absolved the socialists of other countries from honouring the pledges they had made to the International. The intended victims of German aggression not merely had a natural right to defend themselves, they had an imperative obligation to fight to the death against Prussian militarism and the expansionist ambitions of the German state. Germany's suzerainty over Europe and European Russia would, Plekhanov maintained, represent an enormous historical setback for the cause of democracy and socialism. The development of industry would be greatly retarded in the tributary states. The revolutionary labour movement would be crushed and pliant right-wing social democrats would everywhere gain the ascendancy. The cause of socialism, he concluded, would be set back by several decades. Given this awful prospect, the working classes of all the threatened countries must do their utmost for the war effort and inaugurate a period of civil peace until the danger was past.[16] The arch-revolutionary now found himself compelled to restrain the growing restiveness and revolutionary temper that infected Russia as the continuation of the war brought military defeat, economic collapse and general privation. In all this, as his biographer observes, one is hard put to recognise Plekhanov, the militant soldier of revolutionary social democracy . . .

> The Plekhanov of the war period supported class collaboration instead of class struggle; a war among nations instead of international proletarian solidarity. He counselled the necessity of defending the existing state, instead of preparing for its overthrow, since that would bring unintended and undesirable results.[17]

His apostasy, in Lenin's eyes, could go no further; his position was the logical, consistent outcome of *all* apologies for defencism. There were, however, between the two extremes of Lenin's militant defeatism and Plekhanov's patriotic defencism, an almost infinite number of intermediary positions within Russian social democracy. Akselrod, though agreeing with Plekhanov about the right of French and Belgian socialists to assist the war efforts of their countries against German aggression, refused to sanction any support of the Tsar by Russian socialists. Such support, he maintained, would simply be used to prop up the autocratic regime and the power of the landlords and right-wing bourgeoisies.[18] Like the majority of Russian socialists, he rather forlornly 'hoped for a speedy negotiated peace providing for a return to the status quo ante bellum'.[19] Potresov took a similar line. In France and England, he maintained, socialist participation in the war was entirely justified in terms of the preservation of hard-won freedoms. This argument could not, in his view, be transferred to Russia which, through the accident of power politics, found itself allied with democratic Britain and republican France. Only if the whole structure of government in Russia were democratised would Russian socialists be justified in lending it their support.[20] Potresov and his influential group of supporters in Russia believed nonetheless that, for the time being at least, their duty lay in not actively opposing Russian efforts to win the war.

It was, however, the centrist argument which won by far the greatest support among the so-called Internationalist Mensheviks both within Russia and in the emigré movement. Neither side, the centrists argued, merited the support of socialists whose proper duty it was to assist the socialist International in its efforts to bring the war to an end on the basis of a just peace. This view was shared too by many of the Bolsheviks (at least by those who had not gone over, with G. A. Aleksinsky, the former Bolshevik leader in the Duma, to a position as stridently patriotic as Plekhanov's).

The longer the war continued, the more the initial patriotic fervour with which it had been greeted died down. It died with the millions of dead and maimed. In Russia especially the prodigious loss of human life consequent upon repeated military defeats, coupled with the progressive breakdown of transport and the economy generally, resulted in the rapid growth of the internationalist or centrist position among socialists of all varieties.

Socialist Revolutionaries, Mensheviks and Bolsheviks alike, took up the cry of a just peace without annexations or indemnities. They called for concerted action by the proletariat of all countries to bring pressure to bear upon their governments for the speedy cessation of hostilities on the basis of such a platform.

14

This was, in essence, the position adopted by the Menshevik and S.R. leaders of the soviets in the period from March to November 1917.

CONCLUSION

The war presented Lenin with enormous theoretical and practical problems. Organisationally, the Bolshevik Party in Russia lay in ruins. What few activists remained had little contact with each other and less with Lenin. Even within the emigré Bolshevik camp there were grave differences of opinion and Lenin was in a small minority among his own followers. His chances of winning substantial international support seemed even more remote. His personal situation was, moreover, desperate. Throughout the war years he did not have enough money to sustain himself and Krupskaya, let alone to finance publishing ventures and the restitution of the Party. His position seemed hopeless.

Theoretically, he had to attempt to understand and characterise the war in Marxist terms. He had also to construct a coherent Marxist account of the collapse of the Second International and the willingness of its leaders to come to the aid of the bourgeois states they had pledged themselves to destroy.

CHAPTER 2

Lenin on the War

From the very onset of hostilities Lenin knew with absolute certainty that the old order of the bourgeois world had arrived at its final impasse and equally that the old order of international socialism represented by the Second International had passed away never to be re-established. Even while he was in Galicia, arrested, imprisoned, then given leave to make his way to neutral Switzerland, Lenin was already formulating the stridently categorical theses which were to distinguish his policies throughout the war years.

It would be foolish to ignore the sense of personal commitment Lenin felt for the anti-war resolutions of the International. He himself, as a member of the International Socialist Bureau, had, along with Martov and Luxemburg, been responsible for drafting the most specific formulation of the obligations of member parties in the event of war ever produced by the Second International. At the instance of these three, the International unanimously adopted a resolution, at its Stuttgart Congress of 1907, which stipulated that:

> If an outbreak of war appears imminent, the workers and their parliamentary representatives in the countries concerned must do everything in their power to prevent war breaking out, using suitable measures which will differ and increase according to the intensifying of the class struggle and the general political situation. If war should still break out, they must take all steps to bring it to a speedy conclusion and make every possible effort to exploit the economic and political crisis brought about by the war to rouse the people and thereby accelerate the downfall of the rule of the capitalist class.[1]

This resolution formed the basis of the International's attitude

16

towards the war; it was reaffirmed in Copenhagen in 1910 and again in the last Congress to convene before the war, in Basle in 1912. Lenin, in all his writings on the war, returned to it again and again. It was for him the yardstick by which the treachery of socialist parties and leaders could be measured. Throughout his political career, Lenin was a fundamentalist. Nowhere was this clearer than in his attitude towards the war. All around him he saw the great leaders of mighty socialist parties, lured by the spell of patriotism, seduced by the offers of cabinet office and recognition by the state, totally committing themselves to their countries' war efforts. Strikes and industrial militancy ceased overnight, labour leaders, from being tribunes of the class war, suddenly became apostles of industrial harmony and increased productivity, and advocates of a general class truce—the celebrated *Burgfrieden*. All of this, Lenin argued, had nothing to do with socialism. Socialism, he maintained with all the authority of numberless resolutions of the International to back him up, was not about class harmony but class war, it was not about seeking recognition by the bourgeois state but replacing that state, above all it was not about a sense of identity with a national community but with an international one. On all these scores he was adamant about the treachery of the old leaders of the national parties and, from the outset, he anathemised them in language more venomous and savage than he had ever resorted to before.

Lenin's position was made brutally clear in his first considered statement on the war written not later than 24 August and submitted by him to a group of Bolsheviks on his arrival in Berne. Lenin had written not only the obituary notice for the Second International, but the coroner's report of the causes of death as well.

The betrayal of socialism by most leaders of the Second International (1889–1914) signifies the ideological and political bankruptcy of the International. This collapse has been mainly caused by the actual prevalence in it of petty-bourgeois opportunism, the bourgeois nature and the danger of which have long been indicated by the finest representatives of the revolutionary proletariat of all countries. The opportunists had long been preparing to wreck the Second International by denying the socialist revolution and substituting bourgeois reformism in its stead, by rejecting the class struggle with its inevitable conversion at certain moments into civil war, and by preaching class collaboration; by preaching bourgeois chauvinism under the guise of patriotism and the defence of the fatherland ... instead of recognising the need for a revolutionary war by the proletarians of all countries, against the bourgeoisie of all countries; by making a fetish of the necessary utilisation of bourgeois parliamentarianism and bourgeois legality, and forgetting that illegal forms of organisation and agitation are imperative at times of crises.[2]

Lenin's conclusion was that a new International would have to be formed cleansed of 'this bourgeois trend in socialism'. He had arrived at an identification which was to have profoundly important repercussions on the subsequent development of his thought. *All* of those socialists who, whatever their reservations, supported the defence of their own country in the war, were objectively bourgeois. They could not be counted in any way as misguided fighters for the proletarian cause. They had become agents of the bourgeoisie within the labour movement. The economic basis of this bourgeois fifth column was still unelaborated, but their treachery undoubted. The chauvinist and patriotic leadership was, Lenin contended, a very influential stratum but it was nonetheless comparatively small in numbers. The revolutionaries must expose the social chauvinists at every step and appeal to the mass of the working population which still retained its revolutionary internationalism. The central axiom of Lenin's policy throughout the war years, one which he did not question for it made his whole political strategy intelligible, is the presumption of a widespread revolutionary consciousness and mass antagonism to opportunism and chauvinism.[3]

The argument of the social patriots that they just were not strong enough to do anything positive to resist the wave of patriotism was, Lenin maintained, no defence for actually voting *in favour* of war credits and actually assisting the process of mobilisation of the masses for the slaughter.

Even given the total *incapacità* and impotence of the European Socialists, the behaviour of their leaders reveals treachery and baseness: the workers have been driven into the slaughter, while their leaders vote *in favour* and join *governments*! Even with their total impotence, they should have voted *against*, should *not have joined* their governments and uttered chauvinist infamies; should *not* have shown solidarity with their 'nation', and should *not* have defended their 'own' bourgeoisie', they should have unmasked its vileness.

Everywhere there is the bourgeoisie and the imperialists, everywhere the ignoble preparations for carnage.[4]

The only socialist policy, in Lenin's view, was to urge the defeat of one's own government: in practical terms that was the only policy compatible with genuine internationalism. A radical implementation of this policy demanded widespread illegal propaganda canvassing civil war in all the armies of the belligerent countries 'for the socialist revolution and the need to use weapons, not against their brothers, the wage slaves in other countries, but against the reactionaries and bourgeois governments and parties of all countries . . .'[5]

The tactical slogans that Lenin gave out at the very onset of the war were to remain substantially unchanged throughout it, though the rationale behind them became more sophisticated: **defeat of one's own country in this war as the lesser evil**, fraternisation at the front and active preparation for civil war in all countries, merciless struggle against chauvinists of all hues, propaganda for an end to monarchical rule in Germany, Poland and Russia and the slogan of a republican United States of Europe, for socialist republics in Europe and a radical democratic revolution in Russia, for a new revolutionary workers' international and the recognition that the old Second International was utterly dead and discredited.

These were the slogans that Lenin tirelessly repeated in clandestine meetings wherever he could find an audience, in his letters to those few individuals who supported him, and in his theses, manifestoes and speeches to the two international socialist conferences called to discuss the best means of ending the war. It was at those two conferences, at Zimmerwald in September 1915 and Kienthal in April 1916, that Lenin first put himself forward as the leader of the revolutionary left on an international scale. He exerted all his efforts to ensure beforehand that the left was well represented, he held long meetings with individual leaders whose support he hoped to win, he organised separate meetings of the left faction within these conferences and took upon himself the task of drafting their resolutions and manifestoes. Despite all his efforts, the volume of support he secured was, in practical terms, insignificant. Even among the anti-war minority socialist groups and factions represented (for the terms of reference of both conferences excluded all those parties offering support to their governments) Lenin frequently found himself quite isolated. At Zimmerwald, for instance, his was the sole dissenting vote on many issues.[6]

The great majority of the anti-war left minority groups in 1915 and in 1916 rejected as quite impracticable Lenin's call to turn the imperialist war into a civil war. They were equally emphatic that there should be no break with the Second International, though they became increasingly critical and impatient at the failure of the International Socialist Bureau to elaborate a plan for a peace without annexations or indemnities and based upon the right of nations to self-determination.[7] At Kienthal, Lenin did rather better, but even here only twelve of the forty-four delegates supported his draft manifesto.[8] Lenin's self-appointed task was daunting indeed; to convert a world immersed in madness with but twelve disciples to help him. It was precisely the sort of task which he delighted in.

LENIN'S CHARACTERISATION OF THE WAR

For most socialist leaders the war was an embarrassment and an encumbrance – an embarrassment in that it obliged them to attempt some sort of justification of their defencist or openly patriotic policies which so flagrantly conflicted with their most solemn previous promises – an encumbrance in that the universal crisis severely interfered with three decades of patient work building up the vote-catching and welfare facilities of their parties. Crisis was for Lenin his natural milieu. Just as he had seen the war and revolution of 1905 as a welcome quickening of the pace of social and political development after what he termed the philistine years of humdrum change proceeding at cart-horse pace, so now he was aware of the enormous potential for revolution that lay locked up in the European war. As 1905 represented the maturation of the development of economic and social contradictions within emergent Russian capitalism, so 1914 represented for Lenin the maturation of the contradictions of the highest and final phase of capitalism on a world-wide scale. As the crisis of 1905 portended the final collapse of feudalism in Russia, so this global crisis of 1914 portended the death agony of world capitalism. The opportunities which the war would offer for the realisation of socialism would be immense and therefore the obligations imposed on socialist leaders would be equally huge. It was precisely because so many of the socialist leaders of Europe could not, or would not, comprehend these opportunities for the realisation of socialism that Lenin became so enraged.

The war, according to Lenin, was 'no chance happening'.[9] It had been engendered by imperialism and was incomprehensible unless seen as the product of this final and moribund epoch of capitalism.

> The present war is imperialist in character. This war is the outcome of conditions in an epoch in which capitalism has reached the highest stage in its development; in which the greatest significance attaches, not only to the export of commodities, but also to the export of capital; an epoch in which the cartelisation of production and the internationalisation of economic life have assumed impressive proportions, colonial policies have brought about the almost complete partition of the globe, world capitalism's productive forces have outgrown the limited boundaries of national and state division, and the objective conditions are perfectly ripe for socialism to be achieved.[10]

In this the final epoch of capitalism, Lenin argued that the cartels, trusts and great corporations intimately inter-linked with the big banks had, since the turn of the century, established monopolies over whole sectors of production in many of the industrialised countries. Their insatiable thirst for profits, for a market for their goods, for the acquisition of monopoly rights to the sources of raw materials, and especially the need to export super-abundant capital, had driven the monopolies into foreign colonial expansion on the most grandiose scale.

The characterisation of the war as being a necessary product of a specific epoch of capitalist advance is crucial to an understanding of Lenin's political strategy at this time. The war was the culmination of the contradictions besetting international finance capitalism or imperialism which was the *last* historical phase in the career of capitalism, the phase in which it was to be supplanted by socialism.

Basically the war was a war about who should dominate what, it was a slave-holder's war which had everything to do with oppression, domination and exploitation and nothing whatever to do with liberation.

> From the liberator of nations, which it was in the struggle against feudalism, capitalism in its imperialist stage has turned into the greatest oppressor of nations. Formerly progressive, capitalism has become reactionary . . . Mankind is faced with the alternative of adopting socialism or experiencing years and even decades of armed struggle between the 'Great' Powers for the artificial preservation of capitalism by means of colonies, monopolies, privileges and national oppression of every kind.[11]

The war, Lenin concluded, was 'a continuation of the politics of a rotten-ripe reactionary bourgeoisie which has plundered the world, seized colonies, etc.'.[12]

The drive for colonial expansion had assumed an especially frenzied character in the last decades of the nineteenth century. In the period 1884 to 1900, Britain and France, Lenin pointed out, had increased the land area under their control by 3.7 and 3.6 million square miles respectively.[13] This process had continued until virtually the whole economic territory of the world available for seizure, or too weak to withstand the enforcement of concessions, had been annexed. 'For the first time the world is completely divided up, so that in the future *only* redivision is possible.'[14] In this division of the world, Britain and France had acquired an enormously greater share than other countries, and this was no more than a fairly accurate mirror-image of the relative economic power of the industrial nations at a particular moment of their development. The problem was that, once effected, the territorial division of the world remained static and unresponsive to subsequent changes in the economic development and demands of the great powers. It became an institutional framework inappropriate to the pattern of a more developed world economy and was seen as a positive fetter to the further progress of younger, more virile economies. These fresher, more rapidly developing economies, like Germany, Japan and America, also eventually reached the stage where the export of capital and the securing of convenient stocks of raw material became imperative. Their drive for economic territory was, however, frustrated at every turn by the established division of the world. The only way now open to effect a redivision of economic territory which would more accurately correspond to relative economic powers of the industrialised countries was through the trial of arms. Crises resulting in wars were, according to Lenin's analysis, endemic in the structure of international finance capitalism – a product of its uneven development.

At the centre of Lenin's analysis of the war lies his singular and highly important concept of the uneven development of capitalism. This above all gave his analysis of the war and of imperialism a distinctive stamp. It had always been a part of Lenin's general analysis of capitalism that a fundamental imbalance between differing sectors of production – especially that between agriculture and machine industry – made crisis and anarchy inevitable. In the epoch of imperialism he conceded that the anarchy of production in certain spheres of industry could be almost overcome through the establishment of complete monopolies which could appraise total demand fairly accurately and plan the extraction of raw materials and provision of finished goods to meet it. The more that one sphere of industry became the preserve of a single monopoly, the more that it 'rationalised' production and socialised labour, the more the primitive level of technological development and organisation of other sectors was highlighted, the greater became the dislocation and anarchy within the system of social production taken as a whole. Monopolies did not therefore eliminate the anarchy of production in the economy; on the contrary, they emphasised it and raised it to a new level.

In the same way, Lenin argued, the establishment of international monopolies did not, thereby, eliminate the anarchy of

international trade and competition between nations and international trusts; on the contrary, they emphasised the extreme
unevenness of capitalist development among the great powers in
the imperialist epoch.[15]

Part of Lenin's objective in positing an entirely new epoch in
the development of capitalism was to deprive his opponents of
the arguments used by Marx to justify 'progressive' wars which
promoted the process of national consolidation or brought
vegetative hydraulic societies into the maelstrom of world history.
Of course, Lenin argued, so long as capitalism had been
progressive there had been occasions when its wars had assisted
the onward march of history. According to the periodisation
which Lenin now adopted, capitalism had moved through three
principal epochs. The first saw its consolidation and triumph over
feudalism and this was the heroic epoch of its virility which lasted
from 1789 to 1871. The second epoch, which lasted until the
outbreak of the Great War, was that of its late maturity and
approaching senility. The final epoch was that of the evident
moribund nature and degeneration of capitalism which had
lately set in:

> The first epoch from the Great French Revolution to the
> Franco-Prussian war is one of the rise of the bourgeoisie, of
> its triumph, of the bourgeoisie on the upgrade, an epoch
> of bourgeois-democratic movements in general and of
> bourgeois-national movements in particular, an epoch of the
> rapid breakdown of the obsolete feudal-absolutist institu-
> tions. The second epoch is that of the full domination and
> decline of the bourgeoisie, one of transition from its progres-
> sive character towards reactionary and even ultra-reactionary
> finance capital. . . . The third epoch, which has just set in,
> places the bourgeoisie in the same 'position' as that in which the
> feudal lords found themselves during the first epoch. This is
> the epoch of imperialism and imperialist upheavals . . . [16]

The most serious and devastating of the upheavals caused by
putrescent capitalism was, of course, war. War in the epoch of
imperialism was no aberrant or simply ill-fated occurrence. It
was, on the contrary, endemic, unavoidable and would

repeatedly recur so long as the third phase lasted. The whole of European culture was at risk and the imperialist bourgeoisie was set to plunge the world into barbarism from which there could be no escape except via revolution. Anticipating the conclusions which Rosa Luxemburg was to arrive at in her famous Junius pamphlet, Lenin exhorted the European proletariat:

> Do not trust any high-sounding programmes. We say to the masses: rely on your own mass revolutionary action against your governments and your bourgeoisie and try to build up such action; there is no escape from barbarism, no possibility of progress in Europe, without a civil war for Socialism.[17]

The severity of the crisis and the prognosis of recurrent and worsening catastrophes which could only result in deepening oppression made it imperative that all socialists should act to prepare for the revolution which the suffering of the war itself was hastening.

It was precisely commitment to revolutionary action against the imperialist war which now defined a socialist in Lenin's eyes. All those who, for whatever reason, supported the defence of their own fatherland or even took an apparently impartial pacifist stance, were directly or indirectly assisting their general staffs. All those who, for whatever reason, were prepared to support revolutionary action against the war, even if they had hitherto styled themselves anarchists or syndicalists or even Fabians, proved themselves much better socialists than all the pedants of Marxism, 'who know the "Texts" by heart but are now busy . . . justifying social-chauvinism of every kind'.[18]

Directly echoing Sorel and his supporters, Lenin argued that the distinctive characteristic of a socialist, especially in times of crisis, is 'intransigence, a readiness for rebellion' and heroic commitment to act. With Sorel, Lenin agreed that 'Strong ideas are those that shock and scandalise, evoke indignation, anger and animosity in some, and enthusiasm in others'.[19] The war had at least this to commend it – it had brought the crisis not only of capitalism but also of the socialist movement to a head. It had, in Lenin's view, finally presented socialists and labour leaders with an inescapable choice: either they were for the defence of their own country and alliance therefore with their own bourgeoisie, or they stood for turning the imperialist war into a civil war for the triumph of socialism.

CHAUVINISTS, DEFENCISTS, OPPORTUNISTS AND PACIFISTS

Lenin's analysis of the nature of the disease from which social democracy was suffering had, by this time, come very close to the one which the anarchists and syndicalists had been arguing for some considerable time. It was what Lenin took to be the apostasy of the great majority of the leaders of social democracy (nine-tenths of them, he estimated, had sold out to the bourgeoisie) in 1914 that obliged him to undertake an unremitting critique of the whole history and structure of European social democracy. Naturally enough, he set the historical growth of social democracy firmly in the context of his new version of the epochal development of capitalism.

In the first epoch of the rise of capitalism the proletariat had played an outstanding and heroic role as the foremost fighters for progressive ideals. Their political as well as their trade union organisations had been prosecuted and oppressed but had emerged stronger, more militant and more resolute from each bout of persecution. This heroic era came to an end in 1871 with the attempt of the Paris proletariat to 'storm the gates of heaven'. Thereafter the trade union and political organisations of the proletariat had lived a generally legal and uneventful life, patiently building up their strength and exercising increasing influence in the state. Each accretion of strength necessitated new organisational arrangements, more paid functionaries, more offices and officers, more welfare and social activities which further enhanced the prestige, reputation and membership of social democracy. All of this had occurred in the second, comparatively peaceful period of expanding capitalism.

> Peaceful decades, however, have not passed without leaving their mark. They have of necessity given rise to opportunism in all countries, and made it prevalent among parliamentarian, trade union, journalistic and other 'leaders'.[20]

Lenin's analysis bore a striking resemblance to the one which

Michels had elaborated in his *Political Parties*. There he had maintained, following his teacher, Max Weber, that the bureaucratic organisational structure which mass political parties were obliged to create made them, of necessity, conservative in their ethos and activities. German social democracy was the first modern mass political party. It was the laboratory in which Weber and Michels tested and established their iron law of oligarchy – the ever-growing power of the leadership group in putting down any challenge to their authority from the more radical rank and file. Michels, in particular, showed how the very growth of an efficient bureaucracy within German social democracy produced a stable career structure for men of talent and ability within the working class. It also, definitionally, established settled procedures, policies and expectations habituating its officials to a settled style of working. The officials therefore acquired direct interest in the preservation of the existing *status quo*. Lenin had read Michels, but it is doubtful if his own analysis was directly indebted to his work since, to the end of his life, Lenin displayed an aversion, bordering almost on contempt, for sociology.[21] It is also obvious that Lenin could hardly accept Michels' *general* conclusions about the dialectics of success of *all* mass political parties – the thesis that to be politically effective the mass had to be organised, that efficient organisation spawned a bureaucracy with its own conservative values which inevitably corroded whatever radical objectives the party might have initially espoused. It is sufficient for us to note that in the particular case of the German Social Democratic Party during this period, Lenin's views came close to those of Michels and that his analysis was essentially confirmed by Carl Schorske's brilliant book on *German Social Democracy, 1905–1917*.[22]

The final result of this process was that the organisation – as Bernstein frankly admitted – became an end in itself. Its continued existence was practically identified with the triumph of socialism itself. The heroic revolutionary mission of the proletariat had been traduced and in its place there had appeared a servile, place-seeking parliamentary social democracy[23] anxious to preserve its organisational gains at no matter what cost to its ideals.

... decades of a so-called peaceful epoch have allowed an

27

accumulation of petty-bourgeois and opportunist junk *within* the Socialist parties of all the European countries.... There is hardly a single Marxist of note who has not recognised many times and on various occasions that the opportunists are in fact a non-proletarian element hostile to the socialist revolution. The particularly rapid growth of this social element of late years is beyond doubt: it includes officials of the legal labour unions, parliamentarians and the other intellectuals, who have got themselves easy and comfortable posts in the legal mass movement, some sections of the better paid workers, office employees, etc. etc.[24]

These elements who, Lenin maintains, are quite alien to the goals and mission of the proletarian revolution, insinuate themselves into the workers' movement during periods of peace and lie low until times of crisis when, by virtue of their entrenched positions in the leadership of the movement, they are able to paralyse its ability to develop the revolutionary potential of crises.

The opportunists are bourgeois enemies of the proletarian revolution, who in peaceful times carry on their bourgeois work in secret, concealing themselves within the workers' parties, while in times of crisis they *immediately* prove to be open allies of the *entire* united bourgeoisie...[25]

The political disposition of opportunism was then, in Lenin's view, a product of the second era of the development of capitalism so, by extension, its economic roots were discerned in the development of imperialism. The acquisition of protected markets for the export of goods and of capital, the monopolising of sources of raw materials, the brutal exploitation of colonial labourers unprotected by effective laws or defensive associations, all of these features of imperialism ensured that the return on capital invested was much larger than normal. The 'super-profits' obtained in this way could be used not only to arrest the tendency for the rate of profit in the exploiting countries to decline but also to buy off or bribe a certain influential sector of the working-class movement. Colonial expansion, Lenin maintained:

... meant a sum of super-profits and special privileges for the bourgeoisie. It meant, moreover, the possibility of enjoying crumbs from this big cake for a small minority of the petty-bourgeois, as well as for the better-placed employees, officials of the labour movement, etc. . . .

In a word, the 'all-pervading gradualism' of the second epoch (the one of yesterday) has created . . . an entire opportunist *trend* based on a definite social stratum within present-day democracy, and linked with the bourgeoisie of its own national 'shade' by numerous ties of economic, social and political interests – a trend directly, openly, consciously, and systematically hostile to any idea of a 'break in gradualness'.[26]

The second epoch in the development of capitalism provided both the subjective as well as the objective conditions for the development of an extensive opportunist trend in social democracy. Subjectively, the seeming success of the peaceful, responsible tactics of the movement caused them to be raised to the status of a fetish. Objectively, part of the fruits of imperialist superprofits were used to improve the living conditions of a small stratum of the labour aristocracy who therefore themselves participated in colonial exploitation and would have a vested interest in the preservation of their country's empire.

Lenin's verbal assaults on the opportunists became progressively more vicious as the war progressed. All of those leaders of the socialist and labour movements who supported the defence of their own country became, in Lenin's eyes, agents of the bourgeoisie. Their 'formal membership in workers' parties by no means disproves their objectively being a political detachment of the bourgeoisie, conductors of its influence, and its agents in the labour movement'.[27] It was the identification of opportunist social democracy with bourgeois politics that, whilst quite intelligible in the structure of Lenin's ideas, was to have such appalling practical results in the 1920s and 1930s. It formed the basis of the simplistic and tragic equation which the Comintern operated on during that period, that social democracy and fascism were both species of bourgeois politics and that, if a choice had to be made between them, the latter was in some respects preferable for being more frank and open about its objectives.

It was one of the more positive functions of the war that it, like

29

any profound crisis, revealed the essential contradictions of contemporary society.

> The European war is a tremendous historical crisis, the beginning of a new epoch. Like any crisis the war has aggravated deep-seated antagonisms and brought them to the surface, tearing asunder all veils of hypocrisy, agitating all conventions and deflating all corrupt or rotting authorities.[28].

Of all the erstwhile authorities which had been tried in the storm none had been blown to shreds so easily as social democracy. The war demonstrated that opportunism nurtured on the legalism of the 1880s and 1890s had, in the twentieth century, matured to full-blown chauvinism. Out of its humble beginnings in nagging doubts about the possibility or desirability of revolutionary change, opportunism developed to challenge, then to reject, both the class war and the internationalist soul of socialism.

> By social-chauvinism we mean acceptance of the idea of the defence of the fatherland in the present imperialist war, justification of an alliance between socialists and the bourgeoisie and the governments of their 'own' countries in the war, a refusal to propagate and support proletarian-revolutionary action against one's 'own' bourgeoisie, etc. It is perfectly obvious that social-chauvinism's basic ideological and political content fully coincides with the foundations of opportunism. It is *one and the same* tendency. In the conditions of the war of 1914–15, opportunism leads to social-chauvinism. The idea of class collaboration is opportunism's main feature. The war has brought this idea to its logical conclusion, and has augmented its usual factors and stimuli with a number of extraordinary ones; through the operation of special threats and coercion it has compelled the philistine and disunited masses to collaborate with the bourgeoisie . . .
> Opportunism means sacrificing the fundamental interests of the masses to the temporary interests of an insignificant minority of the workers, or in other words, an alliance between a section of the workers and the bourgeoisie. The war has made

such an alliance particularly conspicuous and inescapable. Opportunism was engendered in the course of decades by the special features in the period of the development of capitalism, when the comparatively peaceful and cultured life of a stratum of working men 'bourgeoisified' them, gave them crumbs from the table of their national capitalists, and isolated them from the suffering, misery and revolutionary temper of the impoverished and ruined masses.[29]

The objective economic basis of opportunism and social chauvinism is precisely the same, the attitude of class collaboration is common to both, both were nurtured on legalism which fostered a greater concern for the integrity of the organisation than the realisation of the goals of socialism. Defence of one's own country, open collaboration with one's own bourgeoisie and general staff is the end result of this gradual process of deserting socialism. Social chauvinism is, as Lenin frequently repeats, consummated opportunism – the open exposure of an expressly bourgeois trend within the labour and socialist movements.

The objective roots of this 'bourgeoisification' of a small but important stratum of the 'labour aristocracy' have already been alluded to. The function it performed was, according to Lenin, that of the cleric or priest. In order to secure its social dominance, the bourgeoisie needed not only the coercive machinery of police, courts, prisons and hangmen, it also needed cohorts of propagandists able to reconcile the masses to their dismal lot and buy them off with promises of plenty in the land beyond.[30]

The renegade labour and socialist leaders had, in Lenin's view, prostituted their Marxism and made of it not a combative militant doctrine of international class war but a comfortable plaint plea for social harmony: 'they take from Marxism all that is acceptable to the liberal bourgeoisie . . . they cast aside "only" the living soul of Marxism, "only" its revolutionary content'.[31] Kautsky, the pope of the movement and one-time verbal scourge of the bourgeoisie, had now, in Lenin's estimation, become no more than a street walker, a bourgeois whore, a *Mädchen für alle*.[32] His special contribution to the service of the bourgeoisie was to develop a brand of Marxism on credit. The time for revolution, indeed the time to prepare for revolution, was never now, it was always tomorrow, always a constantly receding mirage which, by

31

the nature of things, could never be attained. Lenin does, very perceptively, get to the heart of Kautsky's ambivalent commitment to revolution. In 1909, Lenin recalls, Kautsky himself had accurately predicted the coming 'acute and cataclysmic epoch' in which the day of reckoning with capitalism would finally come. When the cataclysm arrived, however, Kautsky stalled again. He introduced the possibility of yet another period of potential respite for capitalism which he dubbed the epoch of ultra-imperialism.[33] The possibility at least existed, he now argued, that the fierce rivalries of the imperialist epoch would subside and the imperialist countries would decide upon a peaceful rational carve-up of the world.

> The subsidising of the Protectionist movement in Britain; the lowering of tariffs in America; the trend towards disarmament; the rapid decline in the export of capital from France and Germany in the years immediately preceding the war; finally, the growing international interweaving between the various cliques of finance capital – all this has caused me to consider whether the present imperialist policy cannot be supplanted by a new, ultra-imperialist policy, which will introduce the joint exploitation of the world by internationally united finance capital, in place of the mutual rivalries of national finance capital. Such a phase of capitalism is at any rate conceivable. Can it be achieved? Sufficient premises are still lacking to enable us to answer this question.[34]

The significance of Kautsky's sudden discovery of a new epoch was not lost on Lenin. He had repeatedly insisted that an adequate Marxist characterisation of the contemporary phase of capitalist development was absolutely inseparable from, was indeed the prior condition for the formulation of, correct proletarian tactics.

> Only an objective consideration of the sum total of the relations between absolutely all the classes in a given society, and consequently a consideration of the objective stage of development reached by that society and of relations between it and other societies, can serve as a basis for the correct tactics of an advanced class.[35]

The significance of Kautsky's new 'possible' epoch of further capitalist development was that it provided, in Lenin's view, yet another convenient bolt-hole for those who had peddled revolution in the great bye-and-bye simply as a soporific, as a kind of opiate for present sufferings which on the great day would be redeemed. Kautsky, Lenin maintained,

> ... promises to be a Marxist in *another* epoch, not now, not under present conditions, not in this epoch! Marxism on credit, Marxism in promises, Marxism tomorrow, a petty-bourgeois, opportunist theory – *and not only a theory* – of blunting contradictions today.[36]

The theory of ultra-imperialism admirably fitted the bill in providing a justification for prevarication and inaction; it was but a revised recipe for the perennial and ubiquitous dish of the opportunists – the revolution of infinite regress. That at least was how Lenin appraised it.

> From the necessity of imperialism the Left wing deduces the necessity of revolutionary action. The 'theory of ultra-imperialism', however, serves Kautsky as a means *to justify the opportunists*, to present the situation in such a light as to create the impression that they have not gone over to the bourgeoisie but simply 'do not believe' that socialism can arrive immediately, and expect that a new 'era' of disarmament and lasting peace 'may be' ushered in ... Kautsky is exploiting the *hope* for a *new* peaceful era of capitalism so as to justify the adhesion of the opportunists and the official Social-Democratic parties to the bourgeoisie and their rejection of revolutionary, i.e. proletarian, tactics in the *present stormy era*, this despite the solemn declarations of the Basle resolution.[37]

Almost all the main leaders of European social democracy had, in one way or another, reneged on the obligations which the resolutions of the Second International clearly laid upon them, according to Lenin. Few were as devious as Kautsky and few were therefore as dangerous. Hyndman, for instance, and many of the Fabians as well as the French *possiblistes*, openly declared their support for their governments and saw no real need to justify their patriotism. They had, Lenin reminds his readers, for years past never pretended they would do anything else. Culpable they might be, but they were not hypocritical; they did not, like many of the centrists and defencists, attempt to dress their patriotism in threadbare socialist garb. They openly sided with their own bourgeoisie in the war-time crisis and made no bones about it. Their position was obvious and they were on that score not accounted dangerous by Lenin. Out and out chauvinism would, he felt, naturally discredit itself as the horrors of the war dragged on. More dangerous by far were those like Kautsky who objectively supported their own country and yet contrived to pretend that they were socialists or Marxists.[38]

The only way to expose these hypocrites, these traitors to all the resolutions of the Second International, was to work for a complete organisational break from them and an unremitting ideological attack on their defencist or pacifist positions. Whatever sophisms they advanced to justify their case; that their country was attacked, not an attacker, that Cossack barbarism had to be stopped, that an alliance with France signified an alliance with revolutionary progress, that 'little Belgium' had to be defended; all these paper-thin pretexts had to be mercilessly exposed for what they were. They were but the rationalisations of traitors, the flimsy excuses of leaders who had deserted the mass movement in its hour of supreme crisis. To plead in mitigation that the masses would never have gone along with a militant internationalist line was, Lenin maintained, a pathetic attempt to transfer responsibility from the leaders to the led, and this would never do for the simple reason that in the abruptness of the final crisis, in the discussions on whether to vote war credits, there was no time to consult the mass. The *leaders* were asked for *their* opinions, they were called upon to provide a lead, *their* votes were called for, not those of the mass.[39] Of course, once the leaders had meekly acquiesced to government pressure, the mass followed them. The masses could do no other since they could not act without 'their' organisation:

> The masses could not act in an organised fashion because their previously created organisation, an organisation embodied in a 'handful' of Legiens, Kautsky's and Scheidemann's, had betrayed them. It takes time to create a *new* organisation, as well as

determination to consign the old, rotten, and obsolete organisation to the scrap heap.[40]

It was a central axiom of Lenin's political strategy during and
after the First World War that the political centres of almost all
the social democratic parties had betrayed, confused and disorganised the proletariat.

The war, and the actions of the treacherous leaders, had 'split
and corrupted the proletariat',[41] they 'found themselves disunited and helpless amid a spate of chauvinism and under the
pressure of martial law and the war censorship'.[42]

The prime condition for the re-emergence of the proletariat as
a powerful revolutionary and international force demanded first
and foremost a complete break with the old socialist leadership. It
demanded the recognition that they had now become agents of
the bourgeoisie within the labour movement grown fat on
super-profits and quiescent after decades of peaceful legal
existence. With more than a smack of Old Testament wrath,
Lenin rains down his anathemas on the degeneration and
putrefaction of social democracy.[43] This 'foul and festering
abscess', with its 'unbearably putrid stench' which had developed
in most of the socialist parties, would have to be completely cut
out in order that the healthy parts of socialism might survive.
Only swift decisive surgery could save socialism; any other
treatment would lead to total infection. The chauvinist and
defencist leaders were, Lenin tirelessly repeated, quite beyond
the pale, there could be no hope of bringing them back into the
fold,[44] there could be no conciliation with evil or negotiation with
traitors.[45]

In such conditions, it is our duty, not only to 'blame', but to ring
the tocsin, ruthlessly unmask, overthrow and oust this parasitic
stratum from their posts, and destroy their 'unity' with the
working-class movement, because such 'unity' means, in practice, unity of the proletariat with the national bourgeoisie and a
split in the international proletariat, the unity of lackeys and a
split among the revolutionaries.[46]

Splits would have to be organised in all the European parties, illegal revolutionary Marxist parties would have to be established. The old Second International which had bred the nest of chauvinist vipers and continued to be their haunt must, Lenin argued, be consigned to the scrap heap and a new revolutionary International established in its place. 'It would,' he insisted, 'be a harmful illusion to hope that a genuinely socialist International can be restored without a full organisational severance from the opportunists.'[47]

There was, in Lenin's view, a dialectical process at work which the war had served to emphasise and accelerate. On the negative side, the war had undoubtedly split up the European proletariat, demoralised and disorganised it. It had also revealed the depths of corruption, opportunism and chauvinism of the old leadership of the social democratic parties. On the positive side, however, the war was undoubtedly preparing a revolutionary crisis of unprecedented dimensions. 'All governments,' Lenin declared, 'are sleeping on a volcano.'[48] In June 1915, Lenin had already arrived at a surprisingly accurate and prophetic projection of what the social consequences of continuing the war – or even the securing of a peace settlement – would be.

> The conflagration is spreading; the political foundations of Europe are being shaken more and more; the sufferings of the masses are appalling, the efforts of governments, the bourgeoisie and the opportunists to hush up these sufferings proving ever more futile . . . the smouldering indignation of the masses, the vague yearning of society's downtrodden for a kindly ('democratic') peace, the beginning of discontent among the 'lower classes' – all these are facts. The longer the war drags on and the more acute it becomes, the more the government themselves foster – and must foster – the activity of the masses, whom they call upon to make extraordinary effort and self-sacrifice. The experience of the war, like the experience of any crisis in history, of any great calamity and any sudden turn in human life, stuns and breaks some people, *but enlightens and tempers others* . . . Far from 'immediately' ending all these sufferings and all this enhancement of contradictions, the conclusion of peace will, in many respects, make those sufferings more keenly and immediately felt by the most backward masses of the population.

In a word, a revolutionary situation obtains in most of the advanced countries and the Great Powers of Europe.[49]

In this same article, Lenin outlined quite what he meant by a revolutionary situation. It exhibited, in his account, three main symptoms:

(1) When it is impossible for the ruling classes to maintain their rule without any change; ... For a revolution to take place, it is usually insufficient for the 'lower classes to not to want' to live in the old way; it is also necessary that 'the upper classes should be unable' to live in the old way.

(2) When the suffering and want of the oppressed class have grown more acute than usual.

(3) When, as a result of the above causes, there is a considerable increase in the activity of the masses, who ... in turbulent times, are drawn both by all the circumstances of the crisis, and by the *'upper classes' themselves* into independent historical action.... The totality of these objective changes is called a revolutionary situation.[50]

All the signs pointed, in Lenin's view, to an imminent revolutionary explosion. All the objective conditions for socialist revolution in Europe had already matured and the subjective transformation of mass consciousness was rapidly developing. The one crucial element that was lacking was a united international revolutionary movement. The one-time revolutionaries had deserted their posts and ran to the aid of their bourgeois states. The task now, as Lenin conceived it, was to forge a new revolutionary international, totally committed to the overthrow of the existing imperialist states. This objective necessarily entailed the further theoretical problem of outlining the form of social organisation by which they would be replaced. The basis of Lenin's answer to this problem emerged in the fuller analysis of imperialism which he now began to undertake.

CONCLUSION

Nowhere does the myth of Lenin the pragmatic, calculating power-seeker receive such comprehensive refutation as in his activities during the war and his appraisal of it. His was the stance of a radical intransigent for whom the basic theses of Marxism could not be discreetly shelved because they were out of accord with popular patriotic fervour. As ever, Lenin proclaimed the duty of a Marxist to be that of guiding and developing popular consciousness, not passively reflecting it. In 1914, Lenin refused outright to make the slightest concession to the near-universal patriotic infatuation of socialists and working people throughout Europe. In the early months of jingoist propaganda and heady nationalism, the preaching of pacificism, or reminding the workers of the socialist case against an imperialist war was a hazardous venture. But to argue the case for the defeat of one's own country, to urge that the international war be turned into a civil war in all belligerent countries, this seemed beyond treason. To many it seemed that Lenin had finally gone mad. Certainly if uniqueness be a mark of insanity, there were grounds for suspicion, for he stood almost alone in the extreme radicalness of his policies.

Lenin, in his reactions to the war and to other socialist groups and parties, remained true to the fundamentalist Marxism he had always espoused. If Marxism meant anything to him it meant the inescapable reality of permanent class war within capitalist society. Social democratic proponents of a civil peace for the duration of the war had become mere liberals. Indeed, they had become far more malign for they tried to disguise their class treachery as 'socialism', thereby confusing and deceiving the working class. If Marxism meant anything to Lenin it meant that the workers of any country had more in common with their fellows in other lands than with their own bourgeoisie. When social democrats voted war credits, participated in national governments and encouraged the workers of their own country to go forth to kill those of another, they not only forfeited any claim to call themselves socialist or Marxist, they had to be ruthlessly exposed, ruthlessly vilified and deprived of any influence over the working class. To these fundamentals, Lenin stood firm to the time of his death. His bitter rage against the socialist defencists was that of the fundamentalist who, sticking firm to the precepts of his doctrine, saw all around him his erstwhile brethren cracking when put to the test, yet hypocritically trumpeting their apostasy as orthodoxy.

Lenin's intransigence was staggering in its implications. He wrote off all the leading groups of all the major parties of the Socialist International as lost to the cause, as accomplices of the bourgeoisie. Nor was this a fleeting judgement. On the contrary, it formed the basis of his appraisal of class allegiances and political alliances to the time of his death. It is absolutely central to an understanding of his attitudes towards the Mensheviks and S.R.s (Socialist Revolutionaries) in 1917 and after. Since these parties had, during the war, revealed themselves as bourgeois there could be, in Lenin's view, no possibility of any meaningful collaboration with them.

It could, of course, be argued that Lenin was able to take this principled fundamentalist stand precisely because he was an exile, isolated from the sorts of pressures which most other European socialist leaders were constantly subjected to. There is, moreover, the obvious point that it was far easier for a Russian to dissociate himself completely from any obligation to defend his state than it was for most other Europeans. In Russia, after all, there was no democracy, no legally recognised political parties or trade unions. There the alienation between socialism and the labour movement on the one hand, and the state on the other, had always been more total than anywhere else. These reasons no doubt go some way to explaining why Lenin was able to be so uncompromising in his attitude towards the war and towards all those socialists who had reneged on their duties and earlier pledges. It may also partially explain the bitterness of the post-revolutionary theoretical controversies when those whom Lenin now decried as traitors seized their chance to condemn his 'opportunist manipulation' of Marxism.

Throughout this chapter we have noticed how central the specification of a new and final epoch in the development of capitalism was to Lenin's whole political analysis. The war itself was held to be a direct product of capitalism in its moribund imperialist phase; it could not therefore be defended by utilising Marx's arguments about progressive wars which related to the epoch of capitalism's first, heroic epoch. Imperialism, and the profits it bore, was the objective basis of opportunism and chauvinism, but if it had nurtured treachery of world-wide dimensions it had also inevitably produced crises and revolutionary opportunities on a global scale. 'The epoch of capitalist imperialism,' Lenin maintained, 'is one of ripe and rotten-ripe capitalism which is about to collapse, and which is mature enough to make way for Socialism.'[51] Imperialism, therefore, had through the world war it had produced, created the objective and the subjective conditions for the advance to socialism. It had also, as we will go on to explore in the next chapter, indicated to Lenin the essential outlines of the *content* of socialist reconstruction as well as the *forms* it would assume.

CHAPTER 3

The Theoretical Basis – the Economic and Social Analysis of Imperialism

The central theme of Volume 1 of this study was that Lenin's expressly political recommendations, his ideas on the practice of social democracy, could only be made intelligible by reconstructing the theoretical rationale which underlay them. That theoretical rationale was set out in considerable detail by Lenin in his economic and social analysis of Russian society. It was argued that Lenin's theory not only dictated the limits to social democratic practice by indicating the democratic revolution as the immediate goal of Russian Marxists, but also indicated the form which the democratic revolution might assume in Russia. In addition, the theoretical analysis provided Lenin with a methodology which he consistently applied to the ascending phases of class, consciousness and political organisation. It is the argument of this volume that Lenin's theory of imperialism occupies an exactly similar position in his later thought. We have seen in the previous chapter that in order to make sense of the war and to account for the collapse of the International and the treachery of its leaders, Lenin had employed the Marxist theory of imperialism. This had been first developed in 1910 by Rudolf Hilferding in his book *Finanz Kapital*. It had been further elaborated and given a Bolshevik stamp by Nikolai Bukharin in his *The World Economy of Imperialism* published (with a foreword by Lenin) in 1914. By the time Lenin published his own account in 1916, the general precepts of the Marxist theory of imperialism, as he himself frequently pointed out, had become commonplace tools of analysis. By late 1915, Lenin had already begun work on his own *Imperialism the Highest Stage of Capitalism*. With his usual thoroughness, he prepared his *Notebooks*, making notes and extracts from the available German, French, British and American literature, combing 148 books and 232 articles for material.[1] The text was written in the period January to June 1916.[2]

Lenin's fundamental premiss was that capitalism had changed in nature. From being competitive, thrusting and progressive, it had become monopolistic, passive and degenerate. At the same time, however, finance capital had carried the socialisation of the productive process to its ultimate extent and had created, in the banks, cartels and trusts, mechanisms through which social control of production and distribution could easily be achieved. The obverse of the degenerate, parasitic side of imperialism was that it had finally established the objective basis for an advance to socialism in all the industrially developed countries.

Any adequate definition of imperialism would have to embrace, according to Lenin's specification, the following five of its basic features:

(1) the concentration of production and capital has developed to such a high stage that it has created monopolies which play a decisive role in economic life; (2) the merging of bank capital with industrial capital and the creation, on the basis of this 'finance capital', of a financial oligarchy; (3) the export of capital as distinguished from the export of commodities acquires exceptional importance; (4) the formation of international monopolist capitalist associations which share the world among themselves, and (5) the territorial division of the whole world among the biggest capitalist powers is completed.[3]

The structure of Lenin's *Imperialism the Highest Stage of Capitalism* follows this general progression and we will stick to it in the exposition which follows (save for a minor adjustment, namely that points four and five will be considered together.)

1. THE CONCENTRATION OF PRODUCTION AND THE CREATION OF MONOPOLIES

It was an essential part of Marx's account of the development of capitalism that it contained an inherent tendency for capital to become concentrated in fewer and fewer hands. Faced with a falling rate of profit, it was always the largest enterprises with the biggest reserves, the highest organic composition of capital and the most efficient division of labour which were best equipped to ride out the deepening and recurrent crises capitalism produced. With each crisis, Marx noted, increasing numbers of small establishments were forced out of business and absorbed by the big concerns. One capitalist always killed off many and this, to an extent, was an essential and progressive phenomenon for in the war of each against all only the strongest, best organised and most efficient enterprises would survive. It also, by this very process, lengthened the odds against the future survival of bourgeois dominance for this was the process whereby the vast majority of the population were disinherited and precipitated into the ranks of the proletariat. The process of concentration of production and capital was, at the same time, the process of the class formation of the proletariat. As Marx put it in his ringing conclusion to Volume 1 of *Capital*:

Along with the constantly diminishing number of the magnates of capital, who usurp and monopolise all advantages of this process of transformation, grows the mass of misery, oppression, slavery, degradation, exploitation; but with this too grows the revolt of the working-class, a class always increasing in numbers, and disciplined, united, organised by the very mechanism of process of capitalist production itself.[4]

But, if the structure of capitalist free competition had its progressive tendencies, it equally displayed, in Marx's account, a tendency to destroy the very foundations of free competition which was central to its progressive role. The logical outcome of the process of concentration of production and of capital seemed to be the eventual dominance of a single giant enterprise over a whole sector of industry (or, what amounted to the same thing, the dominance of a small group of enterprises which could compact together to restrict or eliminate competitive pressures from within and outside the group). According to Lenin it was Marx's 'theoretical and historical analysis of capitalism' which itself demonstrated 'that free competition gives rise to the concentration of production which, in turn, at a certain stage of development, leads to monopoly'.[5]

Though it was intrinsic to his account, Marx himself never developed his views on the monopolistic tendencies of capitalist accumulation for, after all, he was writing his critique during the heyday of competition and *laisser-faire* capitalism. It was left to his disciples in the early part of the twentieth century to develop what has undoubtedly become the single most important elaboration of the theory of Marxism. This came to be known as the theory of finance capital or imperialism. The fundamental thesis of the new theory was that by the turn of the century the logical outcome of the process of concentration of production and of capital had substantially been achieved.

> ... the rise of monopolies, as the result of the concentration of production, is a general and fundamental law of the present stage of development of capitalism.
> For Europe, the time when the new capitalism *definitely* superseded the old can be established with fair precision; it was the beginning of the twentieth century.[6]

In many of the most highly developed sectors of industry, it was argued, monopoly had become an established fact. This process had, moreover, taken place not only within particular national economies but had led to the establishment of monopolies on an international scale. From this seemingly modest empirical observation the theorists of finance capital were led to very varying conclusions. In Lenin's case, as we shall see, the consequences were to be quite staggering in their implications.

Lenin began the substantive part of *Imperialism the Highest Stage of Capitalism* with a chapter on 'Concentration of Production and Monopolies'. He cited evidence from German statistics of 1907 to demonstrate that less than 1 per cent of the large-scale enterprises accounted for almost 40 per cent of the total industrial workforce and for more than 75 per cent of steam and electricity consumption, concluding that 'Tens of thousands of huge enterprises are everything; millions of small ones are nothing.'[7] His American sources told much the same tale. In 1909, just over 1 per cent of American enterprises employed 30 per cent of the industrial workforce and produced more than 48 per cent of the value of total industrial production. 'Almost half the total production of all the enterprises of the country was carried on by *one hundredth part* of those enterprises.'[8] Lenin's conclusion was that 'Individual enterprises are becoming larger and larger. An ever-increasing number of enterprises in one, or in several, industries join together in giant enterprises. . . .'[9]

Lenin's evidence for the enormously rapid concentration of production and the disproportionate significance of the few largest enterprises in terms of their contribution to the gross national product could not of themselves directly support the contention that modern capitalism had become positively monopolistic. What he had to establish was the mechanisms and devices through which these very large enterprises compacted together to eliminate competition.

The chosen mechanism which they established to achieve this end was, according to Lenin, the cartel. The rise of the cartel was, he argued, coincident with the rise of finance capitalism and necessarily so, since this was the principal means of establishing monopolies in the sphere of production. According to Lenin:

> Cartels come to an agreement on the terms of sale, dates of payment etc. They divide the markets among themselves. They fix the quantity of goods to be produced. They fix prices. They divide the profits among the various enterprises, etc.[10]

The very large enterprises were, as we have seen, to some extent protected from competition by their very size and the sophistication of their productive techniques. The volume of capital necessary to commence production at a comparable level of scale, integration and technological sophistication grew from year to year, making it enormously difficult for newcomers to break in. Apart from these natural defences, the cartels raised their own artificial fortifications to protect their members' monopolistic position. They evolved a whole range of punitive devices to ward off competition:

> It is instructive to glance at least at the list of the methods the monopolist associations resort to in the present day, the latest, the civilised struggle for 'organisation': (1) stopping supplies of raw materials . . . ; (2) stopping the supply of labour by means of 'alliances' . . . ; (3) stopping deliveries; (4) closing trade outlets; (5) agreements with the buyers, by which the latter

undertake to trade only with the cartels; (6) systematic price cutting (to ruin 'outside' firms, i.e., those which refuse to submit to the monopolists . . .); (7) stopping credits; (8) boycott.

Here we no longer have competition between small and large, between technically developed and backward enterprises. We see here the monopolists throttling those who do not submit to them, to their yoke, to their dictation.[11]

Added to this formidable list, there was another device which the big firms and cartels resorted to on a large scale. This was the tactic of pre-empting competition, and the possible need for expensive retooling to meet the improved technique of potential competitors, by wholesale buying up of the patents which might affect their sphere of production. Thus the United States Tobacco Trust in 1906 established two subsidiary companies 'solely to acquire patents'.[12] There was evidence enough, Lenin asserted, to justify the contention that under monopoly conditions the imperative constantly to revolutionise the forces of production, which had constituted the central progressive role of capitalism, had ceased to operate: 'the tendency to stagnation and decay, which is characteristic of monopoly, continues to operate, and in some branches of industry, in some countries, for certain periods of time, it gains the upper hand.'[13] The extinction of free competition signified the end of the essential progressive role of capitalism in history. Its role in augmenting and constantly refining the productive forces had, under monopoly capitalism, ceased to apply. Worse still were the evident facts, as Lenin saw them, of the positively retrogressive character of finance capital:

. . . like all monopoly, it inevitably engenders a tendency to stagnation and decay. Since monopoly prices are established, even temporarily, the motive cause of technical and, consequently, of all other progress disappears to a certain extent and, further, the *economic* possibility arises of deliberately retarding technical progress.[14]

There were, finally, two other more direct means of discouraging competition, bribery and bombs. 'Monopoly hews a path for

46

itself everywhere without scruple as to the means, from paying a "modest" sum to buy off competitors, to the American device of employing dynamite against them.'[15]

The cumulative effects of these various devices to deter competition were predictable enough. The giant trusts and cartels came to dominate whole branches of industry and, 'The monopoly so created assures enormous profits and leads to the formation of technical production units of formidable magnitude.'[16] It was, in part, the punitive devices employed by the monopolists which guaranteed them profits far above the norm. In part it was the natural superiority flowing from economies of size, ability to finance extensive research and development, and the rational restructuring of the work process in a whole sector of industry in which the consecutive stages in the processing of raw materials and the production of a range of finished goods from these raw materials were brought under unified management and concentrated in one place. In this way, as Hilferding had noticed, the 'combination' of enterprises 'has the effect of rendering possible technical improvements, and, consequently, the acquisition of super profits over and above those obtained by the "pure" [i.e. non-combined] enterprises'.[17]

It was precisely the concentration of production which constituted, in Lenin's view, the single most important progressive attribute of monopoly or finance capital as compared with the earlier phase of large-scale industrial capitalism. Huge numbers of workers had now been aggregated into gigantic plants. The smaller workshops which kept the workers isolated and inhibited the development of their consciousness were being extinguished with increasing rapidity. Monopoly capitalism was progressive in that it had developed a highly integrated, efficient and well-planned productive process in many branches of industry. Above all, the process of monopolisation of production had, to quite a large extent, eliminated the endemic anarchy of production by discovering mechanisms whereby the market demand for particular commodities, and the production of them, could be harmonised. It was in this way, Lenin argued, that production, in the era of imperialism, had become 'socialised'. It was, he maintained, a kind of hybrid form of eminently social production taking place within the framework of private property and individual appropriation. It was almost a half-way house to socialism itself – certainly the material preconditions for the full socialisation of industry had matured.

> When a big enterprise assumes gigantic proportions, and, on the basis of an exact computation of mass data, organises according to plan the supply of primary raw materials to the extent of two-thirds, or three-fourths, of all that is necessary for tens of millions of people; when the raw materials are transported in a systematic way and organised manner to the most suitable place of production, sometimes situated hundreds of thousands of miles from each other; when a single centre directs all the consecutive stages of processing the material right up to the manufacture of numerous varieties of finished articles; when these products are distributed according to a single plan among tens and hundreds of millions of consumers ... then it becomes evident that we have socialisation of production and not mere 'interlocking'; that private economic and private property relations constitute a shell which no longer fits its contents, a shell which must inevitably decay if its removal is artificially delayed, a shell which may remain in a state of decay for a fairly long period (if, at worst, the cure of the opportunist abscess is protracted), but which will inevitably be removed.[18]

Lenin was here following very closely the earlier analysis of Hilferding, which had concluded that, 'In carrying out the function of socialising production, finance capital enormously simplifies the overthrow of capital'.[19] There can be no doubt whatsoever that he believed that monopoly capitalism had now created the objective conditions, the economic basis, for an immediate advance to socialism on a world-wide scale. Elsewhere in *Imperialism the Highest Stage of Capitalism*, he expressed it in this way:

> Capitalism in its imperialist stage leads directly to the most comprehensive socialisation of production; it, so to speak, drags the capitalists, against their will and consciousness, into some sort of a new social order, a transitional one from complete free competition to complete socialisation.[20]

Later, in May 1917, exactly the same sentiment recurred: 'Imperialism is a continuation of the development of capitalism, its highest stage – in a sense, a transition stage to socialism.'[21] The Mensheviks, the Kautskyites, the Centrists and opportunists in general, all the host of permanent postponers of the socialist revolution, shut their eyes to the evident facts and continued their endless vigil for the objective conditions to mature. Still, in September 1917 they were waiting:

> They picture socialism as some remote, unknown and dim future.
> But socialism is now gazing at us from all the windows of modern capitalism; socialism is outlined directly, *practically*, by every important measure that constitutes a forward step on the basis of this modern capitalism.[22]

We have seen that, in Lenin's view, one aspect of the phenomenal growth of the concentration of production and of monopolies was progressive; indeed, in this respect it was establishing the objective preconditions for an immediate advance to socialism. This did not mean, however, that the advent of a more efficient, rationalised, unified and planned organisation of production in some spheres of industry thereby contributed to the stability of imperialism (a conclusion which Bukharin came perilously close to accepting). On the contrary, it was an essential part of Lenin's case aganist imperialism that these very developments enormously accentuated a basic and irremediable flaw in the structure of capitalism generally, namely the acute imbalances between differing sectors of industry (and, in the imperialist stage, the vast differences in levels of economic developments between differing countries) which it necessarily produced. 'The uneven and spasmodic development of individual enterprises, individual branches of industry and individual countries is inevitable under Capitalism.'[23] The concentration of production might, to a large extent, do away with the anarchy of production in certain advanced sectors of industry but only at the cost of highlighting the backwardness of others which, ultimately, would severely retard the growth of the most advanced sectors. The anarchy of production within the national economic structure was not, therefore, overcome: on the contrary, it became more and more acute. (Still more was this the case internationally, as we shall see.)

> The statement that cartels can abolish crises is a fable spread by bourgeois economists who at all costs desire to place capitalism in a favourable light. On the contrary, the monopoly created in *certain* branches of industry increases and intensifies the anarchy inherent in capitalist production *as a whole*. The disparity between the development of agriculture and of industry, which is characteristic of capitalism in general, is increased. The privileged position of the most highly cartelised, so-called *heavy* industry, especially coal and iron, causes 'a still greater lack of co-ordination' in other branches of industry . . .[24]

The new barons of the cartels in the heavy industries, insulated as they were from competition, naturally charged inflated monopoly prices for their products which, in one form or another, almost all the enterprises in all other sectors of industry were obliged to purchase. In this way, 'the "heavy industries" exacted tribute from all other branches of industry'[25] and inhibited their growth.

2. THE MERGER OF BANK CAPITAL WITH INDUSTRIAL CAPITAL

The process of the concentration of industry was exactly matched, according to Lenin's account, by the simultaneous concentration of the capital resources of the imperialist states in the hands of a tiny number of huge banks. The whole role and nature of the banking system had, in Lenin's view, radically altered since 1900.[26] Prior to that time, the banks had acted as mere intermediaries in the financial transactions between individuals and industrial concerns. After that time they had increasingly involved themselves in the direct financing, management and amalgamation of huge industrial concerns. They had finally usurped the role of the Stock Exchange as the principal means of raising finance for industry[27] and had effectively brought the whole economic life of the advanced industrial countries under their exclusive control.

As banking develops and becomes concentrated in a small

number of establishments, the banks grow from modest middlemen into powerful monopolies having at their command almost the whole of the money capital of all the capitalists and small businessmen and also a large part of the means of production and sources of raw materials in any one country and in a number of countries. This transformation of numerous modest middlemen into a handful of monopolists is one of the fundamental processes in the growth of capitalism into capitalist imperialism. . . .[28]

It was through the agency of the banks that the enormous concentration of industry had been accomplished, and nowhere was this dramatic concentration of resources more evident than in the rise of the big banks themselves. Through simple absorption or annexation via holdings, the big banks in Germany, France, America and Britain had, in the period from 1890 to 1910, rapidly concentrated the financial resources of their countries into their own hands. Reviewing the evidence for this, Lenin observed:

We see the rapid expansion of a close network of channels which cover the whole country, centralising all capital and all revenues, transforming thousands and thousands of scattered economic enterprises into a single national capitalist, and then into a world capitalist economy.[29]

In this way, he argued, 'Scattered capitalists are transformed into a single collective capital'[30] and this process was assisted rather than hampered by the advent of the joint-stock companies and the one-pound share. These innovations, far from democratising the financial structure, gave further power to the arm of the financial barons. Through the system of holdings in subsidiary companies they were able to spread the dominion of their capital much further.

In this way, it is possible with a comparatively small capital to dominate immense spheres of production. Indeed, if holding 50 per cent of the capital is always sufficient to control a company, the head of the concern needs only one million to control eight million in the second subsidiaries.[31]

The banks, of course, played a preponderant role in this constant manoeuvring of finance capital to achieve its sway. They had increasingly taken over the very lucrative business of issuing bonds;[32] in times of depression they bought out the smaller and less efficient enterprises 'for a mere song or to participate in profitable schemes for their "reconstruction" and "reorganisation" ',[33] and, no matter how unsuccessful some of their investments might prove to be, they were unlikely to be unduly affected for they would be the first to know when an enterprise was in difficulties and, through adroit transfer of assets from one subsidiary to another, could minimise their losses and offload them on to the smaller investors.

The banks naturally sought the maximum return on the vast volumes of capital they now disposed of and, equally naturally, they used their huge powers to establish, in those industries in which they were investing their capital, the same monopolistic protection they had achieved in their own sphere. By the same techniques of absorption and annexation, they established their hold on whole sectors of industry. Their power to supply or deny credits and finance were, of course, crucially important in establishing their dominance over even the largest of concerns:

> ... for they are enabled – by means of their banking connections, their current accounts and other financial operations – first, to *ascertain exactly* the financial position of the various capitalists, then to *control* them, to influence them by restricting or enlarging, facilitating or hindering credits, and finally to *entirely determine* their fate, determine their income, deprive them of capital, or permit them to increase their capital rapidly and to enormous dimensions, etc.[34]

The intimate connection between banking and industrial capital was, according to Lenin, made abundantly clear in the interchange of top personnel between the two spheres. Bank directors typically sat on the boards of large industrial enterprises and the big industrialists joined the boards of the big banks.[35] It was reflected too in the structural organisation and division of labour within the banks themselves. Specialised departments, headed by a bank director, were quickly developed to assume 'the supervision of several separate enterprises in the same branch of industry or having similar interests . . . (Capitalism has already reached the stage of organised supervision of individual enterprises.)'[36]

Lenin's final parenthetical comment was later to assume a very considerable importance in his conception of the mechanisms through which a properly socialist administration of the economy could be established. The later argument is indeed already explicit in *Imperialism the Highest Stage of Capitalism*. Lenin had derived it from Rudolf Hilferding's study *Finance Capital*.[37]

Hilferding had been the first to establish a convincing Marxist account of the new phase of capitalist development which he termed finance capital. The characteristics which he ascribed to it – massive concentration of production and of capital, the growth of monopolies, trusts and cartels, the merger of banking or finance capital with industrial capital, the extinction of competition, the merger of industrial and finance capital – the imperative to export capital and establish colonies and the growth of militarism – were all taken up in Lenin's theory of imperialism. It is not too extravagant to maintain that Hilferding's analysis, together with Bukharin's refinements to it, constituted the economic bedrock of Lenin's own theory of imperialism. The connection between the views of Hilferding and Lenin is particularly strong though ignored by those who grossly exaggerate the impact of John Hobson's book on *Imperialism* on Lenin.

According to Hilferding, finance capital, through its chosen instrument, the banks, had transformed the latter 'into institutions of a truly universal character',[38] overseeing and controlling the whole economic life of society. The imperialist epoch had therefore realised (albeit in a perverted form) Marx's prediction in Volume 3 of *Capital* that the banking system 'possesses, indeed the form of universal book-keeping and distribution of means of production on a social scale, but solely the form'.[39] Within the context of capitalism, of course, this universal social potential could never be realised for the banking system had to subserve

the interests of big capital, and primarily, of huge, monopoly capital, which operates under conditions in which the masses live in want, in which the whole development of agriculture hopelessly lags behind the development of industry . . .[40]

The great promise and potential of the system could not therefore be developed within the framework of capitalism, for within that framework 'the "conscious regulation" of economic life by the banks consists in the fleecing of the public by a handful of "completely organised" monopolists'.[41]

It is nonetheless perfectly clear that Lenin believed that just as the concentration of industry in general provided the objective basis for an immediate transition to socialism, so the banking system through which that concentration had largely been accomplished had already created a ready-made instrument for the 'universal book-keeping and distribution of means of production on a social scale' which Marx had envisaged.

3. EXPORT OF CAPITAL

Lenin's analysis of the reasons for the export of capital is surprisingly brief and ill-developed. Indeed, the actual motive for the dramatic upsurge in capital export at the end of the nineteenth and beginning of the twentieth centuries is nowhere given in *Imperialism the Highest Stage of Capitalism*. In this respect, even bourgeois theorists like Hobson and Brailsford had been more 'Marxist' in pointing to the inherent tendency for the rate of profit to decline as capitalism became more developed as the principal causal factor explaining the flight of capital from the metropolitan countries.

Lenin's explanation for the huge increase in the export of capital is closely bound up with his account of the uneven development of capitalism, especially in its imperialist phase. His argument here is, once again, not very well developed. He seems to be arguing that certain advanced sectors of industry, through concentration of production, technical innovation and their virtual monopolistic position, amass huge volumes of surplus capital which can find no sufficiently profitable employment in the metropolitan countries.

The need to export capital arises from the fact that in a few countries capitalism has become 'overripe' and (owing to the backward state of agriculture and the poverty of the masses) capital cannot find a field for 'profitable' investment.[42]

They cannot dispense these profits in the form of increased wages, which would generate increased demand and thus more extensive production and increased profit, for to do this would run directly counter to Marx's whole account of the *raison d'être* of the capitalist system and affront the foundation premisses of the labour theory of value. Lenin's analysis rested upon certain unspoken assumptions or axioms derived from Marx, and a brief (and necessarily simplified) digression into Marxian economics will be necessary to make it intelligible.

According to Marx's definition, commodities were objects with use value offered for sale on the market. In the market-place, however, some measure had to be adopted whereby the value of differing commodities could be measured one against the other. The only universal standard for measuring the value of commodities was, Marx believed, the one element they all shared in common – the labour time they all embodied. Marx's eleboration of the labour theory of value up to this point was, of course, far from unique to him. It had formed the foundation of classical political economy. Marx's fundamental originality consisted in taking this respectable notion one very large step forward. He argued that, at a certain stage of commodity production, labour power itself became a commodity; that is, men were increasingly obliged to hire themselves out as labourers in return for a wage. They were forced to offer their labour power for sale on the market. Labour power, having become a commodity was, according to Marx, governed by the same measure of value as all other commodities. Its value was determined by the cost, in terms of labour time, required in its production. The cost of production of a labourer was therefore that minimum of food, shelter and clothing required to keep him in a position to be able to work, with an additional modicum to allow him to reproduce his kind and thus assure the future supply of labour power. In return for his labour power, therefore, the labourer could expect no more than that bare minimum of subsistence requisite to keep him in his condition as a labouring being. Nor could the capitalist pay him more, for to do so would undermine his competitiveness *vis-à-vis* other employers and undermine his own *raison d'être* which was the maximisation of his profit.

It was on the basis of these impeccably Marxian theses that Lenin emphatically rejected the 'solutions' of liberals and radicals like Hobson and Brailsford. They had argued that the surplus capital generated in the advanced sectors of industry could easily be absorbed by directing it into agriculture and by raising wages and purchasing power. In this way, by raising the general level of well-being, the purchasing power of the market would be greatly extended and the crises of over-production of commodities and of capital would be overcome. There would in that case be no need for the enormous export of capital which brought no benefits to the mass of the people either of the exporting countries or of those countries which received it. By an internal redistribution of income, Hobson argued, 'the economic taproot of imperialism', the inability of the home market to assimilate the products of capitalist industry, would at one stroke be severed.

> It is not industrial progress that demands the opening up of new markets and new areas of investment, but mal-distribution of consuming power which prevents the absorption of commodities and capital within the country.[43]

Lenin's response was that such solutions were at best wishful thinking, at worst self-deception. So long as capitalism survived, they could not be applied:

> It goes without saying that if capitalism could develop agriculture, which today is everywhere lagging terribly behind industry, if it could raise the living standards of the masses, who in spite of the amazing technical progress are everywhere still half-starved and poverty-stricken, there could be no question of a surplus of capital. This 'argument' is very often advanced by the petty-bourgeois critics of capitalism. But if capitalism did these things it would not be capitalism; for both uneven development and a semi-starvation level of existence of the masses are fundamental and inevitable conditions and constitute the premises of this mode of existence. As long as capitalism remains what it is, surplus capital will be utilised not for the purpose of raising the standard of living of the masses in a given country, for this would mean a decline in profits for the capitalists, but for the purpose of increasing profits by exporting capital abroad to the backward countries. In these backward countries profits are usually high, for capital is scarce, the

price of land is relatively low, wages are low, raw materials are cheap.[44]

The distinguishing feature of imperialism was, therefore, that the trade in goods typical of the old capitalism had been replaced by the export of capital. Internationally as well as internally, the financier and usurer had taken the place of the entrepreneur. The separation of money or finance capital from industrial or productive capital was now made manifest on a world scale. Just as the rentier, the man who took no active part whatsoever in the production or distribution of goods but lived entirely off the dividends from his investments, had displaced the entrepreneur internally, so now in the final phase of international finance capitalism there had arisen a tiny number of rentier states living predominantly from the tribute levied on the states who had become financially dependent upon them.[45]

Hence the extraordinary growth of a class, or, rather, of a stratum of rentiers, i.e., people who live by 'clipping coupons', who take no part in any enterprise whatever, whose profession is idleness. The export of capital, one of the most essential economic bases of imperialism, still more completely isolates the rentiers from production and sets the seal of parasitism on the whole country that lives by exploiting the labour of several overseas countries and colonies.[46]

Citing Hobson's evidence and conclusions to substantiate his case, Lenin pointed to the example of Britain which, even in 1899, had seen its income from capital invested abroad exceed by five times its income from foreign trade – it had become a rentier state.[47]

The rentier state is a state of parasitic, decaying capitalism, and this circumstance cannot fail to influence all the socio-political conditions of the countries concerned, in general, and the two fundamental trends in the working-class movement, in particular.[48]

The enervating effects of imperialist super-profits were not confined to the idle rentiers living in ostentatious luxury surrounded by their retinues of servile menials in the south-east of

57

England, the grouse moors of Scotland and in their villas on the French Riviera, they weighed too upon the working class of the rentier states, for a section of them also shared in the easy bounty. 'Imperialism,' Lenin found, 'has the tendency to create privileged sections also among the workers, and to detach them from the broad mass of the proletariat.'[49] It was able to do this, of course, precisely because of the abnormally high profits it reaped and this 'makes it economically possible to bribe the upper strata of the proletariat, and thereby fosters, gives shape to, and strengthens opportunism'.[50] To Lenin, it appeared that the prophetic diagnosis of the roots of British working-class opportunism, which Engels had arrived at in 1858, 'that the English proletariat is actually becoming more and more bourgeois, so that this most bourgeois of all nations is apparently aiming ultimately at the possession of a bourgeois aristocracy and a bourgeois proletariat *alongside* the bourgeoisie',[51] had finally been vindicated and brought into high relief in the epoch of imperialism – and not only in Britain.

Lenin's analysis of the effects of the wholesale export of capital on the imperialist states had extremely important repercussions for the structure of his political thought, in particular for the strategy for world revolution which he was beginning to elaborate. In the first place, it had become clear that capitalism had definitely become parasitic and usurious, the vast legions of rentiers had no role to play in the productive process: on the contrary, they had become mere leeches sucking away its life-blood. Monopoly capitalism, moreover, did not, like the earlier epochs of capitalist development, carry within it the imperative for technological innovation. On the contrary, it tended to stagnation and decay. By these tokens imperialism, and the class of rentiers it spawned, had no progressive role to play in history; they had become degenerate and threatened to infect even the healthy and virile elements of society. The imperative to place socialist revolution on the immediate agenda was, therefore, in Lenin's view inescapable.

The analysis also provided Lenin with a coherent account of the economic roots of working-class opportunism and jingoism in the imperialist countries. Lenin was to conclude from this that it would be unrealistic to expect the world revolution for socialism to *begin* in the metropolitan heartland. The system would break down at its weakest link and this was most likely to occur in those exploited countries where the working class and its leadership had not been bought off by the imperialists.

4. AND 5. THE DIVISION OF THE WORLD BY MONOPOLIST TRUSTS AND THE IMPERIALIST POWERS

There was, according to Lenin, a fundamental contradiction locked within world imperialism fraught with the most awful and bloody prospects for the future of mankind. This was the contradiction between the tendency of finance capital cartels and modern means of communication to internationalise the world economic structure on the one hand, and the equally (perhaps more) pronounced tendency for powerful imperialist nations to fight all others for predominance in the world market and the territorial division of the globe.

> The epoch of the latest stage of Capitalism shows us that certain relations between capitalist associations grow up, *based* on the economic division of the world; while parallel to, and in connection with it, certain relations grow up between political alliances, between states, on the basis of the territorial division of the world, of the struggle for colonies, of the 'struggle for spheres of influence'.[52]

The one tendency portended, at least theoretically, the emergence of a single, universal, all-powerful imperialist trust. The other proclaimed the prospect of a world empire established by the armed might of the most powerful imperialist country. Neither of these theoretical prospects could, in Lenin's view, be realised for, in the one case, the growing disparity between the obviously social and international structure of production and the private and nationally exclusive structure of appropriation, as well as the high monopoly prices which the trusts charged for their products which inevitably depressed living standards, would inevitably cause the class struggle to boil over into social revolution. In the other case, the prospect of interminable wars and bloodshed on a massive scale would finally convince even the proletariat of the exploiting countries that the rewards from colonial exploitation were as nothing compared to the costs involved. Both tendencies, in their differing ways, led therefore to the maturation of the objective and subjective conditions for social revolution on an international scale which would consume imperialism long before it arrived at its theoretical terminus.[53]

The role of the international trusts and cartels in monopolising the world market is no more than touched on in *Imperialism the Highest Stage of Capitalism*. Lenin mentions the cases of the two great electrical companies, the two oil trusts and the International Rail Cartel to demonstrate his case that international trusts existed and exerted a dominating control over sections of the world market. He also used them to illustrate his other major point, that whatever agreements the international trusts and cartels arrived at were always conditional and subject to sudden alteration or collapse dependent upon the relative strength of the parties to the agreement.[54] International trusts and cartels were, therefore, by their nature, fluid and unstable organisations and this made a nonsense of Kautsky's pious hopes for international peace being constructed on this basis.[55] Equally utopian and spurious, in Lenin's opinion, were Kautsky's claims that it was at least possible to envisage an international compact amongst imperialist states which would eliminate costly armed rivalries and peacefully settle the problem of the division of the world and allocation of markets. This theory of ultra-imperialism or super-imperialism was, in Lenin's view, yet another opiate or soporific, the intention of which was to lull the masses into the comfortable belief that lasting peace under capitalism was still possible.[56] 'Instead of showing the living connections between periods of imperialist peace and periods of imperialist war, Kautsky presents the workers with a lifeless abstraction in order to reconcile them to their lifeless leaders.'[57]

The central reason which Lenin advanced to support his contention that international peace in the era of imperialism was unattainable derived once again from his analysis of the uneven pace of capitalist development on the global level. Those countries which had been the first to experience the massive concentration of capital of the final phase of capitalist development were, therefore, also the first to seek secure markets for the export of goods and especially for the export of capital. The monopolies within the first capital-exporting countries quickly realised, however, that the only effective guarantee of the security of their investments lay in actual annexation of the creditor countries by their own state. It was therefore far from accidental, in Lenin's view, that the great age of colonial expansion of the West European states again coincided with the period of the consolidation of finance capital and monopolies within each of them. In the years from 1884–1900, according to Hobson's estimates which Lenin cites:

Great Britain . . . acquired 3,700,000 square miles of territory with 57,000,000 inhabitants; France, 3,600,000 square miles with 36,500,000; Germany, 1,000,000 square miles with 14,700,000; Belgium, 900,000 square miles with 30,000,000; Portugal 800,000 square miles with 9,000,000 inhabitants.[58]

It was precisely in the period immediately after the extinction of the competitive phase of capitalism, in the period of the growth of finance capital and monopoly, that the great colonial boom had occurred: 'It is beyond doubt, therefore, that capitalism's transition to the stage of monopoly capitalism, to finance capital, is *connected* with the intensification of the struggle for the partitioning of the world.'[59] By the turn of the century, according to Lenin, this territorial division of the world had been virtually completed.[60] There remained no substantial economic territory available; all the countries of the world had been reduced to the status of colonies or (as was the case with Persia, China and Turkey)[61] semi-colonies.

In this great scramble for colonies and protected markets it was, naturally enough, the countries that, in the 1880s and 1890s were most powerful economically and militarily that had seized the lion's share. Indeed, the share which each country obtained was broadly commensurate with its strength *during this particular period*. The insoluble problem which then arose for international finance capital and international relations generally was that, by the end of that period, and emphatically by the end of the first decade of the twentieth century, the territorial division of the world that had been so finally accomplished no longer bore any relation to the changed balance of economic power in the world. Germany, the United States and Japan had been much later than Britain, France and Belgium to embark on capitalist industrialisation. The imperative to seek markets for the export of capital also

61

therefore occurred later. By the time their rapidly developing economies (which, in terms of productivity, concentration of labour and of capital, generally exceeded their rivals) began to seek secure markets they discovered that the time was already too late. The early starters had virtually absorbed the available economic territory of the whole world. There thus arose a world situation in which 'the relative strength of the empires founded in the nineteenth century is totally out of proportion to the place occupied in Europe by the nations which founded them'.[62] Nowhere, in Lenin's view, was the uneven pace of capitalist development made more manifest and nowhere was it fraught with so many dangers for the future of mankind.

> Finance capital and the trusts do not diminish but increase the difference in the rate of growth of the various parts of the world economy. Once the relation of forces is changed, what other solution of the contradictions can be found *under Capitalism* than that of *force*?[63]

Any new redivision of the world, to bring colonial possessions into line with actual economic strength and broadly commensurate with the demands of each economy for markets for the export of capital, could only be achieved through main force.

> The question is: what means other than war could there be under Capitalism to overcome the disparity between the development of productive forces and the accumulation of capital on the one side, and the division of colonies and spheres of influence for finance capital on the other?[64]

Lenin shared with Hobson, Hilferding and Bukharin the view that in the epoch of imperialism, capitalism had undergone a profound and fundamental change of ethos. Once it had appeared as the standard-bearer not only of freedom for the individual from the yoke of feudal bondage and patriarchal narrowness, but also of the right of each country to self-determination. Now it had become reactionary in both spheres. Its dominant characteristics had now become internal oppression and external aggression.[65] The world had been divided into oppressor and oppressed states.[66] A tiny handful of creditor countries, having established their suzerainty by force of superior arms over the colonised world, lived by parasitically drawing tribute from it. To the extent that the super-profits obtained from colonial investment did temporarily shore up the rate of profit and did allow the metropolitan countries to buy off sections of their own working class, the division of the world among the imperialist powers tended to soften some of the contradictions of world finance capital. This was, however, achieved at the cost of universalising the general contradictions of capitalism and, in particular, of stimulating the movement for national liberation. The subjugated colonies of the world would not, Lenin argued, long endure the ignominy of foreign control and merciless exploitation. Following Hilferding's analysis, Lenin argued that finance capital was itself reproducing on a world scale the very conditions which promoted the emergence of conscious and organised classes which could not fail to demand national independence. The intrusion of finance capital into pre-capitalist societies inevitably disrupted the ancestral immobility, the small-scale and isolated productive units, the web of local, tribal and status subdivisions which had made them 'nations without history'.

> ' . . . they are drawn into the capitalist whirlpool. Capitalism itself gradually provides the subjugated with the means and resources for their emancipation and they set out to achieve the goal which once seemed highest to the European nations: the creation of a united national state as a means to economic and cultural freedom. This movement for national independence threatens European capital in its most valuable and most promising fields of exploitation, and European capital can maintain its dominance only by continually increasing its military forces'.[67]

Directly out of his economic analysis, Lenin here arrived at an idea which was to assume cardinal importance in his overall revolutionary strategy. The movement for national liberation in the colonies threatened the whole basis of imperialist super-profits. It therefore threatened the continued existence of capitalism itself. Even if it did not immediately succeed, the movement would oblige the imperialists to increase their military expenditure. In either case, the living standards of the metropolitan workers would suffer. The spiralling crises induced by the falling rate of profit would lead to a revolutionising of the temper of the Western workers and the creation of the subjective conditions for socialism.

The intimate connection between socialist revolution in the advanced countries and the democratic movement for national liberation in the colonies became the pivot of Lenin's world revolutionary strategy. Both movements, he argued, complemented each other. Both would serve to undermine the world economic hegemony of the imperialist states and both must therefore be actively promoted by socialists. This strategy was not, as many commentators have argued, yet another instance of Lenin's opportunistic appropriation of any movement of discontent which he adroitly annexed to his cause. On the contrary, it expressly derived from his analysis of the uneven pace of capitalist development.

Lenin's argument was a continuation of the one he had earlier engaged in with Rosa Luxemburg. Luxemburg's line on the irrelevance of the movement for national liberation in the epoch of international finance capital[68] had been taken up and extended by Bukharin. Bukharin's book *Imperialism and World Economy* had argued the case that modern finance capital had so enmeshed the world in an integrated web of financial relations that it had become impossible to talk any longer of the autonomy of national economies. The whole world, Bukharin argued, had now become a single integrated economic organism. Given this fact, and given that socialism alone could solve the contradictions which finance capital had reproduced on a global scale, only the world socialist revolution, international in scope and universal in its relevance, could be considered in any way progressive. Bukharin, Pyatakov and the so-called Baugy Group had, by 1916, emerged as prominent and influential spokesmen of these views within the Bolshevik Party. Their arguments were all the more seductive to young radicals in the time of international war who felt that any concessions to the national principle would merely sow the seeds of future conflicts.

It was primarily against Bukharin, whose views on imperialism generally came so close to his own, and whose deviations were therefore all the more dangerous, that Lenin developed his own ideas on the necessity of integrating the socialist and national liberation movements. The crux of Bukharin's errors which 'have *nothing in common either with Marxism or revolutionary Social-Democracy*'[69] was, Lenin argued, the simplistic reductionism which failed to distinguish between a tendency and an accomplished fact. That there was a tendency for imperialism to eliminate national distinctions and draw all the countries of the world into common economic relations Lenin did not doubt – his own theoretical analysis emphatically confirmed this process. The strength, sophistication and flexibility of Lenin's analysis *vis-à-vis* that of Luxemburg and Bukharin was that he employed this as a concrete rather than an abstract principle. In other words, Lenin recognised that this general tendency was in practice very unevenly developed. The processes which imperialism or finance capital signified – the immense socialisation of labour and concentration of capital, the wholesale export of capital, the capture of the home and then the international market by monopolies– these were already overdeveloped in some parts of the world, unconsummated in others and barely emerging elsewhere. Levels of economic development remained very variegated. It was indeed a premiss of the Marxist analysis of imperialism that this had to be the case otherwise there could be no explanation for the flight of capital from regions with a high organic content of capital, and therefore a low return in surplus value or profit, to areas where the organic content of capital was low and the profits high.

Given that the contemporary world was comprised of countries at very differing phases of economic development, given further the thesis which Lenin had earlier maintained against Rosa Luxemburg that capitalism (and alongside it the proletarian movement) had first to become consolidated and organised on the national plane, it followed that where this had not yet occurred the national movement retained its progressive significance. Consequently:

... not less than *three* different types of countries must be distinguished when dealing with self-determination. ... First type: the advanced countries of Western Europe (and America), where the national movement is a thing of the *past*. Second type: Eastern Europe, where it is a thing of the *present*.

Third type: semi-colonies and colonies, where it is largely a thing of the *future*.[70]

Wherever capitalism had not consolidated itself internally, had not established a national market, had not finally destroyed feudal privileges and the medieval partitions of a country, there it continued to have progressive significance. 'There the "defence of the fatherland" can *still* be defence of democracy, of one's native language, of political liberty against oppressor nations, against mediaevalism.'[71] '*Objectively*, these nations still have general national tasks to accomplish, namely, democratic tasks, the tasks of *overthrowing foreign oppression*.'[72] The movement for national self-determination and democracy was, Lenin seemed to be arguing, all the more progressive when compared with the degenerate form of capitalism – imperialism. At least it was not parasitic, it had life and vigour, it had not become despotic and reactionary but stood for democracy, and the freedom and autonomy of the individual and the nation state.

There was therefore, in Lenin's view, a clear bond of unity between the objectives of the socialist and the national liberation movements. Both were concerned to smash the economic and political despotism which the imperialist states exercised over the world. Both movements would go at least part of the way together in a fighting alliance; indeed, the cementing of such an alliance was the *sine qua non* for the success of both movements.

The social revolution can come only in the form of an epoch in which are combined civil war by the proletariat against the bourgeoisie in the advanced countries and a *whole series* of democratic and revolutionary movements, including the national liberation movement, in the undeveloped, backward and oppressed nations.

Why? Because capitalism develops unevenly, and objective reality gives us highly developed capitalist nations side by side with a number of economically slightly developed, or totally undeveloped countries.[73]

It was precisely Bukharin's error that in the abstract reductionism of his theoretical schema 'he cannot solve the problem of *how to link the advent of imperialism with the struggle for reforms and democracy. . . .'[74]*

One of the important political consequences of Lenin's application of the law of uneven development was that it dismissed as utopian and unrealistic the expectation that socialist revolution would arrive simultaneously on a world-wide scale.[75] It would occur first in those advanced countries where the objective and subjective conditions had fully matured and where the national democratic revolution had long been accomplished. 'Hence only in these countries is it possible *now* to "blow up" national unity and establish class unity.'[76]

> The development of capitalism proceeds extremely unevenly in different countries. It cannot be otherwise under commodity production. From this it follows irrefutably that socialism cannot achieve victory simultaneously *in all* countries. It will achieve victory first in one or several countries, while the others will for some time remain bourgeois or pre-bourgeois.[77]

The character of imperialism as the realm of domination rather than of freedom was inevitably projected on to the world stage. Inevitably, too, the techniques and habits of colonial domination had its repercussions on the internal politics of the imperialist states themselves. The reactionary ethos of capitalism in its final degenerate phase was manifested not only in its foreign policy but in its domestic politics as well:

> Both in foreign and home policy imperialism strives towards violations of democracy, towards reaction. In this sense imperialism is indisputably the 'negation' of *democracy in general*, of *all democracy*, and not just of *one* of its demands, national self-determination.[78]

The growth of militarism and habituation to solving social and political problems with violence began to corrode public life. The jingoist ideology of the monopolists, who were intimately linked with governing circles, with its emphasis on the grandeur of the national role and destiny, tended to forge a spurious unanimity of purpose in which any dissent was seen as treason to the national cause. It was, Lenin maintained, part and parcel of imperial ideology to foster the beliefs that the interests of finance capital, euphemistically called trade, were identical to the aims of the state which itself embodied the mission of the entire national group in history. Before this monolith, the individual as the repository of inalienable rights began to count for just as little as the individual entrepreneur beside the new corporations, trusts and cartels of finance capital – both belonged to a different epoch, both had now become anachronistic.

> The political structure of this new economy, of monopoly capitalism (imperialism is monopoly capitalism) is the change *from* democracy *to* political reaction. Democracy corresponds to free competition. Political reaction corresponds to monopoly. 'Finance capital strives for domination, not freedom', Rudolf Hilferding rightly remarks in his *Finance Capital*.[79]

It was in the light of these conclusions and under the immediate influence of Bukharin's nightmarish vision of the superordinate powers which the modern unified state capitalist trust was beginning to assume, that Lenin himself began to appreciate the need for a thoroughgoing revision of the prevalent Marxist attitude towards the state. Lenin's new analysis of the proper Marxist attitude towards the state is, in this account, quite unintelligible unless seen as a direct continuation of his economic analysis of imperialism. In this respect, as we shall see in the next chapter, the evolution of his thought not only followed the logical sequence of Bukharin's ideas but was also deeply indebted to them.

CONCLUSION

The object of Lenin's *Imperialism the Highest Stage of Capitalism* was to provide a coherent Marxist economic analysis for the overtly socialist and international revolutionary strategy which he had begun to develop in the first days of the war. He sought in particular to demonstrate that capitalism was not only in decline, not only had it exhausted its progressive role in history, it had become, in its imperialist phase, positively retrogressive, parasitic and oppressive. In Lenin's historical perspective, the imperialist bourgeoisie now occupied the same place which the nobility and landowners had occupied *vis-à-vis* the thrusting inventive entrepreneurs in the early phases of capitalist development. Superfluous to the modern productive process, bereft of energy or ideas, their only recourse was to conserve their huge privileges by employing a battery of monopolistic practices, none of which served to develop the productive forces of mankind. They also increasingly relied upon the naked power of a vastly augmented militarised state and administrative machine to protect their narrow interests. Far from being the vehicle of civic and individual freedom, the bourgeoisie had now become monolithically reactionary in their internal politics and parasitic and oppressive in their foreign policy. The recklessness of imperialist aggrandisement portended nothing but war upon war, the destruction of productive forces and of man on a huge scale, and the progressive degeneration not only of the imperialist bourgeoisie but even of the proletariat of the advanced countries.

These were, of course, far from academic points. Lenin's concern was not to construct an abstract historiography of the development of capitalism: it was rather to convince all those who called themselves Marxists that the time had now arrived when revolutionary action to overthrow capitalism had become imperative. His primary intention was to impress upon all the faint-hearted who had consistently blenched at the immediate prospect of revolutionary action, who had ever and anon invoked the concept of unripe time, arguing that capitalism had not yet exhausted its progressive potential, that time had run out for capitalism. His object was to convert the faint-hearted and, as important, to seal off once and for all the bolt-holes down which the waverers ran to hide themselves from the actuality of the revolutionary situation. All the proponents of the possibility of a post-war peaceful imperialism, the pacifist dreamers of a democratic peace without annexations, the Lib-Lab. philanthropists who envisaged a gradual redistribution of income as the solution to imperialism; all of them, Lenin argued, saw revolution staring them in the face. All of them must have been aware of the maturation of the objective and subjective conditions for socialist revolution and it was precisely that which terrified them. Their palliatives, Lenin repeatedly argued, were but the sophisms of men terrified by the duty which Marxism, at this critical juncture of world history, imposed upon them. In desperation they cast

69

about them for some hope, however remote, that things might improve, that the use of the ultimate weapon of revolution might yet for a short time at least be postponed, that the cup might be taken from their lips. Lenin's paramount concern was to deny the title 'Marxist' to all those who, at this world war crisis point of imperialism, promised only to be Marxists tomorrow. *Imperialism the Highest Stage of Capitalism* was intended, therefore, finally to deprive the waverers, opportunists and social chauvinists of any warrant for their policies in Marxist theory. At the same time, it explained the economic roots of their apostasy. The Communist International was created to deprive these men, whom Lenin now called traitors to Marxism, of their organisational base within the working class and to coordinate the assault of the revolutionary people on moribund world finance capital.

It is in this light, I believe, that we can best understand Georg Lukacs's somewhat elusive description of Lenin's thought as encapsulating the actuality of the revolution. The revolution was an actuality for Lenin in the literal sense that it was an imperative of the present moment. It could not be put off to a more propitious time, it was not a beautiful dream – the surrogate heaven that it had become for Western social democracy – it was staring the world in the face. All the preconditions for socialism had been established and the alternative to revolution was nothing short of a relapse into barbarism.

Lenin was, at the time, almost alone amongst the prominent Marxist leaders to have arrived at the unshakeable conviction of the immediacy or actuality of the socialist revolution. The object of this chapter has been to establish the theoretical rationale on which this conviction was based.

CHAPTER 4

The Revolutionary Imperative

The continuation of the imperialist war, according to Lenin's analysis, spelt economic ruin. The longer the war progressed the more severe the economic crisis would become and the more obvious would it appear to the mass of the population that the bourgeois economic structure could not possibly rescue mankind from impending economic catastrophe on a prodigious scale. By May of 1917, Lenin reached the conclusion that Russia was already sliding into ruin. Money had lost its value, the distributive mechanism had collapsed, essential goods were unobtainable and the whole structure of capitalism was in an advanced state of collapse. It was not, be argued, dogmatic adherence to the principles of socialism that made revolution necessary, it was not the activities of revolutionaries that had undermined capitalism – history itself had revealed its bankruptcy.[1]

Unless the Soviets took power and assumed effective control over the whole system of production and distribution,

> ... tens of millions of people will go hungry, without clothes and boots. Tens of millions of people are facing disaster and death; safeguarding the interest of the capitalists is the last thing that should bother us.[2]

In June 1917, Lenin insisted that the situation had reached such an impasse that disaster was inevitable.

> The complete disruption of Russia's economic life has now reached a point where catastrophe is unavoidable, a catastrophe of such appalling dimensions that a number of essential industries will be brought to a standstill, the farmer will be prevented from conducting farming on the necessary scale, and railway traffic will be interrupted with a consequent

71

stoppage of grain deliveries to the industrial population and the cities, involving millions of people. What is more, the break-down has already started, and has affected various industries.[3]

His words were of course prophetic: this is exactly what did occur in the autumn of 1917. It was precisely the disruption of industrial and agricultural production and the collapse of the railway network that brought hunger and bread queues to the cities and very considerably raised the revolutionary temperature. Surprisingly, however, Lenin's point is not to gloat over the impending collapse or to make plans for profiting from the débâcle which was at hand. On the contrary, the urgency for the immediate introduction of revolutionary measures and the assumption of power by the soviets was precisely that the sooner this happened the less the economic disorganisation of the country and the less the suffering of the people would be.

By July almost every one of Lenin's articles repeated the indictment – capitalism had manifestly collapsed and the attempts of the Provisional Government to shore it up had proved totally ineffective. Economic dislocation and imminent starvation were staring the Russian people in the face. 'Economic dislocation is getting worse. A crisis is imminent. Disaster is drawing irresistibly near.'[4] 'A crisis of unprecedented scale had descended upon Russia and the whole of humanity.'[5] 'Catastrophe will not wait. It is advancing with terrific speed.'[6]

To Lenin it appeared that the prognosis that he had arrived at in the first days of the war was at last being realised. The barbarism and butchery of the war was now being complemented by famine and economic crisis of unparalleled severity and intensiveness. The effects both of war and economic collapse were bound to raise the level of revolutionary consciousness and then the knell of capitalism itself would be tolled. Both had now become enormous 'accelerators' of the development of popular consciousness 'that may make a month or even a week equal to a year'.[7]

Even in this situation, however, there was no absolute certainty that a socialist revolution would occur or, even if it did, that it would be successful. The maturation of the objective and subjective conditions for a socialist revolution was certainly necessary but still not sufficient for its success. To these conditions would have to be added another which might be summarised as the purposive organisation of the force that would accomplish the revolution. The revolution was not like a plum falling into the hand when fully ripe without so much as a shake of the tree. It was, to characterise Lenin's account, more like a turnip. It would swell and ripen in the ground but would take a stout pull to harvest it – otherwise the action of the elements and of parasites would combine to rot it away. And so in late 1916 and 1917 Lenin conceived two possible outcomes of the revolutionary crisis which he was convinced was maturing. Either the soviets would seize power and organise production and distribution in the interests of the mass of the people and liberate their creative and organisational talents; or the capitalists would, by combining the power of the military and the greatly expanded state machine with that of capital, create a new kind of militarist state capitalist trust with the object of enmeshing and controlling every sector and facet of social life. Let us for a moment examine this latter alternative.

The war had, according to Lenin, imposed upon all belligerent countries the necessity of eliminating much of the anarchy of capitalist production. The state had more and more intruded itself as an agency in overall command of the capitalist economy, planning and co-ordinating its production and dictating its priorities through an increasingly complex system of controls. In this connection, Lenin argued,

> ... the war has done more than was done for twenty-five years. State control of industry has made progress in Britain as well as in Germany. Monopoly, in general, has evolved into state monopoly.[8]

The state had been obliged to intervene not merely in controlling the heights of the economy – the banks, the insurance agencies and the big capitalist monopolies[9] – it had also intervened directly in the distributive process by inaugurating comprehensive schemes of rationing. Finally, the imperialist states had even assumed control over the allocation and distribution of labour by introducing universal labour conscription.[10] It could therefore no longer be said that capitalism was anarchic and devoid of

73

direction or plan. In its new phase of state monopoly capitalism it had developed into an enormously powerful instrument of political, economic and military control over all of society.

> Engels remarked that 'when we came to the trust, then planlessness disappears', though there is capitalism. This remark is all the more pertinent today, when we have a military state, when we have state monopoly capitalism. Planning does not make the worker less of a slave, but it enables the capitalist to make his profits 'according to plan'. Capitalism is now evolving directly into its higher, regulated, form.[11]

The enormous expansion of state activity into every aspect of production, distribution and control of labour did not, of itself, signal the advent of socialism. So long as the objective of state capitalism was the protection of profits, it remained an exploitative system and the worker remained a wage slave. What the opportunists called 'war-time socialism' was, according to Lenin, in fact war-time state-monopoly capitalism, or, to put it more simply and clearly, war-time penal servitude for the workers and war-time protection for capitalist profits.[12]

Lenin's case was that capitalism, in the final perfected form of regulated state monopoly capitalism, had itself introduced all the material pre-requisites for socialism. For the realisation of socialism, however, the huge complexus of economic and political control mechanisms, which presently lay in the hands of the capitalists and was directed in the interests of their profits, would have to be seized by popular organs of self-government and directed in the interests of the mass of the people.[13]

> Objective conditions make it the urgent task of the day to prepare the proletariat in every way for the conquest of political power in order to carry out the economic and political measures which are the sum and substance of the socialist revolution.[14]

By September 1917, Lenin was even more emphatic that the development of state capitalism during the war had itself created all the material preconditions for socialism:

The dialectics of history is such that the war, by extraordinarily expediting the transformation of monopoly capitalism into state-monopoly capitalism, has *thereby* extraordinarily advanced mankind towards socialism.

Imperialist war is the eve of socialist revolution. And this not only because the horrors of the war give rise to proletarian revolt – no revolt can bring about socialism unless the economic conditions for socialism are ripe – but because state-monopoly capitalism is a complete *material* preparation for socialism, the *threshold* of socialism, a rung on the ladder of history between which and the rung called socialism *there are no intermediate rungs*.[15]

In a striking phrase, Lenin concluded that 'socialism is now gazing at us from all the windows of modern capitalism'.[16]

This did not, however, mean that socialism, particularly in Russia, could be introduced *immediately* in the sense that the whole economy could be instantaneously transferred to social owner-ship and control. On the contrary, Lenin repeatedly inveighed against the nonsense of immediate socialism and its ancillary notion of permanent revolution.[17] 'Everybody agrees,' Lenin argued in June 1917, 'that the immediate introduction of socialism in Russia is impossible.'[18] The objectives of the revolu-tion, according to Lenin, at this time were far more modest; they were generally presented as radical democratic rather than expressly socialist. The principal task was to deal urgently with averting economic catastrophe and mass famine. Unless there was a transfer of power from the state capitalist clique, which purposefully bottled up the creative potential of the masses, this would be impossible. Unless the wholesale plunder of the economy by the trusts and the state capitalist monopolies was brought to an immediate end, catastrophe was inevitable.

Let's not talk about the 'introduction' of socialism, which 'everybody' rejects. Let's talk about the exposure of plunder.[19]

... it is not a question of introducing socialism now, directly, overnight, but of *exposing plunder of the state*.[20]

Instead of the purposeful restriction of the people's initiative and energy and their repression by an all-powerful militarist state capitalism, the urgent demands of economic life made it imperative that popular involvement, direction and control over every aspect of the economy, exercised through a wide variety of organs of popular self-government, be encouraged. For Russia, as for other belligerent countries on the precipice of ruin, this was the only available solution. The popular organs of power which Lenin had in mind were many and varied. He proposed that congresses of all the employees of the big banks, the trusts, syndicates and of the workers in all large enterprises should be convened, with the object of keeping the management and owners under the strictest control and supervision. They would examine all the books and prevent any sabotage of the economy or any defrauding or plundering of the government by keeping managers and shareholders directly accountable to their workers. At the end of May 1917, Lenin insisted that the Soviets should issue a decree

> ... immediately convening:
> (1) Councils and congresses of bank employees, both of individual banks and on a national scale, to work out immediate practical measures for amalgamating all banks and banking houses into a single State Bank, and exercising precise control over all banking operations, the results of such control to be published forthwith.
> (2) Councils and congresses of employees of all syndicates and trusts to work out measures for control and accountancy; the results of such control to be published forthwith.
> (3) This decree should grant the right of control not only to the Soviets of Workers' Soldiers' and Peasants' Deputies, but also to councils of the workers at every large factory, as well as to the representatives of every large political party ...
> (5) The decree should call upon the people to establish immediately, through the local organs of self-government, universal labour service, for the control and enforcement of which a universal people's militia should be established (in the rural districts directly, in the cities through the workers' militia).

Without universal labour service, the country *cannot be saved* from ruin; and without a people's militia, universal labour service cannot be effected.[21]

It was only through these organs of popular power that the productive energy of the masses could be mobilised. Only through them, according to Lenin, was it possible to prevent the wholesale fraud and plunder of the state which the capitalists were perpetrating. The objective of those measures was not yet, in Lenin's view, the introduction of socialism. Control over industry and the banks, he repeatedly maintained, should in no way be confused with changes in the existing patterns of ownership. The intention of workers' control was to resuscitate production, ensure equitable distribution and to make sure that both were directed in the interests of the mass of the people. These were, Lenin insisted, democratic not socialist measures. They did not threaten one kopek of invested capital in the banks or elsewhere.

> The ownership of the capital wielded by and concentrated in the banks is certified by printed and written certificates called shares, bonds, bills, receipts, etc. Not a single one of these certificates would be invalidated or altered if the banks were nationalised, i.e. if all the banks were amalgamated into a single state bank.[22]

Only the machinery for the effective supervision of the economy, not the assets of the owners, would be taken over. This was, nonetheless, undoubtedly the single most important measure in Lenin's proposed package. Just as the power of the finance capitalists had been built up and exercised through the banks, so now the consolidated banking system was seen as *the* mechanism to effect the transformation of the economy in a radically popular direction and with radically democratic control and accountancy over it.

> Only by nationalising the banks *can* the state put itself in a position to know where and how, whence and when, millions and billions of rubles flow. And only control over the banks, over the centre, over the pivot and chief mechanism of capitalist circulation, would make it possible to organise real

77

and not fictitious control over all economic life, over the production and distribution of staple goods, and organise that 'regulation of economic life' which otherwise is inevitably doomed to remain a ministerial phrase designed to fool the common people. Only control over banking operations ... would make it possible ... to organise the effective collection of income tax in such a way as to prevent the concealment of property and incomes ... No special machinery, no special preparatory steps on the part of the state would be required, for this is a measure that can be effected by a single decree, 'at a single stroke'. ... *All* that is required is to *unify accountancy* ... this reform would be carried out in a few weeks ... there is not the slightest technical difficulty in the way of the amalgamation of the banks.[23]

Consistently, throughout 1917, Lenin is concerned to bring home this message to all the waverers and faint-hearted in his own party and in the Soviets. The mechanisms for the control of the economy and for a national structure of book-keeping and accountancy already exist. They do not have to be created. No particular effort is demanded from the Soviets and the new popular organs of self-administration. All that is required is that *they* should take over the ready-made machinery of control which finance capital has created.

... the development of capitalism, which resulted in the creation of banks, syndicates, railways and so forth, has greatly facilitated and simplified the adoption of measures of really democratic control by the workers and peasants over exploiters, the landowners and capitalists.[24]

They must displace the boards of directors of the banks, trusts and cartels and the whole apparatus of economic dominance will in this way be transferred to the popular masses.

All that remains to be done here is to transform reactionary – bureaucratic regulation into revolutionary – democratic regulation by simple decrees providing for the summoning of a congress of employees, engineers, directors and shareholders, for the introduction of uniform accountancy, for control by the workers' unions, etc. This is an exceedingly simple thing, yet it has not been done![25]

Lenin's plan for taking over the ready-made economic machinery of bourgeois dominance had its obverse side in his recommendations *vis-à-vis* the political machinery of coercion exercised by the capitalist state. As 1917 progressed and as Lenin became more and more insistent upon the need to capture the *economic* mechanisms of control, so he more and more rejected the view that the Party or the popular mass should take over the *political* or *coercive* mechanisms which the bourgeoisie had also created as vehicles of their domination. Lenin's rapid shift in this connection is unmistakeable and dramatic. State monopoly capitalism had, in his view, created the potential for an immediate transition to socialist construction, but only the potential. Whether that potential would be realised or whether it would atrophy depended now on whether the organs of popular government seized the initiative and grasped the opportunities which the war and the development of state monopoly capitalism had produced. Either they would go forward to smash capitalism or military state monopoly capitalism would rally to smash them. He insisted that there could be no middle course, no possibility of a peaceful cohabitation of the two, for they each stood in flat contradiction to the other. The contest had to be resolved in one way or the other:

> Either in the interest of the landowners and capitalists, in which case we have not a revolutionary-democratic, but a reactionary-bureaucratic state, an imperialist republic.
>
> Or in the interest of revolutionary democracy – and then *it is a step towards socialism.*
>
> For socialism is merely the next step forward from state-capitalist monopoly. Or, in other words, socialism is merely state-capitalist monopoly *which is made to serve the interests of the whole people* and has to that extent *ceased* to be capitalist monopoly.
>
> There is no middle course here. The objective process of development is such that it is *impossible* to advance from *monopolies* (and the war has magnified their number, rule and importance tenfold) without advancing towards socialism.

Either we have to be revolutionary democrats in fact, in which case we must not fear to take steps towards socialism. Or we fear to take steps towards socialism, condemn them . . . in which case we inevitably sink to the level of Kerensky, Milyukov and Kornilov, i.e., we in a *reactionary* – bureaucratic way suppress the 'revolutionary democratic' aspirations of the workers and peasants.

There is no middle course.

And therein lies the fundamental contradiction of our revolution.

It is impossible to stand still in history in general, and in war-time in particular. We must either advance or retreat.[26]

Once again there is an implacable Marxist logic lying behind Lenin's strategy throughout 1917. He was in no doubt that a revolutionary situation obtained in Europe generally and in Russia in particular. In Russia, the emergence of the Soviets signified that the proletariat had already developed the embryonic forms of its own form of state power as distinct from the bourgeois Provisional Government which was striving to preserve intact the power of the old state machinery and the classes which dominated it. The issue of the revolution was, however, the question of the *transfer* of state power from one class to another. Lenin constantly repeated this axiom of Marxism which had, as we have seen, dictated his strategy in 1905:

The basic question of every revolution is that of state power. Unless this question is understood, there can be no intelligent participation in the revolution, not to speak of guidance of the revolution.[27]

The passing of state power from one *class* to another is the first, the principal, the basic sign of a *revolution*, both in the strictly scientific and in the practical political meaning of that term.[28]

It was not enough for the proletarian organs of self-government merely to be tolerated and allowed a legal existence, it was not enough that in a certain sense they stood in a situation of dual power exercised alongside of the Provisional Government. The question was which would gain the ascendancy, which would impress the stamp of its class authority over all other classes. Simply to assent to the continued existence of the soviets and the situation of dual power was not therefore, in Lenin's eyes, an option open to revolutionaries for this entailed acquiescing in the gradual strengthening of the bourgeois-capitalist forces in the Provisional Government which would, as soon as they were sufficiently powerful, destroy their soviet competitors.

> There is no other way out. Either we go back to supreme rule by the capitalists, or forward towards real democracy, towards majority decisions. This dual power cannot last long.[29]

CONCLUSION

By the spring of 1917 Lenin had effectively closed the gaps in his revolutionary strategy. By confronting the arguments of the vacillators, the pacifists and revisionists, he had forged a cohesive set of arguments which demonstrated, against all their misgivings, the imminence, urgency or actuality of the revolution. His theoretical work on the nature of imperialism had established the objective possibilities of socialist revolution. His analysis of threatening economic catastrophe demonstrated the urgent need for popular control of the administration and the economy. His review of the class dynamics of the revolutionary situation showed it to be an immediate political necessity. Only two tasks remained. The first was that of organising and enthusing a sufficient mass following and a sufficient armed force to accomplish the revolutionary transfer of power from one class to another. The other no less important task was to construct some sort of model which would serve to guide the proletariat and its Party in establishing a properly socialist administration. The issue of what the socialist state would look like and what principles ought to inform its construction inescapably presented themselves. Seen in this light it is not in the least surprising that Lenin should have busied himself, in the revolutionary months of spring and summer of 1917, with seemingly abstruse researches into Marxism and the state. The product of his work was, of course, the unfinished book *State and Revolution*. Our argument is that this book, far from being the enigma or pipe-dream which many commentators make it out to be, is an immediate, direct complement

81

to Lenin's theory of imperialism and the whole battery of arguments he advanced for believing socialist revolution to be on the immediate agenda. Lenin's ideas on the nature of the Soviet state are not only complementary to his theoretical (or socio-economic) analysis of finance capital in the sense that there is a temporal progression from the finding that the objective conditions for socialist revolution had matured to the attempt to construct a model for the socialist state; they are complementary in the more intrinsic sense that we cannot understand the *content* of his ideas on the state and administrative forms appropriate to socialist construction *apart from* his theoretical analysis of imperialism.

CHAPTER 5

Theory of the State

Perhaps the most puzzling and inexplicable period of Lenin's life, from the standpoint of those exponents of the 'basic position'[1] who would have us believe that he was pre-eminently an instinctive practical politician, are his activities during the turbulent months following the downfall of the autocracy in February 1917. According to their accounts, we should have expected Lenin to have been exclusively concerned with the immediate tactical concern of maximising his own power and that of the Bolsheviks. We might have expected him therefore to have gone along with what was clearly the majority view of his party in Russia, that the Bolsheviks should themselves participate in the horse trading that was going on, secure an alliance with the Mensheviks and the left S.R.s in order to become a central force in a new coalition Provisional Government. Lenin would have none of this. Instead of devoting his time to political wheeler-dealing to achieve immediate tactical advantage to his party in Russia, he concentrated his energies on an almost academic, exhaustive study of Marx and Engels on the question of the state with a view to outlining the long-term strategic objectives of the global socialist revolution.

The economic and social analysis of imperialism and of the imperialist war had, as we have seen, asserted the imperative of socialist revolution on a global scale. The slide into economic ruination and general famine made it doubly urgent. The problem which now posed itself was to specify guidelines for socialist practice. How would people relate one to another under socialism, through what sorts of organs would the mass exercise its power and what was to become of the state – these questions now absorbed Lenin and in the hope of answers he turned avidly to the texts of Marx and Engels. We should perhaps note in passing that in posing these questions Lenin went considerably beyond Bukharin at this time. Bukharin's progression of thought proceeded from the location and characterisation of a new phase of capitalism to the hypothesis that historically the state changes in nature to correspond to changes in the structure of capitalism to the finding that the economic structure of imperialism begets its own specific form of state. At this point Bukharin stops. Certainly his characterisation of the imperialist state carried with it the imperative to destroy it through socialist revolution, but he made no attempt to specify the positive content of socialism itself. His was a powerful and coherent destructive criticism of the existing structure of imperialism but it contained nothing in the way of principles or proposals which might guide future socialist society. Lenin's *State and Revolution*, by contrast, has an emphatically practical objective. It is an attempt to uncover the principles and forms of organisation appropriate to the construction of socialism and as such it is the practical complement to his economic theory of imperialism. *Imperialism the Highest Stage of Capitalism* was Lenin's *theoretical* justification for socialist revolution, *State and Revolution* was his attempt to establish a yardstick for socialist *practice*.

THE BACKGROUND IN MARX AND ENGELS

The problem which Lenin confronted, and had to attempt to overcome, was that Marx and Engels at different times adopted quite different stances with regard to the state. At times they argued that socialists must take over the existing state machine and utilise it to wrest, by degrees, all capital from the bourgeoisie, to centralise all instruments of production in the hands of state, that is, of the proletariat organised as the ruling class; and to increase the total of productive forces as rapidly as possible.[2] Throughout the critical years 1848 to 1850, Marx and Engels repeatedly emphasised this theme of determined centralisation of political, coercive and economic power, in the hands of the state which was to be dominated by the proletariat. *The Address of the Central Committee to the Communist League*, written in March 1850, insisted that the workers

> ... must not only strive for a single and indivisible German republic, but also within this republic for the most determined

centralisation of power in the hands of the state authority. They must not allow themselves to be misguided by the democratic talk of freedom for the communities, of self-government etc . . . it must under no circumstances be permitted that every village, every town and every province should put up a new obstacle in the paths of revolutionary activity, which can proceed with full force only from the centre. . . . As in France in 1793 so today in Germany it is the task of the really revolutionary party to carry through the strictest centralisation.[3]

The utilisation and huge extension of the powers of the existing state by the proletariat seems to encapsulate much of what Marx and Engels had in mind when they recommended the dictatorship of the proletariat as the state form appropriate to the newly-triumphant working class. According to the programme spelt out in *The Manifesto of the Communist Party*, the proletariat would utilise the coercive agencies of the state to put down its opponents and would presumably create a new administrative machine to centralise all property in the hands of the state. In *The Class Struggles in France*, Marx himself invites us to make the comparison between the seizure of power which the Communists projected and the centralist schema associated with Louis Auguste Blanqui:

> the *proletariat* rallies more and more round *revolutionary socialism*, round *communism*, for which the bourgeoisie has itself invented the name of *Blanqui*. This socialism is the *declaration of the permanence of the revolution*, the class dictatorship of the proletariat as the necessary transit point to the abolition of class distinctions generally . . .[4]

Two years later (1852), in a letter to Weydemeyer, Marx equally briefly referred to the dictatorship of the proletariat, again stressing its transitional features.[5] The only other reference of any significance Marx made was his famous and unelaborated comment in his *Critique of the Gotha Programme* of 1875:

> The question then arises: what transformation will the state undergo in communist society? In other words, what social

functions will remain in existence that are analogous to present functions of the state?

Between capitalist and communist society lies the period of the revolutionary transformation of the one into the other. There corresponds to this also a transitional period in which the state can be nothing but *the revolutionary dictatorship of the proletariat*.[6]

In Marx's view, therefore, the dictatorship of the proletariat was to be a fairly prolonged transitional period during which the proletariat would exercise its hegemony over the possessing classes through its capture of the centralised coercive agencies of the state whilst simultaneously using its power 'to centralise all instruments of production in the hands of the state'. Amongst the ten measures which Marx recommended in *The Manifesto* for all 'the most advanced countries' were the following:

5. Centralisation of credit in the hands of the State, by means of a national bank with State capital and an exclusive monopoly.
6. Centralisation of the means of communication and transport in the hands of the State.
7. Extension of factories and instruments of production owned by the State ...
8. Equal liability of all to labour. Establishment of industrial armies, especially for agriculture.[7]

From this it is transparently clear that, in this model, initiative in both the political and the economic spheres was to proceed from the top downwards. Local or regional agencies of self-government, as well as partial and localised economic associations like co-operatives, were all seen as obstacles 'in the path of revolutionary activity which can proceed with full force only from the Centre', and impediments to the objective of centralising all production 'in the hands of a vast association of the whole nation'.[8]

Unless we took this to be their position at that time we would be unable to explain their contemporaneous controversies with the anarchist Bakunin, nor would we be able to explain why Marx and Engels felt the need to propose a self-conscious and almost complete renunciation of this attitude towards the state after the Paris Commune of 1871. The only substantial amendment to the *Manifesto* they felt obliged to make concerned precisely the role of the state, and it was emphatically the experience of the Commune which impelled them to introduce it. In the Preface to the German edition of 1872 they entered the following reservation:

> ... some parts of this programme have become antiquated. One thing especially was proved by the Commune, viz., that 'the working class cannot simply lay hold of the ready-made State machinery and wield it for its own purposes'.[9]

Clearly, this reservation would make no sense unless we assume that hitherto Marx and Engels *had* advocated the capture of the existing state machine as essential to the dictatorship of the proletariat. We should furthermore be clear that Marx and Engels expressly draw our attention to the fact that certain *parts* of the programme no longer apply and not, as the mistaken English translation of this Preface puts it, 'this programme has in some details become antiquated'.[10] If Marx and Engels were maintaining that the Communists should no longer put the capture of the existing state machine at the very centre of their political tactic then, clearly, they were dramatically re-defining their whole political strategy.

There can be no doubt that Marx's writings on the commune do represent an abrupt change of stance on the question of the state. The state, Marx argued in his *The Civil War in France*, was not to be taken over and utilised by the socialists. The instruments of coercion of the old state were not to be used to put down the challenges of hostile classes nor was its machinery to be used to centralise the forces of production in the hands of the proletariat. State power was to be smashed and the entire significance of the commune, in Marx's view, was that it stood in flat contradiction to the oppressive, parasitic, hierarchical and centralised character of state power *per se*. In his first draft of the *Civil War in France*, Marx was more candid on this point than he dared be in the finished version, bowdlerised as it had to be for the consumption of the august British trades unionists of the General Council of the International Working Men's Association. Here, replete with the gallicisms and odd expressions of Marx's manuscript, is his characterisation of the commune as anarchy:

> The true antithesis to the *Empire itself* – that is to the state power, the centralised executive, of which the Second Empire was only the exhausting formula – was *the Commune*. This state power forms in fact the creation of the middle class, first a means to break down feudalism, then a means to crush the emancipatory aspirations of the producers, of the working class. All reactions and all revolutions had only served to transfer the organized power – that organized force of the slavery of labour – from one hand to the other, from one faction of the ruling classes to the other. It had served the ruling classes as a means of subjugation and of pelf. It had sucked new forces from every new change. It had served as the instrument of breeding every popular rise [rising] and served it to crush the working classes after they had fought and been ordered to secure its transfer from one part of its oppressors to the others. This was, therefore, a Revolution not against this or that, legitimate, constitutional, republican, or Imperialist form of State Power. It was a Revolution against the *State* itself, of this supernaturalist abortion of society, a resumption by the people for the people of its own social life. It was not a revolution to transfer it from one faction of the ruling class to the other, but a Revolution to break down this horrid machinery of Class-domination itself.[11]

The force of Marx's principled opposition to the state nonetheless shone through every page of the final draft of *The Civil War in France*. The commune, Marx insisted, was 'the direct antithesis to the empire' and imperialism itself was but 'the most prostitute and the ultimate form of the State power'.[12] Its first decree 'was the suppression of the standing army, and the substitution for it of the armed people'.[13] All those public functions which the state had arrogated to itself were in Marx's account to be reintegrated with the self-acting mass of the people acting through their local communes for, as Marx insisted, 'the Commune was to be the political form of even the smallest country hamlet'.[14] All functionaries were to be elected, all were to be directly accountable to the people and revocable at any time and all were to be paid at workmen's wages. 'The unity of the nation', Marx claimed,

> was not to be broken, but on the contrary, to be organised by
> the Communal Constitution and to become a reality by the
> destruction of the State power which claimed to be the
> embodiment of that unity independent of, and superior to,
> the nation itself, from which it was but a parasitic excre-
> sence.[15]

> The Communal Constitution would have restored to the social
> body all the forces hitherto absorbed by the State parasite
> feeding upon, and clogging the free movement of, soci-
> ety ... The very existence of the Commune involved, as a
> matter of course, local municipal liberty, but no longer as a
> check upon the, now superseded, State power.[16]

This extremely decentralised social–political structure was,
Marx maintained, a truly universal discovery of the revolutionary
genius of the French working class. It was none other than 'the
political form at last discovered under which to work out the
economic emancipation of labour'.[17] The road to economic
emancipation was itself premised not upon the centralisation of
resources in the hands of the state which had been the leitmotif of
Marx's description of the dictatorship of the proletariat, but upon
a much more variegated and decentralised plan in which 'united
cooperative societies are to regulate production upon a plan, thus
taking it under their control . . .'[18]

We should, at this point, briefly summarise the major differences between Marx's characterisation of the commune and his
earlier account of the dictatorship of the proletariat. In the first
place, the commune was no longer a state in the usual Marxian
definition of that term. Consistently, Marx and Engels defined
the state in terms of separate bodies of armed men (separate, that
is, from the mass of the unarmed populace). It was pre-eminently
a coercive instrument used by one class for retaining its superiority over all other classes. Insofar as the commune moved *immediately*
to disband the standing army and to reintegrate the functions of
the police with the people in arms, the state ceased to exist. Marx
clearly recognised this when he spoke, in *The Civil War in France*,
about 'the now superseded state power'. Moreover, even Engels

89

appeared to have recognised the implications of this in writing to Bebel when he maintained that:

> The whole talk about the state should be dropped, especially since the Commune, which was no longer a state in the proper sense of the word . . . We would therefore propose to replace the word 'State' everywhere by the word Gemeinwesen (Community), a good old German word which can very well represent the French *commune*.[19]

The dictatorship of the proletariat, by contrast, was emphatically a state form even if it was only anticipated that the utilisation of coercion by separate bodies of armed proletarians was to be but a transitional measure. In this connection we should notice that there was nothing *transitional* about Marx's characterisation of the commune. On the contrary, its *first* act was to declare the abolition of the standing army and the police in their old forms; their functions were *immediately* reintegrated with the self-acting armed population. The commune was not a preparation for something more perfected, it was itself, as we have seen, 'the political form at last discovered under which to work out the economic emancipation of labour'.

Finally, it is quite clear that in terms of its political constitution as well as in its projected economic organisation, the commune was to reflect and promote the utmost possible decentralisation, whereas the dictatorship of the proletariat in both political and economic spheres was to press for the most determined centralism.

In taking note of these very large differences we need not necessarily conclude that Marx was quite incoherent in his recommendations to his followers on the question of what was to be done with the state. We must, however, say that (apart from a tantalisingly brief statement in 1852 where he reflected that 'All revolutions perfected this machine instead of smashing it')[20] by 1871 his whole attitude towards the state had undergone a profound change. It may well be that there are good reasons for the change. Perhaps it was appropriate that in the period 1848–51 when Germany had not emerged as a nation-state, when petty-princedoms and internal barriers everywhere presented obstacles to the development of modern productive forces, in that environment and at that time, determined centralism alone was progressive in Marxian terms. It may equally well be the case that by 1871, with the rise of a monstrously swollen executive under Louis Bonaparte in France (which had its origin in the unresolved class conflicts of 1848–51) which grew into an 'appalling parasitic body, which enmeshes the body of French society like a net and chokes all its pores',[21] by that time it had become apparent to Marx that in its final perfected form the state had finally made manifest its own degeneration and had to be destroyed.

To attempt an explanation of why Marx offered different accounts at differing times on what was to be done with the existing state is, however, a very different exercise from that of attempting to integrate his two widely differing models or to try and maintain that really the two were identical. Marx himself never asserted that they were the same, he *never* identified the commune as the dictatorship of the proletariat. It was Engels long after Marx's death who, in an access of rhetoric, posed to all subsequent Marxists the insuperable problem of reconciling, indeed identifying, the commune with the dictatorship of the proletariat. His 1891 Introduction to *The Civil War in France* ended with the ringing and bemusing paragraph:

Of late, the Social-Democratic philistine has once more been filled with wholesome terror at the words: Dictatorship of the Proletariat. Well and good, gentlemen, do you want to know what this dictatorship looks like? Look at the Paris Commune. That was the Dictatorship of the Proletariat.[22]

No small part of Lenin's theoretical difficulties in *State and Revolution*, as we shall see, arose from his inclination to take Engels seriously and therefore from his endeavour to square the circle which Engels had sketched.[23] Lenin never resolved the problem Engels bequeathed him, nor could he. His attempted resolution followed the lines implicit in Engels' identification, that is he characterised the dictatorship of the proletariat, for the moment at least, in terms of the commune. There was, however, always lurking in the immediate background, an alternative model which stressed centralisation against initiative from below, emphasised the need for a transitional period as against an immediate reappropriation by society of the powers arrogated by the state, and separate bodies of armed men under the guidance of the Party as against the self-activity of the people in arms. It was not to be long, a matter of six months to a year, before this background model of the dictatorship of the proletariat emerged to the centre of the stage and drove the commune form into the wings. The important point to note is that, from the outset, Lenin had available an alternative characterisation of the dictatorship of the proletariat should the commune form prove unsatisfactory. The unresolved dualism in the Marxist theory of the state was, as we shall see, to be replicated and thrown into high relief by the actual practice of Soviet government in the first year of its existence.

THE INFLUENCE OF BUKHARIN

Lenin seems to have been prompted to start a thoroughgoing review of his attitude towards the state by an article which Bukharin published under the rather obvious pseudonym Nota-Bene (N.B. were, of course, his initials) in the left-wing journal *Die Jugend Internationale* in 1916. The article, in Lenin's view at that time, merely reiterated the false conclusions which Bukharin had set out earlier in the year in his article 'On the Theory of the Imperialist State'. Bukharin had, in mid-1916, submitted the latter article to Lenin who was editing a collection of programmatic articles entitled *Sbornik Sotsial Demokrat*. Lenin's first inclination was to publish the essay as 'a discussion article'. But, incensed by their other differences, he soon changed his mind and decided that it was 'undoubtedly not suitable'.[24] We must remember that, at this time, Lenin's relationship with Bukharin and the Baugy group had been strained almost to breaking point over the national question.

Lenin was therefore, at this point, ill-disposed to acknowledge that Bukharin had emerged with a stunningly original re-definition of the proper attitude for revolutionary Marxists to adopt towards the bourgeois state. In early September, Lenin wrote to Bukharin rejecting his article and his new formulations. According to Lenin, what Bukharin had to say about the growth of state capitalism was sound enough; where he was in error was in his theoretical analysis of the state in general. Not only had this part been 'insufficiently thought out'[25] it was, Lenin pointed out to Bukharin, wrong on a crucial and fundamental point:

> The distinction between the Marxists and the anarchists on the question of the state . . . has been defined *absolutely incorrectly*: if you are to deal with this subject, you must speak *not* in that way; you *must not* speak in that way. The conclusion (the author gives it in italics): 'Social Democracy must intensively underline its hostility in principle to the state power' . . . is also either supremely inexact, or incorrect.[26]

Lenin made public his critique of Bukharin's ideas in the self-same *Sbornik* for which Bukharin had written his original article. He was no doubt incensed that, in spite of his earlier letter of censure, Bukharin had nonetheless published an abstract of his heresies in the *Jugend Internationale*. There he had, in Lenin's view, persisted in his false view that both revolutionary Marxists and anarchists were united in their resolve to proceed immediately with the destruction or shattering of the existing state. Where the socialists differed from the anarchists was, in Bukharin's account, not in their attitude towards the state but in their rival conceptions of the future organisation of economic life.

At this time (December 1916) Lenin was in no doubt that Bukharin was mistaken. 'This is wrong.'[27] For the moment Lenin held fast to the old social Democratic orthodoxy which had it that socialists would, for a more or less prolonged transitional period, have to make use of the coercive power of the existing state machine in order to put down their opponents and consolidate the power of the proletarian dictatorship. On this point, Lenin was quite unequivocal.

> Socialists are in favour of utilising the present state and its institutions: the struggle for the emancipation of the working class, maintaining also that the state should be used for a specific form of transition from capitalism to socialism. This transitional form is the dictatorship of the proletariat, which is *also* a state.
>
> The anarchists want to 'abolish' the state, 'blow it up' (*sprengen*) as Comrade Nota-Bene expresses it in one place erroneously ascribing this view to the socialists.[28]

93

We shall shortly see how Lenin was to modify his views very considerably in respect of the state, so much so indeed that, according to Bukharin, on his return from America, Krupskaya's first words to him were 'V.I. asked [me] to tell you that on the question of the state he now has no disagreements with you. In tackling the question Ilyich had arrived at the same conclusions concerning the "blowing up"[29] but he developed this theme and then the teaching on dictatorship, so that he took a whole historical epoch in the development of theoretical conceptions in this direction.'[30]

In order to appreciate how important an influence Bukharin's ideas had upon Lenin in the critical first six months of 1917 we must first reconstruct Bukharin's attitude to the state as developed in his masterly article 'On the Theory of the Imperialist State'.[31]

BUKHARIN ON THE NATURE OF THE IMPERIALIST STATE

Bukharin had already in 1914, in his *Imperialism and World Economy*, begun to develop his ideas on the intimate connection between the evolution of finance capital and the changing character of the bourgeois state. According to his economic analysis, the process of concentration and monopolisation had gone so far that the giant cartels, trusts and banks had increasingly merged with the power of the state.

> Thus various spheres of the concentration and organisation process stimulate each other, creating a very strong tendency towards transforming the entire national economy *into one gigantic combined enterprise under the tutelage of the financial kings and the capitalist state, an enterprise which monopolises the national market and forms the prerequisite for organised production on a higher non-capitalist level.*[32]

The state, according to Bukharin, had in the imperialist epoch undergone a metamorphosis akin to that which the banks had undergone. From being modest intermediaries they had emerged as the organising and controlling forces and in like fashion the state, which had hitherto posed as the impartial arbiter of competing interests, now displayed itself as the most comprehensive and powerful organiser and director of the entire complex of finance capital exploitation.

> State power has become the domain of a financial oligarchy; the latter manages production which is tied up by the banks into one knot. This process of the organisation of production has proceeded from below; it has fortified itself within the framework of modern states, which have become the exact expression of the interests of finance capital. Every one of the capitalistically advanced 'national economies' has turned into some kind of 'national' trust.[33]

Within each advanced national economy, Bukharin argued, competition had effectively been done away with and a single capitalist trust had been formed backed by the ever-growing coercive and military power of the state, bent on securing for itself a monolithic unity within the frontiers of the state and an ever larger share of the economic territory of the world in its external policies. Internal unanimity of purpose and elimination of competition was, in the imperialist phase, the necessary complement of the heightened confrontation and competition between state capitalist trust on the international plane.

> Combines in industry and banking syndicates unite the 'national' production which assumes the form of a company of companies thus becoming a state capitalist trust. Competition reaches the highest, the last conceivable state of development. It is now the competition of state capitalist trusts in the world market. Competition is reduced to a minimum within the boundaries of 'national' economies, only to flare up in colossal proportions, such as would not have been possible in any of the preceding historic epochs . . . the centre of gravity is shifted to the competition of gigantic, consolidated, and organised economic bodies possessed of a colossal fighting capacity in the world tournament of 'nations'.[34]

Repeatedly, Bukharin employs the same loaded metaphors 'the iron fist of the military state',[35] the 'iron grip' of finance capital,[36] 'the mailed fist of state power'[37] to express his conviction that the imperialist state had now become a monstrous force which had appropriated to itself a totality of economic and political power. The government, he argued, is *de facto* transformed into a 'committee' elected by the representatives of entrepreneurs' organisations, and becomes the highest guiding force of the state capitalist trust.[38]

> Being a very large shareholder in the state capitalist trust, the modern state is the highest and all-embracing organisational culmination of the latter. Hence its colossal, almost monstrous power.[39]

The ideology of *laisser-faire*, appropriate to the free play of a competitive market structure, which presumed and legitimised the clash of multifarious interests, had long since been replaced by 'the new "mercantilism" of imperialism'.[40] The variety of parties characteristic of the epoch of free competition had given way to the reactionary unanimity of all the ruling groups seeking to preserve their power through their monopolistic hold on the economy integrated with the dictatorship they exercised through the state machine.

> In former times parliament served as an arena for the struggle among various factions of the ruling group (bourgeoisie and landowners, various strata of the bourgeoisie themselves, etc.). Finance capital has consolidated almost all of their varieties into one 'solid reactionary mass' united in many centralised organisations. 'Democratic' and 'liberal' sentiments are replaced by open monarchist tendencies in modern imperialism, which is always in need of a state dictatorship.[41]

With the imperialist war, and in the preparations for it, Bukharin argued, the 'old bourgeois individualism' had been destroyed completely.[42] The ruling groups did not, however, stop there. They recognised full well that a necessary part of their self-preservation lay in putting down the threat which the labour movement presented. As monopoly became transparently obvious, as monopoly prices eroded working-class standards of living, as the state intervened with massive taxation to finance the huge increases in its budget, especially to sustain its expanded army and navy, 'there takes place, not a relative but also an *absolute* worsening of the situation of the working class. Class antagonisms become inevitably sharpened.'[43]

The response of the imperialist state was to introduce draconian legislation which effectively destroyed the hard-won freedom of the workers.

> The workers are deprived of the freedom to move, the right to strike, the right to belong to the so-called 'subversive' parties, the right to choose an enterprise, etc. They are transformed into bondsmen, attached, not to the land, but to the plant. They become white slaves of the predatory imperialist state, which has absorbed into its body all productive life.[44]

The flimsy illusion of neutrality in which the bourgeois state had hitherto draped itself was, in Bukharin's view, at last stripped away. The state in its final imperialist form revealed itself as naked coercive force, itself supervising the exploitation of the workers and acting as the guardian of all other exploiters. The true nature of the bourgeois state in its ultimate perfected form could not fail, therefore, to impress itself upon the minds of the masses.

> Thus the principles of class antagonisms reach a height that could not have been allowed hitherto. Relations between classes become clear, most lucid; the mythical conception of a 'state elevated above classes' disappears from the people's consciousness, once the state becomes a direct entrepreneur and an organiser of production. Property relations, obscured by a number of intermediary links, now appear in their pristine nakedness.[45]

The experience of the senseless butchery of world war would, Bukharin believed, at last reveal to the masses the fact that they would have to destroy the state power of the imperialist bourgeoisie before any advance towards socialism could be made. The workers of the advanced capitalist countries had for some time been 'chained to the chariot of the bourgeois state power'[46] in that they had benefited from 'The additional pennies ... from the colonial policy of imperialism'.[47] Small wonder then that they, and especially their leaders, had come to the aid of the state in its hour of need. As the agony of war continued, however, as the oppressive nature of the imperialist state increasingly revealed itself, the value of the additional pennies received by European workers would be seen in proper perspective:

– what do they count compared to millions of butchered workers, to billions devoured by the war, to the monstrous pressure of brazen militarism, to the vandalism of plundered productive forces, to the high cost of living and starvation!

The war severs the last chain that binds the workers to the masters, their slavish submission to the imperialist state. The last limitation of the proletariat's philosophy is being overcome; its clinging to the narrowness of the national state, its patriotism.[48]

There would, Bukharin proclaimed, at last be realised Marx's insistence, which his socialist epigones had all forgotten, that the bourgeois state had to be opposed with a furious hatred and that the objective of Marxists was to usher in a society in which the state would entirely disappear.[49]

HILFERDING ON THE IMPERIALIST STATE

Bukharin's ideas on the nature of the imperialist state, to this point at least, were little more than a repetition of those of Rudolf Hilferding. Just as Bukharin's appraisal of the changed economic structure of capitalism in its imperialist phase, as set out in his *The World Economy of Imperialism*, was clearly and obviously indebted to Hilferding's analysis in *Finance Capital*, so too were his reflections on the changed nature of the imperialist state. Bukharin and, following him, Lenin, did no more than elaborate the terse and incisive appraisal of the imperialist state sketched out by Hilferding in 1910. Hilferding had argued that coincidentally with the rise of monopoly capitalism, and causally related to that process, there had proceeded a fundamental change in the world-view of the bourgeoisie. 'It had ceased to be peace-loving and humanist. ... The ideal of peace withered away, the ideal of the grandeur and power of the state took the place of the idea of the humanists. And the contemporary state arose as the realisation of the urge of nations towards unification . . . at the present time, the national idea has turned itself into the idea of the domination of one's own nation over all others.'[50]

The stages in this progress were clear in Hilferding's mind. In the era of the rise of capitalism the entrepreneurs had seen the interventionist policy of the feudal state as inimical to their own interests. Their slogan of *laisser-faire* carried with it an assumption that the free play of economic forces was governed by an inherent harmony which the meddling of the state could only disrupt. The complement of *laisser-faire* was, therefore, minimal government.

> In the battle against economic mercantilism and political absolutism the bourgeoisie was the representative of a hostile attitude towards the state. Liberalism really was devastatingly powerful, it really did signify 'the overthrow' of the power of the state, the dissolution of the old ways . . . The victory of liberalism meant, above all, a huge reduction of the forces of governmental power. Economic life, in principle at least, should be completely freed from governmental regulation, and the political state should limit itself to taking care of security and the establishment of civic equality.[51]

This situation could not, in Hilferding's account, long survive the advent of monopoly capitalism. The financial magnates in control of the trusts and cartels quickly appreciated the importance to them of an all-powerful state machine. They needed state intervention in the first place to establish high protective tariffs around the spheres of industry they controlled. In this way their monopoly prices were guaranteed against foreign competition and, with the super-profits yielded by the internal market, they could pay export premiums to buyers abroad. Tariffs thus became vitally important to the trusts and cartels as a principal means of cheapening the export prices of their goods, as a means therefore of dominating the world market. Consequently the striving to increase customs duties becomes as boundless as the urge to profit.[52]

Equally boundless was the striving of the new barons of the trusts and cartels to expand the economic territory of their state. With every expansion of economic territory, the market was extended, unit costs were reduced and the competitiveness of the trust on the international market thereby enhanced. Each step in this process necessarily involved vastly increased expenditure on the army and navy for subject people would have to be forcibly deprived of their land and traditional modes of production as a precondition to their availability as a labour force and as potential consumers. Each expansion of economic territory would, moreover, have to be protected against the hostile intentions of competitive states.

Just as the leaders of the trusts and cartels had eliminated competition in the economic sphere so, too, they were bent upon eliminating political differences within the imperialist state. The present level of the competitive struggle carried with it, in Hilferding's account, the need for positive national unity and identification of all with the interests of the imperialist state as the champion of the 'national interest' in the battle for supremacy in the world market.

> But in order to accomplish this, in order to secure and extend its predominance, it needs a state whose customs and tariff policies must guarantee the internal market and facilitate the conquest of external markets. It has need of the political power of a state which in its trading policy takes no account of the contradictory interests of other states. Finally a powerful state which would secure recognition abroad of its financial interests is essential to it, which would employ its political power in order to compel small states [to accept] favourable agreements on orders and favourable agreements on trade. It needs a state which is able to back up its intervention anywhere in the world, so that the whole world is converted into a sphere of interest for its finance capital.[53]

The epoch of finance capital therefore brought with it a total transformation of the bourgeois state. The old liberal suspicion of the state and insistence on its minimal role had, Hilferding maintained, long since ceased to be the dominant view. The greater international competition became, the more extensive the imperialist state grew in power. The more it grew in power, the more the effects of its protectionist tariff policies and its enormously increased internal taxation weighed upon the working class.

The more internal class contradictions were exacerbated, the more oppressive the imperialist state became in its home policies and the more it insisted on the unity of the whole nation in face of hostile competition externally. In order to subdue the threatening revolt of the working class and in order to secure the profits of the cartels and trusts, the imperialist state took on an increasingly positive role in the actual organisation of industry and the supervision of labour conditions. It thereby revealed itself, according to Hilferding, as the undisguised vehicle of power of a particular class. The illusory universality of the bourgeois state which, in the period of liberalism had retained a degree of plausibility for the simple reason that the state was not directly involved in the economic and productive process, was now finally stripped away. The state was revealed not as an impartial arbiter of competing interests but as the guarantor of the particular interests of the financial barons dominating the banks, the trusts and cartels and the entire fiscal and foreign policies of the country.

> So long as the principle of *laisser-faire* held sway, so long as the intervention of the state in economic life and along with this also the character of the state as an organisation of class domination was still disguised, it required considerable farsightedness in order to be able to understand the necessity of the political struggle and, especially, the necessity of the ultimate political aim – the conquest of state power. . . . Now all that has changed. The capitalist class directly, undisguisedly, tangibly seizes the state organisation and converts it into an instrument of its exploitative interests in such a manner that even the most backward proletarian inevitably becomes conscious that the seizure of political power by the proletariat represents his immediate personal interest. Obviously the seizure of the state by the capitalist class directly compels every proletarian to strive for the conquest of political power as the sole means of putting an end to exploitation.[54]

Hilferding's argument, which was to be refined and extended first by Bukharin and later by Lenin, was that the very success of the imperialists in capturing state power, enormously extending it and using it as a direct means of guaranteeing their power, was

101

of profound importance in transforming the consciousness of the proletariat. They would be confronted with the inescapable and obvious fact that the imperialist state was nothing more or less than the vehicle of the dictatorship of the magnates of capital. They would, therefore, Hilferding asserted in the militant conclusion of his book, be directly confronted with the task of transforming this dictatorship into the dictatorship of the proletariat.

> Finance capital in its perfected form – is the highest stage of complete economic and political power concentrated in the hands of capitalist oligarchies. It consummates the dictatorship of the magnates of capital ... In the mighty confrontation of opposed interests the dictatorship of the magnates of capital will, finally, be transformed into the dictatorship of the proletariat.[55]

Neither Bukharin nor Lenin fully acknowledged their debt to Hilferding in their appraisals of the imperialist state, no doubt because, by 1914, Hilferding had become more moderate in his policies, taking a centrist line on the war. He had, by that fact, ceased to be a revolutionary Marxist as far as Bukharin and Lenin were concerned. Indeed, Lenin now described him as 'the ex-Marxist Hilferding'. Small wonder that the debt to the basic outline of the changed character of the bourgeois state in its imperialist phase, established in 1910 by Hilferding, was unacknowledged by Bukharin in 1916 and by Lenin in 1917. I do not, of course, wish to suggest that Bukharin and Lenin simply laid claim to Hilferding's analysis as their own. In the remainder of this chapter and in Chapter 6, their particular additions to the history of the imperialist state are set out. All that this section sets out to establish is that there is a clear line of filiation on this question from Hilferding to Bukharin to Lenin. Hilferding is not only the fountain-head of subsequent *economic analyses of imperialism* carried out by Marxists, he also first outlined *the implications for political practice* which flowed from those theoretical analyses.

BUKHARIN TOWARDS A THEORY OF THE IMPERIALIST STATE

In his article 'Towards a Theory of the Imperialist State',

Bukharin repeats many of the points of his earlier indictment of the bourgeois state (which Lenin had not, in 1914, dissented from). What is new about his analysis is his attempt to present an integrated sociological and historical justification for his conviction that revolutionary socialists must concentrate all their energies on destroying this predatory force which threatened to absorb into itself all the spheres of economic political and social life which had hitherto enjoyed a certain autonomy. The process of *étatisation (ogosudarstvlenie)*, the swallowing up of every aspect of social life by the militarist state was, Bukharin repeatedly insisted, already well advanced.

A huge role in this growth of the budget is, of course, played by militarism which appears as one of the aspects of imperialist politics which, in its turn necessarily follows from the specific structure of finance capital. But not simply militarism in the narrow sense of the word. As a consequence of it there appears the growth of state intervention in every branch of social life, beginning with the sphere of production and ending with the highest form of ideological creativity. If the pre-imperialist period, the period of liberalism which was the political expression of manufacturing capitalism, was characterised by the non-intervention of state power and the laissez faire formula was an article of faith for the leading circles of the bourgeoisie which allowed 'free play to the economic forces', then our time is characterised by exactly opposite tendencies which has state capitalism as its objective limit, absorbing within the domain of state regulation everyone and everything.[56]

The entire national economy had, Bukharin argued, been militarised, brought under the control of state capitalist trusts and everywhere subjected to the state exercising its power directly, or through its banks,[57] or through the host of quasi-governmental bodies exercising control over whole spheres of production.[58] The first sphere to suffer this drive towards the omnipotence of the state had been what Bukharin described as 'the technico-material framework of the process of circulation: the railroads, telegraph, telephone, underwater cables, and the postal organisation as a whole'.[59] *Etatisation* occurred here earlier than in other spheres for the simple reason that, added to the

103

economic motives, military – strategic demands insisted on their incorporation into the power of the state. Progressively the same rationale was used to justify the further erosion of the autonomy of economic and social life until even the host of voluntary organisations of society became absorbed by the state. In the process of mobilising society behind its predatory objectives

> *the state absorbs into itself a whole series of bourgeois organisations.*
> In this respect too, the war provided a huge stimulus. Philosophy and medicine, religion and ethics, chemistry and bacteriology – all were 'mobilised' and 'militarised' exactly in the same way as industry and finance.[60]

> Thus there arises the finished form of the contemporary imperialist robber state, an iron organisation, which envelops the living body of society with its tenacious grasping claws. It is – The New Leviathan, beside which the fantasy of Thomas Hobbes seems but a child's plaything.[61]

The theoretical analysis, which substantiated this nightmare vision of an omnipotent state swallowing up every aspect of life, Bukharin had developed in the first part of his article. His argument appeared to be sound enough in Marxist terms in that it proceeded from Engels's own authoritative findings in his *The Origin of the Family Private Property and the State*. Bukharin took Engels's basic thesis – that the state was the product and reflection of class differentiation within society[62] – and extended it.

The state therefore, according to Bukharin, only arose when society became divided into classes. Its whole *raison d'être* was to defend, with the authority of the law and the power of the army and the police, the particular economic interests of the dominant class. The essence of the state was therefore, in Bukharin's view, to be grasped as a relationship among men rather than as a complex of institutions or a set of constitutional arrangements. Those latter, he argued, could be and were, subject to enormous variation according to time and place, but so long as relations of class domination and subordination existed the state would endure. As he later put it:

The state is a specific human organisation. It is in this way the expression not of the technical relationships of man to nature but of the *social* relationship of men among each other, of man to man. It would be entirely wrong to seek the 'essence' of the state in its technical – organisational definitions . . .[63]

It did not, of course, follow that the relationship of ruled to ruler remained constant over time. On the contrary, it altered constantly in character. The smaller the dominant social class, the more it felt itself threatened by the propertyless, the more it would be impelled to strengthen the power and prerogatives of the state to sustain its own domination. It followed, therefore, that in the era of finance capital, in which the tendency towards concentration of capital in the hands of a tiny minority had been carried to its utmost possible extent, the power and extensiveness of the state would attain its maximum extension.

As the economic analysis of *The World Economy of Imperialism* had demonstrated that the continued existence of a class-riven society militated against the development of the productive forces, so Bukharin's political analysis showed how the state itself had become a parasite clogging up the pores of society and stifling all progress. The time had now come – as Engels had earlier insisted it would have to come – when the whole structure of class differentiation would have to be destroyed and along with it the entire structure of the state would have to be consigned to the museum of antiquities.

> We are now rapidly approaching a stage of evolution in production in which the existence of classes has not only ceased to be a necessity, but becomes a positive fetter on production. Hence these classes must fall as inevitably as they once arose. The state must irrevocably fall with them. The society that is to reorganise production on the basis of the free [and equal] association of the producers, will transfer the machinery of the state where it will then belong: into the Museum of Antiquities by the side of the spinning wheel and bronze axe.[64]

Capitalism itself, Bukharin argued, had undergone a series of metamorphoses, it had its own history, it passed in succession through the phases of merchant, manufacturing and, finally, finance capital. Each of these different phases of development

105

embodied differing patterns of social relationships, differing patterns of class differentiation which found their reflection in differing forms of the bourgeois state.

> The foregoing general theses with regard to the class character of the state still does not answer the question of the character of the concrete historical types of state organisation. But economic evolution, which creates a definite form of production relations, also creates at the same time a type of state organisation appropriate to them. The feudàl organisation of the state, for example, differs from the general-capitalist [form]. Moreover, even within the bounds of capitalism, to the extent that capitalism passes in succession through the phases of merchant, manufacturing and, finally, finance capital, it is also possible to trace important changes in its state superstructure. Our epoch, the epoch of finance capital, which both within and between states creates specific relations with a sharply defined historical character, has also given a new shape to state power.[65]

The bourgeois state was, therefore, not an immutable, changeless phenomenon; it had, on the contrary, a concrete historical character which altered according to the phases of class differentiation which occurred over time. The state was not, Bukharin reminded his readers, a power existing independently of society; it was, rather, 'a product of that society at a definite stage of its development'.[66] The apogee of development of capitalism was, of course, finance capital. In this epoch the class differentiation of society had reached its ultimate possible extension. Bukharin's analysis showed how the development of the imperialist state had mirrored this process. It too had been extended to the limits of its power and, like the economic structure it served and bolstered, it had become a monstrous force inhibiting economic and social progress. It took Bukharin's theoretical audacity to insist that, within the logical structure of Marxism, the point at which classes become superfluous to the progress of history signified also the redundancy of the state.

Bukharin's point was that just as the workers' practical experience of the imperialist war had severed the last chain that bound them to the state, so the revolutionary Marxists had to purge themselves of their own dogmatic adherence to the idea of the eternal necessity of the state. It was imperative and urgent that they should relearn the essential point of the teaching of Marx and Engels on the state which had become over-simplified and grossly distorted. In their anxiety to distinguish their position from that of the anarchists, Bukharin maintained, social democrats had too glibly insisted that they stood for the preservation and utilisation of the state machine whereas their anarchist opponents stood for its destruction. This line of argument had been elevated to the status of a dogma and for decades it had gone unnoticed that Marx and Engels had repeatedly insisted that the state would cease to have a role to play as soon as class differentiation was done away with.

> The distinction between the Marxists and anarchists is not at all that the Marxists are statists and the anarchists anti-statists, as many assert. The real difference in their views on the structure of the future consists in the following, that for the socialists social economy flows out of the tendency towards concentration and centralisation occurring as essential concomitants of the development of the productive forces, it is a completely technical and centralised economy just as the economic utopia of the anarchist-decentralisers turns us back to pre-capitalist forms and renders any sort of economic progress impossible. Only in the transitional moment of the dictatorship of the proletariat will the state form of power be preserved, because that is the form of class domination where the dominating class is the proletariat. With the disappearance of the proletarian dictatorship there disappears also the final form of existence of the state.[67]

There could be no doubting that Bukharin's logic was impeccable. His account of the genesis of the state as a product of the class differentiation of society – an aspect of man's alienation – was a central axiom of Marx's and Engels's teaching on the state. What Bukharin did was to trace how, within the historical epoch of capitalism, the progress of class differentiation went through phases of development and this phasal progress was therefore mirrored in differing forms of the bourgeois state. Given that finance capital represented the apogee of the development of class polarisation in which the continued existence of classes rendered the further development of the productive forces impossible, it followed that the eminently social *form* of production which monopoly capitalism had created would have to be complemented by social *ownership* of the productive forces. Class differentiation had served its purpose in history, it had become not only redundant but actually malignant. It followed, therefore, that the imperialist state, which directly reflected this final phase of class differentiation of society, had likewise become a positively retrogressive institution. The final form of the capitalist state would necessarily disappear when the perfected form of class differentiation on which it was based was overthrown.

Bukharin not only had logic on his side, he also had the direct authority of Marx and Engels behind him. He brought back to life some long-forgotten quotations from their writings which exhibited their animosity to the state as such and which clearly prescribed the withering away of the state in socialist society.[68] Bukharin's argument was that it was precisely this Marxist revolutionary attitude towards the state which the latter-day social democrats had preferred to ignore. Captivated as they were by electoral politics and the implicit notion that they would fall heir to the power of the bourgeois state at its moment of collapse, it was small wonder that they had conveniently forgotten the teaching of Marx and Engels. In the situation where social democrats had actually come to the assistance of the bourgeois state in its hour of greatest peril – with the outbreak of the world war – the need to ignore the revolutionary hostility of Marx and Engels towards the bourgeois state became even more pronounced. Many of them had indeed so inverted Marxist teaching that they now represented the etatisation of society by the imperialist state as some form of 'state socialism'.[69] The social democrats, in Bukharin's view had, in the course of the war, meekly assigned themselves to the role of a mere appendage of the imperialist state. Even the proletariat, it seemed, was threatened by absorption into its all-embracing apparatus of power.

Theoretically there are two possible alternatives: either the workers' movement, in the same way as all the organisations of the bourgeoisie, becomes an organisation of the universal state and converts itself into a mere appendage of the state apparatus, or it outgrows the limitations of the state and blows it up from the inside, organising its own state power (dictatorship). The first road along which the cowardly social-democrats have travelled, the Guesdes, the Plekhanovs, the Scheidemanns, the Hendersons, the Brantings and similar company, is the path of converting the revolutionary party of the proletariat into a servile mechanism of the imperialist state, into its 'labour department', the second road – this is the road of Liebknecht, Hogland, MacLean and Muranov and other comrades, is the path of revolutionary social-democracy.[70]

This path, Bukharin goes on to explain, seeks to free the proletariat from its national and imperialist politics and to teach it to concentrate 'its principled hostility to state power'.[71]

CHAPTER 6

The State and Revolution

Lenin's starting point in beginning his re-evaluation of the proper attitude of Marxists towards the state was not the expressly theoretical and logical progression of argument which seems to have inspired Bukharin. Bukharin, as we have seen, proceeded from first principles to establish a kind of historical sociology of the state. The state, he argued, was a product and reflection of the degree of class differentiation within society. When class differentiation reached its ultimate extensiveness and, by that very fact, inhibited the further development of the productive forces, it would have to be done away with and along with it the state too would perish. Lenin, by contrast, began by seeking the solution to an immediate and pressing practical need. He had argued, as we saw in the previous chapter, that the world was teetering on the brink of disaster. Many countries, Russia included, had indeed slipped over the edge and were falling at appalling speed into economic ruination.

The response of the bourgeoisie to this imminent and actual crisis was to place an ever-greater reliance on state power, to organise and direct the entire economic life of society through the state's control over the banks and through them its control over the trusts and cartels. Lenin concluded, following Bukharin, that capitalism in the course of the war had evolved into state monopoly capitalism. This was the last desperate stand of finance capital to regulate production according to plan and, more importantly, to guarantee its profits even in the midst of the deepening crisis.[1]

The very mechanisms which state monopoly capitalism had devised to protect its own narrow interests – the omnipotent role of the banks, the nationalisation of the communications structure, the interlocking of the state with the banks, cartels and trusts, the introduction of universal labour conscription – all of these were, Lenin argued, double-edged weapons. They could continue to be used for the purposes for which they were perfected, that is the defence of monopoly profits. Or they could be transferred into the hands of the organs of popular self-administration which the revolution would create. If they continued to operate under the aegis of the imperialist state, then only the interests of the capitalists would be served and the decline into disaster was inevitable. Only if these mechanisms of control were taken over by the masses themselves, acting through new popular revolutionary agencies of power and directed towards the welfare of the masses and not to the profits of the few, only in this way could catastrophe be averted.

What now emerged from Lenin's analysis was the conclusion that no salvation from ruination was conceivable so long as the imperialist state maintained its stranglehold over the economic life of society. New forms of administration which would unleash and encourage popular initiative were needed. The imperialist state, resting as it did on its coercive apparatus of standing army and police to guarantee the servility and passivity of the masses, could not possibly be the agency of regeneration. Only the organisations of the masses themselves, organisations such as the workers' militia and workers' and soldiers' soviets which had been spontaneously produced by the February Revolution in Russia, could, in Lenin's view, provide a solution to the crisis.

The February Revolution which finally overthrew the Tsar had taken all the emigré Russian Marxists completely by surprise. Neither the Bolsheviks nor the majority 'internationalist' Mensheviks had taken any prominent role in it. It had rather been the product of a near universal disgust at the clear ineptitude of the Tsar and his administration in conducting the war, at the scandalous powers of Rasputin, at the 'German' Empress in intervening in affairs of state and, especially, at the failure of the régime to feed the urban population. It was the Workers Group of the War Industries Committees which emerged as the organising centre of worker unrest. This group, rejected by both Bolsheviks and internationalist Mensheviks alike because of its collaboration with liberals and other patriots in helping to boost production, was the principal inspiration behind the formation of the Petrograd Soviet which convened for the first time on 25 February.

The situation which emerged after the abdication of the Tsar on 28 February was that Russia had two potential centres of power – the Soviet and the newly-born Provisional Government existing in uneasy alliance one with another. From the outset, the Petrograd Soviet disclaimed any intention of becoming the government. It was, indeed, largely at the prompting of Kerensky and Chkheidze, prominent members of the Soviet, that the Duma Committee was itself persuaded to form a Provisional Government and take upon itself the task of governing the country. Nonetheless, the Petrograd Soviet which, by this time, embraced representatives not only of the main industrial plants but also from the principal army units, swiftly made it clear that on the crucial issues of economic policy and the deployment of army units, it intended making full use of the popular authority it enjoyed.

Initially, the relatively inexperienced Bolsheviks on the editorial board of *Pravda* fiercely attacked the new liberal and capitalist Provisional Government, but with the return from exile of the more senior Stalin, Muranov, Kamenev and Sverdlov, *Pravda's* line abruptly changed. More senior they might have been, but it quickly became apparent that the previous editors, especially Molotov and Shlyapnikov, were far more *au fait* with Lenin's own views than the exiles who had lost contact in their years in Siberia. Stalin and Kamenev now urged a rapprochement between the left Mensheviks and the Bolsheviks and tentative support for the Provisional Government on the grounds that the old defeatist line had lapsed with the advent of a popular democratic and free government. The workers, they argued, now had a genuine interest in preserving their revolutionary gains against the threat of a German invasion.

Part of Lenin's object in writing *State and Revolution* was undoubtedly to break the widespread support these notions clearly had, not only amongst the revolutionary democracy in general, but amongst large sections of the Bolsheviks too. His immediate practical objective was to show the Bolsheviks that no lasting revolutionary gains could be achieved by working side by side with the Provisional Government. His concern was to demonstrate that the whole structure of the bourgeois state machine had to be destroyed. It could not be built upon, adapted or transmuted in any way into an agency of socialist advance; it would have to be smashed. Far from encouraging the self-denying ordinance of the Executive Committee of the Soviets by endorsing the governmental authority of the Provisional Government, the Bolsheviks would have to agitate for its overthrow and to press the reluctant Soviets into assuming all power in Russia.

The February Revolution had therefore produced, in embryonic form, the organs of popular self-government which, by asserting their power over the simplified mechanisms of economic control which state capitalism had introduced, could revivify the economic life of society and lead Russia on to the path of socialism. This was, however, only a potential. To realise this potential the coercive power of state capitalism would have to be smashed, for the capitalists would not voluntarily relinquish the very structures which alone guaranteed their profits. Furthermore, Lenin argued, unless the power of the police and standing army was broken the embryonic forms of popular self-administration would inevitably fall prey to the counter-revolution.

The Provisional Government, Lenin argued, was a capitalist government. It was a government bent on guaranteeing profits to the bourgeoisie and protecting the state capitalist complex of economic domination. It was a government pledged to the continuation of the imperialist war and bent upon putting down any opposition to the war. It could not therefore tolerate for long the existence of popular organs of self-government which threatened all of these goals. In Lenin's perspective there were, therefore, two alternatives. Either the Provisional Government, sustained by a false patriotism and an inadequate development of class consciousness, continued the war, accelerated the slide to economic catastrophe and preserved the coercive power available to the ruling classes in the guise of a parliamentary democracy; or the working class and poor peasants would take power, end the war, galvanise popular initiative to restore the economy through new institutions, and establish via the Soviets a state form of the commune type through which they might inaugurate a world revolution.[2]

It is already clear that Lenin's analysis of the state had proceeded far beyond Bukharin's. Unlike Bukharin, Lenin was not merely a theorist; he was the leader of a political party as well.

113

Whereas Bukharin could rest content with the theoretical adequacy of his proposition that the time had now arrived at which the bourgeois state had outlived its purpose in history, Lenin was obliged to explore the concrete forms of association which might replace the state and guide society in the direction of socialism. He was obliged above all to examine the significance of the Soviets and their relation to the commune form which Marx had asserted was destined to replace the parasitic bourgeois state.

That Bukharin's analysis of the nature of the imperialist state had a huge influence on Lenin cannot seriously be doubted. Lenin's Preface to the first edition of *State and Revolution* took up precisely the themes we have noted above. 'The question of the state,' Lenin insisted, 'is now acquiring particular importance both in theory and in practical politics.'[3] The practical importance of the issue had been raised in high relief (exactly as Bukharin had maintained) by the treachery of the opportunist and chauvinist social democrats coming to the aid of their states in the war-time crises. 'The base, servile adaptation of the "leaders of Socialism" to the interests not only of "their" national bourgeoisie but of "their" state'[4] was precisely the canker which Lenin's book sought to remove. Lenin was quite explicit about the immediate practical political objective of his book, it was to wage war 'against opportunist prejudices concerning the "state" '.[5]

In this Preface, as in the whole course of the book, Lenin quite clearly follows Bukharin not merely in his emphasis upon the changed character of the bourgeois state in the epoch of imperialism but even in the terminology he now employed to describe this metamorphosis.

> The imperialist war has immensely accelerated and intensified the process of transformation of monopoly capitalism into state-monopoly capitalism. The monstrous oppression of the working people by the state, which is merging more and more with the all-powerful capitalist associations, is becoming increasingly monstrous. The advanced countries – we mean their hinterland – are becoming convict prisons for the workers.[6]

Constantly throughout *State and Revolution*, Lenin returns to Bukharin's central thesis that the state, in its imperialist form, had become a monstrous predator threatening to swallow up social life in its entirety:

> The turn towards imperialism – meaning the complete domination of the trusts, the omnipotence of the big banks, a grand-scale colonial policy, and so forth . . . has brought the 'swallowing' of all the forces of society by the rapacious state power close to complete catastrophe.[7]

Lenin now emphatically shared Bukharin's conviction that imperialism had given rise to an historically specific form of the bourgeois state, its final perfected form, in which the bureaucracy of the state capitalist trust, bolstered by the swollen military apparatus it had created, exercised untrammelled power. For this very reason, Lenin was led to exactly the same conclusion that Bukharin had earlier arrived at. The survival of the brutal and oppressive state in its imperialist form threatened war upon war and threatened too to absorb or vanquish the proletarian movement itself. In this process, of course, the servile social democrats, who prettified state monopoly capitalism by calling it 'state socialism',[8] acted the role of pliant accomplices of the imperialist state. Against them, Lenin now threw in his hand with Bukharin. The imperative to revolt, to rouse the masses to heroic action to smash the state, was directly derived from this analysis of imperialism and its state form. Either social democrats would aid and abet the process of absorption of the proletarian movement into the consolidated 'unity' of the state – capitalist trust or they would bend every effort towards the destruction of it.

> Imperialism – the era of bank capital, the era of gigantic capitalist monopolies, of the development of monopoly capitalism into state-monopoly capitalism – has clearly shown an extraordinary strengthening of the 'state machine' and an unprecedented growth in its bureaucratic and military apparatus in connection with the intensification of repressive measures against the proletariat both in the monarchical and in the freest, republican countries.
>
> World history is now undoubtedly leading, on an incomparably larger scale than in 1852, to the 'concentration of all the forces' of the proletarian revolution on the 'destruction' of the state machine.[9]

Lenin's reference to 1852 and the subsequent quote clearly shows that he had been doing his homework on the Marxian analysis of the state. It was indeed Marx's analysis of the genesis and consolidation of the regime of Louis Bonaparte which appeared to give him a warrant in Marx's own texts for adopting Bukharin's slogan – smash the bourgeois state. Marx's analysis was, very briefly, that the class equilibrium which followed the revolution of 1848 had been exploited by Bonaparte and had allowed him to establish a huge executive which appeared to be independent of class support. In 1848 the workers had gone to the barricades and brought down the monarchy. The fruits of their struggle were, however, appropriated not by themselves but by the petty bourgeoisie which swiftly turned its savage hatred against the proletariat in the slaughter of the July Days. In its turn, the petty bourgeoisie found itself defenceless and without friends when the financiers and bankers moved against them, and the bankers themselves, to guarantee order, installed their tame dictator Louis Bonaparte. Once installed however Bonaparte, by careful balancing of one class against another, by flattering the army and building up a vast bureaucratic administrative structure, was able to establish himself independent of any firm class support. In this, the final perfected form of the bourgeois state, according to Marx, all its parasitic oppressive and reactionary attributes were grotesquely developed. Lenin notes approvingly Marx's account of how Bonaparte's imperial regime had hugely extended the power of the bureaucracy and the standing army in order to attempt to hold in check the internal antagonisms of French society. The end result had been the stultification of all social life for the parasitic executive succeeded in choking all the vital pores of French society.[10] Marx's conclusion, Lenin notes, was that

> This course of events compels the revolution '*to concentrate all its forces of destruction*' against the state power, and to set itself the aim, not of improving the state machine, but of *smashing and destroying* it.[11]

It seems clear that Lenin's new-found preparedness to support Bukharin's position *vis-à-vis* the smashing of the existing state stemmed directly from his reading of Marx. His read-

116

ing of Marx's accounts of Louis Bonaparte's imperial regime and of the Paris Commune finally convinced him that if Marx and the Communards had thought the time was ripe to proceed with the destruction of the swollen empire state of Louis Bonaparte, how much more apposite were their conclusions in the epoch of the imperialist state proper.[12]

Bukharin's conclusion that the bourgeois state had, in the epoch of imperialism, become a dangerous anachronism which needed to be smashed was based, as we have seen, on a brilliant extrapolation from his own theory of imperialism and his observations on the character of the war-time state in the belligerent countries. It was admittedly supported by texts, all drawn from Engels's *Origin of the Family Private Property and the State*, which pointedly reminded Marxists of the fact that according to Marxism there could come a day when the state, as an instrument of class oppression, would have to be consigned to the museum of antiquities. These texts were, however, couched in terms of the broadest historical generality. Even the most revisionist social democrats might accept them as statements of ultimate intent, as an integral part of the beautiful distant vista of the realm of harmony. The problems which Bukharin did not answer and the problems which Lenin took as central in *The State and Revolution* were, in the first place, was there guidance in the writings of Marx and Engels for deciding the point at which the state could and should be dispensed with and, secondly, was there any firm advice on the form of association with which to replace it? It is in a way astonishing that Bukharin made little attempt to deal with these problems and that may have partly accounted for Lenin's initial reluctance to accept his principal conclusion. It was Lenin who found, in Marx's *Eighteenth Brumaire*, guidance on the first problem and, in *The Civil War in France*, advice on the second.

It was the resolution of the second problem that was crucial to Lenin. For him it was of little avail to canvass Bukharin's destructive slogan 'smash the bourgeois state' unless and until revolutionary socialists had some positive ideas on the forms of social, political and economic organisation which were to take its place. On these questions, on the problem of the positive content of the socialist revolution, Bukharin had contributed next to nothing. It was entirely characteristic of Lenin before committing himself to a revolutionary assault against the existing state, he felt obliged to demonstrate:

(i)   That the general outlines of these forms of socialist organisation had been established by Marx in his account of the Paris Commune.

(ii) That the concrete organisational forms which Marx had outlined were mirrored in the soviets.

(iii) That not only were the organisational foci for the reintegration of public functions with the whole of society to hand in Russia, the feasibility of such a reintegration was assured by the simplified economic/administrative mechanisms which imperialism itself had produced.

The originality of Lenin's *The State and Revolution* lies principally in his integration of these three features which we must now examine in more detail.

(i) AND (ii) THE COMMUNE AND THE SOVIETS

It is clear that already by April 1917, in his famous theses on 'The Tasks of the Proletariat in the Present Revolution', Lenin had digested and become a convert to Marx's account of the commune and it is equally clear that he was already beginning to graft the features characteristic of the commune on to the soviets. He insisted that a return to a parliamentary republic would be a most retrograde step, that the proletariat must press instead for a republic of Soviets and for the

> Abolition of the police, the army and the bureaucracy.
>   The salaries of all officials, all of whom are elective and displaceable at any time, not to exceed the average wage of a competent worker.[13]

As to Party tasks, the order in which Lenin sets them is particularly instructive for those who would have us believe that he was pre-eminently a practical man:

(a) Immediate convocation of a Party congress;

(b) Alteration of the Party Programme, mainly

(1) On the question of imperialism and the imperialist war.
(2) On our attitude towards the State and *our* demand for a 'commune state'.[14]

In his 'Notes in Defence of the April Theses', Lenin for the first time makes explicit his identification of the commune with the soviets:

> We must ably, carefully, clear people's minds and lead the proletariat and poor peasants *forward*, away from 'dual power' *towards the full power* of the Soviets of Workers' Deputies, and this is the commune in Marx's sense, in the sense of the experience of 1871.[15]

In fact, according to Lenin, the commune form existed not merely as a potential in Russia but in such places as Petrograd it had become a living reality 'because *there is no* police, *no* army standing apart from the people, *no* officialdom standing all-powerful *above* the people'.[16]

Throughout the spring and summer of 1917, when Lenin was preparing *State and Revolution*, article after article repeats his insistence that only a state of the commune type could possibly deliver Russia from economic catastrophe and only a state of this type could provide the basis for the socialist transformation of the country. These objectives could, however, only be realised if the soviets brought the situation of dual power to an immediate end. Only if the soviets took over all power in the state could they hope to encourage, direct and train the initiative and spontaneous creativity of the popular masses. Every effort must be bent upon stimulating that chief symptom of every red revolution:

> On the unusually rapid, sudden and abrupt increase in the number of 'ordinary citizens' who begin to participate actively, independently and effectively in political life and in the *organisation of the state*.[17]

On the one hand, they must be patiently propagandised and strengthened in the organisations which expressed their interests and their objectives. On the other hand, the Provisional Government must be ruthlessly criticised at every turn so that the pathetic faith of the masses in 'the government' and 'their unreasoning trust in the capitalists'[18] instilled for generations might at last be broken. If it was not, if the Soviets did not seize all the power which was theirs for the asking, if through inertia or generations of conditioning they allowed the Provisional Government to continue in existence and firmly establish a parliamentary democracy – then the relapse into a restoration of the monarchy would, in Lenin's view, be unavoidable. The Russian Revolution, Lenin firmly believed, would issue either in a victory for the reaction or in the establishment of a thoroughgoing socialist democracy exercised through a commune state.

The destruction of the standing army and the police and the reintegration of their functions with society at large was not merely a doctrinal article of faith enjoined upon proponents of the commune. It was at the same time a pre-eminently practical objective of the utmost importance. It was vital to Lenin's objective that the coercive, military power of the Provisional Government should be comprehensively eroded for only in this way was it possible to prevent the slide from reaction to restoration. The whole object of the commune was to take power-coercive, administrative and economic out of the hands of the state and place it in the hands of the armed people:

> It is quite easy (as history proves) to revert from a parliamentary bourgeois republic to a monarchy, for all the machinery of oppression – the army, the police, and the bureaucracy – is left intact. The Commune and the Soviets *smash* that machinery and do away with it.
>
> The parliamentary republic hampers and stifles the independent political life of the *masses*, their direct participation in the *democratic* organisation of the life of the state from the bottom up. The opposite is the case with the Soviets.
>
> The latter reproduce the type of state which was being evolved by the Paris Commune and which Marx described as 'the political form at last discovered under which to work out the economic emancipation of labour.'[19]

It is hardly accidental that the main agency which he concentrates upon as embodying the heart and soul of the commune is the people's militia. The functions of the militia, in Lenin's account, were manifold and, we might add, monumental. The militia becomes, in Lenin's account, the coercive, executive and organising arm of the Soviet/commune state. In and through it the public functions arrogated by the state become the property of the people in arms.

> Democracy must be *built* at once, from below, through the initiative of the masses themselves, through their effective participation *in all* fields of state activity without 'supervision' from above, without the bureaucracy.
>
> Replacement of the police, the bureaucracy, and the standing army by the universal arming of the whole people, by a universal *militia* of the entire people, women included, is a practical job that can and should be tackled immediately. The more initiative, variety, daring and creativeness the masses contribute to this, the better . . .
>
> Our proposals are:
> – not to allow the restoration of the police;
> – not to allow the restoration of the absolute powers of officials who, in effect, are undisplaceable and who belong to the landowner or capitalist class;
> – not to allow the restoration of a standing army separate from the people, for such an army is the surest guarantee that attempts of all kinds will be made to stamp out freedom and restore the monarchy;
> – to teach the people, down to the very bottom, the art of government not only in theory but in practice, by beginning to make immediate use everywhere of the experience of the masses.
>
> Democracy from below, democracy without an officialdom, without a police, without a standing army; voluntary social duty guaranteed by a *militia* formed from a universally armed people – this is a guarantee of freedom which no tsars, no swash-buckling generals and no capitalists can take away.[20]

It was the militia which was to take over the functions of officials and deputies of 'all and every kind'.[21] It was, moreover, to take on tasks immeasurably larger than any attempted by the old state apparatus. It was to become, in Lenin's plan, the organising and enforcement agency of universal labour-service;[22] in addition, it was to enforce workers' control over the whole of the productive and distributive processes. 'A people's militia would mean that control (over factories, dwellings, the distribution of products, etc.) would be *real* and not merely on paper.'[23] As far as the economic crisis was concerned, Lenin clearly believed that only the enthusiasm and popular initiative which a people's militia alone could harness, only an equitable pattern of distribution which it alone could supervise, would be capable of arresting the slide into ruin:

> I 'build' *only* on this, *exclusively* on this – that the workers, soldiers and peasants will deal better than the officials, better than the police, with the difficult, *practical* problems of producing more grain, distributing it better and keeping the soliders better supplied etc. etc.[24]

Marx's whole conception of the commune form was, as we have seen, extremely decentralised, even the smallest country hamlet was to organise itself as an autonomous unit – a fact which Marx (and Bakunin!) noted did not preclude communes compacting together to engage in common tasks or meet a common danger. The initiative in the scheme was always from the bottom upwards, from the periphery to the centre. Lenin's plan at this time was every bit as decentralist and equally emphatic on the proposition that the initiative and autonomy of local organs of power had to be the decisive characteristic of the commune form. 'A commune,' he insisted, 'means complete self-government, the absence of any supervision from above.'[25] It meant that 'All power in the state from the bottom up, from the remotest little village to every street of Petrograd, must belong to the Soviets of Workers', Soldiers', Agricultural Labourers', Peasants' and other deputies'.[26] It meant an end to bossing, an end to the ancestral relation between those whose profession it was to direct and those whose lot it was to be directed:

> Officials 'appointed' from above to 'direct' the local population have always been a sure step towards the restoration of the monarchy, in the same way as the standing army and the police . . . The introduction of 'appointed' officials should not be tolerated. Only such bodies in the local areas should be

recognised as have been set up by the people themselves.

The idea of 'direction' by officials 'appointed' from above is essentially false and undemocratic, it is Caesarism, Blanquist *adventurism*.[27]

This was, of course, entirely consonant with Lenin's view of the essential function of the commune which was precisely to train the mass of the people themselves to undertake all the coercive and administrative functions hitherto alienated to the state: 'to teach the people, down to the very bottom, the art of government, not only in theory but in practice, by beginning to make use everywhere of the experience of the masses.'[28] The commune was in this sense a kind of re-creation of the idealised Athenian *polis* in which all would participate in public deliberations and all would play their part in the carrying out of public functions. For this to be possible, the units of government clearly had to be comparatively small. The educative role of the commune in inducting the whole mass of the people into the arts of governing made it, in Lenin's view, infinitely more democratic than the régime of parliamentary democracy:[29]

Not the police, not the bureaucracy, who are unanswerable to the people and placed above the people, not the standing army, separated from the people, but *the people themselves, universally armed* and united in the Soviets, must run the state . . . get together, unite, organise, yourselves, trusting no one, depending only on your own intelligence and experience . . .[30]

(iii) THE COMMUNE STATE AND IMPERIALISM

Repeatedly Lenin worked upon the theme of mass participation in government through the Soviets and through the militia. 'We need,' he asserted, '*not only* representation along democratic lines, but the building of the entire state administration from the bottom up by the masses themselves, their effective participation in all of life's steps, their active role in the administration.'[31] Here is the heroic activist in Lenin, the promethean conception of man as an actor forging his own destiny and asserting his control over his environment. It is, of course, exactly the vision of man which Marx had espoused in the 1844 Manuscripts – a vision of man which is logically required by the ideal of overcoming alienation in which the transcendence of the state played so large a part. It is the conception of man enclosed in Lenin's ringing words which appear as the prefatory text to this volume:

> But we are out to rebuild the world . . .
> Yet we are afraid of our own selves. We are loth to cast off the 'dear old' soiled shirt . . .
> But it is time to cast off the soiled shirt and to put on clean linen.[32]

It was precisely this theme of the desirability and necessity of inducting the mass of the people into the arts of government which Lenin elaborated in *The State and Revolution*. What was new to his analysis in this work was his concern to demonstrate this to be not only desirable and necessary but also practicable. It was, in any case, the only available solution to the mounting economic catastrophe. The militaristic state capitalist trust, that final perfected form of the bourgeois state, had proven itself woefully inadequate. The very mechanisms which it had devised in its last desperate stand to protect the narrow interests of the imperialist bourgeoisie – the omnipotent role of the banks, the nationalisation of the communications structure, the interlocking of the state with the banks, cartels and trusts, the introduction of universal labour conscription – all of these were, Lenin argued, double-edged weapons. They could continue to be used for the purposes for which they had been perfected, that is the subjection of the mass of the people and the defence of monopoly profits. Or they could be transferred to the hands of the organs of popular self-administration which the revolution had called forth. It was precisely the enormous simplifications of the productive and distributive mechanisms, the simplification of the entire business of administration, which capitalism in its imperialist phase had produced, which at last made feasible the ideal of popular self-administration.

Lenin's argument was that the whole technological and administrative structure of socialism had been laid and fully developed during the epoch of finance capital. It was there ready-made and available for the Soviets to take over and direct in the interests of the mass of the people:

Capitalism differs from the old, pre-capitalist systems of economy in having created the closest inter-connection and interdependence of the various branches of the economy. Were this not so, incidentally, no steps towards socialism would be feasible. Modern capitalism, under which the banks dominate production, has carried this interdependence of the various branches of the economy to the utmost.[33]

In place of the great mass of petty producers competing one with another in the anarchy of the market, finance capital had produced the monopolistic trust which, as we have seen, eliminated duplication of effort and resources, concentrated production in huge rationalised units and planned production according to carefully calculated projections of the likely market. Finance capital had thereby enormously simplified the problem of the transfer of the productive forces from private to public control. It had, moreover, created simplified administrative structures through which popular control over the whole business of production and distribution could at last be realised.

We the workers, shall organise large-scale production on the basis of what capitalism has already created, relying on our own experience as workers, establishing strict, iron discipline backed up by the state power of the armed workers. We shall reduce the role of state officials to that of simply carrying out our instructions as responsible, revocable, modestly paid 'foremen and accountants' . . . This is *our* proletarian task, this is what we can and must *start* with in accomplishing the proletarian revolution. Such a beginning, on the basis of large-scale production, will of itself lead to the gradual 'withering away' of all bureaucracy, to the gradual creation of an order . . . bearing no similarity to wage slavery – an order under which the functions of control and accounting, becoming more and more simple, will be performed by each in turn, will then become a habit and will finally die out as the *special* functions of a special section of the population.[34]

The instruments of control and accounting through which the mass was to reappropriate the functions hitherto arrogated to the bureaucracy and the management boards of the trusts lay

125

immediately to hand; they had of necessity been created by capitalism itself in its imperialist phase. The tasks of control and accountancy had been so simplified that they could now be performed by any average worker:

> Capitalist culture has *created* large-scale production, factories, railways, the postal service, telephones, etc., and *on this basis* the great majority of the functions of the old 'state power' have been so simplified and can be reduced to such exceedingly simple operations of registration, filing and checking that they can be easily performed for ordinary 'workmen's wages,' and that these functions can (and must) be stripped of every semblance of 'official grandeur'.[35]

There can be no doubt that Lenin greatly exaggerated the ease with which these large organisations could be taken over by the armed workers. There is no doubt either that he had an equally exaggerated view of the simplicity of the organisational structures through which they operated. His advent to power swiftly disabused him of the utopian vision of an immediate transition to popular participation in and control over what he discovered to be exceedingly complex structures. Part of the measure of the post-revolutionary disillusionment of the industrial workers was precisely the discrepancy between the ideal of mass participation and control of the state and of industry, which Lenin was pressing at this time on the basis of his extravagant appraisal of the degree of simplicity which finance capitalism had itself introduced, and the actual complexity of the state, administrative and economic control mechanisms which began to dawn on Lenin after the seizure of power. This complexity, coupled with the comparatively low educational and cultural attainments of the average Russian worker, appeared to necessitate and justify the swift re-introduction of specialists and one-man management. The point to be made here is that the subsequent disillusion was bound to be proportionate to the extravagance of Lenin's pre-revolutionary appraisals and the enormous expectations he expressly sought to arouse.

Lenin's projections were, in a way, intensely theoretical or dialectical. Throughout his writings in the period 1916–17 one encounters the central theme that capitalism in its imperialist phase not only carried the parasitism of the state machine to its highest possible extent, it also simultaneously created the conditions for the transcendence of the state as such. It was, for Lenin, a dialectical act of faith that, locked within imperialism, existing in inverted form admittedly, were the very structures through which capitalism and the state were to be transcended. Capitalism was its own gravedigger not only in the sense that it necessarily produced the class which was to destroy it but in the additional sense that it found itself obliged to perfect the very mechanisms of administrative and economic control which the proletariat could take over as ready-made instruments for the realisation of socialism:

> A witty German Social-Democrat of the seventies of the last century called the *postal service* an example of the socialist economic system. This is very true. At present the postal service is a business organised on the lines of a state-*capitalist* monopoly. Imperialism is gradually transforming all trusts into organisations of a similar type, in which, standing over the 'common' people, who are overworked and starved, one has the same bourgeois bureaucracy. But the mechanism of social management is here already to hand. Once we have overthrown the capitalists, crushed the resistance of these exploiters with the iron hand of the armed workers, and smashed the bureaucratic machine of the modern state, we shall have a splendidly equipped mechanism, freed from the 'parasite', a mechanism which can very well be set going by the united workers themselves who will hire technicians and accountants, and pay them *all*, as indeed *all* 'state' officials in general, workmen's wages . . .
>
> To organise the *whole* economy on the lines of the postal service . . . this is our immediate aim. This is the state and this is the economic foundation we need.[36]

The situation that Lenin was aspiring to, the situation that he clearly considered was more or less immediately realisable, was the transcendence not only of the state *qua* separate bodies of armed men, but of the state *qua* separate bodies of men endowed with rights to decide upon and to see to the implementation of public policy. His proposals were even more radical for he

127

considered that the alienation of decision-making and controlling functions within the entire economic substructure of society could now be overcome by a thoroughgoing democratisation of the administrative mechanisms which bourgeois society in its imperialist phase had finally produced. 'Power to the Soviets means the complete transfer of the country's administration and economic control into the hands of the workers and peasants.'[37] All of this emphatically represented a qualitative transformation or transcendence of democracy and even in some respects of the state itself. The extent to which, within the logic of Marxism, it was proper to call the resultant pattern of social organisation a 'state' at all will concern us later. For the moment, let us notice the extreme radicalism of Lenin's proposals to reintegrate all public functions with the people in arms and how intimately these proposals derived from his analysis of finance capitalism or imperialism:

> ... *only* socialism will be the beginning of a rapid, genuine, truly mass forward movement, embracing first the *majority* and then the whole of the population, in all spheres of public and private life.
>
> Democracy is a form of the state, one of its varieties. Consequently, like every state, it represents, on the one hand, the organised, systematic use of force against persons; but, on the other hand, it signifies the formal recognition of equality of citizens, the equal right of all to determine the structure of, and to administer, the state. This, in turn, results in the fact that, at a certain stage in the development of democracy, it first welds together the class that wages a revolutionary struggle against capitalism – the proletariat, and enables it to crush, smash to atoms, wipe off the face of the earth the bourgeois, even the republican – bourgeois, state machine, the standing army, the police and the bureaucracy and to substitute for them a *more* democratic state machine, but a state machine nevertheless, in the shape of armed workers who proceed to form a militia involving the entire population.
>
> Here 'quantity turns into quality': *such* a degree of democracy implies overstepping the boundaries of bourgeois society and beginning its socialist reorganisation. If really *all* take part in the administration of the state, capitalism cannot retain its

hold. The development of capitalism, in turn, creates the *preconditions* that *enable* really 'all' to take part in the administration of the state. Some of these preconditions are: universal literacy, which has already been achieved in a number of the most advanced capitalist countries, then the 'training and disciplining' of millions of workers by the huge complex, socialised apparatus of the postal service, railways, big factories, large-scale commerce, banking, etc. etc.

Given these *economic* preconditions, it is quite possible, after the overthrow of the capitalists and the bureaucrats, to proceed immediately, overnight, to replace them in the *control* over production and distribution, in the work of *keeping account* of labour and products, by the armed workers, by the whole of the armed population. . . .

Accounting and control – that is *mainly* what is needed for the 'smooth working', for the proper functioning, of the *first phase* of communist society. *All* citizens are transformed into hired employees of the state, which consists of the armed workers. *All* citizens become employees and workers of a *single* country-wide state 'syndicate'. All that is required is that they should work equally, do their proper share of work, and get equal pay. The accounting and control necessary for this have been *simplified* by capitalism to the utmost and reduced to the extraordinarily simple operations – which any literate person can perform – of supervising and recording, knowledge of the four rules of arithmetic, and issuing appropriate receipts.[38]

It was in his important articles 'The Impending Catastrophe and How to Combat It'[39] and 'Can the Bolsheviks Retain State Power',[40] which Lenin wrote at exactly the same time as the final chapters of *State and Revolution*, that he most fully and explicitly developed the necessary relation between his conception of socialism and the economic base of finance capital or imperialism from which it was but the next step forward.

For socialism is merely the next step forward from state-capitalist monopoly. Or, in other words, socialism is merely state-capitalist monopoly *which is made to serve the interests of the whole people* and has to that extent *ceased* to be capitalist monopoly.

There is no middle course here. The objective process of development is such that it is *impossible* to advance from monopolies (and the war has magnified their number, role and importance tenfold) without advancing towards Socialism . . .

The dialectics of history is such that the war, by extraordinarily expediting the transformation of monopoly capitalism into state-monopoly capitalism, has *thereby* extraordinarily advanced mankind towards socialism.

Imperialist war is the eve of socialist revolution. And this not only because the horrors of the war give rise to proletarian revolt . . . but because state-monopoly capitalism is a complete *material* preparation for socialism, the *threshold* of socialism, a rung on the ladder of history between which and the rung called socialism *there are no intermediate rungs*.[41]

The development of capitalism in its imperialist phase provided, therefore, not merely the occasion and imperative for the socialist revolution, it also established, in Lenin's account, the content of socialist reconstruction.

Lenin's ideas on the nature of the socialist state and its relationship to the structures of state monopoly capitalism were finally drawn together in the most emphatic way in his article *Can the Bolsheviks Retain State Power*, written just a month before the Bolshevik seizure of power. This article is of exceptional importance for it was the last one Lenin wrote prior to the revolution, where he spelt out in some detail the type of state that he felt appropriate for the transition to socialism. The direct continuity between Lenin's economic analysis of imperialism and his conception of the content and mechanisms of socialist construction is immediately apparent in his emphasis upon the role of the big banks. Just as they had been the organisational foci of finance capital so, under the direction of the socialist state, they would be transformed into a single universal agency of accounting and control over the entire system of production and distribution. The single state bank was represented as *the* means of control 'created *not* by us but by capitalism in its military and imperialist stage'.[42] It was indeed, according to Lenin's extraordinary assertion, 'nine-tenths of the socialist apparatus':

Capitalism has created an accounting apparatus in the shape of the banks, syndicates, postal service, consumers' societies, and office employees' unions. Without big banks socialism would be impossible.

The big banks are the 'state apparatus' which we need to bring about socialism, and which we take ready-made from capitalism; our task here is merely to lop off what capitalistically mutilates this excellent apparatus, to make it even bigger, even more democratic, even more comprehensive. Quantity will be transformed into quality. A single State Bank, the biggest of the big, with branches in every rural district, in every factory, will constitute as much as nine-tenths of the socialist apparatus. This will be country-wide book-keeping, country-wide accounting of the production and distribution of goods, this will be, so to speak, something in the nature of the skeleton of socialist society.

We can 'lay hold of' and 'set in motion' this 'state apparatus' (which is not fully a state apparatus under capitalism, but which will be so with us, under socialism) at one stroke, by a single decree, because the actual work of book-keeping, control, registering, accounting and counting is performed by employees, the majority of whom themselves lead a proletarian or semi-proletarian existence.[43]

Even the machinery for obliging the bourgeois specialists to work for the new regime lay ready to hand. It was not enough, Lenin maintained, to terrorise them as the guillotine had done during the French Revolution, their active assistance *'in the service of the new state'* would have to be secured.

And we have the means to do this, The means and instruments for this have been placed in our hands by the capitalist state in the war. These means are the grain monopoly, bread rationing and labour conscription. 'He who does not work neither shall he eat' – this is the fundamental, the first and most important rule the Soviets of Workers Deputies can and will introduce when they become the ruling power.[44]

The imperialist state, once again, furnished the social means of control to ensure that specialists and bourgeois experts were kept firmly accountable for the conscientious performance of the work allotted to them – their alternative was to be deprived of 'bread ration cards or provisions in general'.[45]

Lenin then goes on to give an example of the way in which the proletarian 'state' will run its affairs. We put 'state' in inverted commas since from the example given it is clear that any idea of central direction, 'official sanction' or legal norms in any conventional sense have no bearing upon the issue. The problem cited is that of moving a poor family into a rich man's flat. What will happen, Lenin asserted, is that a squad of the workers' militia containing a nice balance of 'two sailors, two soldiers, two class-conscious workers . . . one intellectual and eight from the poor working people, of whom at least five must be women, domestic servants, unskilled labourers, and so forth'[46] simply arrives and informs the incumbents that they will temporarily 'have to squeeze up a little' to accommodate others, their phone will be shared with ten families and the unemployed members of their family will be set useful tasks. 'The student citizen in our squad will now write out the state order in two copies and you will be kind enough to give us a signed declaration that you will faithfully carry it out.'[47] A 'state order' is of course appropriate here even if it sounds a little strange for, as we have seen, the workers' militia *was* the state. Any squad of the workers' militia, expressly encouraged by Lenin to exercise the maximum initiative to learn from its own experience and not to tolerate direction from above, was itself a law-making body, a self-acting armed vehicle of state power. The whole idea of the state has clearly undergone a profound metamorphosis. The executive and coercive functions of state power, together with the responsibility for regulating production and distribution, are to be devolved upon the whole of the population. In exactly the same way as Lenin's armed squad dealt with the particular housing problem of a poor family, so the entire business of administration, production and distribution is to be reabsorbed by the people in arms. It is worth quoting at length Lenin's last extended reflections on the nature of the socialist state prior to the revolution of 7 November:[48]

> In our opinion, to ease the incredible burdens and miseries of the war and also to heal the terrible wounds the war has inflicted on the people, *revolutionary* democracy is needed,

revolutionary measures of the kind described in the example of
the distribution of housing accommodation in the interests of
the poor. *Exactly the same* procedure must be adopted in both
town and country for the distribution of provisions, clothing,
footwear, etc., in respect of the land in the rural districts, and so
forth. For the administration of the state in *this* spirit we can *at
once set in motion a state* apparatus consisting of ten if not twenty
million people, an apparatus such as no capitalist state has ever
known. We alone can create such an apparatus, for we are sure
of the fullest and devoted sympathy of the vast majority of the
population. We alone can create such an apparatus, because we
have class-conscious workers disciplined by long capitalist
'schooling' (it was not for nothing that we went to learn in the
school of capitalism), workers who are capable of forming a
workers' militia and of *gradually* expanding it (beginning to
expand it at once) into a militia *embracing the whole people*. The
class-conscious workers must lead, but for the work of
administration they can enlist the vast mass of the working and
oppressed people.

It goes without saying that this new apparatus is bound to
make mistakes in taking its first steps. But did not the peasants
make mistakes when they emerged from serfdom and began to
manage their own affairs? Is there any way other than practice
by which the people can learn to govern themselves and to
avoid mistakes? Is there any way other than by proceeding
immediately to genuine self-government by the people? The
chief thing now is to abandon the prejudiced bourgeois-
intellectualist view that only special officials, who by their very
social position are entirely dependent upon capital, can
administer the state.... The chief thing is to imbue the
oppressed and the working people with confidence in their
own strength, to prove to them in practice that they can and
must themselves ensure the *proper*, most strictly regulated and
organised distribution of bread, all kinds of food, milk,
clothing, housing, etc., *in the interests of the poor*. Unless this is
done, Russia *cannot* be saved from collapse and ruin. The
conscientious, bold, universal move to hand over administrative work to proletarians and semi-proletarians, will, however,
rouse such unprecedented revolutionary enthusiasm among
the people, will so multiply the people's forces in combating

distress, that much that seemed impossible to our narrow, old, bureaucratic forces will become possible for the millions, who will *begin to work for themselves* and not for the capitalists, the gentry, the bureaucrats, and not out of fear of punishment.[49] [Emphasis added]

With the writing of *The State and Revolution* and of his other contemporaneous articles dealing with the character of the socialist state, Lenin's thought reached its culminating point. As a structure of ideas it was coherent and complete. *Imperialism the Highest Stage of Capitalism* had shown that capitalism had gone beyond the apogee of its development. It had sunk into decline and would have to be replaced by socialism. Lenin's later writings on the state proceeded to establish the guidelines for immediate socialist practice. Marx's account of the commune was fused with the practice of the Russian Soviets and shown to be viable by pointing to the simplified mechanisms of accountancy and control which the imperialist state had itself created. Not only was the project of reintegrating all the functions of the state with the self-acting groups of the armed population declared to be viable, it was imperative that it should be immediately accomplished. Lenin's views on the commune state were, quite clearly, not intended as abstract projections for a remote 'communist' future. They were, on the contrary, repeatedly insisted upon as the only way to save Russia from immediate ruination, the only way to train the people for socialism, the only organisational forms appropriate to the transitional period of building up a socialist society.

SEMANTIC PROBLEMS: THE COMMUNE, THE STATE AND THE DICTATORSHIP OF THE PROLETARIAT

As was indicated in the previous chapter, there was a large unresolved problem at the very centre of Marx and Engels's recommendations with regard to the state. Part of Lenin's difficulty in *The State and Revolution* stemmed from his self-imposed need to distil a single coherent Marxist account of the state from the very differing characterisations of the commune and the dictatorship of the proletariat.

Lenin begins his reconstruction of the proper Marxist attitude towards the state with the conventional Marxian hypothesis that: 'The state is a product and manifestation of the *irreconcilability* of class antagonisms.'[50] It is pre-eminently a coercive agency comprising 'special bodies of armed men having prisons, etc. at their command'[51] used to defend the interests of a specific class. According to Engels's account, there had been a time when the functions of policing and defending society had been assumed by the entire population organised as an armed force. With the division of society into classes, this arrangement was replaced and the state arrogated these functions to itself and progressively absorbed all the public functions of society. 'This special, public power is necessary because a self-acting armed organisation of the population has become impossible since the split into classes.'[52] There are two things which we might note at this point. In the first place, it is clear that in this account 'the self-acting armed organisation of the population' is emphatically *not* a characterisation of a form of state. On the contrary, here the notion 'state' is only intelligible in terms of its being counterposed to, and declared to be incompatible with, such an arrangement. The state is *special* bodies of armed men, acting separate from the people in arms under the control of a specific class. It is a 'special force' for the suppression of the oppressed class.[53] The second factor to note is that since the state is the product and reflection of class antagonisms within society, it follows that, the more acute and irreconcilable these become, the more the power of the state has to be augmented to hold them in check. This inference was, as we have seen, clear in Marx's account of Louis Bonaparte's regime and developed further by Bukharin in his account of the historical evolution of the state to its final perfected form as the imperialist state. The longer the state survives, the more perfected it becomes as an instrument of ensuring bourgeois 'order' within society; the more it is compelled to arrogate to itself *all* public functions, the greater therefore becomes the imperative to destroy it, for socialism signified for Marx, Bukharin and Lenin, the restoration to society of *all* the functions absorbed by the parasitic state. This, quite clearly, was the substance of Marx's account of the commune and was echoed in Lenin's vision of the role of the soviets and the militia. The objective of Marxists, according to Lenin, was to smash the state:

All previous revolutions perfected the state machine, whereas it must be broken, smashed.

This conclusion is the chief and fundamental point in the Marxist theory of the state.[54]

The words, 'to smash the bureaucratic – military machine' briefly express the principal lesson of Marxism regarding the tasks of the proletariat during the revolution in relation to the state.[55]

The positive content of the alternative social organisation which was to replace the state was of course the commune or Soviet form. In both Marx's and Lenin's account, *the* central feature of this organisational form was that it proceeded immediately to eliminate the standing army and the police. The coercive policing functions of society were absorbed by the people in arms and all officials reduced to responsible, recallable executors of the popular will. Logically, Lenin has to concede, as Marx had, that this form of organisation cannot qualify as a 'state' form since the state, as we have seen, consists of special bodies of armed men standing over the mass of the people.

The Commune, therefore, appears to have replaced the smashed state machine 'only' by fuller democracy: abolition of the standing army; all officials to be elected and subject to recall. But as a matter of fact this 'only' signifies a gigantic replacement of certain institutions by the institutions of a fundamentally different type. This is exactly a case of 'quantity being transformed into quality': democracy, introduced as fully and consistently as is at all conceivable, is transformed from bourgeois into proletarian democracy; from the state (in a special force for the suppression of a particular class) into something which is no longer the state proper.[56]

Lenin was nonetheless constrained for two reasons to refer to the commune or soviet type of organisation as a 'state'. In the first place, there was the conventional need for the Marxists to distinguish their position from that of the anarchists who had, after all, canvassed the slogan 'smash the state' for far longer than the revolutionary Marxists. In the second place, Lenin recognised the obligation, imposed by Engels, of identifying the commune as the dictatorship of the proletariat, and the dictatorship of the proletariat was emphatically a state form in the Marxian account of it. Thus, in April 1917, whilst conceding that 'we Marxists are opposed to *every kind* of state' and that, furthermore, the February Revolution had already established a 'new type of "state" which is not a state in the proper sense of the word', that is 'domination' over the people by contingents of armed men divorced from the people, nonetheless Lenin insisted that the proletariat still needed a 'state' of some sort:

> Our *emergent*, new state is also a state, for we too need contingents of armed men, we too need the *strictest* order, and must *ruthlessly* crush by force all attempts at either a tsarist or a Guchkov-bourgeois counter-revolution.
>
> But our *emergent*, new state is *no longer* a state in the proper sense of the term, for in some parts of Russia these contingents of armed men are *the masses themselves*, the entire people, and not certain privileged persons placed over the people, and divorced from the people, and for all practical purposes undisplaceable.[57]

There is clearly some confusion here. On the one hand, Lenin felt obliged to repeat the old orthodoxy that Marxists needed to utilise a transitional form of the state. On the other, he had to concede that, in terms of Marxian definition, the commune and the soviet forms could not properly be embraced by the term for their principal objective was the transcendence precisely of separate bodies of armed men and irresponsible officials. In the sense that 'the majority of the people *itself* suppresses its oppressors, a "special force" for suppression *is no longer necessary!* In this sense the state *begins to wither away*.'[58] Even Engels, as Lenin noticed, had been obliged to concede that where the power of the standing army and the police has been broken and their functions reappropriated by the mass, it made no sense to talk of the state.

> 'The Commune was no longer a state in the proper sense of the word' – this is the most theoretically important statement Engels makes . . . It had smashed the bourgeois state machine.

137

In place of a *special* coercive force the population itself came on the scene. All this was a departure from the state in the proper sense of the word.[59]

It was for this reason that, in the light of the experience of the commune, Engels 'in his own as well as in Marx's name suggests to the leader of the German workers' party that the word "state" *be struck out of the programme* and replaced by the word "community" '.[60]

In spite of all these admonitions, Lenin returns repeatedly to the task of reconciling the commune, 'community' form of organisation with that of the dictatorship of the proletariat. He insists that, given Marx's characterisation of his system of thought in his 1852 letter to Weydemeyer, where he pointed out that the analysis of history as class struggle was far from unique or original to him but that he had shown 'that the class struggle necessarily leads to the *dictatorship of the proletariat*',[61] therefore Lenin maintained, 'Only he is a Marxist who *extends* the recognition of the class struggle to the recognition of the *dictatorship of the proletariat* . . . This is the touchstone on which the *real* understanding and recognition of Marxism should be tested.'[62]

This was, furthermore, in Lenin's view the particular factor in the revolutionary Marxist account of the state which marked it off both from the gradualist 'revolution on credit' socialism of opportunists like Kautsky and Bernstein, as well as from the anarchist project of moving immediately to the 'abolition of the state'. On the latter distinction Lenin insisted that the revolutionary Marxists still stood for the temporary utilisation of state power.

> We do not at all differ with the anarchists on the question of the abolition of the state as the *aim*. We maintain that, to achieve this aim, we must temporarily make use of the instruments, resources and methods of state power *against* the exploiters, just as the temporary dictatorship of the oppressed class is necessary for the abolition of classes . . . But what is the systematic use of arms by one class against another if not a 'transient form' of state?[63]

Here the semantic problem is raised in high relief. If Lenin, in his efforts to square the commune form with that of the dictatorship of the proletariat, is reduced to maintaining that the state is no more than 'the systematic use of arms by one class against another', then the disagreement with the anarchists would appear to be founded on a very exiguous basis, for the majority of anarchists, certainly of those in Russia, would have had no qualms about the systematic use of arms by the workers to crush bourgeois resistance. They had, ever since Bakunin, accepted the role of stimulating and organising the violent overthrow of the bourgeoisie and all its institutions. The degree of Lenin's uncertainty on this crucial point is demonstrated a little further on in *State and Revolution* where he returned to the theme of preserving 'A special apparatus, a special machine for suppression, the "state" ' as necessary for the suppression of the minority by the majority. He went on:

> ... but *the people* can suppress the exploiters even with a very simple 'machine', without a special apparatus by the simple *organisation of the armed people* ...[64]

Even this attenuated paper-thin distinction between the Marxists and the anarchists could not however be consistently maintained. As we have already noticed, Lenin had elsewhere in *State and Revolution* committed himself to the view that as soon as the coercive power of society was vested in the people at large, in the majority of the population, in a popular militia under the direction of the soviet (or the commune form), at that moment it became superfluous to talk of the state at all for, definitionally, the state entailed separate bodies of armed men standing over and outside of the majority:

> It is still necessary to suppress the bourgeoisie and crush their resistance ... The organ of suppression, however, is here the majority of the population, and not a minority ... And since the majority of the people *itself* suppresses its oppressors, a 'special force' for suppression *is no longer necessary*.[65]

At this point, clearly, Lenin's previous distinction between Marxism and anarchism disappeared entirely. He tried diligently to solve the conundrum, which Engels bequeathed, of reconciling

139

and identifying the commune and the dictatorship of the proletariat. That the effort merely sowed confusion throughout *State and Revolution* should not surprise us.

CONCLUSION

In spite of the recurrent definitional confusion foisted on Lenin by Engels, we are justified in regarding *State and Revolution* as the crowning achievement of Lenin's political thought in the latter period of his life. It was the practical complement to *Imperialism the Highest Stage of Capitalism* and many of its themes were explicitly derived from that theoretical analysis. As Lenin's theory of imperialism demonstrated the necessity and urgency of socialist revolution from an analysis of the economic structure of international finance capital, his theory of the state, set out in numerous articles throughout 1917 and in his *State and Revolution*, sought to establish a coherent set of guidelines which would guide socialists in the practical tasks of establishing a socialist society.

In this Lenin went far beyond anything which Bukharin or, for that matter any Marxist, had hitherto attempted. The seriousness with which he undertook his task, the constant attempt to relate his scholar's knowledge of the utterances of Marx and Engels with the concrete organisational forms that the Russian Revolution had thrown up, gives the lie to those who assert that Lenin was pre-eminently concerned with the tactical manipulation of power. Lenin was, above all else, a doctrinaire politician. On more than one occasion he proudly accepted the accredition 'dogmatist'. He acted only when he was convinced that the objectives he had in view had firm theoretical and practical foundation. It was precisely this profound conviction that he was theoretically right, that his course of action was, in terms of theory, *necessary*, that gave his actions their quality of unquenchable irreconcilable determination.

There was another more immediate sense in which *The State and Revolution* was explicitly intended as a treatise on socialist practice. Its declared objective was to free Marxists from their superstitious, ingrained regard for the existing institutions of state power. It was, in other words, the culminating point of

Lenin's remorseless polemic with all those socialists who had meekly acquiesced to the demands of their national states at the outbreak of war and who had continued to support their national governments during the hostilities. To win such people round to the revolutionary cause, Lenin recognised that it was not enough to present them (as Hobson, Hilferding, Bukharin, and he himself had done) with a withering critique of imperialism as a degenerate economic and political structure. It was not enough to castigate them as traitors to the decisions of the Second International. It would have to be demonstrated that there were alternative, properly socialist structures of organisation available to revolutionary parties through which the transcendence of the existing state could be accomplished. It had to be demonstrated, furthermore, that these alternative structures not only had a warrant in Marx's writings but represented the essence of his positive ideas on the form of organisation at last discovered to work out the economic emancipation of labour. It was Lenin who, in *State and Revolution*, rescued the commune from oblivion. It was he who integrated Marx's account of the commune with the soviet form which the Russian Revolution had created. His object was clear. It was to cut the ground from under the feet of all those timorous Marxists (not least in his own party) who felt that they had no option but to support their existing governments and who considered that no alternative, short of chaos and anarchy, existed which might take the place of their existing states. Such an attitude, Lenin maintained, merely served to augment the power of the imperialist state at this the war-time crisis of its very existence. It served therefore to arrest the advent of socialist revolution which had become imperative if the butchery of war and the slide to economic disaster was to be overcome. It was precisely on this immediate, practical note that Lenin ended *The State and Revolution*:

> The distortion and hushing up of the relation of the proletarian revolution to the state could not but play an immense role at a time when states, which possess a military apparatus expanded as a consequence of imperialist rivalry, have become military monsters which are exterminating millions of people in order to settle the issue as to whether Britain or Germany – this or that finance capital – is to rule the world.[66]

141

CHAPTER 7

The Art of Insurrection

The period from April to October 1917 was the testing time for Lenin. From the outset he knew that the whole fate of the revolution in Russia would be sealed in a matter of months. His prognosis was based upon the same class analysis that he had employed in the revolution of 1905–6. After the eclipse of tsarism, the Cadets would step into the shoes of the autocracy. They would rally all the right-wing forces behind them, the urban bourgeoisie, the bureaucracy and the gentry. They would become the 'Party of Order', striving to placate the moderate petty-bourgeois parties for the time being, even admitting them into the government, in order to isolate the revolutionaries and suppress the organs of proletarian insurgency. Having assumed the mantle of the monarchy and being bound to the interests of international finance capital, the Cadets were obliged to honour the tsarist commitment to the imperialist war using the slogan of the nation in danger to quell resistance to their Provisional Government and attaching the title of traitor to any who challenged their power. In this way they hoped to hide capitalist self-interest under the mask of patriotism and the defence of 'national interest'. The shoes of the Cadets would, in their turn, be filled by the irresolute and wavering parties of the petty-bourgeoisie whose political line, as ever, mirrored the precariousness of their economic situation. These parties, the Mensheviks and the moderate Socialist Revolutionaries, would quickly lose their revolutionary commitment, just as they had done in 1905–6. They were destined to take the place of the Cadets as 'statesmanlike' and 'responsible' opposition parties or even members of a governing coalition, whose self-appointed role it was to scrutinise, advise and, if necessary, criticise the bourgeois government in order to defend the interests of the common people. Lenin's policy, as in 1905, was based upon a profoundly pessimistic scenario. Economic crisis and dislocation would grow, the bourgeois Provisional Government was, he argued, inherently incapable of introducing the radical measures that alone could lead to recovery. The population of the urban centres, and of Russia as a whole, would rapidly reach that point of desperation at which only a radical revolution would satisfy them. The war would continue and the obligations entered into by the autocracy would be honoured because the bourgeoisie was so dependent upon foreign capital. Dislocation of the entire transportation and distributive system was the inevitable outcome of prolonging the war. Defeat would follow defeat at the front and disaffection amongst the soldiery would soon, if properly channelled, swell the forces of revolution. In the countryside, the Provisional Government, bound to the remnants of landlordism and fearful of usurping the prerogatives of the forthcoming Constituent Assembly, would attempt to buy time and stymie the insistent radical demands of peasants. The peasants would not wait however: they would seize the land and give power to those who would guarantee their possession of it. The Provisional Government was, in Lenin's view, doomed. Its whole class composition and objectives made it impossible for it to deal with *any* of the basic problems facing Russia. All those associated with it, its loyal opposition and, subsequently, its fellow members in the coalition government; all would find themselves compromised in the eyes of the people for their chronic inability to act. They would be shown to be incapable of providing bread, peace or land and the Russian people, driven to despair, would eventually cast them aside and give power to those who were prepared for decisive radical action.

Bolshevik strategy must therefore, Lenin insisted, be based upon a prescient awareness of the changing class patterns of the Russian Revolution. The bourgeoisie would move to the right and its place would be taken by the petty-bourgeois parties – the Mensheviks and the Socialist Revolutionaries. Meanwhile the proletariat, the army and a large part of the peasantry, would move sharply to the left and would be looking for a party which would reflect their impatient desire for resolute action, not endless talk. On this objective basis (which was itself a recapitulation of Lenin's analysis of 1905 and of Marx's analysis of 1848) Lenin premissed the Bolshevik strategy of 1917:

We have always condemned, and as Marxists we must condemn, the tactics of those who live 'from hand to mouth' . . . We must constantly test ourselves by a *study* of the chain of political events in their entirety, in their causal connection, in their results . . . .

A new revolution is obviously maturing in the country, a revolution of *other* classes (other than those that carried out the revolution against tsarism) . . .

The revolution now maturing is one of the proletariat and the majority of the peasants, more specifically, of the poor peasants, against the bourgeoisie, against its ally, Anglo-French finance-capital and against its government apparatus headed by the Bonapartist Kerensky.[1]

Tactically, the Bolsheviks must be guided by the complementary slogans 'Down with the Ten Capitalist Ministers' and 'All Power to the Soviets'. The immediate task in hand was to pursue a ruthless and utterly remorseless critique of the Provisional Government and its petty-bourgeois so-called socialist supporters. More positively, the immediate task of the Bolsheviks was to win over the majority of the people to the view that only the soviets could solve the problems of the economy, of the land and of peace which so desperately needed resolution.

So long as the petty-bourgeois parties, the Mensheviks and Socialist Revolutionaries, commanded a majority in the Soviets there could be no possibility of a socialist revolution in Russia for these parties insisted that the present stage of the revolution was the democratic stage; that, therefore, the bourgeoisie must exercise political power in the country. It followed, moreover, that the appropriate vehicle for bourgeois political power could not be the soviet form, restricted as it was to the lower classes. It could only be a government enjoying the authority of a Constituent Assembly elected on a national rather than on a class basis. The Mensheviks and the S.R.s were taking up once again their self-denying ordinance of 1905 when they had insisted that the proletarian party could play no part in the exercise of political power during the democratic stage of the revolution. To such lengths did they carry this tactic that when, in the governmental crisis of May 1917, they were exhorted to strengthen the government and to fill part of the vacuum caused by the admitted incapacity of the Cadets to run the country, the reaction of the Mensheviks was to turn the idea down on principle. Only grudgingly, only as the result of direct pressure from delegations from the fronts which insisted that the Mensheviks must join the government if they wished to preserve the last remnants of morale and discipline among the soldiers, only then did the Mensheviks agree to participate in a coalition government.

Menshevik abstentionism was, according to most of the scholarly analysis of the Russian Revolution, based on the rock of Marxist orthodoxy whereas Lenin's drive for power, according to an equally imposing consensus, was based on the shifting sands of Lenin's imperious personality and his ability to exploit a chaotic situation. Lenin, it is widely maintained, openly and obviously flouted the Marxian laws of economic determinism in engineering a socialist revolution in Russia. Let us pause for a moment to examine more carefully the terms of this argument.

There is, in the first place, evidence enough that initially the overwhelming majority of Russian Marxists rejected outright Lenin's aggressive plans, first sketched in the *April Theses*, for pressing ahead with a socialist revolution. Goldenberg declared that Lenin was laying claim to a throne vacant in Europe for thirty years – the throne of Bakunin. Plekhanov regarded Lenin as 'depraved' and his *April Theses* no more than the 'ravings' of a madman,[2] he was an 'alchemist of revolution'.[3] Akselrod branded his slogans as 'criminal'[4] and meant what he said. Until September 1917, the key leaders of the Soviets, the men who were undoubtedly the most influential men in Russia (despite their assurances to the contrary and their heart-felt wish that the cup be taken from them), were almost unanimous in their view that Russia was only ripe for the democratic revolution.

This was not only the Menshevik view. It had also, as we saw in Volume 1, been Lenin's view up to 1914. Until Lenin's arrival in Petrograd in April 1917 (indeed for some time thereafter), most of the Russian Bolsheviks continued to maintain it. Paradoxically it was Lenin himself who had, in his *The Development of Capitalism in Russia*, most fully established the objective basis for the democratic limitation to the revolutionary process. In that massive study he had established that by the turn of the century Russia was, overall, in the comparatively early stages of capitalist development. On this basis there could therefore be no talk of proceeding towards socialism. This position Lenin had pointedly maintained against the (Menshevik) proponents of permanent revolution in 1905. In 1917, Plekhanov and all the Mensheviks maintained that the basic economic structure of Russian life had not altered so substantially as to render the further progress of capitalism impossible, unproductive or reactionary. On the contrary, they could point to evidence enough to support their view that Russia remained comparatively backward by comparison with the developed industrialised West. The overwhelming majority of the population remained peasants whose productive techniques, as Lenin's meticulous studies themselves demonstrated, were antiquated and pre-capitalist. In such a country at such a level of economic development the attempt to leap straight into socialism flagrantly transgressed Marx's well-known specifications which Plekhanov repeatedly threw in the face of his Bolshevik opponents:

> No social order ever perishes before all the productive forces for which there is room in it have developed; and new, higher relations of production never appear before the material conditions of their existence have matured in the womb of the old society itself.[5]

This quotation, for Plekhanov, as for many latter-day commentators, clinched the argument. There was nothing left to be said since it was self-evident, and admitted by Lenin's own economic analysis, that there was still room a-plenty for the further development of capitalism in Russia. The Menshevik *Rabochaya gazeta* of 6 April 1917 rebutted Lenin's *Theses* in exactly similar terms:

> The developing revolution is always menaced by danger not only from the right, but from the left as well. The revolution can successfully struggle against reaction and force it out of its position only so long as it is able to remain within the limits which are determined by the objective necessity (the state of productive forces, the level of mentality of the masses of people corresponding to it, etc.). One cannot render a better service to reaction than by disregarding those limits and by making attempts at breaking them.

Lenin arrived in our midst in order to render this service to reaction. After his speech, we can say that each significant success of Lenin will be a success of reaction, and all struggle against counter-revolutionary aspirations and intrigues will be hopeless until we secure our left flank, until we render politically harmless, by a decisive rebuff, the current which Lenin heads. The principal danger, the Mensheviks immediately realised, was on the left.[6]

The problem is, however, that their position had nothing whatever to say about Lenin's justificatory arguments for proceeding towards socialism in Russia in 1917. As we have seen, these justificatory arguments proceeded from his analysis of imperialism. In other words, the 'society' which was the subject of Lenin's investigation was no longer Russia, or for that matter any particular country; it was, rather, the 'society' of international finance capitalism. The question which Lenin asked was is *this* society in any meaningful sense developing productive forces and encouraging the progress of humanity? He concluded that it was not developing the productive forces but actually retarding them and that, moreover, far from leading mankind on the path of progress, it was perpetrating carnage on the most grandiose scale ever witnessed and portended war upon war of ever-increasing dimensions. This society was, according to Lenin's analysis, rotten ripe: its continued existence threatened civilisation itself. Moreover his analysis (and, as we have seen, the analyses of Hilferding and of Bukharin) had amply demonstrated that 'the material conditions' for 'new higher relations of production' had already appeared and were to hand in all the industrially advanced countries. Those 'material conditions' through which to accomplish the transition to socialism had emphatically 'matured in the womb of the old society itself'. Imperialism, or finance capitalism, had itself at last produced precisely those mechanisms which for the first time enabled the administration of things to be accomplished by the mass of the people in and through their own self-activity. The big banks had concentrated production, rationalised the productive base of society and provided the means for a truly universal form of book-keeping and accounting. The cartels and trusts had concentrated and socialised production, pointed the way to overcoming the anarchy of production and simplified enormously the task of socialising the basic structure of the economy. The Post Office, telegraph and railroads had established the infrastructure of communications necessary to accomplish the task. Within *this* society, Lenin argued, the material conditions had long previously matured not only for the overthrow of capitalism as an economic structure but, in certain senses, for the transcendence of the state which socialism entailed.

The 'argument' between Lenin and the Mensheviks was, on this plane, no argument at all. The parameters of their economic analyses and therefore of their political strategies were, by this time, quite different. The Mensheviks remained rooted in the social and economic analysis which they had arrived at in 1905. Their political strategy was similarly unchanged. In 1917 as in 1905 they insisted that the revolution was the democratic revolution whose natural leaders must be the bourgeoisie. The gravest danger to the revolutionary cause in 1917 (as in 1905) for both Plekhanov and Akselrod was that the impatient, aggressive and extravagant demands of the working class and poor peasantry might drive the liberal bourgeoisie into alliance with the forces of the counter-revolution. Both Plekhanov and Akselrod further insisted that so long as revolutionary Russia was faced by the imminent danger of being overrun by reactionary Germany there could be no talk of any radical 'internal reconstruction'.[7] The war, in the opinion of most Mensheviks and most of the S.R.s, had now become a just war for the defence of the revolution, for the defence of a free democratic Russia. It followed, therefore, that the obligations Russia had entered into with her allies would have to be honoured. There could be no possibility of a separate peace with Germany. Their whole analysis of the war as, basically, a confrontation between 'reactionary' and 'progressive' states came home to roost in their political strategies. Since the war was now a just war, it was imperative to secure the maximum possible political cohesion of the nation in the immediate task of defending the democratic revolution in Russia. For Lenin, in contrast, the war was emphatically an imperialist war in which *all* the participants were reactionary. It was, according to his view, a conflict in which no country could claim to be fighting a 'just' war. Consistently the Mensheviks and S.R.s preached restraint, restraint and once again restraint. Plekhanov as ever was the most extreme of the Mensheviks. 'In 1917 Plekhanov did everything he could to stem the class struggle that he had devoted his life to promoting.'[8] 'In truth, the policies he advanced in 1917 were almost indistinguishable from the Cadets.'[9] Akselrod was only a little less extreme, 'Just as in 1905 Akselrod urged the Mensheviks to shun policies likely to cause a break with the progressive middle classes'.[10] 'The entire world proletariat would come to the conclusion that support of the bourgeoisie in time of war was the correct policy.'[11] Potresov, similarly, insisted upon the paramount need of securing the unity of all the patriotic democratic forces behind the Provisional Government and, in order to accomplish this, the Mensheviks would be obliged to put down 'the anarchy which is penetrating and disorganising the revolutionary movement, aided by increasing economic chaos and the irresponsible agitation of certain political groups'. The party was obliged 'to combat that rebellious and predatory tendencies of an unenlightened section of the working class which is disturbing the regular and democratic advancement of its cause'.[12]

In summary, both the Mensheviks and the S.R.s agreed that the outcome of the war could not be settled by Russia alone. Revolutionary democratic Russia was now fighting a just war and therefore any attempts to disorganise or disparage the war effort represented a direct stab in the back of those who were perishing by the thousands on the battlefields. National unity was therefore imperative and, since the revolution was in its democratic stage, this entailed support for the bourgeoisie as leaders of the Provisional Government. The slogan 'All Power to the Soviets' was, necessarily, a divisive slogan since the soviets were exclusively organs of working-class democracy. The Constituent Assembly, elected on the basis of universal suffrage, was the only deliberative body appropriate to the present phase of the revolution and it alone would be endowed with sufficient authority to settle the land question and the demands of the workers. Their interest and obsession was not in fomenting the class struggle but in dampening it down. Their principled rejection of the possibility of an advance towards socialism compelled them to adopt the paradoxical position of actively campaigning against the increasingly militant socialist demands of the urban workers, the sailors and the soldiery.

On all these issues, Lenin had arrived at diametrically opposite conclusions. We have already examined at some length the set of arguments behind his uncompromisingly radical conclusions. Let us merely repeat, at this point, that Lenin had elaborated a far more consistent theoretical justification for his new political strategies than the Mensheviks had for their old ones. It was not the case that Lenin, in 1917, acted in a purely opportunistic fashion, seizing every opportunity for maximising his own power by disorganising the government and his opponents. It certainly was not the case that he quite ignored the constraints which a Marxist economic analysis ought to have imposed upon his political goals; it was, rather, that he had elaborated a new Marxist analysis which justified an advance towards socialism. It was not Lenin who ignored the Menshevik and S.R. argument about the intractable reality of Russia's level of economic development; on the contrary, he constantly tried to convince them of the new realities of international finance capital. It was, rather, the Mensheviks who signally failed to take issue, at the theoretical level, with Lenin's whole analysis of imperialism and the imperialist war. None of the prominent theorists of Menshevism even attempted to keep pace with, or offer substantial criticism of, the theoretical premisses which Bukharin and Lenin elaborated in the period 1914 to 1917. The Mensheviks remained rooted in the synthesis of 1905 (economic analysis – comparatively low development of Russian capitalism, derivative political practice – the realisation of the democratic revolution). In 1917 they bitterly criticised Lenin's proposals for an advance to socialist practice but made little or no attempt to confront the theoretical basis from which this was derived. It was they who bucked the argument.

From the time of his arrival in Russia in April 1917, Lenin took it as axiomatic that the European revolution against imperialism was on the immediate agenda. He believed, as we have seen, that Europe was, in terms of its objective economic base, fully ripe for socialism. He believed, furthermore, that three years of bloodletting and suffering on an unprecedented scale had induced a mood of desperation. The popular masses, he believed, were not simply passively worn out with war-weariness, they were rapidly becoming conscious of the need for the overthrow of the entire system which had brought them death and ruination. The first socialist revolution, overthrowing the power of monopoly capital and the omniscient power of the imperialist state and preaching an end to this and all wars would have immense repercussions throughout Europe. It would be the detonator of a general European socialist explosion. On these basic positions, Lenin based his whole political strategy not only in 1917 but for some time thereafter.

Throughout 1917, Lenin constantly had to rebuff the allegation that the Bolsheviks, in pressing and preparing for a rising against the Provisional Government, had become Blanquists – the apostles of a sudden coup at the centre effected by a small group of dedicated and disciplined men who would proceed to impose socialism upon the population as a whole. The Mensheviks, who laid claim to representing Marxist orthodoxy in this respect, maintained that, since the objective conditions for a socialist revolution were absent in Russia (that is, the economic substructure of society, the productive forces were still ill-developed) it followed that the subjective conditions must also be absent. The mass of the population, they argued, was as yet unprepared in its consciousness for the transition to socialism. Only in and through a long period of struggle within the phase of bourgeois democracy would the working class enjoy conditions of freedom through which to learn the skills of organising themselves and articulating their own interests. Only by going through the hard school of advanced industrial capitalism would the workers acquire confidence in their concentrated strength and be disciplined for the arduous task of taking over the running of the economy and the state. It was, they argued, suicidal folly to attempt a minoritarian coup at the centre in the expectation of inaugurating genuine socialist self-activity before the Russian proletariat had gone through either the school of bourgeois democracy or that of advanced industrial capitalism.

Part of Lenin's response to this position we have already noted. The working class comes to consciousness, it acquires its organisational forms, only in the course of its own self-activity. Properly, socialist consciousness could therefore only be a product of socialist practice. Moreover, imperialism itself on a global basis had furnished the simplified mechanisms of control which enormously facilitated the transition to socialism. As far as Russia itself was concerned, its proletariat had, quite spontaneously, produced the soviet form which was the embryo of a socialist system of administration. Only in the course of the struggle to build socialism would the initiative and creative genius of the people be unleashed and their organisational forms perfected. Only as they actually undertook the battle to create new institutions, reflecting new conceptions of how men should relate one to another as citizens, neighbours, producers and consumers, would consciousness be transformed. Lenin was, therefore, committed to the view that fully socialist consciousness and properly socialist institutions would only be produced *after* the revolution. This did not, however, mean that their embryonic forms had not arisen prior to the revolution. Nor did it follow that the revolution must therefore be effected by a minoritarian conspiratorial group. On the contrary, according to Lenin's projections, the bourgeoisie would increasingly reveal its incompetence in dealing with the crucial issues which demanded resolution in Russia. The vacillating middle-of-the-road parties, the Mensheviks and right S.R.s would, similarly, be compromised by their allegiance to an ineffectual government and hamstrung by their own timorousness in taking power for themselves. The tide would turn, Lenin predicted, and it would turn in the Bolsheviks' favour. The Russian people would at last recognise the incapacity of the other parties to act. They would be driven to acknowledge the impotence of the Provisional Government and to demand the transfer of all power to the Soviets as the only possible alternative to military dictatorship and economic disaster.

The Bolsheviks must therefore seriously prepare themselves and their followers for the revolutionary conquest of power. The conquest of power they aspired to was not, and could not be, according to Lenin's repeated insistence, the work of a small group or even a large political party. It could only be carried out with the support of the majority of the people, especially that of the workers and soldiers. Unless and until the revolutionaries won this support, as expressed in the composition of the Soviets, there could be no transfer of power. The task of the Bolsheviks therefore, as Lenin conceived it between April and November 1917, was to convince the mass of the people that only a revolutionary transfer of power could solve Russia's problems. This task carried with it the further very delicate and difficult problem of enthusing his supporters that immediate resolute action was required to save Russia from chaos yet, at the same time, restraining precipitate action until majority support had been won over. Lenin's difficulty, one which he was constantly aware of and which dominated his tactical moves from April to November, was to keep the revolutionary preparedness of his most ardent supporters on the boil whilst simultaneously holding them back until the optimum point of mass enthusiasm for revolution had been attained. The basic problem was that revolutionary consciousness developed at an uneven rate. To delay too long would sap the morale of his fighting forces and dangerously expose the Bolsheviks to the attacks of activists who would maintain that the Bolsheviks, like the other talking-shop parties, were mere windbags incapable of action. To proceed too early would, equally, alienate the mass of the people and leave the revolutionaries, even if temporarily successful, powerless before the inevitable reaction.

To avert the possibility of a premature rising, and to advertise to the militants the point at which they were to proceed with the insurrection, Lenin attempted to establish general and particular guidelines. In 'Marxism and Insurrection',[13] he specified the general conditions he had in mind.

> To be successful, insurrection must rely not upon conspiracy, and not upon a party, but upon the advanced revolutionary class. That is the first point. Insurrection must rely upon a *revolutionary upsurge of the people*. That is the second point. Insurrection must rely upon that *turning-point* in the history of the growing revolution when the activity of the advanced ranks of the people is at its height, and when the *vacillations* in the ranks of the enemy and *in the ranks of the weak, half-hearted and irresolute friends of the revolution* are strongest. That is the third point. And these three conditions for raising the question of insurrection distinguish *Marxism from Blanquism*.[14]

Just a week before the Bolshevik seizure of power, Lenin again took issue with those outside the Party who levelled the accusation of Blanquism against it and with those inside the Party who, in Lenin's view, had recourse to the same taunt to justify their own spinelessness. He now specified the particular guidelines, the necessary and sufficient conditions for distinguishing the Marxist appraisal of the maturity of a revolutionary situation from Blanquism or any other adventurist schema. 'Military conspiracy', Lenin maintained,

> is Blanquism, *if* it is organised not by a party of a definite class, *if* its organisers have not analysed the political moment in general and the international situation in particular, *if* the party has not on its side the sympathy of the majority of the people, as proved by objective facts, *if* the development of revolutionary events has not brought about a practical refutation of the conciliatory illusions of the petty-bourgeoisie, *if* the majority of the Soviet-type organs of revolutionary struggle that have been recognised as authoritative or have shown themselves to be such in practice have not been won over, *if* there has not matured a sentiment in the army (if in war-time) against the government that protracts the unjust war against the will of the whole people, *if* the slogans of the uprising (like 'All power to the Soviets', 'land to the peasants', or 'Immediate offer of a democratic peace to all the belligerent nations, with an immediate abrogation of all secret treaties and secret diplomacy', etc.) have not become widely known and popular, *if* the advanced workers are not sure of the desperate situation of the masses and of the support of the countryside, a support proved by a serious peasant movement or by an uprising against the landowners and the government that defends the landowners, *if* the country's economic situation inspires earnest hopes for a favourable solution of the crisis by peaceable and parliamentary means.
> This is probably enough.[15]

In July, when many Bolshevik supporters had been urging a coup and had, in a rather anarchic way, attempted one, these conditions had been absent. To have attempted a revolutionary seizure of power at that time would have been Blanquist adventurism. It would, Lenin argued, have been folly to have gone along with the demands of Bolshevik rank and file extremists and of anarchists who demanded in July that the transfer of power should be immediately effected. The armed demonstrations on 3–4 July were premature and ill-advised because:

(1) We still lacked the support of the class which is the vanguard of the revolution. We still did not have a majority among the workers and soldiers of Petrograd and Moscow.

(2) There was no country-wide revolutionary upsurge at that time.

(3) At that time there was no *vacillation* on any serious political scale among our enemies and among the irresolute petty-bourgeoisie.[16]

As a result of these armed demonstrations of the 'July Days', the Bolsheviks suffered a very considerable setback. The Provisional Government, backed by the Mensheviks and the S.R.s, moved in earnest against the Bolsheviks. Bolshevik leaders (including Trotsky and Stalin) were imprisoned, others forced to flee (Lenin went to Finland), their press was closed down and official sanction was given to the persistent rumour that Lenin was a German agent. Bolshevik fortunes were at their lowest ebb. It was only the attempted putsch by the Commander-in-Chief of the army, General Lavr Kornilov, in late July which restored and indeed greatly extended Bolshevik influence and prestige. Faced with what was interpreted as a right-wing coup preparatory to a restoration of the monarchy, the Provisional Government (now dominated by Mensheviks and S.R.s since the cabinet reshuffle of May) were obliged to rally all available forces to defend the gains of the February Revolution. They could not ignore the considerable fighting forces which the Bolsheviks had been organising in the Red Guard nor could they afford to ignore the influence which the Bolsheviks had on the garrisons of Petrograd and Moscow. By their disciplined work in preparing and organising the armed force to defend the revolution against a putative dictator, the Bolsheviks greatly enhanced their reputation. They had, moreover, in the process very considerably extended the force of armed men under their direct control. They could, finally, add weight and conviction to their propaganda that so long as the fate of the revolution lay in the hands of the bourgeoisie and their vacillating socialist supports it would not be safe from Bonapartism. Only the transfer of power to the Soviets, only resolute action by the proletariat in power, could put down the threat of a restoration of the old regime or the rise of a dictator.

The Kornilov affair was, therefore, in Lenin's view precisely the watershed, the turning point in the revolution.

> We could not have retained power politically on July 3–4 because, *before the Kornilov revolt*, the army and the provinces could and would have marched against Petrograd.
> Now the picture is entirely different.
> We have the following of the majority of a *class*, the vanguard of the revolution, the vanguard of the people which is capable of carrying the masses with it.
> We have the following of the *majority* of the people . . .[17]

There can be no doubt at all that at the time this was written (September) there was a considerable element of truth in Lenin's words. The Bolshevik Party in the months from the end of July to the end of 1917 enjoyed a quite astounding increase in support. In the space of three months it emerged from the defeats it had suffered during and after the July Days to become the largest political party in Russia – at least as measured by the elections to the Second Congress of Soviets which was the most reliable means then available for measuring support. From being a noisy but easily contained minority in the major Soviets, by September they dominated the composition of these key bodies in Petrograd and Moscow. From that moment, Lenin insisted in letter after letter of the Central Committee of his Party, 'The Bolsheviks . . . can and *must* take state power into their own hands.'[18]

The situation had, Lenin realised, been quite transformed by the Kornilov putsch and its aftermath. The seizure of power which was out of the question in July had become imperative by October. The subjective conditions for a rising had now matured:

> On the one hand, a conscious, firm and unswerving resolve on the part of the class conscious elements to fight to the end; and on the other, a mood of despair among the broad masses who *feel* that nothing can now be saved by half-measures, that you cannot 'influence' anybody; that the hungry will 'smash everything, destroy everything, even anarchically,' *if* the Bolsheviks are not able to lead them in a decisive battle.

The development of the revolution has in practice brought *both* the workers *and* the peasantry to precisely this combination of a tense mood resulting from experience among the class conscious and a mood of hatred towards those using the lockout weapon and the capitalists that is close to despair among the broadest masses.[19]

The support of the peasants was crucial to Lenin's strategy for the revolution. He recognised that only if the peasants supported a proletarian seizure of power would it have any hope of success.

Russia is a country of the petty bourgeoisie, by far the greater part of the population belonging to this class. Its vacillations between the bourgeoisie and the proletariat are inevitable, and only when it joins the proletariat is the victory of the revolution, of the cause of peace, freedom and land for the working people assured easily, peacefully, quickly and smoothly.[20]

As in 1905, so now in 1917, Lenin maintained the same class analysis of the peasants. As a group they were incapable of political initiative, their mode of production and their precarious economic situation prevented them from emerging as a class properly so-called. They were incapable either of organising themselves cohesively on a national basis or of articulating their own interest. They could only respond to the political initiatives of the major class forces, the initiatives of the bourgeoisie or those of the proletariat. Lenin believed that by October, the peasantry was fully prepared to acknowledge proletarian leadership. 'Objective conditions showed that the peasantry must be led; they would follow the proletariat.'[21] It had grown weary of the endless postponement of the land question and the ambiguous position of the Provisional Government in respect of compensation for the expropriated landlords. It had long become weary of the war and wanted the peasant army back where it belonged – on the land. Most of all it wanted title to *all* the land, the estates of the landowners, the crown and the Church. Lenin recognised that it feared above all the restoration of the landlords and the monarchy; its only salvation, the only hope of implementing its radical demands lay in a victory for soviet power.[22]

By October the people had, Lenin asserted, been driven to desperation by the prevarications of the Provisional Government, its constant declarations of its own incapacity to settle the vital issues of peace and the land and its repeated postponement of elections for the Constituent Assembly which was *supposed* to be the body which would settle them. All the while the economic situation became worse, factories were closing and unemployment spreading rapidly, exchange between town and country was breaking down and bread was already in short supply. All these urgent problems demanded immediate action. They could not be put off until the convocation of the Constituent Assembly in January nor even until the meeting of the Second Congress of Soviets at the end of October. 'The famine will not wait. The peasant uprising did not wait. The war will not wait.'[23] The Russian people, Lenin believed, had had enough of debates, resolutions, pre-parliaments, democratic conferences and all the other devices used by the bourgeoisie to stall to buy time in which to regroup their forces and allow the steam to run out of the revolution.[24] All of Kerensky's schemes for pre-parliaments and democratic conferences were no more than a re-run of the tsarist ploy of the Dumas. The Bolsheviks, Lenin insisted, must have no truck with these fraudulent and impotent institutions which had been designed to hoodwink the revolutionary people. It was disgraceful, Lenin maintained, that the Bolsheviks had even sent delegations to these farcical bodies. The time for parliamentary activity of this sort was when the revolutionary tide was ebbing and in periods of reaction.[25] The tide, however, was now flowing ever fuller, ever more rapidly, and this the Bolshevik leaders had failed to grasp. They were lagging behind the masses just as they had done in 1905. They had quite failed to recognise the crucial importance of the Kornilov watershed and were abnegating their responsibilities to lead the people to provide them with a way out of the impasse and a plan of resolute action relevant to their immediate problems.

The Party failed to keep pace with the incredibly fast tempo of history at this turning-point. The Party allowed itself to be diverted, for the time being, into the trap of a despicable talking shop.

They should have left one hundredth of their forces for that talking shop and devoted ninety-nine hundredths to the masses.[26]

The time for speeches, Lenin insisted, was over.[27] The people had become desperate, only immediate decisive action could save the revolution.[28] 'In a revolution, the masses demand action, not words from the leading parties, they demand victories in the struggle, not talk. The moment is approaching when the people may conceive the idea that the Bolsheviks are no better than the others since they were unable to *act* when the people placed confidence in them . . .'[29] The imperative now was to organise the forces for revolutionary action. The place of the Bolsheviks must therefore be in factories and in the barracks. 'Their place is there, the pulse of life is there, there is the source of salvation for our revolution.'[30]

Since all vital questions in class-bound society were only resolvable by force, since the class war within society necessarily led to civil war and since this moment of decision had now arrived, the Bolsheviks, Lenin insisted, were obliged to treat insurrection as an art. They must take the business of organising and concentrating the coercive power of the proletariat in the right places at the right time with absolute seriousness. 'History,' Lenin wrote to Smilga, 'has made the *military* question now the fundamental *political* question.[31] A secret committee of absolutely reliable men must therefore be formed which would act as the headquarters of the insurgency. It must collect precise data on all troops and Red Guard detachments available to the revolution[32] and draw up a plan for the capture of all the most important strategic points in Petrograd; the telephone and telegraph exchanges, the Peter and Paul Fortress, the railway stations and the bridges.[33] The actual coordination and execution of this work was of course left to Trotsky and his fellow members of the Military Revolutionary Committee of the Petersburg Soviet.

The revolutionary situation had by October, Lenin argued, reached its climax. To delay now would not only mean to betray the peasants, workers and soldiers of Russia who had placed their faith in the Bolsheviks, it would also be tantamount to betraying the international proletariat. 'History will not forgive us if we do not assume power now.'[34]

In invoking the larger historical obligations of the Russian

159

Revolution, Lenin had in mind the duty which the Russians owed to the cause of the international socialist revolution against imperialism. That the world-wide socialist revolution was maturing Lenin was in no doubt. It had begun with the brave action of isolated individuals undertaking a ruthless critique of 'decayed official "socialism" which is in reality social-chauvinism'.[35] Its second stage was the growth of mass discontent 'expressing itself in the split of the official parties, in illegal publications and in street demonstrations'.[36]

> The third stage has now begun. This stage may be called the eve of revolution. Mass arrests of party leaders in free Italy, and particularly the beginning of *mutinies* in the German army, are indisputable symptoms that a great turning-point is at hand, that we are *on the eve of a world-wide revolution* ...
>
> Doubt is out of the question. We are on the threshold of a world proletarian revolution. And since of all the proletarian internationalists in all countries only we Russian Bolsheviks enjoy a measure of freedom – we have a legal party and a score or so of papers, we have the Soviets of Workers' and Soldiers' Deputies of both capitals on our side, and we have the support of a *majority* of the people in a time of revolution – to us the saying, 'To whom much has been given, of him much shall be required' in all justice can and must be applied.[37]

Repeatedly, Lenin came back to the same point in his writings in the month prior to the Bolshevik seizure of power. The Russian revolutionaries, because they enjoyed freedoms conspicuously absent elsewhere to propagandise, organise and even arm themselves, because they commanded the sympathy and support of a majority of the workers and of the soldiers, therefore had a huge responsibility to commence the international proletarian revolution. This was one of the main arguments Lenin utilised to press his point that the Bolsheviks must not postpone an attempt at power until the convocation of the Second All-Russian Congress of Soviets scheduled to take place on 20 October. To delay the revolution until then, as the majority of the Party wanted to, would, in Lenin's view, seriously jeopardise the prospects of a successful international proletarian revolution. All the signs were, he insisted, that the general European revolution was on the immediate agenda. Revolutionary outbreaks had already occurred in many countries, though on a sporadic and piece-meal basis. What was now vital was that a successful precedent be created:

> ... the existence of revolutionary and socialist proletarian masses in all the European states is a fact; the maturing and the inevitability of the world-wide Socialist revolution is beyond doubt, and such a revolution can be seriously aided only by the progress of the Russian revolution ... [38]

It fell to the Russian proletariat to serve as the detonator which would spark the fissile material throughout Europe into a general explosion.[39]

Outbreaks had occurred in Czechoslovakia, in Italy and, most importantly, in Germany. 'It cannot be doubted that the revolt in the German navy is indicative of the great crisis – the growth of the world revolution.'[40] In this situation, Lenin argued, to delay seizing power in Russia would be a shameful betrayal of responsibilities. It would allow the imperialists to cut down piece-meal the partial attempts at revolutionary action in Europe. It would deprive the European workers of confidence in their own cause when the Russians, who enjoyed all the necessary conditions for a successful seizure of power, still refused to act. 'Yes, we shall be real traitors to the International if, at such a moment and under such favourable conditions, we respond to this call from the German revolutionaries with ... *mere* resolutions.'[41]

> The crisis has matured. The whole future of the Russian revolution is at stake. The honour of the Bolshevik Party is in question. The whole future of the international workers' revolution for socialism is at stake.
> The crisis has matured ... [42]

> The success of both the Russian and the world revolution depends on two or three days' fighting.[43]

In the month prior to the October Revolution, Lenin's emphasis was less on the European revolution as a precondition for the completion of socialism in Russia and far more on the Russian Revolution as precondition for the beginning of the socialist revolution in Europe.

There was another facet of the international context which Lenin, and Bolshevik propaganda generally, made the greatest play with immediately prior to the seizure of power. The imperialist powers, Lenin contended, had compacted together to put down the threat of a genuinely proletarian rising in Russia. The Provisional Government, as ever the agent of imperialist designs, was a party to this conspiracy – it was giving up the defences to Kronstadt and Petrograd without a fight as its part in the imperialist design to put down proletarian insurgency in its most powerful centres. On 7 October Lenin wrote:

> The absolute inaction of the British fleet in general, and also of British submarines during the occupation of Esel by the Germans, coupled with the government's plan to move from Petrograd to Moscow – does not all this prove that the Russian and British imperialists, Kerensky and the Anglo-French capitalists *have conspired to surrender* Petrograd to the Germans and *thus* stifle the Russian revolution? . . .
>
> The conclusion is clear.
>
> We must admit that unless the Kerensky government is overthrown by the proletariat and the soldiers in the near future the revolution is ruined. The question of an uprising is on the order of the day.[44]

On the very day of the Bolsheviks' seizure of power, Lenin insisted in *Pravda*:

> Kerensky will surrender Petrograd to the Germans, that is now as clear as daylight. No assertions to the contrary can destroy our full conviction that this is so, for it follows from the entire course of events and Kerensky's entire policy.
>
> Kerensky and the Kornilovites will surrender Petrograd to the Germans. And it is in order to save Petrograd that Kerensky must be overthrown and power taken by the *Soviets of both capital cities*. The Soviets will immediately propose a peace to all the nations and will thereby fulfil their duty to the German revolutionaries. They will thereby also be taking a decisive step

towards frustrating the criminal conspiracies against the Russian revolution, the conspiracies of international imperialism.[45]

Clearly Lenin was attempting to stimulate a feeling of outrage amongst the workers, sailors and soldiers of Petrograd, a feeling that their revolutionary 'Peter' was being sold out by a perfidious government and that they were being handed over bound, trussed and defenceless to the Germans. Lenin's fairly obvious assumption is that only the soviets possessed of full power and commanding the fierce loyalty of the masses could or would defend Petrograd. He was almost explicitly appealing to the revolutionary patriotism of the Kronstadt and Petrograd workers, sailors and soldiers to defend their revolutionary strongpoints.

Perhaps the most surprising omission in Lenin's account of the importance of the international context in justifying the Bolshevik seizure of power was that the very generalised theory of imperialism was never applied at all seriously to the particular case of Russia. It appears to be an essential part of Lenin's argument that a socialist revolution in Russia would deprive the metropolitan imperialist countries of an important source of super-profits obtained through the export of capital and of goods on preferential terms. It was an equally important (if unelaborated) proposition that this must have a considerable impact on the general rate of profit within the imperialist economies. Faced with the reassertion of the Marxian law for the rate of profit to decline, the imperialists would be obliged to react in the way which Marx had predicted. They would be forced to adopt a combination of measures to increase the rate of profit, decreasing the pay of the workers, increasing the hours of work and the intensity of labour and greatly augmenting the industrial reserve army of the unemployed. These measures would, in their turn, lead to increased consciousness amongst the working class and impel it to discard revisionism and become frankly revolutionary. That these implications formed the basis of Lenin's analysis of the chain reaction which would follow a successful socialist revolution in Russia seems clear. This was the 'objective basis' of his theory of the spark, the idea that the chain of imperialism would break at its weakest link. The problem is that these implications of the theory of imperialism were never fully articulated by Lenin. They were inferences which have to be assumed to make his ideas intelligible. There are, in any case, further problems which this progression made no attempt to resolve.

It would, in the first place, have to be demonstrated that Russia, as a source of super-profits, was crucial to the general rate of profit in the imperialist countries. Since the whole future of socialism in Russia was premissed upon the more or less immediate repercussions the Russian Revolution would have in the rest of Europe, we might have expected an attempt at demonstrating the centrality of Russia in the general nexus of international finance capital. We might, furthermore, have expected some attempt at specifying the rapidity with which the impact of its withdrawal from the international structure of finance capital would make itself felt. These, after all, were not merely academic questions. On their outcome, on Lenin's repeated insistence, the whole project for creating socialism in Russia directly depended. It may well have been the case that Lenin did not pursue these problems for the good reason that he recognised that they were irresolvable. They involved so many variables that their outcome was inherently impossible to assess. There was, as we have mentioned, the impossibility of setting a timetable for the chain reaction theory insofar as it affected the economic base of the imperialist countries. To have assessed the impact of Russian withdrawal from the international system of finance capital would have presumed access to the appropriate economic data, much of which was either unobtainable or else outdated. In this respect, Lenin would in any case have encountered a fundamental and intractable problem of the Marxian revolutionary method. The problem in brief is that immediate political tactics, especially one so vital as an attempted seizure of power, have to be predicated upon the basis of what is, and is necessarily, a very imperfect and more or less outdated knowledge of the development of the economic base of society. Another factor which tends to exacerbate this gap between the planning of strategy and tactics and knowledge of developments in the base is that it is precisely during times of economic, political and military crises that developments in the economic base are most rapid. It is, however, precisely during such crises that accurate statistical data on such changes are likely to be most sparse and, probably, kept secret by companies or governments. It follows, therefore, that there can be no scientifically exact method of appraising the point at which the forces of production of a given society have outgrown the property relations in which they were hitherto developing. It follows that not only were the Mensheviks utopian in imagining that this exercise *was* possible but also that Lenin could do no more than rely upon projections from a very generalised scheme which could not, by their nature, be verified by empirical evidence. This, it might be felt, is typical of 'Leninism'; it also happens to be an intrinsic and irreducible problem of the Marxian theory of revolution. Engels, perhaps unaware of the deep implications his remarks had for the whole viability of the Marxian theory of revolution, put the problem clearly enough in his Introduction to *The Class Struggles in France*:

A clear survey of the economic history of a given period can never be obtained contemporaneously, but only subsequently, after a collecting and sifting of the material has taken place. Statistics are a necessary auxiliary means here, and they always lag behind. For this reason, it is only too often necessary, in current history, to treat this, the most decisive factor, as constant, and the economic situation existing at the beginning of the period concerned as given and unalterable for the whole period, or else to take notice of only such changes in this situation as arise out of the patently manifest events themselves, and are, therefore, likewise patently manifest. Hence, the materialist method has here quite often to limit itself to tracing political conflicts back to the struggles between the interests of the existing social classes and fractions of classes created by the economic development, and to prove the particular political parties to be the more or less adequate political expression of these same classes and fractions of classes.

It is self-evident that this unavoidable neglect of contemporaneous changes in the economic situation, the very basis of all the processes to be examined, must be a source of error. But all the conditions of a comprehensive presentation of current history unavoidably include sources of error – which, however, keeps nobody from writing current history.

When Marx undertook this work, the source of error mentioned was even more unavoidable. It was simply impossible during the period of the Revolution of 1848–49 to follow up the economic transformations taking place at the same time or even to keep them in view.[46]

It is rather disingenuous of Engels to conclude that the unavoidable source of error in 'the very basis of all the processes to be examined' kept nobody from writing current history, for what Marxists were exhorted to do was not to write history but to make it and there is clearly a world of difference between the two activities. Precisely the same strictures might be levelled against Lenin's theory of imperialism and his directly related theory of the state. As a structure of ideas, as propositions about current history, they undoubtedly had an impressive force and coherence which has been too lightly dismissed by latter-day critics. The point is, however, that this structure of ideas was the premiss for action, for a revolution which sought to transform society utterly, entirely and universally. The success of this audacious enterprise was, however, wholly dependent not upon the logical integrity or coherence of Lenin's ideas about the contemporary world but upon how accurate a picture it embodied of that world, especially of its economic substructure. The fate of Lenin's project from the moment he seized power hung on the truth of his economic analysis, and its truth content in this respect, as we have noticed, was impossible to ascertain beforehand. Marxism in this crucial area was like the owl of Minerva, it flew only at dusk. It could only offer *retrospective* vindication of action already undertaken since 'A clear survey of the economic history of a given period can never be obtained contemporaneously, but only subsequently . . .' This does not, of course, mean that Lenin was therefore unjustified in taking the action he did in 1917. Engels's comments merely suggest that either all action is impossible because the information on which it is based is necessarily inadequate (a position he clearly did not wish to sustain), or else that justification of this sort must always appear some time after the event. Marxist revolutionary action *must* in other words be based upon a series of more or less well-informed predictions or inferences from a more or less accurate analysis of a relatively antiquated economic structure. Such a formulation clearly involves a whole host of imponderables and uncontrollable variables. And yet the action itself, in Lenin's case the project for a socialist transformation of

Russia, clearly and emphatically depended upon the set of predictions and inferences he had made actually coming true within a very short period of time – of months rather than years.

As Lenin wrote two days after the Bolshevik seizure of power in his Foreword to the second edition of *Can The Bolsheviks Retain State Power?*

> The 25 October Revolution has transferred the question raised in this pamphlet from the sphere of theory to the sphere of practice.
> This question must now be answered by deeds, not words.[47]

CHAPTER 8

The Project for Socialism in Russia

'It is not the gods who make pots' – this is the truth that the workers and peasants should get well drilled into their minds. They must understand that the whole thing now is *practical work*; that the historical moment has arrived when theory is being transformed into practice, vitalised by practice, corrected by practice, tested by practice; when the words of Marx, 'Every step of real movement is more important than a dozen programmes' become particularly true... For, 'theory, my friend, is grey, but green is the eternal tree of life.'[1]

With the assumption of power by the Bolsheviks, the relationship between theory and practice obviously underwent a profound change. In the chapters above I have tried to demonstrate that Lenin had pressed the theory of imperialism to its final, most radical conclusion. He had found that not only had imperialism created all the necessary and sufficient conditions for socialism: its degeneracy and military destructiveness made its immediate supersession imperative. The world was not merely *ready* for socialist revolution: it could only save itself from barbarism thereby. Theory therefore had already, in 1916, with the publication of *Imperialism the Highest Stage of Capitalism*, reached its terminus. The generalised implications for practice, spelt out in *The State and Revolution*, presumed the maturity of the objective and subjective conditions for socialism and set out the yardstick to measure attempts at implementing it. The seizure of power itself was based directly on an assessment of Russian and international maturity for socialism and a prediction about the impact the Russian Revolution would have on the Russian people and, as important, on the rest of the world.

168

Let us look in the first place at the impact which Lenin expected the revolution to have upon the lives of the people of Russia. Let us begin at the proper beginning with Lenin's project for socialism in Russia as he conceived it in the first six months of the revolution. It was a project which in retrospect appears stupendous, breathtaking in its breadth and scope. From everything he wrote at this time it is absolutely clear that Lenin was not concerned with establishing a Party dictatorship (even the *guiding* role of Party is rarely mentioned), still less was he concerned with building up a huge centralised apparatus arrogating all decision making in every sphere of life to itself. On the very contrary, he was striving to erect, in Russia, a state form of the commune type. Far from forgetting his vision of *State and Revolution* on assuming power it was, quite clearly, precisely the ideas expressed there which served as his consistent yardstick to measure the attainment of socialist goals. It is perhaps entirely natural that most Western accounts of Lenin's activity at this time, as well as most Soviet histories, should obscure or ignore this crucial period of Lenin's thought and activity. For most Western commentators, Lenin was a superbly adroit political practitioner, an organisation man whose Jacobin schemes fitted closely with his domineering personality. There is, in addition, another enormously important factor to bear in mind. This is that Western commentators and historians have been obsessed with the search for 'origins'. The historian's role, therefore, is conceived of as the search for the beginnings or origins of contemporary totalitarianism, or authoritarian centralist collectivism in the early history of the Soviet régime. To imagine therefore that Lenin could seriously fall prey to utopian illusions about the dissolution of the power of the state and the project of initiating *all* the people of Russia into *all* the tasks of political and economic administration, exceeds the bounds of credibility. The evidence that he did take such things seriously is therefore not looked for since it could not be accommodated in the tale that is to be told. It would neither square with the received view of the sort of man Lenin was nor with the implicit determinism of the backward view which seeks the origins of the present in the past. There are even more pressing reasons why Soviet accounts should distort and travesty Lenin's visionary project for socialism in Russia. To reconstruct it accurately could prove the gravest threat to the legitimacy of the

169

present régime which purports to be based on his teaching since it is clear that what the Soviet régime has become is the dialectical inverse of what Lenin initially aspired to. This does not mean to say that Lenin did not later substantially change his view of what it was possible to achieve in Russia, nor does it mean that he himself did not bear the major responsibility for initiating the move away from the commune form to the authoritarian state. Later chapters will deal with the circumstances in which these revisions to the original project were made. For the moment let us attempt to reconstruct Lenin's forgotten vision of the socialist society he aspired to in the first six months of the Russian Revolution.

SOCIALIST CONSCIOUSNESS AND SELF-ACTIVITY

As we have repeatedly noted, Lenin's theoretical analysis of finance capitalism had demonstrated to him that the simplified mechanisms of control created by the trusts, cartels and banks, now made it possible for the people as a whole to engage in the administration of things. Theory postulated the possibility which the carnage of the world war converted into an imperative. In December 1917 in his brief article *For Bread and Peace*, Lenin expressed this theoretical and practical imperative with admirable conciseness:

> The imperialist war, the war between the biggest and richest banking firms, Britain and Germany ... this horrible criminal war has ruined all countries, exhausted all peoples, and confronted mankind with the alternative – either sacrifice all civilisation and perish or throw off the capitalist yoke in the revolutionary way, do away with the rule of the bourgeoisie and win socialism and durable peace .... Capitalism had developed into imperialism, i.e. into monopoly capitalism, and under the influence of the war it has become state monopoly capitalism. We have now reached the state of world economy that is the immediate stepping stone to socialism.[2]

In Russia, specifically, the failure of all options successively tried in the period from February to October 1917 impressed upon all the politically conscious people of Russia the need for a radical new beginning. The fact that all other options had been tried and found wanting, the fact that the great mass of the politically conscious people of Russia supported the Soviet assumption of power still did not mean, in Lenin's view, that they had finally arrived at adequate socialist consciousness. For socialist consciousness to develop, for it to spread to *all* the inhabitants of Russia it was imperative, Lenin believed, that all without exception should engage in socialist practice; that all, therefore, should participate in the administration of the state and of the economy.

Lenin's view of the centrality of practice in the development of consciousness can hardly surprise us. In Volume 1 of this study, considerable space was given to Lenin's accounts of how the primary consciousness of a shared community of economic interest was forged only in and through the industrial practice of the working class and how, further, the development of political consciousness was seen to be dependent upon the political activity of the class. In exactly the same way, Lenin now insisted that only through the practical activity and spontaneous organisation of the whole mass of the people reabsorbing the powers hitherto arrogated to the state and the institutions of monopoly capitalism, only thus could socialist consciousness arise. Only in proportion as these forms of activity were universalised would socialist consciousness dawn and the régime be secure.

> The bourgeoisie admits a state to be strong only when it can, by the power of the government apparatus, hurl the people wherever the bourgeois rulers want them hurled. Our idea is different. Our idea is that a state is strong when the people are conscious. It is strong when the people know everything, can form an opinion of everything and do everything consciously.[3]

> This our union, our new state is sounder than power based on violence which keeps artificial state entities hammered together with lies and bayonets in the way the imperialists want them.[4]

There was and could be no other way for the whole population to become conscious socialists, Lenin argued, apart from their own immediate participation in organising their own economic and political life. This then, as Lenin conceived it in this period, was no distant nebulous goal; it was, on the contrary, *the means to attain the goal and the goal itself.* Lenin's view of communism or socialism (for there was, at this stage, no clear delineation in his mind between the two) as an essentially negative movement of the present rather than a distant utopian construct was, in many ways, very similar to that propounded by Marx and Engels in *The German Ideology.* Communism, they maintained, was

> not a *state of affairs* which is to be established, an *ideal* to which reality will have to adjust itself. We call communism the *real* movement which abolishes the present state of things.[5]

The role of the Party and of the central apparatus of the Council of People's Commissars in this process was simply to enthuse the mass of the people with the confidence to undertake this momentous transformation and to break down all the obstacles which hindered their free creative activity. The role of the centre was, therefore, a positive one only insofar as it inspired, enthused and encouraged the mass of the people to organise and experiment with their own political and economic forms. It emphatically was not positive in the sense that it should, in Lenin's view, issue instructions or specify procedures, norms or standardised patterns for the mass to follow. This is so important an aspect of Lenin's thought and has been so neglected by the commentaries that we must spend some time reviewing some of his major statements on this theme. In November 1917 he declared:

> Creative activity at the grass roots is the basic factor of the new public life. Let the workers set up workers' control at their factories. Let them supply the villages with manufactures in exchange for grain.... Socialism cannot be decreed from above. Its spirit rejects the mechanical bureaucratic approach; living, creative socialism is the product of the masses themselves.[6]

In December 1917 in his article *How to Organise Competition*, Lenin made it abundantly clear that in his view the greatest variety of experiments at organising state and economic forms in the localities, the most manifold variations in establishing popular control over production and distribution were the surest signs of advance towards socialism:

Every attempt to establish stereotyped forms and to impose uniformity from above, as intellectuals are so inclined to do, must be combated. Stereotyped forms and uniformity imposed from above have nothing in common with democratic and socialist centralism. The unity of essentials, of fundamentals, of the substance, is not disturbed by *variety* in details, in specific local features, in methods of *approach*, in *methods* of exercising control, in *ways* of exterminating and rendering harmless the parasites (the rich and the rogues, slovenly and hysterical intellectuals, etc. etc.).

The Paris Commune gave a great example of how to combine initiative, independence, freedom of action and vigour from below with voluntary centralism free from stereotyped forms. Our Soviets are following the same road.[7]

Variety, Lenin insisted, was 'a guarantee of effectiveness, a pledge of success'.[8] Here indeed is an extraordinary interpretation of what democratic centralism should mean in a socialist society. Its model was explicitly the Paris Commune which, as Lenin had noted in his *State and Revolution*, preserved the unity of the state by allowing autonomy to all the local communes and by relying upon their *voluntary* collaboration from below upwards for the maintenance of defence needs and communications. In this guise the whole pattern of what was later to be called democratic centralism is quite inverted. Initiative clearly rests with the local communes, their agreement to pursue common goals is voluntary, the centre must never impose its will on the localities for, as we have seen, the vitality of the socialist project, indeed its whole viability, rests upon the widest variety, the broadest experimentation with differing forms of self-administration. The role of the central administration is merely to help clear the path of mass creativity of the obstacles it encounters.

It may perhaps be objected that this extraordinary version of the principle of democratic centralism was merely a hasty and unconsidered utterance. On the contrary. Not only was this the only formulation of appropriate organisational forms consonant with Lenin's view of socialism at that time, it was also elaborated at length in his original version of the article 'The Immediate Tasks of the Soviet Government' written in March 1918. In this article, Lenin was obviously recapitulating and reinforcing what he had written in the article 'How to Organise Competition'. In view of what was later to become of the concept of democratic central- ism, and in order to confirm the picture so far presented in this chapter of Lenin's view of the proper relationship between centre and periphery in socialist society, we will quote him at length.

We are for democratic centralism. And it must be clearly understood how vastly different democratic centralism is from bureaucratic centralism on the one hand, and from anarchism on the other. The opponents of centralism continually put forward autonomy and federation as a means of struggle against the uncertainties of centralism. As a matter of fact, democratic centralism in no way excludes autonomy; on the contrary, it presupposes the necessity of it . . . Under a really democratic system, and the more so with the Soviet organis- ation of the state, federation is very often merely a transitional step towards really democratic centralism. . . .

And just as democratic centralism in no way excludes autonomy and federation, so, too, it in no way excludes, but on the contrary presupposes, the fullest freedom of various localities and even of various communes of the state in developing multifarious forms of state, social and economic life. There is nothing more mistaken than confusing demo- cratic centralism with bureaucracy and routinism. Our task now is to carry out democratic centralism in the economic sphere, to ensure absolute harmony and unity in the functioning of such economic undertakings as the railways, the postal telegraph services, other means of transport, and so forth. At the same time, centralism, understood in a truly democratic sense, presupposes the possibility, created for the first time in history, of a full and unhampered development not only of specific local features, but also of local inventiveness, local initiative, of diverse ways, methods and means of progress to the common goal. The task of organising competition, therefore, has two aspects: on the one hand, it requires the carrying out of democratic centralism as described above, on the other hand it makes it possible to find the most correct and most economical way of reorganising the economic structure of Russia. In general terms, this way is known. It consists in the transition to large-scale economy based on machine industry, in the transition to socialism. But the concrete conditions and forms of this transition are and must be diverse, depending on the conditions under which the advance aiming at the creation of socialism begins. Local distinctions, specific economic formations, forms of everyday life, the degree of preparedness of the population, attempts to carry out a particular plan – all these are bound to be reflected in the specific features of the path to socialism of a particular labour commune of the state. The greater such diversity – provided, of course, that it does not turn into eccentricity – the more surely and rapidly shall we ensure the achievement of both democratic centralism and a socialist economy.... Crushed by the capitalist system, we cannot at present even imagine at all accurately what rich forces lie hidden in the mass of the working people, in the diversity of labour communes of a large state, in the forces of the intelligentsia, who have hitherto worked as lifeless, dumb executors of the capitalists' predetermined plans, what forces are lying hidden and can reveal themselves given a socialist structure of society. What we have to do is only to clear the way for these forces.[9]

Hitherto the principle of democratic centralism had been applied by Lenin solely to the structure of the Party – it would, at the time it was formulated in 1905, have been premature to project it on to the grander scale of society and state. We should notice, however, that the 1905 formulation breathed the same spirit as the passages we have looked at from 1917 and 1918. According to the 1905 specification, social democrats were:

to apply the principle of democratic centralism in Party organisation, to work tirelessly to make the local organisations the principal organisational units of the Party, in fact and not merely in name, and to see to it that all higher-standing bodies are elected, accountable, and subject to recall.... The autonomy of every Party organisation, which hitherto has been largely a dead letter, must become a reality.'[10]

Intrinsic to Lenin's plan for the reorganisation of the Party permitting the broadest diversity and autonomy to the local organisations was his optimistic belief that in the revolution of

175

1905 the predictions of theory were actually being realised in the activity and direct experience of the mass. A firm belief in the theoretical correctness of Bolshevik theory was, therefore, the sure basis for welcoming, promoting and encouraging the mass participation of workers in social democratic activity. The relatively undeveloped consciousness of the mass could not, in this situation, possibly be used as a pretext for excluding them, for only by participating, only through their own revolutionary practice, could the mass become consciously aware of their larger objectives. If then the theoretical basis of the Party's strategy was correct, in a revolutionary situation it would have nothing to fear and everything to gain from spontaneous mass activity.

> Forward, then, more boldly; . . . extend your bases, rally all the worker Social-Democrats round yourselves, incorporate them in the ranks of the Party organisations by hundreds and thousands. Let their delegates put new life into the ranks of our central bodies, let the fresh spirit of young revolutionary Russia pour in through them. So far the revolution has justified all the basic theoretical propositions of Marxism, all the essential slogans of Social-Democracy. And the revolution has also justified our hope and faith in the truly revolutionary spirit of the proletariat. Let us, then, abandon all pettiness in this imperative Party reform; let us strike out on the new path at once.[11]

In 1905 and 1906, Lenin had proposed a transformation of the structure of the Party to accommodate the upsurge of political activity through which alone the mass could come to political consciousness. In 1917 and 1918, the project was far more ambitious and extensive. Theory had now indicated that the essential task in hand was not a political transformation for now the object of mass activity was to destroy the state and reintegrate its powers with society. In this situation the Party, whose function it had been to represent the proletariat in its relations with other classes and with the state, ceased to have the prominence which it had once enjoyed. It was of course an axiom of Marx's class analysis that within class-ridden, state-dominated society the proletariat could exist as a class properly so-called only to the extent that it could organise nationally and articulate its grievances and mission in history. In class-ridden, state-dominated society the class articulated itself in and through the proletarian party. The situation of the Party after the revolution was, however, left far more obscure. The theoretical findings of Bukharin and of Lenin with regard to imperialism and the imperialist state were bound to lead to a further reappraisal of the proper role of the Party in a post-revolutionary situation. In this situation, as we have seen above, *the* condition of success of the project for socialism was that the mass of the population should themselves, in their own localities, in their trade unions, in their co-operative farms and workshops, in their militia groupings and people's courts, build their own communes, their own agencies of state power:

> Each factory, each *artel* and agricultural enterprise, each village that goes over to the new agriculture by applying the law on socialisation of the land, is now, as one of the democratic bases of Soviet power, an independent commune with its own internal organisation of labour.[12]

Only in proportion as they did so would they become conscious socialists and only thus was the project for socialism to be made secure. The Party as we have seen took its cue from the most advanced and conscious proletarians and only from them. Its object and historical mission was to raise the less advanced to that degree of consciousness which the implementation of socialism demanded by providing a correct strategy of advance for the advanced workers through which they would lead the mass into action and, through practice, to more elevated consciousness. The theory of imperialism and Lenin's analysis of the imperialist war had, however, led him to assert that all the objective and subjective conditions for socialism had now been created on a global scale. The consciousness of the mass had, therefore, been adequately prepared. The issue now was, therefore, not that of leading the advanced workers into political action in order to raise the general level of political consciousness. The issue was to draw the entire mass of the population, all without exception, into the tasks of social and economic administration through which they would acquire socialist consciousness. At this level of activity the mass needed no mediating agency; the whole success of the project was based upon their immediate activity. There was a

177

congruence between the type of consciousness aimed at and the organisational structures Lenin recommended. In socialist society the people at large had to become conscious of their own talents and abilities to order and direct all their own affairs. The domain of politics, expressive of class-riven society and the direction of the passive majority by a dominant minority, was at an end. It could only be transcended by mass self-activity. The forms of organisation appropriate to the forging of socialist consciousness were, therefore, not political but administrative, economic, cultural and educational. These were the multiform communes and soviets, agencies of the popular mass reabsorbing the prerogatives arrogated by the state and training the mass to resume direct control over all their affairs. The Party therefore receded into the background, for how could it represent the interests of the class to the state if the whole mass of the people in their plethora of organisations themselves developed 'multifarious forms of state, social and economic life'?

For good reason therefore Lenin, during this period, never applied his idea of democratic centralism to the Party – the Party was seldom mentioned in his writings at this time. The idea was, rather, applied to the relations between the multiform communes which the revolution had thrown up and the voluntary federation of different national groupings. Always it insisted upon the utmost local independence or autonomy and the widest possible variety of the forms of self-administration. It therefore stood implacably opposed to regulation from the centre, the imposition of stereotyped forms and all types of bureaucratic centralism. It was an extraordinarily loose organisational framework and this because it was only such an organisational scheme which was compatible with Lenin's theoretical findings. In this, above all, Lenin displays himself as a revolutionary thinker and activist of extraordinary audacity and consistency. For six months at least, Lenin set himself the task of encouraging a revolution more radical than any the world has seen before or since. The stated object of that revolution was emphatically not the capture and consolidation of state power but rather the dissolution of the state itself.[13] This was the central objective of the project for socialism in Russia, an objective largely forgotten or ignored by commentators of most persuasions, but an objective which, as we have seen, flowed directly out of Lenin's most basic theoretical analysis.

Viewed apart from that theoretical analysis, Lenin's practical work in these early months is quite inexplicable.

THE FORMS OF SELF-ADMINISTRATION

We have seen that a constant feature of Lenin's thought was his belief that the process of knowing of the mass, its route of consciousness, lay not in theoretical induction but in its own practical experience. The value of theoreticians was that they, through study of the laws of history and detailed economic and social analysis of the present, could appraise the potential for socialist transformation and guide the masses into paths of activity through which the transformation might be realised. They could not, however, prescribe the actual concrete forms through which the transformation would be accomplished and, even if they could apprehend such forms beforehand, to dictate them to the masses would of itself frustrate the whole venture. Only by experimenting, only therefore by encouraging the widest diversity of organisations of the power of the people, would the best forms emerge. At the Second Congress of Soviets, Lenin declared:

> Experience is the best teacher and it will show who is right. . . .
> Experience will oblige us to draw together in the general
> stream of revolutionary creative work, in the elaboration of
> new state forms. We must be guided by experience; we must
> allow complete freedom to the creative faculties of the mas-
> ses.[14]

One of the most important aspects of the work of the Council of People's Commissars was therefore to fire the mass of the people with the necessary confidence to begin their momentous task:

> At all costs we must break the old, *absurd*, savage, despicable
> and disgusting prejudice that only the so-called 'upper classes',
> only the rich and those who have gone through the school of
> the rich, are capable of administering the state and directing
> the organisational development of socialist society . . . But
> every rank and file worker and peasant who can read and write,
> who can judge people and has practical experience, is capable
> of *organisational* work.[15]

179

The workers and peasants were, however, still too timid and insufficiently resolute, too much habituated to their servile role to be able to make proper use of the new conditions for self-organisation. They had not acquired 'sufficient confidence in their own strength; age-old tradition has made them far too used to waiting for orders from above . . . there are still elements among them who are frightened and downtrodden and who imagine that they must pass through the despicable school of the bourgeoisie'.[16]

Lenin, addressing the Third Congress of Soviets in January 1918, recalled his embarrassment at meeting delegations of workers and peasants who had come to him as chairman of the Council of People's Commissars for advice on what to do on various issues:

> And I said to them: you are the power, do all you want to do, but take care of production, see that production is useful. Take up useful work, you will make mistakes but you will learn.[17]

The task therefore of the conscious revolutionaries and of the government was, in Lenin's view of this time, one of enthusing the mass, giving it new confidence in its own abilities and clearing away the obstacles to the free development of its initiative: 'What we have to do is only to clear the way for these forces.'[18] Lenin's advice to the intellectual supermen both within and outside his own Party who believed that they had a detailed prospectus on how to create socialism was to put away

> . . . the old, shabby little book carefully stowed away under the pillow, the unwanted book that serves them as a guide and manual in implementing official socialism. But the minds of tens of millions of those who are doing things create something infinitely loftier than the greatest genius can foresee.[19]

We should be quite clear that, when talking about the imperative need to involve the mass of the people in the task of socialist construction and the organisation of agencies of state power, Lenin was not referring exclusively to the proletariat. His project was, and had to be, universal in its social scope. Certainly he expected the proletariat, followed by the working peasants, to demonstrate the greatest initiative, but other social groups were emphatically not precluded from playing their part.

> All citizens must take part in the work of the courts and in the government of the country. It is important for us to draw literally all working people into the government of the state. It is a task of tremendous difficulty. But socialism cannot be implemented by a minority, by the Party. It can be implemented only by tens of millions when they have learned to do it themselves.[20]

THE DISSOLUTION OF THE COERCIVE AGENCIES OF THE STATE

The courts had, of course, been a central part of the old coercive structure which stood at the heart of the bourgeois state. Separate bodies of magistrates were now done away with. Separate bodies of armed men, that other prop of bourgeois dominance, were also to be done away with and, in Lenin's project, the defence and police functions were henceforth to be exercised by the armed people. We have seen how, in *State and Revolution*, Lenin, following Marx, had characterised the essence of the state as the existence of bodies of armed men separate from, and alien to, the mass of the people. We further saw how, in his examination of the Paris Commune, Lenin had emphasised precisely its attempt to do away with the standing army and the police by reintegrating their functions with the armed people. The model of the commune, Lenin declared in March 1918, remained the model for Soviet power:

> Because we are standing on the shoulders of the Paris Commune and the many years of development of German Social-Democracy, we have conditions that enable us to see clearly what we are doing in creating Soviet power ... that Soviet power is a new type of state without a bureaucracy, without police, without a regular army, a state in which bourgeois democracy has been replaced by a new democracy, a democracy that brings to the fore the vanguard of the working people, gives them legislative and executive authority, makes them responsible for military defence and creates a state machinery that can re-educate the masses.[21]

181

Soviet power, Lenin declared, was the embodiment of a new type of democracy which 'has its prototype only in the Paris Commune', and the commune, precisely because its first actions were aimed at the dissolution of the coercive agencies of the old state machine,

> ... was not a state in the proper sense of the word. In short, since the working people themselves are undertaking to administer the state and establish armed forces that support the given state system, the special government apparatus is disappearing, the special apparatus for a certain state coercion is disappearing.[22]

From the start Lenin had proclaimed this dissolution of the coercive force of the state as the Soviet objective. In November 1917 he declared that, 'The wholesale arming of the people and the abolition of the regular army is a task which we must not lose sight of for a single minute.'[23] In his 'Theses on Soviet Power' of March 1918, the same objective is held constant, indeed the Soviet form is identified as the elimination of separate bodies of armed men and the self-activity of the people in arms.

> (5) creation of an armed force of workers and peasants, one least divorced from the people (Soviets = armed workers and peasants). Organised character of nation-wide arming of the people, as one of the first steps towards arming the whole people.[24]

Soviet power would, of course, still have to rely on force to keep order and to put down bourgeois speculators and counter-revolutionaries, but Lenin's advice remained consistent: do not come running to the People's Commissars for assistance or expect help at every turn from the centre – you are the power, do it yourselves. The police, Lenin asserted in February 1918, were dead and buried,[25] the masses could only rely on their own organisations and their own initiative: 'The exploiters must be suppressed, but they cannot be suppressed by police, they must be suppressed by the masses themselves.'[26]

WORKERS' CONTROL AND ECONOMIC SELF-ADMINISTRATION

Lenin's accounts of workers' control prior to the October Revolution can be seen as responses to a complex and confused political and economic situation. In part, no doubt, Lenin's advocacy of the factory committees, which sprang up like mushrooms after the February Revolution, was a tactical ploy designed to offset the sudden and dramatic increase of Menshevik influence on the newly re-formed trade unions. Since the Mensheviks dominated the trade unions, it was natural that Lenin should give the more radical and Bolshevik-dominated factory committees a central role in his strategy. It was, of course, via the factory committees that the Red Guard was created. Still, however, in the pre-October days, workers' control was given a rather modest administrative role to fulfil in Lenin's structure of thought. It was, above all (as we noticed above[27]), emphatically the function of *control* of the capitalists *not their expropriation* which Lenin had in mind for the factory committees. Control, in this sense, meant access to all papers, prevention of sabotage or provocative closure of plants by the capitalists and ensuring that they did not swindle the workers' state. It was in this spirit that Lenin, on the very day that the Second Congress of Soviets approved the formation of a Workers' and Peasants' Government, promulgated his Draft Regulations on Workers' Control.

1. *Workers' control* over the production, storage, purchase and sale of all products and raw materials shall be introduced in all industrial, commercial, banking, agricultural and other enterprises.
2. Workers' control shall be exercised by all the workers and office employees of an enterprise, either directly, if the enterprise is small enough to permit it, or through their elected representatives.
3. Unless permission is given by the elected representatives of the workers and office employees, the suspension of work of an enterprise or an industrial establishment of state importance, . . .or any change in its operation is strictly prohibited.
4. The elected representatives shall be given access to *all* books

and documents and to *all* warehouses and stocks of materials, instruments and products without exception.
5. The decisions of the elected representatives are binding upon the owners of enterprises and may be annulled only by trade unions and their Congresses.[28]

Lenin's more radical proposals for economic self-administration after October were the product of an equally complex situation. In the practical sphere the Soviet régime met with much greater resistance not only from the employers but also from the managers, engineers and specialists, than Lenin had anticipated. The wholesale closure of plants in the early months of the new régime was partly the result of a continuing process of economic dislocation, which had been clearly evident since late 1916, occasioned by the breakdown of the transportation system and the impossibility of obtaining raw materials or of distributing the finished product. In part it was exacerbated by the positive refusal of manufacturers to continue in business given the uncertainty of their position under the new régime. The shades of difference between these reasons for plant closures were often impossible to tell apart and they were in any case a matter of little significance to workers faced with unemployment or the threat of it. Their response was to take over the plants and to exercise the power which, they believed, the Bolsheviks were encouraging them to seize. Once started, the movement of factory committees and local soviets to expropriate the owners and to administer the industrial enterprises assumed its own unstoppable momentum.

> The bourgeoisie was spoiling everything, sabotaging everything, in order to wreck the working-class revolution. And the task of organising production devolved entirely on the working class.[29]

Step by step with this actual process taking place in Russia, Lenin's reflections on the role of the unions and factory committees became increasingly radical. He began, in these first six months, to integrate these and the other economic organisations of the working people into his vision of the soviet/commune administrative form. Just as the coercive agencies of the old state were to be reintegrated with the people in arms, so the forms of economic administration, hitherto standing as alien oppressive structures, were to be taken over and humanised by the working people themselves. The expropriation of the capitalists and the establishment of genuine workers' control created the conditions

> ... in which the working man can reveal his talents, unbend his back a little, rise to his full height and feel that he is a human being. For the first time after centuries of working for others, of forced labour for the exploiter, it has become possible to work for oneself and moreover to employ all the achievements of modern technology and culture in one's work.[30]

The workers would organise themselves in the most varied productive industrial and distributive organisations, each one of which was to operate as an independent commune and an executor of state power (in the rather odd sense, from the theoretical point of view, that each was engaged in the administration of things). Thus 'each factory, each *artel* and agricultural enterprise, each village' was to become 'one of the democratic bases of soviet power, an independent commune with its own internal organisation of labour'.[31] 'Every factory committee', Lenin insisted, must become 'an organisation nucleus helping arrange the life of the state as a whole'.[32] The trade unions, from being defensive organisations protecting the working class against predatory finance capitalism and pre-eminently concerned with negotiating better terms for the sale of labour power, were to undergo an abrupt and radical transformation. The responsibilities which Lenin now laid upon them were awesome: if implemented, they would have made the trade unions by far the most important agencies of Soviet power – of what Lenin called the state. In March 1918 he wrote:

> The trade unions are becoming and must become state organisations which have prime responsibility for the reorganisation of all economic life on a socialist basis.[33]

Similarly the retail co-operatives, extended to embrace the whole population, were to become *the* distributive mechanism of socialist society. Under capitalism the co-operatives had, according to Lenin, been one of the strongest refuges of utopian socialists. They had hitherto catered almost entirely for the upper stratum of the workers and the petty bourgeoisie.

> The co-operative, as a small island in capitalist society, is a little shop. The co-operative, if it embraces the whole of society, in which the land is socialised and the factories nationalised, is socialism.[34]

Not only the co-operatives, which had served as the organisational foci of the petty-bourgeoisie, but even 'the nerve centres of capitalist life'[35] – the banks – could be transformed and made amenable to control by the masses:

> Here we shall present the concrete task of organising distribution, unifying the banks into one universal type and converting them into a network of state institutions covering the whole country and providing us with public book-keeping, accounting and control carried out by the population itself and forming the foundations for further socialist steps.[36]

'Workers' control and **the nationalisation** of the banks' were, in Lenin's view, the two central facets of the new economic model; together, they comprised 'the first steps towards socialism'.[37] Elsewhere, as early as November 1917, Lenin expressed the same idea but added a third highly significant component of a properly socialist economic structure. The victory of socialism, he maintained, was equivalent to

> ... **workers' control over the factories, to be followed by their** expropriation, the nationalisation of the banks and the creation of a Supreme Economic Council for the regulation of the entire economic life of the country.[38]

This was Lenin's first mention of the Supreme Economic Council and it is at this point that a new element enters our story, an element which we have so far neglected.

DISCIPLINE, CENTRALISM AND SELF-ADMINISTRATION

To this point I have presented a purposefully one-dimensional analysis of Lenin's thought in the first six months of Soviet power. I have attempted to establish the fact that the entailments for political practice derived from Lenin's theory of imperialism, his analysis of *The State and Revolution* and of the commune form, that all this was no mere pipe-dream which immediately died the death when Lenin was confronted with the reality of power. On the contrary, what I have argued is that one part of him at least remained obsessed with the audacious project of directly proceeding with and actually encouraging the dissolution of the state. In this period, therefore, when Lenin talks of the dictatorship of the proletariat, he never mentions Marx's references to it in the period 1848–51 with all their centralist overtones: his reference is invariably to Engels's identification of the dictatorship of the proletariat with the Paris Commune. In this respect, Lenin's reflections on practice, which we have quoted above, are clearly derived from his analysis of the state in *The State and Revolution*.

In examining *The State and Revolution*, however, we noticed how, at this level of abstraction, Lenin's analysis of the state reflected a deep ambivalence in the writings of Marx and Engels between the dictatorship of the proletariat and the commune form. Lenin's exegesis, we concluded, necessarily reflected this ambivalence and that, whilst it set the commune in the forefront, there were nonetheless certain undercurrents of the alternative highly centralised structure of power. Exactly the same duality runs through Lenin's recommendations for practice during these first six months. It is indeed the contention of the remaining chapters of this book that this duality or tension pervades all of Lenin's thought in the period 1917–24. At one level this tension might be expressed as that between the commune form and the dictatorship of the proletariat, at another between workers' control and one-man management, at another between the trade unions and the Supreme Economic Council, at another between the Council of People's Commissars and the soviets; and so on.

Let us for the moment examine how the tension was reflected in Lenin's writings in the first six months of the Soviet régime. Predictably enough, it appeared for the first time in the sphere of economic management. To put the matter simply and bluntly,

Lenin quickly became aware of the impossibility in Russian conditions of saving the country from the rapid slide towards economic ruination through authentically socialist forms of administration. He had, as we have seen, earlier justified the revolution precisely on the grounds that *only* socialist forms of economic management and administration could arrest the impending economic catastrophe. By this he meant, as we have seen above, *not* the imposition of stereotyped forms, *not* a centrally dictated and closely supervised plan, but rather the encouragement of the utmost local initiative, the widest variety of forms and the broadest autonomy to local productive and distributive communes. Socialism as self-activity was therefore described precisely as *the means* of overcoming the grave economic crisis, the only means left since all other expedients had been tried and found wanting. Socialism thus conceived was not, therefore, a distant aim to be attained only through a long transitional period. It was an immediate practical imperative.

Lenin's belief in his own schema declined step by step with the catastrophic deterioration of the economy in those early months and as it became increasingly clear to him that the European Revolution, which he had expected as an almost immediate repercussion of the Russian Revolution, was not maturing as expected and would not therefore bale Russia out of her acute economic difficulties.

Lenin's first notice of the 'low cultural level' of the Russian proletariat as a factor inhibiting the progress of socialism came in January 1918 but, at this stage, his optimism was undaunted. This factor, he maintained, simply meant that 'for the success of socialism in Russia a certain amount of time, several months at least, will be necessary'. This projection was clearly and explicitly bound up with Lenin's prediction that the European revolution was imminent:

> That the socialist revolution in Europe must come, and will come, is beyond doubt. All our hopes for the *final* victory of socialism are founded on this certainty and on this scientific prognosis.[39]

It was the rapidly worsening economic situation that dictated a rapid shift of emphasis in Lenin's thought and an overt retreat from his initial project for socialism in Russia. He had invoked the heroic promethean values as the only way to arrest the slide into chaos. He had conjured up the vast creative spontaneity of the mass as Russia's only road to economic redemption, but the hard inescapable facts of accelerating economic decline could not be avoided. In the very article we have quoted, where Lenin waxed most enthusiastic about the variety and autonomy of the organisation of self-management (original version of the article 'The Immediate Tasks of the Soviet Government'), he introduced a new note into the discussion. Let there be endless discussion, meetings and commissions, for they are necessary to awaken the masses from 'historical somnolence to new historical creativeness'.[40] Let variety flourish and autonomy to the multiform communes of economic and political organisation be guaranteed by a loose and permissive interpretation of democratic centralism[41] but, Lenin insisted, let us remember our 'extremely critical and even desperate situation' and let us remember our first, most basic priority is to provide the means of subsistence to the population. To accomplish even this most modest task will require discipline, accountability and efficient economic machinery. In the next four crucially important pages of the text, dictated in late March 1918, Lenin introduced his proposals for dealing with the critical situation in food supply and distribution caused by the collapse of the railway and transport mechanism.[42] These policy proposals and organisational suggestions were to characterise the entire subsequent attitude of the Bolsheviks towards the economy. Many commentators assume that they had always been part and parcel of Lenin's 'organisational scheme'; they had not. They were radical revisions of his initial project and incompatible with it however desperately Lenin sometimes sought to square the circle and make them appear as one. He conceded nonetheless, as he had to, that a 'turning-point' had been reached and that a change of attitude which must be the pivot of subsequent reform had to be produced.

> Now has come the turning-point when – without in any way ceasing to prepare the masses for participation in state and economic administration of all the affairs of society, and without in any way hindering their most detailed discussion of the new tasks . . . we must at the very same time begin strictly to separate two categories of democratic functions: on the one

hand, discussions and the airing of questions of public meetings, and, on the other hand, the establishment of the strictest
responsibility for executive functions and absolutely business-
like, disciplined, voluntary fulfilment of the assignments and
decrees necessary for the economic mechanism to function
really like clockwork. It was impossible to pass to this at once;
some months ago it would have been pedantry or even
malicious provocation to demand it. Generally speaking, the
change cannot be brought about by any decree, by any
prescription. But the time has come when the achievement of
precisely this change is the pivot of all our revolutionary
reforms.[43]

The crucial distinction which Lenin was here introducing, and
which he went on to emphasise as his central point, was the
distinction between the functions of consultation and control
which the mass would continue to exercise and the executive
function which one man was henceforth to be entrusted with.
The masses would continue to choose their leaders, replace them
and check up on their every activity:

But this does not at all mean that the process of collective labour
can remain without definite leadership, without precisely
establishing the responsibility of the person in charge, without
the strictest order created by the single will of that person.
Neither railways nor transport, nor large-scale machinery and
enterprises in general can function correctly without a single
will linking the entire working personnel into an economic
organism operating with the precision of clockwork.[44]

Nothing could be more mistaken, Lenin now asserted, than the
very widely held opinion that 'one-man dictatorial authority is
incompatible with democracy, the Soviet type of state and
collective management'.[45] Lenin can hardly have forgotten that,
according to his own description, it was precisely the superiority
of the soviet form that it transcended the specious separation of
consultative, legislative and executive powers typical of bourgeois
democratic régimes. The virtue of the soviet and commune form,
in Lenin's earlier accounts, was that it combined all these
functions and did not arrogate them to separate bodies of men

with different spheres of jurisdiction. The soviets themselves, as well as the workers' councils and multitudinous labour communes, were now enjoined to separate 'the necessary, useful preparation of the masses for executing a certain measure and checking up on its execution, which is fully recognised by every soviet, from the actual execution itself'.[46]

The sphere of self-activity and its scope had, quite clearly, been dramatically curtailed in its most central aspect, for as we have seen in the quotations cited earlier, Lenin had maintained that only in the activity of deliberating and actually executing their own decisions was it possible for the mass to come to socialist consciousness. Lenin, moreover, strongly hints that it would not necessarily be the outstanding and conscious *workers* who were to be the most likely candidates for wielding the dictatorial powers of one-man management. Quite reversing his earlier stand of principled hostility to the 'absurd, savage, despicable and disgusting prejudice' that only the rich and the educated were capable of administering state and economic affairs,[47] he now insisted upon the active recruitment of the bourgeois intelligentsia who were shortly to be known as the *spetsy*.

> The chief and urgent requirement now is precisely the slogan of practical ability and businesslike methods. It follows that it is now an immediate, ripe and essential task to draw the bourgeois intelligentsia into our work. It would be ludicrously stupid to regard the drawing in of the intelligentsia as some kind of weakening of the Soviet system, some kind of departure from the principles of socialism or some kind of inadmissible compromise with the bourgeoisie. To express such an opinion would be a meaningless repetition of words that refer to a quite different period of activity of the revolutionary proletarian parties.[48]

Lenin's final cautionary words would appear to have been directed towards those who chose to invoke his earlier remarks about absurd prejudices and his own constantly repeated invective about the wrecking activities of the old officials, clerks and specialists,[49] and his characterisations of the 'drooping intellectuals' as 'the spineless hangers-on' and servile accomplices of 'The grasping, malicious, frenzied filthy avidity of the money-bags'.[50]

191

To their challenge that 'You cannot do without us', Lenin, in December 1917, had responded by invoking the great pool of talented organisers among the workers and peasants who were 'only just beginning to become aware of themselves, to awaken, to stretch out towards the great, vital, creative work, to tackle with their own forces the task of building socialist society'.[51] The way to deal with such a threat was clear enough to Lenin in December 1917:

> No mercy for these enemies of the people, the enemies of Socialism, the enemies of the working people. War to the death against the rich and their hangers-on, the bourgeois intellectuals; war on the rogues, the idlers and rowdies. All of them are of the same brood – the spawn of capitalism, the offspring of aristocratic and bourgeois society; the society in which a handful of men robbed and insulted the people . . .[52]

By the time Lenin came to present the second draft of this article to the Party's Central Committee on 26 April 1918, his views on the necessity of dictatorial one-man management and the recruitment of specialists at 'extremely high salaries' had dramatically hardened. Now Lenin no longer contested the view, which a month previously he had castigated as 'ludicrously stupid', that the recruitment of bourgeois specialists at very high wages was indeed 'some kind of departure from the principles of Socialism'. It was, he now conceded, 'a retreat from the principles of the Paris Commune', a 'step backward', a 'retreat' which could not be concealed from the people.[53] It would in all conscience have been extremely difficult for Lenin to have concluded otherwise for on this point Marx's account of the commune, which had been faithfully retailed in *The State and Revolution*, was definite and precise. 'From the Members of the Commune downwards, the public service had to be done at *workmen's wages*.'[54] Looking back on the period, in October 1921, Lenin openly conceded that exceptionally high remuneration for specialists 'did not originally enter into the plans of the Soviet government, and even ran counter to a number of decrees issued at the end of 1917'. At that time, Lenin went on, 'We assumed that we could proceed straight to Socialism without a preliminary period in which the old economy would be adopted to Socialist economy.'[55] That, precisely, is the point. Despite what many commentators maintain, Lenin in these first six months had *not* embarked upon the establishment of some sort of transitional or preparatory régime. His model was the commune model and not the dictatorship of the proletariat, and the commune, as we saw in Chapter 4, was emphatically not a transitional or preparatory régime.

These two measures were now to be supplemented by others, all of which were inspired by the sole aim of increasing productivity and efficiency regardless of their impact on properly socialist self-administration. Thus, for the first time, Lenin talks of the necessity for introducing and applying Taylorism,[56] for introducing the piece-work system[57] and bonuses of different kinds for exemplary labour communes. The need for discipline was constantly invoked and it was coupled with an insistence that friendly competition between productive units was no longer sufficient. Compulsion would have to be used 'so that the slogan of the dictatorship of the proletariat shall not be desecrated by the practice of a lily-livered government'.[58]

> Dictatorship, however, is a big word and big words should not be thrown about carelessly. Dictatorship is iron rule, government that is revolutionarily bold, swift and ruthless in suppressing exploiters and hooligans. But our government is excessively mild, very often it resembles jelly more than iron.[59]

On the question of granting unlimited dictatorial powers to individuals, however, Lenin was less inclined to acknowledge that soviet power had suffered a setback. On the contrary, he confronted his critics head-on in a series of extreme propositions which proved the swansong of mass self-administration. These propositions were themselves no more than a recognition of what had already been decided upon and actually implemented in certain sectors of the economy – especially the railways. The citadels of capitalism had now been stormed, the land and almost all the large factories had been expropriated. The heroic period of the revolution, Lenin seemed to be saying, which *condoned* the unleashing of the elemental force of the masses, was over. The tasks of the second period were quite different. They were pre-eminently the tasks of stocktaking, introducing efficient management within the enterprises and coordinating relations between them in a planned way. Above all, the task was to improve productivity. For these new tasks quite new qualities and virtues were needed. Audacity, heroism, rough enthusiasm and spontaneous organisation became, in the period of consolidation, not simply insufficient but quite inappropriate. What was now needed, Lenin insisted, was discipline, discipline and yet more discipline. Discipline to accept the superior technical abilities of the specialists. Discipline to accept the dictatorial 'or unlimited powers'[60] of individual executives, and discipline to accept the leading role of the Bolshevik Party. We have arrived at the beginning of a progression which was to characterise the entire subsequent development of Lenin's thought and indeed the subsequent development of the Soviet régime. It was a progression which was to be fatal to the original project for socialism through self-administration and to conclude this chapter we must briefly examine the rationale which underlay it.

Lenin set out to rebut the arguments of those 'representatives of petty bourgeois laxity' who argued that the granting of unlimited dictatorial powers was incompatible with the collegiate principle, with democracy and 'the principles of Soviet government'.[61] The problems raised were, Lenin admitted, 'of really enormous significance' which therefore merited thorough treatment. His first thesis is more of an assertion than an argument, namely:

That in the history of revolutionary movements the dictatorship of individuals was very often the expression, the vehicle, the channel of the dictatorship of the revolutionary classes has been shown by the irrefutable experience of history. Undoubtedly, the dictatorship of individuals was compatible with bourgeois democracy.[62]

Here, no doubt, Lenin had in mind the experience of France and the classic example of the French Revolution. But if Robespierre and Saint Just were his models, what was to become of the hallowed distinction between Marxism and Jacobinism? What was to become of the distinction between the dictatorship of particular individuals and the dictatorship of the entire *class* which the dictatorship of the proletariat was supposed to implement?[63] There is, further, the whole question of whether the state forms through which individuals exercised their dictatorships during the bourgeois period were appropriate to the realisation of *socialism?* The Paris Commune, which Lenin had hitherto adopted as his model was, after all, in Marx's account the direct antithesis of the huge bureaucratic executive state machine that the bourgeois dictator Louis Bonaparte had established to exercise his imperial power:

> The true antithesis to the *Empire itself* – that is to the state power, the centralised executive, of which the Second Empire was only the exhaustive formula – was *the Commune*.[64]

The commune model, certainly, said nothing about individuals exercising superordinate powers: on the very contrary, all officials were to be elected and subject to recall at any time. They could therefore exercise only such powers as their constituents bestowed upon them.

Lenin's second argument was the same as the one Engels had earlier employed against the anarchists, namely that large-scale industrial organisation was, by its very nature, authoritarian, demanding 'absolute and strict *unity of will* . . . But how can strict unity of will be ensured? By thousands subordinating their will to the will of one.'[65] Initially, of course, Lenin had optimistically assumed that this unity of will would be spontaneously generated in the course of socialist practice. In December 1917, Lenin had insisted that no amount of direction, orders from above or enforced discipline could lead the mass to socialist consciousness.

> . . . we do not expect the proletariat to mature for power in an atmosphere of cajoling and persuasion, in a school of mealy sermons or didactic declamations, but in the school of life and struggle . . . The proletariat must do its learning in the struggle, and stubborn, desperate struggle in earnest is the only teacher.[66]

The mass, through its own experience, through its blunders and mistakes, would voluntarily come to accept the discipline necessary. That would, according to his initial analysis, be self-imposed, conscious and genuinely socialist discipline evolved only in and through the practice of the mass. Now Lenin

195

introduced a fundamental alteration to this optimistic scenario.

> Given ideal class-consciousness and discipline on the part of those participating in the common work, this subordination would be something like the mild leadership of a conductor of an orchestra. It may assume the sharp forms of a dictatorship if ideal discipline and class consciousness are lacking. Be that as it may, *unquestioning subordination* to a single will is absolutely necessary for the success of processes organised on the pattern of large-scale machine industry.[67]

The unspoken assumption which has now intruded itself was that we cannot wait until the experience of the mass brings it to adequate class consciousness and socialist discipline, things are too desperate to allow the continuation of confusion, wastage and costly errors. Discipline must be enforced. What is omitted and has to be omitted in this resolution of the problem is Lenin's whole sociology of consciousness. He had consistently and properly maintained that *only* through their own experience, *only* from making costly mistakes and learning from them, could the mass arrive at adequate consciousness. Lenin could no longer even pose the question of how the mass was to come to socialist consciousness when they were denied access to executive functions. It is hardly a coincidence that the 'sharp forms of a dictatorship' which he now advocated as the only means of short-circuiting the long arduous path to ideal self-consciousness was for the first time explicitly linked with the leading role of the Communist Party. The whole task of the Party, Lenin now insisted, was to grasp this fundamental reorientation of political practice:

> ...to stand at the head of the exhausted people who are wearily seeking a way out and lead them along the true path, along the path of labour discipline...of unquestioningly obeying the will of the Soviet leader, of the dictator during the work.[68]

For the first time in Lenin's post-revolutionary writings the Party was given an emphatically positive role in administration. Lenin clearly had a good deal more in mind for the Party to do than simply break down the obstacles to mass activity. It was to be an organiser, director, disciplinarian and executive and had to train itself in these new skills. The slogans which Lenin now gave out to the Party mirrored this new orientation: 'manoeuvre, retreat, wait, build slowly, ruthlessly tighten up, rigorously discipline, smash laxity . . .'[69]

CONCLUSION

By the end of April 1918, Lenin had realised that his initial project for proceeding immediately to properly socialist forms of political, economic and social self-management based on the model of the commune could not save Russia from the appalling economic crisis which she was facing. The project itself had been based upon a number of theoretical projections or predictions which the actual experience of these early months had failed to vindicate. It was premissed, in the first place, on the theoretical projection that finance capitalism had so developed the productive forces and so simplified the processes of administration that all, literally all literate workmen could immediately proceed with the task of administering the economy. Experience had proved that the structures involved were a good deal more complicated than Lenin had initially supposed. It had shown in the stark irrefutable statistics of industrial production and productivity that the self-organisation of the culturally backward Russian workers had led, not to a resurgence of economic activity, but to its virtual atrophy. Lenin, as government leader, was forced to resort to measures which Lenin, as theorist of the socialist revolution, found difficult to stomach. The harsh realities of governmental responsibilities intruded themselves as they could not have done before. As government leader he recognised that the primary and basic responsibility of government was to secure the livelihood of the people under its jurisdiction. A large part of Lenin's case against the Provisional Government was that it failed in this primary task. Now he had to concede that breaking down the obstacles to mass spontaneous creativity in the economic sphere had also failed to produce the goods. Nor could it be given more time to learn through costly experiment for, as government leader, Lenin recognised that an *immediate* restitution of order, planning, discipline, expertise and efficient distribution was

197

imperative if millions and tens of millions were not to starve.

> ... the extremely critical and even desperate situation the country is in as regards ensuring at least the mere possibility of existence for the majority of the population, as regards safeguarding it from famine – these economic conditions urgently demand the achievement of definite practical results.[70]

If mass self-activity had literally failed to produce the goods then, Lenin insisted, other expedients would have to be tried. The state and its central planning agencies, the Party as the organiser of labour discipline, the bourgeois specialists with their fund of experience and expertise would have to step into the breach. Coincidentally, Lenin begins to alter the model upon which he had been operating. The commune, the model appropriate to the immediate implementation of socialism, begins to be displaced by the dictatorship of the proletariat – signifying a transitional régime whose objectives were more modestly conceived as creating the conditions for an *eventual* transition to socialist practice. Still, however, Lenin was aware of the inherent dangers of the new course he was plotting. He was aware, in particular, of the danger that commensurate with the diminution of the sphere of self-activity and the increasing power of the centre, there would arise a body of irresponsible functionaries whose activities might subvert the whole future of socialism in Russia. His rather forlorn response was to encourage control from below, but he has nothing to say on the obvious problem of how on the one hand the dictatorial authority of individual executives was to be encouraged and preserved, whilst *at the same time* these same individuals were to be made permanently accountable to, and controlled by, the popular masses. Precisely the same problem recurs in Lenin's last writings and we should notice his first attempt to resolve it:

> The more resolutely we now have to stand for a ruthlessly firm government, for the dictatorship of individuals *in definite processes of work*, in definite aspects of *purely executive* functions, the more varied must be the forms and methods of control from below in order to counteract every shadow of a possibility

of distorting the principles of Soviet government, in order repeatedly and tirelessly to weed out bureaucracy.[71]

The second major theoretical prediction upon which the immediate advance to socialism had been attempted was, of course, the imminent outbreak of the European revolution. In his political report to the Seventh Congress of the Party, in March 1918, Lenin declared in unequivocal terms that 'it is the absolute truth that without a German revolution we are doomed .... At all events, under all conceivable circumstances, if the German revolution does not come we are doomed.'[72] Without a European revolution, Lenin insisted, the Russian Revolution would inevitably suffer recurrent defeats and forced retreat, 'I repeat, our salvation from all these difficulties is an all-Europe revolution.'[73] It was precisely because the European revolution was taking longer to mature than Lenin had anticipated that he felt it all the more necessary to moderate his sweeping plan for the immediate introduction of socialism in Russia. Genuinely socialist practice in Russia had, after all, been premissed upon the prediction that Russia's economic and cultural backwardness would be almost immediately redeemed by the accession of the more developed European countries to the revolutionary cause (though how exactly this was to happen was nowhere elaborated by Lenin). By April 1918 Lenin was beginning to realise that the isolation of the Soviet régime in Russia might be much more prolonged than he had imagined. He resolved, faced with this situation, that if Russia could not of her own resources build a state form of the commune type, she could nonetheless preserve some of the gains of the revolution. In the international sphere, Lenin conceded, 'things did not go according to the book'. This did not mean, however, that the revolution was doomed to perish, as many of Lenin's critics maintained. It meant that the ambitious project for socialism in Russia would have to be moderated. It meant that a hybrid transitional régime preparatory to socialism would have to be established. Soviet power, according to Lenin's new conspectus, would have to drop its claim to represent the realisation of socialism and accept that it represented no more than a holding operation, an attempt to conserve some at least of the gains of the revolution as the basis for a future advance when the European revolution finally broke out:

> ... our task, since we are alone, is to maintain the revolution, to preserve for it at least a certain bastion of socialism, however weak and moderately sized, until the revolution matures in other countries, until other contingents come up to us.[74]

Until that time came, 'however distressing it may be, however repugnant to revolutionary traditions, the only tactics are: to wait, manoeuvre and retreat'.[75]

By the end of April 1918 Lenin had, quite clearly, altered his perspective of what the Russian Revolution was capable of and this re-assessment was itself based on a surprisingly hard-headed appraisal of the prospects for a European revolution. The integration of these two factors and the new note of moderation and realism which had entered his thought is evident enough in his Conclusion to his pamphlet 'The Immediate Tasks of the Soviet Government'.

> An extraordinarily difficult, complex and dangerous situation in international affairs; the necessity of manoeuvring and retreating; a period of waiting for new outbreaks of the revolution which is maturing in the West at a painfully slow pace; within the country a period of slow construction and ruthless 'tightening-up', of prolonged and persistent struggle waged by stern, proletarian discipline against the menacing element of petty-bourgeois laxity and anarchy – these in brief are the distinguishing features of the special stage of the socialist revolution in which we are now living.[76]

CHAPTER 9

The Dictatorship of the Proletariat

GENERAL THEORY – THE DIALECTICAL CHOICE

During the first six months of Soviet power, Lenin rarely mentioned the dictatorship of the proletariat. As we saw in the previous chapter, on the infrequent occasions he did so it was identified with the commune form. From April 1918 onwards, faced with obvious chaos on the railways with the consequent disruption of food and fuel supply to the urban population and to the factories, Lenin did indeed call for increased discipline, one-man management and iron government. It was not, however, until nearly a year after the Bolshevik seizure of power that he discussed the notion of the dictatorship of the proletariat at any length[1] and only from that time onwards did he consistently use the term to characterise the Soviet régime. Coincidentally, Lenin's usage of the term commune became less frequent, more guarded and qualified until, by late 1920, it had virtually disappeared from his vocabulary. There was then no abrupt or self-conscious change in Lenin's views but rather a gradual and constant shift from the ideal of the commune to the idea of the dictatorship of the proletariat. What he now asserted was the need for a transitional régime which would represent not so much the transcendence of the state *per se* as the antithesis of the bourgeois imperialist state. The commune remained the goal but the road to its realisation, Lenin now came to believe, could only lie in the temporary strengthening of the state as the dictatorship of the proletariat. Only such a state could survive in the world environment of encirclement by hostile imperialist states. So long as predatory imperialism survived, any localised attempt to dissolve the state would fall easy prey to its military might. Lenin

201

was led to a reformulation of Marx's dictum that communism could only exist 'world historically', that is, universally.[2]

Lenin was, in effect, tacitly admitting that the localised attempt to establish communism in Russia had been a precocious and rather utopian error. An error in the sense that it was out of step with his basic theoretical analysis. That analysis had shown international finance capitalism to be a highly integrated world system, rent with contradictions admittedly, but united in the savagery of its opposition to communism. As a world system imperialism would stand or fall, and as a world system it would co-ordinate its attacks on any attempts at realising socialism. The force of these propositions became increasingly apparent to Lenin with the imperialist intervention in the civil war in Russia and bolstered his conviction that, in the final battle between international imperialism and the international proletariat, the choice before mankind was either the dictatorship of the imperialist bourgeoisie or the dictatorship of the proletariat. Success over one's native bourgeoisie, he was now saying, did not mean the advent of communism: on the contrary, it meant the redoubled armed intervention of international finance capital to stamp out each and every attempt at socialist revolution. Simply to engage in the battle, the proletariat needed an offensive organisation, a centralised coercive state structure to fight for the destruction of imperialism and that structure was, Lenin maintained, the dictatorship of the proletariat. Until imperialism was defeated on a world-wide scale there could be no possibility of an advance to communism.

In this sense, Lenin's 'rediscovery' of the idea of the dictatorship of the proletariat represents a reversion to the first principles of his theoretical analysis of imperialism. Time and again he returned to the theses he had developed in the period between 1914 and 1916. The imperialist war had made manifest the contradictions of imperialism and was raising the class struggle to its climactic point of civil war between the proletariat and bourgeoisie. Following Bukharin's analysis, Lenin repeatedly emphasised how, in its final death throes, the imperialist state had become ever more oppressive, militaristic and dictatorial. The old distinctions between republican, liberal and conservative bourgeois régimes had, he maintained, now disappeared – they had all become monolithically dictatorial.

The imperialist war of 1914–18 conclusively revealed even to backward workers the true nature of bourgeois democracy, even in the freest republics, as being a dictatorship of the bourgeoisie.[3]

Even in Germany, the most advanced capitalist country in Europe, the first few months of the republican régime headed by the social democrats had, in Lenin's view, degenerated into a tyranny where leaders of the proletariat could be murdered with impunity.

In these circumstances, proletarian dictatorship is not only an absolutely legitimate means of overthrowing the exploiters and suppressing their resistance, but also absolutely necessary to the entire mass of working people being their only defence against the bourgeois dictatorship which led to the war and is preparing new wars.

. . . in capitalist society, whenever there is any serious aggravation of the class struggle intrinsic to that society, there can be no alternative but the dictatorship of the bourgeoisie or the dictatorship of the proletariat. Dreams of some third way are reactionary, petty-bourgeois lamentations.[4]

Lenin's argument was strikingly reminiscent of his analysis of 1905–6. When the class war reaches its climax, politics reduces itself to the struggle of two armed camps locked in irreconcilable conflict.[5] In this situation, neutrality is impossible, claims of independence from the struggle or talk about abstract democracy 'is self-deception or deception of others'.[6] One dictatorship or the other:

> Either – or
> There is no middle course.[7]

The experience of Soviet power confirmed, according to Lenin, the dialectical choice which world history had presented to mankind for there could be no doubt that the dictatorship of the proletariat was not simply a Russian expedient – it was a universal requirement of revolutionary struggle applicable everywhere:

Either the dictatorship (i.e. the iron rule) of the landowners and capitalists, or the dictatorship of the working class.

There is no middle course. The scions of the aristocracy intellectualists and petty gentry, badly educated on bad books, dream of a middle course. There is no middle course anywhere in the world, nor can there be.[8]

It was, of course, precisely the error of Kautsky, according to Lenin's account, that he continued to dream of some kind of peaceful polite and civilised settling of the differences between the proletariat and the bourgeoisie. What he, and all the 'comical pedants' of the Second International, always refused to acknowledge was that the logic of the class struggle led eventually to civil war and that civil wars were decided by fighting not voting.[9]

What Kautsky and his like-minded social pacifists of the Second International never learned was that monopoly capitalism differed fundamentally from competitive capitalism and that, therefore, the form and nature of the bourgeois state had undergone an equally fundamental change. The imperialist state as distinct from the liberal bourgeois state was characterised by 'a minimum fondness for peace and freedom, and by a maximum and universal development of militarism'.[10] For Kautsky, to use Marx's hypothetical comments about the possibility for a peaceful transition to socialism in what were, in the early 1870s, comparatively free, non-bureaucratic and non-militaristic régimes such as Holland, Britain and America, as a general argument in favour of the 'democratic solution', quite ignored the immense changes which had occurred in the meanwhile. It was, Lenin maintained, a fallacious and dishonest juggling with quotations because:

Firstly, Marx regarded it as an exception even then. Secondly, in those days monopoly capitalism, i.e. imperialism, did not exist. Thirdly, in England and America there was no militarist clique then – *as there is now* – serving as the chief apparatus of the bourgeois state machine.[11]

The experience of history, Lenin asserted, demonstrated beyond doubt that dictatorship was necessary to *all* ascendant classes.[12] It was, in Lenin's view, 'an inevitable, essential and absolutely indispensable means of emerging from the capitalist system'.[13] The issue of the dictatorship of the proletariat was then the central question of the proletarian revolution,[14] it expressed the essence of Marxism and served therefore as a means of distinguishing revolutionary Marxists from social patriots on the international plane.

> Anyone who has read Marx and failed to understand that in capitalist society, at every acute moment, in every serious class conflict, the alternative is either the dictatorship of the bourgeoisie or the dictatorship of the proletariat, has understood nothing of either the economic or the political doctrines of Marx.

At this level of abstraction, therefore, Lenin's argument was that the epoch of world history in which he was living was a transitional one. It was the period of the armed battle between two irreconcilable world systems.

For both systems this was a fight for domination and survival on a world scale, for neither the one nor the other could exist on a merely local basis. Both parties to the conflict were therefore obliged to arm themselves, strengthen the power of the state and exercise class dictatorships over those states. The issue now became, in Lenin's view, either the dictatorship of the majority in the interests of peace and socialism, or the dictatorship of the small minority in the interests of militarism and imperialism:

> ... there is no *other* alternative: *either* Soviet government triumphs in every advanced country in the world, *or* the most reactionary imperialism triumphs, the most savage imperialism, which is throttling the small and weak nations and reinstating reaction all over the world.
> One or the other.
> There is no middle course.[15]

RUSSIAN SPECIFICS – CLASS ANALYSIS

It was towards the end of April 1918 that Lenin published his 'The Immediate Tasks of the Soviet Government' which signalled the beginning of a new orientation away from the commune form towards the dictatorship of the proletariat. It is highly significant that in his next major piece of writing, 'Left-Wing Childishness and the Petty-Bourgeois Mentality', completed in early May 1918, Lenin reverts to elements of his *initial* theoretical analysis (that is, his analysis of the development of capitalism in Russia developed in the 1890s) to substantiate his new emphasis on the need for a resolute proletarian dictatorship. This he had to do since the class analysis which formed the basis of his theory of imperialism and which was the premiss for an advance towards the commune form would hardly serve. That class analysis had assumed the socialisation of labour on a vast scale and that the mass of the people had been prepared for an advance to properly socialist self-administration. It is hardly surprising that when talking about the commune form, Lenin gave no special prominence to the role of the urban factory proletariat nor to the role of the Communist Party. Lenin's abstract formulations about the general nature of class dispositions under finance capitalism (*Imperialism the Highest Stage of Capitalism*) and generalised projections on the transcendence of the state (*The State and Revolution*) could not long survive the fact of Russian isolation. Russian economic backwardness was not immediately redeemed by the accession to the revolutionary cause of advanced Europe: on the contrary, war and civil war and the breakdown of transport threatened the total eclipse of all industry. The cultural barbarity of the Russian peasant mass was not rendered a cipher by the disciplined might of the Western proletariat; on the contrary, 'the million tentacles of this petty-bourgeois hydra ... forces its way into every pore of our social and economic organism'.[16] Until the European revolution broke out and redeemed all the pledges placed on it the Russians would have to rely on their own resources to meet the challenge from their own bourgeoisie and petty-bourgeoisie. This meant, according to Lenin, that a sober and realistic appraisal of the basic economic forms and corresponding class forces, as they actually existed in Russia, would have to form the basis of all Soviet political and economic strategies.

In Lenin's view, the transitional character of the epoch of global struggle of nascent socialism with dying capitalism had to be examined in its concrete Russian configuration. The global struggle in this transitional period was, as we have seen above, not the struggle for the immediate introduction of socialism, but rather for the complete physical dominance of the one system over the other. This transitional epoch would therefore be characterised by a struggle within each country between the forces in favour of a proletarian dictatorship and those who stood for a bourgeois dictatorship.

No one, I think, in studying the economic system of Russia, has denied its transitional character. Nor, I think, has any communist denied that the term Socialist Soviet Republic implies the determination of Soviet power to achieve the transition to socialism, and not that the new economic system is recognised as a socialist order.

But what does the term 'transition' mean? Does it not mean, as applied to an economy, that the present system contains elements, particles, fragments of *both* capitalism and socialism? Everyone will admit that it does. But not all who admit this take the trouble to consider what elements actually constitute the socio-economic structures that exist in Russia at the present time. And this is the crux of the question.

Let us enumerate these elements:

1. patriarchal, i.e. to a considerable extent natural peasant farming;
2. small commodity production (this includes the majority of those peasants who sell their grain)
3. private capitalism;
4. state capitalism;
5. socialism.

Russia is so vast and so varied that all these different types of socio-economic structure are intermingled. This is what constitutes the specific feature of the situation.[17]

Quite clearly Lenin's economic analysis had become more complex and complicated. In dealing with the peculiarities of the Russian situation he had to graft on to his analysis of international finance capitalism large elements of his original theoretical analysis of the development of capitalism in Russia. He was obliged to admit that the disposition of class forces, corresponding to the five economic forms he enumerates, had not substantially changed since 1905. The peasantry then, as in 1918, still constituted the immense majority. The bourgeoisie still retained a power out of all proportion to its numbers, but so too did the urban proletariat. The contest then, as in 1918, Lenin maintained, reduced itself to the question of which of those two classes would win sufficient power and support to vanquish the other. In all essentials, Lenin's class analysis of the dictatorship of the proletariat revives his arguments of 1905 and these in turn, as we saw in Volume 1, can be traced back to 1894. Lenin now reverted to his old argument that the proletariat could only establish its pre-eminence by becoming the political vehicle and vanguard of all Russia's exploited. Only through an alliance with the poor peasantry and wage-working artisans could the proletariat achieve a radical democratic revolution. Only by splitting the peasantry, by organising the poor peasants under the leadership of the proletariat would it be possible to establish and maintain the dictatorship of the proletariat and to prepare the foundations of socialism.

THE PEASANTRY AND THE DICTATORSHIP OF THE PROLETARIAT

According to the progression which Lenin now began to sketch, the October Revolution was to be regarded more as the radical realisation of the democratic revolution than the accomplishment of the socialist revolution. The October Revolution was democratic in nature precisely because its objective had been the radical destruction of landlordism and for that reason it had united, and had been supported by, the whole of the peasantry. The fundamental condition for proceeding further, for attempting to lay the foundations for socialism and consolidating the transitional régime of the proletarian dictatorship, was the splitting of the peasantry into its class components. The enemies of socialist advance – the rich peasants, the bourgeoisie and the old landlords – would have to be isolated, the poor peasants and rural proletarians won over to the side of the urban proletariat, and the middle peasants kept neutralised by concessions and cautious regard for their interests.

The victorious Bolshevik revolution meant the end of vacillation, meant the complete destruction of the monarchy and of the landlord system (which had *not* been destroyed before the October Revolution). We carried the *bourgeois* revolution *to its conclusion*. The peasants supported us *as a whole*. Their antagonism to the socialist proletariat could not reveal itself all at once. The Soviets united the peasants *in general*. The class divisions among the peasants had not yet matured, had not yet come into the open. *That* process took place in the summer and autumn of 1918... The poor peasants learned, not from books or newspapers, *but from life itself*, that their interests were irreconcilably antagonistic to those of the kulaks, the rich, the rival bourgeoisie.[18]

The only way, therefore, in which the proletarian dictatorship could hope to survive was in splitting the peasants and securing the support of the rural proletarians and poor peasants. The problem, however, was that in the countryside there had not been the extensive preparation for socialism and class organisation which capitalism had provided for the urban workers.[19] Proletarian influence upon the peasantry was slight and, of course, Bolshevik organisational strength was practically insignificant, 'In the first year the urban proletariat still had no firm foothold in the countryside'.[20] Consequently, as Lenin admitted, 'only an insignificant number of enlightened peasants might support us, while the vast majority had no such object in view'.[21] The poor and even the middle peasants, Lenin insisted, would learn to accept the dictatorship of the proletariat, and to support it, not so much from propaganda for socialism, certainly not from the establishment of ill-prepared collective farms, but from the hard school of kulak exploitation and, especially, from experiencing the restoration of the landlords and big bourgeoisie in the White Guard regions of Russia. The proletariat would only begin to win the support of the poor and middle peasants by dealing ruthlessly with the White Guards and their bourgeois and kulak supporters. Only after destroying the power of these social groups would the rural petty-bourgeoisie be prepared to follow the leadership of the socialist proletariat. Another link was therefore added to the strategic chain: the dictatorship of the proletariat could only be consolidated with the support of the rural poor. That support could, however, only be won by the proletarian state exercising the most severe and ruthless dictatorship over the big bourgeoisie and the kulaks. The state itself (which was the principal vehicle of the dictatorship of the proletariat) became, in this increasingly precarious analysis, the main weapon for securing the class support upon which the proletarian dictatorship was based.

> Only the proletariat could rout the bourgeoisie, and only after routing the bourgeoisie could the proletariat definitely win the sympathy and support of the petty-bourgeois strata of the population by using an instrument like state power.[22]

The initially minoritarian status of the dictatorship did not disturb Lenin. It was, he argued, a necessary and irrefutable fact of history that on the morrow of a successful revolution, every dominant class would be faced with minority support for the good reason that the *ancien régime* had possessed a monopoly over the means of communication and propaganda. Every dominant class had, on coming to power, utilised the state machinery, its coercive agencies and the educational and legal systems to express its *particular* interest as the *general* interest and in this way had won the support it needed. State power, he maintained, 'is simply an *instrument* which *different* classes can and must use (and know how to use) *for their class aims*'.[23] It was, he asserted, a mockery of Marxism perpetrated by opportunists like Kautsky, to maintain

> that the proletariat must first win a majority by means of universal suffrage, then obtain state power, by the vote of that majority, and only after that, on the basis of 'consistent' (some call it 'pure') democracy, organise socialism.
> But we say, on the basis of the teachings of Marx and the experience of the Russian revolution:
> the proletariat must first overthrow the bourgeoisie and win *for itself* state power, and then use that state power, that is, the dictatorship of the proletariat, as an instrument of its class for the purpose of winning the sympathy of the majority of the working people.[24]

The dictatorship of the proletariat, according to Lenin's interpretation, was far from having a purely negative and coercive role to play in the advance towards socialism. Certainly *one* of its main roles would remain that of coercing the remnants of the bourgeoisie and its supporters, but this was by no means its only, perhaps not even its most important function in history. Its positive mission was much more extensive: it was to act as the means through which the proletariat would win the support of all the exploited masses:

> *State power in the hands of one class, the proletariat, can and must become an instrument for winning to the side of the proletariat the non-proletarian working masses, an instrument for winning those masses from the bourgeoisie and from the petty-bourgeois parties.*[25]

All of this quite clearly rested upon precisely the same theoretical projection which had formed the heart of Lenin's idea of the vanguard role of the proletariat, namely his conception of the urban factory proletariat as the political vehicle and articulator of the ill-formed consciousness of the unorganised rural wage workers. The proletariat was once more represented as the natural representative of all Russia's exploited, expressing not merely its own particular interest but also the real interests of all those who exist wholly or partly through the sale of wage-labour. The dictatorship of the proletariat would therefore, in Lenin's account, by ruthlessly suppressing the exploiters and by exposing the petty-bourgeois political leaders who had hitherto duped the rural poor, win a majority for itself by showing the mass of the rural proletariat and semi-proletariat that its true interests were expressed by its vanguard and natural representative – the urban proletariat.

> The dictatorship of the proletariat implies and signifies a clear concept of the truth that the proletariat, because of its objective economic position in every capitalist society, *correctly* expresses the interests of the *entire mass* of working and exploited people, all semi-proletarians (i.e., those who live partly by the sale of their labour-power), all small peasants and similar categories.
>
> These sections do not follow the bourgeois and petty bourgeois parties (including the 'socialist' parties of the Second International) by the free expression of their will (as petty-bourgeois democrats assume) but because they are directly deceived by the bourgeoisie, because of pressure by capital and because of the self-deception of the petty-bourgeois leaders.
>
> The proletariat will attract these sections of the population

211

(semi-proletarians and small peasants) on to its side, and can attract them to its side, only *after* it has achieved a victory, only after it has won state power, that is, after the proletariat has overthrown the bourgeoisie, and emancipated *all* working people and *shown* them in practice the benefits (the benefits of freedom from the exploiters) accruing from proletarian state power.

This is the concept that constitutes the basis and essence of the idea of the dictatorship of the proletariat . . .[26]

In terms of class analysis Lenin had returned to his fundamental standpoint of the 1890s which had remained constant up to 1905. The peasantry as a whole was incapable of political initiative. Its isolated mode of production, lack of mobility and communications, severely restricted the development of consciousness and organisation in its midst. All the while, through the progress of capitalist economic relations, it was being rendered down into its modern class components – rural proletariat and rural bourgeoisie. For all these reasons the peasantry was fated, in Lenin's view, to remain a body of followers not of leaders. Itself incapable of articulation or organisation, it was compelled to choose either the leadership of the proletariat or that of the bourgeoisie. Being partly wage-labourers and partly independent small-scale commodity producers, the rural poor were, necessarily, unstable and ambiguous in their consciousness and political allegiance. Only determined leadership by the urban proletariat could resolve this dualism in the peasants' make-up, obliging them to jettison prejudice for sound judgement.

The peasant has his *prejudice* which makes him inclined to support the capitalist, the Socialist Revolutionary, and 'freedom to trade', but he also has his *sound judgement*, which is impelling him more and more towards an alliance with the workers.[27]

A large part of the objective of the proletarian dictatorship was therefore, in Lenin's words, 'to make [their] reason stronger than their prejudices'.[28] We are back to the category of immanence. The proletariat is already what the rural poor are destined to become. Though exploited, the rural poor cannot adequately apprehend the nature of the exploitation to which they fall prey, they cannot yet see the way to overcome their exploitation nor organise themselves to overcome it. Their inchoate consciousness and ill-formed 'reason' must therefore be refined and articulated by the urban proletariat – their champions in the class struggle.

Throughout the period from mid-1918 to late 1920, Lenin returned to this central precept of his first theoretical analysis.

Owing to their economic status in bourgeois society the peasants must follow either the workers or the bourgeoisie. *There is no middle way* . . . There is not, nor can there be, a middle course.[29]

Until such time as 'the peasantry should, through their own experience, by their own organisational work, arrive at the same conclusions'[30] as their urban vanguard, the workers must, Lenin insisted, be extremely cautious in their dealings with the countryside. For the first two years of Soviet power at least, Lenin constantly warned against the use of coercion towards the poor and middle peasants. He warned too against the over-hasty and ill-prepared attempts to introduce state farms and agricultural communes. Repeatedly he insisted that the grain requisitioning squads sent out by the urban workers should be composed only of the staunchest, most disciplined elements who would not resort to the looting drunkenness these squads all too often fell prey to. Above all, he insisted that coercion should not be used against the poor and middle peasants but only against the overt enemies of the régime, the kulak grain hoarders.

In practice, Lenin's policy proved impossible to apply. In the first place, it was virtually impossible clearly to distinguish in any given locality exactly who were the rich peasants. The poor peasants shaded imperceptibly into the middle peasants and they, in turn, into the rich peasants. There was a continuum of social status and of economic power in every village which tended to beget a natural community of interest within it – a community of interest emphatically hostile to the armed requisition squads of urban workers. There was, in practice, no other way in which the peasants could be persuaded to give up their surplus grain for no return (apart from worthless paper money with which they could buy nothing – mere promissory notes which, Lenin acknowledged, would not be redeemed for some considerable time to come) without coercion or the threat of it.

Lenin's rather pious words about minimising the recourse to force in dealing with the peasants were, in any case, at odds with his appraisal of the fundamental economic problem confronting the régime in its first two years. That fundamental economic problem around which all else revolved was how to obtain grain for the towns and for the army when the regime had nothing to offer in exchange for it. Expressed in another way, the problem was how to convince the peasants of their own long-term interests in the rehabilitation of urban industry and to show them that this very rehabilitation required them to continue making a loan of grain.[31] Lenin's initial and highly idealist solution to this problem of persuading the peasants of the justice of the grain monopoly and the continuing requisitions was to appeal to their reason and especially to their humanitarian feelings. If the appalling predicament of the urban workers was properly explained, he felt confident that the peasants would respond with generosity.[32] This initial optimism was extremely short-lived. It vanished when severe famine began to affect the urban areas in the spring and summer of 1918 and famine, as Lenin remarked, sweeps away all other questions.[33]

The fundamental issue now became the preservation of the working class itself. The preservation of industry, the preservation of any sort of urban life was seriously thrown into question. Therewith the thin veneer of civilisation in Russia appeared to Lenin to be on the verge of being swept away by the narrow selfishness of the peasant masses. For industry to survive, for the towns and civilised life to continue, the working class had to be fed, and for the working class to be fed the grain monopoly would have to be preserved and strengthened as would the dictatorship of the proletariat. The objective now was the bare minimal one of saving the working class from starvation and fighting for at least the possibility of restoring industry:

> ... the main, the fundamental, the root 'economic condition' is to *save the workers*. If the working class is saved from death, from starvation, saved from perishing, it will be possible to restore disrupted production. But in order to save the working class it is necessary to have the dictatorship of the proletariat ...[34]

The primary task in a ruined country is to save the working people. The primary productive force of human society as a whole, is the workers, the working people. If they survive, we shall save and restore *everything* ... We must save the workers even if they are unable to work. If we keep them alive for the next few years we shall save the country, save society and socialism.[35]

In the resolution of this question, no majority vote or broad inclusive labour democracy could decide the issue, no peasant majority, however vast, had the right to starve the workers to death. In this situation only the preservation of the grain monopoly in the hands of a ruthlessly severe proletarian dictatorship could save the proletariat. This, for Lenin, was the irreducible essence of the dictatorship of the proletariat.

Should the sixty peasants have the right to decide and the ten workers be obliged to obey? The great principle of equality, unity of labour democracy and deciding by a majority vote!

That is what they tell us. [The Social Democrats, that is] And we tell them that they are mere clowns who confuse the hunger problem and obscure it with their high-sounding phrases.

We ask you whether the workers in a ruined country where factories are idle ought to submit to the decision of the majority of peasants when the latter refuse to deliver their surplus stocks of grain. Have they the right to take these surplus stocks, by force if necessary, if there is no other way? Give us a straightforward answer.[36]

It was the desperate economic situation of the country, the reality of widespread famine in the urban centres above all which, for Lenin, made coercion towards the countryside inescapable. To feed the workers, the grain monopoly and the requisition squads had to be maintained for otherwise profiteering and hoarding of grain would have put paid to the régime's attempts to feed the towns and the army. The devastation of the war and the profiteering of the peasants could only be overcome by the most determined centralisation and equitable distribution of all resources.[37] There would, inevitably, Lenin recognised, be huge numbers of people who would fight for their 'purely local interests', for their right to hoard and profit from the famine and argue for the re-establishment of 'freedom to trade' in grain. Precisely for these reasons, the dictatorship of the proletariat would have to be strengthened. It was from his appraisal of the basic economic issues confronting Russia that Lenin emerged with his most cogent reasons for increasing the power of the centralised dictatorship. His tone had clearly changed. The point now was not so much to win over that majority of the peasants who, according to theory, shared the same interests as the proletariat, the point was to ensure the continued survival of the proletariat by forcing the peasants as a whole to disgorge their surplus.

In Lenin's initial scenario, an immense role in securing the social base of the dictatorship of the proletariat was to be played by the Poor Peasants' Committees which the Bolshevik Party set out to organise in May 1918. These committees were established not only to act as the principal agencies of the régime in locating and requisitioning the hidden grain stocks of the kulaks, but clearly and obviously they were intended as the foci, the organisational rallying points of the poor peasants. They were to be, in Lenin's plan, the organisational means for splitting the peasants and securing the following of the overwhelming majority of them behind the leadership of the proletariat. It was precisely for this reason that in his periodisation of the revolution, Lenin maintained that the summer of 1918 was the point of transition from the radical democratic to the beginning of the socialist phase of the revolution.

It was, paradoxically, the very success of the Bolsheviks' radical democratic solution to the agrarian question which cut the ground from under the attempt at class differentiation of the peasantry. In abolishing private ownership of the land and legitimising a vast redistribution of the old landed estates and the lands of the Crown and Church, the Bolshevik Decree on Land had fundamentally altered the balance of class forces in the countryside. Back in 1905, Lenin had held up the carrot of nationalisation before the peasant nag. He had produced figures to show that the holdings of the poor peasants could be doubled at a stroke by the nationalisation and redistribution of the landed estates. The effect of the decree on land and the redistribution of land it legitimised and further encouraged was, above all, to reduce the numbers both of the rich and of the poor peasants very considerably.[38] The elements of class antagonism within the countryside had been decidedly reduced and, for the most part, the erstwhile poor peasants shaded imperceptibly into the category of middle peasants.

The truth of Lenin's proposition that only the peasants had profited from the revolution became only too apparent in the career of the Poor Peasants' Committees. They were, from first to last, an ignominious failure. They were poorly and hurriedly organised, they suffered from the almost complete lack of dedicated and capable Bolshevik leaders in the countryside and, above all, they suffered from the almost universal peasant resentment of the activities of the expropriation squads dispatched by the urban workers and the Party to secure grain wherever and however they could.

The Poor Peasants' Committees were, for all these reasons, effectively scrapped in late 1918. Therewith the major component of Lenin's class analysis of the social basis of the dictatorship of the proletariat abruptly vanished. Lenin's theoretical projections, derived from his socio-economic analysis of the 1890s, to the effect that experience would show the poor peasants that the proletariat really was their natural representative had not materialised. In proportion as the class base of the régime shrank, Lenin waxed ever more lyrical about the staunchness, heroism and revolutionary ardour of those who remained as the shock forces of the revolution, the iron battalions of the proletariat.

As 1920 progressed, Lenin's attitude towards the peasantry became distinctly tougher. By the middle of the year he had largely dispensed with the niceties of class analysis of the different strata of the peasantry and the need for a policy of differentiating them organisationally. The tendency now in his writing was to lump them all together as a bad lot and a lost cause. 'The peasants,' he now baldly asserted, 'are not socialists. To base our socialist plans on the assumption that they are would be building on sand.'[39] The solution to the agrarian question which he began to put forward at this time was much more radical and was closely bound to his utopian project for the electrification of Russia.

Lenin's line of argument had, as ever, a certain logic. The peasants as a whole, he acknowledged, were 'Sick at heart because there is no fodder, livestock is perishing, and taxation is so heavy'[40] and forced requisitions of grain continued, but they must be made to understand that the necessary condition for the repayment of the forced loan they were making to the industrial workers was the rehabilitation of industry. Only on the basis of a thriving industrial base could the exchange between town and country be established. The rehabilitation of industry on a modern and technologically sound basis in its turn, in Lenin's view, demanded a comprehensive plan for the electrification of Russia. 'Communism is Soviet power plus the electrification of the whole country, since industry cannot be developed without electrification.'[41] The question then arose of how this huge plan was to be financed, who was to do the paying? Lenin was in no doubt that the surplus product of the peasantry was the only secure source to finance this far-reaching national plan.

> We admit that we are in debt to the peasant. We have had grain from him in return for paper money, and have taken it from him on credit. We must repay that debt, and we shall do so when we have restored our industry. To restore it we need a surplus of agricultural products.[42]

The object of the rehabilitation of industry was not, however, to be the alleviation of the situation of the peasant farmers but rather their elimination as a social group: 'the proletariat will restore large-scale industry and the national economy so that the peasants can be transferred to a higher economic system'.[43]

'Peasant farming,' Lenin concluded, 'cannot continue in the old way.'[44] On the basis of electrification and the new 'electricity consciousness' it would bring,[45] on the basis of the huge industrial machine with plants of gigantic size which would, consequently, be established, the economic base would be created for the elimination of the distinction between town and country:

> The peasants, as petty proprietors, and the workers are two different classes, and we shall abolish the difference between them when we abolish the basis of small-scale production, and create a new basis of gigantic, large-scale machine production.[46]

The elimination of small-scale commodity production and its supersession by large-scale productive units centrally placed and directed was precisely what electrification signified and what the transition to a properly socialist economic base entailed, according to Lenin.

Lenin's progression of thought was then that the repayment of the forced loan levied on the peasantry necessitated the rehabilitation of industry which in turn required the electrification of Russia which could only be accomplished by requisitioning the surplus of peasant production for years to come. The rehabilitation of industry though electrification of industry and the creation of a national plan would, of itself, eliminate the small-scale nature of peasant production and the petty producer as a social class. In the meantime, Lenin frankly conceded, the peasants would have to be treated to alternate doses of encouragement and compulsion and 'the entire male and female population of workers and peasants without exception' would have to be mobilised.[47]

Immediately prior to the Tenth Party Congress, which was of course to initiate the New Economic Policy with its very considerable concessions to peasant demands, Lenin had, as we have seen, elaborated a hard uncompromising stand on the agrarian question. Faced with the inescapable facts of widespread peasant revolts, refusal to sow the available crop areas and slaughter of livestock, faced in other words with the active and passive resistance of the peasantry to the dictatorship of the proletariat, his inclination was to write off the peasantry as a whole as a class lost to socialism. He swept the problem under the carpet by invoking the grandiose plan for the electrification of Russia which would finally dispose of the problem of the petty producer. He was shortly forced to realise and acknowledge the hopeless impracticability of such utopian determinism.

CHAPTER 10

The Proletariat and the Dictatorship

We have seen how, by March/April 1918, faced with incontrovertible evidence of the effective breakdown of transport and of industrial production generally, Lenin began to insist on discipline, one-man responsibility and accountability to the centre. As 1918 progressed, as the Soviet power was faced with kulak revolts, grain crises, fuel crises and full-scale civil war, Lenin's demands for discipline, centralisation and accountability became ever more strident and insistent, and the commune model increasingly receded into the background to be replaced by the dictatorship of the proletariat. The proletariat featured now not simply as the leader of the mass but as the sole repository of administrative skills, the only class with a title to govern. The sphere of self-activity and self-administration was dramatically narrowed from the popular mass to the class, from the people at large to the proletariat. This was the crucial significance of the dictatorship of the proletariat.

Lenin's analysis of the necessity for the dictatorship of the proletariat rested, as we have seen, on a reversion to his old class analysis of the 1890s in which the proletariat was portrayed as the natural representative and vanguard of all Russia's exploited. Equally important in this context was Lenin's view of the dictatorship of the proletariat as a transitional régime which would endure for a considerable period of time. As early as June 1918, Lenin was clear that the 'severe and very painful period of transition from Capitalism to socialism . . . will inevitably be a very long one in all countries'.[1] Its ultimate objective remained the same as the objective of the commune – the 'smashing' of the bourgeois state machine.[2] The difference was that now a whole historical epoch was to be devoted to preparing the ground for the elimination of the state. Furthermore, Lenin now specified that as a precondition for the emergence of socialism proper, classes would have to be abolished.[3] Put in another way, it was the historical function of the dictatorship of the proletariat to oversee the immense task of dissolving the social and economic bases of classes as a precondition for the emergence of socialism.

And classes still *remain* and *will remain* in the era of the dictatorship of the proletariat. The dictatorship will become unnecessary when classes disappear. Without the dictatorship of the proletariat they will not disappear.[4] The abolition of classes, as Lenin candidly admitted, itself entailed fundamental and unprecedented changes in the economic, social and cultural life of the country which would take a very long time to accomplish.

Socialism means the abolition of classes.

In order to abolish classes it is necessary, first, to overthrow the landowners and capitalists. This part of our task has been accomplished, but it is only a part, and moreover, *not* the most difficult part. In order to abolish classes it is necessary, secondly, to abolish the difference between factory worker and peasant, to make *workers of all of them*. This cannot be done all at once. This task is incomparably more difficult and will of necessity take a long time. It is not a problem that can be solved only by the organisational reconstruction of the whole social economy, by a transition from individual, disunited, petty commodity production to large-scale social production. This transition must of necessity be extremely protracted.[5]

There was yet another condition which Lenin specified before the state could be smashed and this followed from the theory of imperialism. So long as imperialism existed, the proletariat would have to maintain its vigil, it would indeed have to take up the armed offensive against predatory imperialism and this meant the maintenance of a powerful centralised coercive machine – or state.

So far we have deprived the capitalists of this machine and have taken it over. We shall use this machine, or bludgeon, to destroy all exploitation. And when the possibility of exploitation no longer exists anywhere in the world, when there are no longer owners of land and owners of factories, and when there is no longer a situation in which some gorge while others starve, only when the possibility of this no longer exists shall we consign the machine to the scrap heap. Then there will be no state and no exploitation.[6]

It is curious (and many would say significant) that Lenin never attempted properly to answer the question which Bakunin first posed and which was later reformulated by the Workers' Opposition and the left wing in the Communist International: that question was how is it possible for a class millions strong to rule and what mechanisms could enable such a large group to exercise its own dictatorship?[7] According to Marxist theory, as Lenin was well aware, it was precisely the class nature of the dictatorship which distinguished the Marxist transitional régime from the 'adventurist' and 'elitist' transitional dictatorship advocated by Jacobins and Blanquists. The closest Lenin comes to offering an answer to the question is in his Draft Programme of; the R.C.P. (b.) written in the spring of 1919. Enumerating the advantages of the soviet structure as the organisational form of 'a new type of state that is transitional', he asserted that it

... gives a certain actual advantage to that section of the working people that all the capitalist developments that preceded socialism has made the most concentrated, united, educated and steeled in the struggle, i.e. to the urban industrial proletariat.[8]

It did this primarily 'by making the economic, industrial unit (factory) and not a territorial division the primary electoral unit and the nucleus of the state structure under Soviet power'.[9] In this same Draft Programme, however, immediately after the passage cited above, Lenin introduces a theme which recurs time and time again in his writings in the period from mid-1918 to late 1920. He adds a well-worn cautionary note to the effect that capitalism had fostered among the workers 'narrow guild and narrow trade interests' which 'split them up into competitive groups'. About a year previously he had reflected that no Chinese wall separated the proletariat from the old bourgeois society, its rotting corpse poisoning the whole atmosphere of the new order.[10]

Having begun the communist revolution, the working class cannot instantly discard the weaknesses and vices inherited from the society of landowners and capitalists, the society of exploiters and parasites, the society based on the filthy selfishness and personal gain of a few and the poverty of the many.[11]

We come to another crucially important facet of Lenin's conception of the dictatorship of the proletariat – the task of re-educating and reforming the working class itself. Before socialism could be introduced, the proletariat would have to be purged of all the pernicious values and habits it had absorbed under capitalism.

The workers were never separated by a Great Wall of China from the old society. And they have preserved a good deal of the traditional mentality of capitalist society. The workers are building a new society without themselves having become new people, or cleansed of the filth of the old world; they are still standing up to their knees in that filth. We can only dream of cleaning the filth away. It would be utterly utopian to think this could be done all at once.[12]

Here with a vengeance was another Herculean task for the proletarian dictatorship – the cleansing of the Augean stables of capitalism.

The urban factory workers were not and could not be immune to the narrow sectarian and self-seeking attitudes to which generations of bourgeois dominance had habituated them. If this was true in general, it was especially true of Russia where the working class formed only a small proportion of the total population and was therefore far more vulnerable to the narrow selfishness of the petty-bourgeoisie. More than anywhere else in Europe it had been deprived of education, leisure and culture and consequently, as Lenin lamented:

we ... felt acutely how heavy the task of re-educating the masses was, the task of organisation and instruction, spreading knowledge, combating the heritage of ignorance, primitiveness, barbarism and savagery that we took over.[13]

223

The brutalisation of a generation which the world war produced was bound to leave its imprint on even the most conscious and committed working men.

> Detachments of Red Army men leave the capital with the best intentions in the world, but, on arriving at their destination, they sometimes succumb to the temptations of looting and drunkenness. For this we have to blame the few years of carnage, which kept men in trenches for so long and compelled them to slaughter each other like wild beasts. This bestiality is to be observed in all countries. Years will pass before men cease to act like wild beasts and resume human shape.
> We appeal to the workers to let us have men.[14]

In Russia too the proletariat had only emerged as an organised and conscious class in the mid-1890s and even then, right down to February 1917, it had suffered mightily from the proscription of its organisations and its press and the exile or execution of its leaders. In the war it had lost millions as cannon-fodder to the grand designs of the tsar and the Entente. After the war, depleted, maimed and brutalised by the immense blood-letting, the working class suffered prolonged unemployment and starvation in its urban strongholds due to the collapse of transport and the effective demise of industrial production. After the revolution its situation became even worse, real wages declined, unemployment grew, exchange between town and country virtually ceased and the kulaks refused to part with their grain at what they considered unfair prices, for money which was devaluing with staggering rapidity, which in any case was useless to them since there were almost no industrial commodities to purchase. On top of all these calamities came the Civil War. Large areas of the country were removed from Bolshevik control. Vital raw materials were denied to those factories still in production, oil and coal were for some time unobtainable and grain procurements slumped dramatically. To meet each of these recurrent crises (and the period of the dictatorship of the proletariat seemed to be, from a reading of Lenin's works, the period of permanent crises) Lenin responded with the same clarion call – factory workers of Russia, the régime is in danger, despatch your staunchest, most organised and class conscious forces for the last struggle on the Kolchak/Denikin/Wrangel fronts, the grain front, the fuel front, the railway front. It sometimes appeared that Lenin considered the battered and depleted proletariat of Russia to be an inexhaustible fount of heroism and devotion. He was, however, fully aware of the enormous privations which the dictatorship of the proletariat had brought upon the proletariat itself. The proletariat had had to endure cold, suffering and starvation more than any class of the population.

> Since the Bolshevik revolution the Russian peasants, for the first time in thousands of years, are working for themselves and can feed better. Yet at the same time, during these two years of struggle the workers, the proletariat, while exercising their dictatorship, have been suffering untold torments of hunger.[15]

The proletariat had, then, reaped no material benefit from its dictatorship. On the contrary, it had been repeatedly mobilised to face death on the fronts of the civil war and enjoined to attempt to restore production and the railway network in unheated workshops on starvation rations. Conditions might well have been peculiarly severe in Russia, but Lenin warned his foreign comrades to make no hedonistic overtures to lure their workers into establishing the dictatorship of the proletariat with promises of a land flowing with milk and honey: ' . . . all Communist parties should inculcate in the industrial proletariat a realisation of the need for sacrifices, and be prepared to make sacrifices so as to overthrow the bourgeoisie and consolidate proletarian power.'[16] Revolution everywhere, he reminded them, meant merciless class struggle, civil war, disruption and dislocation. It was, he maintained, a general rule that at the beginning of the transitional period the workers would be faced with a decline in production and therefore a diminished standard of living.[17]

In the face of all these calamities it was small wonder that Lenin found many of the industrial workers to be unequal to the demands of constant heroism and selfless devotion to the cause of socialism which the régime expected of them. 'Many members of the working masses,' he noted already in June 1918, 'gave way to despair.'[18] Famine was already beginning to bite hard and despair was 'temporarily in the ascendant' in every factory.[19] By December 1919, he conceded that 'the working class is exhausted and is naturally weak in a country that is in ruins'.[20] How then did Lenin hope to maintain the dictatorship of the proletariat?

It is quite clear that from the very time that the dictatorship of the proletariat began to displace the commune as a model, Lenin simultaneously began to exalt the role of the small politically-conscious vanguard of the proletariat as the only reliable social base of the new régime. His analysis once again was strongly reminiscent of his reflections on 1905–6. Then, as in 1918, the small conscious advanced contingent of the proletariat of the capitals would provide the initiative. They would lead the more backward urban workers into the struggle and after them, in turn, the mass of Russia's exploited would be mobilised. Through experience of struggle under the leadership of the advanced workers, by learning in practice who their friends were and who their enemies were, by observing which strata supported which policies, the whole mass of the exploited would gradually acquire adequate consciousness. It would, Lenin asserted, be ridiculous to expect that capitalist society

> ... could at one stroke create a complete appreciation of the need for socialism and an understanding of it. This cannot be. The appreciation comes only at the end of the struggle which has to be waged in the painful period in which our revolution has broken out before the rest and gets no assistance from the others, and when famine approaches. Naturally, certain strata of the toilers are inevitably overcome by despair and indignation and turn away in disgust from everything.[21]

Large-scale factories and socialisation of labour under capitalism did not, of itself, Lenin now argued, automatically or spontaneously generate socialist consciousness. The fact of being a factory worker did not by any means make a man a socialist.

> It is understandable that among the broad masses of the toilers there are many (you know this particularly well; every one of you sees this in the factories [Lenin was addressing trade union leaders]) who are not enlightened socialists and cannot be such because they have to slave in the factories and have neither the time nor opportunity to become socialists.[22]

Even among the proletariat, therefore, adequate consciousness would only appear at the end of the long transitional period of struggle called the dictatorship of the proletariat. The development of adequate consciousness, however, even among the proletariat, was dependent upon the organisation, commitment, loyalty and heroism of the advanced contingent of class-conscious workers. They, Lenin insisted, must be organised into exemplary detachments, iron shock battalions to be dispatched wherever the battle was fiercest and wherever the exhausted mass gave way to despair:

The weary must be encouraged, sustained and led. The comrades themselves see that every class-conscious worker leads scores of tired people. We say this and we demand it. This is exactly what the dictatorship of the proletariat means – one class leads the other, because it is more organised, more solid and more class-conscious. The ignorant masses fell to every bait and because of their weariness are ready to yield to everything.[23]

The basis of the régime during the transitional period could only be the advanced section of the proletariat. Already in May 1918 Lenin had come to the conclusion that, 'We can count on the politically conscious workers alone; the remaining mass, the bourgeoisie and petty proprietors are against us'.[24] The sphere of self-administration was narrowing even further. Already Lenin made his first substitution of the advanced section for the class. A regressive notion of virtual representation was being invoked. The first stage of this we have already noticed – the sense in which all of Russia's toiling and exploited population found its representative, the articulator of its 'sound judgement' as distinct from its 'prejudice', in the urban proletariat. The second stage, which is clearly being introduced here, is contained in the assertion that the essential proletarian role is fulfilled only by its advanced conscious vanguard. As the proletariat 'represents' the exploited mass, so the advanced urban workers 'represent' the proletariat. The 'small section of advanced and politically conscious workers in Russia' must, Lenin asserted in May 1918, recognise its responsibilities and its duties.

227

It is a question of every politically conscious worker feeling that he is not only the master in his own factory but that he is also a representative of the country, of his feeling his responsibility. The politically conscious worker must know that he is a representative of his class.[25]

It was, in particular, to the Petrograd factory workers that Lenin looked whenever a crisis threatened the régime. They, in his idealised view, encapsulated all the qualities the proletariat ought to exhibit, 'the advanced, most class-conscious, most revolutionary, most steadfast detachments of the working class . . . least liable to succumb to empty phrases, to spineless despair and to the intimidation of the bourgeoisie'. Such small exemplary detachments had frequently, he reflected, saved critical situations in the life of nations by firing the masses with revolutionary enthusiasm.[26] 'The country and the revolution can be saved only by the mass effort of the advanced workers.'[27] In the battle for grain, only the advanced workers, especially the workers of Petrograd, could rally the poor peasants and defeat the kulaks. '*Nobody* but the workers of Petrograd can do this, for there are no other workers in Russia as class conscious as the Petrograd workers.'[28] On the changing fronts of the civil war it was the Petrograders who were dispatched to the points of gravest crisis, steeling the unstable elements in the army and guiding 'the wavering sections of the working population.'

The Petrograd proletariat has suffered more than the proletariat in other localities from famine, the perils of war and the withdrawal of the best workers for Soviet duties throughout Russia.

Yet we see that there has been not the slightest dejection, not the slightest diminution of energy among the Petrograd workers. On the contrary, they have become steeled, they have found new strength and have brought new fighters to the fore. They are excellently fulfilling the duty of a leading contingent, sending aid and support where it is most needed.[29]

It was partly, no doubt, through observing the undoubted heroism of the Petrograd and Moscow workers that Lenin was prompted to review an important element of his analysis of

1905–6, namely the central importance of the capital cities in revolutionary struggle. In the period of transition especially: 'The town inevitably *leads* the country. The country inevitably *follows the town*.'[30] This was, in a sense, a reformulation of Lenin's view that the proletariat must lead the poor peasants, but the insistence with which he repeats his formulation and the arguments he uses to sustain it bring him perilously close to Jacobin propositions:

> An overwhelming superiority of forces at the decisive point, this 'law' of military success is also a law of political success, especially in that fierce seething class war which is called revolution.
>
> Capitals, or, in general, big commercial and industrial centres . . . to a considerable degree decide the political fate of a nation, provided, of course, the centres are supported by sufficient local, rural forces, even if that support does not come immediately.[31]

The crucial factor, Lenin insisted, was not a majority vote throughout the country. Elections were significant to the extent that they indicated the volume of support for the revolutionary party amongst the proletariat, and especially amongst the proletariat (and sections of the army) in or near the capitals. Once sure of the capitals, the victorious proletariat would thereby have secured control over the state apparatus and could then proceed to use that apparatus of power to win support from the peripheral regions of the country.

> And being certain of winning the two metropolitan cities, the two centres of the capitalist state machine (economic and political), by a swift decisive blow, we . . . were able with the aid of the central apparatus of state power to *prove by deeds* to the *non*-proletarian working people that the proletariat was their only reliable ally, friend and leader.[32]

The strategic disposition of the proletariat, concentrated in and around the metropolitan nerve centres of bourgeois political and economic dominance, was then of crucial importance in the first stage of the proletarian dictatorship. It enabled them to seize state power. We should note that Lenin has now reverted to Marx's initial vision of the dictatorship of the proletariat as outlined in the period 1848–51. It was, in Marx's description, emphatically a seizure of state power at the centre. The proletariat was to dispose of, build up and utilise state power in order to spread the revolution outwards from the centre to the periphery. And it was exactly these centralist, étatist notions which characterised the dictatorship of the proletariat which Marx reversed after the Paris Commune, enjoining his followers not to seize state power but to smash it. Lenin also had to studiously ignore the words of Engels (with which he was quite familiar) to the effect that the commune demonstrated finally that the age of surprise attacks at the centre, the age when Paris could dominate France, was finally over.[33]

Lenin's account of the class dynamics of the transitional period and his justification for the proletarian dictatorship can best be summarised in a series of theses:

(1) The town dominates the country, the capitals must lead the periphery.
(2) The strategic concentration of the proletariat assures it command over the capitals.
(3) The advanced, class-conscious detachment of the urban proletariat alone expresses the essential interests of the proletariat as a whole.
(4) The proletariat expresses the real interests of all the exploited and toiling masses.
(5) The advanced contingent leads the rest of the proletariat and, after them, the broad mass of the exploited into struggle and from this experience the general level of consciousness is progressively raised.
(6) The critical factor enabling the advanced, politically conscious workers to mobilise the exploited mass and to win them to socialism is its possession of state power – its exercise of the dictatorship of the proletariat. Not through a majority to state power but through state power to win the majority.

Lest it be thought that this cryptic presentation overschematises or traduces Lenin's intentions, let us conclude this section with a quotation which neatly summarises these points:

The strength of the proletariat in any capitalist country is far greater than the proportion it represents of the total population. That is because the proletariat economically dominates the centre and nerve of the entire economic system of capitalism, and also because the proletariat expresses economically and politically the real interests of the overwhelming majority of the working people under capitalism.

Therefore, the proletariat, even when it constitutes a minority of the population (or when the class-conscious and really revolutionary vanguard of the proletariat constitutes a minority of the population), is capable of overthrowing the bourgeoisie, and, after that, of winning to its side numerous allies from a mass of semi-proletarians and petty bourgeoisie who never declare in advance in favour of the rule of the proletariat, who do not understand the conditions and aims of that rule, and only by their subsequent experience become convinced that the proletarian dictatorship is inevitable, proper and legitimate.[34]

CHAPTER 11

The International Dimension of the Revolution

We have already, in the discussion of Lenin's theory of imperialism, established the fundamentals of his outlook on international affairs. Finance capital, being inherently international in its scope and strivings, spread its contradictions throughout the world and fought them out in global war. As a world system it would stand or fall and therefore the forces ranged against it would have to be assessed and organised on a global and not a narrowly national basis. 'Capitalism,' Lenin maintained in August 1918, 'is an international force, and it can therefore be completely destroyed only through victory in all countries not in one alone.'[1]

The belief that the structure of world finance capitalism would shortly come tumbling down was absolutely crucial to Lenin's whole project for socialism in Russia. It was, Lenin maintained, quite accidental that Russia found herself the initiator of the world revolutionary movement, but this was to be attributed more to the backwardness of her capitalism than to any pretensions to be more advanced than others.[2] In Russia, due to a peculiar combination of circumstances, it had been comparatively easy to start the world socialist revolution but, Lenin added, because of her backwardness, it would be inordinately difficult to continue. In Western Europe, by contrast, 'it will be immeasurably more difficult to begin but immeasurably easier to go on'.[3] Once the revolutionary process had been started, however, it would, Lenin believed, acquire an unstoppable momentum of its own, it would scatter its sparks over the great mass of combustible material throughout Europe. Changing the metaphor, Lenin insisted that it was impossible to climb out of war without starting an avalanche.[4] The existence of one régime which promised and secured for its people peace, bread and workers' power, would

232

galvanise the workers of Europe. It would prove to them that they need no longer suffer death on the battlefield and starvation at home, that there was a real practicable alternative to the miseries which they had to suffer and the barbarism to which civilisation had been reduced.

It is perhaps too little noticed how closely Lenin's justification for revolution in Russia, and his projections about the international spread of the revolution, are bound up with his indictment of the savagery and butchery of the First World War. Bukharin's analysis had convinced him of the nightmare which the survival of the imperialist state entailed. All these states were being reduced to the same despotic level. The war had finally wiped out the remnants of liberalism in the capitalist state:

> The imperialist war is so steeped in blood, so predatory and so bestial, that it has effaced even these important differences, and in this respect it has brought the freest democracy of America to the level of semi-militarist, despotic Germany.[5]

The progress of the war itself reinforced his view that imperialism was bringing the world to the brink of barbarism. Just as old Engels had predicted, a war between the big capitalist countries had become a global war and, just as Engels had foretold, that global war had brought death, famine and pestilence, 'hopeless confusion to our artificial machinery in trade, industry and credit, ending in general bankruptcy in collapse of the old states and their traditional state wisdom to such an extent that crowns will roll by dozens on the pavement and there will be nobody to pick them up'. Exactly as Engels had foretold, 'only one result is absolutely certain: general exhaustion and the establishment of the conditions for the ultimate victory of the working class'.[6] These brilliant predictions had, Lenin maintained, been realised 'to the letter'. The war, its unbearable sufferings and wanton destruction of productive capacities, and the impossibility of ending it under the capitalist system, were the imperatives which would impel the workers of the world to follow the Russian example. The Russians, therefore, had done their international duty as no other Party had done[7] and could feel justifiably proud to be the first detachment to fell 'that wild beast capitalism, which has reduced humanity to starvation and demoralisation and

which will assuredly perish soon, no matter how monstrous and
savage its frenzy in the face of death'.[8]

> This war, which has affected almost the whole of the globe,
> which has destroyed not less than ten million lives not counting
> the millions of maimed, crippled and sick, this war which, in
> addition, has torn millions of the healthiest and best forces
> from productive labour – this war has reduced humanity to a
> state of absolute savagery ... Capitalism has led to such a
> severe and painful disaster that it is now perfectly clear to all
> that the present war cannot be ended without a number of most
> severe and bloody revolutions, of which the Russian revolution
> was only the first, only the beginning.[9]

Lenin's was an apocalyptic view. The revolution was not the
apocalypse the continued existence of imperialism was, for it
threatened a world already 'drenched in blood',[10] nothing but
war upon war, insanity and butchery of ever-increasing extensiveness. Crucial to his analysis of imperialism, crucial therefore
to his projections about the spread of the revolution, was his belief
that, so long as finance capitalism continued to exist, constant war
was inevitable. There was then, according to Lenin, no way that
the capitalist countries could agree terms of peace for 'even if
some imperialist countries were to stop fighting, others could
continue ... it is impossible to end this bloody war under the
capitalist system'.[11] Driven beyond the limits of endurance,
increasingly aware of the senselessness of imperialist wars and
inspired by the example of Russia, the workers of the world
would overthrow the imperialists and establish a world federal
republic of socialist states in which the comparative backwardness
of Russia would be redeemed by her more developed neighbours.
These were the predictions stemming from Lenin's analysis of
imperialism, upon which the spread of the revolution, and
therefore the fate of the Russian Revolution, was based. And
Lenin was clear that in the international arena, just as in the
sphere of internal class analysis, the Russian Revolution was
premissed upon the predictive capacity of theory:

> When, over two years ago, at the very beginning of the Russian
> revolution, we spoke about the approaching international,

world revolution, it was a prevision, and to a certain extent a prediction.[12]

At the time of the Brest negotiations, Lenin later recalled:

> ... we were groping, guessing when the revolution in Europe might break out – we presumed, on the basis of our theoretical conviction, that the revolution must take place . . .[13]

This prediction could not, however, have an elastic timescale attached to its realisation. This did not mean, Lenin hastened to add, that the spread of the revolution could be exactly predicted to the day or the hour, but it certainly meant that the time scale he had in mind was to be reckoned in weeks and months rather than years. In July 1921 he conceded that:

> Before the revolution, and even after it, we thought: either revolution breaks out in the other countries, in the Capitalistically more developed countries, immediately, or at least very quickly, or we must perish.[14]

We must now explore the circumstances in which this world view was radically changed.

THE RUSSIAN REVOLUTION AS AN INTERNATIONAL MODEL

Initially, Lenin was extremely modest about the relevance of the Russian Revolution to revolutionaries in other countries. As we have already noticed, he recognised that, although it had been easy for Russia to begin the world revolution, it would be extremely difficult for her to proceed far with the building of socialism due to her relatively backward economy. From the point of view of creating a genuinely socialist society, Russia could in no sense be a model for other countries to follow. The more developed countries would, Lenin felt sure, proceed at a faster pace and avoid the errors into which the Russians had been forced. As late as March 1919 he reminded the Eighth Party Congress of the need for the Russians to retain a proper modesty about the universality of their experience.

235

It would be absurd to set up our revolution as the ideal for all countries, to imagine that it has made a number of brilliant discoveries and has introduced a heap of socialist innovations. I have not heard anybody make this claim and I assert that we shall not hear anybody make it. We acquired practical experience in taking the first steps towards destroying capitalism in a country where specific relations exist between the proletariat and the peasants. Nothing more.[15]

At exactly the same time, he radioed Bela Kun that 'It is altogether beyond doubt that it would be a mistake merely to imitate our Russian tactics in all details in the specific conditions of the Hungarian revolution. I must warn you against the mistake . . .'.[16] In this very same radio message, however, Lenin requests (and clearly expects) 'guarantees' from Kun about the relationship between communists and socialists in the government, the attitude of the latter to the dictatorship of the proletariat and the proposed convocation of a Congress of Soviets.

It might well have been the case that Lenin did enjoin his foreign comrades not to slavishly follow the Russians 'in all details'. It is equally true that he did not hesitate, almost from the outset, to issue them with advice, which had the tone more of instructions than suggestions. It is also quite clear that very early on in the career of Soviet power in Russia he came to the conclusion that the essential features of the Russian road to power and the basic institutions established by the Russian Revolution were of general applicability. The longer the period of Russian isolation lasted, the more frequent the failures of revolutionary movements elsewhere, the more insistently and stridently Lenin portrayed the Russian model as universal in its relevance.

In July 1918, Lenin for the first time resorted to an identification which the Communist International was later to adopt as its own. Upon the outcome of the civil war in Russia, he asserted, 'the fate of the Russian and world revolution now depends'. The task of the Russians was 'to maintain, protect and uphold this force of socialism, this torch of socialism, this source of socialism which is so actively influencing the whole world'.[17] A few days later he declared, 'The Russian revolution has charted the road to socialism for the whole world . . .'.[18]

It is significant that Lenin's first identification of the Russian Revolution as the world model of revolutionary development came at about the same time as the changeover from the commune form to the dictatorship of the proletariat. The dictatorship of the proletariat was, indeed, a major element of the Russian model which Lenin now insisted was of general applicability. In an important sense the projection of the Russian experience as a universal form was based on the same rationale as that which had formed the basis of the dictatorship of the proletariat. The Russian experience, Lenin now maintained, simply confirmed the general theoretical finding that the whole world was presented with a choice – either the dictatorship of the imperialist bourgeoisie or the dictatorship of the proletariat. There was not and could not be, in Lenin's mind, any third course anywhere in the world. The dictatorship of the proletariat was not therefore a peculiarly Russian feature, it was the necessary and only available form of rule which the proletariat could avail itself of in its battle with imperialism. Acceptance of its necessity was the mark which everywhere distinguished genuine revolutionaries from traitorous social democrats.

The universalisation of Russian revolutionary experience did not, however, stop there. Not only the dictatorship of the proletariat but even its uniquely Russian form – the Soviets – was asserted to be of general relevance. The dictatorship of the proletariat everywhere signified, according to Lenin, the redundancy of the old bourgeois democratic forms of government with their separation of legislative and executive powers, bicameral legislatures and independent judiciaries. The Soviet form, the spontaneous creation of the Russian revolutionary masses, transcended this formal legalistic dilution of democracy and was destined to replace it everywhere:

> . . . the revolutions now starting up in the West are taking place under the slogan of Soviet government and we are setting up Soviet government. Soviets are the distinguishing feature of the revolution everywhere . . . That means that the historical collapse of bourgeois democracy was an absolute historical necessity, not an invention of the Bolsheviks.[19]

By mid-1920, Lenin had indeed come to the conclusion that the Soviet form was not only applicable to the developed countries of the West, it had an immediate relevance to the situation of the underdeveloped countries of the East. It was time to consider, he told the Second Congress of the Communist International:

> ... how the foundation-stone of the organisation of the Soviet movement can be laid in the *non*-capitalist countries. Soviets are possible there; they will not be workers' Soviets, but peasants' Soviets, or Soviets of working people.[20]

The idea of Soviets as the organisations of the exploited masses was, Lenin felt, hardly a complex one, it was 'becoming accessible to hundreds of millions of people oppressed by the exploiters all over the world'.[21]

By this time, Lenin had become convinced that not only was the Russian state form of the dictatorship of the proletariat of universal relevance but that the party structure which inspired and directed that state form would also have to be adopted by all revolutionary Marxists. This was one of the main conclusions which Lenin arrived at in his celebrated reflections and instructions on the proper character of the international revolutionary movement spelt out in *Left Wing Communism an Infantile Disorder*. The whole 'general plan' of this lengthy pamphlet was explicitly 'aimed at applying to Western Europe whatever is universally practicable, significant and relevant in the history and the present-day tactics of Bolshevism'.[22] It might be added that the practical objective of the pamphlet was to serve notice to would-be affiliates to the Communist International that the Russian Bolshevik Party structure was to be made obligatory at the forthcoming Second Congress of the Comintern. The twenty-one Conditions for Admission to the Communist International formulated by Lenin, and imposed at the Second Congress, were but an abstract of this pamphlet.

Significantly enough, the first chapter of the pamphlet was entitled 'In What Sense We Can Speak of the International Significance of the Russian Revolution'. In formulating his answer, it is obvious that Lenin had by this time forgotten his earlier pleas for modesty.

We now possess quite considerable international experience, which shows very definitely that certain fundamental features of our revolution have a significance that is not local, or peculiarly national, or Russian alone, but international. I am not speaking here of international significance in the broad sense of the term: not merely several but all the primary features of our revolution, and many of its secondary features, are of international significance in the meaning of its effect on all countries. I am speaking of it in the narrowest sense of the word, taking international significance to mean the international validity or the historical inevitability of a repetition, on an international scale, of what has taken place in our country. It must be admitted that certain fundamental features of our revolution do possess that significance.[23]

In this extreme formulation, the Russian Revolution is projected not simply as the general model adaptable to local conditions but as the stereotype which will inevitably be reproduced elsewhere. This is bound up with Lenin's enthusiastic acceptance of a queer kind of revolutionary ethnicity in which he subscribes to the profoundly Romantic notion that different epochs of world revolutionary development have been defined by the dominance of successive revolutionary nations.

Marx himself had, of course, fallen prey to very similar ideas and Lenin's periodisation is clearly indebted to Marx's. Writing to Engels on the outbreak of the Franco-Prussian war in 1870, Marx asserted that 'the French need a thrashing' and that:

German predominance would also transfer the centre of gravity of the workers' movement in Western Europe from France to Germany, and one has only to compare the movement in the two countries from 1860 till now to see that the German working class is superior to the French both theoretically and organisationally. Their predominance over the French on the world stage would also mean the predominance of *our* theory over Proudhon's, etc.[24]

Lenin followed Marx in dating the beginning of the international predominance of the Germans from 1871. The previous epoch, according to Lenin's chronology, had been a French epoch, when the model of the Great French Revolution blazed the path for the revolutionaries of the world. From 1871 to 1914, for almost half a century, the German working class was a model of socialist organisation for the whole world.[25] The present epoch, Lenin had no doubt, was the one in which the Russians had advanced to the centre of the stage, in which 'the revolutionary spirit of the Russian proletariat would provide a model to Western Europe'. This was not a new idea for Lenin. Reviewing the historical significance of the Communist International he had, in 1919, resorted to the same chronology, typifying epochs of revolutionary development by the national group that was in the ascendancy.[26] In 1919, as in 1921, Lenin pointed with approval to the finding of Karl Kautsky ('when he was still a Marxist') that in the twentieth century, leadership was likely to pass to the Slavs. With clear satisfaction, Lenin quoted Kautsky's words of 1902:

> At the present time it would seem that not only have the Slavs entered the ranks of the revolutionary nations, but that the centre of revolutionary thought and revolutionary action is shifting more and more to the Slavs. The revolutionary centre is shifting from the West to the East ... Russia, which has borrowed so much revolutionary initiative from the West, is now perhaps herself ready to serve the West as a source of revolutionary energy. The Russian revolutionary movement that is now flaring up will perhaps prove to be the most potent means of exorcising the spirit of flabby philistinism and coldly calculating politics that is beginning to spread in our midst, and it may cause the fighting spirit and the passionate devotion to our great ideals to flare up again. To Western Europe, Russia has long ceased to be a bulwark of reaction and absolutism. I think the reverse is true today. Western Europe is becoming Russia's bulwark of reaction and absolutism ... In 1848 the Slavs were a killing frost which blighted the flowers of the people's spring. Perhaps they are now destined to be the storm that will break the ice of reaction and irresistibly bring with it a new and happy spring for the nations.[27]

The Russians, Lenin acknowledged, had acquired incomparable revolutionary experience in the twentieth century and 'a wealth of international links and excellent information on the forms and theories of the world revolutionary movement such as no other country possessed'.[28] Having experienced the revolution of 1905 and the two revolutions of 1917, they had the unique opportunity of developing, testing and refining their revolutionary theory and tactics. By contrast, 'Hardly anyone in Western Europe has experienced anything like a big revolution. Here the experience of great revolutions has been almost entirely forgotten . . .'[29]

Throughout *Left-Wing Communism an Infantile Disorder*, indeed throughout the many pieces of advice to the parties of the Communist International, Lenin was insistent that foreign revolutionaries must study, assimilate and apply the lessons of the Russian revolutionary movement. And the principal lesson to be learned was that 'the Bolsheviks . . . *came closest* to being the party the revolutionary proletariat needs in order to achieve victory'.[30] Addressing the Second Congress of the Comintern, he insisted (against the strong opposition of the Italian and other parties) that the Communist International, like the Bolshevik Party, would have to be a centralised and unified body. It would not content itself, as the Second International had done, with passing vague resolutions which carried no binding obligations for its constituent parties. The Communist International would have to issue directions to its member parties, and in formulating these directives Lenin was clear that the revolutionary experience of the Russian Party must play a preponderant role:

Directives must be issued by the Communist International and the comrades must be made more familiar with the experience of Russia, with the significance of a genuinely proletarian political party. Our work will consist in accomplishing this task.[31]

A 'genuinely proletarian political party' was not, however, to be appraised simply in terms of its class composition. It was not, Lenin insisted, proletarian membership which made a proletarian party for if that were the case the British Labour Party would qualify. More important were 'the men that lead it, and the content of its actions and its political tactics'[32] and by these criteria the Labour Party, though overwhelmingly proletarian in composition, was irredeemably bourgeois in its politics. It was, there-fore, the character of the leadership, the theory and tactics they subscribed to and the kinds of actions they engaged in which defined a genuinely proletarian party. Already in October 1918, however, Lenin had become convinced that in all these respects the Bolsheviks led the world; it was to be adherence to *their* model which defined a genuinely proletarian movement.

> Bolshevism has become the world-wide theory and tactics of the international proletariat! It has accomplished a thorough going socialist revolution for all the world to see. To be for or against the Bolsheviks is actually the dividing line among socialists.[33]

Bolshevism, Lenin maintained, had created the ideological and tactical foundations of the Communist International and must therefore serve as a model to all member parties.[34]

As with all discussions of definitions, an extremely important role was played by the terms, conventions and precedents which were held to be appropriate. Repeatedly, Lenin utilised the particular experience of the Russian Bolsheviks as sufficient proof of the correct resolution of a general problem. In dis-cussing the respective roles of the trade unions and the Party, for instance, he begins with the phrase 'To make this clear, I shall begin with our own experience'.[35] Similarly, in dealing with the general attitude to be adopted to bourgeois parliaments he reviews the Russian experience of the Dumas and the Constituent Assembly, concluding that the general lessons to be drawn are thereby made clear and 'absolutely incontrovertible'.[36]

Lenin not only universalised the Russian experience as contain-ing the appropriate precedents to be referred to, he also internationalised the Russian terminology in which the discussion was to be couched. Thus, as we have already noticed, 'Bolshevism' had acquired the status of a complete international programme, so too had the term 'Soviets'.[37] 'Menshevism' had also become an international term, 'a generic term for all allegedly socialist, Social-Democratic and other trends that are hostile to Bolshev-ism'.[38] Even the Russian revolutionary calendar, like the calendar of the French Revolution, was pressed into service as a sort of universal sequence through which all were fated to progress.

As the French revolutionary tradition had its Brumaires and Thermidors, the Russian had its Februarys and Octobers. Nor was this merely rhetoric, it was intrinsic to a mode of analysis which Lenin increasingly came to adopt, a mode of analysis which urgently sought, and therefore discovered, elements of similarity between the situation in particular countries and the situation which had led to revolution in Russia.

A good example of the disposition to see foreign phenomena through Russian eyes, in the light of Russian precedent, calling them by their Russian names, and setting them in their Russian calendar, is Lenin's analysis of the Council of Action established by the British trade unions in 1920. This Council of Action 'has presented an ultimatum to the government on behalf of the workers. This is a step towards dictatorship and there is no other way out of the situation.' 'Its significance to Great Britain is as great as the revolution of February 1917 was to us.' 'It is the same kind of dual power as we had under Kerensky from March 1917 onwards.' The Council of Action meant the Soviets as the bourgeois press correctly realised. The only real difference in the situation was that 'the British Mensheviks' had been obliged to act unconstitutionally.[39]

It is perhaps one of the larger paradoxes of Lenin's writings in the last three or four years of his life that the more he commended the Russian experience for international consumption the more bitterly he came to criticise the internal composition and activities of the Russian Party and state. There may perhaps have been a distinction in his mind between the Russian road to revolution and the international significance of the institutions it produced on the one hand, and the style of work and the substantive policies which the Russians were obliged to implement, which were not meant for emulation elsewhere. This distinction was, however, never properly articulated.

GEO-POLITICS, IMPERIALISM AND DIPLOMATIC MANOEUVRES

From about the middle of 1920 onwards there was a perceptible shift in Lenin's international analysis. The essence of this change was that Lenin no longer operated on an exclusively class-based analysis of the prospects for the revolutionary overthrow of imperialism. His initial view, as we saw above, was that the contradictions between the imperialist states were so acute that there was no prospect of them being reconciled in any peace settlement. War upon war and the rapid descent into barbarism and famine would therefore drive the workers of the world to revolution and this movement would be stimulated and organised by the Communist International. This was the period of the offensive, the period of the final death throes of capitalism. Given that the imperialist states were locked in desperate battle for the redivision of the world, they would not be able to combine their forces against the Soviet régime in Russia and this was *the* central international fact which allowed it to exist.

> That we were able to survive a year after the October Revolution was due to the split of international imperialism into two predatory groups ... Neither group could muster large forces against us, which they would have done had they been in a position to do so.[40]

By mid-1920 it had become perfectly clear that this series of predictions from theory had not materialised. In particular, a peace settlement had been arrived at. However savage and fraught with future wars its provisions might have been, it was a peace of sorts. The clear and obvious danger now existed that the victorious imperialist powers of the Entente could at last concentrate their attention on smashing the infant Soviet Republic. The very conclusion of peace was, moreover, bound to undermine the imperative for revolution in Western Europe. In December 1920, Lenin observed that 'It was evident that the revolutionary movement would inevitably slow down when the nations secured peace'.[41] By July 1921, Lenin openly recognised that the conclusion of peace had fundamentally altered the prospects for revolution in the capitalist countries. 'It becomes clear at the first glance that after the conclusion of peace, bad as it was, it proved impossible to call forth revolution in other Capitalist countries.'[42] His conclusion, bolstered by the repeated failure of revolutionary attempts in Germany, Hungary and Bavaria, was that the period of the revolutionary offensive was now over. A new strategy would have to be evolved and new tactics devised to meet this new unforeseen situation. As far as the Communist International was concerned, Lenin felt that a fairly prolonged period of preparation for revolution was now at hand. During the coming period, the objectives should therefore be to compromise and expose the social-democratic leaders as agents of the bourgeoisie in order to win the masses from their influence, and to build a strong united leadership within each Party by combating both revisionist and left-wing deviations. 'We must now thoroughly prepare for revolution', Lenin told the Third Congress of the Comintern, and that involved first and foremost 'winning over the majority of the population'[43] which he clearly felt would take some considerable time.

If then there was very little immediate prospect of proletarian revolution in the West, and if, furthermore, the securing of peace allowed the imperialists to combine their forces against the Soviet régime, did not this mean that socialism in Russia was bound to perish? According to Lenin's repeated earlier pronouncements, this was bound to happen.

The way out, the only way out which might guarantee the survival of the Soviet state, was to exploit the contradictions amongst the imperialist powers which the peace settlement had exacerbated rather than resolved.

> What then is the Treaty of Versailles? It is an unparalleled and predatory peace, which has made slaves of tens of millions of people, including the most civilised. This is no peace, but terms dictated to a defenceless victim by armed robbers . . . That is why this international system in its entirety, the order based on the Treaty of Versailles, stands on the brink of a volcano, for the enslaved seven-tenths of the world's population are waiting impatiently for someone to give them a lead in a struggle which will shake all these countries.[44]

As a result of the war, 'all capitalist contradictions have become immeasurably more acute'. Russia, Austria-Hungary and Bulgaria had been reduced by the Treaty of Versailles 'to a state of colonial dependence, poverty, starvation, ruin and loss of rights . . . placing them in conditions that no civilised nation has ever lived in'. Germany and the other defeated countries had been stripped of their national rights, humiliated and reduced to a position 'that makes their economic existence physically impossible'.[45]

As far as Europe was concerned, this meant, in Lenin's acutely realistic appraisal, playing upon the enormous grievances the Germans had against the Treaty of Versailles. The terms of that iniquitous treaty were, Lenin correctly saw, incompatible with Germany's continued existence as a modern industrial state: 'her existence has been made impossible by the conditions in which the Entente has placed her'.[46] 'The Peace of Versailles ... in robbing Germany of coal, robbing her of milch herds, and in reducing her to an unparalleled and unprecedented state of servitude.'[47] Germany would therefore be obliged to fight against the ignominious position allotted to her by the victorious Entente as would all the other countries so harshly treated at Versailles. It followed, therefore, that for Germany 'her only means of salvation lies in an alliance with Soviet Russia, a country towards which her eyes are therefore turning'.[48]

Lenin's international policy had become more 'realist' or Machiavellian, based more on the national aspirations of those countries which had a clear interest in revising the Versailles settlement than upon class analysis. Russia's objective must be, he now maintained, to establish herself as the main protagonist and leader of these revisionist countries so that 'in all these countries the people can now see that Soviet Russia is a force that is smashing the Peace of Versailles'.[49] As far as Europe was concerned, 'Our policy is grouping around the Soviet Republic those capitalist countries which are being strangled by imperialism'.[50] Germany, of course, remained the key, the revisionist power par excellence, and her situation naturally impelled her 'towards *rapprochement* with Soviet Russia'.[51]

The necessity of taking advantage of the contradictions of the Versailles peace settlement, and of establishing Russia as the vanguard of those opposed to it, entailed, as Lenin recognised, a considerable change in the methods of conducting international relations. Revolutionary propaganda conducted by the communist parties of Europe might have been sufficient to advertise the Soviet view of the world during the period of the offensive: now, however, it would have to be supplemented by the conventional skills of diplomacy. Trade agreements and the granting of economic concessions within Russia must, Lenin now insisted, be adroitly utilised to exacerbate tensions in the imperialist camp. Agricultural concessions, he admitted in December 1920, had already been offered to Germany.[52] Lenin was beginning the strategic change of direction which was to be consummated with the Treaty of Rapallo in 1922 and the restoration of full diplomatic relations between Germany and Russia. In this diplomatic attempt to split the West, Russia proved eminently more successful than in her revolutionary attempts at overthrowing it. As Kennan remarks, 'Rapallo could justly be described as the first great victory for Soviet diplomacy. It successfully split the Western community in its relation to Russia.'[53] That, precisely, had been the objective of Lenin's policy in Europe since mid-1920.

The contradictions of imperialism encapsulated in the Versailles Treaty were, however, very far from being restricted to Europe. With the recurrent failures of revolutionary attempts in Europe and with the equally perennial problems of sectarianism and internal divisions within the European communist parties, Lenin's attention turned increasingly towards the East.

The basic fact of post-war international politics was, according to Lenin, the new balance between oppressor and oppressed nations which had resulted from the redivision of the world. According to his figures, the total population of the world was about 1750 million. Of these America, Japan and Britain had benefited considerably from the war and they, together with their lesser imperialist allies, comprised some 500 million. All the rest of the world's population in the colonies (and in the defeated countries which had been reduced to colonial status) comprised the remaining 1250 million people.[54]

> I would like to remind you of this picture of the world, for all the basic contradictions of imperialism, which are leading up to revolution, all the basic contradictions in the working-class movement . . . are all connected with this partitioning of the world's population.[55]

Apart from the contradiction between Germany and the Entente, which we have already looked at, the two other principal contradictions which Lenin noticed were the incompatibility of the interests of America with those of Japan and the antagonism between America and the rest of the capitalist world. The object of the foreign policy of the Soviet Union was to utilise these contradictions, exacerbate the differences between the imperial-ist states, 'to play one off against the other', in order 'to take advantage of every hour granted it by circumstances in order to gain strength as rapidly as possible'.[56]

America, according to Lenin's reasoning, being without col-onies, having a larger population and more dynamic economy than Japan, was bound to covet the rich pickings which the Japanese had obtained from the war. America and Japan were bound to come into conflict over the right to loot China and Korea. One of the ways to precipitate their conflict would be 'to lease to America Kamchatka, which legally belongs to us but has actually been seized by Japan'.[57] The mere offer of such a concession had 'set Japan and America at loggerheads'.[58]

The antagonism between America and the rest of the capitalist world was, according to Lenin's analysis, based upon the fact that, of all the imperialist powers, America alone had emerged from the war enriched, solvent and therefore independent as an actor in international affairs. 'America alone is absolutely independent financially.' Britain, by contrast, was 'already half way to becoming a debtor nation'[59] and France, the money-lender of the pre-war world, had liabilities three times larger than her assets.[60] In November 1919, Lenin had seized upon British and French dependence on America and resentment at their loss of status as politically explosive factors in the post-war world.

> Britain and France are the victors but they are up to their ears in debt to America, who has decided that the French and British may consider themselves victors as much as they like, but that she is going to skim the cream and exact usurious interest for her assistance during the war.[61]

Britain and France, he concluded, were economically bankrupt, envious of America's new-found financial dominance, and Britain in particular was bound to be bitterly apprehensive about the rise of American naval strength which was rapidly overhaul-ing her own and would overtake her by 1923.[62] All three potent sources of grievance and resentment should be utilised so that 'if the least opportunity arises of aggravating the differences between America and the other capitalist countries, it should be grasped with both hands'.[63]

Again and again, Lenin repeated his central message. In comparison to the economic and military resources of the combined imperialist powers, Soviet Russia was inordinately weak. Nor could Russia any longer expect immediate assistance from revolutions in the advanced capitalist countries. Simply in order to exist as a weakened beleaguered fortress of socialism, surrounded by more powerful and hostile states, the Soviet Union's only hope lay in the skilful exploitation of the differences or contradictions within the imperialist camp. The strategic line which Lenin dictated for Soviet foreign policy was therefore brutally simple and unambiguous.

> If we are obliged to put up with such scoundrels as the capitalist robbers, each of whom is ready to knife us, it is our prime duty to make them turn their knives against each other.[64]

THE TEMPORARY STABILISATION OF CAPITALISM

By December 1920, Lenin was faced with a severe internal crisis. Peasant revolts against the harsh system of grain requisitioning were growing; famine was hitting the urban areas and the whole of the Volga region; strikes of increasing size were being mounted even by his favourite sons, the Petrograd workers. Worst of all, the Party had been split down the middle by the trade union question. Faced with all these problems, Lenin recognised that a considerable retreat would have to be made. In particular, the grievances of the peasants would have to be met and the attempts to introduce socialism in the countryside temporarily reversed.

It followed that, faced with such a host of internal crises (which reached their apogee with the Kronstadt rebellion in March 1921), the régime could not, at the same time, support a belligerent foreign policy. In any case Lenin had, as we have seen, recognised that the period of the revolutionary assault was now over. In December 1920 he went a good deal further. He asserted that Russia had won 'something more than a breathing space: we have entered a new period, in which we have won the right to our fundamental international existence in the network of capitalist states'.[65] 'Today,' he went on, 'we can speak, not merely of a breathing space, but of a real chance of a new and lengthy period of development.'[66]

By May 1921, Lenin had formally recognised that the revolutionary wave during and immediately following the war had come to an end. It had been followed by what he termed 'some sort of a temporary, unstable equilibrium, but equilibrium for all that'.[67] This finding coincided, almost exactly, with the introduction of the New Economic Policy – a forced retreat specifically introduced to stabilise the Soviet economy. In the New Economic Policy (hereafter NEP), Lenin acknowledged the fact that internally the Bolsheviks had pressed ahead too fast and too furious with the attempt to socialise the economy. The theory of the temporary stabilisation of international capitalism was its complement in the international arena. The two were complementary. NEP signified the realisation by the Russians that a prolonged period of isolation lay ahead of them; that, therefore, the advance towards socialism would have to be slowed down and partly reversed. The temporary stabilisation of capitalism thesis for its part signified the acceptance by the Russians that the period of revolutionary assault was over. It therefore legitimised the conventional diplomatic moves being made to secure international recognition for the Soviet régime. Formal recognition was vital to the securing of concessions and trade agreements with Western capitalist countries which Lenin now saw as absolutely vital for the rehabilitation of the Soviet economy. The likelihood of securing concessions and trade agreements rested in turn upon the creation of stability within the Soviet economic and political structure and it was precisely the object of NEP to provide such stability:

> We, too, are acting like merchants. But every merchant takes some account of politics. If he is a merchant from a not altogether barbarous country, he will not enter into transactions with a government unless it shows considerable signs of stability, unless it is very reliable.[68]

According to Lenin's revised perspective, the Soviet Union could not expect assistance to redeem its backwardness from revolutionary Europe in the foreseeable future. The peasants would not part with their grain surpluses unless offered goods in exchange. The problem was, how to produce these goods when industry was still in ruins, requiring massive injections of capital and the introduction of new machinery, neither of which the Soviet Union had at its disposal. The capital and technology would have to come from the imperialist countries, there was no other source. The only inducement Russia could offer was to lease agricultural, forest, mineral and industrial resources, which she could not work herself, to the foreign capitalists. They would, of course, reap their enormous profits but Russia would at least get a share. She would obtain her rent, she would ensure that at least some of her workers were well fed, she would above all learn how to exploit her resources in a modern way. The concessionaires could, moreover, be used as import houses, contractually obliged to bring into Russia double the machinery they envisaged needing. In this way they could be used to obtain vitally important modern machinery.

A situation of deadlock obtained in international affairs. Neither 'the Russian Soviet Republic or the capitalist world – has gained victory or suffered defeat' but the main thing had been achieved, 'the possibility has been maintained of the existence of proletarian rule and the Soviet Republic even in the event of the world Socialist revolution being delayed'.[69] The workers of the West had not, Lenin admitted, fulfilled his earlier predictions. They had not risen in revolt, but they had extended their support and sympathy and had effectively prevented their governments from undertaking an all-out war on Soviet Russia, 'In fact, they went half way in their support, for they weakened the hand raised against us, yet in doing so they were helping us'.[70]

The objectives of the Communist International in this period of temporary stabilisation were spelt out at its Third World Congress in the summer of 1921. Lenin's policies of 'winning the masses', concentrating on economic rather than expressly revolutionary grievances, winning the workers from their social democratic leaders and supporting the isolated Soviet state, were endorsed despite the murmurings of its left wing that such policies amounted to forsaking the revolution which the Comintern had been established to pursue. For many on the left these policies amounted to the simple prostitution of the Comintern to the present state interests of Russia. Their forebodings greatly increased when, in December 1921, the Executive Committee of the Communist International instructed its national sections to collaborate with the socialist parties in a United Front to improve the material conditions of life of the working class. It was hoped that through this tactic the Western workers would come to appreciate who their most devoted and uncompromising champions were and would come over to the communist side.[71] Simultaneously the Executive Committee of the Comintern made approaches to their opposite numbers in the Second International and the so-called Two and a Half International which resulted in a top-level but abortive meeting of communist and socialist leaders in Berlin in April 1922. This was the United Front from Above, a rapprochement between socialists and communists which, for many communists, undermined the very *raison d'être* of the Comintern. Large and vociferous sections of the German, French and Italian parties at first refused to implement the policy on the grounds that it merely sowed confusion in the communist ranks to attempt to convince them of the need to collaborate with people whom Lenin had hitherto condemned as the vilest traitors of the working class.

Towards the end of his life, when Lenin was assailed by the most serious doubts about what had been implemented, and the future prospects for socialism in Russia, he fitted in the other side of the equilibrium balance. If capitalism had been weakened by the worker allies of the Soviet Republic, so too had capitalism wrecked its vengeance on Russia. If capitalism had been unable to defeat Russia it had, at the least, been able to stunt its development. It had effectively prevented the realisation of the glittering prospects socialism had in view and it had, thereby, destroyed the chance of the first socialist republic becoming an exemplary socialist régime of irresistible appeal.

They argued somewhat as follows: 'If we fail to overthrow the revolutionary system in Russia, we shall, at all events, hinder its progress towards socialism' . . . They failed to overthrow the new system created by the revolution, but they did prevent it from at once taking the step forward that would have justified the forecasts of the socialist, that would have enabled the latter to develop the productive forces with enormous speed, to develop all the potentialities which, taken together, would have produced socialism; socialists would thus have proved to all and sundry that socialism contains within itself gigantic forces and

that mankind had now entered into a new stage of development of extraordinarily brilliant prospects.[72]

All of Lenin's last writings, as we shall see, tell the same sombre
tale of the vision withering, of his agonising awareness that the
brilliant prospects he predicted in 1917 had somehow turned
sour. The failure of his international predictions, he was now
painfully aware, had played a leading role in the tragedy. And yet
even now, even in his last extended article, he saw some rays of
light piercing the general gloom. And those rays of light came
from the East.

RUSSIA: THE VANGUARD OF THE WORLD'S EXPLOITED

We are now led back to Lenin's earlier analysis of the implications
of the peace settlement which reflected the global relationship of
oppressors to oppressed in the post-war world. Russia, Lenin
insisted, must not only take upon herself the leadership of all the
European countries robbed of their national integrity by the
Treaty of Versailles, she must also become the representative of
all the world's exploited. Only the Soviet Republic could act as the
inspirational force and organisational centre of the movement of
all the colonial peoples against their imperialist exploiters. 'We
now stand, not only as the representatives of the proletarians of
all countries but as representatives of the oppressed peoples as
well.'[73] The oppressed peoples everywhere, he maintained, were
seething with discontent at the harsh arrogance of the Entente,
the rapacity of the Japanese and Americans: 'As a result, they
have made Russia the immediate representative of the entire
mass of the oppressed population of the earth.'[74] The banner and
programme of Bolshevism had therefore become 'an emblem of
salvation, 'an emblem of struggle' to the workers and to the
peasants of all lands.[75]

However bleak the prospects for socialism might appear,
however forlorn the chances of revolution in Europe, in the last
resort, Lenin argued, sheer weight of numbers must carry the
day. The 1250 million oppressed would prevail over their 500
million exploiters. In terms of sheer numbers Russia, India and
China were incomparably mightier than the imperialist countries
of the West. All that they lacked was culture and civilisation and to
Russia, as their vanguard, fell the responsibility of raising the

cultural level of its people so that, after the titanic battle with reactionary Western imperialism which lay ahead, the backward countries would be able to proceed to the building of socialism. This was the vision which sustained Lenin in the last years of his life. Socialism in Russia was in desperate straits. Stunted by imperialist intervention and harassment, restricted by the petty-bourgeois milieu of Russia and the absorption of the old tsarist bureaucratic ways, and hampered by the lack of disciplined capable cadres, socialism was struggling to survive. But survive it must and the condition for its survival was no less than a cultural revolution to raise the level of education and administrative and economic expertise. Only if Russia dramatically improved her state machinery, only if she quickly restored her productive forces on the basis of the electrification of industry and agriculture, only then would she be able to realise her role of vanguard of all the oppressed peoples of the world against imperialism. And unless she was actually able to fulfil that vanguard role her fate was sealed. At the end of the last article he wrote, 'Better Fewer but Better', the interweaving of these themes comes through with remarkable clarity.

> In the last analysis, the outcome of the struggle will be determined by the fact that Russia, India, China etc., account for the overwhelming majority of the population of the globe. And during the past few years it is the majority that has been drawn into the struggle for emancipation with extraordinary rapidity, so that in this respect there cannot be the slightest doubt what the final outcome of the world struggle will be. In this sense, the complete victory of socialism is fully and absolutely assured ... To ensure our existence until the next military conflict between the counter-revolutionary imperialist West and the revolutionary and nationalist East, between the most civilised countries of the world and the orientally backward countries which, however, comprise the majority, this majority must become civilised. We, too, lack enough civilisation to enable us to pass straight on to socialism ...
>
> We must reduce our state apparatus to the utmost degree of economy. We must banish from it all traces of extravagance, of which so much has been left over from tsarist Russia, from its bureaucratic capitalist state machine.

254

Will not this be a reign of peasant limitations?

No. If we see to it that the working class retains its leadership over the peasantry, we shall be able, by exercising the greatest possible thrift in the economic life of our state, to use every saving we make to develop our large-scale machine industry, to develop electrification, the hydraulic extraction of peat, to complete the Volkhov Power Project, etc.

In this, and in this alone, lies our hope.[76]

CHAPTER 12

The Trade Union Debate

In May 1920 Trotsky, with his usual zeal, had taken his turn in the polemical ping-pong with Kautsky who had replied to Lenin's *The Proletarian Revolution and the Renegade Kautsky* with his book *Terrorism and Communism*. Trotsky responded with a lengthy pamphlet with the same title in the course of which he reflected on his own experience of organising labour as Commissar for War, generalising from that experience to construct a plan for the mobilisation and militarisation of the entire Soviet workforce. According to Trotsky's profoundly authoritarian Saint Simonian scheme, 'the one unchanging end' of the organisation of labour was to maximise its productivity.[1] Since, however, 'As a general rule, man strives to avoid labour',[2] it followed that the availability of labour where and when it was required, particularly in the inhospitable and ravaged areas of Russia, could only be secured by state compulsion. Of all state institutions, Trotsky went on, the army was, by its nature a vehicle of compulsion, 'endowed with powers of demanding from each and all complete submission to its problems, aims, regulations, and orders'.[3] Only the army had, moreover, the experience and resources 'in the sphere of the registration, mobilisation, formation and transference from one place to another of large masses'.[4] It followed therefore, according to this view, that the only salvation for Russia's economic crisis lay in the mobilisation and militarisation of the entire workforce with the object of securing the goals of a single national economic plan.

In Trotsky's account of the militarised productive state, the trade unions could not expect to enjoy any autonomous role. They were to be directly subordinate to the Party and were to act as the auxiliaries and instruments of the state and the army. Their continued 'independence' was an impossibility. In the era of the dictatorship of the proletariat they, like all other sections of the 'heavy masses', had to acknowledge the supremacy of the revolutionary vanguard 'which ... obliges the backward tail to dress by the head. This refers also to the trade unions.'[5] Their function was not to oppose the state nor to see themselves as the representative champions of the workers' grievances but, on the contrary, to identify with their workers' state and 'become the organisers of labour discipline'.[6]

> ... the young Socialist State requires trade unions, not for a struggle for better conditions of labour – that is the task of the social and State organisations as a whole – but to organise the working class for the ends of production, to educate, discipline, distribute, group, retain certain categories and certain workers at their posts for fixed periods – in a word, hand in hand with the State to exercise their authority in order to lead the workers into the framework of a single economic plan.[7]

With a perverse vengeance, the very features of the state capitalist trust, the Leviathan state arrogating to itself and subordinating all the independent organisations of society, this nightmare vision which had inspired both Bukharin and Lenin to make the socialist revolution, now were lauded by Trotsky as essential elements of the dictatorship of the proletariat. The swallowing up of society by the state, in particular the threatened prostitution of the labour movement as the mere labour department of the state, against which both Bukharin and Lenin had sounded the alarm, was now represented as essential for the realisation of socialism. Trotsky now emerged with the most stridently statist formulations which read almost word for word like Bukharin's characterisation, not of socialism, but of that which socialism sought to destroy; the militarist, omnipotent, servile, productive state of monopoly capitalism. The wheel had turned full circle. What the revolution aspired to negate was presented as the only road to the realisation of socialism. The final bitter paradox was that just these formulations, in almost the same words, were to be used by Stalin to justify his ruthless dictatorship. The road to socialism, Trotsky maintained:

> lies through a period of the highest possible intensification of the principle of the State. ... Just as a lamp, before going out,

257

shoots up in a brilliant flame, so the State, before disappearing, assumes the form of the dictatorship of the proletariat; i.e., the most ruthless form of State, which embraces the life of the citizens authoritatively in every direction.[8]

Trotsky's views on the étatisation of the trade unions (and every other organisation) were, unfortunately, not merely academic projects. They were generalisations from his own experience in organising large-scale labour armies, especially for the rehabilitation of transport, in the latter part of the civil war. They acquired quite a new significance, however, when in 1920 he was appointed to head the newly-formed Tsektran organisation which had sweeping powers to supervise the rehabilitation of rail and water transport. Trotsky and his lieutenants set about their task with customary brusqueness and panache, brooking no opposition to their draconian methods. Conflicts between the overlapping jurisdictions of Tsektran and the transport unions inevitably developed which Trotsky attempted to resolve by threatening imprisonment for the union officials who stood in his path and by promising a general 'shake-up' of the unions' staffs. This was, of course, entirely consonant with the ideas of his *Terrorism and Communism* where he had maintained that 'not only questions of principle in the trade union movement, but serious conflicts of organisation within it, are decided by the Central Committee of our Party'.[9] It was, moreover, unquestionably the case that ever since October 1917, the Party had insisted on its right to install its appointees to the executive committees of the major unions. It was not so much what he said as the manner in which he said it that set the hackles of the trade union leadership rising. They were still smarting from their failures in the recurrent battle to preserve the collegiate system of management which, for many of the rank and file unionists, represented the single most important victory of the revolution. Under intense Party pressure, workers' control and the collegiate system had been replaced by strict one-man management – generally in the person of one of the tsarist managers or specialists. In this campaign for one-man management, Trotsky had also been vociferous, vaunting in almost Platonic tones the role of specially trained and educated specialists, experts and administrators, and pouring scorn on the collegiate system which, he maintained, was simply a shield for general ignorance and typical of the herd mentality of the Russian workers. The form of administration was, according to Trotsky (and here again he provided Stalin with a justificatory rationale), a matter of irrelevance so long as ownership was vested in the state:

> The dictatorship of the proletariat is expressed in the abolition of private property in the means of production, in the supremacy over the whole Soviet mechanism of the collective will of the workers, and not at all in the form in which individual economic enterprises are administered.[10]

At the Ninth Party Congress, March/April 1920, Trotsky had again pursued his favourite themes of militarisation of labour, one-man management, Taylorism and the introduction of bonuses and labour incentives to encourage the assiduous exemplary workers.[11] Too obviously he delighted in his role as the gadfly stinging the old trade union carthorse into action.

By December 1920 the trade union leadership, even the pliant Tomsky, had decided that they had had enough of Tsektran and Trotsky's immoderate interference. Indeed, they went a good deal further, complaining bitterly about bureaucratic interference in the work of the unions, the Party's appointments system, and the complete failure of the régime to move towards the promise of the constitution that the trade unions would become the supreme policy-making body for the whole economy. They went to Lenin with their complaints and he was left in no doubt that relations between the Party and the trade unions had been strained to breaking point. A split with the unions at that critical point would, Lenin believed, have brought about the downfall of the régime.[12] In spite of the fact that he himself had expressly approved Trotsky's policies, he now came to the conclusion that Trotsky would have to be disowned. The trade unions had to be assuaged and Trotsky's head was part of their price.

> ... I decided there and then that policy [that is, the Party's trade union policy] lay at the root of the controversy, and that Comrade Trotsky, with his 'shake-up' policy against Comrade Tomsky, was entirely in the wrong. For, *even if the 'shake-up' policy were partly justified* by the 'new tasks and methods' ... it

259

cannot be tolerated at the present time and in the present situation, because it threatens a split.[13]

The basic theoretical error which Trotsky had made was, according to Lenin, his proposal to absorb the unions into the Party/state machine. He thereby failed to distinguish properly between the class and its vanguard. The trade unions were mass organisations embracing, or striving to do so, the entire class. They could not therefore themselves exercise leadership functions nor should they. Their role, Lenin argued in December 1920, was to act as the all-important 'link between the vanguard and the masses'.[14] Under Trotsky's proposal, these links or 'transmission belts' would have lost their organisational integrity and a large part of their effectiveness as vehicles of the Party's influence and mobilisers of the mass behind the Party's goals. Trotsky's proposal threatened, moreover, to submerge the conscious vanguard beneath the mass of the backward, degraded and corrupted workers:

But the dictatorship of the proletariat cannot be exercised through an organisation embracing the whole of that class, because in all capitalist countries (and not only over here, in one of the most backward) the proletariat is still so divided, so degraded, and so corrupted ... that an organisation taking in the whole proletariat cannot directly exercise proletarian dictatorship. It can be exercised only by a vanguard that has absorbed the revolutionary energy of the class. The whole is like an arrangement of cog wheels. It cannot work without a number of 'transmission belts' running from the vanguard to the mass of the advanced class, and from the latter to the mass of the working people.[15]

As Lenin reflected some time later, without such 'links' or 'transmission belts' the danger existed that the vanguard might isolate itself and run too far ahead of the masses.[16]

There was a further serious defect in Trotsky's reasoning, according to Lenin. This lay in his simple equation that since the state was a workers' state its policies reflected the real interests of the working class, therefore the workers could not have interests against or apart from those of the state. It therefore followed that the trade unions should be absorbed into the state as subordinate parts of its administrative machinery. The mistake here, Lenin maintained, was to assume that the Soviet régime represented a perfected workers' state. It did not. 'For one thing, ours is not actually a workers' state but a workers' and peasants' state.'[17] This new formulation, which obviously recalled Lenin's 'democratic dictatorship of the proletariat and poor peasantry' of the 1905 revolution, might have been consistent with Lenin's reversion to his earlier economic analysis (as we demonstrated in Volume 1, this was the most radical form of the *democratic* state which could be aspired to give the level of capitalist development in Russia), but it certainly had not been used by Lenin since the October Revolution. An amazed Bukharin immediately questioned Lenin's formulation, but Lenin made no attempt to respond, though later he conceded that he had been in error. Lenin went on to broach a theme which was to become absolutely central to his last writings – the problem of bureaucracy. 'Our Party Programme... shows that ours is a workers' state *with a bureaucratic twist to it*.'[18] The workers' organisations had to preserve their own separate organisational identity in order 'to protect the workers from their state, and to get them to protect our state'.[19] One of the principal functions which Lenin now allotted to the unions was the job of 'combating bureaucratic distortions of the Soviet apparatus, safeguarding the working people's material and spiritual interests in ways and means inaccessible to the apparatus, etc.'.[20]

We should at this point note that it was only the outspoken critique of bureaucratic practices voiced by the trade union movement which led Lenin to focus his attention upon the problem. Hitherto it had featured only marginally in his writings. We should, in the second place, notice how adroit Lenin was in attempting to turn what he took to be negative criticism of the régime into positive involvement. To the trade unionists, and the Workers' Opposition for whom the critique of the bureaucratic distortions of the régime was the rallying point, Lenin's disarming response was, 'Yes, you're right, we deserve your reproaches, but what are you doing to combat bureaucracy? Come and help the Party root it out!' The all-important question, to which he could give no response, was how was this to be done without seriously undermining the prerogatives and authority of the Party which were inseparably entwined with the state bureaucracy.

One way out of the problem might have been to attempt a separation and clear demarcation of the respective spheres of Party and state and for a short time, as we shall see later, Lenin flirted with this idea. By that time, however, the Communist Party had no other prop but state power to retain its control. It had long lost the support of the peasants, indeed in early 1921, Victor Serge recalled, 'We knew of fifty rallying-points for peasant insurrection in European Russia alone'.[21] In Tambov, tens of thousands of peasants were organised into a formidable insurgent army. By early 1921 the situation with regard to the urban workers was little better. Their resentment took tangible form in the series of strikes which swept the industrial region of European Russia in January and February, culminating in the near general strike in Petrograd in late February and the immediately following rising in Kronstadt.

The self-styled spokesmen of this proletarian discontent within the Party were the members of the Workers' Opposition. Like many of the active and conscious worker activists, the Workers' Opposition was struck by the disparity between promise and performance. As Kollontai put it in the platform of the Workers' Opposition, 'A great deal was said and well said, but from words to deeds there is a considerable distance'.[22] They were unambiguous champions of the values which had originally inspired the revolution and to a large extent their popularity rested on their conscious evocation of the 'golden age' of the first six months of Soviet power. That first heroic period of the revolution had, by this time, acquired almost mythological status in the minds of many workers and union activists. That was their realm of freedom when workers' control had brought them a new sense of dignity, a sense of the significance of the rank and file worker as master of his own destiny. For many industrial workers, probably for the great majority, that, primarily, was what the revolution had been all about – an end to bossing, as Lenin himself had once put it. Its theoretical expression was Lenin's own *State and Revolution*, and its organisational expression the multiform agencies of workers' control, producers' and consumers' communes and the plethora of local Soviet organisations and committees. With the coming of the civil war the workers had, without too much protest, acquiesced in the temporary supersession of workers' control by the system of collegial administration. Under this system, plants were run by a team of five men, generally three workers and two specialists. Still the workers felt they had the whip hand. It was when the Party, at the insistent promptings of Lenin and Trotsky, began to press for the abolition of collegial management and its replacement by one-man management that signalled, in the opinion of many workers, the final extinction of the workers' gains in the revolution. The trade union leadership knew, as did their membership, that the one man who would emerge as manager would not be a worker but a specialist. In the popular mind this simply meant a reversion to the old system of industrial relations with the old personnel directing and controlling affairs, with the important difference that now the manager was to enjoy even greater arbitrary or dictatorial power than he ever had before.

The plan of Lenin, Trotsky and the Central Committee to restore discipline and improve productivity did not, however, end there. The elimination of collegial management was but the necessary precondition for the assault which immediately followed – the Party's plan for the comprehensive mobilisation and militarisation of the entire workforce and economy. At this point the trade union controversies, which had been simmering for so long, boiled over with threatening force. For the last time, Lenin was forced to back-pedal for a brief period though, as we shall see, when the steam had all evaporated away he proceeded with his draconian policies of putting the screw on the trade unions.

Contrary to some popular legends, Lenin did not encourage nor approve of the heated debate on the trade union question. He was, from the outset, furious that things should have come to such a pass that the Party was seen to be openly squabbling with the unions and rent with internal disputes. He had for some time believed that the time for wrangling over issues of principle had long gone, it belonged to the infancy of the Party and had no place in its actual exercise of power. The crucial thing in the new phase was not theoretical precision but practical ability to organise and get things moving. Lenin's intemperance with the ideologues and windbags in his own Party, those indefatigable composers of endless wordy resolutions, theses enough to give one a headache and amendments to amendments, was clear and obvious. 'We have so many resolutions that nobody even takes the trouble to file them, let alone read them. We must devote our attention to business not resolutions.'[23] Opening the fateful Tenth Party Congress, he declared:

> Comrades, we have passed through an exceptional year, we have allowed ourselves the luxury of discussions and disputes within the Party. This was an amazing luxury for a Party shouldering unprecedented responsibilities and surrounded by mighty and powerful enemies uniting the whole capitalist world.[24]

It was not, however, merely the fact of a hostile imperialist encirclement which made Lenin condemn the luxury of open debate within the Party. Indeed, this could not have been his primary reason for, by this time, all foreign troops had left Russia and it was clear that the imperialist powers were moving towards a grudging acceptance of the Soviet régime. A far more important consideration was Lenin's realisation that the social base of the régime had all but vanished. The proletariat, upon which the régime had relied and in whose name it presumed to govern, had been thoroughly decimated by civil war, famine and the break-down of industry. It had, moreover, been a purposive part of government policy, actively encouraged by Lenin, to close all but the most important industrial plants and to sack all but the most industrious workers in order to relieve pressure on food supplies. The remnants of the urban proletariat were, as Lenin was well aware, bitterly critical of the Bolshevik Party. They resented the elimination of workers' control and the eclipse of collegial administration of the factories. They resented the authority of the specialists and, even more, their high wages and privileges of all sorts. They resented too the reintroduction of the piece-work and bonus systems. They had been prepared to tolerate hunger and cold and an attenuation of what they saw as the gains of the revolution, so long as everyone else shared their lot, so long as the civil war seemed to justify exceptional measures. Now, however, in late 1920 and early 1921, they had reached the limits of their tolerance. Their grievances were vented and articulated by the group within the Party called the Workers' Opposition.

It was Alexandra Kollontai, one of Lenin's most trusted and

talented lieutenants before the revolution, one of the few within the Bolshevik Party who had immediately supported his April Theses, who hastily compiled the platform of the Workers' Opposition. It was the last time that the régime allowed so comprehensive and scathing a critique of its policies and its underlying assumptions to be published. Kollontai faithfully recorded the catalogue of grievances voiced by the trade unions and worker activists, but she went a good deal further. She directed the main thrust of her attack at what she knew was the weak spot of the policies of the Politburo: its assumption that rational expertise and administrative efficiency were the only ways out of Russia's difficulties. The prevalence of this attitude and of policies based on it represented, according to Kollontai, the greatest threat to the development of proletarian consciousness and organisation and threatened the destruction of socialism in Russia. Nor would the rule of the expert and the militarisation and coercion of labour lead to an increase in productivity. It had, on the contrary, according to Kollontai, led to the extinction of initiative, passivity among the mass who had resigned themselves to being controlled at every turn by Soviet officials, and open rebellion among the advanced workers who had not. The Party had lost faith in the working class. It had elevated specialists, bureaucrats and administrators to take all decisions. 'Some third person decides your fate; that is the whole essence of bureaucracy.'[25] Bureaucracy was then, in Kollontai's account, the inevitable result of the régime's constant move away from proletarian self-activity. The workers were, of course, constantly exhorted by the régime to display their creative initiative and assist the Soviet régime, but every time they did so, when the 'workers themselves attempted to organise dining-rooms, day nurseries for children, transportation of wood etc.', the bureaucrats immediately closed in, claimed jurisdiction, issued regulations 'or refusals, new requirements etc.' and killed the initiative stone dead.[26] 'Bureaucracy,' Kollontai concluded, 'as it is, is a direct negation of mass self-activity.'[27] By the same token, mass self-activity was its only antidote.

Only the working class was the creator of material values in society. Only the working class had an unambiguous interest in the building of a properly socialist society. Only the working class itself could, through its own self-activity, its initiative, its disagreements, its mistakes and errors, learn how to construct patterns of socialist relations in industry and in society as a whole. On these impeccably Leninist propositions, Kollontai rested her case.

> It is impossible to decree Communism. It can be created only in the process of practical research, through mistakes, perhaps, but only in the creative powers of the working class itself.[28]

It followed, from Kollontai's analysis, that there could be no end to the 'bureaucratic twist' in the workers' state so long as the régime continued to rely on specialists and one-man management, so long as it remained infatuated solely with administrative efficiency and the 'scientific' resolution of policy decisions which therefore dismissed political controversy as redundant. Such attitudes necessarily led, in Kollontai's analysis, to the extinction of working-class initiative, increased coercion against the working class, led to the resurgence of bourgeois dominance over the state and the Communist Party, the atrophy of both the political (Soviet) and class (trade union) organisations of the working class, and the elimination of controversy and democracy in the Party itself. All these elements were, in her view, reciprocally connected. The choice before the Party was either to foster and promote working-class self-activity to resurrect the unions not merely as 'schools of communism' but as 'the managers and creators of the Communist economy',[29] or to perpetuate and legitimise the authoritarian administrative attitudes and organisational structures which had emerged during the civil war. 'Whether it be bureaucracy or self-activity of the masses. This is the second point of the controversy between the leaders of our Party and the Workers' Opposition.'[30] Either rely on working-class self-activity or suffer full-blown bureaucracy and the degeneration of the Party and the whole régime. That was the sum and substance of the platform of the Workers' Opposition:

> There can be no self-activity without freedom of thought and opinion, for self-activity manifests itself not only in initiative, action and work, but in independent thought as well. We give no freedom to class activity, we are afraid of criticism, we have ceased to rely on the masses, hence we have bureaucracy with us. That is why the Workers' Opposition considers that

bureaucracy is our enemy, our scourge, and the greatest danger to the future existence of the Communist Party itself.

In order to do away with the bureaucracy that is finding shelter in the Soviet institutions, we must first get rid of all bureaucracy in the Party itself. That is where we face the immediate struggle against this system. As soon as the party – not in theory but in practice – recognises the self-activity of the masses as the basis of our State, the Soviet institutions will again automatically become those living institutions which are destined to carry out the Communist project, and will cease to be the institutions of red tape, laboratories for still-born decrees, into which they have very rapidly degenerated.[31]

The practical remedies proposed by the platform of the Workers' Opposition were simple and forthright; they undoubtedly had widespread appeal both within the Party and outside it. They were the more difficult to rebut because they were entirely faithful to Lenin's initial project for socialism in Russia.

They recommended the formation of 'a body from the worker-producers themselves for administering the people's economy'. They conceded that this might take some time and require considerable preparation, but it was imperative, they felt, to resolve the existing dualism of the Supreme Economic Council and the All-Russian Executive Committee of the Trade Unions in favour of the latter. All union appointments were to be made with union consent: 'All candidates nominated by the union are non-removable. All responsible officials appointed by the unions are responsible to it and may be recalled by it.'[32]

In Party and political life they recommended the same principles:
(1) Return to the principle of election all along the line with the elimination of the bureaucracy, by making all responsible officials answerable to the masses.
(2) Introduction of wide publicity within the Party . . . paying more attention to the voice of the rank and file . . . establishment of freedom of opinion and expression (giving the right not only to criticise freely during discussions, but to use funds for publication of literature proposed by different Party factions).

(3) Making the Party more of a workers' party, with limitations imposed on those who fill offices, both in the Party and the Soviet institutions at the same time.[33]

Lenin was, as we shall see, later to go part of the way towards meeting some of the popular grievances voiced by the Workers' Opposition. He was to become even more bitter in his denunciation of bureaucracy than they had ever been. He was shortly to insist upon admission procedures to the Party which were weighted heavily in favour of workers and against the intelligentsia. But, on the crucial question of the relative roles of the specialists and of working-class self-activity, he gave not an inch. His response to the threat of bureaucracy was to call for the formation of a small élite corps of irreproachable communists. To them and to them alone was the administration to be answerable. In any case, Lenin undertook none of these moves until after he had crushed the Workers' Opposition at the Tenth Party Congress where he insisted that membership of it be declared incompatible with membership of the Party.

There can be little doubt that the publication and widespread discussion of the platform of the Workers' Opposition played its part in creating a milieu of forthright criticism of the régime which culminated in the great tragedy of the Kronstadt Commune. There were, of course, other contributory factors. The Party was split wide open over the trade union controversy. Zinoviev, in charge of the Petrograd Party organisation, had deviously encouraged the climate of criticism as a means of undermining Trotsky's authority over the Baltic Fleet stationed at Kronstadt. Zinoviev himself had promised the Eighth All-Russia Congress of Soviets, at the end of December 1920, that

We will establish more intimate contacts with the working masses. We will hold meetings in the barracks, in the camps and in the factories ... it is no jest when we proclaim that a new era is about to start, that as soon as we can breathe freely again we will transfer our political meetings into the factories ... We are asked what we mean by workers' and peasants' democracy. I answer: nothing more and nothing less than what we meant by it in 1917. We must re-establish the principle of election in the workers' and peasants' democracy ... If we have deprived ourselves of the most elementary democratic rights for workers and peasants, it is time that we put an end to this state of affairs.[34]

Zinoviev was shortly to reap the whirlwind. The Kronstadt sailors took his words seriously and, with their customary despatch, were unwilling to wait for the Party to usher in the promised new era. They did it themselves. They reconstituted their Soviet, dissolved the power of the irresponsible appointees of the government in the fleet and in the Soviet administration, and established themselves as an autonomous commune after the model of 1917. More ominously, they began cultivating their links with the Petrograd workers who were in the grip of a mounting wave of strikes. In a very real sense the Kronstadt rising was inspired precisely with the desire of the Kronstadt sailors to come to the aid of the Petrograd strikers. The lock-outs, withdrawal of rations, attempts to starve the workers into submission and the intimidation of their leaders carried out by the Petrograd Soviet were well known in Kronstadt. Rumours were rife that worse yet was in store. It was, therefore, to the Petrograd workers and the other workers of Russia, as much as to the Party, that the Kronstadters announced their demands:

(1) Immediate new elections to the Soviets. The present Soviets no longer express the wishes of the workers and peasants. The new elections should be by secret ballot, and should be preceded by free electoral propaganda.

(2) Freedom of speech and of the press for workers and peasants, for the Anarchists, and for the Left Socialist parties.

(3) The right of assembly, and freedom for trade union and peasant organisation.

(4) The organisation, at the latest on 10th March 1921, of a Conference of non-Party workers, soldiers and sailors of Petrograd, Kronstadt and the Petrograd District.

(5) The liberation of all political prisoners of the Socialist parties, and of all imprisoned workers and peasants, soldiers and sailors belonging to working class and peasant organisations.

(6) The election of a commission to look into the dossiers of all those detained in prisons and concentration camps.

(7) The abolition of all political sections in the armed forces. No political party should have privileges for the propagation of its ideas, or receive State subsidies to this end ...

(8) The immediate abolition of the militia detachments set up between towns and countryside.

(9) The equalisation of rations for all workers, except those engaged in dangerous or unhealthy jobs.

(10) The abolition of Party combat detachments in all military groups. The abolition of Party guards in factories and enterprises ...

(11) The granting to the peasants of freedom of action on their own soil, and of the right to own cattle, provided they look after them themselves and do not employ hired labour.

(14) We demand the institution of mobile workers' control groups.

(15) We demand that handicraft production be authorised provided that it does not utilise wage labour.[35]

The Kronstadters, if they had any strategy at all, clearly hoped that their display of solidarity with the Petrograd workers would be reciprocated and that, in a general rising, a régime of free Soviets cleansed of the bureaucratic and authoritarian practices of the communists would be created. The Kronstadt programme was the last gasp of the powerful popular belief that the basic meaning of the revolution was power to the people. For a brief period in Kronstadt, the revolution renewed itself by going back to its roots. It was 'a throwback to the ebullience and excitement of 1917. For the sailors who styled themselves "Communards", 1917 was the Golden Age, and they longed to recapture the spirit of the revolution.'[36] As in 1917, so in Kronstadt, a host of organisations staffed by the sailors, the garrison and the townspeople were created. New life breathed in the Soviet which once again became the vibrant centre of political and administrative life. Great open-air meetings were held, as of old, in Anchor Square. As in 1917, the rallying cry was 'All Power to the Soviets' but now, by March 1921, the Bolsheviks regarded this as a slogan of the counter-revolution. So in a sense it was. It was emphatically a self-proclaimed third revolution against the Bolshevik perversion of the ideals of 1917. It was a revolution to restore 'power to the soviets but not to parties', a revolution to inaugurate a toilers' republic in which working people would be freed of the despotic control of centralised government and free (so long as they employed no hired labour) to dispose of their produce as they saw fit. It was, as Avrich observes, a naive mixture of anarchist and Maximalist (extreme left SR) views which inspired the insurgents, their programme and the leading articles of the Kronstadt *Izvestiia*. Many times in earlier revolutions the cry had gone up, *la révolution trahie, la révolution est à refaire* and, if the revolution was to be made again, the Kronstadters had no false modesty about where it should begin.

> The autocracy has fallen, The Constituent Assembly has departed to the region of the damned. The commissarocracy is crumbling. The time has come for the true power of the toilers, the power of the soviets.[37]

The response of the Communist Party to this the most critical threat posed to it was swift and decisive. A campaign of calumny and lies about the nature and motives of the Kronstadters was carefully orchestrated. Lenin, Trotsky, Zinoviev and virtually all the ranking communist leaders declared that the Kronstadt rebellion was a carefully prepared White Guard plot, directed by White Guard generals and having expressly counter-revolutionary objectives. The campaign of intimidation and coercion of the Petrograd workers was immediately reversed. Emergency food supplies were immediately rushed to the capital and distributed.[38] Zinoviev now accepted many of the workers' grievances and promised them early redress. Meanwhile the government faced the problem of mobilising Red Army units to fight against the *Bratchiki*, the sailors of Kronstadt who had during the revolution and civil war acquired for themselves a reputation synonymous with revolutionary audacity and fortitude. Regiments had to be regrouped and reorganised, forces had to be brought in from the distant lands of the Kirghiz and Bashkir, and still units refused to fight. Many indeed had to be disarmed and arrested, many more were machine-gunned by their own officers for refusing to continue the fight. Party organisations throughout the country were mobilised and the Tenth Party Congress then in session dispatched 300 delegates to stiffen the resolve of the dubious, near mutinous, Red Army.[39]

On 7 March 1921, military operations under Tukhachevsky were begun: eleven days the Kronstadt fortress held out, but by 18 March resistance had been crushed and the Bolshevik Revolutionary Tribunals exacted their vengeance on those who remained.

Lenin's own response to the Kronstadt uprising was confused and contradictory. Addressing the Tenth Party Congress the day after military operations had been started against the sailors, he saw in the revolt 'the familiar figures of whiteguard generals', then went on to declare that the movement had been inspired by a 'motley crowd or alliance of ill-assorted elements, apparently just to the right of the Bolsheviks, or perhaps even to their "left" – you can't really tell'. He was nonetheless certain that an unlikely combination of White Guard emigrés, socialist revolutionaries, petty-bourgeois counter-revolutionaries and anarchists were at the back of it. Lenin nonetheless conceded that the anarchist slogans of freedom of trade and hostility to the dictatorship of the proletariat 'has had a wide influence on the proletariat. It has had an effect on factories in Moscow and a number of provincial centres.' It was, he warned, a threat 'more dangerous than Denikin, Yudenich and Kolchak put together'.[40] By 15 March, Lenin was prepared to be even more candid, cutting the ground from under his earlier insistence that the Kronstadters were willingly following the lead of the White Guards. He told the Tenth Congress,

> The experience of Kronstadt proves this. There they do not want either the White Guards or our government – and there is no other.[41]

There is little doubt that Lenin firmly believed that, regardless of their reputation and traditions, regardless of their proletarian/sailor leadership, regardless of their socialist and revolutionary sincerity, the Kronstadters would eventually have become a powerful prop to the counter-revolution. The whole of his political strategy had, as we have seen, been based upon his either/or analyses. If not the iron dictatorship of the proletariat exercised by its vanguard, then the restoration of capitalism, dictatorship of the imperialist bourgeoisie and restoration of the monarchy.[42] There was, and could be in Lenin's mind, no alternative.

Both the Workers' Opposition and the Kronstadt rising were, in Lenin's account, aspects of the same general phenomenon. Both stemmed from a flagging of resolve among the workers and peasants as a result of their years of suffering and privation under the dictatorship of the proletariat. Both reflected the rise of petty-bourgeois anarchist sentiments which had arisen in this milieu of desperation, hunger and demoralisation. It was evident, Lenin told the Tenth Party Congress, that the syndicalist, anarchist deviation of the Workers' Opposition 'has been penetrating into the broad masses'.[43] Lenin went on to explain the objective reasons for the broad currency of this trend:

> The workers have simply abandoned their factories; they have had to settle down in the country and have ceased to be workers.... That is the economic source of the proletariat's declassing and the inevitable rise of petty-bourgeois, anarchist trends.[44]

This was Lenin's first reference to the declassing of the proletariat. It was made on 9 March 1921, two days after the assault on Kronstadt had begun. It was at this same Tenth Congress of the Party that Bukharin's faith in the working class as an inexhaustible fount of revolutionary energy finally snapped. He too conceded that the working class as a whole had become contaminated by its petty-bourgeois surroundings and thoroughly saturated with peasant attitudes. For Bukharin too the proletariat had been declassed.[45] We should notice too that the declassing of the proletariat was inseparably bound up, in Lenin's analysis, with the acceptance of anarchist and syndicalist ideas even by 'the revolutionary elements'.[46] The implications of this persistent theme in Lenin's later writings of the declassing of the proletariat were to be very considerable. They will be pursued in the next chapter.

Having located the Workers' Opposition and Kronstadt as stations on a continuum of petty-bourgeois anarchist demoralisation, Lenin had little difficulty in putting down Shlyapnikov, Medvedev, Kollontai and their adherents at the Tenth Party Congress. The resolutions of Kronstadt and those of the Workers' Opposition, he asserted, amounted to the same thing.[47] The awesome results of their propaganda were clear for all to see, across the ice in Kronstadt. All Party members had their choice to make, either with the insurgents or with the dictatorship of the proletariat exercised by the Bolsheviks. The only response to the sort of critique which Shlyapnikov made of the Party and state apparatus was, Lenin maintained with a personal savagery rare in his writings, a gun.[48]

The final paradoxical result of the Kronstadt rising was that it created within the Bolshevik ranks a painful awareness of the fragility of the régime and the isolation of the Party. It was, according to Bukharin, the moment of 'the collapse of our illusions'.[49] It provided the milieu of acute crisis in which Lenin was able to push through the Tenth Congress his Resolution on Party Unity which took the fateful step not only of banning the Workers' Opposition, but of proscribing all groups and factions within the Party 'formed on the basis of "platforms" etc....'[50]

> The Congress, therefore, hereby declares dissolved and orders the immediate dissolution of all groups without exception formed on the basis of one platform or another (such as the Workers' Opposition group, the Democratic Centralist group, etc.). Non-observance of this decision of the Congress shall entail unconditional and instant expulsion from the Party.[51]

Lenin had finally 'put the lid on' all opposition within the Party. The objective of Kronstadters to revive the reality of Soviet democracy for the population as a whole had been answered by its effective proscription in the last small island where it had hitherto enjoyed some sort of existence.

CHAPTER 13

The Declassing of the Proletariat

Lenin's response to the criticisms voiced by the Workers' Opposition and those taken up more stridently but more incoherently by the Kronstadters was *the* crucial turning point in the history of the Russian Revolution. There could be no doubt that the Workers' Opposition group did faithfully resurrect the original goals of the movement and pointed precisely to the ills which Lenin himself later sought to remedy. There is, equally, no less doubt that the demands of the Kronstadters, for free soviets and the guarantee of the rights of all socialist parties, were consonant with the original goals. Lenin himself had, after all, justified the repression of other socialist parties on the grounds that these were exceptional and temporary measures forced upon the régime by the exigencies of the moment. Nor could Lenin plead that the economic demands made by the Kronstadters were out of order for they formed the backbone of the New Economic Policy which was adopted immediately after the Kronstadt rising was suppressed. Why then did Lenin reject the theses of the Workers' Opposition and condemn membership of it as incompatible with membership of the Party? Why did he, for the first time, resort to the tactic of the big lie in labelling the Kronstadt revolt a White Guard uprising intent on the restoration of capitalism?

The brutally simple answer was that Lenin recognised perfectly clearly that the Party could not possibly grant the demands either of the Workers' Opposition or of the Kronstadters and still retain its undivided power over the state and the economy. He further believed that, without the Communist Party at the helm, the cause of socialism in Russia would die a swift death. Lenin was thus reduced to the bizarre position of arguing that, if the Party had to govern without proletarian support, so much the worse for the proletariat. Part of his rationalisation for this situation was to argue the even more extraordinary thesis that the proletariat had quite ceased to exist in Russia and, therefore, the dictatorship of the proletariat would have to be exercised without it. This was, quite clearly, a moment of critical importance in the disintegration of Lenin's structure of thought which demands examination in closer detail.

The narrowing down of the social base of the régime and the increasing animosity directed against it by the urban workers left its clear imprint on Lenin's thought, in particular upon his conception of the dictatorship of the proletariat.

By late 1920 he emphasised more and more the proposition that the dictatorship could not be exercised by the whole class of urban workers, but would have to be the property of the Party. 'What happens is that the Party, shall we say, absorbs the vanguard of the proletariat, and this vanguard exercises the dictatorship of the proletariat.'[1] It was an illusion, Lenin now maintained, to imagine that every worker was capable of helping to run the state. They would have to learn, slowly and painfully, to acquire all the arts of administration. Many were illiterate, many were still in touch with peasants and 'liable to fall for non-proletarian slogans'. Few had had any sort of practical experience in government and administration: 'A few thousand throughout Russia and no more.'[2] The proletariat was 'still so divided, so degraded, and so corrupted in parts' that its dictatorship would have to be exercised by the vanguard 'that has absorbed the revolutionary energy of the class'.[3]

There were, to be sure, objective causes for this degradation of the proletariat. The hard years of Soviet power had left it exhausted.[4]

> In those three and a half years, it has suffered distress, want, starvation and a worsening of its economic positions such as no other class in history has suffered. It's not surprising that it is uncommonly weary, exhausted and strained.[5]

Even the vanguard of the proletariat had lapsed into passivity and despair and in such a situation, with little hope of relief at hand, it was dangerous and absurd, Lenin maintained, to propose great extensions of the powers of the unions in economic administration or of the workers in industrial management. The extravagant plans of the Workers' Opposition were therefore, in his view, based upon a chimerical view of an ideal proletariat which was conspicuously absent in Russia. That precisely was the problem:

> Are we so childish as to think that we can complete the process so quickly at this time of dire distress and impoverishment, in a country with a mass of peasants, with workers in a minority, and a proletarian vanguard bleeding and in a state of prostration?[6]

Lenin concluded that not even the advanced workers, the vanguard of the proletariat, were capable of performing their historic role.

The sphere of self-activity had now been narrowed down from mass, to class, to vanguard, to Party, and it became increasingly difficult therefore to understand how Lenin anticipated the development of mass consciousness. Such consciousness could, according to Lenin's model, arise only as a product of practice, but all save the Party had now been reduced to spheres of activity so restricted and trivial that consciousness would be similarly cramped in its confines. After the Kronstadt rising, Lenin became even more pessimistic and bitter about the urban workers. Faced with the evident and obvious disaffection of the workers, their pronounced sympathies for syndicalism and open hostility to the Bolsheviks, Lenin responded by pronouncing that the proletariat in Russia had ceased to exist.

There is a curious logic behind Lenin's position. In a certain sense it was merely the adumbration of some of his central ideas on consciousness, class and political organisation. In 1900–3, Lenin had, as we saw in Volume 1, spelt out the orthodox social democratic idea that the working class does not spontaneously develop towards socialism; indeed, the production of socialist ideas was not part of the properly proletarian sphere of activity but was necessarily the domain of the radical intelligentsia. It was they who defined the goals of the movement and only insofar as the working class worked to fulfil those goals did it exist as a proletariat. If, like the English labour movement, the working class became infected with petty-bourgeois eclecticism, the pursuit of gradualism and political accommodation, then, by those tokens, it was not proletarian. As Lenin had earlier insisted, it was not the class composition of a party which determined its proletarian character, but its objectives and activity. It followed, therefore, that not *all* the projects, ideas and plans of the working class could be characterised as proletarian. Insofar as the working class moved away from the goals of the movement established by its vanguard – the Party – to that extent it ceased to be pro-letarian. The Russian workers, infatuated with petty-bourgeois syndicalism and even turning towards Menshevism, faced Lenin with an acute problem. Faced with the inescapable disjunction between the goals of the Party and those articulated by the workers in 1921, Lenin had two alternatives. He could have maintained that the Party had been wrong, that it had miscalcu-lated the needs and goals of the class. Or he could assert that the workers had misestimated the needs and goals of the class which were only kept alive by the Party. In putting down the Workers' Opposition with theses and administrative manoeuvres and in putting down the Kronstadters with lies and bullets, Lenin made the fateful decision – the workers were wrong, not the Party. They had become declassed, they no longer existed as a pro-letariat properly so-called. Only *after* Kronstadt did these extreme propositions about the declassing of the proletariat appear in Lenin's writings and it was symptomatic that in Lenin's first formulation, at the Tenth Party Congress, it was directly linked to the spread of anarchist and syndicalist ideas.

> The theses of the Workers' Opposition fly in the face of the decision of the Second Congress of the Comintern on the Communist Party's role in operating the dictatorship of the proletariat. It is syndicalism because – consider this carefully – our proletariat has been largely declassed; the terrible crises and closing down of the factories have compelled people to flee from starvation. The workers have simply abandoned their factories; they have had to settle down in the country and have ceased to be workers . . . That is the economic source of the proletariat's declassing and the inevitable rise of petty-bourgeois, anarchist trends.[7]

The petty-bourgeois milieu of Russia was bound to infect the proletariat in a situation where the autonomy of its social existence had been destroyed. In the years of civil war, the workers found it impossible to live in an exclusively urban environment. They were obliged to forage for food in the countryside. They were obliged, simply in order to stay alive, to become petty-traders and to cultivate whatever links they preserved with the village. The petty-bourgeois element had consequently penetrated 'deep into the ranks of the proletariat, and the proletariat is declassed, i.e. dislodged from its class groove. The factories and mills are idle – the proletariat is weak, scattered, enfeebled.'[8]

> After an enormous, unparalleled exertion of effort, the working class in a small-peasant, ruined country, the working class which has very largely become declassed, needs an interval of time in which to allow new forces to grow and be brought to the fore, in which the old and worn-out forces can 'recuperate'.[9]

It had, as we have seen, been part of the purposive policy of the régime to reduce the numbers of the urban workers and to reduce the numbers of plants kept running. Lenin himself had strongly encouraged the move to feed only the most essential workers, only the most exemplary. He himself could not shake off some of the responsibility for the dissolution of the industrial proletariat. Nor could he absolve himself from responsibility for the spread of petty-bourgeois tendencies in the ranks of the remaining workers. Against the fierce opposition of the rank and file, large differentials had been introduced, piece-work reestablished and, worst of all, bonuses in kind promoted, at the insistence of Lenin and Trotsky, to stimulate competition and provide direct material incentives for increased productivity.[10] Bonuses in kind were particularly corrosive of proletarian values for under this system the exemplary worker received part of his produce in addition to his food ration and pay (if any). This system endorsed and encouraged the widespread development of petty-trading between town and country conducted on a thoroughly wasteful individual basis. Only at the Tenth Party Congress did Lenin recognise the dangers posed by the spread of this petty-trading and profiteering:

Owing to our present deplorable conditions, proletarians are obliged to earn a living by methods which are not proletarian and are not connected with large-scale industry. They are obliged to procure goods by petty-bourgeois profiteering methods, either by stealing, or by making them for themselves in a publicly-owned factory, in order to barter them for agricultural produce – and that is the main economic danger, jeopardising the existence of the Soviet system. The proletariat must now exercise its dictatorship in such a way as to have a sense of security as a class, with a firm footing. But the ground is slipping from under its feet.[11]

Lenin's forebodings became ever more acute. By the summer of 1921 he finally accepted the fact that the time was too late, the proletariat had, in the awful severities it had suffered, quite lost its footing in Russia and had become declassed. The implication was that the whole process of generating a new and genuine proletarian working class, purged of its petty-bourgeois Menshevik, anarchist, and profiteering tendencies, would have to start all over again.

It was, paradoxically, the capitalists who were to be the main force in re-creating an authentic Russian proletariat purged of the petty-bourgeois habits which they had acquired under Soviet rule. A central part of Lenin's justification of NEP and the granting of concessions to both foreign and Russian capitalists was that only in this way could large-scale industry be revitalised and the vanished proletariat restored. In the meantime the dictatorship of the proletariat would have to be exercised exclusively by the Party, which had become the sole repository of proletarian values and goals. The main function of the proletarian state in the period of NEP was, therefore, that of supervising the capitalists in the re-creation of the proletariat which had, for the time being, ceased to exist.

The capitalists will gain from our policy and will create an industrial proletariat, which in our country, owing to the war and to the desperate poverty and ruin, has become declassed, i.e. dislodged from its class groove, and has ceased to exist as a proletariat. The proletariat is the class which is engaged in the production of material policies in large-scale capitalist industry. Since large-scale capitalist industry has been destroyed, since the factories are at a standstill, the proletariat has disappeared.

The restoration of capitalism would mean the restoration of socially useful material values in big factories employing machinery, and not in profiteering, not in making cigarette-lighters for sale, and in other 'work' which is not very useful, but which is inevitable when our industry is in a state of ruin.

The whole question is who will take the lead? We must face the issue squarely – who will come out on top? Either the capitalists succeed in organising first – in which case they will drive out the Communists and that will be the end of it. Or the proletarian state power, with the support of the peasantry, will prove capable of keeping a proper rein on those gentlemen, the capitalists, so as to direct capitalism along state channels and to create a capitalism that will be subordinate to the state and serve the state.[12]

A few months earlier, in May 1921, reporting on the Tax in Kind to the Tenth All-Russia Conference of the Party, Lenin had conceded that, 'It would be absurd and ridiculous to deny that the fact that the proletariat is declassed is a handicap'.[13] It could nevertheless, 'fulfil its task of winning and holding state power'[14] by keeping its grip on the few very large works still under its control and retaining possession of the transport system. This small but strategically vital economic base, in conjunction with command over the state machine, would be sufficient to maintain the 'dictatorship of the proletariat'. The entire responsibility for the fate of the revolution hung therefore upon the Party, and especially upon the quality and unity of its leading cadres. Isolated from class support, the significance of personal factors assumed enormous importance in Lenin's last writings.

Lenin was hanging on by his fingernails. His theoretical position, once so impregnable, now seemed to have about the tensile strength of wet tissue. Almost nothing of his original project for socialism remained. He had begun by arguing that only the reintegration of the state with society at large could save the world from barbarism, liberate the proletariat and usher in socialism. Now he was obliged to argue the case, which Stalin was to appropriate as his own, that only the state could reform and direct the economy and society so as to establish the basic preconditions for an eventual advance towards socialism. Lenin it was who first proclaimed the superiority of the political superstructure over the economic and social base and therewith the whole pattern of coherence, which ran through both moments of his thought, quite collapsed.

CHAPTER 14

The Degeneration of the Party

The Bolshevik Party was the party of Lenin in a way that was unique. He had played the most conspicuous role both as an organiser and as a theoretician from the very beginnings of the organised socialist movement in Russia. After the Bolshevik/ Menshevik split it was his indomitable will that had held the Bolsheviks together, dictated their tasks in 1905 and kept the radical flame burning in the years of reaction which followed. Above all it had been Lenin who had, immediately on the outbreak of the war, coined the aggressive defeatist slogans which were to sweep through Russia in 1917. In 1917 itself he had almost single-handedly changed the entire perspective of his party, committing it to a revolutionary seizure of power. At every point in its history to date it had been Lenin's will, Lenin's theoretical arguments and Lenin's prestige which had always prevailed. From the very outset he had an exalted view of the qualities necessary to be a good Party man and an equally high estimation of the duties of a Party member.

All of this stemmed, of course, from Lenin's basic distinction between party and class, and his analysis of the various strata which composed the class itself. The class was, he argued, made up of a large mass of backward and average workers who ascended to more adequate consciousness and organisation by following the lead of the advanced workers. It was, Lenin had always insisted, the advanced workers to which the Party addressed itself. The Party was the vanguard of the advanced workers in that it could anticipate theoretically the next stage of their struggle and was duty bound to provide them with guidance. The title of vanguard belonged to the Party only insofar as it provided the advanced workers with prescient guidance on the next phase of the struggle, and only insofar as Party members always proved themselves the most united, efficient and steadfast of activists in the sphere of organisation and practical leadership.

Lenin's view of the proper role and duties of Party membership did not change after the revolution – they just became even more extensive and demanding. The duties of Party membership changed naturally according to the principal problems confronting it. At different times, different qualities were called for. The character of any organisation was, as Lenin declared, determined by the nature of its tasks and objectives. During the revolution a degree of courage was called for, if not for the actual fighting at least to throw aside fears of the consequences of failure. During the civil war, Party members were required to be heroes. The Party made no secret of the fact that its members would be concentrated wherever the battle was hottest and danger most acute. There was, in the situation of imminent danger and real self-denial, no danger that the Party would be contaminated by self-seeking careerists. Lenin therefore called on the Party to open wide its doors and actively assisted the Party Week recruitment campaigns in Moscow and other centres which resulted in the enrolment of 200,000 new recruits in the period between October and November 1919, so that by the time of the Ninth Congress in March 1920 its size was given as 611,978.[1]

By late 1920, however, the civil war was over, the danger to the régime was no longer military but the threat of the total breakdown of the economy and, therewith, of peasant insurgency and proletarian disaffection. By the spring of 1921 it had become plainly apparent that these threats had indeed materialised. The economy was in a state of acute collapse. Peasant rebellions were spreading uncontrollably and the disaffection of the urban workers was clear from the widespread support enjoyed by the Workers' Opposition; it recorded itself in strikes in Petrograd and in Moscow, and reached its climacteric in Kronstadt.

In this situation, Lenin insisted, new tasks were imposed on the members of the Party. They *had* to learn how to manage the economy or else they would, and would deserve to be, swept away. They *had* to re-establish their links with the peasants and workers which years of privation and suffering had severed. They *had* to purge their ranks of the place-seekers and parasites who had joined when the period of immediate danger was over. New times, Lenin declared, imposed new tasks and responsibilities on the Party and called for new skills from the membership. Either

284

they rapidly acquired these skills or the régime would be toppled. Pointedly he reminded Party members that for all their dialectical expertise the country was still not emerging from economic crisis, the Party was still 'a drop in the ocean' of an increasingly hostile population. Repeatedly he suggested that they would do well to learn the new skills of administration, accountancy and control. They must learn from the specialists, they must carefully and scrupulously collect and study factual data on production methods in the best plants and take concrete action to improve efficiency. The press should learn that it too had a new role to play in the building of socialism. It too must turn its head away from the fireworks of political controversy, confrontations and discussion of rival platforms or theses. It would be far more valuable, Lenin suggested, if instead of digging around for sensational stories about prominent leaders and their clashes one with another, the press devoted itself to economic education. Its job, as conceived by Lenin, was to seek out the exemplary administrative and productive units, publish their results and commend their concrete measures. It should, equally, investigate and expose bad management, red tape, bribery and corruption. It should communicate the government's plans to the masses and help to enlist their support in carrying them out. The era of politics was, in Lenin's view, over and done with, it had been superseded by an administrative era where the first priority had to be the learning of proper business-like methods.

> We don't know how to collect evidence of practical experience and sum it up. We indulge in empty 'general arguments and abstract slogans', but we do not know how to utilise the services of competent teachers, in general, and of competent engineers and agronomists for technical education, in particular; we don't know how to utilise factories, state farms, tolerably well-organised enterprises and electric power stations for the purpose of polytechnic education.[2]

One of the problems which confronted the régime, a problem of which Lenin was constantly aware, was that the attributes of a good industrial manager or those of an efficient state administrator were, in general, precisely the inverse of those qualities which made men good revolutionaries. Intransigence, heroism, impatience and enthusiasm were precisely the qualities Lenin had looked for in the pre-revolutionary period, during the seizure of power and in the civil war. In the period of painstaking reconstruction which lay ahead, however, these qualities became not merely redundant but positively mischievous. What Lenin now sought were men who would not

> turn their backs on and wave aside the humble, many years difficult work in economic management, which demands forbearance, bitter experience, long effort, punctuality and perseverance. ... [3]

He doubted very much whether the Bolshevik Old Guard had these qualities and he doubted even more their preparedness to acquire them. There was a constant refrain running through his writings of 1921–2 lamenting the fact that his colleagues were full of endless bustle, constantly reorganising administrative structures in an ever more grandiose scheme justified to the nth degree by theses of impeccable Marxian foundation – but achieving nothing, checking up on nothing, learning nothing.

'Men's vices', Lenin reflected, 'are for the most part bound up with their virtues.'[4] The Bolshevik activists had excelled themselves in bravery in the face of danger, they had taken by storm the positions of the enemy, put down the bourgeoisie and crushed the resistance of the specialists. Now, in spring 1921, they had been forced into retreat. The Party must learn to accept that retreat was necessary because of its own bad management, its incompetence and arrogance. Now in the spring of 1921 the Party had to learn new ways. It had to learn to trade and to administer. To learn these things it would have to reverse its earlier attitudes. From the merchants, the Party would have to learn the elements of how to trade.

> The whole point is that the responsible Communists, even the best of them, who are unquestionably honest and loyal, who in the old days suffered penal servitude and did not fear death, do not know how to trade, because they are not business-men, they have not learnt to trade, do not want to learn and do not understand that they must start learning from the beginning.[5]

Even the best communists, Lenin reflected, were useless in matters of business, in matters of economic management and administration, by comparison with the average tsarist salesman.[6] From the specialists they would have to learn how to run factories, railways and offices. They would have to discipline themselves not to meddle with matters of which they had no experience, to give fewer orders to the specialists and to be more modest, much more modest, in their attitudes for they had, Lenin insisted, a very great deal to be modest about. The long and the short of it was that 'we have given Communists, with all their splendid qualities practical executive jobs for which they are totally unfitted'.[7] The plain unvarnished truth of the matter, Lenin told the Eleventh Congress of the Party in April 1922, was 'That in ninety-nine cases out of a hundred the responsible Communists are not in the jobs they are now fit for; that they are unable to perform their duties, and that they must sit down and learn'.[8]

The basic cause of this situation was their lack of culture. Political power they had in plenty[9] and boundless talents in drawing up theses, decrees and platforms, but these talents were superannuated, they were relevant only to a bygone era and even possession of political power was no sufficient guarantee of survival. The cultural backwardness of the communists threatened now to be their Achilles heel. The old culture, miserable and povertystricken as it was, was infinitely superior to that of the communist officials. Consequently, large numbers of the administrators of the *ancien régime* had been recruited into the Soviet state apparatus. This was in accord with Lenin's view of the necessity, during the dictatorship of the proletariat, of making use of all the scarce talent and experience available and pressing it into the service of building the basis for socialist advance. So long, in other words, as the specialists were firmly directed by the proletarian state and its governing Party, acting under their orders according to a definite plan, they would constitute no danger. They were indeed vital to the reconstruction of industry and the machinery of state during the transition period. Lenin, by 1922, had come to the conclusion that due to the cultural superiority of the old tsarist specialists the pattern of relationships between them and the state and Party had in practice been reversed. The communists, he concluded, 'are not directing, they are being directed'.[10]

> Will the responsible Communists of the R.S.F.S.R. and of the Russian Communist Party realise that they cannot administer; that they only imagine they are directing, but are, actually, being directed. If they realise this, they will learn, of course; for the business can be learnt. But one must study hard to learn it, and our people are not doing this. They scatter orders and decrees right and left, but the result is quite different from what they want.[11]

As a result, because people did not know what they were doing, because nobody would take responsibility even for the most mundane things like ordering cans of meat, nothing in fact got done.

> Think of it! How could 4,700 responsible officials ... decide a matter like purchasing food abroad without the consent of the Political Bureau of the Central Committee? This would be something supernatural, of course.[12]

It had taken two investigations, the intervention of Lenin, a meeting between Krasin and Kamenev and the instructions of the Politburo to send off one order to buy canned goods from France.[13] The régime had collapsed into a state of administrative atrophy. Everything was referred to the Politburo. The agencies of state had become so fat that it was more than they could do to support their own weight.

In the past, Lenin had responded to crises with a clarion call to the proletariat to swell the ranks of the Party with fresh forces. Now he knew that such a course would be to no avail. The proletariat had become declassed, it was alienated from the régime. In any case it could not bring to the Party the skills and expertise it so desperately needed. Instead of broadening the Party, Lenin decided that it would have to be drastically purged. The petty-bourgeois and anarchist element, which had corrupted the proletariat, was corrupting the Party too.[14] A Commission for Purging the Party was established with the object of reducing membership by 100,000, though Lenin himself was in favour of doubling that figure.[15] He further suggested far more rigorous terms of probation before aspiring members could be admitted, stipulating that a sliding scale ranging from six months for industrial workers with at least ten years' experience (earlier he had insisted upon eighteen months' probation even for this category),[16] to three years, for applicants who were neither bona fida workers nor soldiers, should be introduced.[17]

Lenin was still sufficiently in control of the Party to carry out his plan for purging it. The reduction in numbers which resulted was indeed greater than he had anticipated. Membership of the Party was reduced from the peak of three-quarters of a million, which it had attained in March 1921 at the time of the Tenth Party Congress, to 485,500 in January 1923.[18] Whether the objective of the purge – to purify the Party by cutting down its non-proletarian elements – was achieved is far from clear. The opposition elements within the Party, the Democratic Centralists and the Workers' Opposition, certainly suffered, particularly at the lower levels. There is evidence too that worker activists resigned from the Party in considerable numbers during this period, angered at the way in which the trade union issue had been settled, the proscription of debate within the Party and the large concessions which had been made to the peasants in NEP.

It was consistently Lenin's view in the period 1921–3 that the Party had degenerated. It had been contaminated by the petty-bourgeois milieu in which it had to operate. Its level of culture was too low, its expertise too ill-developed for it to be able to administer the state or organise production. It had fallen prey to the worst forms of the old tsarist style of work – red tape, high-handedness and arrogance.

The only way out of the morass was to ensure that the most talented and efficient individuals should be placed in the right jobs at the right time. The fetish for the reorganisation of Party or state administration, the concern with 'politics' and resolutions; all these things were, Lenin asserted, very largely irrelevant. What counted was the quality of personnel, in particular the abilities and initiative of the top man. 'In the present situation the key feature is people, the proper choice of people.'[19]

The key feature is that we have not got the right men in the right places; that responsible Communists who acquitted themselves magnificently during the revolution have been given commercial and industrial functions about which they know nothing; and they prevent us from seeing the truth for rogues and rascals hide magnificently behind their backs.[20]

In the planned reorganisation of the state apparatus, as well as in his recommendations for refurbishing the Party, Lenin exhibits precisely the same absorption with the proper training and allocation of the leading personnel. That, he insisted, had become 'the pivot of our work.'[21] Lenin's last major speech to the Party, 'on the Political Report of the Central Committee', at its Eleventh Congress perfectly typifies the new approach. In the past he had used the Political Report to Congress to review the events of the year in a very general way and used his analysis to make propositions about what lay immediately ahead. He would, earlier, have felt it quite unnecessary and improper to discourse to the Party as a whole on the strengths and weaknesses of particular members. In this, his last major speech to the Party, Lenin was little concerned with general analysis: he was almost wholly absorbed with personality problems which were indissolubly bound up with interdepartmental rivalries. He concentrated his fire on the deficiencies of those who still presumed to criticise the overall line of the Party – Shlyapnikov, Preobrazhensky (who 'comes along and airily says that Stalin has jobs in two Commissariats. Who among us has not sinned this way?'). Next Lenin turned his fire against Kosior and then Osinsky, followed by a dispute between Larin and Preobrazhensky, to end with bitter words against Myasnikov and Medvedev. It was not a political report Lenin had made, it was a recitation of personality defects and a strong plea that the Party should have the resolve to expel the fractious troublemakers whom Lenin had been trying to dispose of for some time.

The same absorption with character strengths and weaknesses runs through Lenin's so-called Testament, the series of notes he dictated for the Thirteenth Congress of the Party in late December 1922. Above all he feared that 'conflict between small sections of the C.C.' would acquire excessive importance for the future of the Party.[22] In the continuation of the notes he explained that what he had in mind was the danger of a split between Trotsky and Stalin. Lenin went on to dictate his now famous characterisation of the principal members of the Central Committee:

Comrade Stalin, having become Secretary-General, has un-limited authority concentrated in his hands, and I am not sure that he will always be capable of using that authority with sufficient caution. Comrade Trotsky, on the other hand, as his struggle against the Central Committee on the question of the People's Commissariat for Communications has already proved, is distinguished not only by outstanding ability. He is personally perhaps the most capable man in the present Central Committee, but he has displayed excessive self-assurance and shown excessive preoccupation with the purely administrative side of the work.[23]

Zinoviev, Kamenev, Bukharin and Pyatakov then passed under his scrutiny, the last two being singled out as youngsters of outstanding ability. In a further addition to the notes, Lenin observed that, given the existing state of the Party, what might appear as 'A negligible detail' in one man's make-up might assume 'decisive importance' for the Party. He was referring, prophetically, to Stalin's rudeness and intolerance and rec-ommended 'that the comrades think about a way of removing Stalin from that post [of Secretary-General] and appointing another man in his stead'.[24]

To remedy this state of affairs Lenin, in his last despairing letter to the Party Congress, proposed increasing the number of Central Committee members 'to a few dozen or even a hundred'.[25] In this way he hoped that the dangerous deficiencies of personalities and the threat of a split would be reduced: 'the more members there are in the Central Committee, the more men will be trained in Central Committee work and the less danger there will be of a split due to some indiscretion'.[26] The new members, Lenin felt, 'must be mainly workers of a lower station than those promoted in the last five years of work in Soviet bodies; they must be people close to being rank-and-file workers and peasants. . . . '[27] This was Lenin's last token enrolment of the working class into the affairs of state – the final proxy form of worker self-administration. But the time was now too late. The Party with Lenin at its head had quite consciously refused to democratise its structure or revivify the soviets. At the Eighth Party Congress back in 1919, the leaders of the Democratic Centralists, Sapronov and Osinsky, had made these demands and had, specifically, recommended that the composition of the Central Committee be radically changed to make it a broader, far more proletarian centre, making it more in touch with the felt needs of the working class. The response of the Party even then had been to retreat into an even more rigidly centralised administrative structure. This was the Congress which confirmed the existence of the select Politburo and instituted the Orgburo and the Secretariat of the Central Committee. The same sorts of demands for increased worker participation and for free soviets had been voiced by the Workers' Opposition and by the Kronstadt insurgents and had been summarily rejected as petty-bourgeois anarchist slogans. Then, finally, had come Lenin's declaration that the proletariat had been declassed. It followed that only the Party or, more properly, a small section of it, was fit to exercise the dictatorship of the proletariat.

The last bitter paradox was that, in putting down and discrediting the Democratic Centralists and Workers' Opposition, Lenin had effectively destroyed the bases within the Party which might have rallied to his call for its regeneration. Even more ominously, in crushing these groups, new Party institutions – the Orgburo, the Secretariat, and Central Control Commission – had been established with plentiful powers to break up centres of opposition and dissent, especially by 'exiling' their leaders. Then these institutions had served Lenin's purpose but now, now that his control over the Party apparatus had been eroded, now that he wanted to shake up the leading cadres of the Party and transform its institutions, these same institutions could be and were used to isolate Lenin himself. Inexorably the power of the Central Committee as *the* authoritative guiding centre responsible to the Congress of the Party was eaten away. It met less and less frequently. By contrast, the Politburo and the Orgburo, working closely together, met with ever-increasing frequency. The apparatus of Party control was becoming increasingly sophisticated. Separate departments for Organisation and Instruction and for Records and Assignment were also created by the Eighth Congress and these, under the general control of Stalin as General Secretary of the Party, swiftly emerged as bodies of enormous importance since they had overall responsibility for checking up on the performance of all Party units and for seeing to the placement of all Party cadres. It was these departments which so efficiently dispersed the centres of opposition to the policies of Lenin and the Politburo in 1920 and 1921. The boot was, however, to be on the other foot when, in 1922, Lenin became ever more scathing in his attack on the ineptitude of the Party and state apparatuses, when in particular he was finally alerted to the rudeness and high-handedness of Stalin. He came to regret his earlier defence of Stalin's multiple job-holding but, by that time., ill health had slackened his grip on the Party and Stalin was able without much difficulty to isolate Lenin and prevent the publication of Lenin's damning final testament. The machine which Lenin himself had created was now quite strong enough to mute all his stormy criticisms and insistent demands for radical change.

CHAPTER 15

The Reform of the State Apparatus

We have seen in the previous chapters how the state had emerged from a position of comparative insignificance to one of cardinal importance in Lenin's thought. This was the obverse side of the constant whittling down of the sphere of self-activity and the bridling of all spontaneous and voluntary organisations. Since state power was, as it were, 'hanging in the air', with the Party as its sole executor, paramount importance now attached to the unity and cohesion of the Party and to the personal qualities of its top leadership. It also became vitally important that the machinery of state was up to the enormous tasks which Lenin had in mind for it. It was, according to Lenin, along with the Party, the last bastion of socialism in Russia. To it attached the great responsibility of keeping the torch of socialism flickering, however fitfully, until Russia was finally joined by the forces of the international revolution.

The problems which confronted him were daunting. There was, above all, the problem of controlling the size of the bureaucratic apparatus. Whilst the economic basis of the régime had remained static or had actually shrunk, the bureaucracy had grown at a dizzy speed. In December 1920, Lenin quoted with approval Radzutak's thesis that 'the state apparatus of economic management, gradually gaining in size and complexity, has been transformed into a huge bureaucratic machine which is out of all proportion to the scale of industry'.[1] Apart from sheer numbers, there was also the question of its responsibility and accountability. Some remedy had to be found to the abuses which the Workers' Opposition had vociferously pointed to, if only because, as Lenin recognised, their criticisms were widely shared and were a major cause of disaffection from the régime. There was a very

294

widespread popular feeling that the government apparatus had become a nest of bourgeois place-seekers riding rough-shod over ordinary people and, like their tsarist predecessors, amenable only to bribes.

Lenin was sensitive to this mood of public disenchantment and extremely adroit at using the threat of a popular rising against the régime to stymie criticism within the Party. Thus he warned Bukharin and the advocates of 'industrial democracy' that the masses might well interpret the slogan in their own syndicalist way to mean the ousting of the bureaucrats and the dismantling of the central boards.[2] Too aggressive and open a critique of the present régime would, Lenin warned, merely aid the anarchist element, 'the most dangerous enemy of the proletarian dictatorship'.[3] Lenin was never, it seems, consciously aware of the ambiguities of his own position. He had insisted upon the suppression of factions and the publication of separate platforms within the Party, yet he wanted criticism and informed discussion of alternatives. He repeatedly insisted that it was the duty of every communist to expose bureaucracy and red tape wherever it was found, yet he warned against the dangerous demagogy of those like Shlyapnikov who called on the Party to 'put a stop to bureaucratic practices'. Indeed, at the Tenth Party Congress he threatened Shlyapnikov with the weapon of Party criticism – the machine gun.[4] This was demagogy because it was a task which could not be immediately accomplished yet it incited people to believe that it could. There were, incidentally, many times when Lenin used almost identical language to Shlyapnikov's, indeed his critique of the state apparatus was more bitter and trenchant than that set out by the Workers' Opposition group, membership of which had, at Lenin's insistence, been declared inconsistent with membership of the Party. This made the dividing line he was trying to establish even more blurred, indistinct and, therefore, arbitrary. The point at which sincere constructive criticism became demagogy could never be defined. It was, moreover, a distinction which, in Lenin's view, was very much contingent upon the situation in which the régime found itself, the audience being addressed and the occasion for the utterance. Lenin insisted that critics should be sensitive to all these factors; furthermore, he insisted that firm action be taken against anyone lodging unjustified complaints[5] and yet he simultaneously reproved his colleagues for not doing enough to expose red tape and to bring the culprits to court.

The root problem in reforming the state apparatus was, in Lenin's view, the problem of raising the cultural level of the population generally and of the government functionaries especially. This factor would, Lenin believed, directly determine the quality of the administration, and the general level of culture, even among the communist vanguard was, he found, lamentably, deplorably low.

The problem was, how to remedy these obvious abuses? The state apparatus had clearly developed a vested interest in preserving its present size and its *modus operandi*. It was, moreover, strongly identified at all levels with the Communist Party. The organs of popular government, the Soviets, had long lost their vitality and were now quite subordinated to the central government bodies. They could not therefore be used as agencies for the regeneration of the state. Nor could they be revived on a popular basis, for to allow free soviets, as the Kronstadters had demanded, would have meant the eclipse of Bolshevik power. Lenin was, moreover, constantly aware of the fact that, in undertaking his censure of the bureaucracy, he was walking a tightrope. Too virulent a critique would simply lend credence to the complaints of emigré Marxists and threaten to unleash within Russia a popular movement which would sweep the entire administration away.

For a brief moment Lenin flirted with the idea of effecting a separation between Party and state. He briefly urged a clear specification and demarcation of the respective spheres of each and proposed that the organs of the state be given much greater autonomy and freedom from Party interference. Very similar proposals have, of course, lately come into fashion with Eurocommunists, and for very similar reasons. If the Party and state machines were to be kept separate then the Party itself could act as the agency of criticism and benefit from pressing for the remedying of popular grievances against the bureaucracy. Lenin never fully elaborated his proposals for he recognised almost instantly that they could not work. They were impractical above all because, as he constantly reminded his colleagues, the communists were but a tiny drop in the vast ocean of the people. They had, moreover, forfeited what mass support they had enjoyed.

The régime was fragile and only the most determined combination and centralisation of its resources would preserve it. The Bolsheviks had little else to lean on except the organising and punitive power of the state. Lenin accepted, therefore, that the interweaving of state and Party machines would have to continue, indeed his final recommendation was that the highest body of each should be fused together in one exemplary all-powerful directorate. The crucial problems remained. How to promote much-needed criticism of the state apparatus without this becoming corrosive of Party authority? How to encourage prominent Party officials to join in the campaign for the reduction in numbers of commissariats and the staffs they employed, when these very Party officials were simultaneously commissars with empires to protect? Above all, how was the state machine to be made accountable and responsible to the views and feelings of the mass of the people in a situation where other parties had been proscribed? Even factions within the Party had now been banned *precisely because* one of them, the Workers' Opposition, had been adjudged too virulent in its critique of place-seekers, bureaucracy, and the irresponsibility of the régime.

The paradox is that having put down the Workers' Opposition, Lenin's own critique of the state machine becomes sharper by the month. It became an obsession with him and virtually all his last writings, in the period 1922–3, were concerned with purging the state of the canker of bureaucracy. Only intermittently did he have the strength to dictate to his secretaries. He was, besides, denied access to his secretaries and to important materials by his fellow commissars who pleaded they were merely safeguarding his health. They had reason enough to fear the candour of the leader who knew he was dying, who had set himself this one last vital task of reforming the Soviet state apparatus before it was too late, and who brought to his task a mind still sharp and inventive and a determination to tell the truth no matter how unpleasant.

The starting point of Lenin's analysis of the bureaucratic distortion which threatened to subvert the workers' state was, as ever, his socio-economic analysis of Russian society. The predominant form of economic relations under the Soviet régime remained the same as that under tsarism: small-scale relatively isolated productive units in industry as well as in agriculture remained the prevalent economic form. It was also quite clear from Lenin's economic analysis, and patently obvious to everyone, that even the degree of centralisation of capital and socialisation of labour characteristic of the pre-revolutionary economy had drastically declined during the war and civil war. Following Marx, Lenin argued that it was precisely this structure of small-scale, isolated units of production which had formed the social basis of despotism and the growth of an all-powerful bureaucracy. The economic level of society was intimately related to its cultural level. Small-scale isolated productive units perpetuated antiquated methods, inhibited the spread of enlightenment and education, restricted horizons and led to a primitive conception of individual rights. Illiteracy was, in particular, the seemingly immovable rock upon which all attempts to improve the state machine threatened to founder. Illiterates, Lenin argued, stood outside politics, they existed in the realm of gossip, fairy tales and rumour.[6] Being unaware of their rights, unable to record their grievances, let alone get proper redress for them, the only recourse of the illiterate was the old traditional manner of greasing the machinery – *blat* – bribes. But the system of bribery itself was outside politics, being a person-to-person not a class-to-class transaction, being covert and inarticulate, not open and reasoned: 'if such a thing as bribery is possible it is no use talking about politics. Here we have not even an approach to politics; here it is impossible to pursue politics.'[7] The one thing which the people of Russia lacked and which even the high state officials lacked was culture.[8] Until the level of culture was raised, until a cultural revolution brought the people at least up to *bourgeois* standards, then all the huffing and puffing, all the reorganisations, all the theses, declarations and legislation would be in vain.

The problem which now emerged, the problem which stands out agonisingly in Lenin's writings in 1922–3, is that the level of culture is determined by the economic level of society. The economic level would, however, as NEP made clear, rise only very gradually. Only in the distant future would the cultural backwardness of Russia's vast hinterland be overcome by the complementary forces of electricity and education. In the meanwhile the Party and the state stood guardian over socialist values. Here was the rub. Lenin recognised full well that even the highest Party and state officials were not immune to the cultural milieu which surrounded them. They too rode rough-shod where they could, took bribes and gained material advantage, hid behind red tape and often acted with rudeness, even brutality. In short, the Party/state apparatus had taken on all the modes of behaviour attitudes and conventions of the old tsarist bureaucratic structure:

> With the exception of the People's Commissariat of Foreign Affairs, our state apparatus is to a considerable extent a survival of the past and has undergone hardly any serious change. It has only been slightly touched up on the surface, but in all other respects it is a most typical relic of our old state machine.[9]

The first of the two main tasks which constituted the epoch of NEP was, Lenin argued, 'to reorganise our machinery of state, which is utterly useless, and which we took over in its entirety from the preceding epoch'.[10] These were hard words for all those with a mind to remember that the primary project of the revolution, the central goal which Lenin held up to the communists in order to distinguish their position from the social democrats, the insistent goal of state and revolution, had been that of smashing the existing state machine and replacing it with one which would be radically free and democratic in quite a new way. But worse yet was to come. Lenin castigated this 'utterly impossible, indecently pre-revolutionary form'[11] of the state which had survived and fortified itself in the years of Soviet rule. 'Our state apparatus is so deplorable, not to say wretched, that we must first think very carefully how to combat its defects.'[12] A necessary precondition of combating its many defects and gross deformities was to foster a general awareness of their existence. The smug complacency of the communists and bureaucrats was Lenin's first target.

> It is time we learned to put a value on science and got rid of the 'communist' conceit of the dabbler and bureaucrat; it is time we learned to work systematically, making use of our own experience and practice.[13]

The communists would have to 'stop substituting intellectualist and bureaucratic profiteering for vibrant effort'.[14] They would have to be prepared to go back to square one, acknowledge their ignorance and learn from the experts. Above all, they would have to accept the fact that what had been built up so far was not only useless it was positively harmful to the cause of preserving socialism in Russia and would have to be radically reconstructed. First of all, as a precondition for everything else, Lenin insisted that the communists acknowledge their profound ignorance and acknowledge that their work to date had been quite futile.

In 'Better Fewer, But Better', the last article he wrote, this was his considered overview of the development of the Soviet state, the legacy he feared to bequeath to his followers:

> The most harmful thing would be to rely upon the assumption that we know at least something, or that we have any consider-able number of elements necessary for the building of a really new state apparatus, one really worthy to be called Socialist, Soviet, etc.
>
> No, we are ridiculously deficient of such an apparatus, and even of the elements of it, and we must remember that we must not stint time on building it, and that it will take many, many years.[15]
>
> We have been bustling for five years trying to improve our state apparatus, but it has been mere bustle, which has proved useless in these five years, or even futile or even harmful. This bustle created the impression that we were doing something, but in effect it was only clogging up our institutions and our brains.
>
> It is high time things were changed.
> We must follow the rule: Better fewer, but better.[16]

The first imperative was to reduce the number of central state institutions and to cut the staffs of all of them. 'We have eighteen People's Commissariats of which not less than fifteen are no use at all – efficient People's Commissars cannot be found anywhere,'[17] Lenin declared to the Eleventh Congress of the Party. A little later he told the Central Executive Committee of Soviets, 'We are convinced that our machinery of state, which suffers from many defects, is inflated to more than twice the size we need, and often works not for us, but against us.'[18] As early as May 1921 he had written to Krzhizhanovsky as chairman of the State Planning Commission asking him to enquire into the feasibility of reducing Soviet office staffs by 25 or 50 per cent.[19] The inevitable consequence of this situation was 'that our vital affairs became submerged in a deluge of paper'.[20] To the All-Russia Congress of the Soviet Employees Union he was equally blunt:

Dear Comrades,

The primary, immediate task of the present day, and of the next few years, is systematically to reduce the size and the cost of the Soviet machinery of state by cutting down staffs, improving organisation, eliminating red tape and bureaucracy, and by reducing unproductive expenditure.[21]

Hardly words to gladden the hearts of the Praesidium of the union of state employees.

Reduction in the number, size and costliness of the central commissariats was to be complemented, in Lenin's plan, by a new emphasis on local initiative. The role of the commissariat, he suggested, was not that of drawing up plans which were then to be uniformly imposed on all localities. It was rather to encourage local initiatives, observe and encourage the efficient and inventive and persuade others in a similar situation to follow their example.[22]

Exemplary organisation in this respect, even in a single volost, is of far greater national importance than the 'exemplary' improvement of the central apparatus of any People's Commissariat; over the past three and half years our central apparatus has been built up to such an extent that it has managed to acquire a certain amount of harmful routine; we cannot improve it quickly to any extent, we do not know how to. Assistance in the work of radically improving it, securing an influx of fresh forces, combating bureaucratic practices effectively and overcoming harmful routine must come from the localities and the lower ranks, with the model organisation of a 'complex', even if on a small scale.[23]

In the meanwhile those 'doomed to work in the centre', in Moscow where all the abuses were most concentrated, and which was therefore 'the worst city' and, in general, the worst 'locality' in

301

the Republic,[24] would just have to grin and bear it. For a brief time, in April 1921, perhaps on the basis of an exaggerated optimism about the new popularity the regime was to enjoy with the introduction of NEP, Lenin partially revived his 'mass line'. The Party must seize the chance to encourage initiative and fresh forces in every locality instead of stifling them as it had done.[25] Lenin had clearly altered his mind very considerably since arguing with and proscribing the Workers' Opposition for it had been a central plank in their platform that the Party had smothered all local initiatives and failed to encourage young rank and file enthusiasts. At that time, a month or so earlier, Lenin had maintained that there *were* no such forces, that the Communist Party was only too willing to encourage and promote them but none were coming forward. This had been the main brunt of his argument declaring that the Workers' Opposition were, therefore, hopelessly utopian premissing the transformation of the régime on an idealised and non-existent proletariat. The proletariat, he frequently reminded them, had been declassed and dislodged from its class groove, it had been decimated, scattered and corrupted. After the defeat of the Workers' Opposition we see Lenin, for a time at least, waxing as enthusiastic as they had done about enlisting the support of the non-party rank and file.

> We must do more to promote and test thousands and thousands of rank-and-file workers, to try them out systematically and persistently, and appoint hundreds of them to higher posts, if experience shows they can fill them.[26]

This was, however, a short-lived remembrance of things past. Lenin soon became totally committed to his new schema for the regeneration of the régime, one which owed nothing to faith in the rank and file, one which was supercentralising rather than decentralising. It was a plan which rested entirely upon the exemplary qualities of what he recognised to be a tiny handful of able, devoted, totally uncorruptible men grouped in one exemplary all-powerful institution. Here, at the last, was the Jacobin solution, the rule of the men of Virtue.

The main thrust of Lenin's proposals to reorganise the state machinery lay in his suggestion that a single truly exemplary Party/state body, recruited from the best of the best and endowed with enormous jurisdiction should, as a matter of supreme urgency, be formed to purge the state machine and set it moving at last upon the right rails. The reorganised Workers and Peasants Inspectorate, fused with the Central Control Commission of the Party, was to save the soul of socialism in Russia. Lenin's new plan superseded and flatly contradicted his earlier projects for dealing with the problem of bureaucracy through separation of Party and state and through decentralisation. His final solution, to which he devoted virtually all his remaining energies in 1922 – 3, was to merge the most authoritative bodies of Party and state to supervise, control and hold to account all agencies of the administration, at all levels, in all localities.

The state body which he proposed elevating to this awesome role was the Workers and Peasants Inspectorate, known by its Russian acronym Rabkrin. It had been established in 1919 for the purpose of guaranteeing the immediate representatives of the workers and peasants a direct role in overseeing the affairs of all departments of state. It had never had much more than a token existence and by the beginning of the 1920s it had virtually ceased to function. As Lenin admitted in March 1923, it had become the most deplorably organised of the People's Commissariats and it enjoyed no authority whatever.[27] This was, no doubt, intended as a stab at Stalin who had been in charge of it until the very end of 1922,[28] but there was little doubt that the substance of Lenin's remarks was justified.

Lenin's package of proposals to revitalise Rabkrin and to make of it the supreme organ in the Soviet state tell us a good deal about the cast of his mind in these his last years. He had, as we have seen, become convinced that in the era of the dictatorship of the proletariat, politics would be replaced by administration. Great debates about the direction and goals of the régime would yield place to expert technical discussion about alternative means of achieving agreed ends. Democracy therefore, in the sense of great controversy between competing political parties, was irrelevant. Parties represented classes and the ascendant proletariat would not and should not tolerate the wrecking and insurrectionary activities of bourgeois parties. There is plenty of evidence to suggest that even within the Party, Lenin considered that the airing of great theoretical debates was an antediluvian throwback to an earlier period. Certainly Lenin made no attempt to conceal his impatience and anger at Party members who ventured to disagree with him in the period from 1919 onwards. Since the crucial problems which the régime had to resolve were extremely complex and technical in nature, for instance the drawing up of a national economic plan and the electrification of the country, the re-establishment of the transport system, the revitalisation of trade between town and country etc., it was best that their resolution should be left to men with the appropriate expertise. There was behind this the unspoken assumption that large bodies of public representatives, no matter how proletarian, would be quite unable to contribute on these crucial questions. Lenin certainly reminded the communists, the top people in the state and Party that *they* certainly had precious little competence in these fields and that they should therefore do far more listening to the experts.

The central practical problem which Lenin faced was how to ensure the accountability of the administration to the mass in the absence of free press, free Soviets, other political parties or even rival factions within the Party. Recent events had amply demonstrated the dangers to Bolshevik hegemony which arose from any slackening of its monopoly command over the whole political process. But still the state machine ought, in some way, to be made accountable to the interests of the mass of the people; the problem was how to accomplish it? Almost all of Lenin's options had by this time been closed and he himself had been instrumental in sealing them off. Self-activity had been narrowed down from mass to class to political vanguard and even the Party had been found to be corrupted by its petty-bourgeois environment. Criticism of all sorts had been effectively stifled. In this situation the only body which could hope to oversee and bring to account the Party/state bureaucracy, was a special Party/state apparatus composed of the most exemplary and dedicated workers and endowed with superordinate powers. Lenin's solution to the threat of administrative irresponsibility was to create another administrative body.

The Workers' and Peasants' Inspection would, in order to fulfil its tasks, have to set its own house in order and that would require drastic pruning of its staff. They should be reduced to one-sixth, from 12,000 to 2000 staff. Their payroll should, however, be cut by only one-half so that the wages of those remaining would be trebled. Of the surviving staff, 'select a few dozen and later hundreds of the best, absolutely honest and most efficient employees'[29] to be grouped together as the nucleus of the new unit. By January 1923, in his major article 'How We Should Reorganise the Workers' and Peasants' Inspection', Lenin proposed an even more swingeing reduction in the staff complement. He now considered that the staff of the Workers' and Peasants' Inspection should be reduced to three or four hundred persons, specially screened for conscientiousness and knowledge of our state apparatus. They must also undergo a special test as regards their knowledge of the principles of scientific organisation of labour in general, and of administrative work, office work and so forth, in particular. These, clearly, were to be the business efficiency men and exponents of Taylorism, the time and motion, organisation and methods experts whose main object was to give the administration an up-to-date administrative structure. It goes without saying that the sort of education, experience and ability needed to qualify for entrance to this élite corps of Guardians instantly disqualified all but an infinitesimal number of workers and peasants. The Workers' and Peasants' Inspection, by the character Lenin gave it, could only have been the domain of the bourgeois *spetsy*. They were the only ones with the requisite background, as Lenin unflaggingly reminded the communists. The plan to combine Rabkrin with the Central Control Commission and to give the new body plenary powers can only be construed as Lenin's attempt to get the views and skills of the *spetsy* into the very highest organ of government. It was Lenin's attempt finally to eradicate the complaisant arrogance of the communist commissars by forcing them to collaborate in a joint organisation with real experts. Lenin was indeed giving the *spetsy* the whip hand in many respects for they were given powers to investigate all aspects of administration in all the commissariats.

> This can and must be done; if not, it will be impossible to combat departmentalism and red tape, it will be impossible to teach non-Party workers and peasants the art of administration, which is a task that in the present time we cannot shirk either in principle or in practice.[30]

Here is the last glimmer of Lenin's project for socialism in

Russia at the heart of which lay mass participation in self-administration – Rabkrin as surrogate self-administration – its proxy form. Just a very few of the most able, dedicated and honest non-Party mass are to be very gradually and cautiously inducted into the administration, at every stage subject to rigorous examination of their abilities and performance.

In view of the stringent specification which Lenin laid down for the selection of the staff of the Inspectorate and the recurrent tests and examinations he insisted they underwent, it was clear that Lenin's dream of using it to teach 'non-Party workers and peasants the art of administration'[31] could not materialise. He had after all insisted that of the thousand present employees only a few dozen had the qualities needed for the task he had in mind. It is difficult therefore to see how his conclusion that through merger of the CCC with Rabkrin, the Central Committee's contacts with the masses would be greatly improved.[32] For such 'a really exemplary institution, an instrument to improve our state apparatus'[33] only exemplary men would do. The need 'to obtain really exemplary quality' would be put before all other considerations and employees would be selected 'with particular care and only on the basis of the strictest test'.[34]

> For this purpose, we must utilise the very best of what there is in our social system, and utilise it with the greatest caution, thoughtfulness and knowledge, to build up the new People's Commissariat.
>
> For this purpose, the best elements that we have in our social system such as, first, the advanced workers, and, second the really enlightened elements for whom we can vouch that they will not take the word for the deed, and will not utter a single word that goes against their conscience – should not shrink from admitting any difficulty and should not shrink from any struggle in order to achieve the object they have seriously set themselves.[35]

This was the solution of Lenin's last despair. The salvation of the revolution, the redemption of socialism in Russia now was laid in the hands of a few truly exemplary men. These 'irreproachable communists',[36] the Guardians, the sea-green incorruptibles of the revolution, would have to be firmly united and concentrated together in one institution which would serve as a model to all others.[37] Otherwise they would be spread too thinly and, like the rest of the party, would succumb to the petty-bourgeois environment and the all-pervading legacy of the past.

To be effective the new body would have to be given powers to see all papers of the Politburo[38] and call all persons. It would have to investigate the deficiencies of all administrative bodies and make recommendations for their improvement. It would be omni-present and omnipotent:

The functions of the Workers' and Peasants' Inspection cover our state apparatus as a whole, and its activities should affect all and every state institution without exception; local, central, commercial, purely administrative, educational, archive, theatrical, etc. – in short, all without any exception.[39]

It was to be 'an apparatus for investigating and improving all government work'.[40]

Its members would not be restricted by the formal procedures of conducting an investigation which were customary in the West. They should, Lenin felt, be encouraged to use imagination, ruse and trickery to trap the rogues and opportunists hiding in the state machinery.[41]

Here, at the end, in the last pamphlets he wrote in this his political testament, Lenin became a Jacobin. We have seen how initiative and self-activity had been narrowed down from mass to class to party. But even the Party had fallen prey to careerism, the legacy of the past and the cultural level of petty-bourgeois Russia. The Party as a whole could no longer be entrusted with the task of preserving socialism in Russia. That job now passed to a small group of individuals. It therefore became a matter of enormous significance that the right individuals were recruited, that they received the correct training, that they were, in personal make-up, suited to their job and able to collaborate with their colleagues. For these reasons Lenin's last writings, especially of course his 'Testament', repeatedly emphasised the importance of factors of personality and virtually ignored class analysis. As Lenin explained to Stalin:

The purpose is to train by having them tested by you and the

two deputies on *practical* assignments specially and unquestionably reliable people, from among the best workers of the
Workers' and Peasants' Inspection . . .[42]

It was entirely consonant with the Jacobinism of Lenin's last
writings that he should also examine the situation within the Party
from the same vantage point. He became obsessed with discovering and promoting the few men with the right qualities to the
right jobs. This, he declared, was the pivot of the Party's work.
Equally he was obsessed with the strengths and weaknesses of top
Party personnel, assigning to them a crucial importance which
speaks volumes to the collapse of his class analysis.

Conclusion

The argument which runs through both volumes of this study can be summarised simply enough. It is that Lenin's political ideas cannot be grasped, cannot be made intelligible, unless seen in relation to his economic ideas. To this extent I have argued the case that Lenin must be taken seriously as a knowledgeable and dedicated Marxist for it is intrinsic to Marxism that economic and social theory is the *prius* from which ideas on politics or practice derive. Negatively, therefore, my conclusion is that the very prevalent attempts to interpret Lenin as the last gasp of an illustrious tradition of Russian Jacobinism not only tell us nothing about the structure of Lenin's thought but also do violence to the ideas of all the long roster of Russian revolutionaries pressed into service as proto-Bolsheviks, fore-runners or antecedents. Nor is Lenin to be regarded simply as a brilliant politician who unerringly scents where his best course lies. According to this popular pastiche Lenin, like some wily fox, plots his course according to his nose. Only after the event does he use his brain to construct a theoretical justification of actions already undertaken. Theory in this account is, for Lenin, always anterior to action, it flies at dusk. Accounts in this vein are, I have argued, plainly in error for they ignore the fact that Lenin had established the theoretical parameters of the democratic revolution long before 1905 and had spelt out the theoretical basis of the socialist revolution before October 1917. They are therefore too easy and undemanding because they must ignore the fundamental problem of relating Lenin's theory to his practical activity.

The context of Lenin's thought is given in the development of Marxism in Russia and, especially from 1914 onwards, in the development of left-wing Marxism in Europe. These were Lenin's sources and starting points. To these traditions he was

309

consciously contributing and by those traditions he was accepted as a major contributor.

The question which now arises is that, given that Lenin was a Marxist, what *was* the nature of the relationship between his economic and his political ideas? I have, throughout both volumes, reformulated this as the distinction between theory and practice in Lenin's thought. The theoretical part of Lenin's thought is, according to the distinction I have adopted, his analysis of the economic substructure of society, the level of development of productive forces and the corresponding level of development of social classes. This theory, or socio-economic analysis, formed the basis of Lenin's practice, of his political strategies. Clearly we have not yet progressed very far in dealing with the initial question. To say that theory formed the *basis* of practice does not tell us a great deal. It is nonetheless clear that it is of cardinal importance to establish the case that Lenin was in fact preoccupied with the need to examine, as thoroughly as he could, the economic structure of society in the ascending phases of its development. This he did more assiduously than any practising politician and party leader that the present writer is aware of. Clearly it was of central importance to Lenin and we must grasp its importance to him. A major objective of this study has therefore been to reconstruct the sources and content of Lenin's economic or theoretical ideas as a necessary precondition to understanding their entailments for practice. It is symptomatic of the weakness of Lenin studies that this exercise should have to be conducted at all, yet there are some who deny that Lenin ever undertook a serious analysis of economics or society, and many more, even among sympathetic Marxists, who virtually ignore the theoretical underpinnings of Lenin's thought and strive for a flimsy coherence at the level of political tactic.

Lenin, at different stages of his life, elaborated two quite different theoretical analyses from which were derived quite different prescriptions for practice. Volume 1 was devoted to the first moment of theory and practice in Lenin's intellectual evolution and this volume to the second.

Lenin's first theoretical analysis was finally completed with the publication of his massive *The Development of Capitalism in Russia*, in 1899. It was the product of an enormous amount of work and was, in its day, the fullest and most thorough study of Russian economic development available. It charted the development of capitalist economic relations in Russia through their several phases of usury, merchant, manufacturing and industrial capitalism. It located the degree of development of different branches of industry and different regions of the country within this progression. It also traced the patterns of growth and decline of social classes in Russia and showed which of them had an economic interest in the preservation of the autocracy and which of them had an interest in its overthrow. It showed in particular how the feudal system of land holding was the lynchpin of the social structure supporting the autocracy and why, therefore, the dissolution of the landed estates had to be the central objective of the democratic revolution. The redefinition of economic and social relations was the key feature of Lenin's view of the democratic revolution and hence of the political strategy which the social democrats had to pursue. In other words, the economic objectives of the democratic revolution were of primary importance and constitutional rearrangements were decidedly subordinate to them. It was on the basis of this sure theoretical analysis that Lenin therefore dismissed the mania for constitutional projecteering and poured scorn on all those who accepted at face value the tsar's promises to inaugurate a constitutional régime. All of this, Lenin maintained, prior to, during and after 1905, was to no avail whatsoever, was indeed quite illusory, so long as the economic power of the social classes who had an interest in supporting the autocracy remained untouched. All of Lenin's political prescriptions during the period of the struggle for the democratic revolution were expressly derived from his economic analysis of Russian society.

It further followed from Lenin's analysis of the comparatively primitive development of capitalist productive forces in Russia that the social democrats could only aspire to the realisation of a radical democratic republic in Russia. The economic base would not support an advance to socialism and on this secure basis Lenin rejected any talk of skipping phases or the theory of permanent revolution. Nothing but the most absurd and reactionary consequences would attend such attempts to escape the determining influence of the economic structure of society.

The economic analysis did not, however, merely dictate the limits to practice and the objectives at which it should aim: it also

311

provided Lenin with a sophisticated methodology which, it was argued, was applied to almost every significant sphere of practical political activity and gives us the key to the coherence of his writings prior to 1914.

According to Lenin's economic analysis, capitalism moved through a number of phases of development before assuming its developed or perfected form. Thus the typical or essential social contradiction of capitalism, in which the mass of propertyless workers, entirely dependent upon the sale of their labour power, found themselves united and conscious of the irreconcilability of their interests with those comparatively few capitalists who had concentrated all the instruments of production in their own hands; this essential contradiction had its own history. It did not suddenly arise but developed progressively with the evolution of capitalism through its phases of development. Each of the successive phases of the evolution of capitalism; usury, merchant and then manufacturing capital, were but moments in this evolution in which the essential characteristics of capitalism were present only in underdeveloped form. Each phase was necessary to the process but each had to be transcended until the perfected form of industrial capitalism could be arrived at.

A central part of the argument of Volume 1 was that this dialectical methodology which formed the organisational core of Lenin's economic or theoretical work was directly transposed to the sphere of practice. Lenin utilised precisely the same dialectical (and teleological) framework to describe the evolution of social classes, class consciousness and class organisation. Each, according to Lenin's account, moved through distinct phases of development in which its mature form was progressively realised. The task of the social democratic vanguard was always to have the next stage of development in view. It was, as Lenin once put it, 'to see the future in the present'. Theory, far from being retrospective was, for Lenin, valuable only because it was predictive. The claim to authority of the social democrats (and later the communists) was derived from their prescient awareness of the broad outlines of the next phase of the historical progression – they claimed to know what was coming into being.

Each successive phase in the development of the class entailed, according to Lenin, new forms of organisation, new objectives and new forms of struggle. This was part and parcel of what the transcendence of the earlier stage and the ascent from the particular to the general involved. Lenin's changes of stance on tactics, on organisational forms, on the nature of class consciousness are, therefore, quite intelligible. They are not, as so many commentators have been quick to suggest, marks of Lenin's inconsistency and incoherence. They are, on the very contrary, precisely what we must expect from his sophisticated dialectical account. Lenin's political writings during this period display a consistency and coherence for which one would be hard-pressed to find a parallel. And this because they were expressly grounded in a thoroughgoing theoretical analysis more rigorous than any which practising politicians have apparently felt the need to engage in. The unity, coherence and range of Lenin's early writings has, therefore, been grossly misestimated, largely because the theoretical work upon which they were based has, for so long, been almost totally ignored. This ignorance has, in its turn, necessarily fostered a terminological imprecision in which little attempt has been made to refine the meanings of 'theory' and 'practice' or to distinguish between the levels of Lenin's thought.

To some extent the same is true of Lenin's writings in the period from 1914. Critics and commentators have too readily interpreted the 'engineering' of the revolution of 1917 as the proof positive of Lenin's voluntarism, his opportunistic jettisoning of the Marxian deterministic constraints for an advance to socialism or, alternatively, as evidence of Lenin's final conversion to the theory of permanent revolution. None of these judgements tells us anything about the structure of Lenin's thought at the time. Worse, they avert our attention from his own theoretical justification for the socialist revolution. That theoretical justification was spelt out in *Imperialism the Highest Stage of Capitalism*. This work was for Lenin's post-1914 writings what *The Development of Capitalism in Russia* had been for his previous writings. It was the sun around which all other elements of his system revolved.

In the last chapter of Volume 1 I showed how Lenin was presented, in the years from 1908 to 1914, with problems which his first theoretical analysis could not embrace. Problems such as the nationalities question, the colonial question, the drift towards international war and the increasing evidence of revisionist trends in international social democracy. Lenin's original theoretical analysis had been exclusively concerned with outlining the economic basis for the strategy and objectives of the democratic revolution in Russia. On these new problems it could provide no guidance.

It was the outbreak of the First World War which obliged Lenin to undertake a new economic analysis from which entirely new prescriptions for practice were to flow. This was the second moment in the development of Lenin's thought which I have subtitled theory and practice in the socialist revolution. Unless we understand Lenin's new account of capitalism as monopoly capitalism or imperialism, we cannot begin to understand his totally changed recommendations for political practice.

Lenin's theoretical analysis of finance capital, or monopoly capitalism, demonstrated to his satisfaction that capitalism had finally exhausted its historical mission. That historical mission had been progressive insofar as capitalism had augmented and refined the productive forces available to mankind. It did this, however, only insofar as it retained its competitive market structure. As soon as competition within important branches of industry was replaced by monopoly, the imperative constantly to revolutionise the forces of production, to retool and keep in the foreground of technological innovation disappeared. This occurred, according to Lenin, at about the turn of the century.

Monopoly capitalism was, however, not simply retrogressive vis-a-vis the development of the productive forces, it was also parasitic in its relation to the whole world which it had opened up to its exploitation. The metropolitan capitalist countries were forced, by the immanent laws which governed capitalist accumulation and reproduction, to export an ever larger proportion of their total capital to areas where, for the moment at least, it would yield a higher return. The whole world became an extension of their economic territory and in the scramble for imperial domination the roots of wars without end struck deep. Once the economic territory of the world had been divided up according to the relative power of the contestants at a particular stage in history, there could be no redivision to correspond to a new balance of power in which new contestants had taken the field without war.

Monopoly capitalism or imperialism (for the two were identified by Lenin) could survive only by exacting tribute in the form of super-profits from the underdeveloped areas of the world. The problem was, however, that the economic territory of the globe was finite and, once absorbed, annexed or subjugated financially, could only be redistributed subsequently by war amongst the imperialist nations.

On the one hand, therefore, the continued existence of monopoly capitalism threatening the retrogression of the productive forces, relapse into barbarism and recurrent wars of increasing dimensions, made socialist revolution imperative. On the other hand, the very progress of monopoly or finance capitalism had created all the objective conditions to make socialist revolution feasible on an international scale. The trusts and cartels, Lenin argued, had rationalised the productive process, vastly increased the socialisation of labour by aggregating men together in huge numbers in consolidated plants. They had, to a large extent, overcome the anarchy of production and the disjunction between production and consumption in particular branches of industry and had elaborated simplified administrative mechanisms through which whole sectors of industry could be controlled. The huge banks too provided, in his account, ready-made instruments through which social control over the whole of industry could be accomplished by the nationwide system of book-keeping and control of investment which they administered.

As was the case with Lenin's earlier analysis of economic and social life, theory not only specified the imperative for revolution and its feasibility, it also indicated the substantive form which the revolution would assume. The theoretical analysis of finance capitalism not only disclosed for Lenin the objective and subjective conditions for socialist revolution, but also its content.

To this point, Lenin's theoretical justification for socialist revolution relied heavily on the work of Bukharin and Hilferding and, like his predecessors, Lenin came to the conclusion that the huge changes which finance capitalism had produced in the economic base of society had led to equally significant changes on its political superstructure. The nature of the bourgeois state, he argued, had undergone a profound metamorphosis in the transition from competitive to monopoly capitalism. Its minimal role of acting as the guarantor of rights and as the arbiter of the widely differing interests of a socially variegated society was applicable only to the epoch of competitive capitalism. In that epoch, Lenin argued, class differentiation had still not reached its apogee, class conflict could therefore be contained and the potent fiction of the class impartiality of the state could be preserved. The epoch of finance capital, or imperialism, signified the final liquidation of all the intermediate strata between the proletariat and the few financial barons who, through the banks, had concentrated the entire capital of society into their own hands. The ranks of the proletariat had been swollen by the ruination of the small bourgeoisie, and the difference between their conditions of life and those of the tiny handful of the magnates of capital had been pressed to its utmost. Class differentiation and, therewith, class struggle, attained its sharpest most obvious expression. In this situation, Lenin maintained, as had Bukharin before him, that the state became the last bastion of the financial oligarchy. In proportion as the class struggle became more acute, the state became ever more openly an instrument of their interests. Its power was enormously augmented not merely to meet the internal threats to the dominance of the finance capitalists but also to fulfil the enormous burdens of the colonial policies of finance capitalism which were so vital to its continued existence. Competition within the national market was extinguished and assumed the form of competition between huge state capitalist trusts on the international plane.

A corollary of this new pattern of economic relations was the fostering of an imperialist ideology in which national interest was spuriously identified with the interests of trade and colonial aggrandisement. As the imperialist state grew in power, intervening directly in the management of the economy and the control of labour, assimilating to itself the hitherto independent voluntary associations of society, so it developed a monolithic ideology and political structure profoundly corrosive of the pluralism that the liberal state had encouraged. Lenin agreed with Bukharin that a new and mighty Leviathan had arisen of enormous power and with an insatiable appetite to intervene everywhere to subjugate and control everything, to absorb all the vital forces of society into itself. The prospect before mankind, Lenin believed, was the awful prospect of the servility of individuals and groups within society prostrated before the omnipotent power of the state capitalist trust.

It is seldom noticed how closely Lenin's conception of the

objectives of the socialist revolution was bound to this nightmare vision of the servile imperialist state in which even the proletariat was becoming corrupted and docile – the mere labour department of the imperialist state. The whole promethean historical role of the labour movement, the dream of freedom through self-activity and the re-appropriation to society of the powers and prerogatives arrogated by the state – in short the vision of socialism itself – appeared to him to be withering at the very time when the objective and subjective conditions for its realisation were being brought to full maturity. And the worst of all to bear was that the erstwhile leaders of the proletariat, the ex-Marxist luminaries of the Second International, were meekly leading their followers into the thralls of serfdom. By acquiescing in the war and by voting war credits, they placed themselves and the class they once represented at the service of the imperialist state, bolstering its power at its moment of deepest crisis. Lenin's rage with what he took to be this apostasy is therefore quite intelligible in terms of his own structure of thought. It was a rage which never abated and was to leave its deep impress upon the Communist International and the politics of the twentieth century.

The continued existence of imperialism in Lenin's account spelt economic decline, political servitude and a relapse into barbarism resulting from wars of increasing extensiveness and intensity. All of this was, he maintained, endemic to imperialism. The socialist revolution, according to his conceptions of 1916–17, was the only road left open to mankind towards material plenty, social freedom and international sanity. Its first objective must be to smash the huge coercive and bureaucratic structures which formed the core of the imperialist state. Here too Lenin closely followed the evolution of Bukharin's thought. It was in his recommendations on the positive form of the new socialist administration which was to replace the imperialist state that Lenin displayed a genius and audacity which Bukharin never matched.

A large part of the objective of Lenin's writings in 1917, expressed not only in *State and Revolution*, but in almost all his major articles, was to break social democrats of their superstitious regard for the state. To do this he had to offer an alternative which was feasible in the sense that (i) alternative structures for the administration of the economy lay ready to hand, (ii) was also acceptable in terms of Marxist thought and (iii) was seen to be practicable in that existing popular institutions were available for the transcendence of politics and the initiation of the mass of the people into the practice of their own self-government. The first consideration he satisfied by pointing to the banks as agencies potentially capable of providing a universal nationwide system of book-keeping and accountancy. The second he discovered in Marx's account of the Paris Commune which had, for so long, been virtually ignored by Marxists. And the third he found in the soviets – the spontaneous creation of the Russian February Revolution. On all three scores, Lenin found that the time was now ripe for the people in arms to appropriate to themselves the powers and initiatives which the state had progressively taken away from them. Mankind could be saved from economic decline, the barbarism of war and permanent political servitude only by dissolving economic administrative and political power in the mass of the people themselves – that was the express object of the socialist revolution, its occasion, its imperative and its justification. The objective of the socialist revolution was, as Lenin once pithily put it, 'an end to bossing' and this, in a nutshell, was the message of *State and Revolution*. Its challenge was the promethean one, born of the impeccable line of Marx's romantic view of man as actor, the forger of his own world. It ran directly counter to that other Saint Simonian development of social democratic Marxism which saw the individual as the beneficiary of an efficient state-directed philanthropy. To the war-weary, to the hungry, to the indentured workforce and the oppressed peasantry, Lenin projected in 1917 a vision, a challenge whose potency has been much ignored – power is yours, take it and use it; the land is yours, take it and use it; the factories are yours, take them and use them – get off your knees and be men, rule yourselves. This was the message of his newspaper articles of 1917 and of *State and Revolution*, and was encapsulated in his slogan 'All Power to the Soviets'. It was an extraordinary platform which called not for the capture of political power by a political party but for the dissolution of the state in an infinitely varied system of soviets and communes. This was no transitional form which Lenin was recommending, any more than the Paris Commune in Marx's account was. Lenin did not suppose, in 1917, that any transitional economic, political, economic or social measures would be necessary. Indeed, as we have seen, he was later to admit that this was his principal error in October 1917 and in the months thereafter. Like the French communards of 1871, he saw the Bolsheviks and their European comrades directly storming the gates of heaven rather than building a pathway to the portals. There was, at this stage, no distinction in his writings between socialism and communism.

It was without doubt precisely the extreme radicalness of Lenin's proposals which largely accounted for the mushroom growth of Bolshevik influence between July and November 1917. Nor should we underestimate the volume of support which the Bolsheviks won in these turbulent months. In the capitals, among the urban workers and the principal sections of the army they won a majority. It is staggering that on *such* a platform Lenin and the Bolsheviks won control over the principal Soviets in Russia and a majority at the Second All-Russian Congress of Soviets. Theory pressed, as always with Lenin, to its most radical conclusions had, by October/November 1917, become a material force; it had gripped the masses. This was the crowning moment of Lenin's political life. His theoretical findings, his recommendations for practice and the popular mood had come together.

The project for socialism in Russia was explicitly premissed upon two crucial predictions. The first was that the process of class differentiation amongst the peasantry, which had been proceeding rapidly since the Emancipation in 1861, would be given an enormous boost by the revolution. Lenin believed that the poor peasants would rapidly and decisively detach themselves from the rich peasants and from the political leadership of the petty-bourgeois parties. It was a major finding of his earlier theoretical analysis that the peasants were devoid of political initiative. They could not themselves articulate nor represent their interests on the national plane. They were obliged to choose between the leadership of the proletariat and that of the bourgeoisie. Lenin was confident that the poor peasants would, through their own practical experience of the revolution, vindicate his earlier theoretical finding that the proletariat was the natural representative of all Russia's exploited. Consciousness of this identity of interests could, however, dawn only *after* the revolution, only after the poor peasants through their own practical experience had been shown who were their true allies.

319

Socialist consciousness, Lenin argued, could only be the product of socialist practice just as he had earlier argued (in *What Is To Be Done?*) that political consciousness could only arise from political practice. This applied particularly to the peasantry.

The second prediction, intrinsic to the project for socialism in Russia, was that world revolution was imminent. World revolution, or at least a European-wide revolution, was not merely a plus factor or additional bonus, it was from the outset written into the constitution of socialism in Russia. Without the European revolution, as Lenin constantly insisted, socialism in Russia was doomed to die stillborn. Without it the advance to socialist practice through which the poor peasantry would be won over to the proletarian side would be impossible. It was therefore the central projection making sense of the entire venture.

It is, of course, easy to censure Lenin for basing so bold an experiment as the introduction of socialism in the extraordinarily radical form which he proposed, on projections or predictions as to the future. Marxism, many have remarked, pretends to be a science, it ought therefore to tie up all the ends, it ought with certainty to be able to know whether social and political action will be successful. Such a view is no more consistent with the thought and activity of Marx and Engels than it is with Lenin's. Social and historical science, Lenin recognised full well, did not deal in cast-iron certainties but in probabilities established through theoretical analysis of economic and social conditions and the observing of regularities or laws on the basis of which extrapolations could be made as to the future. *All* Marxist revolutions were, he rightly observed, based upon projections as to the future arrived at from the study of present evidence.

There remained, nonetheless, certain crucial problems which Lenin made little attempt to explore. The first problem was, quite simply, the scale of the exercise. The society under examination now became that of international finance capitalism. To examine in detail the intricate patterns of economic relationship between the imperialist countries and between them and their colonial or semi-colonial tributaries would have taken a long, long time. And time, Lenin recognised, was at a premium, for, with the ending of the war, the prospects for revolutionary success would dramatically recede. Lenin never occupied himself with, or did not find the time to explore, such questions as: what size of economic territory in the colonies or semi-colonies would have to be denied to the imperialists in order for the rate of profit to decline so seriously as to cause a severe economic crisis and create a revolutionary situation? What would be the impact of the withdrawal of Germany (the country of which he had highest hopes) from the imperialist camp? Could the imperialists devise means for cushioning the economic impact of the one and of the other? Would the imperialists be able to unite to overwhelm the revolutionary outbreaks before they spread and got out of hand?

There was another acute methodological problem which all Marxist revolutionaries must confront but which they have never (to my knowledge at least) explicitly recognised. That is the problem raised by Engels and referred to in Chapter 7. Marxists, Engels remarked, had no alternative but to take as the base-line of their economic and social analysis a relatively distant socio-economic situation. This arose necessarily because of the temporal gap between the collection of relevant data, their compilation, publication and absorption by the revolutionaries. This unavoidable source of error, he went on to show, was magnified in times of crisis because at such times economic and social changes occur with enormous rapidity. The point can be more concretely made. Lenin premissed the seizure of power precisely during such a period of crisis and rapid change on the basis of his analysis of imperialism completed in 1916. But that work was itself based upon the economic researches of others published largely in the period up to 1910 and they, in turn, relied upon statistical abstracts and economic data which dated generally from the 1890s or the turn of the century. In the meanwhile, of course, economic conditions and the configuration of classes might have changed very considerably. All of this does not mean that Lenin was flouting the canons of Marxism in basing the seizure of power upon a theoretical prediction. On the contrary, it is to say that all Marxists *must* act in such a manner and, as Engels pointed out, there is unavoidably written into the methodology a potential source of error.

There was, finally, no attempt by Lenin to explain how the European or world revolution was to have assisted Russia in her progress towards socialism. It is obvious, of course, that the European or world revolution would have guaranteed the

Russian Revolution in the negative sense that the power of the imperialists to overthrow it would have been sapped. It is, however, far from clear how Lenin conceived of other countries redeeming the backwardness of the immensity of the newborn Soviet Republic. Germany and Austria were, by his own admission, economically ruined. Their industry and transportation systems were in chaos, inflation was rampant and money had lost its value, famine had swept through central and eastern Europe, the proletariat had been decimated on the battlefields and corrupted by its leaders. The huge question arises, therefore, of whether it was consistent with Lenin's own analysis to assume that revolutionary governments in central and eastern Europe (the most obvious possible benefactors) would be in a position to give Russia the enormous volume of material and human resources which would be necessary to overcome her backwardness and enable her to advance towards socialism? Lenin never attempted to specify the sort or the scale of aid which he felt to be the minimum necessary for the realisation of socialism in Russia. Had he done so he might well have questioned the capacity of war-ravaged Europe to provide it. The dialectics of the war-time situation both assisted Lenin and, at the same time, were likely to impede his plans. There is no doubt that the war-time crisis did produce the objective and the subjective preconditions for revolution which he had laid down. At the same time, however, in the particular case of the Russian Revolution, the war and the ruination it had brought made it unlikely that aid would be forthcoming to redeem its backwardness.

I have argued that Lenin did provide a coherent theory and practice for the socialist revolution which rested upon a cogent Marxist basis. Lenin had at least as good a claim to represent revolutionary Marxism as his Marxist critics – Kautsky, Luxemburg and the Mensheviks. This seems paradoxical only if we take the simpliste view that Marxism as a mode of analysis necessarily prescribes a single 'correct' political strategy in any given situation. We do not expect this of contemporary Marxism nor should we of the time at which Lenin was writing. It is a main contention of this book that the integrity and coherence of Lenin's thought prior to the October Revolution – his theory of imperialism and theory of the state, the masterly way in which he brought the two together and integrated them with Marx's conception of the commune and located the soviets as the form through which these conceptions could be realised – all of this has been much under-valued or simply dismissed as an inexplicable lapse into anarchism. It may well be objected that the treatment of these themes in this book, a treatment which takes what Lenin wrote seriously and assumes that what he wrote he believed, is by those very tokens naive and ingenuous. The counter to this rests eventually on one's impression of Lenin's intellectual and political honesty. It is my view that Lenin was generally honest and direct with himself and with his followers. (At least until his class analysis collapsed when, as I point out, he did resort to sophism and misrepresentation.) It is further my view that what he wrote about the state can be shown to be an eminently logical progression out of his theory of imperialism and his continuing problems with the reformists and defencists. I have also argued that his belief in the commune state did not instantly disappear on the morrow of the revolution but continued to inform his activities until the middle of 1918. Those who argue that *The State and Revolution* is merely a 'pipedream', an inexplicable voyage into utopianism and thoroughly inconsistent with Lenin's real Jacobinism, offer, in effect, no explanation at all. The text cannot be squared either with their account of Lenin's personality or with their account of his political thought and activity. It remains for them an uncomfortable enigma. It is also undoubtedly the case that Soviet and some Marxist interpretations of Lenin's thought suffer from the same kind of embarrassment. Lenin's views of self-activity exercised through a multiplicity of independent communes and soviets learning through their own mistakes and experiments how best to resume control over all their affairs – this view of the project for socialism in Russia is so profoundly corrosive of the legitimacy of most of the régimes allegedly building socialism in accordance with his ideas, that it is either discreetly ignored or, in severely bowdlerised form, held out as the very long-term objective of 'full communism'. Both left and right have reason enough to avoid the difficulties of Lenin on the nature of a properly socialist society.

Part of the tragedy of Lenin's thought is that he too was increasingly obliged to discount and deny his initial vision. As his theoretical predictions, upon which the socialist revolution had been based, failed to materialise, as civil war, famine and industrial collapse consumed the country, he was obliged to retreat from his project for socialism in Russia.

With the failure of the international revolution, Lenin was forced back upon his first theoretical analysis. The level of Russian economic and social development, the intractable reality with which the Bolsheviks had to cope in the post-revolutionary period, was certainly no higher than it had been in the 1890s when Lenin had written his meticulous study of it. Indeed, in almost all respects the economic and social situation of post-revolutionary Russia was very considerably worse. The production levels of virtually all raw materials and commodities was lower, even in 1924, than it had been in the 1890s. The proletariat, by Lenin's own admission, had to all intents and purposes ceased to exist by 1921. It had been decimated in war and civil war, absorbed into the new agencies of state, demoralised and atomised by the famines and hardships of the early years of Soviet power. In the 1890s and, consistently up to 1914, Lenin had been perfectly clear that to attempt to build socialism on the basis of Russian economic and social conditions would result in nothing but the most absurd and reactionary conclusions. The situation after 1917, as each successive year confirmed the isolation of the régime, was that Lenin was attempting to implement policies which made sense only in terms of his *second* theoretical analysis in an objective situation which was less developed than his *first* theoretical analysis. He was attempting socialist practice on the basis of a much lower economic and social basis than had obtained when he had denied its possibility. So long as the prospects for revolution in Europe appeared encouraging (and Lenin was obviously inclined to exaggerate any and all revolutionary prospects), the coherence of Lenin's theory and practice could, with very considerable difficulty, be sustained. As each year confirmed Russia's isolation, it was bound to fall apart.

Lenin's response was to re-specify the goals appropriate to the revolution. It was hardly accidental that his first move in this direction coincided with his reversion to the economic and social analysis of the 1890s. The most radical political programme compatible with that analysis was the one elaborated by Lenin in 1905 – the democratic dictatorship of the proletariat and poor peasantry. Its objective was not the implementation of socialism but rather the radical realisation of the democratic revolution and the final destruction of the economic and social bases of feudalism. In mid-1918 Lenin gave it a similar function: not the building of socialism but preparing the path towards socialism. The objective in hand was now declared to be the construction of a powerful centralised state machine as the only means of surviving in the face of hostile encirclement by powerful imperialist states. The project of transcending the state was dropped. The dictatorship of the proletariat was vindicated by Lenin, Trotsky and Bukharin as the antithesis of the imperialist state, not its transcendence. 'Temporary' measures, designed to meet recurrent crises by centralising resources and decision-making, gradually hardened into articles of faith. A style of work emerged which, as Lenin constantly lamented, owed more to tsarist bureaucratic traditions than the ideals of the revolution. A vast bureaucratic and administrative structure was established which was quite independent of Soviet or democratic control and therefore all the more arrogant in its claims and unchecked in its growth. The military methods of the civil war merely led to an accentuation of this centralising and authoritarian approach. The commune vanished from Lenin's vocabulary.

Lenin's adoption of the super-centralist scheme associated with the dictatorship was symptomatic not only of the régime's international isolation but also of its shrinking internal social base. It provided legitimation for the leading role of the proletariat and recognition of the fact that the prospects for assistance and positive support from the poor peasantry had all but vanished. The social base of the régime was narrowed to the proletariat and the sphere of self-activity which had begun by embracing the populace *as a whole* shrank very considerably. It was now to embrace only a tiny and ever-shrinking minority of the population. The goals of the revolution and the meaning attached to socialism had been dramatically redefined. Nor was this the end of the process. The collapse of industry and of the transport system, the recruitment of the proletariat into the Red Army and the state administration, the recurrent famines and dispersal of the urban workers to the countryside combined to reduce the proletariat to a group which was tiny in numbers and was, moreover, by Lenin's own admission, quite demoralised. The proletariat as a whole, Lenin declared, had, in the awful severity of Russian conditions, been dislodged from its class groove. It had been declassed, unable to rise to the tasks which its historical mission imposed upon it. In this situation, in order to keep some flicker of the project for socialism burning, however fitfully, until the European revolution arrived, Lenin turned to the Party. The Party, uniting the advance guard of the conscious workers, would have to act as proxy for the exhausted and scattered proletariat. The sphere of initiative and self-activity was narrowed down to a numerically insignificant group – a mere drop in the ocean of the people, as Lenin reminded his comrades. The collapse of Lenin's class analysis was, by this time, evident enough. The project for universal self-activity transcending the state through a multiplicity of independent communes was replaced by an emphatically centralised dictatorship – the maximisation of the principle of the state exercised exclusively by the single Party. Nor did the progression stop there. As we have seen, Lenin found that even the Party proved unequal to its tasks. It fell easy prey to the traditions of the old bureaucracy. It acquired a high-handedness, what Lenin termed a 'Communist conceit', which blinded it to its own ignorance and made it, therefore, implausible as the vehicle of socialist virtue. Even the Party proved unequal to the task which Lenin had imposed upon it. In the desperation of his last writings, Lenin finally sought the salvation of some remnants at least of the initial vision of socialism in the Jacobin solution. A small band of men, the most resolute, far-seeing and determined men, unsullied by corruption and thoughts of personal advantage, would have to assume the mantle of guardians of the socialist cause. Only at the very end, when all other avenues were closed to him (or had been closed by him), did Lenin become a Jacobin. And yet, even then, in his last writings Lenin did not entirely lose sight of the original project for socialism in Russia. The re-organised Workers' and Peasants' Inspection, all-powerful and carefully chosen as it was to have been, was still presented by Lenin as the rallying of all the sound forces in the Party and the administration to create an embryo out of which the self-administration of the peasants and workers might yet develop. In his final writings Lenin at last became aware of the dangerous narrowing down of the concept of socialism which he himself had come perilously close to accepting during his infatuation with military methods and the dictatorship of the proletariat. He had then, as we have seen, declared that socialism had to do not with a particular pattern of relationships between people but rather with a system of state ownership. So long as the means of production, distribution and exchange was the property of the state, Lenin had declared that the *forms* of administration were a matter of no consequence. The idea of socialism as a relationship amongst people was displaced by the idea of it as a relationship between things. It was this cramped and narrow conception of socialism which Stalin adopted as his own and which subsequent Soviet practice has relied upon. The time was already too late when Lenin finally became aware of the dangers of identifying and defining socialism as state ownership and control of production. He had put down the Democratic Centralists, the left communists and Workers' Opposition and emasculated the unions and the soviets. He was left with no allies to fight the arrogance and narrow ruthlessness of the apparatus men like Stalin whom he himself had promoted and defended. The apparatus now controlled him, dictating his daily regimen, refusing him books and newspapers, forbidding him to communicate. Lenin was trapped and stifled in the web which he himself had spun.

My conclusion is that Lenin's thought is to be understood as an essay in the theory and practice of Marxism. Its difficulties and ambiguities are located within the Marxist tradition itself rather than in Lenin's peculiar character or in the Russian Jacobin tradition. Commentators have too easily and too quickly identified as specifically 'Leninist', elements of thought which, on further examination, prove to be parts of the general currency of Marxism in Russia or which were unresolved and problematic in Marxism itself. The coherence of Lenin's thought is to be found in the relation between his analysis of economic and social conditions and his recommendations on strategy and tactics. He elaborated two such analyses, both of which have been underestimated or even ignored by commentators on his political thought. The first, completed in the late 1890s, was a meticulous study of the levels of capitalist development in Russia and the changing patterns of class forces this development produced. I argued in Volume 1 that this theoretical analysis not only defined the limits to social democratic practice (the democratic revolution), but also provided Lenin with a methodology which he consistently applied to social democratic activity. Thus, just as capitalism, according to Lenin's theoretical analysis, moved through distinct phases of development before attaining its essential form so too did class consciousness and class organisation. Lenin's second theoretical analysis, completed in 1916, served a similar function in the second moment of his intellectual development. It demonstrated that the productive forces and class dispositions of international finance capitalism were ripe for the socialist revolution. The theoretical analysis not only defined a new (socialist) objective for social democratic practice, it also indicated the *content*, the forms of administration, which socialist practice would assume.

The disintegration of the coherence of Lenin's thought after the revolution was, as we have seen, a consequence of the failure of his theoretical predictions to materialise. The revolution was isolated and forced in upon its own ruined resources. Lenin was then faced with the hopeless task of attempting to sustain some part of the socialist objectives, which made sense only in terms of his *second* theoretical analysis, on the socio-economic basis of his *first* theoretical analysis. It proved an impossible task, as the frank and poignant reappraisals of his last writings make so painfully obvious.

Notes and References

Full title, place and date of publication is only given when a work is cited for the first time in the notes. Thereafter only the author's name followed by page number is normally given. In cases where more than one work by the same author are referred to, the author's surname is followed by an abbreviation of the title. As in Volume 1 of this study, Lenin's *Collected Works* in 45 volumes (Moscow, 1960–70) will be abbreviated to *CW* and references will give only the volume number in bold type followed by the page number in plain type.

INTRODUCTION

1. J. Plamenatz, *German Marxism and Russian Communism* (London, 1954) p. 231.
2. See, for example, the series of excellent monographs produced by the Inter-University Project on the History of Menshevism under the general editorship of Leopold Haimson.
3. K. Marx and F. Engels, *Collected Works* [hereafter, MECW], to comprise 50 vols (London, 1975–   ) vol. 3, p. 183.

CHAPTER 1

1. See Volume 1 of this study, pp. 294–5.
2. M. Lair, *Jaurès et l'Allemagne* (Paris, 1935) p. 222.
3. Cited in E. Bevan, *German Social Democracy During the War* (London, 1918) p. 21.
4. Ibid., p. 15.
5. E. Dolléans, *Historie du Mouvement Ouvrier 1871–1936* (Paris, 1939) p. 215.
6. D. W. Brogan, *The Development of Modern France 1870–1939* (London, 1940) p. 529. See also J. Braunthal, *History of the International*, vol. 2, 1914–1943, (London, 1967) p. 22.
7. Bevan, p. 24.
8. B. Wolfe, *Three Who Made a Revolution* (Harmondsworth, 1966) p. 699, cf. Wolfe, 'War Comes to Russia in Exile', *Russian Review*, vol. 20 (October 1961).
9. See Volume 1 of this study, pp. 283–4.
10. S. P. Turin, *From Peter the Great to Lenin. A History of the Russian Labour Movement* (London, 1968) p. 128.

11. See Braunthal, vol. 2, p. 31 and L. B. Schapiro, *The Communist Party of the Soviet Union* (London, 1963) p. 142.
12. Cited in Turin, p. 132.
13. B. D. Wolfe, 'War Comes to Russia in Exile', *Russian Review*, vol. 20 (October 1961) p. 297.
14. S. H. Baron, *Plekhanov The Father of Russian Marxism* (London, 1963) p. 318.
15. Ibid., p. 324.
16. This was the general position Plekhanov argued in a series of articles brought together in his collection *O voine: stati* (Petrograd, 1917).
17. Baron, p. 329.
18. A. Ascher, *Pavel Axelrod and the Development of Menshevism* (Cambridge, Mass., 1972) p. 307.
19. Ibid., loc. cit.
20. Ibid., p. 310.

CHAPTER 2

1. G. Nollau, *International Communism and World Revolution* (London, 1961) pp. 24–5.
2. V. I. Lenin, *Collected Works* (English translation of the fourth Russian edition of the *Sochineniia*) vol. 21, pp. 16–17. Hereafter references to this source will be abbreviated on the following model: *CW*, **21**, 16–17.
3. Ibid., p. 18.
4. Ibid., p. 22.
5. Ibid., p. 18.
6. L. Trotsky, *My Life* (New York, 1930) p. 250.
7. For the 'Manifesto of the International Socialist Conferences at Zimmerwald' and Lenin's rival 'Draft Manifesto' of the left-wing delegates, see H. Gruber, *International Communism in the Era of Lenin* (New York, 1967) pp. 65–9.
8. Braunthal, vol. 2, p. 50.
9. *CW*, **21**, 39.
10. Ibid., p. 159.
11. Ibid., pp. 301–2.
12. *CW*, **22**, 163.
13. Ibid., pp. 255–6.
14. Ibid., p. 254.
15. Ibid., p. 170.
16. *CW*, **21**, 146.
17. Ibid., p. 285.
18. Ibid., p. 354.
19. Ibid., p. 353.
20. Ibid., p. 98.
21. Lenin's most frequent criticism of Bukharin, for instance, was that he fell too easily for the 'modern' sociological jargon of Bogdanov. On this point, as on many others, Lenin agreed with Sorel who

contemptuously dubbed sociology 'the little science' and its practitioners the brahmins of the labour movement.

22. C. E. Schorske, *German Social Democracy 1905–1917* (New York, 1955).
23. *CW*, **21**, 179.
24. Ibid., p. 109.
25. Ibid., p. 110.
26. Ibid., pp. 152–3.
27. Ibid., p. 247.
28. Ibid., p. 98.
29. Ibid., p. 242–3.
30. Ibid., p. 231.
31. Ibid., p. 222.
32. Ibid., pp. 252, 259.
33. *CW*, **22**, 106–7.
34. *Die Neue Zeit*, no. 5 (30 April 1915) p. 144. Cited in *CW*, **21**, 223.
35. *CW*, **21**, 75; cf. p. 145.
36. Ibid., p. 107.
37. Ibid., p. 225.
38. Ibid., p. 257.
39. Ibid., p. 240.
40. Ibid.
41. Ibid., p. 233.
42. Ibid., p. 257.
43. Ibid., p. 271.
44. Ibid., pp. 200–1.
45. Ibid., p. 202.
46. Ibid., p. 356.
47. Ibid., p. 162.
48. Ibid., p. 215.
49. Ibid., pp. 215–16.
50. Ibid., pp. 213–14.
51. *CW*, **22**, 109.

CHAPTER 3

1. Lenin's *Notebooks on Imperialism* are published as Volume 39 of the *Collected Works*.
2. The text of *Imperialism the Highest Stage of Capitalism* is in Volume 22 of the *Collected Works*, pp. 185–304.
3. *CW*, **22**, 266.
4. Marx, *Capital*, vol. 1, p. 763.
5. *CW*, **22**, 200.
6. Ibid., p. 200; cf. p. 241: 'On the threshold of the twentieth century we see the foundation of a new type of monopoly: firstly associations of capitalists in all capitalistically developed countries; secondly, the

monopolist position of a few very rich countries, in which the accumulation of capital has reached gigantic proportions.'

7. Ibid., p. 196.
8. Ibid., p. 197.
9. Ibid., p. 199.
10. Ibid., p. 202.
11. Ibid., p. 206.
12. Ibid., p. 204.
13. Ibid., p. 276.
14. Ibid., p. 276.
15. Ibid., p. 208.
16. Ibid., p. 203.
17. Ibid., p. 198.
18. Ibid., pp. 302–3.
19. R. Hilferding, *Finansovyi kapital*, (Moscow, 1914) p. 475.
20. *CW*, **22**, 205.
21. *CW*, **24**, 464.
22. *CW*, **25**, 363.
23. *CW*, **22**, 241.
24. Ibid., p. 208.
25. Ibid., p. 217.
26. Ibid., pp. 225–6.
27. Ibid., p. 218.
28. Ibid., p. 210.
29. Ibid., p. 213.
30. Ibid., p. 214.
31. Ibid., p. 227.
32. Ibid., p. 233.
33. Ibid., p. 235.
34. Ibid., pp. 214–15.
35. Ibid., pp. 220–1.
36. Ibid., p. 222. Lenin was here quoting from Jeidels' *Das Verhältnis der deutschen Grossbanken zur Industrie* ... (Leipzig, 1905). Jeidels was a main source of Lenin's information on the connection between bank capital and industrial capital. His book, Lenin remarked, was one of the best on the subject (cf. p. 208).
37. R. Hilferding, *Das Finanzkapital* (Wien, 1910).
38. *CW*, **22**, 223.
39. Quoted by Lenin, *CW*, **22**, 216. See Marx, *Capital*, vol. 3 (Moscow, 1962) p. 593.
40. *CW*, **22**, 217.
41. Ibid., pp. 218–19.
42. Ibid., p. 242.
43. J. Hobson, *Imperialism: a Study* (London, 1902) p. 91.
44. *CW*, **22**, 241.
45. Ibid., pp. 238–9.
46. Ibid., p. 277.
47. Ibid., p. 277.

48. Ibid., pp. 278–9.
49. Ibid., p. 283.
50. Ibid., p. 281.
51. Ibid., p. 283.
52. Ibid., p. 253.
53. Ibid., p. 143.
54. Ibid., p. 253.
55. Ibid., p. 252; cf. p. 293.
56. Ibid., p. 294.
57. Ibid., p. 296.
58. Ibid., pp. 255–6.
59. Ibid., p. 255.
60. Ibid., p. 258.
61. Ibid., p. 257.
62. Ibid., p. 265.
63. Ibid., p. 274; cf. p. 295.
64. Ibid., pp. 275–6.
65. *CW*, **21**, 301.
66. Ibid., p. 409.
67. *CW*, **22**, 297. Lenin was here directly quoting Hilferding.
68. See Volume 1 of this study, Chapter 11, pp. 298–305.
69. *CW*, **23**, 14.
70. Ibid., p. 38.
71. Ibid., p. 39.
72. Ibid., p. 59.
73. Ibid., p. 60.
74. Ibid., p. 15.
75. Ibid., pp. 58–9.
76. Ibid., p. 59.
77. Ibid., p. 79.
78. Ibid., p. 43.
79. Ibid., p. 43.

CHAPTER 4

1. *CW*, **24**, 417.
2. Ibid., p. 418; cf. pp. 439–40.
3. Ibid., p. 513.
4. *CW*, **25**, 107.
5. Ibid., p. 112.
6. Ibid., p. 143.
7. Ibid., p. 190.
8. *CW*, **24**, 240.
9. Ibid., p. 307.
10. Ibid., p. 305.
11. Ibid., p. 306.
12. *CW*, **25**, 361.
13. *CW*, **24**, 428.

14. Ibid., p. 460.
15. *CW*, **25**, 363.
16. Loc. cit.
17. See, for example, *CW*, **24**, 24, 53, 73–4; *CW*, **25**, 44, 63, 344.
18. *CW*, **25**, 69.
19. Ibid., p. 68.
20. Ibid., p. 344.
21. *CW*, **24**, 426.
22. *CW*, **25**, 334.
23. Ibid., p. 335.
24. Ibid., p. 346.
25. Ibid., p. 340.
26. Ibid., p. 362.
27. *CW*, **24**, 38.
28. *CW*, **24**, 44; cf. p. 445.
29. Ibid., p. 448.

CHAPTER 5

1. In the Introduction to Volume 1 of this study I gave an account of this prevalent manner of interpreting Lenin's thought and activity.
2. K. Marx and F. Engels, *Selected Works* (hereafter *MESW*) 2 vols (Moscow, 1962) vol. 1, p. 53.
3. Ibid., p. 115.
4. Ibid., p. 223.
5. Karl Marx and Friedrich Engels, *Correspondence 1846–1895* trans. D. Torr (London, 1936) p. 57.
6. *MESW*, vol. 2, pp. 32–3. For a comprehensive check-list of the references to the dictatorship of the proletariat in the writings of Marx and Engels, see H. Draper, 'Marx and the dictatorship of the proletariat', in *Cahiers de l'Institut de Science Economique Appliqué, Série S, Etudes de Marxologie* (Paris, 1962) no. 6, pp. 5–73.
7. *MESW*, vol. 1, p. 53.
8. Ibid., p. 54.
9. *Manifest der Kommunistischen Partei. Vorrede zur deutschen Ausgabe von 1872* (Leipzig, 1971) p. 6.
10. *MESW*, vol. 1, p. 3. The German *stellenweise* clearly suggests that it is in places or parts that the programme has become antiquated, not in 'some details' or particulars. It would make no sense for Marx and Engels to refer to this crucial revision as a 'detail'.
11. Karl Marx, *The Civil War in France* (Peking, 1970) pp. 165–6.
12. *MESW*, vol. 1, p. 518.
13. Ibid., p. 519.
14. Ibid., p. 520.
15. Ibid., p. 520.
16. Ibid., p. 521.
17. Ibid., p. 522.
18. Ibid., p. 523.

19. Marx/Engels, *Correspondence* (trans. Torr.) op. cit., pp. 336–7; cf. A. Bebel, *Aus Meinem Leben, Zweiter Teil* (Stuttgart, 1911) pp. 322–3.
20. *MESW*, vol. 1, p. 333.
21. Ibid., p. 332.
22. Ibid., p. 485.
23. A sophisticated attempt by a contemporary British Marxist to accomplish the same task is Monty Johnstone's 'The Paris Commune and Marx's Conception of the Dictatorship of the Proletariat', in *The Massachusetts Review* (Summer 1971) no. 3, pp. 447–62.
24. S. F. Cohen, *Bukharin and the Bolshevik Revolution* (London, 1974) p. 39.
25. *CW*, **35**, 230.
26. Ibid., p. 231.
27. Cited by Lenin, *CW*, **23**, 165.
28. Ibid., p. 165.
29. The word used, *vzryvat*, is the nearest Russian equivalent of the German *sprengen*.
30. N. Bukharin, 'K teorii imperialisticheskogo gosudarstva', hereafter 'k teorii . . .', *Revoliutsiia Prava, Sbornik pervyi* (Moscow, 1925) pp. 5–32, p. 5.
31. See reference 30 above.
32. N. Bukharin, *Imperialism and World Economy* (London, n.d. [1929?]) pp. 73–4.
33. Ibid., p. 108.
34. Ibid., p. 179.
35. Ibid., p. 112.
36. Ibid., p. 118.
37. Ibid., p. 124.
38. Ibid., p. 128.
39. Ibid., p. 129.
40. Ibid., p. 125.
41. Ibid., p. 128.
42. Ibid., p. 155.
43. Ibid., p. 159.
44. Ibid., p. 160.
45. Ibid., p. 160.
46. Ibid., p. 166.
47. Ibid., p. 107.
48. Ibid., p. 167.
49. Ibid., p. 166.
50. R. Hilferding, *Finansovyi kapital* (Moscow, 1914) p. 433.
51. Ibid., p. 430.
52. Ibid., p. 396.
53. Ibid., p. 433.
54. Ibid., p. 476.
55. Ibid., p. 478.
56. N. Bukharin, 'K teorii . . .', p. 16.

57. Ibid., p. 18.
58. Ibid., pp. 22–3.
59. Ibid., p. 22.
60. Ibid., p. 29.
61. Ibid., p. 30.
62. Ibid., p. 8.
63. N. Bukharin, *Economics of the Transformation Period* (New York and London, 1971) p. 27.
64. F. Engels, *The Origin of the Family* (Chicago, 1902) pp. 211–12. Cited Bukharin, *K teorii* ... op. cit., p. 11. The phrase in square brackets is not given in Bukharin's text.
65. N. Bukharin, *K. teorii* ..., p. 14.
66. Ibid., p. 10.
67. Ibid., p. 13.
68. Ibid., p. 11.
69. Ibid., pp. 26–7.
70. Ibid., p. 30.
71. Ibid., p. 31.

CHAPTER 6

1. *CW*, **24**, 306; cf. Lenin's remarks on German state capitalism, ibid., p. 403.
2. *CW*, **25**, 25.
3. Ibid., p. 387.
4. Ibid., pp. 397–8.
5. Ibid., p. 388.
6. Ibid., p. 387.
7. Ibid., p. 396.
8. Ibid., pp. 447–8.
9. Ibid., p. 415.
10. Ibid., p. 412.
11. Ibid., p. 414.
12. Lenin and Bukharin could hardly have guessed just how close their analyses were to Marx's more candid (and then unpublished) drafts of *The Civil War in France*. There Marx traced the historical progress of the state as a weapon of the bourgeoisie. From being a necessary and progressive institution, it had, he concluded, become quite parasitic and degenerate. The form of the state, in other words, mirrored the history of the bourgeoisie. (See 1970 Peking edition of *The Civil War in France*, especially pp. 247–51.)
13. *CW*, **24**, 23.
14. Ibid., p. 24.
15. Ibid., pp. 32–3.
16. Ibid., p. 46.
17. Ibid., p. 61.
18. Ibid., p. 62.
19. Ibid., p. 69.

20. Ibid., pp. 169–70.
21. Ibid., p. 100.
22. Ibid., p. 426.
23. Ibid., p. 353.
24. Ibid., p. 53.
25. Ibid., p. 150.
26. Ibid., p. 107; cf. p. 149: 'The whole of Russia is already being covered with a network of organs of self-government. A commune may exist also in the form of organs of self-government.'
27. Ibid., p. 322.
28. Ibid., pp. 169–70.
29. Ibid., p. 53; cf. p. 461.
30. Ibid., pp. 107–8.
31. Ibid., p. 181.
32. Ibid., p. 88.
33. *CW*, **25**, 339.
34. Ibid., p. 431.
35. Ibid., pp. 425–6.
36. Ibid., pp. 431–2.
37. Ibid., p. 377.
38. Ibid., pp. 477–8.
39. Ibid., pp. 327–69.
40. *CW*, **26**, 89–136.
41. *CW*, **25**, 362–3.
42. *CW*, **26**, 108.
43. Ibid., p. 106.
44. Ibid., p. 109.
45. Ibid., p. 110.
46. Ibid., p. 112.
47. Ibid., p. 113.
48. To avoid confusion in chronology the Old Style date is given here.
49. *CW*, **26**, 114–15.
50. *CW*, **26**, 392.
51. Ibid., p. 394.
52. Ibid., p. 393.
53. Ibid., p. 403.
54. Ibid., p. 411.
55. Ibid., p. 420.
56. Ibid., p. 424.
57. *CW*, **24**, 85.
58. *CW*, **25**, 424.
59. Ibid., p. 446.
60. Ibid., p. 445. The reference is, of course, to Engels's lengthy letter to Bebel, 18–28 March 1875. See Marx and Engels, *Correspondence* (trans. Torr) pp. 332–9.
61. *CW*, **25**, 416.
62. Ibid., p. 417.

63. Ibid., p. 441; cf. Lenin's lengthier vindication of the dictatorship of the proletariat on p. 409.
64. Ibid., p. 468.
65. Ibid., p. 424.
66. Ibid., p. 496.

CHAPTER 7

1. *CW*, **26**, 52.
2. Baron, p. 347.
3. Ibid., p. 348.
4. Ascher, p. 323.
5. K. Marx, *Preface to the Critique of Political Economy, MESW*, vol. 1, p. 363, cited by Plekhanov in *God na rodine* (Paris, 1924) 2 vols, vol. 1, p. 27.
6. *Rabochaia Gazeta*, no. 24 (6 April 1917). Quoted in R. P. Browder and A. F. Kerensky, vol. 3, p. 1208.
7. Ascher, p. 321.
8. Baron, p. 347.
9. Ibid., p. 350.
10. Ascher, p. 321.
11. Ibid., p. 321.
12. A. N. Potresov, *Posmertnyi sbornik proizvedenii* (Paris, 1937) p. 258. Cited in A. Ascher, *The Mensheviks in the Russian Revolution* (London, 1976) p. 101.
13. *CW*, **26**, 22–7.
14. Ibid., pp. 22–3.
15. Ibid., pp. 212–13.
16. Ibid., p. 23.
17. Ibid., p. 24.
18. Ibid., p. 19.
19. Ibid., p. 210.
20. Ibid., p. 59.
21. Ibid., p. 193.
22. Ibid., p. 231.
23. Ibid., p. 202; cf. pp. 135–6 and 139.
24. Ibid., p. 56.
25. Ibid., p. 50; cf. p. 55.
26. Ibid., p. 48.
27. Ibid., p. 26.
28. Ibid., p. 27.
29. Ibid., p. 184.
30. Ibid., p. 27.
31. Ibid., p. 69.
32. Ibid., p. 70.
33. Ibid., pp. 27, 180.
34. Ibid., p. 21.
35. Ibid., p. 19.

36. Ibid., p. 19.
37. Ibid., pp. 74–7; cf. p. 174.
38. Ibid., p. 40.
39. Ibid., p. 182.
40. Ibid., p. 182.
41. Ibid., p. 183.
42. Ibid., p. 82.
43. Ibid., p. 181.
44. Ibid., p. 145.
45. Ibid., p. 186.
46. *MESW*, vol. 1, p. 119.
47. *CW*, **26**, 89.

CHAPTER 8

1. *CW*, **26**, 413.
2. Ibid., p. 386.
3. Ibid., p. 256. The translation has it that 'a state is strong when the people are politically conscious'. The word 'politically' does not, however, appear in the Russian original. I am indebted to Richard Taylor for drawing this to my attention.
4. Ibid., p. 480.
5. K. Marx and F. Engels, *The German Ideology* (London, 1965) p. 47.
6. *CW*, **26**, 288.
7. Ibid., p. 413.
8. Ibid., p. 414.
9. *CW*, **27**, 207–9.
10. *CW*, **10**, 376, quoted in Volume 1 of this study, p. 232.
11. Ibid., p. 32.
12. *CW*, **27**, 204.
13. Ibid., p. 126.
14. *CW*, **26**, 261.
15. Ibid., p. 409.
16. *CW*, **21**, 469.
17. *CW*, **26**, 468.
18. *CW*, **27**, 209.
19. *CW*, **26**, 474.
20. *CW*, **27**, 135.
21. Ibid., p. 133.
22. Ibid., p. 126.
23. *CW*, **26**, 272.
24. *CW*, **27**, 154.
25. *CW*, **26**, 516.
26. *CW*, **27**, 134.
27. See pp. 76–8.
28. *CW*, **26**, 264.
29. *CW*, **27**, 365.
30. *CW*, **26**, 407.

31. *CW*, **27**, 204.
32. *CW*, **26**, 365.
33. *CW*, **27**, 215.
34. Ibid., pp. 215–16.
35. *CW*, **26**, 466.
36. *CW*, **27**, 136; cf. p. 223.
37. *CW*, **26**, 400.
38. Ibid., p. 336.
39. Ibid., p. 443.
40. *CW*, **27**, 210.
41. Ibid., pp. 207–8.
42. Ibid., pp. 211–15.
43. Ibid., p. 211.
44. Ibid., p. 212.
45. Ibid., p. 212.
46. Ibid., p. 213.
47. *CW*, **26**, 409.
48. *CW*, **27**, 214; cf. Marx in the *Civil War in France* [First Draft]. 'The whole sham of state mysteries and state pretensions was done away with by the Commune which made all the public functions – military, administrative, political – real workman's functions' (Peking edition, 1970, p. 170). There is a compelling resemblance between Lenin's views on the state in the first six months of Soviet power and Marx's extreme libertarianism in the First Draft of *The Civil War in France*.
49. *CW*, **26**, 374–5.
50. Ibid., p. 402.
51. Ibid., p. 409.
52. Ibid., p. 411.
53. *CW*, **27**, 249.
54. *MECW*, vol. 1, p. 519.
55. *CW*, **33**, 88.
56. *CW*, **27**, 259.
57. Ibid., p. 258.
58. Ibid., p. 259.
59. Ibid., p. 265.
60. Ibid., p. 267.
61. Ibid., p. 267.
62. Ibid., pp. 267–8.
63. Bakunin, in his *Gosudarstvennost i anarkhiia*, was the first socialist critic to have the impudence to pose the question of how exactly a class such as the German proletariat, forty million strong, was to exercise dictatorship over itself; if they were all to take part in governing, Bakunin asserted, there would be no one left to govern, there would be no state. What the Marxist really meant, he maintained, was that a despotism of a small directing minority would be hidden behind a system of representative elections and so 'the pseudo people's state would be nothing other than despotic gov-

ernment of the proletarian masses by a new and very restricted aristocracy of real or pretending *savants*. The people not being *savant* would be entirely relieved of governmental concerns and completely integrated into the herd of the governed. A fine liberation!' Bakunin it was who first and most trenchantly seized upon the incompatibility of means and ends in the Marxist schema, and predicted that the 'transitional' dictatorship the Marxists aspired to would prove all too permanent. 'Anarchy or liberty being the goal, the State or dictatorship the means. And so in order to emancipate the popular masses, one must begin by enslaving them.'
Quotes from Michel Bakounine, *Gosudarstvennost i anarkhiia, Archives Bakounine*, vol. III (Leiden, 1967) pp. 148–9.

64. K. Marx, *The Civil War in France* [First Draft] (Peking, 1970) p. 165.
65. *CW*, **27**, 268–9.
66. *CW*, **26**, 402–3.
67. Ibid., p. 269.
68. Ibid., p. 270.
69. Ibid., p. 275.
70. *CW*, **27**, 210–11.
71. Ibid., p. 275.
72. Ibid., p. 98.
73. Ibid., p. 95.
74. Ibid., p. 290.
75. Ibid., p. 292.
76. Ibid., p. 275.

CHAPTER 9

1. The occasion for Lenin's comments was the appearance of Kautsky's *The Dictatorship of the Proletariat* which Lenin reviewed in *Pravda* (11 October 1918) (*CW*, **28**, 105–13).
2. K. Marx and F. Engels, *The German Ideology*, (Moscow, 1965) p. 47.
3. *CW*, **28**, 462.
4. Ibid., pp. 463–4.
5. Ibid., p. 96.
6. Ibid., p. 417.
7. *CW*, **27**, 394.
8. *CW*, **29**, 559.
9. *CW*, **30**, 95.
10. *CW*, **28**, 239.
11. Ibid., p. 108.
12. Ibid., p. 458.
13. *CW*, **29**, 373.
14. *CW*, **28**, 231.
15. Ibid., pp. 189–90.
16. *CW*, **27**, 337.
17. Ibid., pp. 335–6.
18. *CW*, **28**, 301; cf. p. 142.

19. Ibid., p. 171.
20. *CW*, **30**, 133.
21. Ibid., p. 141.
22. Ibid., p. 270.
23. Ibid., p. 263.
24. Ibid., p. 263.
25. Ibid., p. 262, emphasis in original.
26. Ibid., pp. 339–40.
27. *CW*, **29**, 441.
28. Ibid., p. 524.
29. Ibid., p. 370.
30. *CW*, **30**, 133.
31. *CW*, **27**, 469.
32. Ibid., pp. 472–3.
33. Ibid., p. 461.
34. *CW*, **29**, 398.
35. Ibid., p. 364.
36. Ibid., p. 365.
37. *CW*, **28**, 405.
38. There is a useful table demonstrating this point in T. Cliff, *Lenin*, vol. 3 (London, 1978) p. 133.
39. *CW*, **31**, 503.
40. Ibid., p. 336.
41. Ibid., p. 419.
42. Ibid., p. 501.
43. Ibid., p. 418.
44. Ibid., p. 504.
45. Ibid., p. 517.
46. Ibid., p. 523.
47. Ibid., p. 503.

CHAPTER 10

1. *CW*, **27**, 465.
2. *CW*, **28**, 233.
3. *CW*, **30**, 112.
4. Ibid., p. 112.
5. Ibid., p. 112.
6. *CW*, **29**, 488,
7. For Bakunin's formulation, see note 63 to Chapter 8 above.
8. *CW*, **29**, 107.
9. Ibid., p. 108.
10. Ibid., p. 335.
11. *CW*, **27**, 398; cf. *CW*, **28**, 72.
12. *CW*, **28**, 424–5.
13. *CW*, **29**, 335.
14. *CW*, **27**, 452.
15. *CW*, **30**, 397.

16. *CW*, **31**, 162.
17. Ibid., p. 160.
18. *CW*, **27**, 431.
19. Ibid., p. 437.
20. *CW*, **30**, 186.
21. *CW*, **27**, 466.
22. Ibid., p. 466.
23. *CW*, **29**, 301.
24. *CW*, **27**, 402.
25. Ibid., p. 403.
26. Ibid., p. 395.
27. Ibid., p. 396.
28. Ibid., p. 536.
29. *CW*, **30**, 48.
30. Ibid., p. 257.
31. Ibid., p. 258.
32. Ibid., p. 259.
33. *MESW*, Vol. 1, pp. 132–4.
34. *CW*, **30**, 274.

CHAPTER 11

1. *CW*, **28**, 78.
2. *CW*, **30**, 207–8, *CW*, **28**, 138.
3. *CW*, **27**, 291; cf. p. 547.
4. *CW*, **29**, 61.
5. *CW*, **28**, 156.
6. *CW*, **27**, 494–5.
7. *CW*, **28**, 24–5.
8. *CW*, **27**, 499.
9. Ibid., p. 460.
10. *CW*, **28**, 77.
11. Ibid., p. 77.
12. *CW*, **30**, 380.
13. *CW*, **32**, 480.
14. Ibid., p. 480.
15. *CW*, **29**, 192.
16. Ibid., p. 227.
17. *CW*, **28**, 31.
18. Ibid., p. 44.
19. Ibid., p. 206.
20. *CW*, **31**, 232–3.
21. Ibid., p. 233; cf. pp. 47, 62.
22. Ibid., p. 47.
23. Ibid., p. 21.
24. Marx, Engels, *Correspondence* (trans. Torr) p. 292.
25. *CW*, **27**, 484.
26. *CW*, **29**, 309–10.

27. *CW*, **31**, 22–3.
28. Ibid., p. 26.
29. *CW*, **32**, 514.
30. *CW*, **31**, 34.
31. Ibid., p. 231.
32. Ibid., p. 258.
33. *CW*, **28**, 116.
34. Ibid., pp. 292–3.
35. *CW*, **31**, 47.
36. Ibid., p. 60.
37. *CW*, **28**, 484.
38. *CW*, **31**, 229.
39. Ibid., pp. 307–8.
40. *CW*, **28**, 154.
41. *CW*, **31**, 441–2.
42. *CW*, **32**, 480.
43. Ibid., p. 481.
44. *CW*, **31**, 226.
45. Ibid., p. 217.
46. Ibid., p. 476.
47. Ibid., p. 306.
48. Ibid., p. 475.
49. Ibid., p. 329.
50. Ibid., p. 478.
51. Ibid., p. 476.
52. Ibid., p. 479.
53. G. F. Kennan, *Russia and the West under Lenin and Stalin* (London, 1961) p. 222.
54. *CW*, **31**, 217–18.
55. Ibid., p. 218.
56. Ibid., p. 443.
57. Ibid., p. 445.
58. Ibid., p. 446.
59. Ibid., p. 219.
60. Ibid., p. 220.
61. *CW*, **30**, 156.
62. *CW*, **31**, 449; cf. *CW*, **30**, 156.
63. *CW*, **31**, 449.
64. Ibid., p. 448.
65. Ibid., p. 412.
66. Ibid., p. 413.
67. *CW*, **32**, 436.
68. *CW*, **33**, 222.
69. *CW*, **31**, 411.
70. Ibid., p. 414.
71. *CW*, **33**, 334.
72. Ibid., p. 498.
73. *CW*, **31**, 453.

74. Ibid., p. 453.
75. Ibid., p. 330.
76. *CW*, **33**, 500–1.

CHAPTER 12

1. L. Trotsky, *Terrorism and Communism* (Ann Arbor, 1961) p. 146.
2. Ibid., p. 133.
3. Ibid., p. 141.
4. Ibid., p. 133.
5. Ibid., p. 110.
6. Ibid., p. 111.
7. Ibid., p. 143.
8. Ibid., p. 170.
9. Ibid., p. 110.
10. Ibid., p. 162.
11. I. Deutscher, *Trotsky, vol. 1, The Prophet Armed* (London, 1954) p. 487.
12. *CW*, **32**, 58.
13. Ibid., p. 75. Lenin's reference to the 'new tasks and methods' is to Trotsky's theses on the trade union question submitted to the Party under that title.
14. Ibid., p. 20.
15. Ibid., p. 21.
16. *CW*, **33**, 191.
17. *CW*, **32**, 24.
18. Ibid., p. 24.
19. Ibid., p. 25.
20. Ibid., p. 100.
21. V. Serge, *Kronstadt 1921* (Tonbridge, n.d. [Solidarity pamphlet]) p. 5.
22. A. Kollontai, *The Workers' Opposition* (Reading, n.d. [Solidarity pamphlet]) p. 3.
23. *CW*, **32**, 430.
24. Ibid., p. 168.
25. Kollontai, p. 35.
26. Ibid., p. 33.
27. Ibid., p. 34.
28. Ibid., p. 30.
29. Ibid., p. 25.
30. Ibid., p. 32.
31. Ibid., pp. 35–6.
32. Ibid., p. 31.
33. Ibid., p. 40.
34. *Vosmoi Vserossüskii Sezd Sovetov Rabochikh ... Deputatov: Stenografcheskii otchet* (Moscow, 1921) p. 324.
35. Ida Mett, *The Kronstadt Commune* (London, 1967) pp. 6–7.
36. P. Avrich, *Kronstadt 1921* (Princetown N. J., 1970) p. 160.

37. *Pravda o Kronshtadte*, p. 128, cited Avrich, p. 173.
38. L. Schapiro, *The Origin of the Communist Autocracy* (New York, 1965) p. 298.
39. I. Mett, *The Kronstadt Commune* (London, 1967) pp. 21–5.
40. *CW*, **32**, 183–4.
41. Ibid., p. 228.
42. See, for instance, *CW*, **32**, 281 and 360.
43. Ibid., p. 197.
44. Ibid., p. 199.
45. See Bukharin's speech to the Tenth Congress in *Desyatyi Sezd RKP (b)* (Moscow, 1933) pp. 221–5.
46. *CW*, **32**, 282.
47. Ibid., p. 204.
48. Ibid., p. 206.
49. Cohen, p. 107.
50. *CW*, **32**, 243.
51. Ibid., p. 244.

CHAPTER 13

1. *CW*, **32**, 20.
2. Ibid., p. 61.
3. Ibid., p. 31.
4. Ibid., p. 111.
5. Ibid., p. 274.
6. Ibid., p. 254.
7. Ibid., p. 199.
8. *CW*, **33**, 23–4.
9. Ibid., p. 26; cf. p. 29.
10. *CW*, **32**, 31; cf. p. 297.
11. Ibid., p. 411.
12. *CW*, **33**, 66.
13. *CW*, **32**, 412.
14. Ibid., p. 412.

CHAPTER 14

1. L. Schapiro, *The Communist Party of the Soviet Union* (London, 1970) p. 235.
2. *CW*, **32**, 127.
3. *CW*, **33**, 173.
4. *CW*, **32**, 145.
5. *CW*, **33**, 275.
6. Ibid., p. 276.
7. Ibid., p. 224.
8. Ibid., p. 309.
9. Ibid., p. 287.

10. Ibid., p. 288.
11. Ibid., p. 289.
12. Ibid., p. 293.
13. Ibid., p. 292–5.
14. Ibid., p. 75.
15. Ibid., p. 39.
16. Ibid., p. 138.
17. Ibid., p. 224.
18. Schapiro, *C.P.S.U.* (1970) p. 237.
19. *CW*, **33**, 303.
20. Ibid., p. 304.
21. Ibid., p. 321.
22. *CW*, **36**, 593.
23. Ibid., pp. 594–5.
24. Ibid., p. 596.
25. Ibid., p. 593.
26. Ibid., p. 595.
27. Ibid., p. 597.

CHAPTER 15

1. *CW*, **32**, 38.
2. Ibid., p. 34.
3. Ibid., p. 191.
4. Ibid., p. 68.
5. Ibid., p. 427.
6. *CW*, **33**, 78.
7. Ibid., p. 78.
8. Ibid., p. 295.
9. Ibid., p. 481.
10. Ibid., p. 474.
11. Ibid., p. 483.
12. Ibid., p. 487.
13. *CW*, **32**, 142.
14. Ibid., p. 143.
15. *CW*, **33**, 488.
16. Ibid., p. 489.
17. Ibid., p. 307.
18. Ibid., pp. 394–5.
19. *CW*, **32**, 372.
20. *CW*, **33**, 395.
21. Ibid., p. 444.
22. *CW*, **32**, 356.
23. Ibid., p. 355.
24. Ibid., p. 355.
25. Ibid., p. 356.
26. Ibid., p. 363.
27. *CW*, **33**, 490.

28. T. H. Rigby, *Lenin's Government: Sovnarkom 1917–1972* (Cambridge, 1979) p. 220; cf. p. 240.
29. Ibid., p. 354.
30. Ibid., p. 354.
31. Ibid., p. 354.
32. Ibid., p. 484.
33. Ibid., p. 489.
34. Ibid., p. 490.
35. Ibid., p. 489.
36. Ibid., p. 491.
37. Ibid., p. 492.
38. Ibid., p. 494.
39. Ibid., p. 496.
40. Ibid., p. 354.
41. Ibid., pp. 494–5.
42. Ibid., p. 247.

Bibliography

A comprehensive Lenin bibliography would be virtually impossible to compile. Its very bulk would, in any case, diminish its utility. My object here is more modest. I have set out a guide only to the major sources, the principal biographies and commentaries and what impress me as the most important works on the context of Lenin's life and thought. As an undifferentiated list even this might have appeared somewhat daunting. It would not, moreover, have provided obvious guidance to anyone anxious to study a particular period of Lenin's activity or aspect of his thought. I have therefore sacrificed the advantages of an unbroken alphabetical list of authors for an arrangement according to period and topic.

Section 1. Sources
      (a) Bibliographical
      (b) Works, principal editions
      (c) Principal collections by topic
      (d) Materials on particular works

Section 2. General Biography and Commentary

Section 3. Memoirs

Section 4. Life and Thought to 1914
      (a) Family and early years
      (b) The controversy with populism
      (c) Social democracy and the labour movement

Section 5. Life and Thought 1914–24
      (a) The war and theory of imperialism
      (b) 1917
      (c) 1917–24
      (d) Comintern and world revolution

Section 6. Lenin by Topic
      (a) Lenin and philosophy
      (b) Lenin and history
      (c) Lenin and culture
      (d) Lenin and the media
      (e) Lenin and the national question
      (f) Lenin and military matters
      (g) Lenin and places – bibliographical gazeteer
      (h) Lenin and books
      (i) Lenin and statistics
      (j) Miscellaneous

Bibliography

SECTION 1. SOURCES

1(a) Bibliographical

V. Bystrianskii, *Sistematicheskii ukazatel k sochineniiam V. I. Lenina* (Leningrad, 1924).

E. Drahn, *Vladimir Iljich Uljanov. Eine Bio-Bibliographie* (Berlin, 1924).

Institut für Marxismus-Leninismus beim Z. K. der SED, *Lenins Werk in deutscher Sprache. Bibliographie* (Berlin, 1967).

Institut Marksizma-Leninizma pri Ts.K. K.P.S.S., *Bibliografiia proizvedenii V. I. Lenina i literatury o nem 1956–1967 gg*, 2 vols (Moscow, 1971 and 1974). *Biblioteka V. I. Lenina v Kremle: Katalog* (Moscow, 1961).

Leniniana, ed. L. B. Kamenev, 5 vols (Moscow, 1926–30).

Kommunisticheskaia Akademiia, *Lenin i Leninizm: Alfavitno-predmetnyi ukazatel literatury v biblioteke Kommunisticheskoi Akademii* (Moscow, 1928).

N. K. Krupskaya, *Bibliografiia trudov i literatury o zhizni i deiatelnosti*, ed. A. D. Kondakov (Moscow, 1969).

T. N. Lenkov, *Lenin i zheleznodorozhnyi transport. Bibliograficheskii ukazatel* (Moscow, 1971).

L. A. Levin, *Bibliografiia bibliografii proizvedenii K. Marksa, F. Engelsa, V. I. Lenina* (Moscow, 1961).

L. A. Levin, *K. Marks, F. Engels, V. I. Lenin, Ukazatel bibliograficheskikh rabot 1961–72* (Moscow, 1973).

R. M. Savitskaia and Z. L. Fradinka, *Vospominaniia o V. I. Lenine. Annotirovannyi ukazatel knig i zhurnalnykh statei 1954–1961 gg* (Moscow, 1963).

R. Ia. Zuereva (ed.), *Lenin i teper zhivee vsekh zhivykh. Rekomendatelnyi ukazatel memuarnoi i biograficheskoi literatury o V. I. Lenine* (Moscow, 1968).

1(b) Works, Principal Editions

Sobranie sochinenii, 1st edn, ed. L. B. Kamenev, 20 vols (Moscow, 1922–4).

Sochineniia, 2nd edn, 30 vols (Moscow, 1926–1929), eds Bukharin, Molotov, Skvortsov-Stepanov, Adoratskii *et al.*

Sochineniia, 3rd edn, 30 vols (Moscow, 1935). Virtually a reprint of 2nd edn.

Sochineniia, 4th edn, 35 vols (Moscow, 1941–50).

Spravochnyi tom k 4 izdanii sochinenii V. I. Lenina, Parts I and II (Moscow, 1957).

Collected Works (translation of 4th enlarged Russian edition), 45 vols (Moscow, 1960–70).

(The Chronology should be consulted to locate volume number and date of composition of specific texts.)

(1) 1893–4.
(2) 1895–7.
(3) *The Development of Capitalism in Russia.*
(4) 1898–April 1901.
(5) May 1901–February 1902.

(6) January 1902–August 1903.
(7) September 1903–December 1904.
(8) January–July 1905.
(9) June–November 1905.
(10) November 1905–June 1906.
(11) June 1906–January 1907.
(12) January–June 1907.
(13) June 1907–April 1908.
(14) 1908.
(15) March 1908–August 1909.
(16) September 1909–December 1910.
(17) December 1910–April 1912.
(18) April 1912–March 1913.
(19) March–December 1913.
(20) December 1913–August 1914.
(21) August 1914–December 1915.
(22) December 1915–July 1916.
(23) August 1916–March 1917.
(24) April–June 1917.
(25) June–September 1917.
(26) September 1917–February 1918.
(27) February–July 1918.
(28) July 1918–March 1919.
(29) March–August 1919.
(30) September 1919–April 1920.
(31) April–December 1920.
(32) December 1920–August 1921.
(33) August 1921–March 1923.
(34) *Letters* November 1895–November 1911.
(35) *Letters* February 1912–December 1922.
(36) 1900–23 additional materials.
(37) *Letters to Relatives.*
(38) *Philosophical Notebooks.*
(39) *Notebooks on Imperialism.*
(40) *Notebooks on the Agrarian Question 1900–16.*
(41) 1896–October 1917 additional materials.
(42) October 1917–March 1923 additional materials.
(43) December 1893–October 1917.
(44) October 1917–November 1920.
(45) November 1920–March 1923.

Polnoe sobranie sochinenii, 5th edn, 55 vols (Moscow, 1971–5).
Alfavitnyi ukazatel proizvedenii vosshedshikh v Poln. Sobr. Soch. V. I. Lenina (Moscow, 1966).
Spravochnyi tom k Poln. Sobr. Soch, 2 parts (Moscow, 1969, 1970).
Khronologicheskii ukazatel proivvedenii V. I Lenina, 2 vols (Moscow, 1959 and 1962).
Vospomogatelnye ukazateli k khronologicheskomu ukazateliu proivvedenii V. I. Lenina (Moscow, 1963).

Bibliography

1 (c) Principal Collections by Topic

Against Liquidationism, ed. T. Dexter (Moscow, n.d.).
Against Revisionism, compiler N. I. Krutikova *et al.*, 2nd ed. (Moscow, 1966).
Agitation und Propaganda (Vienna, 1929).
Borba s ekonomizmom. Stati i rechi, ed. D. V. Schwartz (Moscow, 1926).
Contre le courant (Essays of Lenin and G. Zinoviev), 2 vols (Paris, 1927).
Correspondence entre Lénine et Camille Huysmans 1905–1914, ed. G. Haupt (The Hague, 1963).
Lenin and Britain (London, 1949).
Lenine et la France (Paris, 1925).
Lenin i 'Pravda' 1912–1962 (Moscow, 1962), ed. Institut Marksizma-Leninizma pri Ts.K. K.P.S.S. (hereafter Inst. M-L).
Lenin on the Jewish Question (New York, 1934).
Lenin on the United States, pref. J. S. Allen (New York, 1970).
Leninskii Sbornik, ed. L. B. Kamenev, N. I. Bukharin and V. M. Molotov, 31 vols (Moscow, 1924–38).
Marks–Engels Marksisme (Moscow, 1934).
O gosudarstve i prave, compilers V. N. Avilkin and A. A. Lipatov (Moscow, 1958).
O mezhdunarodnom rabochem i kommunisticheskom dvizhenii, ed. I. S. Dinerstein (Moscow, 1967).
O natsionalnom i natsionalno-kolonialnom voprose (Moscow, 1956).
O normakh partiinoi zhizni i printsipakh partiinogo rukovodstva, compiler V. Ia. Akomov *et al.* (Moscow, 1969).
O profsoiuzakh 1894–1922, compilers A. P. Troshin and S. F. Naida (Moscow, 1970).
O rukovodiashchei roli partii v sotsialisticheskom stroitelstve, compiler R. A. Lavrov (Moscow, 1969).
O soiuze rabochego klassa i krestianstva, Inst. M-L (Moscow, 1969).
O sovetskoi sotsialisticheskoi demokratii, compiler P. T. Vasilenko (Moscow, 1967).
O vospitanii i obrazovanii, compiler V. P. Gruzdev (Moscow, 1970).
Ob ateizme, religii i tserkvi, ed. I. U. P. Francev *et al.* (Moscow, 1969).
Ob elekrifikatsii, Intro. G. M. Krzhizhanovskii (Moscow, 1930).
Ob ustave partii, compilers B. E. Zaslavskii and M. A. Manarov (Moscow, 1968).
On Religion (New York, n.d.).
On Socialist Ideology and Culture, Inst. M-L (Moscow, n.d.).
On Soviet Socialist Democracy, ed. G. Hanna (Moscow, n.d.).
On the Foreign Policy of the Soviet State, Inst. M-L (Moscow, n.d.).
On the Great October Socialist Revolution, Inst. M-L (Moscow, 1967).
On Utopian and Scientific Socialism, compiler A. Koptsev (Moscow, 1965).
Protiv dogmatizma, sektantstva, 'levogo' opportunizma, Inst. M-L (Moscow, 1967).
Socialism and Religion, Inst. M-L (Moscow, n.d.).
Socialism and War, Inst. M-L (Moscow, n.d.).

Sur la littérature et l'art, ed. J. Freville (Paris, 1957).
The Awakening of Asia (New York, n.d.).
The Paris Commune, Intro. P. Braun (New York, 1931).
The Revolution of 1905 (New York, 1931).
The Teachings of Karl Marx, Pref. A. Trachtenberg (New York, 1937).
The War and the Second International, Pref. A. Trachtenberg (New York, 1931).
The Woman Question, selections from the writings of K. Marx, F. Engels, V. I. Lenin and J. Stalin (New York, 1951).
The Young Generation (New York, 1940).
Über Deutschland und die deutsche Arbeiterbewegung (Berlin, 1976).
War and the Workers (New York, 1940).
Women and Society, Intro. N. K. Krupskaya (New York, 1938).

1(d) Materials on Particular Works

N. N. Akimov, *Metodicheskie sovety po izucheniiu proizvedenii V. I. Lenina* (Moscow, 1972).
M. A. Arzhanov, *O knige V. I. Lenina 'Gosudarstvo i Revoliutsiia'* (Moscow, 1948).
N. I. Gushchin, *Proizvedeniia V. I. Lenina o Novoi Ekonomicheskoi Politike* (Moscow, 1965).
Institut Marksizma – Leninizma – pri Ts.K. K.P.S.S., *Podgotovitelnye materialy k knige 'Razvitie kapitalizma v Rossii',* ed. N. A. Kulagin *et al.* (Moscow, 1970).
M. I. Kalinin, *O rabote Lenina 'Chto takoe druzia naroda'* (Moscow, 1949).
G. I. Kurbatova, *O knige V. I. Lenina, 'Gosudarstvo i Revoliutsiia',* 2nd ed. (Moscow, 1967).
J. J. Marie, *Que Faire?* (Paris, 1966).
T. V. Pavechenko, *Proizvedeniia V. I. Lenina. Pisma iz daleka i Aprelskie tezisy* (Moscow, 1972).
L. Trotsky, *The suppressed testament of Lenin* (London, 1954), and *On Lenin's Testament* (New York, 1946).
A. I. Vasilkovo (ed.), *Kniga V. I. Lenina 'Materializm i empiriokrititsizm'* (Moscow, 1959).
Ia. R. Volin (ed.), *Kniga V. I. Lenina 'Chto delat?' i mestnye partiinye organizatsii Rossii* (Paris, 1972).

SECTION 2. GENERAL BIOGRAPHY AND COMMENTARY

V. K. Adoratskii, *K voprosu o nauchnoi biografii Lenina* (Moscow, 1933).
M. Aldanov, *Lenin* (New York, 1922).
C. Bachmann, *Lénine* (Paris, 1970).
N. A. Barsukov, *K izucheniiu biografii V. I. Lenina,* 5th edn (Moscow, 1972).
A. Beucler and G. A. Aleksinsky, *Les amours secrètes de Lénine* (Paris, 1937).
K. F. Bogdanov and A. P. Iakushin (eds), *Lenin through the eyes of the World* (Moscow, 1969).

Bibliography

N. Boukharine, *Lénine Marxiste* (Paris, 1966).
W. Bringholf, *Lenin. Sein Leben und Werk* (Schaffhausen, 1924).
J. Bruhat, *Lénine* (Paris, 1960).
N. I. Bukharin, *Politicheskoe zaveshchanie Lenina*, 2nd edn (Moscow, 1929).
N. Bukharin, I. Iaroslavskii and L. Kamenev, *Lenin: Leben und Werk* (Vienna, 1924).
E. H. Carr, *A History of Soviet Russia. The Bolshevik Revolution*, 3 vols, *The Interregnum*, vol. 4 (London, 1950–4).
B. A. Chagin, *Lenin: Velikii revoliutsioner i myslitel* (Leningrad, 1949) and *G. V. Plekhanov i ego rol v razvitii marksistskoi filosofii* (Moscow, 1963).
P. Chasles, *La vie de Lénine* (Paris, 1929).
T. Cliff, *Lenin*, 4 vols (London, 1975–9).
G. Cogniot, *Présence de Lénine* 2 vols (Paris, 1970).
R. Conquest, *V. I. Lenin* (London, 1972).
R. V. Daniels, *The Russian Revolution* (Englewood Cliffs, N.J., 1972).
R. P. Dutt, *Lenin* (London, 1933).
B. W. Eissenstadt, *Lenin and Leninism* (Lexington, N.J., 1971).
P. N. Fedoseev, *Marksizm v XX veke. Marks, Engels, Lenin i sovremennost* (Moscow, 1972).
L. B. Fischer, *The Life of Lenin* (New York, 1964).
R. Fox, *Lenin, A Biography* (London, 1933).
R. Fülöp-Miller, *Lenin and Gandhi* (London and New York, 1927).
R. Garaudy, *Lénine* (Paris, 1968).
C-J. Gignoux, *Lénine* (Paris, 1952).
G. N. Golikov (ed.) *et al.*, *Vladimir Ilich Lenin: Biograficheskaia khronika* (Moscow, 1970–   ), 7 vols to November 1919.
    vol. 1 1870–1905 (1970)
    vol. 2 1905–12 (1971)
    vol. 3 1912–17 (1972)
    vol. 4 March – October 1917 (1973)
    vol. 5 October 1917–July 1918 (1974)
    vol. 6 July 1918–March 1919 (1975)
    vol. 7 March – November 1919 (1976).
N. Gourfinkel, *Portrait of Lenin* (New York, 1972).
V. Grigoryan, *Lenin, A Short Biography* (Moscow, 1969).
G. H. Hanna, *About Lenin* (1969).
E. Iaroslavskii, *Biografiia Lenina* (Moscow, 1934).
E. Iaroslavskii, *Lénine, Sa vie. Son oeuvre* (Paris, n.d.).
E. Iaroslavskii, *Mysli Lenina o religii*, 2nd edn (Moscow, 1925).
A. M. Ioffe, *Lenin, der kämpfende Materialist* (Vienna, 1924).
Institut Marksa – Engelsa – Lenina Ts.K. V.K.P.(b). *Daty zhizni i deiatelnosti Lenina. 1870–1924*, ed. Sh. N. Manuchariants (Moscow, 1933).
Institut Marksizma – Leninizma Ts.K. K.P.S.S., *Kratkii biograficheskii ocherk*, 6th ed (Moscow, 1969).
Institut Marksizma – Leninizma Ts.K. K.P.S.S., *Lenin – biograficheskii atlas* (Moscow, 1970).

V. A. Karpinskii, *Vladimir Ilich Lenin: Vozhd, tovarishch, chelovek* (Moscow, 1966).

P. Kerzhentsev, *Life of Lenin* (Moscow, 1937).

P. Lafue, *Lénine, ou le mouvement* (Paris, 1930).

M. A. Landau, *Lenin* (New York, 1922).

W. Laqueur, *The Fate of the Revolution: Interpretations of Soviet History* (London, 1967).

R. Larsson, *Theories of revolution. From Marx to the first Russian Revolution* (Stockholm, 1970).

T. H. von Laue, *Why Lenin? Why Stalin?* (Philadelphia, 1964).

H. F. Lefebvre, *La pensée de Lénine* (Paris, 1957).

N. Leites, *A Study of Bolshevism* (Glencoe, 1953).

P. Lepeshinskii, *Zhiznennyi put Lenina* (Leningrad, 1925).

Z. D. Levine, *The Man Lenin* (New York, 1924).

G. Lichtheim, *Marxism – A Historical and Critical Study* (New York, 1961).

M. Liebman, *Leninism under Lenin* (London, 1975).

L. Lukács, *Lenin: a study on the unity of his thought* (London, 1970).

V. Marcu, *Lenin* (London, 1928).

Marx – Engels – Lenin Institute, C.C. C.P.S.U., *Lenin, A Political Biography* (New York, 1943).

J. Maxton, *Lenin* (London, 1932).

R. H. McNeal, *Bride of the Revolution: Krupskaya and Lenin* (London, 1973).

A. G. Meyer, *Leninism* (New York, 1962).

A. Mikoyan, *Lénine vivant* (Paris, 1970).

D. S. Mirsky, *Lenin* (London, 1931).

M. C. Morgan, *Lenin* (London, 1971).

G. Obuchkin and M. Pankratova, *V. I. Lenin, a Short Biography* (Moscow, 1969).

S. W. Page, *Lenin and World Revolution* (New York, 1972).

R. Payne, *The Life and Death of Lenin* (London, 1964).

R. Pipes, *Revolutionary Russia* (Cambridge, Mass. and London, 1968).

J. Plamenatz, *German Marxism and Russian Communism* (London, 1954).

P. N. Pospelov (ed.) *et al.*, *Lenin, A Biography* (Moscow, 1965).

S. T. Possony, *Lenin: The Compulsive Revolutionary* (Chicago, 1964).

M. P. Prilezhaeva, *V. I. Lenin, The Story of his Life* (Moscow, 1973).

L. B. Schapiro and P. Reddaway, *Lenin: The Man, the Theorist, the Leader* (London, 1968).

P. Scheibert, *Von Bakunin zu Lenin*, vol. 1 (Leiden, 1956).

D. Shub, *Lenin* (Harmondsworth, 1966).

P. Sorlin, *Lénine, Trotski, Staline, 1921–27* (Paris, 1961).

C. Suckert, *Le bonhomme Lenine* (Paris, 1932).

D. P. Sviatopolk-Mirski, *Lenin* (London, 1931).

P. M. Sweezy and H. Magdoff (ed.), *Lenin Today* (N.Y., 1970).

R. H. W. Theen, *V. I. Lenin: The Genesis and Development of a Revolutionary* (London, 1974).

L. Trotsky, *On Lenin: Notes Towards a Biography* (London, 1971).

R. C. Tucker, *The Marxian Revolutionary Idea* (New York, 1969).

Bibliography

A. B. Ulam, *Lenin and the Bolsheviks* (London, 1969).

F. J. Veale, *The Man from the Volga: Lenin* (London, 1932).

G. V. Vernadskii, *Lenin: Red Dictator*, tr. M. W. Davis (1931).

G. Walter, *Lénine* (Paris, 1950).

E. Wilson, *To the Finland Station* (London, 1960).

B. D. Wolfe, *Three Who Made a Revolution* (Harmondsworth, 1966).

B. D. Wolfe, *Marxism: One Hundred Years in the Life of a Doctrine* (New York, 1963).

E. V. Wolfenstein, *The Revolutionary Personality: Lenin, Trotsky, Gandhi* (Princeton, 1967).

V. Zevin and G. Golikov, *Lenin: A Short Biography* (Moscow, 1972).

G. E. Zinoviev, *N. Lenin. Vladimir Ilich Ulyanov: Ocherki zhizni i deiatelnosti* (Petrograd, 1918).

G. E. Zinoviev, *N. Lénine, Sa vie et son activité* (Paris, 1919).

G. E. Zinoviev, *Notre Maître Lénine* (Paris, 1924).

G. E. Zinoviev, *Le léninisme* (Paris, 1926).

SECTION 3. MEMOIRS

B. N. Avilkin, *Lenin v Samare: Vospominaniia Sovremennikov* (Kuibishev, 1969).

A. I. Balabanova, *Impressions of Lenin* (Ann Arbor, 1964).

V. D. Bonch-Bruevich, *Vospominaniia o Lenine* (Moscow, 1965).

V. D. Bonch-Bruevich, *V. I. Lenin v Petrograde i v Moskve 1917–20 gg* (Moscow, 1966).

S. M. Budennyi, *Vstrechi s Ilichem* (Moscow, 1970).

M. M. Essen, *Vstrechi s Leninym* (Moscow, 1966).

L. A. Fotieva, *Iz zhizni V. I. Lenina* (Moscow, 1967).

L. A. Fotieva, *Iz vospominanii o V. I. Lenine. (Dekabr 1922 g-mart 1923 g)* (Moscow, 1964).

B. I. Gorev, *Iz partiinogo proshlogo, Vospominaniia. 1895–1905* (Leningrad, 1924).

M. Gorki, *Days with Lenin* (London, n.d.).

Institut Marksizma – Leninizma pri Ts.K. K.P.S.S., *Vospominaniia o Vladimire Iliche Lenine*, ed. G. N. Golikov et. al., 5 vols (Moscow, 1969–70).

A. M. Kollontai, *Vospominaniia ob Iliche* (Moscow, 1959).

T. Kopelzon, *O Lenine* (Moscow, 1925).

N. D. Kostin, *Iz novykh vospominanii o Lenine* (Moscow, 1967).

G. M. Krzhizhanovskii, *O Vladimire Iliche* (Moscow, 1933).

P. N. Lepeshinskii, *Vstrechi s Ilichem* (Moscow, 1966).

A Mikoyan, *Mysli i vospominaniia o Lenine* (Moscow, 1970).

E. P. Onufriev, *Vstrechi s Leninym* (Moscow, 1966).

R. M. Savitskaia and Z. L. Fradinka, *Vospominaniia o Vl. Il. Lenine. Annotirovannyi ukazatel knig i zhurnalnykh statei 1954–1961 gg.* (Moscow, 1963).

L. Schälike (ed.), *Genosse Lenin. Erinnerungen von Zeitgenossen* (Berlin, 1967).

A. S. Semenov, *Nezabyvaemye vstrechi s V. I. Leninym* (Kishinev, 1965).

E. E. Shteinman (ed.), *Vospominaniia I. V. Babushkina* (Leningrad, 1925).

J. Stalin, M. Gorki, V. Mayakovski *et al.*, *Lénine* (Moscow, 1945).

J. Stalin, V. Molotov and K. Voroshilov, *Lénine tel qu'il fût* (Paris, 1934).

G. E. Titelman (ed.), *Our Lenin* (Moscow, 1970).

A. I. Ulianova-Elizarova, *Vospominaniia ob Iliche* (Moscow, 1934).

D. and M. Ulianov, *O Lenine* (Moscow, 1934).

N. Valentinov, *Encounters with Lenin* (London, 1968).

V. Vodovozov, *Moe znakomstvo s Leninym, Na Chuzhnoi Storone* (Prague, 1925) no. 12.

C. Zetkin, *Reminiscences of Lenin* (London, 1929).

K. Zetkin, *Vospominaniia o Lenine* (Moscow, 1933).

R. Zhak (ed.), *Lenin's Comrades-in-arms* (Moscow, 1969).

SECTION 4. LIFE AND THOUGHT TO 1914

4(a) Family and Early Years (to about 1893)

T. Barkovskaia, *Nachalo bolshogo puti* (Kuibishev, 1964).

A. Beliakov, *Yunost Vozhdia* (Moscow, 1958).

V. Chuev, *V. I. Lenin v Samare* (Moscow, 1960).

I. Deutscher, *Lenin's Childhood* (London, 1970).

B. S. Itenberg and A. Ia. Cherniak, *Aleksandr Ulianov 1866–1887* (Moscow, 1957).

A. I. Ivanskii, *Molodoi Lenin* (Moscow, 1964).

A. I. Ivanskii, *Molodye gody V. I. Lenina po vospominaniiam sovremennikov i dokumentam* (Moscow, 1960).

V. V. Kanivets, *Aleksandr Ulianov* (Moscow, 1961).

R. A. Kovnator, *Olga Ulianova* (Moscow, 1971).

P. E. Nafigov, *Pervyi shag v revoliutsii. V. I. Lenin i kazanskoe studenschestvo 80kh godov XIX veka* (Kazan, 1970).

G. P. Nikiforov, *V. I. Lenin i N. E. Fedoseev* (Iaroslavl, 1969).

R. Pipes, 'The Origins of Bolshevism: The Intellectual Evolution of Young Lenin', in R. Pipes (ed.), *Revolutionary Russia* (London, 1968).

S. N. Semanov, *Vo imia naroda, Ocherk zhizni i borby Aleksandra Ulianova* (Moscow, 1961).

M. I. Semenov, *Staryi tovarishch A. P. Skliarenko* (Moscow, 1922).

M. I. Semenov, *V. I. Lenin v Samare 1889–93* (Moscow, 1933).

M. I. Semenov, *Revoliutsionnaia Samara 80–90 godov* (Kuibishev, 1940).

M. Shaginian, *Semia Ulianovykh* (Moscow, 1958).

G. A. Solomon, *Lenin i ego semia* (Paris, 1931).

V. Sutyrin, *Aleksandr Ulianov, 1866–1887* (Moscow, 1971).

L. Trotsky, *The Young Lenin* (Harmondsworth, 1974).

A. I. Ulianova- Elizarova, *O zhizni Vladimira Ilicha v Kazani*, in *Molodaia Gvardiia* (Moscow, 1924) no. 2–3.

A. E. Ulianova-Elizarova, *Aleksandr Ilich Ulianov i delo 1 marta 1887g* (Moscow, 1927).

N. Veretennikov, *Vospominaniia o detskikh godakh V. I. Lenina v Kokushkine* (Moscow, 1941).

Bibliography

B. Volin, *Lenin v Povolzhe 1870–93* (Moscow, 1956).

4(b) The Controversy with Populism

E. S. Erokhin, *Shchushenskii arsenal* (Moscow, 1971).
B. G. Filov, *V. I. Lenin o klassovom rassloenii v derevne* (Moscow, 1926).
B. P. Kozmin, *Iz istorii revoliutsionnoi mysli v Rossii* (Moscow, 1961).
V. I. Lenin, volumes 1, 2 and 3 of the *Collected Works* contain important
   writings by Lenin countering Populist political and economic analyses.
   See especially:
   What the 'Friends of the People' Are . . .
   The Economic Content of Narodism (vol. 1)
   A Characterisation of Economic Romanticism
   The Heritage We Renounce (vol. 2) and
   The Development of Capitalism in Russia (vol. 3)
A. P. Mendel, *Dilemmas of Progress in Tsarist Russia: Legal Populism and
   Legal Marxism* (Cambridge, Mass., 1961).
I. M. Mrachovskaia, *Razvitie V. I. Leninym marksistskoi teorii vosproizvodstva
   obshchestvennogo kapitala . . .* (Moscow, 1960).
A. I. Pashkov, *Ekonomicheskie raboty V. I. Lenina 90 kh godov* (Moscow,
   1960).
G. Plekhanov, *Socialism and the Political Struggle* (1883). *Our Differences*
   (1884). *Programme of the Social Democratic Group Emancipation of Labour*
   (1884). *The Development of the Monist View of History* (1895). All in
   G. Plekhanov, *Selected Philosophical Works*, vol. 1 (London, 1961).
O. H. Radkey, *The Agrarian Foes of Bolshevism* (New York, 1958).
M. G. Shestakov, *Borba V. I. Lenina protiv idealisticheskoi sotsiologii
   narodnichestva* (Moscow, 1959).
V. V. (pseud. V. P. Vorontsov), *Sudby kapitalizma v Rossii* (St Petersburg,
   1882).
F. Venturi, *Roots of Revolution* (London, 1964).
A. Walicki, *The Controversy over Populism* (Oxford, 1969).
R. Wortman, *The Crisis of Russian Populism* (Cambridge, 1967).
N. Ziber, *Ocherk pervobytnoi ekonomicheskoi kultury* (Moscow, 1883).
N. Ziber, *David Rikardo i Karl Marks v ikh obshchestvenno-ekonomicheskikh
   issledovaniiakh* (St Petersburg, 1897).

4(c) Social Democracy and the Labour Movement to 1914

R. Abramovich, *The Soviet Revolution* (New York, 1962).
V. P. Akimov (pseud. V. P. Makhnovets), *Materialy dlia kharakter-
   istiki razvitiia rossiikoi sotsialdemokraticheskoi rabochei partii* (Geneva,
   1904).
V. P. Akimov (pseud. V. P. Makhnovets), *K voprosu o rabotakh vtorogo sezda
   Rossiiskoi sotsialdemokratischeskoi rabochei partii* (Geneva, 1904). See also
   J. Frankel.
P. B. Akselrod, *Pismo k russkim rabochim. Zadachi rabochei intelligentsii v
   Rossii*, 2nd edn (Geneva, 1893).

358

P. B. Akselrod, *Pismo k redaktsiiu 'Rabochago Dela'* (Geneva, 1889).
P. B. Akselrod, *Rabochee dvizhenie i sotsialnaia demokratiia* (Geneva, 1884).
P. B. Akselrod, *K voprosu o sovremennykh zadachakh i taktike russkikh Sotsial-demokratov* (Geneva, 1898).
P. B. Akselrod, *Narodnaia duma i rabochii sezd* (Geneva, 1905).
Iu. M. Arsenev, *Lenin i sotsial-demokraticheskaia emigratsiia, 1900–1904 gg.* (Moscow, 1971).
A. Ascher, *Pavel Axelrod and the Development of Menshevism* (Cambridge, Mass., 1972).
A. Ascher, *The Mensheviks in the Russian Revolution* (London, 1976).
A. E. Badaev, *The Bolsheviks in the Tsarist Duma* (Moscow, 1933).
A. Balabanova, *My Life as a Rebel* (London, 1938).
S. H. Baron, *Plekhanov, the Father of Russian Marxism* (London, 1963).
N. Baturin, *Ocherki iz istorii rabochego dvizheniia 70 kh; 80 kh godov* (Moscow, Leningrad, 1925).
J. Braunthal, *History of the International*, vol. I, 1864–1914 (London, 1966).
Iu. M. Chernetsovskii, *Borba V. I. Lenina protiv kautskianskoi revizii marksizma* (Leningrad, 1965).
A. G. Chernikh, *V. I. Lenin – istorik proletarskoi revoliutsii v Rossii* (Moscow, 1969).
T. Dan, *The Origins of Bolshevism* (London, 1964).
L. G. Deich, *Gruppa 'Osvobozhdenie truda'*, 6 vols (Moscow, Leningrad, 1924–6).
J. Frankel, *Vladimir Akimov on the Dilemmas of Russian Marxism, 1895–1903* (London, 1969).
M. Futrell, *The Russian Underground* (London, 1963).
P. A. Garvi, *Vospominaniia sotsialdemokrata* (New York, 1946).
I. Getzler, *Martov: A Political Biography of a Russian Social Democrat* (Cambridge, 1967).
D. Geyer, *Lenin in der russischen Sozialdemokratie* (Cologne, 1962).
P. S. Gusiatnikov, *Revoliutsionnoe studencheskoe dvizhenie v Rossii 1899–1907* (Moscow, 1971).
L. H. Haimson, *The Russian Marxists and the Origins of Bolshevism* (Cambridge, Mass., 1955).
S. Harcave, *First Blood* (London, 1964).
N. Harding, *Lenin's Political Thought*, Vol. I, *Theory and Practice in the Democratic Revolution* (London, 1977).
A. P. Iakushina, *Lenin i zagranichnaia organizatsiia R.S.D.R.P. 1905–1917* (Moscow, 1972).
A. P. Ilin, *Rozhdenie partii, 1883–1904* (Moscow, 1962).
Institut Marksa – Engelsa – Lenina pri Ts. Kom. K.P.S.S., *Vsesoiuznaia Kommunisticheskaia partiia bolshevikov v rezoliutsiiakh i resheniiakh sezdov, konferentsii i plenumov Ts.K. 1898–1939*, 4 parts (Leningrad, 1954).
Institut Marksa – Engelsa Lenina pri Ts. Kom. K.P.S.S., *Vtoroi sezd R.S.D.R.P. Materialy i dokumenty* (Moscow, 1938).
Institut Marksa – Engelsa – Lenina pri Ts. Kom. K.P.S.S., *Lenin v epokhe Vtorogo sezda i raskola partii* (Moscow, 1934).

Bibliography

A. G. Ivankov, *Lenin v sibirskoi ssylke 1897–1900* (Moscow, 1962).

N. A. Ivanova, *Lenin o revoliutsionnoi massovoi stachke v Rossii* (Moscow, 1976).

A. I. Ivanskii, *Peterburgskie gody V. I. Lenina* (Moscow, 1972).

A. I. Ivanskii, *Sibirskaia saylka V. I. Lenina* (Moscow, 1975).

J. Joll, *The Second International* (London, 1955).

K. Kautsky, 'Die Differenzen unter den russischen Sozialdemokraten', *Die Neue Zeit*, XXII, part 2, 1905.

P. A. Kazakevich, *Sotsial-demokraticheskie organisatsii Peterburga kontsa 80 kh - nachala 90 kh godov* (Leningrad, 1960).

J. L. H. Keep, *The Rise of Social Democracy in Russia* (London, 1963).

E. S. Khazakhmetov, *Lenin i ssylnye bolsheviki Sibiri* (Novosibirsk, 1971).

R. Kindersley, *The First Russian Revisionists: A Study of 'Legal Marxism' in Russia* (Oxford, 1962).

G. V. Kniazeva, *Borba bolshevikov za sozdanie nelegalnoi i legalnoi partiinoi raboty 1907–1910* (Leningrad, 1964).

Kommunisticheskaia Partiia Sovetskogo Soiuza Kom. po Ist. Okt. Rev. i R.K.P., *Kak rozhdalas partiia bolshevikov. Literaturnaia polemika 1903–04 gg* (Leningrad, 1925).

E. A. Korolchuk, *Severnyi soiuz russkikh rabochikh i rabochee dvizhenie v 70 kh godov v Piter* (Moscow, 1971).

A. F. Kostin, *Lenin – sozdatel partii novogo tipa (1894–1904 gg)* (Moscow, 1970).

A. Kremer and Iu. Martov, *Ob agitatsii* (Geneva, 1896). English translation in N. Harding and R. Taylor, *Marxism in Russia* (London, 1981).

I. M. Krivoguz and Iu. A. Molchanov, *Lenin i borba za edinstvo rabochego dvizheniia* (Leningrad, 1969).

E. E. Kruze, *Peterburgskie rabochie v 1912–1914 godakh* (Moscow, 1961).

O. G. Kutsentov, *Deiateli Peterburgskogo 'Soiuza borby za osvobozhdenie rabochego klassa'* (Moscow, 1962).

Ia. E. Kvachev, *V. I. Lenin i zagranichnie sektsii bolshevikov (1914–1917)* (Minsk, 1971).

D. Lane, *The Roots of Russian Communism* (Assen, 1968).

P. N. Lepeshinskii, *Vladimir Ilich v tiurme* (Moscow, 1934).

P. N. Lepeshinskii, *Na povorote. Ot kontsa 80 kh godov k 1905 g* (St Petersburg, 1922).

M. N. Liadov, *Istoriia rossiiskoi sotsial-demokraticheskoi partii*, 2 vols (St Petersburg, 1906–7).

R. Luxemburg, *Reform or Revolution* (New York, 1970).

Iu. O. Martov, *Borba s 'Osadnym polozheniem'v R.S.D.R.P.* (Geneva. 1904).

Iu.O. Martov, *Klass protiv klassa* (Odessa, 1917).

L. Martov, *Rabochee delo v Rossii* (Geneva, 1899).

L. Martov, *Vpered ili nazad?* (Geneva, 1904).

L. Martov, *Politicheskie partii v Rossii* (St Petersburg, 1906).

L. Martov, *Zapiski sotsialdemokrata* (Moscow, 1922).

M. Martynov (pseud. A. S. Pikker), *Peredovye i otstalye* (Geneva, 1905).

M. Martynov (pseud. A. S. Pikker), *Dve diktatury* (Geneva, 1905).

M. Martynov (pseud. A. S. Pikker), *Rabochie i revoliutsiia* (Geneva. 1902).

N. I. Matiushkin, *Partiia bolshevikov v period reaktsii. 1907–1910 gg* (Moscow, 1968).

E. Mendelsohn, *Class Struggles in the Pale* (Cambridge, 1970).

A. P. Meshcherskii and N. N. Shcherbakov, *V. I. Lenin i politicheskaia ssylka v Sibiri* (Irkutsk, 1973).

C. I. Mitskeevich, *Revoliutsionnaia Moskva 1888–1905* (Moscow, 1940).

M. V. Moskalev, *Lenin v Sibiri* (Moscow, 1957).

N. V. Nelidov, *Leninskaia shkola v Lonzhumo* (Moscow, 1967).

J. P. Nettl, *Rosa Luxemburg*, 2 vols (London, 1966).

V. I. Nevskii, *Ocherki po istorii rossiiskoi sotsial-demokraticheskoi partii* (Moscow, 1925).

V. I. Nevskii, *Deiateli revoliutsionnogo dvizhenii v Rossii: Bibliograficheskii slovar*, 10 vols in 5 (Leipzig, 1974).

A. M. Pankratova, L. M. Ivanov *et al.* (eds), *Rabochee dvizhenie v Rossii v XIX-om veke*, 4 vols (Moscow and Leningrad, 1950–63).

B. Pearce (trans.), *1903. Second Congress of the R.S.D.L.P.*, complete text of the minutes (London, 1978).

O. Piatnitskii, *Zapiski bolshevika* (Leningrad, 1925).

R. Pipes, *Social Democracy and the St. Petersburg Labour Movement 1885–1897* (Cambridge., Mass, 1963).

R. Pipes, *Struve, Liberal on the Left* (Cambridge, Mass., 1970).

Iu. Polevoi, *Zarozhdenie marksizma v Rossii 1883–1894 gg* (Moscow, 1959).

P. N. Pospelov *et al.*, *Istoriia K.P.S.S. Tom pervyi Sozdanie bolshevistskoi partii, 1888 – 1903* (Moscow and Leningrad, 1964).

A. Rosmer, *Le mouvement ouvrier pendant la guerre. tome I: De l'union sacrée à Zimmerwald* (Paris, 1936).

Rossiiskaia sotsial-demokraticheskaia rabochaia partiia. 2d Kongress, *Polnyi tekst protokolov* (Geneva, 1904). See also B. Pearce.

W. B. Scharlau and Z. A. B. Zeman, *Merchant of Revolution:a life of Alexander Helphand [Parvus]* (London, 1965).

C. E. Schorske, *German Social Democracy 1905–1917* (New York, 1965).

J. Seradskii, *Polskie gody Lenina* (Moscow, 1963).

N. L. Sergievskii, *Partiia russkikh sotsial-demokratov, Gruppa Blagoeva* (Moscow, 1929).

M. A. Silvin, *Lenin v period zarozhdeniia partii* (Leningrad, 1958).

E. E. Smith, *The Young Stalin: the early years of an elusive revolutionary* (London, 1968).

N. N. Sarovtseva and R. Z. Iunitskaia (eds), *Vospominaniia o II R.S.D.R.P.* (Moscow, 1973).

K. I. Suvorov, I. I. Groshev i dr, *Bolshevistskaia Partiia v revoliutsii 1905–1907 gg* (Moscow, 1975).

K. M. Takhtarev, *Ocherk Peterburgskogo rabochego dvizheniia 90 kh. godov* (London, 1902).

D. W. Treadgold, *Lenin and His Rivals* (London, 1955).

Bibliography

V. I. Tropin, *Borba bolshevikov za rukovodstvo krestianskim dvizheniem v 1905 g* (Moscow, 1970).

L. Trotsky, *Vtoroi sezd partii: otchet sibirskoi delegatsii* (Geneva, 1903).

R. C. Tucker, *Stalin as a Revolutionary 1879–1929* (New York, 1973).

S. P. Turin, *From Peter the Great to Lenin. A History of the Russian Labour Movement* (London, 1968).

Ukazatel sotsialdemokraticheskoi literatury na russkom iazike. 1883–1905 gg (Paris, 1913).

N. A. Ulianov and V. A. Ulianov, *Ukazatel zhurnalnoi literature. Alfavitnyi, predmetnyi, sistematicheskii, 1896–1910*, 2 vols (Moscow, 1911–13).

S. N. Valk (ed.), *Listovki 'Peterburgskogo soiuza borby za osvobozhdenie rabochego klassa', 1895–1897 gg* (Moscow, 1934).

Ia. R. Volin *et al.* (ed.), *Lenin i mestnye partiinye organizatsii Rossii (1894–1917)* (Perm, 1970).

Ia. R. Volin *et al.* (ed.), *Kniga 'Chto delat? i mestnye partiinye organizatsii Rossii* (Perm, 1972).

Ia. R. Volin *et al.* (ed.), *Vtoroi sezd R.S.D.R.P. i mestnye partiinye organizatsii Rossii* (Perm, 1973).

I. V. Volkovicher, *Nachalo sotsialisticheskogo rabochego dvizheniia v byvshei russkoi Polshe* (Leningrad, 1925).

J. Walkin, *The Rise of Democracy in Pre-revolutionary Russia* (London, 1963).

A. K. Wildman, *The Making of a Workers' Revolution* (Chicago, 1967).

E. Zaleski, *Mouvements Ouvriers et Socialistes. Chronologie et bibliographie. La Russie*, 2 vols (Paris, 1956).

M. N. Zinovev, *Partiia bolshevikov v revoliutsii 1905–1907 godov* (Moscow, 1965).

SECTION 5. LIFE AND THOUGHT 1914–24

5(a) The War and the Theory of Imperialism

G. A. Alexinsky, *Russia and the Great War* (London, 1915).

B. M. Barratt Brown, *Essays on Imperialism* (London, 1972).

E. Bevan, *German Social Democracy During the War* (London, 1918).

N. Bukharin, *Mirovoe khoziaistvo i imperializm* (Moscow, 1917), translated as *Imperialism and World Economy* (London, n.d. (1929 or 1930)).
'Der imperialistische Raubstaat', in *Jugend Internationale*, no. 6 (Dec. 1916) pp. 7–9.
'K teorii imperialisticheskogo gosudarstva', in *Revoluitsiia prava. Sbornik Pervyi*, no. 25 (Moscow, 1925).

V. N. Cherkovets, I. P. Faminskii *et al.*, *Leninskii analiz imperializma i sovremennyi kapitalizm* (Moscow, 1969).

Y. Danilov, *La Russie dans la guerre mondiale 1914–1917* (Paris, 1927).

M. Fainsod, *International Socialism and the World War* (Cambridge, Mass., 1935).

J. Freymond, *Lénine et l'imperialisme* (Lausanne, 1951).

O. H. Gankin and M. H. Fisher (eds), *The Bolsheviks and the World War. The Origins of the Third International* (Stanford, 1940).

M. Gorter, *Der Imperialismus, der Weltkrieg und die Sozial-Demokratie* (Amsterdam, 1975).

R. Hilferding, *Das Finanzkapital* (Vienna, 1910). Russian edition *Finansovyi kapital* (Moscow, 1914).

J. Hobson, *Imperialism. A Study* (London, 1902).

D. Horowitz, *Imperialism and Revolution* (London, 1969).

T. Kemp, *Theories of Imperialism* (London, 1967).

G. B. Khromushin, *Lenin on Modern Capitalism* (1969).

H. Lademacher (ed), *Die Zimmerwalder Bewegung: Protokolle und Korrespondenz* (The Hague, 1967).

V. A. Lavrin, *Bolshevistskaia Partiia v nachale pervoi mirovoi voiny 1914–15 gg* (Moscow, 1972).

A. Leontev, *O Leninskikh tetradakh po imperializmu* (1941).

L. A. Leontev, *Über das Werk W. I. Lenins 'Der Imperialismus als höchstes Stadium des Kapitalismus'* (Berlin, 1951).

V. I. Lenin, *Lenin i iunye internatsionalisty. Sbornik dokumentov i materialov* (Moscow, 1968).

G. Lichtheim, *Imperialism* (Harmondsworth, 1974).

R. Luxemburg, *The Accumulation of Capital* (London, 1963).

R. Luxemburg and N. Bukharin, *Imperialism and the Accumulation of Capital*, ed. K. J. Tarbuck (London, 1972).

L. Martov, *Protiv voiny! Sbornik statei 1914–16* (Moscow, 1917).

I. Menitskii, *Revoliutsionnoe dvizhenie voennykh godov (1914–17)*, 2 vols (Moscow, 1924 and 1925).

C. I. Murashov, *Partiia bolshevikov v gody pervoi mirovoi voiny* (Moscow, 1963).

R. Owen and R. Sutcliffe, *Studies in the Theory of Imperialism* (London, 1972).

G. V. Plekhanov, *O voine: Stati* (Petrograd, 1917).

A. Rosmer, *Le mouvement ouvrier pendant la guerre*, 2 vols (Paris, 1936).

A. W. Senn, *The Russian Revolution in Switzerland 1914–17* (Madison, Wisconsin, 1971).

L. D. Trotsky, *The War and the International* (Welawatte, US, 1971).

E. Varga and L. Mendelsohn (eds), *New Data on V. I. Lenin's Imperialism: the Highest Stage of Capitalism* (London, 1939).

E. G. Vasilevskii, *Razvitie vzgliadov V. I. Lenina na imperializm* (Moscow 1969).

W. F. Walling, *The Socialists and the War* (New York, 1915).

G. Zinoviev and V. I. Lenin, *Socialism and War* (London, n.d.).

5(b) 1917

V. D. Bonch-Bruevich, *V. I. Lenin v Petrograde i Moskve (1917–1920 gg.)* (Moscow, 1966).

V. D. Bonch-Bruevich, *Vsia vlast sovetam. Vospominaniia* (Moscow, 1957).

R. P. Browder and A. F. Kerensky, *The Russian Provisional Government, 1917: Documents*, 3 vols (Stanford, 1961).

J. Carmichael, *The Russian Revolution 1917)* (London, 1955).

Bibliography

W. H. Chamberlin, *The Russian Revolution 1917–21*, 2 vols (New York, 1935).

V. Chernov, *The Great Russian Revolution* (New Haven, 1936).

M. T. Florinsky, *The End of the Russian Empire* (New Haven, 1931).

G. Katkov, *Russia. 1917* (London, 1967).

G. M. Krzhizhanovskii, *Lenin: Myslitel i revoliutsioner* (Moscow, 1960).

K. F. Mailloux and M. P. Mailloux, *Lenin. The Exile Returns* (London, 1971).

J. Marabini, *L'étincelle: Lénine, organisateur de la Révolution russe* (1962).

S. P. Melgunov, *The Bolshevik Seizure of Power* (Santa Barbara and Oxford, 1972).

I. I. Mins (ed.), *Lenin i oktiabrskoe voorzhennoe vostanie v Petrograde* (Moscow, 1964).

R. W. Pethybridge, *The Spread of the Russian Revolution. Essays on 1917* (London, 1972).

J. Reed, *Ten Days That Shook the World* (New York, 1934).

H. Shukman, *Lenin and the Russian Revolution* (London, 1966).

P. N. Sobolev (ed.), *Lenin ob istoricheskom opyte Velikogo Oktiabria. Sbornik statei* (Moscow, 1969).

F. D. Stacey (ed.), *Lenin and the Russian Revolution* (London, 1968).

N. N. Sukhanov, *The Russian Revolution, 1917* (London, 1955).

I. Tsereteli, *Vospominaniia fevralskoi revoliutsii*, 2 vols (The Hague, 1963).

L. Trotsky, *The History of the Russian Revolution*, 3 vols (London, 1934).

L. Trotsky, *Kak vooruzhalas revoliutsiia*, vol. 1 (Moscow, 1923).

Voline (pseud V. M. Eichenbaum), *Nineteen Seventeen* (London, 1954).

5(c) 1917–24

A. Andreev, B. Pankov and E. Smirnova, *Lenin v Kremle* (Moscow, 1960).

P. Avrich, *Kronstadt 1921* (Princeton, N. J. 1970).

C. Bettelheim, *Class Struggles in the U.S.S.R.*, vol. 1 1917–23 (Hassocks, 1977).

N. Bukharin, *Programme of the World Revolution* (Glasgow, 1920).

N. Bukharin, *Ekonomika perekhodnogo perioda* (Moscow, 1920), translated as *Economics of the Transformation Period* (New York, 1971).

N. Bukharin and E. Preobrazhensky, *The A.B.C. of Communism* (London, 1969).

I. M. Chernetsovskii, *Borba V. I. Lenina protiv kautskianskoi revizii marksizma* (Leningrad, 1965).

S. F. Cohen, *Bukarin and the Bolshevik Revolution* (London, 1974).

R. V. Daniels, *The Conscience of the Revolution: Opposition in the Soviet Union, 1917–1929* (Cambridge, Mass., 1961).

I. Deutscher, *The Prophet Armed 1879–1921* (London, 1954).

V. A. Ezhov, *Lenin i problemy stroitelstva sotsializma* (Leningrad, 1970).

L. E. Fain, *Istoriia razrabotki V. I. Leninym kooperativnogo plana* (Moscow, 1970).

E. B. Genkina, *Lenin predsedatel Sovnarkoma i S.T.O. (1921–1922 gg.)* (Moscow, 1960).

E. B. Genkina *Gosudarstvennaia deiatelnost V. I. Lenina* (Moscow, 1969).

Institut Marska – Engelsa – Lenina pri Ts.K. K.P.S.S., *Leninskie Dekrety – 1917–1922. Bibliografiia* (Moscow, 1974).

N. P. Iroshnikov, *Predesedatel Soveta Narodnykh Komissarov VI. Ulianov (1917–1918 gg.)* (Leningrad, 1974).

K. Kautsky, *Die Diktatur des Proletariats* (Vienna, 1918).

E. V. Klopov, *Lenin v Smolnom (Oktiabr 1917g mart 1918g.)* (Moscow, 1965).

A. Kollontai, *The Workers' Opposition* (Reading, n.d.).

A. D. Kosichev, *Teoreticheskoe oboshenie V. I. Lenin i opyta Oktiabrskoi revoliutsii i stroitelstva sotsializma v. S.S.S.R.* (Moscow, 1974).

M. Lewin, *Lenin's Last Struggle* (London, 1969).

M. D. Lutskii, *Voprosy diktatury proletariata v trudakh V. I. Lenina, 1917–24 gg* (Moscow, 1957).

R. Luxemburg, *The Russian Revolution and Leninism or Marxism* (Ann Arbor, 1961).

S. M. Maiorov, *Poslednie pisma i stati V. I. Lenina* (Moscow, 1970).

I. Mett, *The Kronstadt Commune* (London, 1967).

M. A. Moskalev, *Lenin v poslednie gody zhizni 1921–1924 gg* (Simferopol, 1959).

B. E. Nolde, *Lenins Räte-Republik* (Berlin, 1920).

B. E. Nolde, *Le règne de Lenine* (Paris, 1920).

V. V. Platkovskii, *V. I. Lenin o diktature proletariata i sotasialisticheskom gosudarstve* (Moscow, 1975).

E. Pollock, *The Kronstadt Rebellion* (New York, 1959).

T. H. Rigby, *Lenin's Government. Sovnarkom 1917–22* (Cambridge, 1979).

V. V. Romanov, *Borba V. I. Lenina protiv antipartiinoi gruppy demokraticheskogo tsentralizma* (Moscow, 1969).

A. Rosmer, *Moscou sous Lénine*, 2 vols (Paris, 1970).

N. V. Rubon (ed.), *Voprosy strategii i taktiki v trudakh V. I. Lenina posle oktiabrskogo perioda* (Moscow, 1971).

R. M. Savitskaia, *Ocherk gosudarstvennoi deiatelnost V. I. Lenina* (Moscow, 1975).

R. M. Savitskaia, *Deiatelnost V. I. Lenina v oblasti ekonomicheskogo stroitelstva. Oktiabr 1917–iiul 1918 gg* (Moscow, 1975).

V. M. Selunskaia, *Lenin i nekotorye voprosy sotsialnoi struktury sovetskogo obshchestva v perekhodnyi period* (Moscow, 1973).

V. Serge, *Memoirs of a Revolutionary* (London, 1963).

V. Serge, *Year One of the Russian Revolution* (London, 1972).

V. Serge, *Kronstadt, 1921* (Tonbridge, n.d.).

A. A. Timofeevskii (ed.) *et al.*, *Lenin i stroitelstvo partii v pervye gody sovetskoi vlasti* (Moscow, 1965).

L. Trotsky, *Terrorism and Communism* (Ann Arbor, 1961).

G. E. Zinoviev, *Pressing Questions of the International Labour Movement* (Petrograd, 1920).

Bibliography

5(d) Comintern and World Revolution

B. A. Aizin, V. M. Dalin *et al.* (eds), *Lenin v borbe za revoliutsionnii International* (Moscow, 1970).

F. Borkenau, *The Communist International* (London, 1938).

J. Braunthal, *A History of the International 1914–43*, vol. 2 (London, 1967).

J. Degras, *The Communist International, 1919–1943*, documents, 2 vols (London, 1956–60).

M. Djïas, *Lenine et les rapports entre états socialistes* (Paris, 1949).

M. Drachkovitch (ed.), *The Revolutionary Internationals* (Stanford, 1966).

M. Drachkovitch (ed.), *The Comintern. Historical Highlights* (Stanford, 1966).

L. Fischer, *The Soviets in World Affairs*, 2 vols (New York, 1930).

M. T. Florinsky, *World Revolution and the U.S.S.R.* (London, 1933).

J. Freymond, *Contribution à l'histoire du Comintern* (Geneva, 1965).

H. Gruber, *International Communism in the Era of Lenin*, documents.

J. W. Hulse, *The Forming of the Communist International* (Stanford, 1964).

J. Humbert-Droz, *L'Origine de l'Internationale Communistè* (Neuchâtel, 1968).

Institute of Marxism – Leninism of C.C. of C.P.S.U., *Outline History of the Communist International* (Moscow, 1971).

G. F. Kennan, *Russia and the West under Lenin and Stalin* (London, 1961).

N. E. Kordev, *Lenin i mezhdunarodnoe rabochee dvizhenie, 1914–1918 gg* (Moscow, 1968).

B. Lazitch, *Lénine et la III e Internationale* (Neuchâtel, 1951).

B. Lazitch and M. Drachkevitch, *Lenin and the Comintern* (Stanford, 1972).

D. Z. Manuilskii, *Lenin and the International Labour Movement* (London, 1939).

G. Nollau, *International Communism and World Revolution* (New York, 1961).

S. W. Page, *Lenin and World Revolution* (New York, 1972).

L. A. Slepov (ed.), *Lenin i mezhdunarodnoe rabochee dvizhenie* (Moscow, 1969).

L. Trotsky, *The First Five Years of the Communist International* (New York, 1945).

SECTION 6. LENIN BY TOPIC

6(a) Lenin and Philosophy

H. B. Acton, *The Illusion of the Epoch. Marxism – Leninism as a Philosophical Creed* (London, 1955).

G. F. Aleksandrov *et al.*, *Razvitie V. I. Leninym marksistskogo ucheniia o zakonakh dialektiki* (Minsk, 1960).

L. Althusser, *Lénine et la philosophie* (Paris, 1969).

Th. B. M. Brameld, *A Philosophical Approach to Communism* (Chicago, 1933).

D. I. Danilenko, *Razvitie V. I. Leninym dialektiki v posleoktiabrskii period* (Moscow, 1971).

366

A. Deborin, *Lenin, der kämpfende Materialist* (Vienna, 1924).

R. Garaudy, *Lénine* (Paris, 1968).

V. I. Gorbakh *et al.* (eds), *Voprosy marksistskoi filosofii v trudakh V. I. Lenina* (Minsk, 1958).

G. Harmsen, *Lenin. Filosoof van de revolutië* (Baarn, 1970).

B. M. Kedrov, *Iz laboratorii leninskoi mysli (Ocherki o filosofskikh tetradakh V. I. Lenina)* (Moscow, 1972).

P. V. Kopnin, *Filosofskie idei V. I. Lenina i logika* (Moscow, 1969).

V. E. Kozlovskii, *Razvitie V. I. Leninym marksistskogo ucheniia o protivorechiiakh* (Moscow, 1966).

D. Lecourt, *Une crise et son enjeu. Essai sur la position de Lénine en philosophie* (Paris, 1973).

I. K. Luppol, *Lenin und die Philosophie* (Vienna, 1929).

A. Pannekoek, *Lenin as philosopher* (New York, 1948).

T. Pavlov, *Leninskaia teoriia otrazheniia i sovremennost* (Moscow, 1969).

J. Plamenatz, *German Marxism and Russian Communism* (London, 1954).

M. M. Rosental, *Lenin kak filosof* (Moscow, 1969).

L. Sève and G. Labica, *Lénine et la pratique scientifique* (Paris, 1974).

G. A. Wetter, *Dialectical Materialism. A Historical and Systematic Survey of Philosophy in the Soviet Union* (London, 1958).

L. Iu. Zvonev, *Filosofskie tetradi V. I. Lenina* (Leningrad, 1949).

6(b) Lenin and History

V. I. Astokhov and I. L. Serman, *V. I. Lenin – istorik sovetskogo obshchestva* (Kharkov, 1969).

B. A. Chagin, *Lenin o roli subektivnogo faktora v istorii* (Moscow, 1967).

A. G. Chernykh, *V. I. Lenin. Istorik proletarskoi revoliutsii v Rossii* (Moscow, 1969).

V. V. Ivanov *et al., Istoriia i istoriki. Istoricheskaia kontseptsiia V. I. Lenina. Metodologiia* (Moscow, 1972).

M. P. Kim (ed.), *Lenin i istoriia klassov i politicheskikh partii v Rossii* (Moscow, 1970).

S. M. Levin (ed.), *Lenin i russkaia obshchestvenno – politicheskaia mysl* (Leningrad, 1969).

V. V. Marodin, *Lenin i istoricheskaia nauka* (Leningrad, 1970).

N. N. Maslov, *Lenin kak istorik partii* (Leningrad, 1964).

A. A. Matiugin, *V. I. Lenin ob istoricheskoi roli rabochego klassa* (Moscow, 1974).

M. V. Nechkina (ed.), *Lenin i istoricheskaia nauka* (Moscow, 1968).

N. E. Nosov (ed.), *Lenin i problemy istorii* (Leningrad, 1970).

Z. M. Protasenko, *Lenin kak istorik filosofii* (Moscow, 1969).

6(c) Lenin and Culture

G. Besse, J. Milhau and M. Simon, *Lénine, la philosophie et la culture* (Paris, 1971).

Bibliography

V. V. Gorbunov, *V. I. Lenin i Proletkult* (Moscow, 1974).
A. Iufit, *Lenin. Revoliutsiia. Teatr. Dokumenty i vospominaniia* (Leningrad, 1970).
G. G. Karpov, *Lenin o kulturnoi revoliutsii* (Leningrad, 1970).
M. P Kim (ed.), *Lenin i Kulturnaia revoliutsiia khronika sobytii (1917–1923)* (Moscow, 1972).
N. I. Krulikov, *Lenin o literature i iskusstve*, 5th edn (Moscow, 1976).
V. S. Krushkova, *Lenin i iskusstvo* (Moscow, 1969).
I. S. Smirnov, *Lenin i sovetskaia kultura. Gosudarstvennaia deiatelnost V. I. Lenina v oblasti kulturnogo stroitelstva (Oktiabr 1917g.–Leto 1918g)* (Moscow, 1960).
A. Weser and L. Stöhr, *Lenin in Kunst und Literatur* (Berlin, 1969).

6(d) Lenin and the Media

A. F. Berezhnaia, *Lenin – sozdatel pechati novogo tipa* (Leningrad, 1971).
A. F. Berezhnaia, *V. I. Lenin – publitsist i redaktor* (Moscow, 1975).
F. Billoux, *Lénine par l'image* (Paris, 1950).
A. M. Gak (ed.), *Samoe vazhnoe iz vsekh iskusstv. Lenin o kino*, 2nd edn (Moscow, 1973).
A. M. Gak, A. I. Petrov and L. N. Fomicheva (eds), *Lenin: Sobranie fotografii i kinokadrov*, 2 vols (Moscow, 1970–2).
T. H. Guback and S. P. Hill, *The innovation of broadcasting in the Soviet Union and the role of V. I. Lenin* (Lexington, Ky., 1972).
Institut Marksizma – Leninizma pri Ts.K. K.P.S.S., *Lenin i Pravda*, 2nd edn (Moscow, 1967).
A. A. Kruglov, *V. I. Lenin i stanovlenie sovetskoi pressy* (Moscow, 1973).
G. I. Kunitsin, *V. I. Lenin o partiinosti i svobode pechati* (Moscow, 1971).
R. A. Lavrov and B. V. Iakovlev (eds), *Lenin i 'Izvestiia' Dokumenty i materialy 1917–1922* (Moscow, 1975).
V. T. Loginov, *Lenin i 'Pravda', 1912–1914 godov* (Moscow, 1962).
V. T. Loginov, *Leninskaia 'Pravda', 1912–1914 gg* (Moscow, 1972).
A. Z. Okorokov, *Lenin, zhurnalist i redaktor* (Moscow, 1960).
V. S. Panchenko, *Leninskaia nelegalnaia pechat* (Moscow, 1970).
E. B. Strukov *et al.*, *Lenin v 'Pravde'* (Moscow, 1970).

6(e) The National Question

G. Adikhari (ed.) *et al.*, *Lenin and India* (New Delhi, 1970).
P. A. Azibekov and I. A. Gusenov, *Lenin drug narodov vostoka*, 2 vols (Baku, 1967).
T. Iu. Burmistrova, *Razrabotka V. I. Leninym programmy bolshevistskoi partii po natsionalnomu voprosu* (1910–1914 gg.).
G. V. Efimov, *Lenin i problemy istorii stran Azii* (Leningrad, 1970).
B. Gafurov *et al.*, *Lenin and Revolution in the East* (Moscow, 1970).
S. S. Gililov, *V. I. Lenin – organizator sovetskogo mnogonatsionalnogo gosudarstva*, 2nd edn (Moscow, 1972).
A. D. Low, *Lenin on the Question of Nationality* (New York, 1958).

A. N. Mnatskanian, *Lenin i reshenie natsionalnogo voprosa v SSSR* (Erevan, 1970).

S. A. Radzhabov, *Lenin i sovetskaia natsionalnaia gosudarstvennost* (Dushanbe, 1970).

6(f) Lenin and Military Matters

N. N. Azovtzev, *Voennye voprosy v trudakh V. I. Lenina* (Moscow, 1971).

D. M. Grinishin, *Voennaia deiatelnost V. I. Lenina* (Moscow, 1957).

N. I. Podvoiskii *et al.*, *Lenin i krasnaia armiia* (Moscow, 1958).

M. V. Zacharov (ed.), *Lenin i voennaia istoriia* (Moscow, 1970).

A. S. Zheltov, *Lenin i sovetskie vooruzhennye sily* (Moscow, 1969).

6(g) Lenin and Places – Bibliographical Gazeteer

Iu. V. Bernov and A. I. Manusevich, *Lenin v Krakove* (Moscow, 1972).

A. A. Dobrodomov, *Lenin i moskovskie bolsheviki* (Moscow, 1969).

F. Donath, *Lenin in Leipzig* (Berlin, 1958).

C. Feld, *Quand Lénine vivait a Paris* (Paris, 1969).

J. Fréville, *Lénine à Paris* (Paris, 1968).

W. Gautschi, *Lenin als Emigrant in der Schweiz* (Zurich, 1973).

B. V. Iakovlev, *Lenin v Krasnoiarske. Dok. ocherk* (Moscow, 1965).

M. Ivanov, *Lenin v Prage* (Moscow, 1963).

R. F. Ivanov, *Lenin o Soedinennykh Shtatakh Ameriki* (Moscow, 1965).

R. Iu. Kaganova, *Lenin vo Frantsii (Dekabr 1908–iiun 1912)* (Moscow, 1972).

N. B. Karakhan, *Vladimir Ilich Lenin v Londone* (Moscow, 1969).

H. König, *Lenin und der italienische Sozialismus 1915–21* (Tübingen, 1967).

A. S. Kudriavtsev and L. Muravev, *Lenin v Berne i Tsiurikhe* (Moscow, 1972).

A. S. Kudriavchev and L. Muravev, *Lenin v Zheneve* (Moscow, 1967).

London landmarks. A guide with map to places where Marx, Engels and Lenin lived and worked (London, n.d.).

'Moskovskii rabochii', *Lenin i moskovskie bolsheviki* (Moscow, 1969).

P. E. Nikitinikh, *Zdes zhil i rabotal Lenin* (Moscow, 1966).

M. Pianzola, *Lénine en Suisse* (Geneva, 1952).

S. B. Polesev, *Po leninskim adresam* (Moscow, 1969).

A. Reisberg, *Lenin i nemetskoe rabochee dvizhenie* (Moscow, 1974).

L. Riti, *Lenin i vengerskoe rabochee dvizhenie* (Moscow, 1972).

6(h) Lenin and Books

P. A. Chuvikov, *Lenin v pechati* (Moscow, 1972).

Institut Marksa – Engelsa – Lenina pri Ts.K. K.P.S.S., *Izdanie i rasprostranenie proizvedenii V. I. Lenina* (Moscow, 1960).

Institut Marksizma – Leninizma pri Ts.K. K.P.S.S., *Kak V. I. Lenin gotovil svoi trudy* (Moscow, 1969).

Bibliography

Institut Marksizma – Leninizma pri Ts.K. K.P.S.S., *centralnyi Muzei V. I. Lenina. Katalog* (Moscow, 1936).

I. P. Kondakov (ed.) *et al., Lenin i bibliotechnoe delo.* (Moscow, 1969).

N. K. Krupskaia, *How Lenin studied Marx.* (London, n.d.).

N. A. Mikhailov, *Lenin i mir knigi* (Moscow, 1970).

M. Pianzola, *Lénine à la bibliotheque,* Bulletin mensuel des musées et collections de la ville de Genève, llme année, 1954, no. 6.

Vsesoiuznaia knizhnaia palata, *Lenin v pechati* (Moscow, 1969).

6(i) Lenin and Statistics

S. M. Gurevich, *V. I. Lenin i statistika sotsialisticheskogo gosudarstva* (Moscow, 1963).

I. Iu. Pisarev, *Voprosy statistiki truda v rabotakh V. I. Lenina* (Moscow, 1964).

T. V. Riabushkin (ed.), *Razvitie statisticheskoi nauki v trudakh V. I. Lenina* (Moscow, 1969).

T. V. Riabushkin (ed.), *Lenin i sovremennaia statistika,* 3 rols (Moscow, 1970–3).

I. P. Suslov, *Politicheskaia statistika v rabotakh V. I. Lenina* (Moscow, 1968).

6(j) Miscellaneous

T. Brown, *Lenin and Workers' Control* (London, n.d.).

M. Dommanget, *Les grands socialistes et l'éducation: de Platon à Lénine* (Paris, 1970).

V. G. Egorov and N. A. Khvorostovskii, *V. I. Lenin o kommunisticheskom trude* (Leningrad, 1960).

R. Fülöp-Miller, *Lenin and Gandhi* (London, 1927).

A. D. Goncharov and P. I. Luniakov, *V. I. Lenin i krestianstvo* (Moscow, 1967).

E. L. Manevich, *Lenin on work under socialism and communism* (1970).

K. J. Naiakshin, *Krestianskii vopros v trudakh V. I. Lenina* (Kuibishev, 1974).

A. S. Smirnov, *Agitatsiia i propaganda bolshevikov v derevne v period podgotovki Oktiabrskoi Revoliutsii (Mart – Oktiabr 1917)* (Moscow, 1957).

I. N. Volper, *Psevdonimy V. I. Lenina* (Moscow, 1968).

A. A. Voronovich, *Agrarnaia programma partii v trudakh V. I. Lenina* (Moscow, 1971).

H-J. Waldschmidt, *Lenin und Kautsky* (Würzburg, 1966).

Chronology of Major Events and Lenin's Writings and Activities, 1914–24

Dates given are those of the Russian calendar. Not until February 1918 was the New Style or Western calendar adopted; up to that time the Old Style calendar prevailed, which was thirteen days behind the New.

1914	22 July	Social democratic parties of Germany and
	(4 August	France vote for war credits – effective col-
	Western calendar)	lapse of the Second International.
	26 July	Lenin arrested in Novy Targ.
	6 August	Following the intervention of Polish and Austrian socialists, Lenin released from prison.
	Mid August	Receives permission to leave Austria-Hungary for Switzerland.
	23 August	Arrives in Berne and in the following three days delivers his theses on the war to a Bolshevik conference (**22**, 15–19).
	September–December	Participates in numerous discussions and conferences on the war, lectures in Swiss cities and writes the manifesto, 'The War and Russian Social Democracy' (**22**, 27–34) and the lengthy pamphlet 'Socialism and War' (**22**, 295–338). Defends and disseminates his ideas.
	September 1914–May 1915	Engages in study of Feuerbach, Hegel and Aristotle; this material later published as *Philosophical Notebooks* (*CW*, **38**).
	19 October	Resumption of publication of *Sotsial Demokrat* under Lenin's editorship. This journal was the principal vehicle for his views for the next three years.
1915	14–19 February	Conference of R.S.D.L.P. Groups Abroad convened in Berne and directed by Lenin.

371

February–July	Writes a stream of anti-war articles for *Sotsial Demokrat* and strengthens cohesion of Bolshevik emigré groups.
June–July	Lenin begins his study of the literature on imperialism incorporated in *Imperialism the Highest State of Capitalism*. His notes later published as *Notebooks on Imperialism* (*CW*, **39**).
July–August	Begins in earnest to establish international contacts with anti-war groups in preparation for the International Conference of Socialists opposed to the war, to be convened in Zimmerwald.
20–26 August	Lenin in Zimmerwald, rallying left wing, writes 'Draft Resolution Proposed by the left wing at Zimmerwald' (**21**, 345–8) but his appeals are ill-supported.
August–December 1915	Continued journalistic activity, and desperate attempts to disseminate Bolshevik views on the war internationally.
December 1915	Lenin writes preface to Bukharin's *Imperialism and the World Economy* (**22**, 103–8) and begins writing his own book on imperialism.
1916 January–February	Lenin active in organising the Zimmerwald left and founding its journal *Vorbote* for which he writes 'Opportunism and the Collapse of the Second International' (**22**, 108–21) and 'The Socialist Revolution and the Right of Nations to Self-Determination' (**22**, 143–57).
February–June	Polemical articles and organisational manoeuvres to counter the influence of Bukharin and Pyatakov.
11–17 April	Second International Conference of anti-war socialists at Kienthal in which Lenin emerges as principal organiser of the left wing and secures broader support than at Zimmerwald.
19 June	Lenin dispatches the manuscript of *Imperialism the Highest Stage of Capitalism* (**22**, 185–305) to his Russian publishers.
12 July	Maria Ulianova, Lenin's mother, dies in Petrograd.
July	Lenin writes a favourable commentary to Rosa Luxemburg's 'Junius Pamphlet' (**22**, 305–19).
October	Publication of *Sbornik Sotsial Demokrata*, no. 1, edited and largely written by Lenin. Lenin

writes a succinct and important statement of his views 'Imperialism and the Split in Socialism' (**22**, 105–20).

October–
December

Continues correspondence, journalistic and organisational work on behalf of the Zimmerwald left.

December

Publication of *Sbornik Sotsial Demokrata*, no. 2, containing Lenin's 'The Youth International', his short critique of Bukharin on the state.

Lenin begins work in the Zurich Library on Marxism and the state which he pursues until the outbreak of the October Revolution.

1917 9 January

Lenin delivers a 'Lecture on the 1905 Revolution' on the anniversary of 'Bloody Sunday' (**23**, 236–53).

24–8 February

The February Revolution in Russia. Mass strikes and demonstrations throughout Russia joined by the soldiers, the sudden emergence of the powerful Petrograd Soviet followed by others in main cities, the arrest of the Tsar's ministers, establishment of a Provisional Government (Provisional Committee of the Duma).

2 March

The Tsar abdicates in favour of Grand Duke Mikhail. Lenin receives news of February Revolution and begins to make arrangements for a return to Russia.

4–26 March

Lenin defines his attitude towards the February Revolution in his 'Draft Theses' of 4 March (**23**, 287–91), the themes of which were amplified in his five 'Letters from 'Afar' (**23**, 297–342).

12 March

Stalin and Kamenev return from Siberian exile to resume control over *Pravda* and to steer the Bolsheviks into a more conciliatory position *vis-à-vis* the Mensheviks and the Provisional Government.

27 March–
3 April

Lenin and Krupskaya leave Berne for Zurich having earlier completed the arrangements for the 'sealed train' journey during which Lenin prepared his 'The Tasks of the Proletariat in the Present Revolution' (the 'April Theses', **24**, 21–6). They stop in Stockholm for one day and arrive to tumultuous welcome at the Finland Station in Petrograd. In the night, Lenin presents his ideas to the incredulous and unsympathetic Party workers of Petrograd.

29 March	All-Russia Conference of Soviets.
April–May	Furious organisational and journalistic work convincing the Bolshevik Party of his new strategy, undermining the Provisional Government, the influence of the Mensheviks and the continuation of the war. More than ninety articles in *Pravda* and *Soldatskaia Pravda* in these two months.
4 May	Trotsky returns from America and joins forces with Lenin.
5 May	Formation of a new coalition government with participation of socialist and Soviet leaders. Kerensky becomes Minister of War.
3–24 June	First All-Russia Congress of Soviets of Workers' and Soldiers' Deputies.
9 June	Bolshevik call for mass street demonstrations countermanded by Congress of Soviets.
10 June	Large-scale demonstration in Petrograd mounted by rank and file Bolsheviks. Vacillation of Bolshevik leadership.
18 June	Renewed anti-government demonstrations protesting against the Russian offensive in Galicia.
20 June	Lenin elected to Central Executive Committee of All-Russia Congress of Soviets.
3–5 July	Riots and demonstrations in Petrograd against the mobilisation of units for the front supported by Bolshevik rank and file and, initially, by the Central Committee who called up the Kronstadt sailors but failed to provide effective leadership. The improvised coup fizzled out and Lenin was forced to go underground.
7 July	An order for Lenin's arrest issued by the Provisional Government.
8 July	Kerensky becomes head of the Ministry.
10 July– 8 August	Lenin and Zinoviev hiding at Razliv; continues intensive journalistic work and the writing of *The State and Revolution*.
16 July	General Kornilov appointed Commander in Chief of the Army.
23 July	Arrest of Trotsky.
26 July– 3 August	Sixth Congress of R.C.P. (b.).
8–9 August	Lenin moves from Razliv and illegally crosses into Finland.

Late August	The attempted putsch by the Commander in Chief of the Army, Lavr Kornilov. Transformation of Bolshevik fortunes and growth of the Red Guard.
10 August– 17 September	Lenin in Finland.
4 September	Trotsky freed on bail.
15 September	Bolshevik Central Committee discuss Lenin's letters, 'The Bolsheviks Must Assume Power' (**26**, 19–21) and 'Marxism and Insurrection' (**26**, 22–7). By this time the Bolsheviks were in a majority in the Petrograd and Moscow Soviets.
17 September	Lenin moves from Helsingfors in Finland to Vyborg to exert more direct influence on the Party's Central Committee which refused, for the time being, to authorise his return to Petrograd.
22–24 September	Lenin writes the article 'From a Publicist's Diary. The Mistakes of Our Party' (**26**, 52–8).
27 September	Lenin writes to I. T. Smilga on the military aspects of the revolution (**26**, 69–73).
29 September	Lenin writes 'The Crisis has Matured' (**26**, 74–85).
End September– 1 October	Lenin writes his 'Can the Bolsheviks Retain State Power?' (**26**, 89–136).
6–8 October	Lenin writes the article 'Revision of the Party Programme' (**26**, 151–78).
7 October	Lenin returns from Vyborg to Petrograd.
9 October	Formation of the Military Revolutionary Committee of the Petrograd Soviets under Trotsky's energetic leadership.
10 October	At a meeting of the Central Committee, Lenin calls for an armed uprising and the majority formally commits itself to this course of action. Zinoviev and Kamenev abstain.
14 October	Lenin meets leading Bolsheviks to discuss preparations for the rising.
15 October	Petrograd Committee of the Party pessimistic about the prospects for a rising.
17 October	Lenin writes his 'Letter to Comrades' attacking Kamenev and Zinoviev for publicly opposing the uprising (**26**, 195–215).
20 October	The Military Revolutionary Committee begins to muster its forces.
23 October	The Provisional Government orders the closing down of the Bolshevik press.

24 October	Lenin writes the 'Letter to Central Committee Members' urging an immediate armed uprising. In the night, Lenin arrives at Smolny to assist in co-ordinating the revolutionary forces and to prepare the formation of a Soviet Government.
25 October	At 10 am, Lenin issues the announcement 'To the Citizens of Russia' (**26**, 236) proclaiming the overthrow of the Provisional Government and the transfer of power to the Petrograd Soviet and the Military Revolutionary Committee. Attends the Petrograd Soviet and writes the draft decrees on peace, on land and the formation of the Soviet Government (**26**, 249–63). Convocation of the Second Congress of Soviets with Bolshevik majority which approves Lenin's measures and decides to install a new government.
26 October	Installation of a new Government of People's Commissars. Lenin drafts the 'Regulations on Workers' Control' (**26**, 264–5) and attends the meeting of the Central Council of the Petrograd Factory Committees to discuss ways and means for the introduction of workers' control of production.
27 October– 1 November	Kerensky rallies his forces under General Krasnov and marches on Petrograd, is defeated and flees.
29 October	The ultimatum from the Executive Committee of the Railway Union for a united socialist coalition government.
2 November	Bolsheviks seize power in Moscow after considerable fighting.
4 November	Resignation of Nogin, Rykov, Milyutin and Teodorovich from the Council of People's Commissars, protesting against Lenin's refusal to include representatives of other socialist parties in the government.
13 November	Decree establishing workers' control over all industrial enterprises.
15 November	Lenin presides at a government meeting to discuss the establishment of an Economic Council.
29 November	Establishment of Politburo within the Central Committee to deal with urgent matters.
2 December	Lenin addresses the Second All-Russia Congress of Soviets of Peasants' Deputies.
7 December	Establishment of the All-Russia Extraordi-

	nary Commission to Combat Counter-Revolution and Sabotage (Cheka).
9 December	Negotiations begin in Brest Litovsk for a peace settlement with Germany.
14 December	Lenin writes the 'Draft Decree on the Nationalisation of the Banks' (**26**, 391–4).
24–27 December	Lenin on short rest in Finland writes 'How to Organise Competition' (**26**, 404–15).
1918 5 January	Convocation of Constituent Assembly attended by Lenin before Bolshevik walk-out and summary dismissal of the Assembly.
6 January	Lenin writes the 'Draft Decree on the Dissolution of the Constituent Assembly' (**26**, 434–6).
7 January	Lenin writes his 'Theses on the Question of a Separate Peace' (**26**, 442–50).
8–9 January	Central Committee rejects Lenin's proposals for a separate peace and endorses Bukharin's project for a revolutionary war against Germany.
10–18 January	Third Congress of Soviets.
15 and 16 January	Lenin active in mobilising resources to overcome the famine in the capitals.
30 January	Deadlock in peace negotiations. At Brest Litovsk Trotsky refuses to sign peace terms but declares the war ended.
	From the beginning of February, Russia adopted the New Style Calendar; dates hereafter are the same as those prevailing in the West.
18 February	Resumption of German offensive and Lenin's insistence that peace be signed.
20 February	Establishment of Provisional Executive Committee to handle urgent business in between government meetings. Government decree establishing the Red Army.
23 February	The government and the Bolshevik Central Committee agree to sign peace terms.
6–8 March	Seventh Congress of the Russian Communist Party (Bolsheviks) at which Lenin presents the Political Report (**27**, 87–109), the 'Report on the Review of the Programme and on changing the name of the Party' (**27**, 126–30).
3 March	Peace Treaty of Brest Litovsk is signed.
10–11 March	Lenin and the other members of the government move from Petrograd to Moscow.
8 March	The Bolsheviks adopt the title 'Communist'.
14–16 March	Fourth Congress of Soviets.

15 March	Ratification of the peace treaty with Germany and resignation of left SRs and left communists from the government.
23–28 March	Lenin dictates the original version of the article *The Immediate Tasks of the Soviet Government* (**27**, 203–18).
1 April	Establishment of a Supreme Military Council to direct defence and organise the armed forces.
29 April	Decree nationalising foreign trade.
5 May	Writes the article 'Left-Wing Childishness and the Petty-bourgeois Mentality' (**27**, 325–54).
26 May	Convocation of the First All-Russia Congress of Economic Councils.
May–June	Lenin preoccupied with the critical food supply and fuel situation, the mutiny of the Czechoslovak regiments, anti-Soviet rebellion in Tambov and the collapse of the transport system.
4–10 July	Lenin reports to the Fifth All-Russia Congress of Workers, Peasants, Soldiers and Red Army Deputies (**27**, 507–28).
6 July	Assassination of Mirbach, the German Ambassador and revolt of left SRs.
16 July	The tsar and members of his family shot in Ekaterinberg.
30 August	Lenin is shot and wounded by Fanny Kaplan and is critically ill for a fortnight. Uritsky assassinated.
10 September	Red Army takes Kazan.
24 September– Mid October	Lenin convalescing at Gorki.
8 October	Red Army takes Samara.
3 November	The outbreak of the Hungarian Soviet Revolution.
6–9 November	Convocation of the Extraordinary Sixth All-Russia Congress of Soviet Deputies.
10 November	Lenin finishes writing his book *The Proletarian Revolution and the Renegade Kautsky* (**28**, 229–25).
December 1918– January 1919	Lenin drafts theses for the C.C. of the Party 'Tasks of the Trade Unions' (**28**, 382–5).
1919 January	Abortive coup by German Spartacists and subsequent murder of Luxemburg and Liebknecht.
16–25 January	Second Congress of the Trade Unions.
6 February	Red Army takes Kiev.

	22 February	Closure of the remaining Menshevik newspapers (**28**, 447–8).
	2–6 March	First Congress of the Communist International in Moscow for which Lenin prepares 'Theses and Report on Bourgeois Democracy and the Dictatorship of the Proletariat' (**28**, 457–74).
	18–23 March	Eighth Congress of R.C.P.(b). Denikin's advance in the south and Yudenich's advance on Petrograd. Lenin preoccupied with military matters and the strengthening of the Party to meet this threat.
	21 March	Soviet régime headed by Bela Kun established in Hungary.
	September–October	Lenin works on his article 'Economics and Politics in the Era of the Dictatorship of the Proletariat' (**30**, 107–17).
	November–December	Red Army regroups and goes over to successful offensive against Yudenich, Kolchak and Denikin.
	2–4 December	Eighth All-Russia Conference of the Russian Communist Party. Lenin delivers the Political Report of the Central Committee (**30**, 170–88).
	5–9 December	Seventh All-Russia Congress of Soviets. Lenin delivers the report of the Central Executive Committee and the Council of People's Commissars (**30**, 207–31).
	12 December	Red Army takes Kharkov.
	16 December	Lenin writes 'The Constituent Assembly Elections and the Dictatorship of the Proletariat' (**30**, 253–75).
	20 December	Lenin delivers a 'Report on Subbotniks' at the Moscow Conference of the Party (**30**, 283–8).
	30 December	Red Army takes Ekaterinoslav.
1920	Early January	Red Army takes Tsaritsin and Rostov.
	25 January	In a speech to the Third All-Russia Congress of Economic Councils, Lenin vindicates one-man management and the establishment of labour armies (**30**, 309–13).
	February	Units of Red Army translated into 'labour armies'.
	29 March–5 April	Ninth Congress of the Russian Communist Party (Bolsheviks). Lenin gives the 'Report of the Central Committee' (**30**, 443–62). Congress decides to issue Lenin's *Collected Works*.
	3–7 April	Third Congress of Trade Unions addressed by Lenin (**30**, 502–15).

23 April	Lenin celebrates his fiftieth birthday.
April–May	Lenin writes *Left-Wing Communism – an Infantile Disorder* (**31**, 21–117).
1 May	Lenin participates in the first All-Russia May Day Subbotnik.
Beginning of June	Lenin writes his 'Draft Theses on the National and Colonial Questions' and 'Preliminary Draft Theses on the Agrarian Question for the forthcoming Second Congress of the Comintern' (**31**, 144–64). Beginning of war with Poland.
4 July	Lenin Writes his 'Theses on the Fundamental Tasks for the . . . Communist International' (**31**, 184–201).
11 July	Red Army captures Minsk in the offensive against Poland.
19 July–4 August	Second Congress of the Communist International. Lenin delivers a 'Report on the International Situation' (**31**, 215–34). The Congress approves Lenin's Conditions for Admission to the Communist International (**31**, 206–12).
15 August	Polish counter-attack begins – rapid retreat of Red Army.
22–25 September	Ninth All-Russia Conference of the R.C.P.(b.).
12 October	Attends the funeral of Inessa Armand.
20 October	Writes the article 'A Contribution to the History of the Question of the Dictatorship' (**31**, 340–61).
21 November	Lenin addresses the Moscow Party Organisation on 'Our Foreign and Domestic Position and the Tasks of the Party' (**31**, 408–26).
22–29 December	Eighth All-Russia Congress of Soviets. Lenin reports on the work of the Council of People's Commissars on concessions and on electrification (**31**, 461–518, 532–3).
30 December	Lenin delivers a speech on 'The Trade Unions, the Present Situation and Trotsky's Mistakes' to the Bolshevik delegates to the Eighth Congress of Soviets, the members of the All-Russia Central Council of Trade Unions and the Moscow City Council of Trade Unions (**32**, 19–42).
1921 19 January	Lenin writes 'The Party Crisis' (**32**, 43–53).
25 January	Lenin completes his pamphlet *Once Again on the Trade Unions, the Current Situation and the Mistakes of Trotsky and Bukharin* (**32**, 70–107).

End of February	Large-scale strikes in Petrograd and severe reaction of the City Party under Zinoviev. State of siege declared.
8–16 March	Tenth Congress of R.C.P.(b.). Lenin's 'Report of the Political Work of the Central Committee' and Summing Up Speech on the Report (**32**, 170–209). His speech on the Trade Unions (**32**, 210–13). His 'Report on the Substitution of a Tax in Kind for the Surplus-Grain Appropriation System' – the beginnings of the New Economic Policy (**32**, 214–28). His 'Preliminary Draft Resolution … on Party Unity' – banning factionalism and separate 'platforms' (**32**, 241–4).
8 March	The outbreak of the Kronstadt rebellion. The overthrow of Bolshevik power in the Baltic Fleet.
20 March	Petrograd put under martial law at Lenin's instructions.
21 April	Lenin completes the pamphlet *The Tax in Kind* (The Significance of the New Economic Policy and its Conditions) (**32**, 329–65).
26–28 May	Lenin presides at the Tenth All-Russia Conference of the R.C.P.(b.).
22 June– 12 July	Third Congress of the Communist International. Lenin defends the tactics of the Communist International and reports on the tactics of the R.C.P. (**32**, 468–96).
20 August	Lenin writes the article 'New Times and Old Mistakes in a New Guise' in which he bemoans the declassing of the proletariat(**33**, 21–9).
20 September	Lenin writes the article 'Purging the Party' (**33**, 39–41).
27 September	Lenin writes the letter 'Tasks of the Workers' and Peasants' Inspection …' (**33**, 42–8).
17 October	Lenin delivers an important policy statement on 'The New Economic Policy and the Tasks of the Political Education Departments' (**33**, 60–78).
23–28 December	Ninth All-Russia Congress of Soviets. Lenin reports on 'The Home and Foreign Policy of ᵗʰe Republic' (**33**, 143–77).
31 December	The Political Bureau of the Party directs Lenin to take six weeks' leave, extended in February 1922 until the end of March.
1922 12 January	Lenin's 'The Role and Function of the Trade

	Unions under the New Economic Policy' (**33**, 184–96) approved by the Central Committee.
12 March	Lenin writes the article 'on the Significance of Militant Materialism' (**33**, 227–36).
24 March	Lenin submits to the C.C. his proposals for toughening the conditions for admission to the Party (**33**, 254–5).
27 March– 2 April	Eleventh Congress of the R.C.P.(b.). Lenin delivers the 'Political Report of the Central Committee' (**33**, 263–310).
23 May– 1 October	Lenin living at Gorki Near Moscow.
26 May	Lenin suffers his first stroke.
13 July	Lenin instructs his secretary that he is well enough to read.
2 October	Lenin returns to Moscow and resumes work.
5 November– 5 December	Fourth Congress of the Communist International. Lenin reports on 'Five Years of the Russian Revolution and the Prospects of the World Revolution' (**33**, 418–32).
23 December	Lenin suffers his second stroke.
23–26 December	Lenin dictates a 'Letter to The Congress' – his so-called 'Testament' – in which he called for an increase in numbers of the Central Committee, gave an appreciation of its leading personnel and a demand for the removal of Stalin (**36**, 593–7). For the circumstances in which this was dictated, see his secretary's diary (**42**, 481–2).
30 December	Lenin dictates notes on 'The Question of Nationalities or Autonomisation' (**36**, 605–11).
1923 4 and 6 January	Lenin dictates the article 'On Co-operation' calling for a reorganisation of the state machinery and a new emphasis on peasant co-operatives (**33**, 467–75).
9 and 13 January	Lenin dictates the plan of an article 'What should we do with the Workers' and Peasants' Inspection' (**42**, 433–40).
19–23 January	Lenin dictates the article 'How We Should Reorganise the Workers' and Peasants' Inspection' (**33**, 481–6).
2–9 March	Lenin dictates his last article 'Better Fewer, But Better' (**33**, 487–502).
9 March	Lenin suffers a third stroke.
15 May	Lenin is moved to Gorki.

	Second half of July	His health improves.
	19 October	Lenin pays his last fleeting visit to Moscow.
1924	21 January	Lenin dies.
	23 January	Lenin's body is brought to Moscow and lies in state at the House of Trade Unions.
	27 January	Lenin's body is installed in a temporary mausoleum in Red Square.

Index

233, 239: and theory of the state 84–92, 104–5, 107–8; on predicting revolution 165–6

Fabians 33
fascism 29

Guesde, J. 7, 9, 109

Haase, H. 6
Hilferding, R. 41, 47, 48, 141, 147, 315: Lenin's debt to 53–4, 62, 63, 68; on the state 98–102
Hobbes, T. 104
Hobson, J. 53, 54, 61, 62, 141: and imperialist parasitism 56–7
Hyndman, H. M. 33

International: *see* Second International, Communist International

Jacobinism 2–3, 194, 222, 302–3, 306–8, 323, 326–7
Jaurès, J. 6

Kamenev, L. B. 112, 288, 291
Kautsky, K. 256, 322: Lenin's attacks on 31, 34, 60, 138, 204, 210; on Slavs 240
Kerensky, A. F. 80, 112, 144, 158, 162, 243
Kienthal Conference 19–20
Kollontai, A. M. 262: and platform of Workers' Opposition 264–8, 273
Kornilov, L. G. 80, 155–6, 157, 158
Kosior, S. V. 290
Krasin, L. B. 288
Kronstadt 163, 275, 277, 278, 284, 292, 296: rebellion of 249, 268–74
Krzhizhanovsky, G. M. 301
kulaks 209, 213, 216–17, 220, 228
Kun, B. 236

Larin, Iu. 290

Lenin, V. I.: interpretations of his thought 1–3, 37–8, 53, 83, 145, 169–70, 313; Jacobinism of 2–3, 302–3, 306–8, 309, 323, 326–7; and Marxism 37–9, 309–28, 327–8; theory and practice 3–5, 41, 81–4, 140, 168, 170–1, 309–28; and First World War 4, 6, 15, 16–29, 148, 203, 233–4; and peace settlement 245–53; on opportunists and defencists 26–40, 138

theory of imperialism 4–5, 21–6, 41–69, 147–8, 150; on monopoly capitalism 42–50, 314–15; on finance capitalism 50–4, 77–9, 130–1; on state capitalism 73–5, 79; on uneven development of capitalism 23–4, 49–50, 56, 64–7; and national liberation movement 63–7; finance capital as precursor of socialism 46–9, 53–4, 73–5, 77–9, 124–34, 147–8, 168–9; on the imperialist state 73–5, 110–11, 114–15, 124, 127–34, 170, 202–5, 257, 315–19

nature of revolutionary situation 37, 71–3, 79–81, 142–4, 153–7, 159–63; problems of predicting revolution 163–7, 320–2; international dimensions of revolution 159–62, 188, 199–200, 206, 232–55; military aspects of 159, 229–31

theory of the state: background in Marx and Engels 84–92, 116–19, 134–41, 204–5; in Bukharin 67–8, 83–4, 92–8, 102–9, 113–15, 315–17; in Hilferding 98–102; Lenin's analysis in 1917 117–34; semantic difficulties 134–40; on soviet/commune form 71–3, 113, 114, 118–34, 170–86, 187, 193, 318–19; and immediate transition to socialism 192; and workers' control 183–6, 187; and

385

Lenin, V. I. – *continued*

consciousness 153, 170–9, 176–81, 195–6, 226–7; and peasant support 143, 146, 157, 208–19; soviets and Bolshevik strategy 144, 149, 151–3, 155–6; democratic centralism and Party 173–9

revised estimate of soviet/commune form 190–1, 199, 201–2; soviets as dictatorship of the proletariat 207; general theory of dictatorship of the proletariat 134–40, 187, 193–7, 201–31, 324–7; proletarian class domination of 210–12; domination by advanced workers 260, 276–7; as international model 203–5, 236–43; violence in 204–5

domination of dictatorship of the proletariat by Party 196, 198, 277–8, 294; Lenin on the trade-union debate 259–64; on one-man management 190–2; on intellectuals and specialists 191–2; on low cultural level – of Russian people 253–4, 298; and of peasants 206; and of proletariat 189, 222–7; and of Party 288–90; and of government functionaries 296, 299–302

temporary stabilisation of capitalism 244–5, 249–53; New Economic Policy 250, 275, 280–1, 302; on electrification 218–19, 254–5; response to Kronstadt revolt 271–4; ban on factions in Party 274; on bureaucratic distortions in state 260–2, 294–308; on ineptness and need for purge in Party 284–93; and declassing of proletariat 222–7, 275–82, 325–6; on anarchism 92–3, 136–40, 272–3, 280; final proposals to reform state 302–8

works of: *The Development of Capitalism in Russia* 145, 206–7, 310–12; *Imperialism the Highest Stage of Capitalism* 41–70, 168, 206, 313–17, 372; *The Tasks of the Proletariat in the Present Revolution* (the 'April Theses') 145–6, 265, 373; *The State and Revolution* 112, 118–41, 168, 169, 181, 187, 192, 206, 317–19, 323, 374; *Can the Bolsheviks Retain State Power?* 129–34, 167, 375; *The Immediate Tasks of the Soviet Government* 173–5, 189–97, 200, 205, 378; *How to Organise Competition* 172–3, 174, 377; *Left-Wing Communism an Infantile Disorder* 238–9, 241–3, 380; *Letter to Congress* (Lenin's 'Testament') 290–1, 382; *Better Fewer – But Better* 300–8, 382

Liebknecht, C. 109
Lukacs, G. 70
Luxemburg, R. 16, 25, 64–5, 322

MacLean, J. 109
Martov, Iu. 16
Marx, K. 3–4, 24, 143, 163, 165, 168, 172, 183, 187, 202: and concentration of capital 42–4, 53, 54, 55, 83; on the state 84–92, 107, 108, 116–19, 122, 123; on commune and dictatorship of the proletariat 134–41; on violence in revolution 204–5, 229–30
Medvedev, S. 273, 290
Mensheviks 10, 11, 14, 15, 49, 111, 278, 280: contributions to Lenin scholarship 2–3; in 1917 142–52, 155
Michels, R. 27
Military Revolutionary Committee 159
militia 120–2, 133
Millerand, A. 9
Molotov, V. M. 112
Muranov, M. K. 112
Myasnikov, G. I. 290

About Haymarket Books

Haymarket Books is a nonprofit, progressive book distributor and publisher, a project of the Center for Economic Research and Social Change. We believe that activists need to take ideas, history, and politics into the many struggles for social justice today. Learning the lessons of past victories, as well as defeats, can arm a new generation of fighters for a better world. As Karl Marx said, "The philosophers have merely interpreted the world; the point however is to change it."

We take inspiration and courage from our namesakes, the Haymarket Martyrs, who gave their lives fighting for a better world. Their 1886 struggle for the eight-hour day, which gave us May Day, the international workers' holiday, reminds workers around the world that ordinary people can organize and struggle for their own liberation. These struggles continue today across the globe—struggles against oppression, exploitation, hunger, and poverty.

It was August Spies, one of the Martyrs who was targeted for being an immigrant and an anarchist, who predicted the battles being fought to this day. "If you think that by hanging us you can stamp out the labor movement," Spies told the judge, "then hang us. Here you will tread upon a spark, but here, and there, and behind you, and in front of you, and everywhere, the flames will blaze up. It is a subterranean fire. You cannot put it out. The ground is on fire upon which you stand."

Related Titles From Haymarket Books

History of the Russian Revolution
Leon Trotsky I ISBN 9781931859455

Imperialism and War: Classic Writings by V. I. Lenin and Nicolai Bukharin
V.I. Lenin, Nikolai Bukharin, edited by Phil Gasper I ISBN 9781931859660

Lenin Rediscovered: What Is to be Done? *In Context*
Lars T. Lih I ISBN 9781931859509

Revolution and Counterrevolution: Class Struggle in a Moscow Metal Factory
Kevin Murphy I ISBN 9781931859691

Western Marxism and the Soviet Union
Marcel van der Linden I ISBN 9781931859691

State and Revolution
V. I. Lenin, introduction by Todd Chretien I ISBN 9781931859905